Hands-On Microservices with Spring Boot and Spring Cloud

Build and deploy Java microservices using Spring Cloud, Istio, and Kubernetes

Magnus Larsson

Pack<t>

BIRMINGHAM - MUMBAI

Hands-On Microservices with Spring Boot and Spring Cloud

Commissioning Editor: Richa Tripathi
Acquisition Editor: Shriram Shekhar
Content Development Editor: Tiksha Sarang
Senior Editor: Rohit Singh
Technical Editor: Gaurav Gala
Copy Editor: Safis Editing
Project Coordinator: Prajakta Naik
Proofreader: Safis Editing
Indexer: Rekha Nair
Production Designer: Jyoti Chauhan

First published: September 2019

Production reference: 1190919

Published by Packt Publishing Ltd.
Livery Place
35 Livery Street
Birmingham
B3 2PB, UK.

ISBN 978-1-78961-347-6

www.packt.com

Packt>

Packt.com

Subscribe to our online digital library for full access to over 7,000 books and videos, as well as industry leading tools to help you plan your personal development and advance your career. For more information, please visit our website.

Why subscribe?

- Spend less time learning and more time coding with practical eBooks and Videos from over 4,000 industry professionals

- Improve your learning with Skill Plans built especially for you

- Get a free eBook or video every month

- Fully searchable for easy access to vital information

- Copy and paste, print, and bookmark content

Did you know that Packt offers eBook versions of every book published, with PDF and ePub files available? You can upgrade to the eBook version at www.packt.com and as a print book customer, you are entitled to a discount on the eBook copy. Get in touch with us at customercare@packtpub.com for more details.

At www.packt.com, you can also read a collection of free technical articles, sign up for a range of free newsletters, and receive exclusive discounts and offers on Packt books and eBooks.

Contributors

About the author

Magnus Larsson has been in the IT industry for more than 30 years, working as a consultant for large companies in Sweden such as Volvo, Ericsson, and AstraZeneca. He has seen a lot of different communication technologies come and go over the years, such as RPC, CORBA, SOAP, and REST. In the past, he struggled with the challenges associated with distributed systems as there was no substantial help from the software available at that time. This has, however, changed dramatically over the last few years with the introduction of open source projects such as Spring Cloud, Netflix OSS, Docker, and Kubernetes. Over the last five years, Magnus has been helping customers use these new software technologies and has also done several presentations and blog posts on the subject.

I would like to thank the following people:

Shriram Shekhar, Tiksha Sarang, and Gaurav Gala from Packt Publishing for their constant support.

My college Erik Lupander, the technical reviewer of this book and a persistent troubleshooter.

To my wife Maria, thank you for all of your support and understanding throughout the process of writing this book.

And to our daughter Emma, who has reviewed each chapter and helped me to write proper English.

About the reviewer

Erik Lupander is a software architect and developer with over 15 years of professional experience.

He holds an M.Sc. in applied informatics from the University of Gothenburg. While Java Virtual Machine-based languages and architecture have been his bread and butter, Erik is a polyglot software craftsman at heart who, among other technologies, has embraced Go and microservice architecture.

He has spoken at software conferences on topics ranging from OpenGL ES and big data to Go and microservices, and was a technical reviewer for *Building Microservices with Go*, by Nic Jackson.

He lives just outside Gothenburg, Sweden, with his wife and two children, and is currently employed by Callista Enterprise AB, a Swedish consultancy specializing in software architecture.

Packt is searching for authors like you

If you're interested in becoming an author for Packt, please visit `authors.packtpub.com` and apply today. We have worked with thousands of developers and tech professionals, just like you, to help them share their insight with the global tech community. You can make a general application, apply for a specific hot topic that we are recruiting an author for, or submit your own idea.

Table of Contents

Preface

This book is about building production-ready microservices using Spring Boot and Spring Cloud. Five years ago, when I began to explore microservices, I was looking for a book like this.

This book has been developed after I learned about, and mastered, open source software used for developing, testing, deploying, and managing landscapes of cooperating microservices.

This book primarily covers Spring Boot, Spring Cloud, Docker, Kubernetes, Istio, the EFK stack, Prometheus, and Grafana. Each of these open source tools works great by itself, but it can be challenging to understand how to use them together in an advantageous way. In some areas, they complement each other, but in other areas they overlap, and it is not obvious which one to choose for a particular situation.

This is a hands-on book that describes step by step how to use these open source tools together. This is the book I was looking for five years ago when I started to learn about microservices, but with updated versions of the open source tools it covers.

Who this book is for

This book is for Java and Spring developers and architects who want to learn how to break up their existing monoliths into microservices and deploy them either on-premises or in the cloud, using Kubernetes as a container orchestrator and Istio as a service mesh. No familiarity with microservices architecture is required to get started with this book.

What this book covers

Chapter 1, *Introduction to Microservices*, will help you understand the basic premise of the book, microservices, along with the essential concepts and design patterns that go along with it.

Chapter 2, *Introduction to Spring Boot,* will get you introduced to Spring Boot and the other open source projects that will be used in the first part of the book: Spring WebFlux for developing RESTful APIs, SpringFox for producing OpenAPI- or Swagger-based documentation for the APIs, Spring Data for storing data in SQL and NoSQL databases, Spring Cloud Stream for message-based microservices, and Docker to run the microservices as containers.

Chapter 3, *Creating a Set of Cooperating Microservices,* will teach you how to create a set of cooperating microservices from scratch. You will use Spring Initializr to create skeleton projects based on Spring Framework 5.1 and Spring Boot 2.1. The idea is to create three core services (that will handle their own resources) and one composite service that uses the three core services to aggregate a composite result. Toward the end of the chapter, you will learn how to add very basic RESTful APIs based on Spring WebFlux. In the next chapter, more and more functionality will be added to these microservices.

Chapter 4, *Deploying Our Microservices Using Docker,* will teach you how to deploy microservices using Docker. You will learn how to add Dockerfiles and docker-compose files in order to start up the whole microservice landscape with a single command. Then, you will learn how to use multiple Spring profiles to handle configurations with and without Docker.

Chapter 5, *Adding an API Description Using OpenAPI/Swagger,* will get you up to speed with documenting the APIs exposed by a microservice using OpenAPI/Swagger. You will use the SpringFox framework to annotate the services to create OpenAPI- or Swagger-based API documentation on the fly. The key highlight will be how the APIs can be tested in a web browser using SpringFox Swagger UI.

Chapter 6, *Adding Persistence,* will show you how to add persistence to the data of the microservice. You will use Spring Data to set up and access data in a MongoDB document database for two of the core microservices and access data in a MySQL relational database using the **Java Persistence API** (**JPA**) for the remaining microservice.

Chapter 7, *Developing Reactive Microservices,* will teach you why and when a reactive approach is of importance and how to develop end-to-end reactive services. You will learn how to develop and test both non-blocking synchronous RESTful APIs and asynchronous event-driven services. You will also learn how to use the reactive non-blocking driver for MongoDB and use conventional blocking code for MySQL.

Chapter 8, *Introduction to Spring Cloud,* will introduce you to Spring Cloud and the components of Spring Cloud that will be used in this book.

Chapter 9, *Adding Service Discovery Using Netflix Eureka and Ribbon,* will show you how to use Netflix Eureka and Ribbon in Spring Cloud to add service discovery capabilities. This will be achieved by adding a Netflix Eureka-based service discovery server to the system landscape. You will then configure the microservices to use Netflix Ribbon to find other microservices. You will understand how microservices are registered automatically and how traffic through Netflix Ribbon is automatically load balanced to new instances when they become available.

Chapter 10, *Using Spring Cloud Gateway to Hide Microservices Behind an Edge Server,* will guide you through how to hide the microservices behind an edge server using Spring Cloud Gateway and only expose selected APIs to external consumers. You will also learn how to hide the internal complexity of the microservices from external consumers. This will be achieved by adding a Spring Cloud Gateway-based edge server to the system landscape and configuring it to only expose the public APIs.

Chapter 11, *Securing Access to APIs,* will explain how to protect exposed APIs using OAuth 2.0 and OpenID Connect. You will learn how to add an OAuth 2.0 authorization server based on Spring Security to the system landscape, and how to configure the edge server and the composite service to require valid access tokens issued by that authorization server. You will learn how to expose the authorization server through the edge server and secure its communication with external consumers using HTTPS. Finally, you will learn how to replace the internal OAuth 2.0 authorization server with an external OpenID Connect provider from Auth0.

Chapter 12, *Centralized Configuration,* will deal with how to collect the configuration files from all the microservices in one central repository and use the configuration server to distribute the configuration to the microservices at runtime. You will also learn how to add a Spring Cloud Config Server to the system landscape and configure all microservices to use the Spring Config Server to get its configuration.

Chapter 13, *Improving Resilience Using Resilience4j,* will explain how to use the capabilities of Resilience4j to prevent, for example, the "chain of failure" anti-pattern. You will learn how to add a retry mechanism and a circuit breaker to the composite service, and how to configure the circuit breaker to *fast fail* when the circuit is open, and how to utilize a fallback method to create a best-effort response.

Chapter 14, *Understanding Distributed Tracing,* will show you how to use Zipkin to collect and visualize tracing information. You will also use Spring Cloud Sleuth to add trace IDs to requests so that request chains between cooperating microservices can be visualized.

Chapter 15, *Introduction to Kubernetes,* will explain the core concepts of Kubernetes and how to perform a sample deployment. You will also learn how to set up Kubernetes locally for development and testing purposes using Minkube.

Chapter 16, *Deploying Our Microservices to Kubernetes*, will show how to deploy microservices on Kubernetes. You will also learn how to use Kustomize to configure the deployment in Kubernetes for different runtime environments, such as test and production environments. Finally, you will learn how to replace Netflix Eureka with the built-in support in Kubernetes for service discovery, based on Kubernetes services objects and the kube-proxy runtime component.

Chapter 17, *Implementing Kubernetes Features as an Alternative*, will explain how to use Kubernetes features as an alternative to the Spring Cloud services introduced in the previous chapters. You will learn why and how to replace Spring Cloud Config Server with Kubernetes secrets and config maps. You will also learn why and how to replace Spring Cloud Gateway with Kubernetes ingress objects and how to add the Cert Manager to automatically provision and rotate certificates from Let's Encrypt's for HTTPS endpoints.

Chapter 18, *Using a Service Mesh to Improve Observability and Management*, will introduce the concept of a service mesh and will explain how to use Istio to implement a service mesh in runtime using Kubernetes. You will learn how to use a service mesh to further improve the resilience, security, traffic management, and observability of the microservice landscape.

Chapter 19, *Centralized Logging with the EFK Stack*, will explain how to use Elasticsearch, Fluentd, and Kibana (the EFK stack) to collect, store, and visualize log streams from microservices. You will learn how to deploy the EFK stack in Minikube and how to use it to analyze collected log records and find log output from all microservices involved in the processing of a request that spans several microservices. You will also learn how to perform root cause analysis using the EFK stack.

Chapter 20, *Monitoring Microservices*, will show you how to monitor the microservices deployed in Kubernetes using Prometheus and Grafana. You will learn how to use both existing dashboards in Granfana to monitor different types of metrics, and you will also learn how to create your own dashboards. Finally, you will learn how to create alerts in Grafana that will be used to send emails with alerts when configured thresholds are passed for selected metrics.

Assessments, is uploaded on the GitHub repository containing the answers to the questions asked in the respective chapters.

To get the most out of this book

A good understanding of Java 8, along with a basic knowledge of Spring Framework, is required. A general understanding of the challenges of distributed systems, in addition to some experience of running your own code in production, will also be beneficial.

Download the example code files

You can download the example code files for this book from your account at
www.packt.com. If you purchased this book elsewhere, you can visit
www.packtpub.com/support and register to have the files emailed directly to you.

You can download the code files by following these steps:

1. Log in or register at www.packt.com.
2. Select the **Support** tab.
3. Click on **Code Downloads**.
4. Enter the name of the book in the **Search** box and follow the onscreen instructions.

Once the file is downloaded, please make sure that you unzip or extract the folder using the latest version of:

- WinRAR/7-Zip for Windows
- Zipeg/iZip/UnRarX for Mac
- 7-Zip/PeaZip for Linux

The code bundle for the book is also hosted on GitHub at https://github.com/
PacktPublishing/Hands-On-Microservices-with-Spring-Boot-and-Spring-Cloud. In case
there's an update to the code, it will be updated on the existing GitHub repository.

We also have other code bundles from our rich catalog of books and videos available
at https://github.com/PacktPublishing/. Check them out!

Download the color images

We also provide a PDF file that has color images of the screenshots/diagrams used in this
book. You can download it here: https://static.packt-cdn.com/downloads/
9781789613476_ColorImages.pdf.

Code in Action

To see the code being executed, please visit the following: http://bit.ly/2kn7mSp.

Conventions used

There are a number of text conventions used throughout this book.

`CodeInText`: Indicates code words in text, database table names, folder names, filenames, file extensions, pathnames, dummy URLs, user input, and Twitter handles. Here is an example: "To use the local filesystem, the config server needs to be launched with the Spring profile, `native`, enabled"

A block of code is set as follows:

```
management.endpoint.health.show-details: "ALWAYS"
management.endpoints.web.exposure.include: "*"

logging.level.root: info
```

When we wish to draw your attention to a particular part of a code block, the relevant lines or items are set in bold:

```
backend:
  serviceName: auth-server
  servicePort: 80
- path: /product-composite
```

Any command-line input or output is written as follows:

```
brew install kubectl
```

Bold: Indicates a new term, an important word, or words that you see on screen. For example, words in menus or dialog boxes appear in the text like this. Here is an example: "As seen in the preceding screenshot Chrome reports: **This certificate is valid**!"

Warnings or important notes appear like this.

Tips and tricks appear like this.

Get in touch

Feedback from our readers is always welcome.

General feedback: If you have questions about any aspect of this book, mention the book title in the subject of your message and email us at customercare@packtpub.com.

Errata: Although we have taken every care to ensure the accuracy of our content, mistakes do happen. If you have found a mistake in this book, we would be grateful if you would report this to us. Please visit www.packtpub.com/support/errata, selecting your book, clicking on the Errata Submission Form link, and entering the details.

Piracy: If you come across any illegal copies of our works in any form on the internet, we would be grateful if you would provide us with the location address or website name. Please contact us at copyright@packt.com with a link to the material.

If you are interested in becoming an author: If there is a topic that you have expertise in, and you are interested in either writing or contributing to a book, please visit authors.packtpub.com.

Reviews

Please leave a review. Once you have read and used this book, why not leave a review on the site that you purchased it from? Potential readers can then see and use your unbiased opinion to make purchase decisions, we at Packt can understand what you think about our products, and our authors can see your feedback on their book. Thank you!

For more information about Packt, please visit packt.com.

Section 1: Getting Started with Microservice Development Using Spring Boot

1

In this section, you will learn how to use some of the most important features of Spring Boot to develop microservices.

This section includes the following chapters:

Introduction to Microservices

1

This book does not blindly praise microservices. Instead, it's about how we can use their benefits while being able to handle the challenges of building scalable, resilient, and manageable microservices.

As an introduction to this book, the following topics will be covered in this chapter:

- How I learned about microservices and what experience I have of their benefits and challenges
- What is a microservice-based architecture?
- Challenges with microservices
- Design patterns for handling challenges
- Software enablers that can help us handle these challenges
- Other important considerations that aren't covered in this book

Technical requirements

No installations are required for this chapter. However, you may be interested in taking a look at the C4 model conventions, `https://c4model.com`, since the illustrations in this chapter are inspired by the C4 model.

This chapter does not contain any source code.

My way into microservices

When I first learned about the concept of microservices back in 2014, I realized that I had been developing microservices (well, kind of) for a number of years without knowing it was microservices I was dealing with. I was involved in a project that started in 2009 where we developed a platform based on a set of separated features. The platform was delivered to a number of customers that deployed it on-premise. To make it easy for the customers to pick and choose what features they wanted to use from the platform, each feature was developed as an **autonomous software component**; that is, it had its own persistent data and only communicated with other components using well-defined APIs.

Since I can't discuss specific features in this project's platform, I have generalized the names of the components, which are labeled from **Component A** to **Component F**. The composition of the platform into a set of components is illustrated as follows:

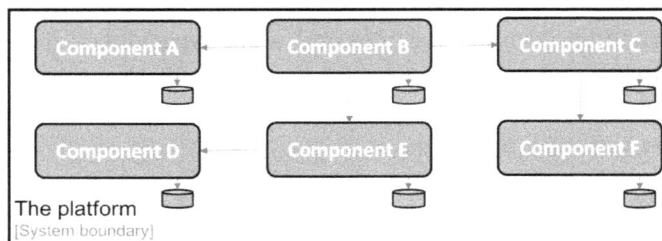

Each component is developed using Java and the Spring Framework, and is packaged as a WAR file and deployed as a web app in a Java EE web container, for example, Apache Tomcat. Depending on the customer's specific requirements, the platform can be deployed on single or multiple servers. A two-node deployment may look as follows:

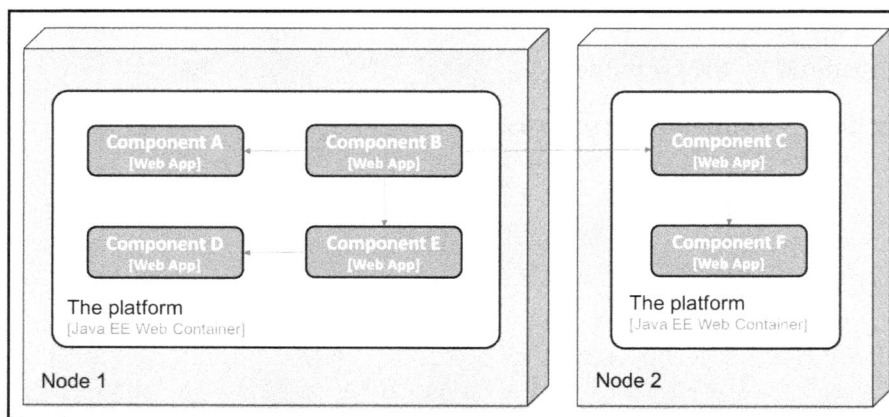

Benefits of autonomous software components

Decomposing the platform's functionality into a set of autonomous software components provides a number of benefits:

- A customer can deploy parts of the platform in its own system landscape, integrating it with its existing systems using its well-defined APIs.
  The following is an example where one customer decided to deploy **Component A**, **Component B**, **Component D**, and **Component E** from the platform and integrate them with two existing systems in the customer's system landscape, **System A** and **System B**:

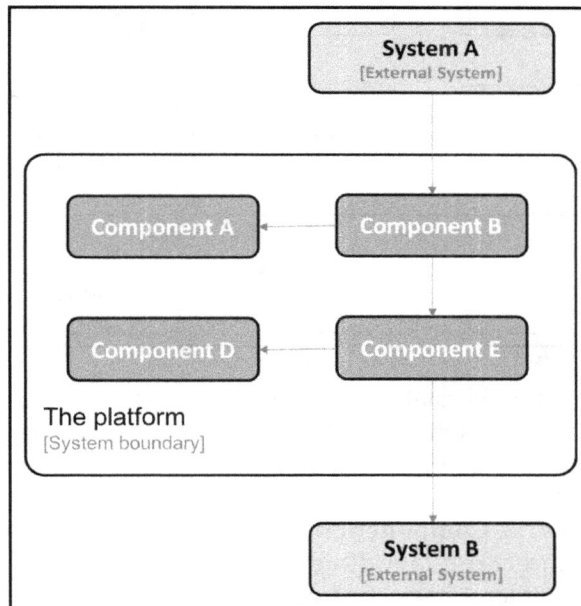

- Another customer can choose to replace parts of the platform's functionality with implementations that already exist in the customer's system landscape, potentially requiring some adoption of the existing functionality in the platform's APIs. The following is an example where a customer has replaced **Component C** and **Component F** in the platform with their own implementation:

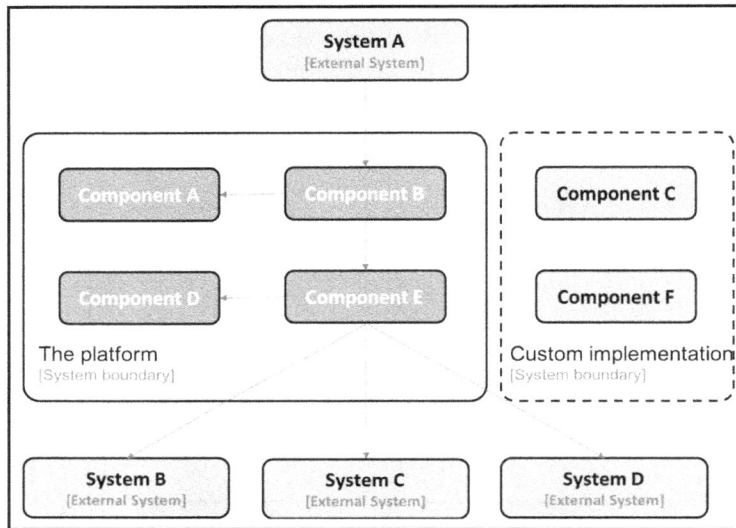

- Each component in the platform can be delivered and upgraded separately. Thanks to using well-defined APIs, one component can be upgraded to a new version without being dependent on the life cycle of the other components. The following is an example where **Component A** has been upgraded from version **v1.1** to **v1.2**. **Component B**, which calls **Component A**, does not need to be upgraded since it uses a well-defined API; that is, it's still the same after the upgrade (or it's at least backward-compatible):

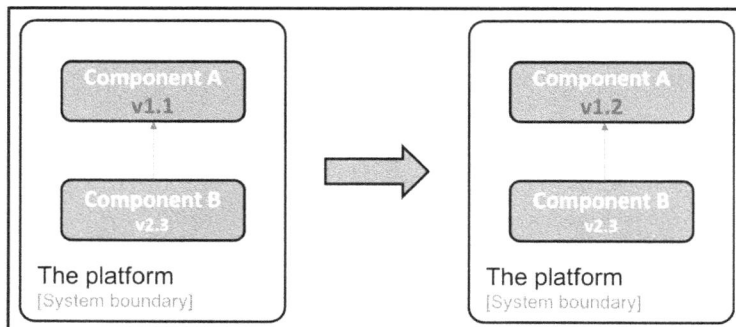

- Thanks to the use of well-defined APIs, each component in the platform can also be scaled out to multiple servers independently of the other components. Scaling can be done either to meet high availability requirements or to handle higher volumes of requests. Technically, this is achieved by *manually* setting up load balancers in front of a number of servers, each running a Java EE web container. An example where **Component A** has been scaled out to three instances looks as follows:

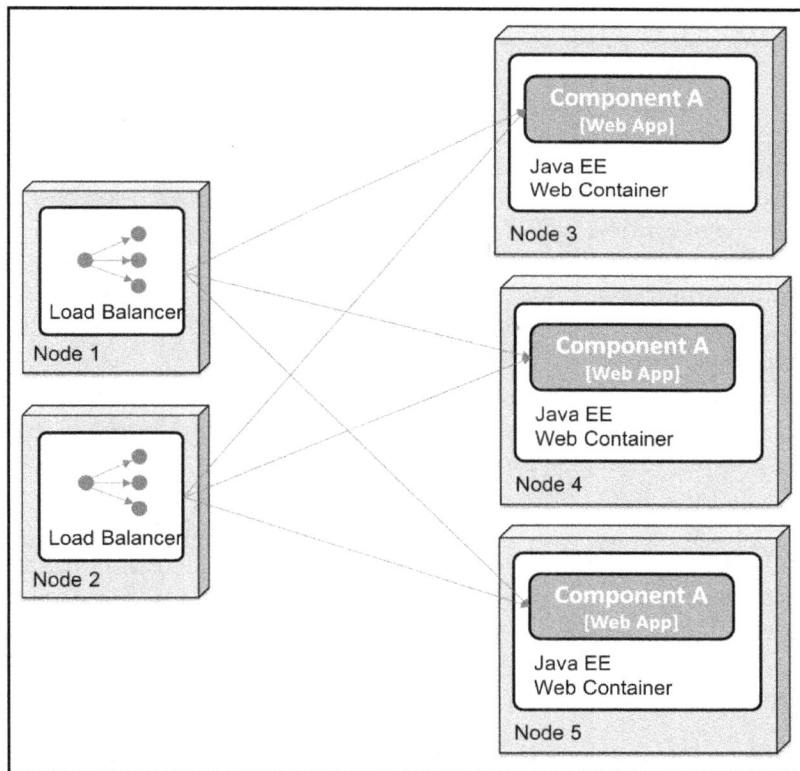

Challenges with autonomous software components

We also learned that decomposing the platform introduced a number of new challenges that we were not exposed (at least not to the same degree) when developing more traditional, monolithic applications:

- Adding new instances to a component required manually configuring load balancers and manually setting up new nodes. This work was both time-consuming and error-prone.
- The platform was initially prone to errors in the other systems it was communicating with. If a system stopped responding to requests that were sent from the platform in a timely fashion, the platform quickly ran out of crucial resources, for example, OS threads, specifically when exposed to a large number of concurrent requests. This caused components in the platform to hang or even crash. Since most of the communication in the platform is based on synchronous communication, one component crashing can lead to cascading failures; that is, clients of the crashing components could also crash after a while. This is known as a **chain of failures**.
- Keeping the configuration consistent and up to date in all the instances of the components quickly became a problem, causing a lot of manual and repetitive work. This led to quality problems from time to time.
- Monitoring the state of the platform in terms of latency issues and hardware usage (for example, usage of CPU, memory, disks, and the network) was more complicated compared to monitoring a single instance of a monolithic application.
- Collecting log files from a number of distributed components and correlating related log events from the components was also difficult but feasible since the number of components was fixed and known in advance.

Over time, we addressed most of the challenges that were mentioned in the preceding list with a mix of in-house-developed tools and well-documented instructions for handling these challenges manually. The scale of the operation was, in general, at a level where manual procedures for releasing new versions of the components and handling runtime issues were acceptable, even though they were not desirable.

Enter microservices

Learning about microservice-based architectures in 2014 made me realize that other projects had also been struggling with similar challenges (partly for other reasons than the ones I described earlier, for example, the large cloud service providers meeting web-scale requirements). Many microservice pioneers had published details of lessons they'd learned. It was very interesting to learn from these lessons.

Many of the pioneers initially developed monolithic applications that made them very successful from a business perspective. But over time, these monolithic applications became more and more difficult to maintain and evolve. They also became challenging to scale beyond the capabilities of the largest machines available (also known as **vertical scaling**). Eventually, the pioneers started to find ways to split monolithic applications into smaller components that could be released and scaled independently of each other. Scaling small components can be done horizontally, that is, deploying a component on a number of smaller servers and placing a load balancer in front of it. If done in the cloud, the scaling capability is potentially endless – it is just a matter of how many virtual servers you bring in (given that your component can scale out on a huge number of instances, but more on that later on).

In 2014, I also learned about a number of new open source projects that delivered tools and frameworks that simplified the development of microservices and could be used to handle the challenges that come with a microservice-based architecture. Some of these are as follows:

- Pivotal released **Spring Cloud**, which wraps parts of the **Netflix OSS** in order to provide capabilities such as dynamic service discovery, configuration management, distributed tracing, circuit breaking, and more.
- I also learned about **Docker** and the container revolution, which is great for minimizing the gap between development and production. Being able to package a component not only as a deployable runtime artifact (for example, a Java, `war` or, `jar` file) but as a complete image ready to be launched as a container (for example, an isolated process) on a server running Docker was a great step forward for development and testing.

- A container engine, such as Docker, is not enough to be able to use containers in a production environment. Something is needed that, for example, can ensure that all the containers are up and running and that they can scale out containers on a number of servers, thereby providing high availability and/or increased compute resources. These types of product became known as **container orchestrators**. A number of products have evolved over the last few years, such as Apache Mesos, Docker in Swarm mode, Amazon ECS, HashiCorp Nomad, and **Kubernetes**. Kubernetes was initially developed by Google. When Google released v1.0, they also donated Kubernetes to CNCF (`https://www.cncf.io/`). During 2018, Kubernetes became kind of a de facto standard, available both pre-packaged for on-premise use and available as a service from most major cloud providers.
- I have recently started to learn about the concept of a **service mesh** and how a service mesh can complement a container orchestrator to further offload microservices from responsibilities to make them manageable and resilient.

A sample microservice landscape

Since this book can't cover all aspects of the technologies I just mentioned, I will focus on the parts that have proven to be useful in customer projects I have been involved in since 2014. I will describe how they can be used together to create cooperating microservices that are manageable, scalable, and resilient.

Each chapter in this book will address a specific concern. To demonstrate how things fit together, I will use a small set of cooperating microservices that we will evolve throughout this book:

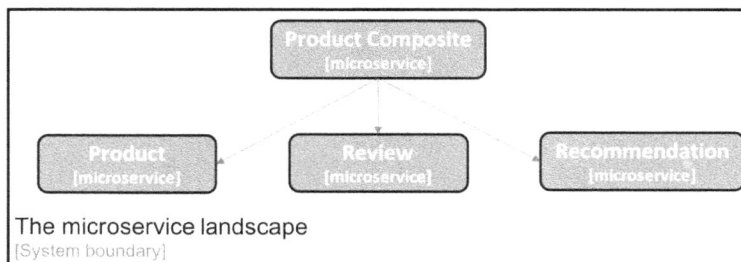

The microservice landscape
[System boundary]

Now that we know the how and what of microservices, let's start to look into how a microservice can be defined.

Defining a microservice

To me, a microservice architecture is about splitting up monolithic applications into smaller components, which achieves two major goals:

- Faster development, enabling continuous deployments
- Easier to scale, manually or automatically

A microservice is essentially an autonomous software component that is independently upgradeable and scalable. To be able to act as an autonomous component, it must fulfill certain criteria as follows:

- It must conform to a shared-nothing architecture; that is, microservices don't share data in databases with each other!
- It must only communicate through well-defined interfaces, for example, using synchronous services or preferably by sending messages to each other using APIs and message formats that are stable, well-documented, and evolve by following a defined versioning strategy.
- It must be deployed as separate runtime processes. Each instance of a microservice runs in a separate runtime process, for example, a Docker container.
- Microservice instances are stateless so that incoming requests to a microservice can be handled by any of its instances.

Using a set of microservices, we can deploy to a number of smaller servers instead of being forced to deploy to a single big server, like we have to do when deploying a monolithic application.

Given that the preceding criteria have been fulfilled, it is easier to scale up a single microservice into more instances (for example, using more virtual servers) compared to scaling up a big monolithic application. Utilizing auto-scaling capabilities that are available in the cloud is also a possibility, but not typically feasible for a big monolithic application. It's also easier to upgrade or even replace a single microservice compared to upgrading a big monolithic application.

This is illustrated by the following diagram, where a monolithic application has been divided into six microservices, all of which have been deployed into one separate server. Some of the microservices have also been scaled up independently of the others:

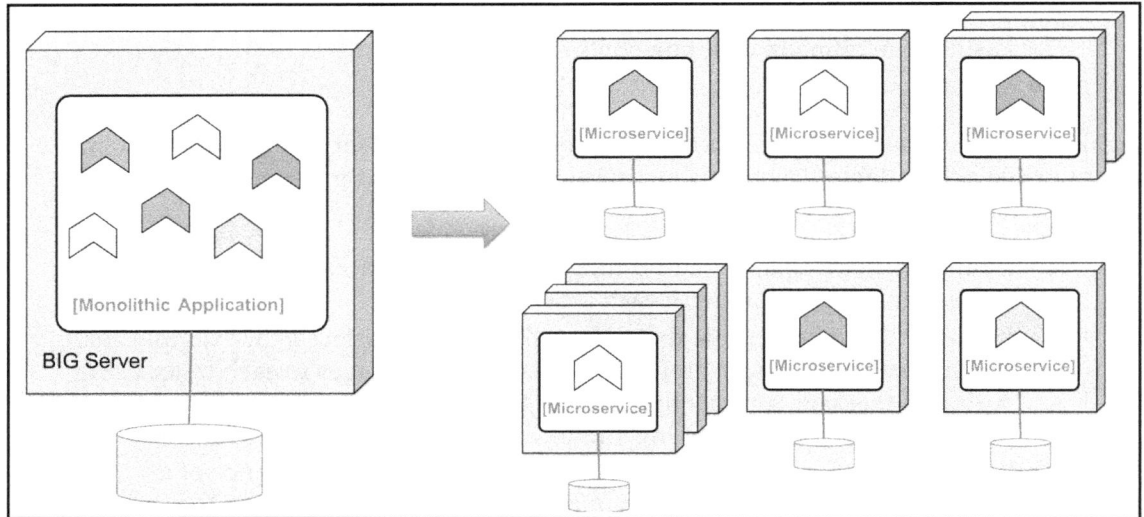

A very frequent question I receive from customers is, *How big should a microservice be?*

I try to use the following rules-of-thumb:

- Small enough to fit in the head of a developer
- Big enough to not jeopardize performance (that is, latency) and/or data consistency (SQL foreign keys between data that's stored in different microservices are no longer something you can take for granted)

So, to summarize, a microservice architecture is, in essence, an architectural style where we decompose a monolithic application into a group of cooperating autonomous software components. The motivation is to enable faster development and to make it easier to scale the application.

Next, we will move on to understand some of the challenges that we will face when it comes to microservices.

Challenges with microservices

In the *Challenges with autonomous software components* section, we have already seen some of the challenges that autonomous software components can bring (and they all apply to microservices as well) as follows:

- Many small components that use synchronous communication can cause *a chain of failure* problem, especially under high load.
- Keeping the configuration up to date for many small components can be challenging.
- It's hard to track a request that's being processed and involves many components, for example, when performing root cause analysis, where each component stores log events locally.
- Analyzing the usage of hardware resources on a component level can be challenging as well.
- Manual configuration and management of many small components can become costly and error-prone.

Another downside (but not always obvious initially) of decomposing an application into a group of autonomous components is that they form a distributed system. Distributed systems are known to be, by their nature, very hard to deal with. This has been known for many years (but in many cases neglected until proven differently). My favorite quote to establish this fact is from Peter Deutsch who, back in 1994, stated the following:

> **The 8 fallacies of distributed computing**: *Essentially everyone, when they first build a distributed application, makes the following eight assumptions. All prove to be false in the long run and all cause big trouble and painful learning experiences:*
>
> 1. *The network is reliable*
> 2. *Latency is zero*
> 3. *Bandwidth is infinite*
> 4. *The network is secure*
> 5. *Topology doesn't change*
> 6. *There is one administrator*
> 7. *Transport cost is zero*
> 8. *The network is homogeneous*
>
> *-- Peter Deutsch, 1994*

> **Note:** The eighth fallacy was actually added by James Gosling at a later date. For more details, please go to `https://www.rgoarchitects.com/Files/fallacies.pdf`.

In general, building microservices-based on these false assumptions leads to solutions that are prone to both temporary network glitches and problems that occur in other microservice instances. When the number of microservices in a system landscape increases, the likelihood of problems also goes up. A good rule of thumb is to design your microservice architecture based on the assumption that there is always something going wrong in the system landscape. The microservice architecture needs to be designed to handle this, in terms of detecting problems and restarting failed components but also on the client-side so that requests are not sent to failed microservice instances. When problems are corrected, requests to the previously failing microservice should be resumed; that is, microservice clients need to be resilient. All of these need, of course, to be fully automated. With a large number of microservices, it is not feasible for operators to handle this manually!

The scope of this is large, but we will limit ourselves for now and move on to study design patterns for microservices.

Design patterns for microservices

This topic will cover using design patterns to mitigate challenges with microservices, as described in the preceding section. Later in this book, we will see how we can implement these design patterns using Spring Boot, Spring Cloud, and Kubernetes.

The concept of design patterns is actually quite old; it was invented by Christopher Alexander back in 1977. In essence, a design pattern is about describing a reusable solution to a problem when given a specific context.

The design patterns we will cover are as follows:

- Service discovery
- Edge server
- Reactive microservices
- Central configuration
- Centralized log analysis
- Distributed tracing
- Circuit Breaker
- Control loop
- Centralized monitoring and alarms

> This list is not intended to be comprehensive; instead, it's a minimal list of design patterns that are required to handle the challenges we described previously.

We will use a lightweight approach to describing design patterns, and focus on the following:

- The problem
- A solution
- Requirements for the solution

Later in this book, we will delve more deeply into how to apply these design patterns. The context for these design patterns is a system landscape of cooperating microservices where the microservices communicate with each other using either synchronous requests (for example, using HTTP) or by sending asynchronous messages (for example, using a message broker).

Service discovery

The **service discovery** pattern has the following problem, solution, and solution requirements.

Problem

How can clients find microservices and their instances?

Microservices instances are typically assigned dynamically allocated IP addresses when they start up, for example, when running in containers. This makes it difficult for a client to make a request to a microservice that, for example, exposes a REST API over HTTP. Consider the following diagram:

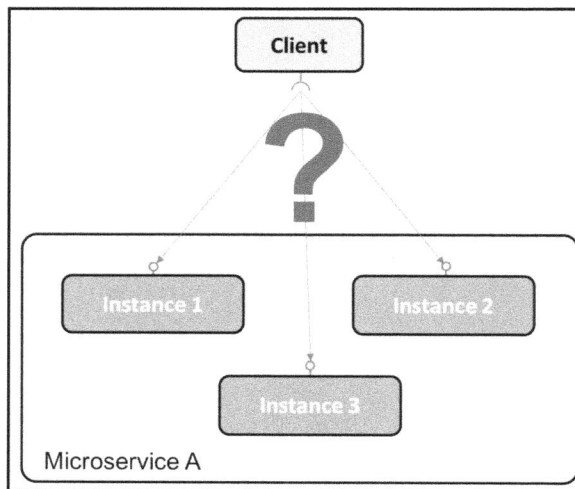

Solution

Add a new component – a **service discovery** service – to the system landscape, which keeps track of currently available microservices and the IP addresses of its instances.

Solution requirements

Some solution requirements are as follows:

- Automatically register/unregister microservices and their instances as they come and go.
- The client must be able to make a request to a logical endpoint for the microservice. The request will be routed to one of the microservices available instances.
- Requests to a microservice must be load-balanced over the available instances.
- We must be able to detect instances that are not currently healthy; that is, requests will not be routed to them.

Implementation notes: As we will see, this design pattern can be implemented using two different strategies:

- **Client-side routing**: The client uses a library that communicates with the service discovery service to find out the proper instances to send the requests to.
- **Server-side routing**: The infrastructure of the service discovery service also exposes a reverse proxy that all requests are sent to. The reverse proxy forwards the requests to a proper microservice instance on behalf of the client.

Edge server

The edge server pattern has the following problem, solution, and solution requirements.

Problem

In a system landscape of microservices, it is in many cases desirable to expose some of the microservices to the outside of the system landscape and hide the remaining microservices from external access. The exposed microservices must be protected against requests from malicious clients.

Solution

Add a new component, an **Edge Server**, to the system landscape that all incoming requests will go through:

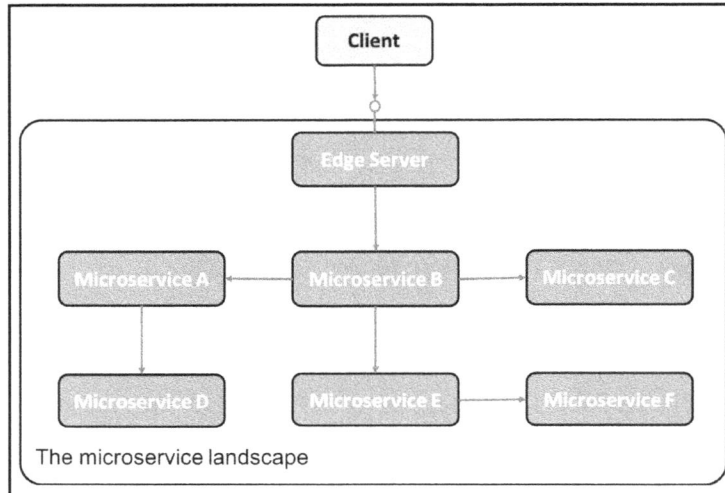

Implementation notes: An edge server typically behaves like a reverse proxy and can be integrated with a discovery service to provide dynamic load balancing capabilities.

Solution requirements

Some solution requirements are as follows:

- Hide internal services that should not be exposed outside their context; that is, only route requests to microservices that are configured to allow external requests.
- Expose external services and protect them from malicious requests; that is, use standard protocols and best practices such as OAuth, OIDC, JWT tokens, and API keys to ensure that the clients are trustworthy.

Reactive microservice

The reactive microservice pattern has the following problem, solution, and solution requirements.

Problem

Traditionally, as Java developers, we are used to implementing synchronous communication using blocking I/O, for example, a RESTful JSON API over HTTP. Using a blocking I/O means that a thread is allocated from the operating system for the length of the request. If the number of concurrent requests goes up (and/or the number of involved components in a request, for example, a chain of cooperating microservices, goes up), a server might run out of available threads in the operating system, causing problems ranging from longer response times to crashing servers.

Also, as we already mentioned in this chapter, overusing blocking I/O can make a system of microservices prone to errors. For example, an increased delay in one service can cause clients to run out of available threads, causing them to fail. This, in turn, can cause their clients to have the same types of problem, which is also known as a chain of failures. See the *Circuit Breaker* section for how to handle a chain-of-failure-related problem.

Solution

Use non-blocking I/O to ensure that no threads are allocated while waiting for processing to occur in another service, that is, a database or another microservice.

Solution requirements

Some solution requirements are as follows:

- Whenever feasible, use an asynchronous programming model; that is, send messages without waiting for the receiver to process them.
- If a synchronous programming model is preferred, ensure that reactive frameworks are used that can execute synchronous requests using non-blocking I/O, that is, without allocating a thread while waiting for a response. This will make the microservices easier to scale in order to handle an increased workload.
- Microservices must also be designed to be resilient, that is, capable of producing a response, even if a service that it depends on fails. Once the failing service is operational again, its clients must be able to resume using it, which is known as self-healing.

In 2013, key principles for designing systems in these ways were established in *The Reactive Manifesto* (`https://www.reactivemanifesto.org/`). According to the manifesto, the foundation for reactive systems is that they are message-driven; that is, they use asynchronous communication. This allows them to be elastic, that is, scalable, and resilient, that is, tolerant to failures. Elasticity and resilience together allow a reactive system to be responsive so that it can respond in a timely fashion.

Central configuration

The central configuration pattern has the following problem, solution, and solution requirements.

Problem

An application is, traditionally, deployed together with its configuration, for example, a set of environment variables and/or files containing configuration information. Given a system landscape based on a microservice architecture, that is, with a large number of deployed microservice instances, some queries arise:

- How do I get a complete picture of the configuration that is in place for all the running microservice instances?
- How do I update the configuration and make sure that all the affected microservice instances are updated correctly?

Solution

Add a new component, a **configuration** server, to the system landscape to store the configuration of all the microservices.

Solution requirements

Make it possible to store configuration information for a group of microservices in one place, with different settings for different environments (for example, `dev`, `test`, `qa`, and `prod`).

Centralized log analysis

Centralized log analysis has the following problem, solution, and solution requirements.

Problem

Traditionally, an application writes log events to log files that are stored on the local machine that the application runs on. Given a system landscape based on a microservice architecture, that is, with a large number of deployed microservice instances on a large number of smaller servers, we can ask the following questions:

- How do I get an overview of what is going on in the system landscape when each microservice instance writes to its own local log file?
- How do I find out if any of the microservice instances get into trouble and start writing error messages to their log files?
- If end users start to report problems, how can I find related log messages; that is, how can I identify which microservice instance is the root cause of the problem? The following diagram illustrates the problem:

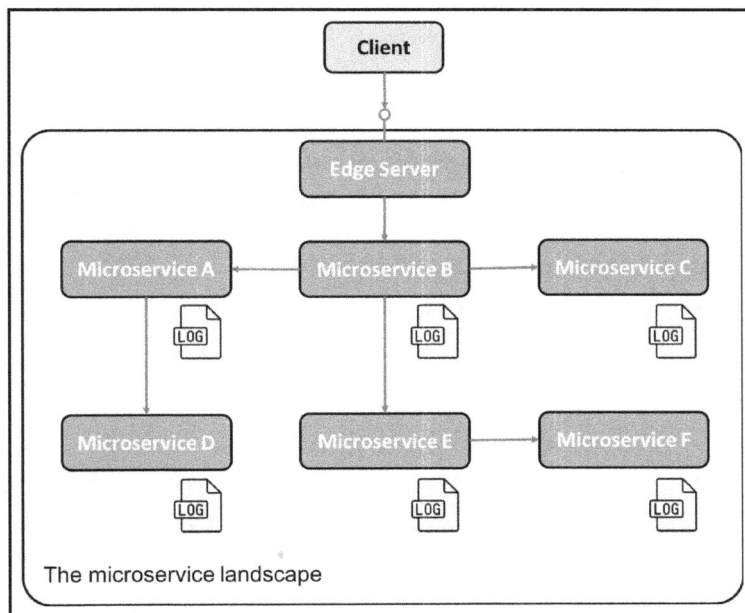

The microservice landscape

Solution

Add a new component that can manage **centralized logging** and is capable of the following:

- Detecting new microservice instances and collecting log events from them
- Interpreting and storing log events in a structured and searchable way in a central database
- Providing APIs and graphical tools for querying and analyzing log events

Distributed tracing

Distributed tracing has the following problem, solution, and solution requirements.

Problem

It must be possible to track requests and messages that flow between microservices while processing an external call to the system landscape.

Some examples of fault scenarios are as follows:

- If end users start to file support cases regarding a specific failure, how can we identify the microservice that caused the problem, that is, the root cause?
- If one support case mentions problems related to a specific entity, for example, a specific order number, how can we find log messages related to processing this specific order – for example, log messages from all microservices that were involved in processing this specific order?

The following diagram depicts this:

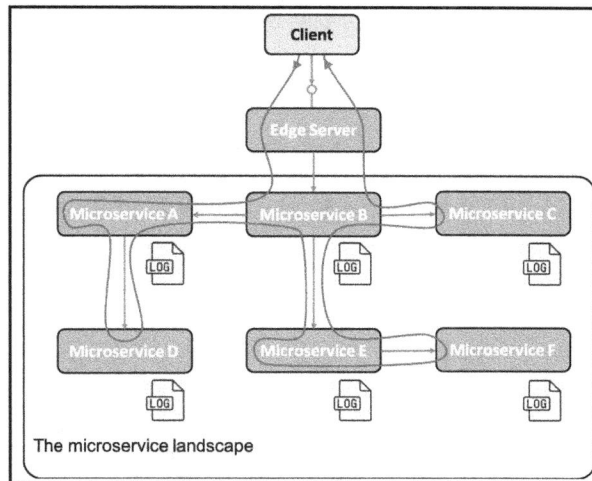

The microservice landscape

Solution

To track the processing between cooperating microservices, we need to ensure that all related requests and messages are marked with a common correlation ID and that the correlation ID is part of all log events. Based on a correlation ID, we can use the centralized logging service to find all related log events. If one of the log events also includes information about a business-related identifier, for example, the ID of a customer, product, order, and so on, we can find all related log events for that business identifier using the correlation ID.

Solution requirements

The solution requirements are as follows:

- Assign unique correlation IDs to all incoming or new requests and events in a well-known place, such as a header with a recognized name.
- When a microservice makes an outgoing request or sends a message, it must add the correlation ID to the request and message.
- All log events must include the correlation ID in a predefined format so that the centralized logging service can extract the correlation ID from the log event and make it searchable.

Circuit Breaker

The Circuit Breaker pattern will have the following problem, solution, and solution requirements.

Problem

A system landscape of microservices that uses synchronous intercommunication can be exposed to a *chain of failure*. If one microservice stops responding, its clients might get into problems as well and stop responding to requests from their clients. The problem can propagate recursively throughout a system landscape and take out major parts of it.

This is especially common in cases where synchronous requests are executed using blocking I/O, that is, blocking a thread from the underlying operating system while a request is being processed. Combined with a large number of concurrent requests and a service that starts to respond unexpectedly slowly, thread pools can quickly become drained, causing the caller to hang and/or crash. This failure can spread unpleasantly fast to the caller's caller, and so on.

Solution

Add a Circuit Breaker that prevents new outgoing requests from a caller if it detects a problem with the service it calls.

Solution requirements

The solution requirements are as follows:

- Open the circuit and fail fast (without waiting for a timeout) if problems with the service are detected.
- Probe for failure correction (also known as a **half-open circuit**); that is, allow a single request to go through on a regular basis to see if the service operates normally again.
- Close the circuit if the probe detects that the service operates normally again. This capability is very important since it makes the system landscape resilient to these kinds of problems; that is, it self-heals.

The following diagram illustrates a scenario where all synchronous communication within the system landscape of microservices goes through Circuit Breakers. All the Circuit Breakers are closed; that is, they allow traffic, except for one Circuit Breaker detected problems in the service the requests go to. Therefore, this Circuit Breaker is open and utilizes fast-fail logic; that is, it does not call the failing service and waits for a timeout to occur. In the following, it immediately returns a response, optionally applying some fallback logic before responding:

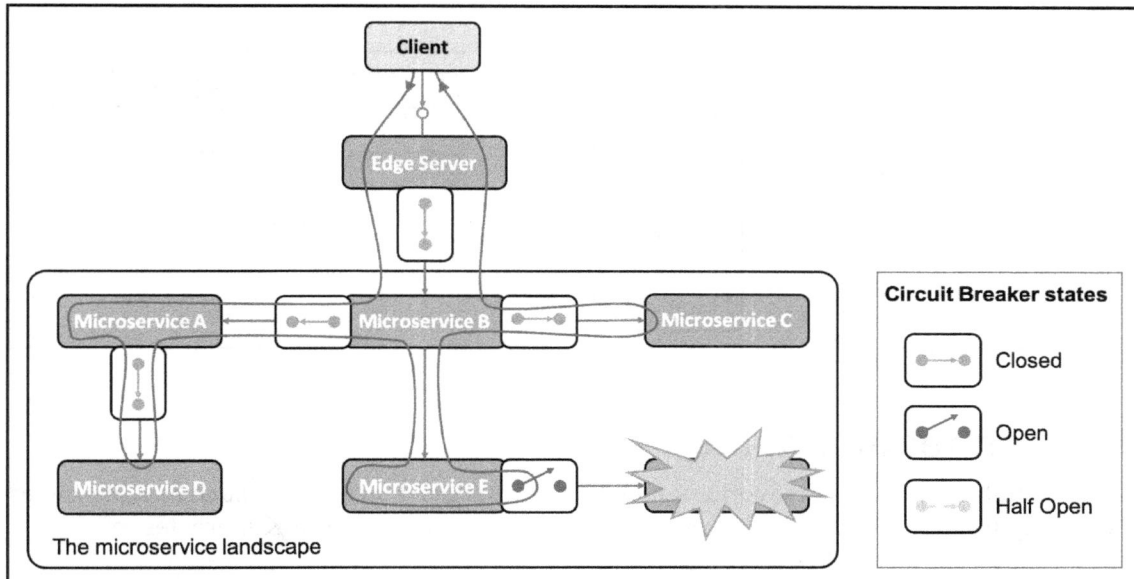

Control loop

The control loop pattern will have the following problem, solution, and solution requirements.

Problem

In a system landscape with a large number of microservice instances spread out over a number of servers, it is very difficult to manually detect and correct problems such as crashed or hung microservice instances.

Solution

Add a new component, a **control loop**, to the system landscape; this constantly observes the actual state of the system landscape; compares it with the desired state, as specified by the operators; and, if required, takes action. For example, if the two states differ, it needs to make the actual state equal to the desired state:

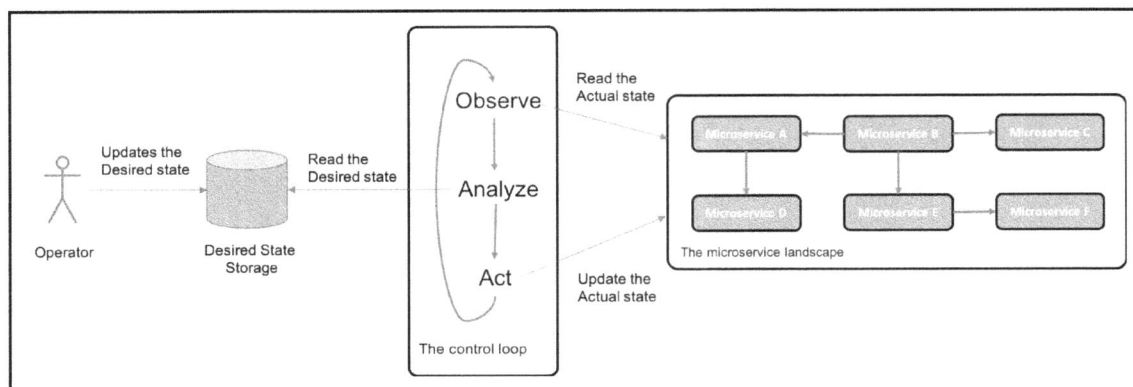

Solution requirements

Implementation notes: In the world of containers, a *container orchestrator* such as Kubernetes is typically used to implement this pattern. We will learn more about Kubernetes in `Chapter 15`, *Introduction to Kubernetes*.

Centralized monitoring and alarms

For this pattern, we will have the following problem, solution, and solution requirements.

Problem

If observed response times and/or the usage of hardware resources become unacceptably high, it can be very hard to discover the root cause of the problem. For example, we need to be able to analyze hardware resource consumption per microservice.

Solution

To curb this, we add a new component, a **monitor service**, to the system landscape, which is capable of collecting metrics about hardware resource usage for each microservice instance level.

Solution requirements

The solution requirements are as follows:

- It must be able to collect metrics from all the servers that are used by the system landscape, which includes auto-scaling servers.
- It must be able to detect new microservice instances as they are launched on the available servers and start to collect metrics from them.
- It must be able to provide APIs and graphical tools for querying and analyzing the collected metrics.

The following screenshot shows Grafana, which visualizes metrics from Prometheus, a monitoring tool that we will look at later in this book:

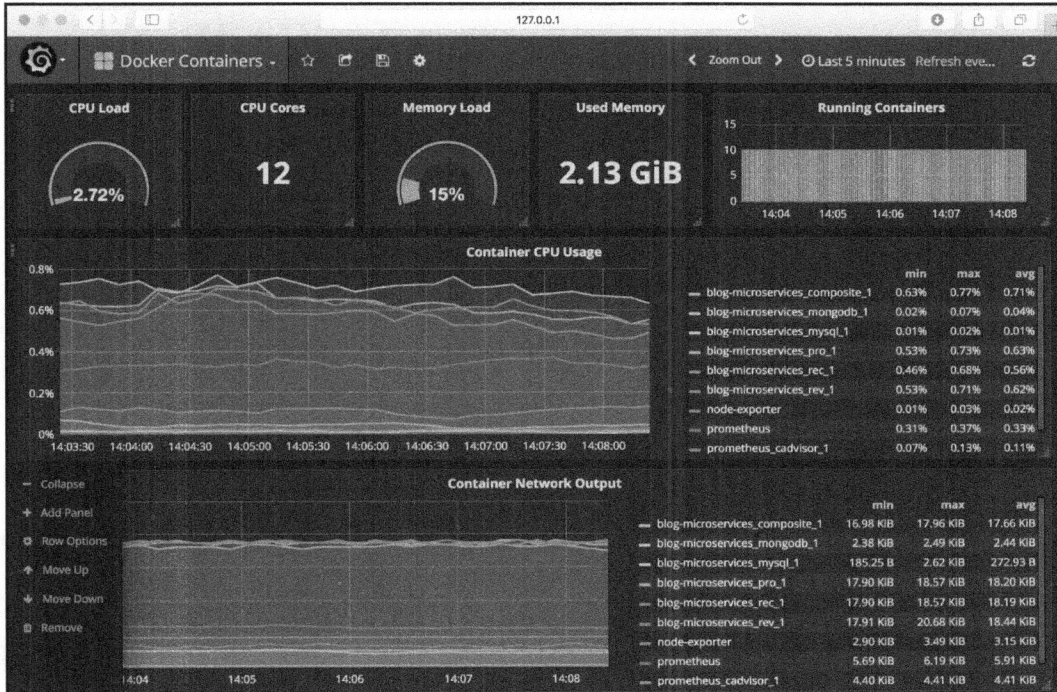

That was an extensive list! I am sure these design patterns helped you understand the challenges with microservices better. Next, we will move on to understand software enablers.

Software enablers

As we've already mentioned, we have a number of very good open-source tools that can help us both meet our expectations of microservices and, most importantly, handle the new challenges that come with them:

- Spring Boot
- Spring Cloud/Netflix OSS
- Docker
- Kubernetes
- Istio (a service mesh)

The following table maps the design patterns we will need to handle these challenges, along with the corresponding open-source tool that implements the design pattern:

Design Pattern	Spring Boot	Spring Cloud	Kubernetes	Istio
Service discovery		Netflix Eureka and Netflix Ribbon	Kubernetes `kube-proxy` and service resources	
Edge server		Spring Cloud and Spring Security OAuth	Kubernetes Ingress controller	Istio ingress gateway
Reactive microservices	Spring Reactor and Spring WebFlux			
Central configuration		Spring Config Server	Kubernetes `ConfigMaps` and Secrets	

			Elasticsearch, Fluentd, and Kibana **Note**: Actually not part of Kubernetes but can easily be deployed and configured together with Kubernetes	
Centralized log analysis			Elasticsearch, Fluentd, and Kibana **Note**: Actually not part of Kubernetes but can easily be deployed and configured together with Kubernetes	
Distributed tracing		Spring Cloud Sleuth and Zipkin		Jaeger
Circuit Breaker		Resilience4j		Outlier detection
Control loop			Kubernetes controller manager	
Centralized monitoring and alarms			Grafana and Prometheus **Note**: Actually not part of Kubernetes but can easily be deployed and configured together with Kubernetes	Kiali, Grafana, and Prometheus

Please note that Spring Cloud, Kubernetes, and Istio can be used to implement some design patterns, such as service discovery, edge server, and central configuration. We will discuss the pros and cons of using these alternatives later in this book.

Now, let's look at some other important things that we need to take into consideration.

Other important considerations

To be successful implementing a microservice architecture, there are a number of related areas to consider as well. I will not cover these areas in this book; instead, I'll just briefly mention them here as follows:

- **Importance of Dev/Ops**: One of the benefits of a microservice architecture is that it enables shorter delivery times and, in extreme cases allows the *continuous delivery* of new versions. To be able to deliver that fast, you need to establish an organization where dev and ops work together under the mantra *you built it, you run it*. This means that developers are no longer allowed to simply pass new versions of the software over to the operations team. Instead, the dev and ops organizations need to work much more closely together, organized into teams that have full responsibility for the end-to-end life cycle of one microservice (or a group of related microservices). Besides the organizational part of `dev/ops`, the teams also need to automate the delivery chain, that is, the steps for building, testing, packaging, and deploying the microservices to the various deployment environments. This is known as setting up a *delivery pipeline*.

- **Organizational aspects and Conway's law**: Another interesting aspect of how a microservice architecture might affect the organization is *Conway's law*, which states the following:

  "Any organization that designs a system (defined broadly) will produce a design whose structure is a copy of the organization's communication structure."

  -- Melvyn Conway, 1967

  This means that the traditional approach of organizing IT teams for large applications based on their technology expertise (for example, UX, business logic, and databases-teams) will lead to a big three-tier application – typically a big monolithic application with a separately deployable unit for the UI, one for processing the business logic, and one for the big database. To successfully deliver an application based on a microservice architecture, the organization needs to be changed into teams that work with one or a group of related microservices. The team must have the skills that are required for those microservices, for example, languages and frameworks for the business logic and database technologies for persisting its data.

- **Decomposing a monolithic application into microservices:** One of the most difficult and expensive decisions is how to decompose a monolithic application into a set of cooperating microservices. If this is done in the wrong way, you will end up with problems such as the following:
    - **Slow delivery**: Changes in the business requirements will affect too many of the microservices, resulting in extra work.
    - **Slow performance**: To be able to perform a specific business function, a lot of requests have to be passed between various microservices, resulting in long response times.
    - **Inconsistent data**: Since related data is separated into different microservices, inconsistencies can appear over time in data that's managed by different microservices.

    A good approach to finding proper boundaries for microservices is to apply **Domain-Driven Design** and its **Bounded Context** concept. According to Eric Evans, a *Bounded Context* is "*A description of a boundary (typically a subsystem, or the work of a particular team) within which a particular model is defined and applicable.*" This means that the microservice defined by a Bounded Context will have a well-defined model of its own data.

- **Importance of API design:** If a group of microservices expose a common, externally available API, it is important that the API is easy to understand and consumes the following:
    - If the same concept is used in multiple APIs, it should have the same description in terms of the naming and data types used.
    - It is of great importance that APIs are allowed to evolve in a controlled manner. This typically requires applying a proper versioning schema for the APIs, for example, `https://semver.org/`, and having the capability of handling multiple major versions of an API over a specific period of time, allowing clients of the API to migrate to new major versions at their own pace.

- **Migration paths from on-premise to the cloud**: Many companies today run their workload on-premise, but are searching for ways to move parts of their workload to the cloud. Since most cloud providers today offer Kubernetes as a Service, an appealing migration approach can be to first move the workload into Kubernetes on-premise (as microservices or not) and then redeploy it on a *Kubernetes as a Service* offering provided by a preferred cloud provider.
- **Good design principles for microservices, the 12-factor app**: The 12-factor app (`https://12factor.net`) is a set of design principles for building software that can be deployed in the cloud. Most of these design principles are applicable to building microservices independently of where and how they will be deployed, that is, in the cloud or on-premise. Some of these principles will be covered in this book, such as config, processes, and logs, but not all.

That's it for the first chapter! I hope this gave you a good basic idea of microservices and helped you understand the large scale topics that will be covered in this book.

Summary

In this introductory chapter, I described my own way into microservices and delved into a bit of their history. We defined what a microservice is, that is, a kind of autonomous distributed component with some specific requirements. We also went through the good and challenging aspects of a microservice-based architecture.

To handle these challenges, we defined a set of design patterns and briefly mapped the capabilities of open source products such as Spring Boot, Spring Cloud, and Kubernetes to them.

You're eager to develop your first microservice now, right? In the next chapter, we will be introduced to Spring Boot and complementary open source tools that we will use to develop our first microservices

Introduction to Spring Boot 2

In this chapter, we will be introduced to how to build a set of cooperating microservices using Spring Boot, focusing on how to develop functionality that delivers business value. The challenges that we pointed out in the previous chapter will be considered only to some degree, but they will be addressed to their full extent in later chapters.

We will develop microservices that contain business logic based on plain Spring Beans and REST APIs using Spring WebFlux, the Swagger/OpenAPI-based documentation of the REST APIs, and SpringFox and data persistence, while using Spring Data to store data in both SQL and NoSQL databases

Since Spring Boot v2.0 was released in March 2018, it has become much easier to develop reactive microservices (refer to `Chapter 1`, *Introduction to Microservices*, the *Reactive microservices* section for more information). Therefore, we will also cover how to create reactive microservices in this chapter, including both non-blocking synchronous REST APIs and message-based asynchronous services. We will use Spring WebFlux to develop non-blocking synchronous REST APIs and Spring Cloud Stream to develop message-based asynchronous services.

Finally, we will use Docker to run our microservices as containers. This will allow us to start and stop our microservice landscape, including database servers and a message broker, with a single command.

That's a lot of technologies and frameworks, so let's go through each of them briefly to see what they are about!

In this chapter, we will cover the following topics:

- Learning about Spring Boot
- Beginning with Spring WebFlux
- Exploring SpringFox

Introduction to Spring Boot

- Understanding Spring Data
- Understanding Spring Cloud Stream
- Learning about Docker

More details about each product will be provided in upcoming chapters.

Technical requirements

This chapter does not contain any source code that can be downloaded, nor does it require any tools to be installed.

Learning about Spring Boot

Spring Boot, and the Spring Framework that Spring Boot is based on, is a great framework for developing microservices in Java.

When the Spring Framework was released in v1.0 back in 2004, it was released in order to fix the overly complex **J2EE** standard (short for **Java 2 Platforms, Enterprise Edition**) with its infamous and heavyweight deployment descriptors. Spring Framework provided a much more lightweight development model based on the concept of **dependency injection** (**DI**). Spring Framework also used far more lightweight XML configuration files compared to the deployment descriptors in J2EE.

To make things even worse with the J2EE standard, the heavyweight deployment descriptors actually came in two types:

- Standard deployment descriptors, describing the configuration in a standardized way
- Vendor-specific deployment descriptors, mapping the configuration to vendor-specific features in the vendor's application server

J2EE was renamed in 2006 to **Java EE**, short for **Java Platform, Enterprise Edition**, and recently, Oracle submitted Jave EE to the Eclipse foundation. In February 2018, Java EE was renamed Jakarta EE.

[42]

Over the years, while the Spring Framework gained increasing popularity, the functionality in the Spring Framework grew significantly. Slowly, the burden of setting up a Spring application using the no-longer-so-lightweight XML configuration file became a problem.

In 2014, Spring Boot v1.0 was released, addressing these problems!

Convention over configuration and fat JAR files

Spring Boot targets the fast development of production-ready Spring applications by being strongly opinionated about how to set up both core modules from the Spring Framework and third-party products, such as libraries that are used for logging or connecting to a database. Spring Boot does that by applying a number of conventions by default, minimizing the need for configuration. Whenever required, each convention can be overridden by writing some configuration, case by case. This design pattern is known as **convention over configuration** and minimizes the need for initial configuration.

> Configuration, when required, is in my opinion written best using Java and annotations. The good old XML-based configuration files can still be used, although they are significantly smaller than before Spring Boot was introduced.

Added to the usage of *convention over configuration*, Spring Boot also favors a runtime model based on a standalone JAR file, also known as a fat JAR file. Before Spring Boot, the most common way to run a Spring application was to deploy it as a WAR file on a Java EE web server, such as Apache Tomcat. WAR file deployment is still supported by Spring Boot.

> A fat JAR file contains not only the classes and resource files of the application itself, but also all the `.jar` files the application depends on. This means that the fat JAR file is the only JAR file required to run the application; that is, we only need to transfer one JAR file to an environment where we want to run the application instead of transferring the application's JAR file along with all the JAR files the application depends on.

Starting a fat JAR requires no separately installed Java EE web server, such as Apache Tomcat. Instead, it can be started with a simple command such as `java -jar app.jar`, making it a perfect choice for running in a Docker container! If the Spring Boot application uses HTTP, for example, to expose a REST API, it will contain an embedded web server.

Code examples for setting up a Spring Boot application

To better understand what this means, let's look at some source code examples.

> We will only look at some small fragments of code here to point out the main features. For a fully working example, you'll have to wait until the next chapter!

The magic @SpringBootApplication annotation

The convention-based autoconfiguration mechanism can be initiated by annotating the application class, that is, the class that contains the static `main` method, with the `@SpringBootApplication` annotation. The following code shows this:

```
@SpringBootApplication
public class MyApplication {

  public static void main(String[] args) {
    SpringApplication.run(MyApplication.class, args);
  }
}
```

The following functionality will be provided by this annotation:

- It enables component scanning, that is, looking for Spring components and configuration classes in the package of the application class and all its sub-packages.
- The application class itself becomes a configuration class.
- It enables autoconfiguration, where Spring Boot looks for JAR files in the classpath that it can configure automatically. If you, for example, have Tomcat in the classpath, Spring Boot will automatically configure Tomcat as an embedded web server.

Component scanning

Let's assume we have the following Spring component in the package of the application class (or in one of its sub-packages):

```
@Component
public class MyComponentImpl implements MyComponent { ...
```

Another component in the application can get the component automatically injected, also known as **auto-wiring**, using the @Autowired annotation:

```
public class AnotherComponent {

  private final MyComponent myComponent;

  @Autowired
  public AnotherComponent(MyComponent myComponent) {
    this.myComponent = myComponent;
  }
}
```

> I prefer using constructor injection (over field and setter injection) to keep the state in my components immutable. The immutable state is important if you want to be able to run the component in a multithreaded runtime environment.

If we want to use components that are declared in a package outside the applications package, for example, a utility component shared by multiple Spring Boot applications, we can complement the @SpringBootApplication annotation in the application class with a @ComponentScan annotation:

```
package se.magnus.myapp;

@SpringBootApplication
@ComponentScan({"se.magnus.myapp","se.magnus.utils"})
public class MyApplication {
```

We can now auto-wire components from the se.magnus.util package in the application code, for example, a utility component, as follows:

```
package se.magnus.utils;

@Component
public class MyUtility { ...
```

This utility component can be auto-wired in an application component like so:

```
package se.magnus.myapp.services;

public class AnotherComponent {

 private final MyUtility myUtility;

 @Autowired
 public AnotherComponent(MyUtility myUtility) {
   this.myUtility = myUtility;
 }
```

Java-based configuration

If we want to override Spring Boot's default configuration or if we want to add our own configuration, we can simply annotate a class with @Configuration and it will be picked up by the component scanning mechanism we described previously.

If we, for example, want to set up a filter in the processing of HTTP requests (handled by Spring WebFlux, which is described as follows) that writes a log message at the beginning and at the end of the processing of the request, we can configure a log-filter, as follows:

```
@Configuration
public class SubscriberApplication {

  @Bean
  public Filter logFilter() {
    CommonsRequestLoggingFilter filter = new
        CommonsRequestLoggingFilter();
    filter.setIncludeQueryString(true);
    filter.setIncludePayload(true);
    filter.setMaxPayloadLength(5120);
    return filter;
  }
```

> We can also place the configuration directly in the application class since the @SpringBootApplication annotation implies the @Configuration annotation.

Now that we have learned about Spring Boot, let's talk about Spring WebFlux.

Beginning with Spring WebFlux

Spring Boot 2.0 is based on Spring Framework 5.0, which came with built-in support for developing reactive applications. Spring Framework uses **Project Reactor** as the base implementation of its reactive support, and also comes with a new web framework, Spring WebFlux, which supports the development of reactive, that is, non-blocking, HTTP clients and services.

Spring WebFlux supports two different programming models:

- An annotation-based imperative style, similar to the already existing web framework, Spring Web MVC, but with support for reactive services
- A new function-oriented model based on routers and handlers

In this book, we will use the annotation-based imperative style to demonstrate how easy it is to move REST services from Spring Web MVC to Spring WebFlux and then start to refactor the services so that they become fully reactive.

Spring WebFlux also provides a fully reactive HTTP client, `WebClient`, as a complement to the existing `RestTemplate` client.

Spring WebFlux supports running on a servlet container (it requires Servlet v3.1 or higher), but also supports reactive non-servlet-based embedded web servers such as Netty (`https:/ /netty.io/`).

Code examples of setting up a REST service using Spring WebFlux

Before we can create a REST service based on Spring WebFlux, we need to add Spring WebFlux (and the dependencies that Spring WebFlux requires) to the classpath for Spring Boot to be detected and configured during startup. Spring Boot provides a large number of convenient *starter dependencies* that bring in a specific feature, together with the dependencies each feature normally requires. So, let's use the starter dependency for Spring WebFlux and then see what a simple REST service looks like!

Starter dependencies

In this book, we will use Gradle as our build tool, so the Spring WebFlux starter dependency will be added to the `build.gradle` file. It looks like this:

```
implementation('org.springframework.boot:spring-boot-starter-webflux')
```

You might be wondering why we don't specify a version number. We will talk about that when we look at a complete example in `Chapter 3`, *Creating a Set of Cooperating Microservices*!

When the microservice is started up, Spring Boot will detect Spring WebFlux on the classpath and configure it, as well as other things that are used to start up an embedded web server. Netty is used by default, which we can see from the log output:

```
2018-09-30 15:23:43.592 INFO 17429 --- [ main]
o.s.b.web.embedded.netty.NettyWebServer : Netty started on port(s): 8080
```

If we want to switch from Netty to Tomcat as our embedded web server, we can override the default configuration by excluding Netty from the starter dependency and add the starter dependency for Tomcat:

```
implementation('org.springframework.boot:spring-boot-starter-webflux')
{
 exclude group: 'org.springframework.boot', module: 'spring-boot-
 starter-reactor-netty'
}
implementation('org.springframework.boot:spring-boot-starter-tomcat')
```

After restarting the microservice, we can see that Spring Boot picked Tomcat instead:

```
2018-09-30 18:23:44.182 INFO 17648 --- [ main]
o.s.b.w.embedded.tomcat.TomcatWebServer : Tomcat initialized with port(s):
8080 (http)
```

Property files

As you can see from the preceding examples, the web server is started up using port `8080`. If you want to change the port, you can override the default value using a property file. Spring Boot application property files can either be a `.properties` file or a YAML file. By default, they are named `application.properties` and `application.yml`, respectively.

In this book, we will use YAML files so that the HTTP port used by the embedded web server can be changed to `7001`. By doing this, we can avoid port collisions with other microservices running on the same server. To do this, add the following line to the `application.yml` file:

```
server.port: 7001
```

Sample RestController

Now, with Spring WebFlux and an embedded web server of our choice in place, we can write a REST service in the same way as when using Spring MVC, that is, as `RestController`:

```
@RestController
public class MyRestService {

  @GetMapping(value = "/my-resource", produces = "application/json")
  List<Resource> listResources() {
    ...
  }
```

The `@GetMapping` annotation on the `listResources()` method will map the Java method to an HTTP `GET` API on the `host:8080/myResource` URL. The return value of the `List<Resource>` type will be converted into JSON.

Now that we've talked about Spring WebFlux, let's see what SpringFox is about.

Exploring SpringFox

One very important aspect of developing APIs, for example, RESTful services, is how to document them so that they are easy to use. When it comes to RESTful services, Swagger is one of the most widely used ways of documenting RESTful services. Many leading API gateways have native support for exposing the documentation of RESTful services using Swagger.

In 2015, SmartBear Software donated the Swagger specification to the Linux Foundation under the OpenAPI Initiative and created the OpenAPI Specification. The name Swagger is still used for the tooling provided by SmartBear Software.

SpringFox is an open-source project, separate from the Spring Framework, that can create Swagger-based API documentation at runtime. It does so by examining the application at startup, for example, inspecting `WebFlux` and Swagger-based annotations.

We will look at full source code examples in upcoming chapters, but for now the following screenshot of this sample API documentation will do:

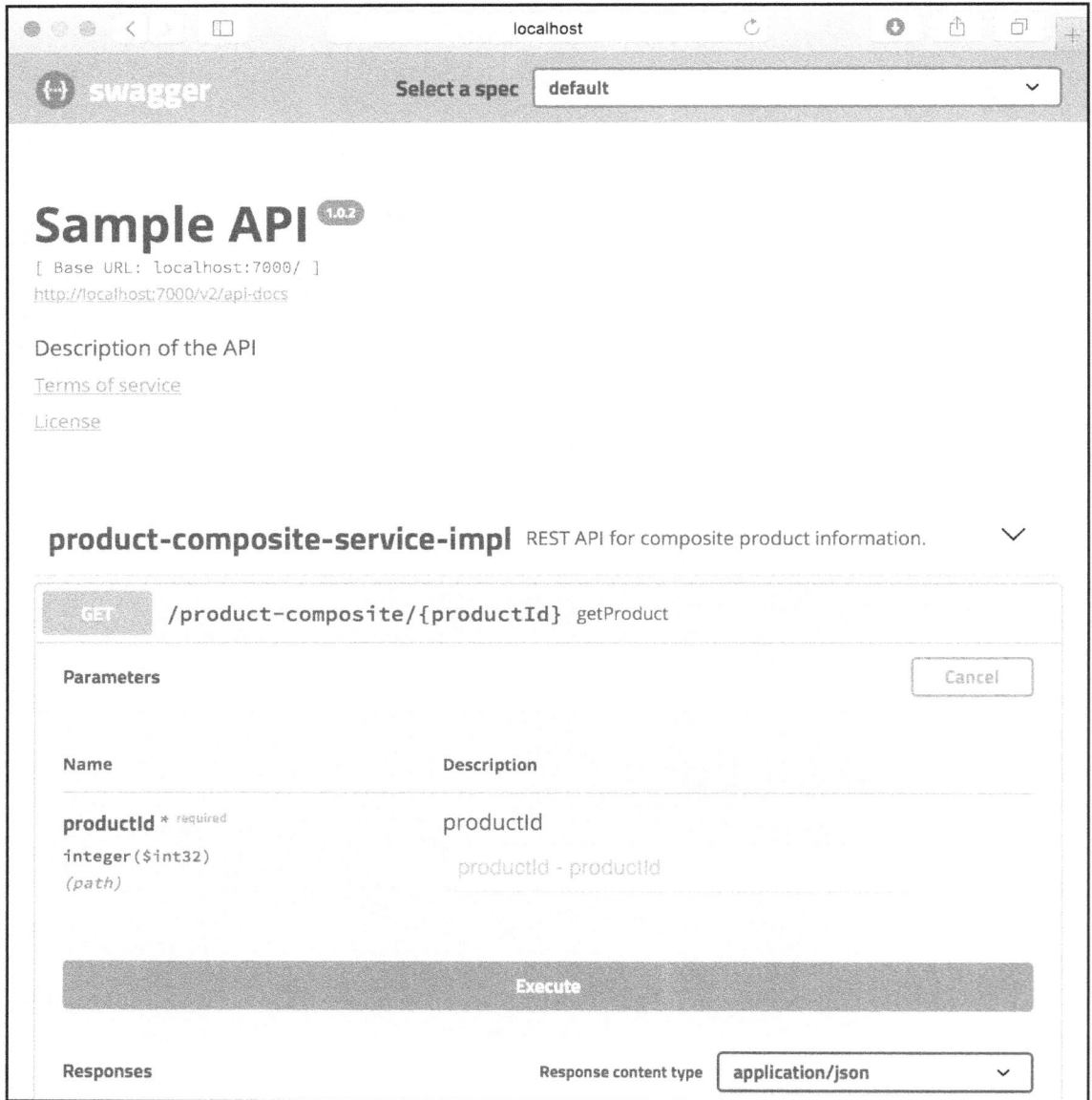

Note the big **Execute** button, which can be used to actually try out the API, not just read its documentation!

SpringFox helped us understand how microservices delved into Spring Framework. Now, let's move on to Spring Data.

Understanding Spring Data

Spring Data comes with a common programming model for persisting data in various types of database engine, ranging from traditional relational databases (SQL databases) to various types of NoSQL database engine, such as document databases (for example, MongoDB), key-value databases (for example, Redis), and graph databases (for example, Neo4J).

The Spring Data project is divided into several subprojects and in this book we will use Spring Data subprojects for MongoDB and JPA that have been mapped to a MySQL database.

JPA stands for **Java Persistence API** and is a Java specification about how to handle relational data. Please go to `https://jcp.org/aboutJava/communityprocess/mrel/jsr338/index.html` for the latest specification, which is JPA 2.2 at the time of writing.

The two core concepts of the programming model in Spring Data are entities and repositories. Entities and repositories generalize how data is stored and accessed from the various types of database. They provide a common abstraction but still support adding database-specific behavior to the entities and repositories. These two core concepts are briefly explained together with some illustrative code examples as we proceed through this chapter. Remember that more details will be provided in the upcoming chapters!

Even though Spring Data provides a common programming model for different types of database, this doesn't mean that you will be able to write portable source code, for example, switching the database technology from a SQL database to a NoSQL database, without changes needing to be made to the source code!

Entity

An entity describes the data that will be stored by Spring Data. Entity classes are, in general, annotated with a mix of generic Spring Data annotations and annotations that are specific to each database technology.

For example, an entity that will be stored in a relational database can be annotated with JPA annotations such as the following:

```
import javax.persistence.Entity;
import javax.persistence.Id;
import javax.persistence.IdClass;
import javax.persistence.Table;

@Entity
@IdClass(ReviewEntityPK.class)
@Table(name = "review")
public class ReviewEntity {
 @Id private int productId;
 @Id private int reviewId;
 private String author;
 private String subject;
 private String content;
```

If an entity is to be stored in a MongoDB database, annotations from the Spring Data MongoDB subproject can be used together with generic Spring Data annotations. For example, consider the following code:

```
import org.springframework.data.annotation.Id;
import org.springframework.data.annotation.Version;
import org.springframework.data.mongodb.core.mapping.Document;

@Document
public class RecommendationEntity {

    @Id
    private String id;

    @Version
    private int version;

    private int productId;
    private int recommendationId;
    private String author;
    private int rate;
    private String content;
```

The @Id and @Version annotations are generic annotations, while the @Document annotation is specific to the Spring Data MongoDB subproject.

> **TIP**
>
> This can be revealed by studying the import statements; that is, the import statements that contain mongodb come from the Spring Data MongoDB subproject.

Repositories

Repositories are used to store and access data from different types of database. In its most basic form, a repository can be declared as a Java interface, and Spring Data will generate its implementation on the fly using opinionated conventions. These conventions can be overridden and/or complemented by additional configuration and, if required, some Java code. Spring Data also comes with some base Java interfaces, for example, CrudRepository, to make the definition of a repository even simpler. The base interface, CrudRepository, provides us with standard methods for create, read, update, and delete operations.

To specify a repository for handling the JPA entity, ReviewEntity, we only need to declare the following:

```
import org.springframework.data.repository.CrudRepository;

public interface ReviewRepository extends CrudRepository<ReviewEntity,
ReviewEntityPK> {
    Collection<ReviewEntity> findByProductId(int productId);
}
```

In this example we use a class, ReviewEntityPK, to describe a composite primary key. It looks as follows:

```
public class ReviewEntityPK implements Serializable {
    public int productId;
    public int reviewId;
}
```

We have also added an extra method, findByProductId, which allows us to look up Review entities based on productId – a field that is part of the primary key. The naming of the method follows a naming convention defined by Spring Data that allows Spring Data to generate the implementation of this method on the fly as well.

If we want to use the repository, we can simply inject it and then start to use it, for example:

```
private final ReviewRepository repository;

@Autowired
public ReviewService(ReviewRepository repository) {
 this.repository = repository;
}

public void someMethod() {
  repository.save(entity);
  repository.delete(entity);
  repository.findByProductId(productId);
```

Also added to the `CrudRepository` interface, Spring Data also provides a reactive base interface, `ReactiveCrudRepository`, which enables reactive repositories. The methods in this interface do not return objects or collections of objects; instead, they return `Mono` and `Flux` objects. `Mono` and `Flux` objects are, as we will see in later chapters, reactive streams that are capable of returning either 0..1 or 0..m entities as they become available on the stream. The reactive-based interface can only be used by Spring Data subprojects that support reactive database drivers; that is, they are based on non-blocking I/O. The Spring Data MongoDB subproject supports reactive repositories, while Spring Data JPA does not.

Specifying a reactive repository for handling the MongoDB entity, `RecommendationEntity`, as described previously, might look something like the following:

```
import org.springframework.data.repository.reactive.ReactiveCrudRepository;
import reactor.core.publisher.Flux;

public interface RecommendationRepository extends
ReactiveCrudRepository<RecommendationEntity, String> {
    Flux<RecommendationEntity> findByProductId(int productId);
}
```

This concludes the section on Spring Data. Now let's see what the Spring Cloud Stream is about.

Understanding Spring Cloud Stream

We will not focus on Spring Cloud in this chapter; we will do that from `Chapter 9`, *Adding Service Discovery Using Netflix Eureka and Ribbon* to `Chapter 14`, *Understanding Distributed Tracing*. However, we will bring in one of the modules that's part of Spring Cloud: Spring Cloud Stream. Spring Cloud Stream provides a streaming abstraction over messaging, based on the publish-and-subscribe integration pattern. Spring Cloud Stream currently comes with support for Apache Kafka and RabbitMQ out of the box. A number of separate projects exist that provide integration with other popular messaging systems. See `https://github.com/spring-cloud?q=binder` for more details.

The core concepts in Spring Cloud Stream are as follows:

- **Message:** A data structure that's used to describe data sent to and received from a messaging system.
- **Publisher:** Sends messages to the messaging system.
- **Subscriber**: Receives messages from the messaging system.
- **Channel:** Used to communicate with the messaging system. Publishers use output channels and subscribers use input channels.
- **Binder:** A binder provides the actual integration with a specific messaging system, similar to what a JDBC driver does for a specific type of database.

The actual messaging system to be used is determined at runtime, depending on what is found on the classpath. Spring Cloud Stream comes with opinionated conventions on how to handle messaging. These conventions can be overridden by specifying a configuration for messaging features such as consumer groups, partitioning, persistence, durability, and error handling, such as retries and dead letter queue handling.

Code examples for sending and receiving messages with Spring Cloud Stream

To better understand how all this fits together, let's look at some source code examples.

Let's assume that we have a simple message class such as the following (constructors, getters, and setters have been left out for improved readability):

```
public class MyMessage {
  private String attribute1 = null;
  private String attribute2 = null;
```

Spring Cloud Stream comes with default input and output channels, `Sink` and `Source`, so we don't need to create our own to get started. To publish a message, we can use the following source code:

```
import org.springframework.cloud.stream.messaging.Source;

@EnableBinding(Source.class)
public class MyPublisher {

 @Autowired private Source mysource;

 public String processMessage(MyMessage message) {
   mysource.output().send(MessageBuilder.withPayload(message).build());
```

To receive messages, we can use the following code:

```
import org.springframework.cloud.stream.messaging.Sink;

@EnableBinding(Sink.class)
public class MySubscriber {

 @StreamListener(target = Sink.INPUT)
 public void receive(MyMessage message) {
 LOG.info("Received: {}",message);
```

To bind to RabbitMQ, we will use a dedicated starter dependency in the build file, `build.gradle`:

```
implementation('org.springframework.cloud:spring-cloud-starter-stream-
rabbit')
```

For the subscriber to receive messages from the publisher, we need to configure the input and output channel to use the same destination. If we use YAML to describe our configuration, it might look like the following for the publisher:

```
spring.cloud.stream:
  default.contentType: application/json
  bindings.output.destination: mydestination
```

The configuration for the subscriber is as follows:

```
spring.cloud.stream:
  default.contentType: application/json
  bindings.input.destination: mydestination
```

We use `default.contentType` to specify that we prefer messages to be serialized in JSON format.

Now that we understand the various Spring APIs, let's understand a concept relatively newer, Docker, in the next section.

Learning about Docker

I assume that Docker and the concept of containers need no in-depth presentation. Docker the concept of containers as a lightweight alternative to virtual machines very popular in 2013. Containers are actually processed in a Linux host that uses Linux **namespaces** to provide between containers of global system resources, such as users, processes, filesystems, and networking. Linux control groups (also known as **cgroups**) are used to limit the amount of CPU and memory that a container is allowed to consume. Compared to a virtual machine that uses a hypervisor to run a complete copy of an operating system in each virtual machine, the overhead in a container is a fraction of the overhead in a virtual machine. This leads to much faster startup times and significantly lower overhead in terms of CPU and memory usage. The isolation that's provided for a container is, however, not considered to be as secure as the isolation that's provided for a virtual machine. With the release of Windows Server 2016, Microsoft supports the use of Docker in Windows servers.

Containers are very useful both during development and testing. Being able to start up a complete system landscape of cooperating microservices and resource managers (for example, database servers, messaging brokers, and so on) with a single command for testing is simply amazing.

For example, we can write scripts in order to automate end-to-end tests of our microservice landscape. A test script can start up the microservice landscape, run tests using the exposed services, and tear down the landscape. This type of automated test script is very useful, both for running locally on a developer PC before pushing code to a source code repository, and to be executed as a step in a delivery pipeline. A build server can run these types of test in its continuous integration and deployment process whenever a developer pushes code to the source repository.

For production usage, we need a container orchestrator such as Kubernetes. We will get back to container orchestrators and Kubernetes later in this book.

For most of the microservices we will look at in this book, a Dockerfile such as the following is all that is required to run the microservice as a Docker container:

```
FROM openjdk:12.0.2

MAINTAINER Magnus Larsson <magnus.larsson.ml@gmail.com>

EXPOSE 8080
ADD ./build/libs/*.jar app.jar
ENTRYPOINT ["java","-jar","/app.jar"]
```

If we want to start and stop many containers with one command, Docker Compose is the perfect tool. Docker Compose uses a YAML file to describe the containers to be managed. For our microservices, it might look something like the following:

```
product:
  build: microservices/product-service

recommendation:
  build: microservices/recommendation-service

review:
  build: microservices/review-service

composite:
  build: microservices/product-composite-service
  ports:
    - "8080:8080"
```

Let me explain the preceding source code a little:

- The `build` directive is used to specify which Dockerfile to use for each microservice. Docker Compose will use it to build a Docker image and then launch a Docker container based on that Docker image.
- The `ports` directive for the composite service is used to expose port `8080` on the server where Docker runs. On a developer's machine, this means that the port of the composite service can be reached simply by using `localhost:8080`!

All the containers in the YAML files can be managed with simple commands such as the following:

- `docker-compose up -d`: Starts all containers. `-d` means that the containers run in the background, not locking the Terminal from where the command was executed.
- `docker-compose down`: Stops and removes all containers.
- `docker-compose logs -f --tail=0`: Prints out log messages from all containers. `-f` means that the command will not complete, and instead waits for new log messages. `--tail=0` means that we don't want to see any previous log messages, only new ones.

This was a brief introduction to Docker. We will go into more detail about Docker in the last few chapters of this book.

Summary

In this chapter, we have been introduced to Spring Boot and complementary open source tools that can be used to build cooperating microservices.

Spring Boot is used to simplify the development of Spring-based, production-ready applications. It is strongly opinionated in terms of how to set up both core modules from the Spring Framework and third-party products.

Spring WebFlux is a new module in the Spring family and is used to develop reactive, that is, non-blocking, REST services. It runs on both lightweight web servers such as Netty and on any Servlet 3.1+ compatible web server. It also supports the programming model from the older Spring MVC module; it is easy to move REST services written for Spring MVC to Spring WebFlux without fully rewriting the code.

SpringFox can be used to create Swagger and OpenAPI-based documentation regarding REST services. It creates the documentation on the fly at runtime by inspecting the annotations for the REST services – both the Spring annotations and some Swagger specific annotations – if used.

Spring Data provides an elegant abstraction for accessing and manipulating persistent data using entities and repositories. The programming model is similar, but isn't portable between different types of database, for example, relational, document, key-value, and graph databases.

Spring Cloud Stream provides a streaming abstraction over messaging, based on the publish and subscribe integration pattern. Spring Cloud Stream comes with out of the box support for Apache Kafka and RabbitMQ but can be extended to support other messaging brokers using custom binders.

Docker makes the concept of containers as a lightweight alternative to virtual machines easy to use. Based on Linux Namespaces and Control Groups, containers provide isolation similar to what traditional virtual machines provide, but with a significantly lower overhead in terms of CPU and memory usage. Docker is a very good tool for development and testing but in most cases requires a container orchestrator such as Kubernetes to be used in a production environment.

Questions

1. What is the purpose of the `@SpringBootApplication` annotation?
2. What are the main differences between the older Spring component for developing REST services, Spring Web MVC, and the new Spring WebFlux?
3. How does SpringFox help a developer document REST APIs?
4. What is the function of a repository in Spring Data and what is the simplest possible implementation of a repository?
5. What is the purpose of a binder in Spring Cloud Stream?
6. What is the purpose of Docker Compose?

Creating a Set of Cooperating Microservices

3

In this chapter, we will build our first couple of microservices. We will learn how to create cooperating microservices with minimalistic functionality. In upcoming chapters, we will add more and more functionality to these microservices. By the end of this chapter, we will have a RESTful API exposed by a composite microservice. The composite microservice will call three other microservices using their RESTful API's to create an aggregated response.

The following topics will be covered in this chapter:

- Introducing the microservice landscape
- Generating skeleton microservices
- Adding RESTful APIs
- Adding a composite microservice
- Adding error handling
- Testing the APIs manually
- Adding automated tests of microservices in isolation
- Adding semi-automated tests to a microservice landscape

Technical requirements

All of the commands that are described in this book are run on a MacBook Pro using macOS Mojave but should be straightforward to modify so that they can be run on another platform such as Linux or Windows.

Tool installation

To be able to execute the commands that are used in this chapter, you need to have the following tools installed on your computer:

- **Git:** Can be downloaded and installed from `https://git-scm.com/downloads`.
- **Java:** Can be downloaded and installed from `https://www.oracle.com/technetwork/java/javase/downloads/index.html`.
- `curl`: This command-line tool for testing HTTP-based APIs can be downloaded and installed from `https://curl.haxx.se/download.html`.
- `jq`: This command-line JSON processor can be downloaded and installed from `https://stedolan.github.io/jq/download/`.
- **Spring Boot CLI**: This command-line tool for Spring Boot applications can be downloaded and installed from `https://docs.spring.io/spring-boot/docs/current/reference/html/getting-started-installing-spring-boot.html#getting-started-installing-the-cli`.

Installing Homebrew

To install these tools on macOS, I recommend that you use Homebrew, `https://brew.sh/`. If you don't have it installed, you can install it with the following command:

```
/usr/bin/ruby -e "$(curl -fsSL
https://raw.githubusercontent.com/Homebrew/install/master/install)"
```

> Installing the command-line tools for Xcode installs Homebrew, so it might take a while if you don't have it installed already.

Verify the installation of Homebrew with the following commands:

```
brew --version
```

Expect a response such as the following:

```
Homebrew 1.7.7
```

Using Homebrew to install Java, curl, jq, and the Spring Boot CLI

On a macOS, `curl` is already preinstalled and `git` was installed as part of the installation of Homebrew. The remaining tools can be installed on a macOS using Homebrew with the following command:

```
brew tap pivotal/tap && \
brew cask install java && \
brew install jq && \
brew install springboot
```

The installation of these tools can be verified by the following commands:

```
git --version
java -version
curl --version
jq --version
spring --version
```

These commands will return something like the following (some extra irrelevant output was removed):

```
6. @b394afed9384:/ (bash)
git version 2.17.1 (Apple Git-112)
openjdk version "11" 2018-09-25
curl 7.54.0 ...
jq-1.5
Spring CLI v2.0.5.RELEASE
```

Using an IDE

I recommend that you work with your Java code using an IDE that supports the development of Spring Boot applications such as Spring Tool Suite or IntelliJ IDEA Ultimate Edition. See the *Testing APIs manually* section to learn how to use the Spring Boot Dashboard. However, you don't need an IDE to be able to follow the instructions in this book.

Accessing the source code

The source code for this chapter can be found in this book's GitHub repository: https://github.com/PacktPublishing/Hands-On-Microservices-with-Spring-Boot-and-Spring-Cloud/tree/master/Chapter03.

To be able to run the commands that are described in this book, download the source code to a folder and set up an environment variable, $BOOK_HOME, that points to that folder. Some sample commands are as follows:

```
export BOOK_HOME=~/Documents/Hands-On-Microservices-with-Spring-Boot-and-
Spring-Cloud
git clone
https://github.com/PacktPublishing/Hands-On-Microservices-with-Spring-Boot-
and-Spring-Cloud $BOOK_HOME
cd $BOOK_HOME/Chapter03
```

The Java source code is written for Java 8 and tested to run on Java 12. To avoid some problems with Spring Boot 2.0 (and Spring 5.0), this chapter uses Spring Boot 2.1.0 RC1 (and Spring 5.1.1), the latest available version of Spring Boot at the time of writing.

The code examples in this chapter all come from the source code in $BOOK_HOME/Chapter03 but are in many cases edited to remove irrelevant parts of the source code, such as comments, imports, and log statements.

With this, we have the required tools installed and the source code for the chapter downloaded. In the next section, we will learn about the system landscape of cooperating microservices that we will create in this chapter.

Introducing the microservice landscape

In Chapter 1, *Introduction to Microservices*, we were briefly introduced to the microservice-based system landscape that we will use throughout this book:

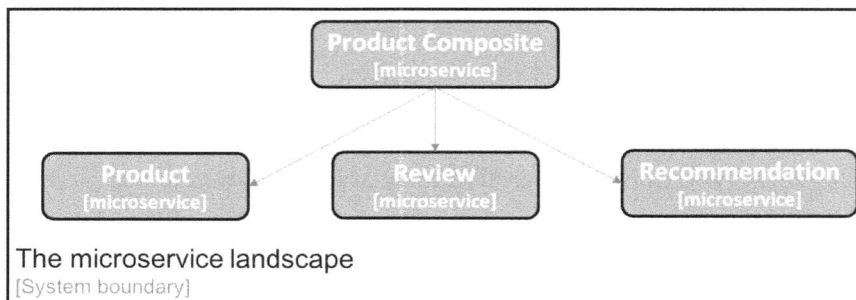

It consists of three core microservices, the **Product**, **Review**, and **Recommendation** services, all of which deal with one type of resource, and a composite microservice called the **Product Composite** service, which aggregates information from the three core services.

Information handled by microservices

To keep the source code examples in this book easy to understand, they have a minimal amount of business logic. The information model for the business objects they process is kept minimal for the same reason. In this section, we will go through the information that's handled by each microservice, plus infrastructure-related information that microservices handle.

Product service

The `product` service manages product information and describes each product with the following attributes:

- Product ID
- Name
- Weight

Review service

The `review` service manages product reviews and stores the following information about each review:

- Product ID
- Review ID
- Author
- Subject
- Content

Recommendation service

The `recommendation` service manages product recommendations and stores the following information about each recommendation:

- Product ID
- Recommendation ID
- Author
- Rate
- Content

Product composite service

The product composite service aggregates information from the three core services and presents information about a product as follows:

- Product information, as described in the `product` service
- A list of product reviews for the specified product, as described in the `review` service
- A list of product recommendations for the specified product, as described in the `recommendation` service

Infrastructure-related information

Once we start to run our microservices as containers that are managed by the infrastructure (first Docker and later on Kubernetes), it will be of interest to track which container actually responded to our requests. To simplify this tracking, we have also added a `serviceAddress` attribute to all our responses, formatted as `hostname/ip-address:port`.

Temporarily replacing a discovery service

Since, at this stage, we don't have any service discovery mechanism in place, we will use hardcoded port numbers for each microservice. We will use the following ports:

- Product composite service: `7000`
- Product service: `7001`
- Review service: `7002`
- Recommendation service: `7003`

> We will get rid of the hardcoded ports later when we start using Docker and Kubernetes!

In this section, we have been introduced to the microservices we are going to create and the information that they will handle. In the next section, we will use Spring Initializr to create skeleton code for the microservices.

Generating skeleton microservices

Now it's time to see how we can create projects for our microservices. The final result for this topic can be found in the $BOOK_HOME/Chapter03/1-spring-init folder. To simplify setting up the projects, we will use Spring Initializr to generate a skeleton project for each microservice. A skeleton project contains the necessary files for building the project, along with an empty main class and test class for the microservice. After that, we will see how we can build all our microservices with one command using multi-project builds in the build tool that we will use, Gradle.

Using Spring Initializr to generate skeleton code

To get started with developing our microservices, we will use a tool called **Spring Initializr** to generate skeleton code for us. It can either be invoked from a web browser using the https://start.spring.io/ URL or by a command-line tool, spring init. To make it easier to reproduce the creation of the microservices, we will use the command-line tool.

For each microservice, we will create a Spring Boot project which does the following:

- Uses Gradle as a build tool
- Generates code for Java 8
- Packages the project as a fat JAR file
- Brings in dependencies for the Actuator and WebFlux Spring modules
- Is based on Spring Boot v2.1.0 RC1 (which depends on Spring Framework v5.1.1)

> Spring Boot Actuator enables a number of valuable endpoints for management and monitoring. We will see them in action later on. Spring WebFlux will be used here to create our RESTful APIs.

To create skeleton code for our microservices, we need to run the following command for product-service:

```
spring init \
--boot-version=2.1.0.RC1 \
--build=gradle \
--java-version=1.8 \
--packaging=jar \
--name=product-service \
--package-name=se.magnus.microservices.core.product \
--groupId=se.magnus.microservices.core.product \
--dependencies=actuator,webflux \
```

```
--version=1.0.0-SNAPSHOT \
product-service
```

> If you want to learn more about the `spring init` CLI, you can run the `spring help init` command. To see what dependencies you can add, run the `spring init --list` command.

If you want to create the four projects on your own instead of using the source code in this book's GitHub repository, try out `$BOOK_HOME/Chapter03/1-spring-init/create-projects.bash`, as follows:

```
mkdir some-temp-folder
cd some-temp-folder
$BOOK_HOME/Chapter03/1-spring-init/create-projects.bash
```

After creating our four projects using `create-projects.bash`, we will have the following file structure:

```
microservices/
├── product-composite-service
├── product-service
├── recommendation-service
└── review-service
```

For each project, we can list the created files. Let's do this for the `product-service` project:

```
find microservices/product-service -type f
```

We will receive the following output:

```
4. bash
$ find microservices/product-service -type f
microservices/product-service/gradle/wrapper/gradle-wrapper.jar
microservices/product-service/gradle/wrapper/gradle-wrapper.properties
microservices/product-service/gradlew
microservices/product-service/.gitignore
microservices/product-service/build.gradle
microservices/product-service/gradlew.bat
microservices/product-service/settings.gradle
microservices/product-service/src/test/java/se/magnus/microservices/core/product/ProductServiceApplicationTests.java
microservices/product-service/src/main/resources/application.properties
microservices/product-service/src/main/java/se/magnus/microservices/core/product/ProductServiceApplication.java
$
```

Spring Initializr created a number of files for Gradle, including a `.gitignore` file and three Spring Boot files:

- `ProductServiceApplication.java`, our main application class
- `application.properties`, an empty property file
- `ProductServiceApplicationTests.java`, a test class that's been configured to run tests on our Spring Boot application using JUnit

The `main` application class, `ProductServiceApplication.java`, looks as we'd expect based on the previous chapter:

```
package se.magnus.microservices.core.product;

@SpringBootApplication
public class ProductServiceApplication {
    public static void main(String[] args) {
        SpringApplication.run(ProductServiceApplication.class, args);
    }
}
```

The test class looks as follows:

```
package se.magnus.microservices.core.product;

@RunWith(SpringRunner.class)
@SpringBootTest
public class ProductServiceApplicationTests {
    @Test
    public void contextLoads() {
    }
}
```

The `@RunWith(SpringRunner.class)` and `@SpringBootTest` annotations will initialize our application in the same way as `@SpringBootApplication` does when running the application; that is, the Spring application context will be set up before the tests are executed using component scanning and auto-configuration, as described in the previous chapter.

Let's also look at the most important Gradle file, `build.gradle`. The content of this file describes how to build the project, for example, compile, test, and package the source code. The Gradle file starts by setting up the conditions for the rest of the build file by declaring the `buildscript` element and listing what plugins to apply:

```
buildscript {
   ext {
```

```
        springBootVersion = '2.1.0.RC1'
    }
    repositories {
      mavenCentral()
      maven { url "https://repo.spring.io/snapshot" }
      maven { url "https://repo.spring.io/milestone" }
    }
    dependencies {
      classpath("org.springframework.boot:spring-boot-gradle-
      plugin:${springBootVersion}")
    }
}

apply plugin: 'java'
apply plugin: 'eclipse'
apply plugin: 'org.springframework.boot'
apply plugin: 'io.spring.dependency-management'
```

Let's explain the preceding source code in more detail:

- The Spring Boot version is set to what we specified when we ran the `spring init` command, `2.1.0.RC1`.
- A number of Gradle plugins are declared. The most important ones are the `org.springframework.boot` and `io.spring.dependency-management` plugins, which together ensure that Gradle will build a fat JAR file and that we don't need to specify any explicit version numbers on our Spring Boot starter dependencies. Instead, they are implied by the `springBootVersion` property.
- Plugins are fetched from the central Maven repository and from Spring's snapshot and milestone repositories since we have specified a release candidate of Spring Boot, v2.1.0 RC1, and not a version that's been released and is available in the central Maven repository.

In the rest of the build file, we basically declare a group name and version for our project, Java version, and its dependencies:

```
group = 'se.magnus.microservices.core.product'
version = '1.0.0-SNAPSHOT'
sourceCompatibility = 1.8

repositories {
  mavenCentral()
  maven { url "https://repo.spring.io/snapshot" }
  maven { url "https://repo.spring.io/milestone" }
}
```

```
dependencies {
  implementation('org.springframework.boot:spring-boot-starter-
  actuator')
  implementation('org.springframework.boot:spring-boot-starter-
  webflux')
  testImplementation('org.springframework.boot:spring-boot-starter-
  test')
  testImplementation('io.projectreactor:reactor-test')
}
```

Let's explain the preceding source code in more detail as follows:

- Dependencies are, as with the preceding plugins, fetched from the central Maven repository and from Spring's snapshot and milestone repositories.
- Dependencies are set up as specified in the Actuator and WebFlux modules, along with a couple of useful test dependencies.

We can build each microservice separately with the following command:

```
cd microservices/product-composite-service;   ./gradlew build; cd -; \
cd microservices/product-service;              ./gradlew build; cd -; \
cd microservices/recommendation-service;       ./gradlew build; cd -; \
cd microservices/review-service;               ./gradlew build; cd -;
```

> Note how we use the gradlew executables that are created by Spring Initializr; that is, we don't need to have Gradle installed!
>
> The first time we run a command with gradlew, it will download Gradle automatically. The Gradle version that's used is determined by the distributionUrl property in the gradle/wrapper/gradle-wrapper.properties file.

Setting up multi-project builds in Gradle

To make it a bit simpler to build all the microservices with one command, we can set up a multi-project build in Gradle. The steps are as follows:

1. First, we create the settings.gradle file, which describes what projects that Gradle should build:

```
cat <<EOF > settings.gradle
include ':microservices:product-service'
include ':microservices:review-service'
```

```
include ':microservices:recommendation-service'
include ':microservices:product-composite-service'
EOF
```

2. Next, we copy the Gradle executable files that were generated from one of the projects so that we can reuse them for the multi-project builds:

```
cp -r microservices/product-service/gradle .
cp microservices/product-service/gradlew .
cp microservices/product-service/gradlew.bat .
cp microservices/product-service/.gitignore .
```

3. We no longer need the generated Gradle executable files in each project, so we can remove them with the following commands:

```
find microservices -depth -name "gradle" -exec rm -rfv "{}" \;
find microservices -depth -name "gradlew*" -exec rm -fv "{}" \;
```

The result should be similar to the code you can find in the folder $BOOK_HOME/Chapter03/1-spring-init.

4. Now, we can build all the microservices with one command:

```
./gradlew build
```

If you haven't run the preceding commands, you can simply go to the book's source code and build it from there:

```
cd $BOOK_HOME/Chapter03/1-spring-init
```

```
./gradlew build
```

5. This should result in the following output:

With skeleton projects for the microservices created using Spring Initializr and successfully built using Gradle, we are ready to add some code to the microservices in the next section.

> From a DevOps perspective, a multi-project setup might not be preferred. Instead, setting up a separate build pipeline for each microservice project would probably be preferred. However, for the purposes of this book, we will use the multi-project setup to make it easier to build and deploy the whole system landscape with a single command.

Adding RESTful APIs

Now that we have projects set up for our microservices, let's add some RESTful APIs to our three core microservices!

The final result of this and the remaining topics in this chapter can be found in the `$BOOK_HOME/Chapter03/2-basic-rest-services` folder.

First, we will add two projects (`api` and `util`) that will contain code that is shared by the microservice projects, and then we will implement the RESTful APIs.

Adding an API and a util project

To add an API, we need to do the following:

1. First, we will set up a separate Gradle project where we can place our API definitions. We will use Java interfaces in order to describe our RESTful APIs and model classes to describe the data that the API uses in its requests and responses. Describing a RESTful API in a Java interface instead of directly in the Java class is, to me, a good way of separating the API definition from its implementation. We will further extend this pattern later in this book when we add more API information in the Java interfaces to be exposed in the Swagger/OpenAPI definition. See `Chapter 5`, *Adding an API Description Using OpenAPI/Swagger*, for more information.

Describing RESTful APIs in Java interfaces wasn't fully supported until Spring Framework v5.1.0. See `https://jira.spring.io/browse/SPR-11055` for details.

It is debatable whether it is good practice to store API definitions for a group of microservices in a common API module. To me, it is a good choice for microservices that are part of the same delivery organization, that is, whose releases are governed by one and the same organization (compare to a *Bounded Context* in *Domain-Driven Design*, where our microservices are placed in one and the same bounded context).

2. Next, we will create a `util` project that can hold some helper classes that are shared by our microservices, for example, for handling errors in a uniform way.

Again, from a DevOps perspective, it would be preferable to build all the projects in their own build pipeline and have version-controlled dependencies for the `api` and `util` projects in the microservice projects; that is, so that each microservice can choose what versions of the `api` and `util` projects to use. But to keep the build and deployment steps simple in the context of this book, we will make the `api` and `util` projects part of the multi-project build.

The api project

The `api` project will be packaged as a library; that is, it won't have its own `main` application class. Unfortunately, Spring Initializr doesn't support the creation of library projects. Instead, a library project has to be created manually from scratch. The source code for the API project is available at `$BOOK_HOME/Chapter03/2-basic-rest-services/api`.

The structure of a library project is the same as for an application project, except that we no longer have the `main` application class, as well as some minor differences in the `build.gradle` file. The Gradle `org.springframework.boot` and `io.spring.dependency-management` plugins are replaced with a `dependencyManagement` section:

```
plugins {
    id "io.spring.dependency-management" version "1.0.5.RELEASE"
}

dependencyManagement {
  imports { mavenBom("org.springframework.boot:spring-boot-
  dependencies:${springBootVersion}") }
}
```

This allows us to retain Spring Boot dependency management while we are replacing the construction of a fat JAR in the build step with the creation of normal JAR files; that is, they only contain the library project's own class and property files.

The Java files in the api project for our three core microservices are as follows:

```
$BOOK_HOME/Chapter03/2-basic-rest-
services/api/src/main/java/se/magnus/api/core
├── product
│   ├── Product.java
│   └── ProductService.java
├── recommendation
│   ├── Recommendation.java
│   └── RecommendationService.java
└── review
    ├── Review.java
    └── ReviewService.java
```

The structure of the Java classes looks very similar for the three core microservices, so we will only go through the source code for the product service.

First, we will look at the ProductService.java Java interface, as shown in the following code:

```
package se.magnus.api.core.product;

public interface ProductService {
    @GetMapping(
        value    = "/product/{productId}",
        produces = "application/json")
      Product getProduct(@PathVariable int productId);
}
```

Let's explain the preceding source code in more detail:

- The product service only exposes one API method, getProduct() (we will extend the API later in this book).
- To map the method to an HTTP GET request, we use the @GetMapping Spring annotation, where we specify what URL path the method will be mapped to (/product/{productId}) and what format the response will be, in this case, JSON.

- The `{productId}` part of the path maps to a `path` variable named `productId`.
- The `productId` method parameter is annotated with `@PathVariable`, which will map the value that's passed in the HTTP request to the parameter. For example, an HTTP `GET` request to `/product/123` will result in the `getProduct()` method being called with the `productId` parameter set to `123`.

The method returns a `Product` object, a plain POJO-based model class with the member variables corresponding to attributes for `Product`, as described at the start of this chapter. `Product.java` looks as follows (with constructors and getter methods excluded):

```
public class Product {
  private final int productId;
  private final String name;
  private final int weight;
  private final String serviceAddress;
}
```

> This type of POJO class is also known as a **Data Transfer Object** (DTO) as it is used to transfer data between the API implementation and the caller of the API. When we get to Chapter 6, *Adding Persistence*, we will look at another type of POJO that can be used to describe how data is stored in the databases, also known as entity objects.

The util project

The `util` project will be packaged as a library in the same way as the `api` project. The source code for the `util` project is available at `$BOOK_HOME/Chapter03/2-basic-rest-services/util`. The project contains the following Java files:

- The `InvalidInputException` and `NotFoundException` exception classes
- The `GlobalControllerExceptionHandler`, `HttpErrorInfo`, and `ServiceUtil` utility classes

Except for the code in `ServiceUtil.java`, these classes are reusable utility classes that we can use to map Java exceptions to proper HTTP status codes, as described in the *Adding error handling* section. The main purpose of `ServiceUtil.java` is to find out the hostname, IP address, and port used by the microservice. The class exposes a method, `getServiceAddress()`, that can be used by the microservices to find their hostname, IP address, and port.

Implementing our API

Now we can start to implement our APIs in the core microservices!

The implementation looks very similar for the three core microservices, so we will only go through the source code for the `product` service. You can find the other files in `$BOOK_HOME/Chapter03/2-basic-rest-services/microservices`. Let's see how we go about this:

1. We need to add the `api` and `util` projects as dependencies in our `build.gradle` file, that is, `$BOOK_HOME/Chapter03/2-basic-rest-services/microservices/product-service/build.gradle`:

   ```
   dependencies {
       implementation project(':api')
       implementation project(':util')
   ```

2. To enable Spring Boot's autoconfiguration feature to detect Spring beans in the `api` and `util` projects, we also need to add a `@ComponentScan` annotation to the `main` application class, which includes the packages of the `api` and `util` projects:

   ```
   @SpringBootApplication
   @ComponentScan("se.magnus")
   public class ProductServiceApplication {
   ```

3. Next, we create our service implementation file, `ProductServiceImpl.java`, in order to implement the Java interface, `ProductService`, from the `api` project and annotate the class with `@RestController` so that Spring will call the methods in this class according to the mappings specified in the `Interface` class:

   ```
   package se.magnus.microservices.core.product.services;

   @RestController
   public class ProductServiceImpl implements ProductService {
   }
   ```

4. To be able to use the `ServiceUtil` class from the `util` project, we will inject it into the constructor, as follows:

   ```
   private final ServiceUtil serviceUtil;

   @Autowired
   public ProductServiceImpl(ServiceUtil serviceUtil) {
   ```

```
this.serviceUtil = serviceUtil;
}
```

5. Now, we can implement the API by overriding the `getProduct()` method from the interface in the `api` project:

```
@Override
public Product getProduct(int productId) {
  return new Product(productId, "name-" + productId, 123,
  serviceUtil.getServiceAddress());
}
```

Since we aren't currently using a database, we simply return a hardcoded response based on the input of `productId`, along with the service address supplied by the `ServiceUtil` class.

For the final result, including logging and error handling, see `$BOOK_HOME/Chapter03/2-basic-rest-services/microservices/product-service/src/main/java/se/magnus/microservices/core/product/services/ProductServiceImpl.java`.

6. Finally, we also need to set up some runtime properties – what port to use and the desired level of logging. This is added to the `$BOOK_HOME/Chapter03/2-basic-rest-services/microservices/product-service/src/main/resources/application.yml` property file:

```
server.port: 7001

logging:
  level:
    root: INFO
    se.magnus.microservices: DEBUG
```

7. We can try out the `product` service on its own. Build and start the microservice with the following commands:

```
cd $BOOK_HOME/Chapter03/2-basic-rest-services
./gradlew build
java -jar microservices/product-service/build/libs/*.jar &
```

8. Wait until the following is printed in the Terminal:

```
                                             4. bash
$ java -jar microservices/product-service/build/libs/*.jar &

     .   __ _ _          _ __          __  _ _ _ \ \ \ \
  ( ( )\__ | '_ | '_| | '_ \/ _` | \ \ \ \
   \\/  __)| |_)| | | | | | (_| |  ) ) ) )
    '  |____| .__|_| |_|_| |_\__, | / / / /
   ======|_|============|___/=/_/_/_/
   :: Spring Boot ::          (v2.1.0.RC1)

...Started ProductServiceApplication in 2.339 seconds (JVM running for 2.771)
```

9. Make a test call to the product service:

   curl http://localhost:7001/product/123

10. It should respond with something similar to the following:

```
                                             4. bash
$ curl http://localhost:7001/product/123
{"productId":123,"name":"name-123","weight":123,"serviceAddress":"Magnus-MBP32.local/192.168.1.185:7001"}
$
```

11. Finally, stop the product service:

   kill $(jobs -p)

We have now built, run, and tested our first single microservice. In the next section, we will implement the composite microservice that will use the three core microservices that we've created so far.

Adding a composite microservice

Now, it's time to tie things together by adding the composite service that will call the three core services!

The implementation of the composite services is divided into two parts: an integration component that handles the outgoing HTTP requests to the core services and the composite service implementation itself. The main reason for this division of responsibility is that it simplifies automated unit and integration testing; that is, we can test the service implementation in isolation by replacing the integration component with a mock.

As we will see later on in this book, this division of responsibility will also make it easier to introduce a Circuit Breaker!

Before we look into the source code of the two components, we need to take a look at the API classes that the composite microservices will use and also learn about how runtime properties are used to hold address information for the core microservices.

The full implementation of both the integration component and the implementation of the composite service can be found in the `$BOOK_HOME/Chapter03/2-basic-rest-services/microservices/product-composite-service/src/main/java/se/magnus/microservices/composite/product/services` folder.

API classes

In this section, we will take a look at the classes that describes the API of the composite component. They can be found in `$BOOK_HOME/Chapter03/2-basic-rest-services/api`. The following are the API classes:

```
$BOOK_HOME/Chapter03/2-basic-rest-services/api
└── src/main/java/se/magnus/api/composite
    └── product
        ├── ProductAggregate.java
        ├── ProductCompositeService.java
        ├── RecommendationSummary.java
        ├── ReviewSummary.java
        └── ServiceAddresses.java
```

The Java interface class, `ProductCompositeService.java`, follows the same pattern that's used by the core services and looks as follows:

```java
package se.magnus.api.composite.product;

public interface ProductCompositeService {
    @GetMapping(
        value    = "/product-composite/{productId}",
        produces = "application/json")
    ProductAggregate getProduct(@PathVariable int productId);
}
```

The model class, `ProductAggregate.java`, is a bit more complex than the core models since it contains fields for lists of recommendations and reviews:

```
package se.magnus.api.composite.product;

public class ProductAggregate {
    private final int productId;
    private final String name;
    private final int weight;
    private final List<RecommendationSummary> recommendations;
    private final List<ReviewSummary> reviews;
    private final ServiceAddresses serviceAddresses;
```

Properties

To avoid hardcoding the address information for the core services into the source code of the composite microservice, the latter uses a property file where information on how to find the core services is stored. The property file can be found in `$BOOK_HOME/Chapter03/2-basic-rest-services/microservices/product-composite-service/src/main/resources/application.yml` and looks as follows:

```
server.port: 7000

app:
  product-service:
    host: localhost
    port: 7001
  recommendation-service:
    host: localhost
    port: 7002
  review-service:
    host: localhost
    port: 7003
```

This configuration will, as already noted, be replaced by a service discovery mechanism later on in this book.

Integration component

Let's look at the integration component, `ProductCompositeIntegration.java`. It is declared as a Spring Bean using the `@Component` annotation and implements the three core services' API interfaces:

```
package se.magnus.microservices.composite.product.services;

@Component
public class ProductCompositeIntegration implements ProductService,
RecommendationService, ReviewService {
```

The integration component uses a helper class in Spring Framework, `RestTemplate.java`, to perform the actual HTTP requests to the core microservices. Before we can inject it into the integration component, we need to configure it. We do that in the `main` application class, `ProductCompositeServiceApplication.java`, as follows:

```
@Bean
RestTemplate restTemplate() {
    return new RestTemplate();
}
```

`RestTemplate` is highly configurable, but we leave it with its default values for now.

We can now inject `RestTemplate`, along with a JSON mapper that's used for error handling and the configuration values that we set up in the property file in the constructor of the integration component. Let's see how this is done:

1. The configuration values we use to set up the URLs for the three core services are injected into the constructor as follows:

```
private final RestTemplate restTemplate;
private final ObjectMapper mapper;

private final String productServiceUrl;
private final String recommendationServiceUrl;
private final String reviewServiceUrl;

@Autowired
public ProductCompositeIntegration(
  RestTemplate restTemplate,
  ObjectMapper mapper,

  @Value("${app.product-service.host}") String productServiceHost,
  @Value("${app.product-service.port}") int productServicePort,
```

```
@Value("${app.recommendation-service.host}") String
recommendationServiceHost,
@Value("${app.recommendation-service.port}") int
recommendationServicePort,

@Value("${app.review-service.host}") String reviewServiceHost,
@Value("${app.review-service.port}") int reviewServicePort
)
```

The body of the constructor builds the URLs based on the injected values, as follows:

```
{
  this.restTemplate = restTemplate;
  this.mapper = mapper;

  productServiceUrl = "http://" + productServiceHost + ":" +
  productServicePort + "/product/";
  recommendationServiceUrl = "http://" + recommendationServiceHost
  + ":" + recommendationServicePort + "/recommendation?
  productId="; reviewServiceUrl = "http://" + reviewServiceHost +
  ":" + reviewServicePort + "/review?productId=";
}
```

2. Finally, the integration component implements the API methods for the three core services by using `RestTemplate` to make the actual outgoing calls:

```
public Product getProduct(int productId) {
 String url = productServiceUrl + productId;
 Product product = restTemplate.getForObject(url, Product.class);
 return product;
}

public List<Recommendation> getRecommendations(int productId) {
    String url = recommendationServiceUrl + productId;
    List<Recommendation> recommendations =
    restTemplate.exchange(url, GET, null, new
    ParameterizedTypeReference<List<Recommendation>>()
    {}).getBody();
    return recommendations;
}

public List<Review> getReviews(int productId) {
    String url = reviewServiceUrl + productId;
    List<Review> reviews = restTemplate.exchange(url, GET, null,
    new ParameterizedTypeReference<List<Review>>() {}).getBody();
    return reviews;
}
```

Let's explain the preceding source code in more detail:

- For the `getProduct()` implementation, the `getForObject()` method can be used in `RestTemplate`. The expected response is a `Product` object, and it can be expressed in the call to `getForObject()` by specifying the `Product.class` class that `RestTemplate` will map the JSON response to.
- For the calls to `getRecommendations()` and `getReviews()`, a more advanced method, `exchange()`, has to be used. The reason for this is the automatic mapping from a JSON response to a model class that `RestTemplate` performs.
- The `getRecommendations()` and `getReviews()` methods expect a generic list in the responses, that is, `List<Recommendation>` and `List<Review>`. Since generics don't hold any type of information at runtime, we can't specify that the methods expect a generic list in their responses. Instead, we can use a helper class from the Spring Framework, `ParameterizedTypeReference`, that is designed to resolve this problem by holding the type information at runtime. This means that `RestTemplate` can figure out what class to map the JSON responses to. To utilize this helper class, we have to use the more involved `exchange()` method instead of the simpler `getForObject()` method on `RestTemplate`.

Composite API implementation

Finally, we will look at the last piece of the implementation of the composite microservice: the `ProductCompositeServiceImpl.java.` implementation class. Let's go through it step-by-step:

1. In the same way that we did for the core services, the composite service implements its API interface, `ProductCompositeService`, and is annotated with `@RestController` to mark it as a REST service:

```
package se.magnus.microservices.composite.product.services;

@RestController
public class ProductCompositeServiceImpl implements
ProductCompositeService {
```

2. The implementation class requires the `ServiceUtil` bean and its own integration component, so they are injected in its constructor:

```
private final ServiceUtil serviceUtil;
private  ProductCompositeIntegration integration;

@Autowired
public ProductCompositeServiceImpl(ServiceUtil serviceUtil,
ProductCompositeIntegration integration) {
    this.serviceUtil = serviceUtil;
    this.integration = integration;
}
```

3. Finally, the API method is implemented as follows:

```
@Override
public ProductAggregate getProduct(int productId) {
    Product product = integration.getProduct(productId);
    List<Recommendation> recommendations =
    integration.getRecommendations(productId);
    List<Review> reviews = integration.getReviews(productId);
    return createProductAggregate(product, recommendations,
    reviews, serviceUtil.getServiceAddress());
}
```

The integration component is used to call the three core services, and a helper method, `createProductAggregate()`, is used to create a response object of the `ProductAggregate` type based on the responses from the calls to the integration component.

The implementation of the helper method, `createProductAggregate()`, is quite lengthy and not very important and so has been omitted from this chapter; however, it can be found in this book's source code.

The full implementation of both the integration component and the composite service can be found in the `$BOOK_HOME/Chapter03/2-basic-rest-services/microservices/product-composite-service/src/main/java/se/magnus/microservices/composite/product/services` folder.

That completes the implementation of the composite microservice from a functional point of view. In the next section, we will see how we can add source code so that we can handle errors.

Adding error handling

Handling errors in a structured and well thought-out way is essential in a microservice landscape where a large number of microservices communicate with each other using synchronous APIs, for example, using HTTP and JSON. It is also important to separate protocol-specific handling of errors, such as HTTP status codes, from the business logic.

> It could be argued that a separate layer for the business logic should be added when implementing of the microservices. This should ensure that business logic is separated from the protocol-specific code, making it easier both to test and reuse. To avoid unnecessary complexity in the examples provided in this book, we have left out a separate layer for business logic, that is, the microservices implement their business logic directly in the @RestController components.

I have created a set of Java exceptions in the util project that are used by both the API implementations and the API clients, initially InvalidInputException and NotFoundException. See $BOOK_HOME/Chapter03/2-basic-rest-services/util/src/main/java/se/magnus/util/exceptions for details.

The global REST controller exception handler

To separate protocol-specific error handling from the business logic in the REST controllers, that is, the API implementations, I have created a utility class, GlobalControllerExceptionHandler.java, in the util project that's annotated as @RestControllerAdvice.

For each Java exception that the API implementations throws, the utility class has an exception handler method that maps the Java exception to a proper HTTP response, that is, with a proper HTTP status and HTTP response body.

For example, if an API implementation class throws InvalidInputException, the utility class will map it to an HTTP response with the status code set to 422 (UNPROCESSABLE_ENTITY). The following code shows this:

```
@ResponseStatus(UNPROCESSABLE_ENTITY)
@ExceptionHandler(InvalidInputException.class)
public @ResponseBody HttpErrorInfo
handleInvalidInputException(ServerHttpRequest request, Exception ex) {
    return createHttpErrorInfo(UNPROCESSABLE_ENTITY, request, ex);
}
```

In the same way, `NotFoundException` is mapped to a `404` (`NOT_FOUND`) HTTP status code.

Whenever a REST controller throws any of these exceptions, Spring will use the utility class to create an HTTP response.

> Note that Spring itself returns the HTTP status code `400` (`BAD_REQUEST`) when it detects an invalid request, for example, if the request contains a non-numeric product ID (`productId` is specified as an integer in the API declaration).

For the full source code of the utility class, see `$BOOK_HOME/Chapter03/2-basic-rest-services/util/src/main/java/se/magnus/util/http/GlobalControllerExceptionHandler.java`.

Error-handling in API implementations

API implementations use the exceptions in the `util` project to signal errors. They will be reported back to the REST client as HTTPS status codes indicating what went wrong. For example, the `Product` microservice implementation class, `ProductServiceImpl.java`, uses the `InvalidInputException` exception to return an error that indicates invalid input, as well as the `NotFoundException` exception to tell us that the product that was asked for does not exist. The code looks as follows:

```
if (productId < 1) throw new InvalidInputException("Invalid productId:
    " + productId);
if (productId == 13) throw new NotFoundException("No product found for
    productId: " + productId);
```

> Since we currently aren't using a database, we have to simulate when to throw `NotFoundException`.

Error-handling in the API client

The API client, that is, the integration component of the `Composite` microservice, does the reverse; that is, it maps the `422` (`UNPROCESSABLE_ENTITY`) HTTP status code to `InvalidInputException` and the `404` (`NOT_FOUND`) HTTP status code to `NotFoundException`. See the `getProduct()` method in `ProductCompositeIntegration.java` for the implementation of this error handling logic. The source code looks as follows:

```
catch (HttpClientErrorException ex) {

    switch (ex.getStatusCode()) {

    case NOT_FOUND:
        throw new NotFoundException(getErrorMessage(ex));

    case UNPROCESSABLE_ENTITY :
        throw new InvalidInputException(getErrorMessage(ex));

    default:
        LOG.warn("Got a unexpected HTTP error: {}, will rethrow it",
        ex.getStatusCode());
        LOG.warn("Error body: {}", ex.getResponseBodyAsString());
        throw ex;
    }
}
```

The error handling for `getRecommendations()` and `getReviews()` in the integration component is a bit more relaxed – classed as best-effort, meaning that, if it succeeds in getting product information but fails to get either recommendations or reviews, it is still considered to be okay. However, a warning is written to the log.

For more details, see `$BOOK_HOME/Chapter03/2-basic-rest-services/microservices/product-composite-service/src/main/java/se/magnus/microservices/composite/product/services/ProductCompositeIntegration.java`.

That completes the implementation of both the code and composite microservices. In the next section, we will test the microservices and the API that they expose.

Testing APIs manually

That concludes the implementation of our microservices. Let's try them out by performing the following steps:

1. Build and start them up as background processes.
2. Use `curl` to call the composite API.
3. Stop them.

First, build and start-up each microservice as a background process, as follows:

```
cd $BOOK_HOME/Chapter03/2-basic-rest-services/
```

```
./gradlew build
```

Once the build completes, we can launch our microservices as background processes to the Terminal process with the following code:

```
java -jar microservices/product-composite-service/build/libs/*.jar &
java -jar microservices/product-service/build/libs/*.jar &
java -jar microservices/recommendation-service/build/libs/*.jar &
java -jar microservices/review-service/build/libs/*.jar &
```

A lot of log messages will be written to the Terminal, but after a few seconds, things will calm down and we will find the following messages written to the log:

This means that they all are ready to receive requests. Try this out with the following code:

```
curl http://localhost:7000/product-composite/1
```

After some log output, we will get a JSON response that looks something like the following:

```
● ○ ●                          4. bash
$ curl http://localhost:7000/product-composite/1
{"productId":1,"name":"name-1","weight":123,"recommendations":[{"recomm
endationId":1,"author":"Author 1","rate":1},{"recommendationId":2,"auth
or":"Author 2","rate":2},{"recommendationId":3,"author":"Author 3","rat
e":3}],"reviews":[{"reviewId":1,"author":"Author 1","subject":"Subject
1"},{"reviewId":2,"author":"Author 2","subject":"Subject 2"},{"reviewId
":3,"author":"Author 3","subject":"Subject 3"}],"serviceAddresses":{"cm
p":"Magnus-MBP32.lan/192.168.1.185:7000","pro":"Magnus-MBP32.lan/192.16
8.1.185:7001","rev":"Magnus-MBP32.lan/192.168.1.185:7003","rec":"Magnus
-MBP32.lan/192.168.1.185:7002"}}$
```

To get the JSON response pretty-printed, you can use the `jq` tool:

```
curl http://localhost:7000/product-composite/1 -s | jq .
```

This results in the following output (some details have been replaced by . . . for increased readability):

```
● ○ ●                          4. bash
$ curl http://localhost:7000/product-composite/1 -s | jq .
{
    "productId": 123,
    ...
    "recommendations": [ ... ],
    "reviews": [ ... ],
    "serviceAddresses": { ... }
}
$
```

If you want to, you can also try out the following commands to verify that the error handling works as expected:

```
# Verify that a 404 (Not Found) error is returned for a non-existing
productId (13)
curl http://localhost:7000/product-composite/13 -i

# Verify that no recommendations are returned for productId 113
curl http://localhost:7000/product-composite/113 -s | jq .

# Verify that no reviews are returned for productId 213
curl http://localhost:7000/product-composite/213 -s | jq .

# Verify that a 422 (Unprocessable Entity) error is returned for a
productId that is out of range (-1)
```

```
curl http://localhost:7000/product-composite/-1 -i

# Verify that a 400 (Bad Request) error is returned for a productId that is
not a number, i.e. invalid format
curl http://localhost:7000/product-composite/invalidProductId -i
```

Finally, you can shut down the microservices with the following command:

```
kill $(jobs -p)
```

If you are using either Spring Tool Suite or IntelliJ IDEA Ultimate Edition as your IDE, you can use their Spring Boot Dashboard to start and stop your microservices with one click.

The following screenshot shows the use of Spring Tool Suite:

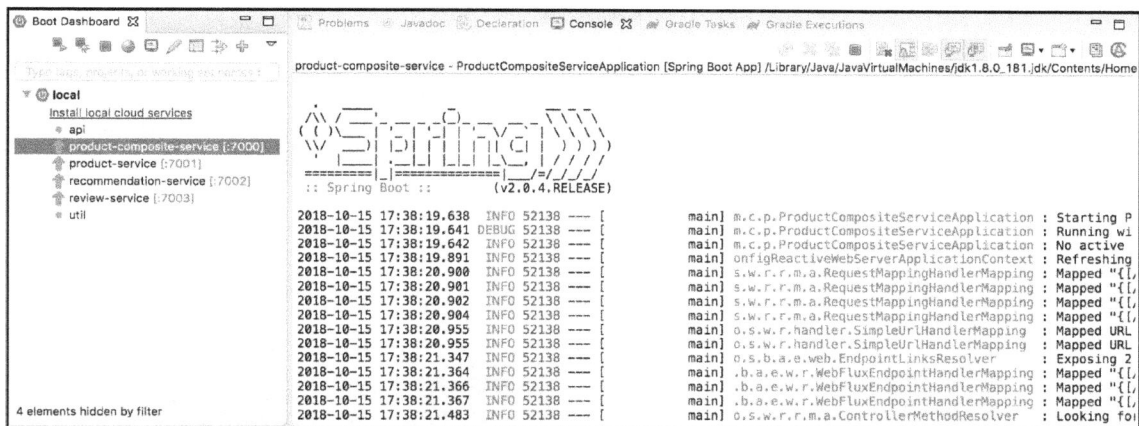

The following screenshot shows the use of IntelliJ IDEA Ultimate Edition:

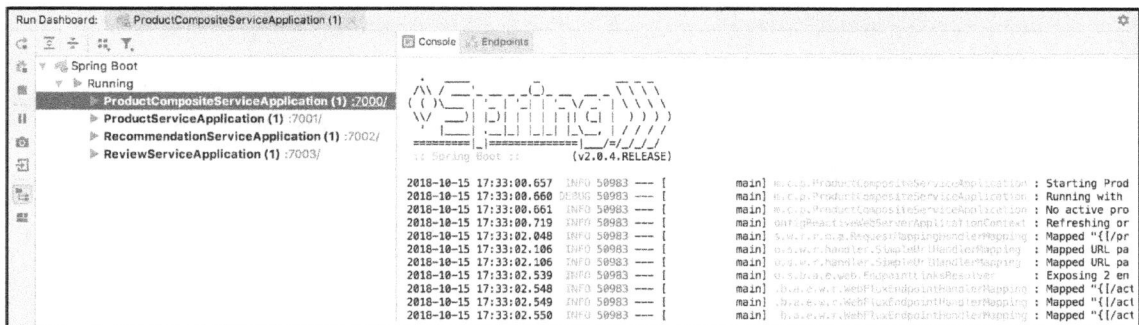

In this section, we have learned how to manually start, test, and stop the system landscape of cooperating microservices. These types of test are time-consuming, so they clearly need to be automated. In the next two sections, we will take our first steps toward learning how to automate testing, testing both a single microservice in isolation and a whole system landscape of cooperating microservices. Throughout this book, we will improve how we test our microservices.

Preventing slow lookup of the localhost hostname

With effect from macOS Sierra, looking up the hostname that's used by the localhost in a Java program on a macOS can take a very long time, that is, 5 seconds, making tests very slow. The problem seems to be fixed when using macOS Mojave, but if you are using an older version of macOS, this can easily be fixed.

First, you need to verify whether the problem affects you by downloading a small tool from GitHub and running it:

```
git clone https://github.com/thoeni/inetTester.git
java -jar inetTester/bin/inetTester.jar
```

Let's say the program responds with something like the following:

```
6. @b394afed9384:/ (bash)
$ java -jar inetTester/bin/inetTester.jar
Calling the hostname resolution method...
Method called, hostname Magnuss-Mac.local, elapsed time: 5010 (ms)
$ 
```

If you have a response time of 5 seconds, then you have a problem!

The solution is to edit the /etc/hosts file and add your local hostname, which is Magnuss-Mac.local in the preceding example, after localhost; for example:

```
127.0.0.1 localhost Magnuss-Mac.local
::1       localhost Magnuss-Mac.local
```

Rerun the test. It should respond with a response time of a few milliseconds, for example:

```
6. @b394afed9384:/ (bash)
$ java -jar inetTester/bin/inetTester.jar
Calling the hostname resolution method...
Method called, hostname Magnuss-Mac.local, elapsed time: 9 (ms)
$
```

Now lets see how to add automated tests in isolation for microservices.

Adding automated microservice tests in isolation

Before we wrap up the implementation, we also need to write some automated tests.

We don't have much business logic to test at this time, so we don't need to write any unit tests. Instead, we will focus on testing the APIs that our microservices expose; that is, we will start them up in integration tests with their embedded web server and then use a test client to perform HTTP requests and validate the responses. With Spring WebFlux came a new test client, `WebTestClient`, that provides a fluent API for making a request and then applying assertions on its result.

The following is an example where we test the composite product API by doing the following:

- Sending in `productId` for an existing product and asserting that we get back 200 as an HTTP response code and a JSON response that contains the requested `productId` along with one recommendation and one review
- Sending in a missing `productId` and asserting that we get back 404 as an HTTP response code and a JSON response that contains relevant error information

The implementation for these two tests is shown in the following code:

```
@Autowired
private WebTestClient client;

@Test
public void getProductById() {
  client.get()
    .uri("/product-composite/" + PRODUCT_ID_OK)
    .accept(APPLICATION_JSON_UTF8)
```

```
.exchange()
.expectStatus().isOk()
.expectHeader().contentType(APPLICATION_JSON_UTF8)
.expectBody()
.jsonPath("$.productId").isEqualTo(PRODUCT_ID_OK)
.jsonPath("$.recommendations.length()").isEqualTo(1)
.jsonPath("$.reviews.length()").isEqualTo(1);
}
```

Let's explain the preceding source code in more detail:

- The test uses the fluent `WebTestClient` API to set up the URL to call `"/product-composite/" + PRODUCT_ID_OK` and specify the accepted response format, JSON.
- After executing the request using the `exchange()` method, the test verifies that the response status is OK (200) and that the response format actually is JSON (as requested).
- Finally, the test inspects the response body and verifies that it contains the expected information in terms of `productId` and the number of recommendations and reviews.

The second test looks as follows:

```
@Test
public void getProductNotFound() {
  client.get()
    .uri("/product-composite/" + PRODUCT_ID_NOT_FOUND)
    .accept(APPLICATION_JSON_UTF8)
    .exchange()
    .expectStatus().isNotFound()
    .expectHeader().contentType(APPLICATION_JSON_UTF8)
    .expectBody()
    .jsonPath("$.path").isEqualTo("/product-composite/" +
    PRODUCT_ID_NOT_FOUND)
    .jsonPath("$.message").isEqualTo("NOT FOUND: " +
    PRODUCT_ID_NOT_FOUND);
}
```

Let's explain the preceding source code in more detail:

- This negative test is very similar to the preceding test in terms of its structure; the main difference is that it verifies that it got an error status code back, Not Found (404), and that the response body contains the expected error message.

To test the composite product API in isolation, we need to mock its dependencies, that is, the requests to the other three microservices that were performed by the integration component, `ProductCompositeIntegration`. We use Mockito to do this, as follows:

```
private static final int PRODUCT_ID_OK = 1;
private static final int PRODUCT_ID_NOT_FOUND = 2;
private static final int PRODUCT_ID_INVALID = 3;

@MockBean
private ProductCompositeIntegration compositeIntegration;

@Before
public void setUp() {

  when(compositeIntegration.getProduct(PRODUCT_ID_OK)).
    thenReturn(new Product(PRODUCT_ID_OK, "name", 1, "mock-address"));
  when(compositeIntegration.getRecommendations(PRODUCT_ID_OK)).
    thenReturn(singletonList(new Recommendation(PRODUCT_ID_OK, 1,
    "author", 1, "content", "mock address")));
     when(compositeIntegration.getReviews(PRODUCT_ID_OK)).
    thenReturn(singletonList(new Review(PRODUCT_ID_OK, 1, "author",
    "subject", "content", "mock address")));

  when(compositeIntegration.getProduct(PRODUCT_ID_NOT_FOUND)).
    thenThrow(new NotFoundException("NOT FOUND: " +
    PRODUCT_ID_NOT_FOUND));

  when(compositeIntegration.getProduct(PRODUCT_ID_INVALID)).
    thenThrow(new InvalidInputException("INVALID: " +
    PRODUCT_ID_INVALID));
}
```

Let's explain the preceding source code in more detail:

- First, we declare three constants that are used in the test class: PRODUCT_ID_OK, PRODUCT_ID_NOT_FOUND, and PRODUCT_ID_INVALID.
- If the getProduct(), getRecommendations(), and getReviews() methods are called on the integration component, and productId is set to PRODUCT_ID_OK, the mock will return a normal response.

- If the `getProduct()` method is called with `productId` set to `PRODUCT_ID_NOT_FOUND`, the mock will throw `NotFoundException`.
- If the `getProduct()` method is called with `productId` set to `PRODUCT_ID_INVALID`, the mock will throw `InvalidInputException`.

The full source code for the automated integration tests on the composite product API can be found in `$BOOK_HOME/Chapter03/2-basic-rest-services/microservices/product-composite-service/src/test/java/se/magnus/microservices/composite/product/ProductCompositeServiceApplicationTests.java`.

The automated integration tests on the API exposed by the three core microservices are similar, but simpler since they don't need to mock anything! The source code for the tests can be found in each microservice's `test` folder.

The tests are run automatically by Gradle when performing a build:

```
./gradlew build
```

You can, however, specify that you only want to run the tests (and not the rest of the build):

```
./gradlew test
```

This was an introduction to how to write automated tests for microservices in isolation. In the next section, we will learn how to write tests that automatically test a microservice landscape. In this chapter, these tests will only be semi-automated. In upcoming chapters, the tests will be fully automated, a significant improvement.

Adding semi-automated tests of a microservice landscape

Being able to automatically test each microservice in isolation is, of course, very useful, but insufficient!

We need a way to automatically test all of our microservices to ensure that they deliver what we expect!

For this reason, I have written a simple bash script that can perform calls to a RESTful API using `curl` and verify its return code and parts of its JSON response using `jq`. The script contains two helper functions, `assertCurl()` and `assertEqual()`, to make the test code compact and easier to read.

For example, making a normal request and expecting 200 as the status code, as well as asserting that we get back a JSON response that returns the requested `productId` along with three recommendations and three reviews, looks like the following:

```
# Verify that a normal request works, expect three recommendations and
three reviews
assertCurl 200 "curl http://$HOST:${PORT}/product-composite/1 -s"
assertEqual 1 $(echo $RESPONSE | jq .productId)
assertEqual 3 $(echo $RESPONSE | jq ".recommendations | length")
assertEqual 3 $(echo $RESPONSE | jq ".reviews | length")
```

Verifying that we get 404 (Not Found) back as an HTTP response code (when we try to look up a product that doesn't exist) looks as follows:

```
# Verify that a 404 (Not Found) error is returned for a non-existing
productId (13)
assertCurl 404 "curl http://$HOST:${PORT}/product-composite/13 -s"
```

The test script implements the manual tests that were described in the *Testing APIs manually* section and can be found in `$BOOK_HOME/Chapter03/2-basic-rest-services/test-em-all.bash`.

Trying out the test script

To try out the test script, perform the following steps:

1. First, start the microservices, as we did previously:

```
cd $BOOK_HOME/Chapter03/2-basic-rest-services
java -jar microservices/product-composite-service/build/libs/*.jar
& java -jar microservices/product-service/build/libs/*.jar &
java -jar microservices/recommendation-service/build/libs/*.jar &
java -jar microservices/review-service/build/libs/*.jar &
```

2. Once they've all started up, run the test script:

```
./test-em-all.bash
```

3. Expect the output to look similar to the following:

```
● ● ●                          6. @b394afed9384:/ (bash)
$ ./test-em-all.bash
Test OK (HTTP Code: 200)
Test OK (actual value: 1)
Test OK (actual value: 3)
Test OK (actual value: 3)
Test OK (HTTP Code: 404, {"timestamp":"2018-10-18T14:00:49.62+02:00","path":"/product-compo
site/13","message":"No product found for productId: 13","status":404,"error":"Not Found"})
Test OK (HTTP Code: 200)
Test OK (actual value: 113)
Test OK (actual value: 0)
Test OK (actual value: 3)
Test OK (HTTP Code: 200)
Test OK (actual value: 213)
Test OK (actual value: 3)
Test OK (actual value: 0)
Test OK (HTTP Code: 422, {"timestamp":"2018-10-18T14:00:49.811+02:00","path":"/product-comp
osite/-1","message":"Invalid productId: -1","status":422,"error":"Unprocessable Entity"})
Test OK (actual value: "Invalid productId: -1")
Test OK (HTTP Code: 400, {"timestamp":"2018-10-18T12:00:49.858+0000","path":"/product-compo
site/invalidProductId","status":400,"error":"Bad Request","message":"Type mismatch."})
Test OK (actual value: "Type mismatch.")
$ ▮
```

4. Wrap this up by shutting down the microservices with the following command:

```
kill $(jobs -p)
```

In this section, we have taken the first steps toward automating testing a system landscape of cooperating microservices, all of which will be improved in upcoming chapters.

Summary

We have now built our first few microservices using Spring Boot. After being introduced to the microservice landscape, which we will use throughout this book, we learned how to use Spring Initializr to create skeleton projects for each microservice.

Next, we learned how to add APIs using Spring WebFlux for the three core services and implemented a composite service that uses the three core services APIs to create an aggregated view of the information in them. The composite service uses the `RestTemplate` class in Spring Framework to perform HTTP requests to APIs that are exposed by the core services. After adding logic for error handling in the services, we ran some manual tests on the microservice landscape.

We wrapped this chapter up by learning how to add tests for microservices in isolation and when they work together as a system landscape. To provide controlled isolation for the composite service, we mocked its dependencies to the core services using Mockito. Testing the whole system landscape is performed by a bash script that uses `curl` to perform calls to the API of the composite service.

With these skills in place, we are ready to take the next step, entering the world of Docker and containers, in the next chapter! Among other things, we will learn how to use Docker to fully automate testing of a system landscape of cooperating microservices.

Questions

1. What is the command that lists available dependencies when you create a new Spring Boot project using the `spring init` Spring Initializr CLI tool?
2. How can you set up Gradle to build multiple related projects with one command?
3. What are the `@PathVariable` and `@RequestParam` annotations used for?
4. How can you separate protocol-specific error handling from the business logic in an API implementation class?
5. What is Mockito used for?

4
Deploying Our Microservices Using Docker

In this chapter, we will start using Docker and put our microservices into containers!

By the end of this chapter, we will have run fully automated tests of our microservice landscape that start all our microservices as Docker containers, requiring no other infrastructure than a Docker engine. We will have also run a number of tests to verify that the microservices work together as expected and finally shut down all the microservices, leaving no traces of the tests we executed.

Being able to test a number of cooperating microservices in this way is very useful. As developers, we can verify that it works on our local developer machines. We can also run exactly the same tests in a build server to automatically verify that changes to the source code won't break the tests at a system level. Additionally, we don't need to have a dedicated infrastructure allocated to run these types of tests. In the upcoming chapters, we will see how we can add databases and queue managers to our test landscape, all of which will run as Docker containers.

> This does not, however, replace the need for automated unit and integrations tests, which test individual microservices in isolation. They are as important as ever.
>
> For production usage, as we mentioned earlier in this book, we need a container orchestrator such as Kubernetes. We will go back to container orchestrators and Kubernetes later in this book.

The following topics will be covered in this chapter:

- Introduction to Docker.
- Docker and Java. Java hasn't been very friendly to containers historically, but that changed with Java 10. Let's see how Docker and Java fit together on this topic!
- Using Docker with one microservice.

- Managing a landscape of microservices using Docker Compose.
- Testing them all together automatically.

Technical requirements

All of the commands that are described in this book are run on a MacBook Pro using macOS Mojave but should be straightforward to modify if you want to run them on another platform such as Linux or Windows.

Apart from the technical requirements from the previous chapter, we need to have Docker installed. Docker Community Edition can be downloaded from `https://store.docker.com/search?type=editionoffering=community`.

To be able to run the examples in this book, it is recommended that you configure Docker so that you can use all the CPUs except one (allocating all CPUs to Docker can make the computer unresponsive when tests are running) and at least 6 GB of memory. This can be configured in the **Advanced** tab in the **Preferences** settings for Docker, as illustrated by the following screenshot:

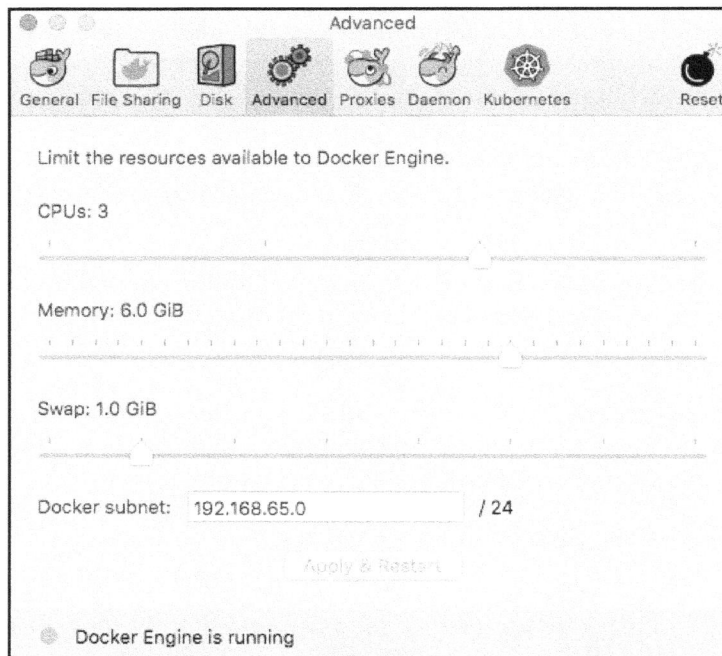

The source code for this chapter can be found in this book's GitHub repository: `https://github.com/PacktPublishing/Hands-On-Microservices-with-Spring-Boot-and-Spring-Cloud/tree/master/Chapter04`.

To be able to run the commands that are described in this book, download the source code to a folder and set up an environment variable, `$BOOK_HOME`, that points to that folder. Some sample commands are as follows:

```
export BOOK_HOME=~/Documents/Hands-On-Microservices-with-Spring-Boot-and-Spring-Cloud
git clone
https://github.com/PacktPublishing/Hands-On-Microservices-with-Spring-Boot-and-Spring-Cloud $BOOK_HOME
cd $BOOK_HOME/Chapter04
```

The Java source code is written for Java 8 and tested to run on Java 12. This chapter uses Spring Boot 2.1.0 (and Spring 5.1.2), the latest available version of Spring Boot at the time of writing this chapter.

The code examples in this chapter all come from the source code in `$BOOK_HOME/Chapter04` but in many cases have been edited to remove irrelevant parts of the source code, such as comments, imports, and log statements.

If you want to see the changes that were applied to the source code in this chapter, that is, see what it took to add support for Docker, you can compare it with the source code for `Chapter 3`, *Creating a Set of Cooperating Microservices*. You can use your favorite `diff` tool and compare the two folders, `$BOOK_HOME/Chapter03/2-basic-rest-services` and `$BOOK_HOME/Chapter04`.

Introduction to Docker

As we already mentioned in Chapter 2, *Introduction to Spring Boot*, Docker made the concept of containers as a lightweight alternative to virtual machines very popular in 2013. Containers are actually processed in a Linux host that uses Linux namespaces to provide isolation between containers of global system resources, such as users, processes, filesystems, and networking. **Linux Control Groups** (also knows as **cgroups**) are used to limit the amount of CPU and memory that a container is allowed to consume. Compared to a virtual machine that uses a hypervisor to run a complete copy of an operating system in each virtual machine, the overhead in a container is a fraction of the overhead in a virtual machine. This leads to much faster startup times and significantly lower overhead in terms of CPU and memory usage. The isolation that's provided for a container, however, is not considered to be as secure as the isolation that's provided for a virtual machine. With the release of Windows Server 2016 and Windows 10 Pro (1607 Anniversary Update), Microsoft supports the usage of Docker on Windows as well. Take a look at the following diagram:

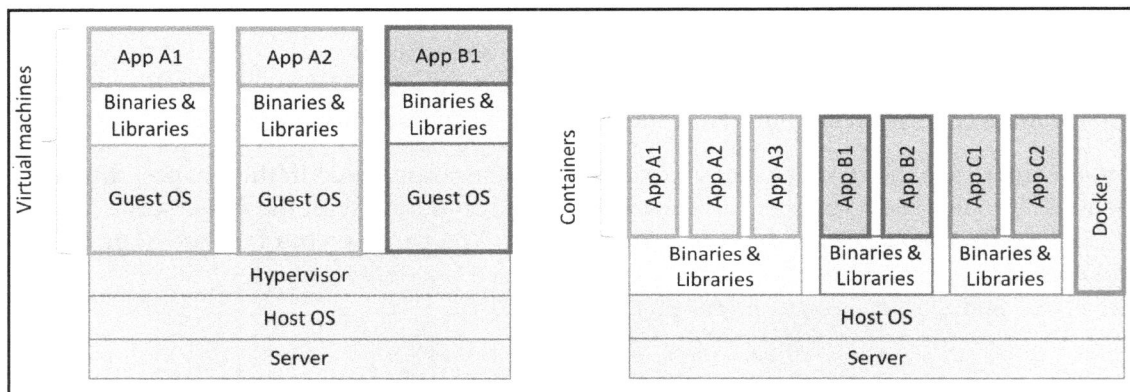

The preceding diagram illustrates the difference between the resource usage of virtual machines and containers, visualizing that the same type of server can run significantly more containers than virtual machines.

Running our first Docker commands

Let's try to start a container by launching an Ubuntu server in one using Docker's `run` command:

```
docker run -it --rm ubuntu
```

With the preceding command, we ask Docker to create a container that runs Ubuntu, based on the latest version that's available of the official Docker image for Ubuntu. The `-it` option is used so that we can interact with the container using Terminal, and the `--rm` option tells Docker to remove the container once we exit the Terminal session; otherwise, the container will remain in the Docker engine with an `Exited` state.

The first time we use a Docker image that we haven't built ourselves, Docker will download it from a Docker registry, which is Docker Hub by default (`https://hub.docker.com`). This will take some time, but for subsequent usage of that Docker image, the container will start in just a few seconds!

Once the Docker image has been downloaded and the container has been started up, the Ubuntu server should respond with a prompt such as the following:

```
4. root@435dc56d39f6: / (docker)
$ docker run -it --rm ubuntu
root@435dc56d39f6:/#
```

We can try out the container by asking what version of Ubuntu it runs:

```
cat /etc/os-release | grep 'VERSION='
```

It should respond with something like the following:

```
4. root@435dc56d39f6: / (docker)
root@435dc56d39f6:/# cat /etc/os-release | grep 'VERSION='
VERSION="18.04.3 LTS (Bionic Beaver)"
root@435dc56d39f6:/#
```

We can leave the container with an `exit` command and verify that the Ubuntu container no longer exits with the `docker ps -a` command. We need to use the `-a` option to see stopped containers; otherwise, only running containers are displayed.

If you favor CentOS over Ubuntu, feel free to try the same with the `docker run --rm -it centos` command. Once the CoreOS server has started running in its container you can, for example, ask what version of CoreOS that it runs with the `cat /etc/redhat-release` command. It should respond with something like the following:

```
4. @700dd0df9ffe:/ (docker)
$ docker run --rm -it centos
[root@700dd0df9ffe /]# cat /etc/redhat-release
CentOS Linux release 7.6.1810 (Core)
[root@700dd0df9ffe /]#
```

Leave the container with the `exit` command to remove it.

> If, at some point, you find that you have a lot of unwanted containers in the Docker engine and you want to get a clean sheet, that is, get rid of them all, you can run the following command:

```
docker rm -f $(docker ps -aq)
```

> The `docker rm -f` command stops and removes the containers whose container IDs are specified to the command. The `docker ps -aq` command lists the container IDs of all the running and stopped containers in the Docker engine. The `-q` option reduces the output from the `docker ps` command so that it only lists the container IDs.

After understanding what Docker is, next we can move on to understand the problems which we might face while running Java in Docker.

Challenges with running Java in Docker

When it comes to Java, over the past few years, there have been a number of attempts to get Java working in Docker in a good way. Currently, the official Docker image for Java is based on OpenJDK: `https://hub.docker.com/_/openjdk/`. We will use Java SE 12 with the Docker tag `openjdk:12.0.2`, that is, Java SE v12.0.2.

Java has historically not been very good at honoring the quotas specified for a Docker container using Linux cgroups; it has simply ignored these settings. So, instead of allocating memory inside the JVM in relation to the memory available in the container, Java allocated memory as if it had access to all the memory in the Docker host, which obviously isn't good! In the same way, Java allocated CPU-related resources such as thread pools in relation to the total number of available CPU cores in the Docker host instead of the number of CPU cores that were made available for the container JVM was running in. In Java SE 9, some initial support was provided, which was also back-ported to later versions of Java SE 8. In Java 10, however, much-improved support for CPU and memory constraints was put in place.

Let's try it out!

First, we will try out Java commands locally, without Docker, since that tells us how much memory and the number of CPU cores that the JVM sees. Next, we will try the commands in Docker using Java SE 12 to verify that it honors the constraints we set on the Docker container it runs in. Finally, we will also try out a Java SE 9 container and see how it fails to honor the constraints and what problems it can result in.

Java without Docker

Before we jump in to Docker, let's try the Java commands without Docker to familiarize ourselves with the Java commands!

Let's start by finding out how many available processors, that is, CPU cores, Java sees when running outside of Docker. We can do this by sending the `Runtime.getRuntime().availableprocessors()` Java statement to the Java CLI tool `jshell`, like so:

```
echo 'Runtime.getRuntime().availableProcessors()' | jshell -q
```

> `jshell` requires Java SE 9 or later!

On my machine, I get the following response:

Okay, `12` cores is as expected, since the processor in my laptop is a six-core Intel Core i9 CPU with hyper-threading (the operating system sees two virtual cores for each physical core).

In terms of the amount of available memory, let's ask the JVM for the maximum size that it thinks it can allocate for the heap. We can achieve this by asking the JVM for extra runtime information using the `-XX:+PrintFlagsFinal` Java option and then using the `grep` command to filter out the `MaxHeapSize` parameter, like so:

```
java -XX:+PrintFlagsFinal -version | grep MaxHeapSize
```

On my machine, I get the following response:

```
                    4. @700dd0df9ffe:/ (bash)
$ java -XX:+PrintFlagsFinal -version | grep MaxHeapSize
     size_t MaxHeapSize = 8589934592 {product} {ergonomic}
...
$
```

`8589934592` bytes happens to be exactly 8 GB, that is, *8 * 1,024^3*. Given that we don't specify any max heap size for the JVM using the −Xmx parameter, the JVM will set the max value to one quarter of the available memory. Since my laptop has 32 GB of memory and *32/4=8*, this is also as expected!

Let's wrap this up by verifying that we can lower the maximum heap size with the −Xmx parameter to, for example, 200 MB:

```
java −Xmx200m −XX:+PrintFlagsFinal −version | grep MaxHeapSize
```

The JVM will respond with *209,715,200* bytes, that is, *200 * 1,024^3* bytes = 200 MB, as expected!

Now that we have seen how the Java commands work without Docker, let's try this with Docker!

Java in Docker

Let's look at how Java SE 12 responds to limits we set on a container it runs in!

Since I'm using Docker for macOS, I'm actually running the Docker engine on a virtual machine on my MacBook Pro as the Docker host. I have configured Docker for macOS so that it allows the Docker host to use all 12 cores in my macOS but only use up to 16 GB of memory. All in all, the Docker host has 12 cores and 16 GB of memory.

CPU

Let's start by applying no constraints, that is, the same test that we did without Docker:

```
echo 'Runtime.getRuntime().availableProcessors()' | docker run --rm -i
openjdk:12.0.2 jshell -q
```

This command will send the
`Runtime.getRuntime().availableProcessors()` string to the
Docker container that will process the string using `jshell`.

It will respond with the same result, that is, `$1 ==> 12` in my case. Let's move on and restrict the Docker container to only be allowed to use three CPU cores using the `--cpus 3` Docker option and ask the JVM about how many available processors it sees:

```
echo 'Runtime.getRuntime().availableProcessors()' | docker run --rm -i --cpus 3 openjdk:12.0.2 jshell -q
```

The JVM now responds with `$1 ==> 3`, that is, Java SE 12 honors the settings in the container and will, therefore, be able to configure CPU-related resources such as thread pools correctly!

Let's also try to specify a relative share of the available CPUs instead of an exact number of CPUs. 1,024 shares correspond to one core by default, so if we want to limit the container to two cores, we set the `--cpu-shares` Docker option to 2,048, like so:

```
echo 'Runtime.getRuntime().availableProcessors()' | docker run --rm -i --cpu-shares 2048 openjdk:12.0.2 jshell -q
```

The JVM will respond with `$1 ==> 2`, that is, Java SE 12 honors the relative `share` option as well!

While the `--cpus` option is a hard constraint, the `--cpu-shares` option only applies when the Docker host is under high load. This means that a container can consume more CPU than what the `share` option indicates whether CPU capacity is available.

Let's try out limiting the amount of memory next.

Memory

With no memory constraints, Docker will allocate one-fourth of the memory to the container:

```
docker run -it --rm openjdk:12.0.2 java -XX:+PrintFlagsFinal -version | grep MaxHeapSize
```

It will respond with 4,202,692,608 bytes, which equals 4 GB, that is, $8 * 1024\^3$. Since my Docker host has 16 GB of memory, this is correct, that is, $16/4 = 4$.

However, if we constrain the Docker container to only use up to 1 GB of memory using the -m=1024M Docker option, we will see a lower memory allocation:

```
docker run -it --rm -m=1024M openjdk:12.0.2 java -XX:+PrintFlagsFinal -
version | grep MaxHeapSize
```

The JVM will respond with 268,435,456 bytes, which equals 256 MB, that is, *2 * 1024^2* bytes. 256 MB is one-fourth of 1 GB, so again, this is as expected.

We can, as usual, set the max heap size ourselves. For example, if we want to allow the heap to use 800 MB of the total 1 GB we have, we can specify that using the -Xmx800m Java option:

```
docker run -it --rm -m=1024M openjdk:12.0.2 java -Xmx800m -
XX:+PrintFlagsFinal -version | grep MaxHeapSize
```

The JVM will respond with 838,860,800 bytes = *800 * 1024^2* bytes = 800 MB, as expected.

Let's conclude with some out of memory tests to ensure that this really works.

Let's allocate some memory using jshell in a JVM that runs in a container that has been given 1 GB of memory; that is, it has a max heap size of 256 MB.

First, try to allocate a byte array of 100 MB:

```
echo 'new byte[100_000_000]' | docker run -i --rm -m=1024M openjdk:12.0.2
jshell -q
```

The command will respond with $1 ==>, meaning that it worked fine!

> Normally, jshell will print out the value resulting from the command, but 100 MB of bytes all set to zero is a bit too much printout, and so we get nothing.

Now, let's try to allocate a byte array that is larger than the max heap size, for example, 500 MB:

```
echo 'new byte[500_000_000]' | docker run -i --rm -m=1024M openjdk:12.0.2
jshell -q
```

The JVM sees that it can't perform the action since it honors the container settings of max memory and responds immediately with Exception java.lang.OutOfMemoryError: Java heap space. Great!

What would happen in this case if we use a JVM that doesn't honor the container settings of max memory?

Let's find out by using Java SE 9!

Problems with Docker and Java SE 9 (or older)

First, try out limiting a Java SE 9 JVM to three CPU cores using `openjdk:9-jdk` image.

Java 9 fails to obey the three-CPU limit:

```
echo 'Runtime.getRuntime().availableProcessors()' | docker run --rm -i --
cpus 3 openjdk:9-jdk jshell -q
```

It responds with `$1 ==> 12` on my machine, that is, it ignores the limitation of three CPU cores.

We will see the same result, that is, `$1 ==> 12`, if we try out the `--cpu-shares` option:

```
echo 'Runtime.getRuntime().availableProcessors()' | docker run --rm -i --
cpu-shares 2048 openjdk:9-jdk jshell -q
```

Now, let's try to limit the memory to 1 GB:

```
docker run -it --rm -m=1024M openjdk:9-jdk java -XX:+PrintFlagsFinal -
version | grep MaxHeapSize
```

As expected, Java SE 9 does not honor the memory constraint that we set in Docker; that is, it reports a max heap size of 4,202,692,608 bytes = *4 GB − 4 * 1024^3* bytes. Here, Java 9 calculated the available memory when given the memory in the Docker host, not in the actual container!

So, what happens if we repeat the memory allocation tests that we did for Java SE 12?

Let's try out the first test, that is, allocating a 100 MB array:

```
echo 'new byte[100_000_000]' | docker run -i --rm -m=1024M openjdk:9-jdk
jshell -q
```

The command responds with `$1 ==> byte[100000000] { 0, 0, 0, ...`, so that worked fine!

Now, let's move on to the really interesting test: what if we allocate a byte array of 500 MB that doesn't fit in the memory that was allocated to the container by Docker?

```
echo 'new byte[500_000_000]' | docker run -i --rm -m=1024M openjdk:9-jdk
jshell -q
```

From a Java perspective, this should work. Since Java thinks the total memory is 16 GB, it has set the max heap size to 4 GB, so it happily starts to allocate 500 MB for the byte array. But after a while, the total size of the JVM exceeds 1 GB and Docker will kill the container with no mercy, resulting in a confusing exception such as State engine terminated. We basically have no clue what went wrong, even though we can guess that we ran out of memory.

So, to summarize, if you plan to do any serious work with Docker and Java, ensure that you use Java SE 10 or later!

> To be fair to Java SE 9, it should be mentioned that Java SE 9 contains some initial support for cgroups. If you specify the Java options – XX:+UnlockExperimentalVMOptions and – XX:+UseCGroupMemoryLimitForHeap, it will honor parts of the cgroup constraints, but not all of them, and it should be noted that this is only experimental. Due to this, it should be avoided in production environments. Simply use Java SE 10 or later in Docker!

Using Docker with one microservice

Now that we understand how Java works, we can start using Docker with one of our microservices. Before we can run our microservice as a Docker container, we need to package it in a Docker image. To build a Docker image, we need a Dockerfile, so we will start with that. Next, we need a Docker-specific configuration for our microservice. Since a microservice that runs in a container is isolated from other microservices, for example, has its own IP address, hostname, and ports, it needs a different configuration compared to when it's running on the same host with other microservices. For example, since the other microservices no longer run on the same host, no port conflicts will occur. When running in Docker, we can use the default port 8080 for all our microservices without any risk of port conflicts. On the other hand, if we need to talk to the other microservices, we can no longer use localhost like we could when we ran them on the same host. The source code in the microservices will not be affected by running the microservices in containers, only their configuration.

To handle the different configurations that are required when running locally without Docker and when running the microservices as Docker containers, we will use Spring profiles. Since Chapter 3, *Creating a Set of Cooperating Microservices*, we have been using the default Spring profile for running locally without Docker, so we will create a Spring profile named docker for when we run our microservices as containers in Docker.

Changes in source code

We will use the product microservice, which can be found in the source code at $BOOK_HOME/Chapter04/microservices/product-service/. In the next section, we will apply this to the other microservices as well.

First, we add the Spring profile for Docker at the end of the property file $BOOK_HOME/Chapter04/microservices/product-service/src/main/resources/application.yml:

```
---
spring.profiles: docker

server.port: 8080
```

> Spring profiles can be used to specify environment-specific configuration, which in this case is a configuration that is to only be used when running the microservice in a Docker container. Other examples are configurations that are specific to dev, test, and production environments. Values in a profile override the default values, that is, values from the default profile. Using .yaml files, multiple Spring profiles can be placed in the same file, separated by `---`.

The only parameter we will change is the port that's being used; that is, we will use the default port 8080 when running the microservice in a container.

Next, we will create the Dockerfile that we will use to build the Docker image, $BOOK_HOME/Chapter04/microservices/product-service/Dockerfile. It looks like this:

```
FROM openjdk:12.0.2

EXPOSE 8080

ADD ./build/libs/*.jar app.jar

ENTRYPOINT ["java","-jar","/app.jar"]
```

Some things to take note of are as follows:

- We will base our Docker image on the official Docker image for OpenJDK and use the Java SE v12.0.2.
- We will expose port `8080` to other Docker containers.
- We add our `fat-jar` file to the Docker image from the Gradle build library, `build/libs`.
- We will specify the command to be used by Docker when a container is started up using this Docker image, that is, `java -jar /app.jar`.

After taking into account these changes in source code

Building a Docker image

To build the Docker image, we need to build our deployment artifact, that is, the fat-file, for `product-service`:

```
cd $BOOK_HOME/Chapter04
./gradlew :microservices:product-service:build
```

> Since we only want to build `product-service` and the projects it depends on, `api` and `util`, we don't use the normal `build` command, which builds all the microservices, but a variant that tells Gradle to only build `product-service`: `:microservices:product-service:build`.

We can find the `fat-jar` file in the Gradle build library, `build/libs`. For example, the `ls -l microservices/product-service/build/libs` command will report something like the following:

```
6. @b394afed9384:/ (bash)
$ ls -l microservices/product-service/build/libs
-rw-r--r--  1 magnus  staff  19618829 Aug 30 18:59 product-service-1.0.0-SNAPSHOT.jar
$
```

> As you can see, the JAR file is close to 20 MB in size – no wonder they are called `fat-jar` files!
>
> If you are curious about its actual content, you can view it by using the `unzip -l microservices/product-service/build/libs/product-service-1.0.0-SNAPSHOT.jar` command.

Next, we will build the Docker image and name it `product-service`, as follows:

```
cd microservices/product-service
docker build -t product-service .
```

Docker will use the Dockerfile in the current directory to build the Docker image. The image will be tagged with the name `product-service` and stored locally inside the Docker engine.

Verify that we got a Docker image, as expected, by using the following command:

```
docker images | grep product-service
```

The expected output is as follows:

```
4. @700dd0df9ffe:/ (bash)
$ docker images | grep product-service
product-service   latest   119a3f98ad0c   9 seconds ago   490MB
$
```

So now that we have built the image, lets see how we can start the service.

Starting up the service

Let's start up the `product` microservice as a container by using the following command:

```
docker run --rm -p8080:8080 -e "SPRING_PROFILES_ACTIVE=docker" product-
service
```

This is what we can infer from the preceding code:

1. `docker run`: The Docker run command will start the container and display log output in Terminal. Terminal will be locked as long as the container runs.
2. We have seen the `--rm` option already; it will tell Docker to clean up the container once we stop the execution from Terminal using *Ctrl + C*.
3. The `-p8080:8080` option maps port `8080` in the container to port `8080` in the Docker host, which makes it possible to call it from the outside. In the case of Docker for macOS, which runs Docker in a local Linux virtual machine, the port will also be port-forwarded to macOS, which is made available on localhost. We can only have one container mapping to a specific port in the Docker host!

4. With the -e option, we can specify environment variables for the container, which in this case is SPRING_PROFILES_ACTIVE=docker.
   The SPRING_PROFILES_ACTIVE environment variable is used to tell Spring what profile to use. In our case, we want Spring to use the docker profile.

5. Finally, we have product-service, which is the name of the Docker image that Docker will use to start the container.

The expected output is as follows:

This is what we infer from the preceding output:

- The profile that's used by Spring is docker. Look for The following profiles are active: docker in the output to verify this.
- The port that's allocated by the container is 8080. Look for Netty started on port(s): 8080 in the output to verify this.
- The microservice is ready to accept requests once the log message Started ProductServiceApplication has been written!

Try out the following code in another Terminal window:

```
curl localhost:8080/product/3
```

Note that we can use port 8080 on localhost, as explained previously!

The following is the expected output:

```
6. @b394afed9384:/ (bash)
$ curl localhost:8080/product/3
{"productId":3,"name":"name-3","weight":123,"serviceAddress":"9dc086e4a88b/172.17.0.2:8080"}
$
```

This is similar to the output we received from the previous chapter, but with one major difference; we have the content of `"service Address":"aebb42b32fef/172.17.0.2:8080"`, the port is `8080`, as expected, and the IP address, `172.17.0.2`, is an IP address that's been allocated to the container from an internal network in Docker – but where did the hostname, `aebb42b32fef`, come from?

Ask Docker for all the running containers:

    docker ps

We will see something like the following:

```
6. @b394afed9384:/ (bash)
$ docker ps
CONTAINER ID   IMAGE             COMMAND              CREATED         STATUS        PORTS                    NAMES
9dc086e4a88b   product-service   "java -jar /app.jar"  3 minutes ago   Up 3 minutes  0.0.0.0:8080->8080/tcp   eloquent_jones
$
```

As we can see from the preceding output that, the hostname is equivalent to the ID of the container, which is good to know if you want to understand what container actually responded to your request!

Wrap this up by stopping the container in Terminal with the *Ctrl + C* command. With this done, we can now move on to running the container detached while being detached.

Running the container detached

Okay, that was great, but what if we don't want to hang the Terminal windows from where we started the container?

It's time to start the container as detached, that is, running the container without locking Terminal!

We can do this by adding the `-d` option and at the same time giving it a name using the `--name` option. The `--rm` option is no longer required since we will stop and remove the container explicitly when we are done with it:

```
docker run -d -p8080:8080 -e "SPRING_PROFILES_ACTIVE=docker" --name my-prd-srv product-service
```

If we run the `docker ps` command again, we will see our new container, called `my-prd-srv`:

```
$ docker ps
CONTAINER ID   IMAGE             COMMAND              CREATED         STATUS          PORTS                     NAMES
f4c8645902c6   product-service   "java -jar /app.jar"  13 seconds ago  Up 11 seconds   0.0.0.0:8080->8080/tcp   my-prd-srv
$
```

But how do we get the log output from our container?

Meet the Docker `logs` command:

```
docker logs my-prd-srv -f
```

The `-f` option tells the command to follow the log output, that is, not end the command when all the current log output has been written to Terminal, but also wait for more output. If you expect a lot of old log messages that you don't want to see, you can also add the `--tail 0` option so that you only see new log messages. Alternatively, you can use the `--since` option and use either an absolute timestamp or a relative time, for example, `--since 5m`, to see log messages that are at most five minutes old.

Try this out with a new `curl` request. You should see that a new log message has been written to the log output in Terminal!

Wrap this up by stopping and removing the container:

```
docker rm -f my-prd-srv
```

The `-f` option forces Docker to remove the container, even if it is running. Docker will automatically stop the container before it removes it.

Now that we know how to use Docker with a microservice, we can now see how to manage a microservices landscape with the help of Docker Compose and see the changes in it.

Managing a landscape of microservices using Docker Compose

We've already seen how we can run a single microservice as a Docker container, but what about managing a whole system landscape of microservices?

As we mentioned earlier, this is the purpose of `docker-compose`. By using single commands, we can build, start, log, and stop a group of cooperating microservices running as Docker containers!

Changes in the source code

To be able to use Docker Compose, we need to create a configuration file, `docker-compose.yml`, that describes the microservices Docker Compose will manage for us. We also need to set up Dockerfiles for the remaining microservices and add a Docker-specific Spring profile to each of them.

All four microservices have their own Dockerfile, but they all look the same as the preceding one. You can find them here:

- `$BOOK_HOME/Chapter04/microservices/product-service/Dockerfile`
- `$BOOK_HOME/Chapter04/microservices/recommendation-service/Dockerfile`
- `$BOOK_HOME/Chapter04/microservices/review-service/Dockerfile`
- `$BOOK_HOME/Chapter04/microservices/product-composite-service/Dockerfile`

When it comes to the Spring profiles, the three core services, `product`, `recommendation`, and `review-service`, have the same `docker` profile, which only specifies that the default port `8080` should be used when running as a container.

For `product-composite-service`, things are a bit more complicated since it needs to know where to find the core services. When we ran all the services on localhost, it was configured to use localhost and individual port numbers, `7001-7003`, for each core service. When running in Docker, each service will have its own hostname but will be accessible on the same port number, `8080`. Here, the `docker` profile for `product-composite-service` looks as follows:

```
---
spring.profiles: docker

server.port: 8080

app:
  product-service:
    host: product
    port: 8080
  recommendation-service:
    host: recommendation
    port: 8080
  review-service:
    host: review
    port: 8080
```

See `$BOOK_HOME/Chapter04/microservices/product-composite-service/src/main/resources/application.yml` for details.

Where did the hostnames, products, recommendations, and reviews come from?

These are specified in the `docker-compose.yml` file, which is located in the `$BOOK_HOME/Chapter04` folder. It looks like this:

```
version: '2.1'

services:
  product:
    build: microservices/product-service
    mem_limit: 350m
    environment:
      - SPRING_PROFILES_ACTIVE=docker

  recommendation:
    build: microservices/recommendation-service
    mem_limit: 350m
    environment:
      - SPRING_PROFILES_ACTIVE=docker

  review:
```

```
    build: microservices/review-service
    mem_limit: 350m
    environment:
      - SPRING_PROFILES_ACTIVE=docker

product-composite:
    build: microservices/product-composite-service
    mem_limit: 350m
    ports:
      - "8080:8080"
    environment:
      - SPRING_PROFILES_ACTIVE=docker
```

For each microservice, we specify the following:

- The name of the microservice. This will also be the hostname of the container in the internal Docker network.
- A build directive that specifies where to find the Dockerfile that was used to build the Docker image.
- A memory limit of 350 MB. This ensures that all containers in this and the upcoming chapters will fit in the 6 GB of memory that we allocated to the Docker engine in the *Technical requirements* section.
- The environment variables that will be set up for the container. In our case, we used these to specify what Spring profile to use.

For the `product-composite` service, we will also specify port mappings, that is, we will expose its port to the outside of Docker. The other microservices will not be accessible from the outside. Next, we will see how to start up a microservice landscape.

Starting up the microservice landscape

With all the necessary code changes in place, we can build our Docker images, start up the microservice landscape, and run some tests to verify that it works as expected. For this, we need to do the following:

1. First, we build our deployment artifacts with Gradle and then the Docker images with Docker Compose:

   ```
   cd $BOOK_HOME/Chapter04
   ./gradlew build
   docker-compose build
   ```

2. Then, we need to verify that we can see our Docker images, as follows:

```
docker images | grep chapter04
```

3. We should see the following output:

```
6. @b394afed9384:/ (bash)
$ docker images | grep chapter04
chapter04_product-composite  latest  a04b5b1cfd4a  19 seconds ago  490MB
chapter04_review             latest  72ca17df2799  21 seconds ago  490MB
chapter04_recommendation     latest  c44e8f50dc51  22 seconds ago  490MB
chapter04_product            latest  a0f9f70b6ed8  24 seconds ago  490MB
$
```

4. Start up the microservices landscape with the following command:

```
docker-compose up -d
```

The -d option means the same as for Docker, as described previously.

We can follow the startup by monitoring the output that's written to each container log with the following command:

```
docker-compose logs -f
```

The docker compose logs command supports the same -f and --tail options as docker logs, as described earlier.

The Docker Compose logs command also supports restricting the log output to a group of containers. Simply add the names of the containers you want to see the log output of after the logs command. For example, to only see log output from the product and review service, use docker-compose logs -f product review.

When all four microservices have reported that they have started up, we are ready to try out the microservices landscape. Look for the following:

```
                            6. @b394afed9384:/ (bash)
$ docker-compose logs -f
...
review_1  | 2018-11-04 09:22:03.618 INFO 1 --- [ main] s.m.m.c.review.ReviewServiceApplication
 : Started ReviewServiceApplication in 6.051 seconds (JVM running for 6.952)
...
product-composite_1 | 2018-11-04 09:22:03.151 INFO 1 --- [ main] m.c.p.ProductCompositeServic
eApplication : Started ProductCompositeServiceApplication in 6.414 seconds (JVM running for 6
.936)
...
recommendation_1 | 2018-11-04 09:22:03.542 INFO 1 --- [ main] m.m.c.r.RecommendationServiceAp
plication : Started RecommendationServiceApplication in 6.199 seconds (JVM running for 7.131)
...
product_1 | 2018-11-04 09:22:04.250  INFO 1 --- [ main] s.m.m.c.p.ProductServiceApplication :
 Started ProductServiceApplication in 6.212 seconds (JVM running for 7.614)
```

> Note that each log message is prefixed with the name of the container that produces the output!

Now, we are ready to run some tests to verify that this works as expected. The only change we need to make when calling the composite service in Docker from when we ran it directly on the localhost, as we did in the previous chapter, is the port number. We now use port 8080:

```
curl localhost:8080/product-composite/123 -s | jq .
```

We will get the same type of response:

```
                            6. @b394afed9384:/ (bash)
$ curl localhost:8080/product-composite/123 -s | jq .
{
    "productId": 123,
    ...
    "recommendations": [ ... ],
    "reviews": [ ... ],
    "serviceAddresses": { ... }
}
$
```

However, there's one big difference – the hostnames and ports reported by `serviceAddresses` in the response:

```
6. @b394afed9384:/ (bash)
"serviceAddresses": {
  "cmp": "98059be902bf/172.21.0.2:8080",
  "pro": "99774d9be7b8/172.21.0.4:8080",
  "rev": "a89da16763d9/172.21.0.5:8080",
  "rec": "2a846794a1d0/172.21.0.3:8080"
}
```

Here, we can see the hostnames and IP addresses that have been allocated to each of the Docker containers.

We're done; now only one step is left:

```
docker-compose down
```

The preceding command will shut down the microservices landscape.

Testing them all together automatically

Docker Compose is really helpful when it comes to manually managing a group of microservices! In this section, we will take this one step further and integrate Docker Compose into our test script, `test-em-all.bash`. The test script will automatically start up the microservice landscape, run all the required tests to verify that the microservice landscape works as expected, and finally tear it down, leaving no traces behind.

The test script can be found at `$BOOK_HOME/Chapter04/test-em-all.bash`.

Before the test script runs the test suite, it will check for the presence of a `start` argument in the invocation of the test script. If found, it will restart the containers with the following code:

```
if [[ $@ == *"start"* ]]
then
    echo "Restarting the test environment..."
    echo "$ docker-compose down"
    docker-compose down
    echo "$ docker-compose up -d"
    docker-compose up -d
fi
```

After that, the test script will wait for the `product-composite` service to respond with OK:

```
waitForService http://$HOST:${PORT}/product-composite/1
```

The `waitForService` bash function can be implemented like so:

```
function testUrl() {
    url=$@
    if curl $url -ks -f -o /dev/null
    then
            echo "Ok"
            return 0
    else
            echo -n "not yet"
            return 1
    fi;
}

function waitForService() {
    url=$@
    echo -n "Wait for: $url... "
    n=0
    until testUrl $url
    do
        n=$((n + 1))
        if [[ $n == 100 ]]
        then
            echo " Give up"
            exit 1
        else
            sleep 6
            echo -n ", retry #$n "
        fi
    done
}
```

Next, all the tests are executed like they were previously. Afterward, they will tear down the landscape if it finds the `stop` argument in the invocation of the test scripts:

```
if [[ $@ == *"stop"* ]]
then
    echo "We are done, stopping the test environment..."
    echo "$ docker-compose down"
    docker-compose down
fi
```

Note that the test script will not tear down the landscape if some tests fail; it will simply stop, leaving the landscape up for error analysis!

The test script has also changed the default port from `7000`, which we used when we ran the microservices without Docker, to `8080`, which is used by our Docker containers.

Let's try it out! To start the landscape, run the tests and tear it down afterward, like so:

```
./test-em-all.bash start stop
```

The following is some sample output from a test run (with output from the specific tests that were deleted):

```
                          6. @b394afed9384:/ (bash)
$ ./test-em-all.bash start stop
Start: Sun Nov 4 13:17:45 CET 2018
HOST=localhost
PORT=8080
Restarting the test environment...
$ docker-compose down
Removing network chapter04_default
WARNING: Network chapter04_default not found.
$ docker-compose up -d
Creating network "chapter04_default" with the default driver
Creating chapter04_product_1 ... done
Creating chapter04_review_1 ... done
Creating chapter04_product-composite_1 ... done
Creating chapter04_recommendation_1 ... done
Wait for: http://localhost:8080/product-composite/1... not yet, retry #1 not yet, retry #2 Ok
...Tests OK...
We are done, stopping the test environment...
$ docker-compose down
Stopping chapter04_recommendation_1 ... done
Stopping chapter04_review_1 ... done
Stopping chapter04_product_1 ... done
Stopping chapter04_product-composite_1 ... done
Removing chapter04_recommendation_1 ... done
Removing chapter04_review_1 ... done
Removing chapter04_product_1 ... done
Removing chapter04_product-composite_1 ... done
Removing network chapter04_default
End: Sun Nov 4 13:18:03 CET 2018
$
```

After testing these, we can now move on to see how to troubleshoot tests that fail.

Troubleshooting a test run

If the tests that were running `./test-em-all.bash start stop` fail, following these steps can help you identify the problem and resume the tests once the problem has been fixed:

1. First, check the status of the running microservices with the following command:

   ```
   docker-compose ps
   ```

2. If all the microservices are up and running and healthy, you will receive the following output:

```
Chapter04 $ docker-compose ps
              Name                    Command           State           Ports
-----------------------------------------------------------------------------------
chapter04_product-composite_1    java -jar /app.jar     Up     0.0.0.0:8080->8080/tcp
chapter04_product_1              java -jar /app.jar     Up     8080/tcp
chapter04_recommendation_1       java -jar /app.jar     Up     8080/tcp
chapter04_review_1               java -jar /app.jar     Up     8080/tcp
Chapter04 $
```

3. If any of the microservices do not have a status of `Up`, check its log output for any errors by using the `docker-compose logs` command. For example, you would use the following code if you wanted to check the log output for the `product` service:

   ```
   docker-compose logs product
   ```

4. If errors in the log output indicate that Docker is running out of disk space, parts of it can be reclaimed with the following command:

   ```
   docker system prune -f --volumes
   ```

5. If required, you can restart a failed microservice with the `docker-compose up -d --scale` command. For example, you would use the following code if you wanted to restart the `product` service:

   ```
   docker-compose up -d --scale product=0
   docker-compose up -d --scale product=1
   ```

6. If a microservice is missing, for example, due to a crash, you start it up with the `docker-compose up -d --scale` command. For example, you would use the following code for the `product` service:

```
docker-compose up -d --scale product=1
```

7. Once all the microservices are up and running and healthy, run the test script again, but without starting the microservices:

```
./test-em-all.bash
```

The tests should run fine!

> Finally, a tip about a combined command that builds runtime artifacts and Docker images from source and then runs all the tests in Docker:
>
> ```
> ./gradlew clean build && docker-compose build && ./test-em-all.bash start stop
> ```
>
> This is perfect if you want to check that everything works before you push new code to your Git repository or as part of a build pipeline in your build server!

Summary

In this chapter, we have seen how Docker can be used to simplify testing a landscape of cooperating microservices.

We learned how Java SE since v10 honors constraints that we put on containers regarding how much CPU and memory they are allowed to use.

We have also seen how little it takes to make it possible to run a Java-based microservice as a Docker container. Thanks to Spring profiles, we can run the microservice in Docker without having to make any code changes.

Finally, we have seen how Docker Compose can help us manage a landscape of cooperating microservices with single commands, either manually or, even better, automatically, when integrated with a test script such as `test-em-all.bash`.

In the next chapter, we will study how we can add a documentation of the API using OpenAPI/Swagger descriptions.

Questions

1. What are the major differences between a virtual machine and a Docker container?
2. What is the purpose of namespaces and cgroups in Docker?
3. What happens with a Java application that doesn't honor the max memory settings in a container and allocates more memory than it is allowed to?
4. How can we make a Spring-based application run as a Docker container without requiring modifications of its source code?
5. Why will the following Docker Compose code snippet not work?

```
review:
  build: microservices/review-service
  ports:
    - "8080:8080"
  environment:
    - SPRING_PROFILES_ACTIVE=docker

product-composite:
  build: microservices/product-composite-service
  ports:
    - "8080:8080"
  environment:
    - SPRING_PROFILES_ACTIVE=docker
```

5
Adding an API Description Using OpenAPI/Swagger

The value of an API, such as a RESTful service, to a large extent depends on how easy it is to consume! Good and easily accessible documentation is an important part of whether an API is useful. In this chapter, we will learn how we can use OpenAPI/Swagger to document APIs that we can make externally accessible from a microservice landscape.

As we mentioned in Chapter 2, *Introduction to Spring Boot*, Swagger is one of the most commonly used specifications when it comes to documenting RESTful services, and many of the leading API gateways have native support for Swagger. We will learn how to use SpringFox to produce such documentation, the kind of changes in source code required to document the eternal API using SpringFox. We will try out Swagger documentation, which shows how to use an embedded Swagger viewer to both inspect the documentation and to try out the API.

By the end of this chapter, we will have Swagger-based API documentation about the external API that's exposed by the product-composite-service microservice. We will be able to use an embedded Swagger viewer to both visualize and test the API.

The following topics will be covered in this chapter:

- Introduction to using SpringFox
- Changes in the source code
- Building and starting the microservice
- Trying out the Swagger documentation

Technical requirements

All of the commands that are described in this book are run on a MacBook Pro using macOS Mojave, but should be straightforward to modify if you want to run them on another platform such as Linux or Windows.

No new tools need to be installed before you can work through this chapter.

The source code for this chapter can be found in this book's GitHub repository: `https://github.com/PacktPublishing/Hands-On-Microservices-with-Spring-Boot-and-Spring-Cloud/tree/master/Chapter05`.

To be able to run the commands that are described in this book, download the source code to a folder and set up an environment variable, `$BOOK_HOME`, that points to that folder. Some sample commands are as follows:

```
export BOOK_HOME=~/Documents/Hands-On-Microservices-with-Spring-Boot-and-Spring-Cloud
git clone
https://github.com/PacktPublishing/Hands-On-Microservices-with-Spring-Boot-and-Spring-Cloud $BOOK_HOME
cd $BOOK_HOME/Chapter05
```

The Java source code in this book has been written for Java 8 and tested on Java 12. This chapter uses Spring Boot 2.1.0 (and Spring 5.1.2), which is the latest available version of Spring Boot at the time of writing this chapter.

The code examples in this chapter all come from the source code in $BOOK_HOME/Chapter05 but have been, in many cases, edited to remove irrelevant parts of the source code, such as comments, imports, and log statements.

If you want to view the changes that were applied to the source code in this chapter, that is, see what it took to create Swagger-based API documentation using SpringFox, you can compare it with the source code for Chapter 4, *Deploying Our Microservices Using Docker*. You can use your favorite diff tool and compare the two folders, that is, $BOOK_HOME/Chapter04 and $BOOK_HOME/Chapter05.

Introduction to using SpringFox

SpringFox makes it possible to keep the documentation of the API together with the source code that implements the API. To me, this is an important feature. If the API documentation is maintained in a separate life cycle from the Java source code, they will diverge from each other over time. In many cases, this is sooner than expected (from my experience). As always, it is important to separate the interface of a component from its implementation. In terms of documenting a RESTful API, we should add the API documentation to the Java interface that describes the API, and not to the Java class that implements the API. To simplify updating the documentation of the API, we can place parts of the documentation in property files instead of in the Java code directly.

In 2015, SmartBear Software donated the Swagger specification to the Linux Foundation under the OpenAPI Initiative and created the OpenAPI Specification. To create the API documentation, we will use **SpringFox**, which can create Swagger-based API documentation at runtime.

It does this based on a configuration that we supply and by inspecting annotations that have been provided by Spring WebFlux and Swagger:

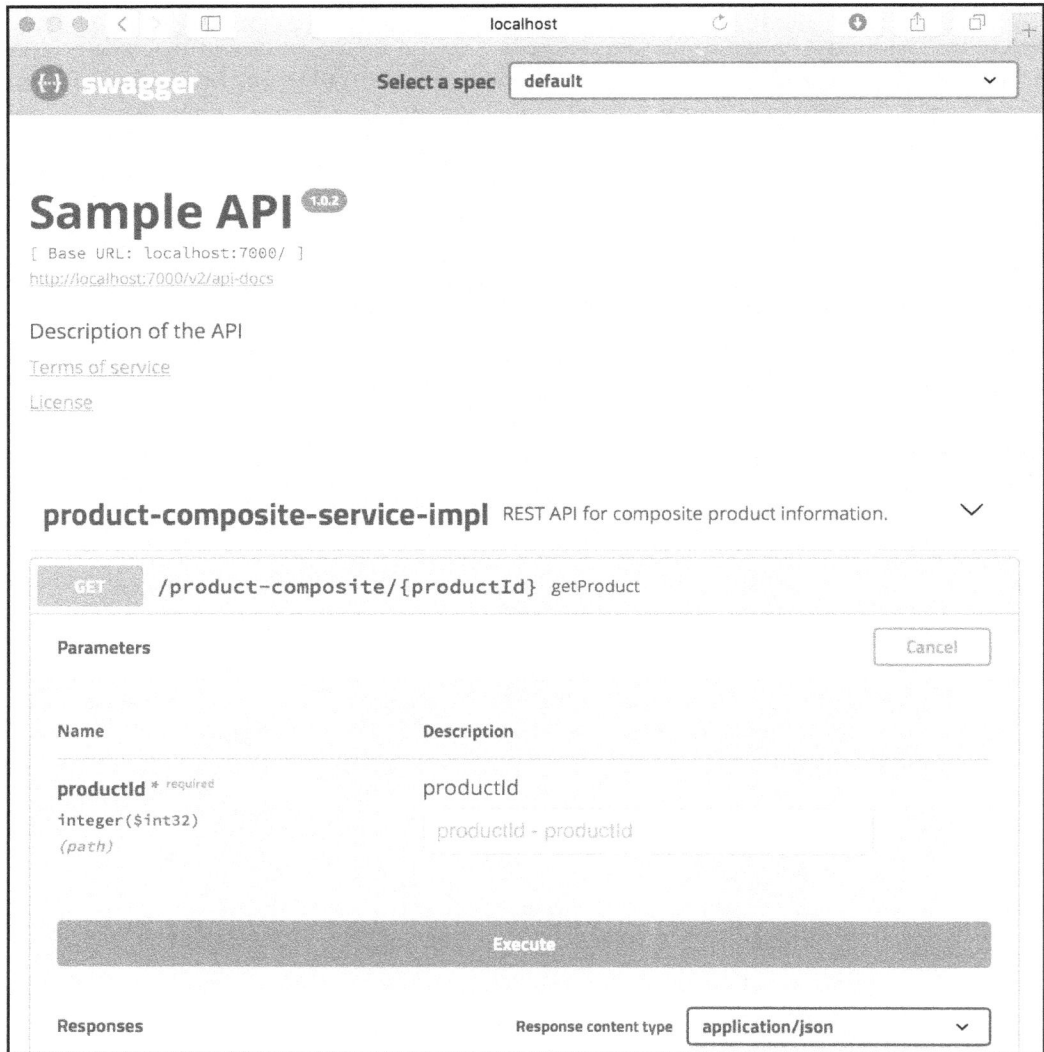

Support for OpenAPI has been planned for v3 of SpringFox. SpringFox V3 was still under development at the time of writing this chapter, so we will use a snapshot version of SpringFox V3 and create the API documentation based on Swagger V2. Once SpringFox V3 has been released, the source code for this book will be updated.

To enable SpringFox so that we can create the API documentation, we will set up a base configuration for SpringFox and add annotations to the Java interfaces that define the RESTful services.

> If parts of the documentation have been placed in property files to simplify updating the API documentation, it is important that the property files are handled in the same life cycle and under the same version control as the source code, otherwise there is a risk that they will start to diverge from the implementation, that is, become out of date.

Changes in the source code

To add Swagger-based documentation about the external API that's exposed by the `product-composite-service` microservice, we need to change the source code in two modules:

- `product-composite-services`: Here, we will set up a SpringFox configuration in the Java application class, `ProductCompositeServiceApplication`, and describe general information about the API.
- `api`: Here, we will add Swagger annotations to the Java interface, `ProductCompositeService`, describing each RESTful service. At this stage, we only have one RESTful service, `/product-composite/{productId}`, which is used for requesting composite information regarding a specific product.

The actual texts that are used to describe the API operation will be placed in the default property file, `application.yml`.

Before we can start using SpringFox, we need to add it as a dependency in the Gradle build files. So, let's start with that!

Adding dependencies to the Gradle build files

As we mentioned previously, we will use a snapshot version of SpringFox V3. The SpringFox product is divided into a number of modules. The modules that we need to specify dependencies are as follows:

- `springfox-swagger2`, so that we can create Swagger 2-based documentation
- `springfox-spring-webflux`, so that we can support the use of Spring WebFlux-based RESTful operations
- `springfox-swagger-ui`, so that we can embed a Swagger viewer in our microservice

We can add these to the Gradle build file, `build.gradle`, for the `product-composite-service` module as follows:

```
implementation('io.springfox:springfox-swagger2:3.0.0-SNAPSHOT')
implementation('io.springfox:springfox-swagger-ui:3.0.0-SNAPSHOT')
implementation('io.springfox:springfox-spring-webflux:3.0.0-SNAPSHOT')
```

The `api` project only needs one dependency for the `springfox-swagger2` module, and so only the following dependency needs to be added to its `build.gradle` file:

```
implementation('io.springfox:springfox-swagger2:3.0.0-SNAPSHOT')
```

The SpringFox project publishes snapshot builds in the Maven repository (`http://oss.jfrog.org/artifactory/oss-snapshot-local/`), so we need to add that as well:

```
repositories {
    mavenCentral()
    maven { url 'http://oss.jfrog.org/artifactory/oss-snapshot-local/' }
}
```

To be able to build the core modules, that is, `product-service`, `recommendation-service`, and `review-service`, we need to add the Maven repository to their Gradle build files, `build.gradle`, as well.

Adding configuration and general API documentation to Product Composite Service Application

To enable SpringFox in the `product-composite-service` microservice, we have to add a configuration. To keep the source code compact, we will add it directly to the `ProductCompositeServiceApplication` application class.

> If you prefer, you can place the configuration of SpringFox in a separate Spring configuration class.

First, we need to add the `@EnableSwagger2WebFlux` annotation in order to get SpringFox to generate Swagger V2 documentation for our RESTful services, which is implemented using Spring WebFlux. Next, we need to define a Spring Bean that returns a SpringFox `Docket` bean, which is used to configure SpringFox.

The source code that we will be adding to `$BOOK_HOME/Chapter05/microservices/product-composite-service/src/main/java/se/magnus/microservices/composite/product/ProductCompositeServiceApplication.java` looks as follows:

```java
@EnableSwagger2WebFlux
public class ProductCompositeServiceApplication {

    @Bean
    public Docket apiDocumentation() {
        return new Docket(SWAGGER_2)
            .select()
            .apis(basePackage("se.magnus.microservices.composite.product"))
            .paths(PathSelectors.any())
            .build()
                .globalResponseMessage(GET, emptyList())
                .apiInfo(new ApiInfo(
                        apiTitle,
                        apiDescription,
                        apiVersion,
                        apiTermsOfServiceUrl,
                        new Contact(apiContactName, apiContactUrl,
                         apiContactEmail),
                        apiLicense,
```

```
                    apiLicenseUrl,
                    emptyList()
                                        ));
    }
```

From the preceding code, we can understand the following:

- The `@EnableSwagger2WebFlux` annotation is the starting point for initiating SpringFox.
- The `Docket` bean is initiated to create Swagger V2 documentation.
- Using the `apis()` and `paths()` methods, we can specify where SpringFox shall look for API documentation.
- Using the `globalResponseMessage()` method, we ask SpringFox not to add any default HTTP response codes to the API documentation, such as `401` and `403`, which we don't currently use.
- The `api*` variables that are used to configure the `Docket` bean with general information about the API are initialized from the property file using Spring `@Value` annotations. These are as follows:

```
@Value("${api.common.version}")            String apiVersion;
@Value("${api.common.title}")              String apiTitle;
@Value("${api.common.description}")        String apiDescription;
@Value("${api.common.termsOfServiceUrl}")  String
                                           apiTermsOfServiceUrl;
@Value("${api.common.license}")            String apiLicense;
@Value("${api.common.licenseUrl}")         String apiLicenseUrl;
@Value("${api.common.contact.name}")       String apiContactName;
@Value("${api.common.contact.url}")        String apiContactUrl;
@Value("${api.common.contact.email}")      String apiContactEmail;
```

After adding a configuration and API documentation, we can now proceed to understand how to add an API specific documentation to ProductCompositeService.

Adding API-specific documentation to ProductCompositeService

To document the actual API, `ProductCompositeService`, and its RESTful operations, we will add an `@Api` annotation to the Java interface declaration so that we can provide a general description of the API. For each RESTful operation in the API, we will add an `@ApiOperation` annotation, along with `@ApiResponse` annotations on the corresponding Java method, to describe the operation and its expected error responses.

SpringFox will inspect the @GetMapping Spring annotation to understand what input argument the operation takes and what the response will look like if a successful response is produced.

In the following example, we have extracted the actual text from the @ApiOperation annotation to a property file. The annotation contains property placeholders that SpringFox will use to look up the actual text from the property files at runtime.

The documentation of the API on the resource level appears as follows:

```
@Api(description = "REST API for composite product information.")
public interface ProductCompositeService {
```

The single API operation is documented as follows:

```
@ApiOperation(
    value = "${api.product-composite.get-composite-
      product.description}",
    notes = "${api.product-composite.get-composite-product.notes}")
@ApiResponses(value = {
    @ApiResponse(code = 400, message = "Bad Request, invalid format
    of the request. See response message for more information."),
    @ApiResponse(code = 404, message = "Not found, the specified id
      does not exist."),
    @ApiResponse(code = 422, message = "Unprocessable entity, input
      parameters caused the processing to fails. See response
      message for more information.")
})
@GetMapping(
    value   = "/product-composite/{productId}",
    produces = "application/json")
ProductAggregate getProduct(@PathVariable int productId);
```

For the values specified in the @ApiOperation Swagger annotation, we can use property placeholders directly, without using Spring @Value annotations. For the description of the expected ApiResponses, that is, the expected error codes, SpringFox currently does not support the use of property placeholders, so in this case, the actual text describing each error code is placed directly in the Java source code.

For details,
see $BOOK_HOME/Chapter05/api/src/main/java/se/magnus/api/composite/produ
ct/ProductCompositeService.java.

Adding textual descriptions of the API to the property file

Finally, we need to add the textual descriptions of the API to the property file,
application.yml. Here, we have @Value annotations, which look as follows:

```
@Value("${api.common.version}") String apiVersion;
```

For each @Value annotation, we need to specify a corresponding property in the YAML
file; for example:

```
api:
  common:
    version: 1.0.0
```

In the same way, we have Swagger annotations, which look as follows:

```
@ApiOperation(value = "${api.product-composite.get-composite-
product.description}")
```

These expect a corresponding property in the YAML file; for example:

```
api:
  product-composite:
    get-composite-product:
      description: Returns a composite view of the specified product id
```

> If you want to find out more about how a YAML file is constructed, view
> the specification: https://yaml.org/spec/1.2/spec.html.

First, the general description of the API, which is configured in the SpringFox Docket bean,
is described as follows:

```
api:
  common:
    version: 1.0.0
    title: Sample API
```

```
description: Description of the API...
termsOfServiceUrl: MINE TERMS OF SERVICE URL
license: License
licenseUrl: MY LICENSE URL
contact:
  name: Contact
  url: My
  email: me@mail.com
```

Next, a detailed description of the actual API operation is given:

```
product-composite:
  get-composite-product:
    description: Returns a composite view of the specified product id
    notes: |
      # Normal response
      If the requested product id is found the method will return
      information regarding:
      1. Base product information
      1. Reviews
      1. Recommendations
      1. Service Addresses\n(technical information regarding the
      addresses of the microservices that created the response)

      # Expected partial and error responses
      In the following cases, only a partial response be created (used
      to simplify testing of error conditions)

      ## Product id 113
      200 - Ok, but no recommendations will be returned

      ## Product id 213
      200 - Ok, but no reviews will be returned

      ## Non numerical product id
      400 - A <b>Bad Request</b> error will be returned

      ## Product id 13
      404 - A <b>Not Found</b> error will be returned

      ## Negative product ids
      422 - An <b>Unprocessable Entity</b> error will be returned
```

Note that SpringFox supports providing a multiline description of an API operation using markdown syntax.

For more details, see `$BOOK_HOME/Chapter05/microservices/product-composite-service/src/main/resources/application.yml`.

Building and starting the microservice landscape

Before we can try out the Swagger documentation, we need to build and start the microservice landscape!

This can be done with the following commands:

```
cd $BOOK_HOME/Chapter05
./gradlew build && docker-compose build && docker-compose up -d
```

You may run into an error message regarding port `8080` already being allocated. This will look as follows:

```
ERROR: for product-composite Cannot start service product-composite: driver
failed programming external connectivity on endpoint chapter05_product-
composite_1
(0138d46f2a3055ed1b90b3b3daca92330919a1e7fec20351728633222db5e737): Bind
for 0.0.0.0:8080 failed: port is already allocated
```

If this is the case, you might have forgotten to bring down the microservice landscape from the previous chapter. To find out the names of the executing containers, run the following command:

```
docker ps --format {{.Names}}
```

A sample response when a microservice landscape from the previous chapter is still running is as follows:

```
chapter05_review_1
chapter05_product_1
chapter05_recommendation_1
chapter04_review_1
chapter04_product-composite_1
chapter04_product_1
chapter04_recommendation_1
```

If you find containers from other chapters in the output from the command, for example, from Chapter 4, *Deploying Our Microservices Using Docker*, as in the preceding example, you need to jump over to that chapter and bring down the containers for that chapter:

```
cd ../Chapter04
docker-compose down
```

Now, you can bring up the missing container for this chapter:

```
cd ../Chapter05
docker-compose up -d
```

Note that only the missing container, product-composite, is started by the command since the other ones were already started successfully:

```
Starting chapter05_product-composite_1 ... done
```

To wait for the microservice landscape to startup and verify that it works, you can run the following command:

```
./test-em-all.bash
```

The successful start-up of this microservice helps us understand its landscape better and also aids in understanding the Swagger documentation which we are about to study in the next section.

Trying out the Swagger documentation

To browse the Swagger documentation, we will use the embedded Swagger viewer. If we open the `http://localhost:8080/swagger-ui.html` URL in a web browser, we will see a web page that looks something like the following screenshot:

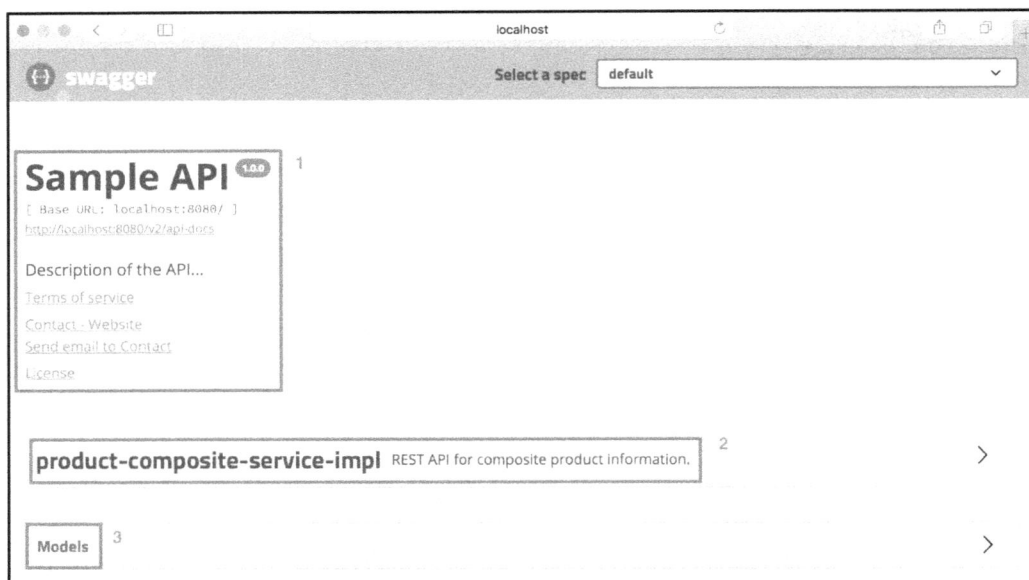

Here, we can find the following:

- The general information we specified in the SpringFox `Docket` bean and a link to the actual Swagger document, `http://localhost:8080/v2/api-docs`
- A list of API resources; in our case, the `product-composite-service` API
- At the bottom of the page, there is a section where we can inspect the models that are used in the API

This is how it works:

1. Click on the `product-composite-service` API resource to expand it. You will get a list of operations that are available on the resource.
2. You will only see one operation, **/product-composite/{productId}**. Click on it to expand it. You will see the documentation of the operation that we specified in the `ProductCompositeService` Java interface:

Here, we can see the following:

- The one-line description of the operation.
- A section with details regarding the operation, including the input parameters it supports. Note how the markdown syntax from the `notes` field in the `@ApiOperation` annotation has been nicely rendered!

If you scroll down the web page, you will also find documentation regarding the expected responses, both a normal **200** response and the various 4xx error responses we defined, as shown in the following screenshot:

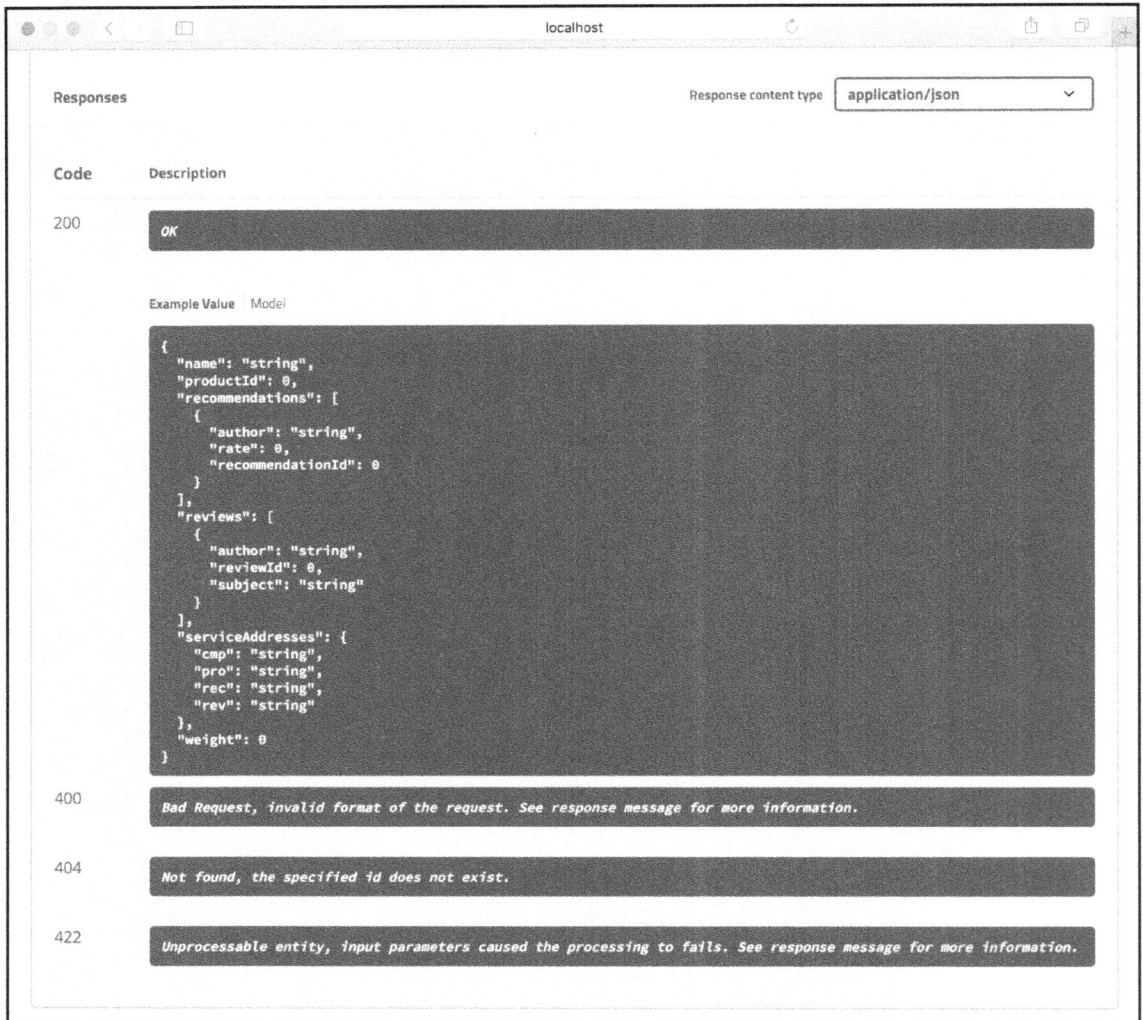

If we scroll back up to the parameter description, we will find the **Try it out!** button. If we click on that, we can fill in actual parameter values and send a request to the API by clicking on the **Execute** button. For example, if we put in **productId** 123, we will get the following response:

We will get an expected **200** (OK) as the response code and a JSON structure in the response body that we already are familiar with!

If we enter an incorrect input, such as −1, we will get a proper error code as the response code and a corresponding JSON-based error description in the response body:

If you want to try out calling the API without using the Swagger UI, you can copy the corresponding `curl` command from the response section and run it in a Terminal window! Look at the following by way of an example:

```
curl -X GET "http://localhost:8080/product-composite/123" -H "accept:
application/json"
```

Great, isn't it?

Summary

Good documenting of an API is essential for its acceptance, and Swagger is one of the most commonly used specifications when it comes to documenting RESTful services. SpringFox is an opensource project that makes it possible to create Swagger-based API documentation on the fly at runtime by inspecting Spring WebFlux and Swagger annotations. Textual descriptions of an API can be extracted from the annotations in the Java source code and be placed in a property file for ease of editing. SpringFox can be configured to bring in an embedded Swagger viewer to a microservice, which makes it very easy to read about APIs that have been exposed by the microservice and also try them out from the viewer.

Now, what about bringing some life to our microservices by adding persistence, that is, the capability to save data in a database? To do this, we need to add some more APIs so that we can create and delete the information that's handled by the microservices. Head over to the next chapter to find out more!

Questions

1. How does SpringFox help us create API documentation for RESTful services?
2. What specifications for documenting APIs does SpringFox support?
3. What is the purpose of the SpringFox `Docket` bean?
4. Name some annotations that SpringFox reads at runtime to create the API documentation on the fly!
5. What does : | mean in a YAML file?
6. How can you repeat a call to an API that was performed using the embedded Swagger viewer without using the viewer again?

6
Adding Persistence

In this chapter, we will learn how to persist data that a microservice is using. As already mentioned in Chapter 2, *Introduction to Spring Boot*, we will use the Spring Data project to persist data to MongoDB and MySQL databases. The project and recommendation microservices will use Spring Data for MongoDB and the review microservice will use Spring Data for the **JPA** (short for the **Java Persistence API**) to access a MySQL database. We will add operations to the RESTful APIs to be able to create and delete data in the databases. The existing APIs for reading data will be updated to access the databases. We will run the databases as Docker containers, managed by Docker Compose, that is, in the same way as we run our microservices.

The following topics will be covered in this chapter:

- Adding a persistence layer to the core microservices
- Writing automated tests that focus on persistence
- Using the persistence layer in the service layer
- Extending the composite service API
- Adding databases to the Docker Compose landscape
- Manual testing of the new APIs and the persistence layer
- Updating the automated tests of the microservice landscape

Technical requirements

All commands described in this book are run on a MacBook Pro using macOS Mojave but should be straightforward to modify to run on another platform such as Linux or Windows.

No new tools need to be installed in this chapter.

To access the databases manually, we will use the CLI tools provided in the Docker images used to run the databases. We will, however, expose the standard ports used for each database in Docker Compose—`3306` for MySQL and `27017` for MongoDB. This will enable you to use your local favorite database tools for accessing the databases in the same way as if they were running locally on your computer.

The source code for this chapter can be found on GitHub: `https://github.com/ PacktPublishing/Hands-On-Microservices-with-Spring-Boot-and-Spring-Cloud/tree/ master/Chapter06`.

To be able to run the commands as described in the book, download the source code to a folder and set up an environment variable, `$BOOK_HOME`, that points to that folder. Following are some sample commands:

```
export BOOK_HOME=~/Documents/Hands-On-Microservices-with-Spring-Boot-and-
Spring-Cloud
git clone
https://github.com/PacktPublishing/Hands-On-Microservices-with-Spring-Boot-
and-Spring-Cloud $BOOK_HOME
cd $BOOK_HOME/Chapter06
```

The Java source code is written for Java 8 and tested on Java 12. This chapter uses Spring Boot 2.1.0 (and Spring 5.1.2)—the latest available version of Spring Boot at the time of writing this chapter.

The source code contains the following Gradle projects:

- `api`
- `util`
- `microservices/product-service`
- `microservices/review-service`
- `microservices/recommendation-service`
- `microservices/product-composite-service`

The code examples in this chapter all come from source code in `$BOOK_HOME/Chapter06` but are, in many cases, edited to remove non-relevant parts of the source code, such as comments and import and log statements.

If you want to see the changes applied to the source code in `Chapter 6`, *Adding Persistence*, which sees what it took to add persistence to the microservices using Spring Data, you can compare it with the source code for `Chapter 5`, *Adding API Description Using OpenAPI/Swagger*. You can use your favorite diff tool and compare the two folders, `$BOOK_HOME/Chapter05` and `$BOOK_HOME/Chapter06`.

But first, let's see where we are heading

By the end of this chapter, we will have layers inside our microservices that look like the following:

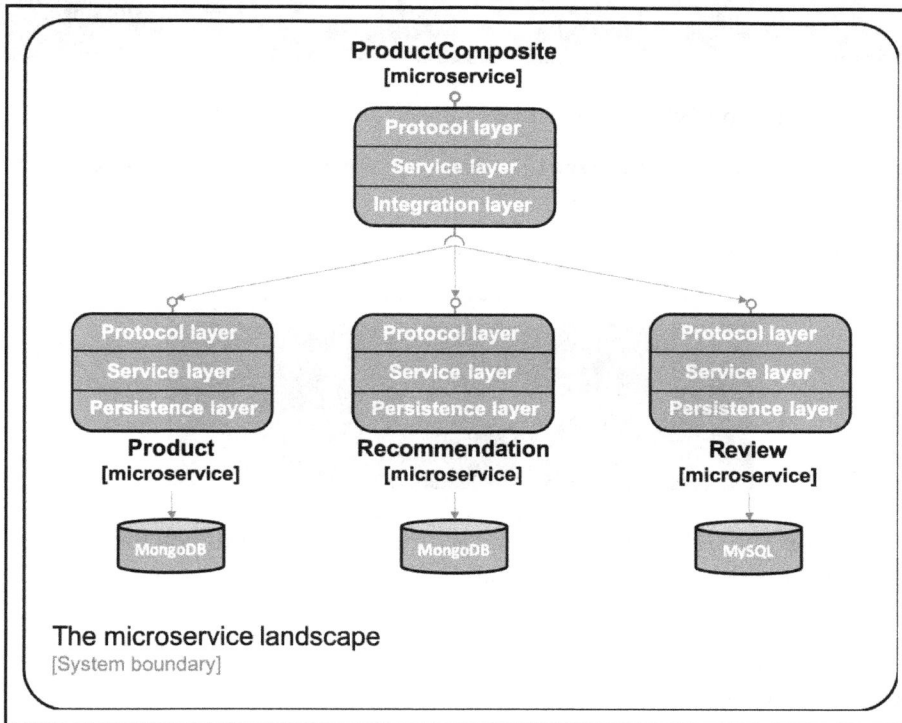

The **Protocol layer** is very thin, only consisting of `RestController` annotations and the common `GlobalControllerExceptionHandler`. The main functionality of each microservice resides in the service layers. The `product-composite` service contains an integration layer to communicate with the three core microservices. The core microservices will all have a **Persistence layer** used for communicating with their databases.

We will be able to see data stored in MongoDB with a command like the following:

```
docker-compose exec mongodb mongo product-db --quiet --eval
"db.products.find()"
```

The result of the command should look like the following:

```
2. bash
{ "_id" : ..., "productId" : 1, "name" : "product 1", "weight" : 1 }
{ "_id" : ..., "productId" : 113, "name" : "product 113", "weight" : 113 }
{ "_id" : ..., "productId" : 213, "name" : "product 213", "weight" : 213 }
$
```

Regarding data stored in MySQL, we will be able to see it with a command like this:

```
docker-compose exec mysql mysql -uuser -p review-db -e "select * from
reviews"
```

The result of the command should look as follows:

```
2. bash
+----+----------+-----------+------------+-----------+
| id | author   | content   | product_id | review_id |
+----+----------+-----------+------------+-----------+
|  1 | author 1 | content 1 |          1 |         1 |
|  2 | author 2 | content 2 |          1 |         2 |
+----+----------+-----------+------------+-----------+
$
```

Note: The output from the `mongo` and `mysql` commands have been shortened for improved readability.

Let's see how to go about this.

Adding a persistence layer to the core microservices

Let's start with adding a persistence layer to the core microservices. Besides using Spring Data, we will also use a Java bean mapping tool, MapStruct, that makes it easy to transform between Spring Data entity objects and the API model classes. For further details, see http://mapstruct.org/.

First, we need to add dependencies to MapStruct, Spring Data, and the JDBC drivers for the databases we intend to use. After that, we can define our Spring Data entity classes and repositories. The Spring Data entity classes and repositories will be placed in their own Java package, `persistence`. For example, for the product microservice, they will be placed in the Java package, `se.magnus.microservices.core.product.persistence`.

Adding dependencies

We will use MapStruct V1.3.0-Beta 2, so we start by defining a variable holding the version information in the build file for each core microservice, `build.gradle`:

```
ext {
 mapstructVersion = "1.3.0.Beta2"
}
```

Next, we declare a dependency on MapStruct:

```
implementation("org.mapstruct:mapstruct:${mapstructVersion}")
```

Since MapStruct generates the implementation of the bean mappings at compile time by processing MapStruct annotations, we need to add an `annotationProcessor` and a `testAnnotationProcessor` dependency:

```
iannotationProcessor "org.mapstruct:mapstruct-
processor:${mapstructVersion}"
testAnnotationProcessor "org.mapstruct:mapstruct-
processor:${mapstructVersion}"
```

To make the compile-time generation work in popular IDEs such as IntelliJ IDEA, we also need to add the following dependency:

```
compileOnly "org.mapstruct:mapstruct-processor:${mapstructVersion}"
```

> If you are using IntelliJ IDEA, you also need to ensure that support for annotation processing is enabled. Open **Preferences** and navigate to **Build, Execute, Deployment | Compiler | Annotations Processors**. Verify that the checkbox named **Enable annotation processing** is selected!

For the `project` and `recommendation` microservices, we declare the following dependencies to Spring Data for MongoDB:

```
implementation('org.springframework.boot:spring-boot-starter-data-mongodb')
testImplementation('de.flapdoodle.embed:de.flapdoodle.embed.mongo')
```

The test dependency to `de.flapdoodle.embed.mongo` enables us to run MongoDB embedded when we run JUnit-based tests.

The `review` microservices will use Spring Data for JPA together with MySQL as its database in runtime and it will use an embedded database, H2, during tests. Therefore, it declares the following dependencies in its build file, `build.gradle`:

```
implementation('org.springframework.boot:spring-boot-starter-data-jpa')
implementation('mysql:mysql-connector-java')
testImplementation('com.h2database:h2')
```

Storing data with entity classes

The entity classes are similar to the corresponding API model classes in terms of what fields they contain—see the Java package, `se.magnus.api.core`, in the `api` project. We will add two fields, `id`, and `version`, in the entity classes compared to the fields in the API model classes.

The `id` field is used to hold the database identity of each stored entity—the primary key when using a relational database. We will delegate the responsibility to generate unique values of the identity field to Spring Data. Depending on the database used, Spring Data can delegate this responsibility to the database engine. In either case, the application code does not need to consider how a unique database `id` value is set. The `id` field is not exposed in the API, as a best practice from a security perspective. The fields in the model classes that identify an entity will be assigned a unique index in the corresponding entity class, to ensure consistency in the database from a business perspective.

The `version` field is used to implement optimistic locking, that is, allowing Spring Data to verify that updates of an entity in the database do not overwrite a concurrent update. If the value of the version field stored in the database is higher than the value of the version field in an update request, it indicates that the update is performed on stale data—the information to be updated has been updated by someone else since it was read from the database. Attempts to perform updates based on stale data will be prevented by Spring Data. In the section on writing persistence tests, we will see tests that verify the optimistic locking mechanism in Spring Data prevent updates performed on stale data. Since we only implement APIs for create, read, and delete operations, we will, however, not expose the version field in the API.

The most interesting parts of the product entity class look like this:

```
@Document(collection="products")
public class ProductEntity {

    @Id
    private String id;

    @Version
    private Integer version;

    @Indexed(unique = true)
    private int productId;

    private String name;
    private int weight;
```

The following are the observations from the preceding code:

- The `@Document(collection="products")` annotation is used to mark the class as an entity class used for MongoDB, that is, mapped to a collection in MongoDB with the name, `products`.
- The `@Id` and `@Version` annotations are used to mark the `id` and `version` fields to be used by Spring Data, as explained previously.
- The `@Indexed(unique = true)` annotation is used to get a unique index created for the business key, `productId`.

The most interesting parts of the `Recommendation` entity class look like this:

```
@Document(collection="recommendations")
@CompoundIndex(name = "prod-rec-id", unique = true, def = "{'productId': 1,
'recommendationId' : 1}")
public class RecommendationEntity {

    @Id
    private String id;

    @Version
    private Integer version;

    private int productId;
    private int recommendationId;
    private String author;
    private int rating;
    private String content;
```

Added to the explanations for the preceding product entity, we can see how a unique compound index is created using the @CompoundIndex annotation for the compound business key based on the fields, productId and recommendationId.

Finally, the most interesting parts of the Review entity class look like this:

```
@Entity
@Table(name = "reviews", indexes = { @Index(name = "reviews_unique_idx",
unique = true, columnList = "productId,reviewId") })
public class ReviewEntity {

    @Id @GeneratedValue
    private int id;

    @Version
    private int version;

    private int productId;
    private int reviewId;
    private String author;
    private String subject;
    private String content;
```

The following are the observations from the preceding code:

- The @Entity and @Table annotations are used to mark the class as an entity class used for JPA—mapped to a table in a SQL database with the name, products.
- The @Table annotation is also used to specify that a unique compound index shall be created for the compound business key based on the fields, productId and reviewId.
- The @Id and @Version annotations are used to mark the id and version fields to be used by Spring Data as explained previously. To direct Spring Data for JPA to automatically generate unique id values for the id field, we are using the @GeneratedValue annotation.

For full source code of the entity classes, see the following:

- se.magnus.microservices.core.product.persistence.ProductEntity in the product project
- se.magnus.microservices.core.recommendation.persistence.RecommendationEntity in the recommendation project

- `se.magnus.microservices.core.review.persistence.ReviewEntity` in the `review` project

Defining repositories in Spring Data

Spring Data comes with a set of base classes for defining repositories. We will use the base classes, `CrudRepository` and `PagingAndSortingRepository`. The `CrudRepository` base class provides standard methods for performing basic create, read, update, and delete operations on the data stored in the databases. The `PagingAndSortingRepository` base class adds support for paging and sorting to the `CrudRepository` base class.

We will use the `CrudRepository` class as the base class for the `Recommendation` and `Review` repositories and the `PagingAndSortingRepository` class as the base class for the `Product` repository.

We will also add a few extra query methods to our repositories for looking up entities using the business key, `productId`.

Spring Data supports defining extra query methods based on naming conventions for the signature of the method. For example, the `findByProductId(int productId)` method signature can be used to direct Spring Data to automatically create a query that returns entities from the underlying collection or table that has the `productId` field set to the value specified in the `productId` parameter when calling the query method. For more details on how to declare extra queries, see `https://docs.spring.io/spring-data/data-commons/docs/current/reference/html/#repositories.query-methods.query-creation`.

The `Product` repository class looks like this:

```
public interface ProductRepository extends
PagingAndSortingRepository<ProductEntity, String> {
    Optional<ProductEntity> findByProductId(int productId);
}
```

Since the `findByProductId` method might return zero or one product entity, the return value is marked to be optional by wrapping it in an `Optional` object.

The `Recommendation` repository class looks like this:

```
public interface RecommendationRepository extends
CrudRepository<RecommendationEntity, String> {
    List<RecommendationEntity> findByProductId(int productId);
}
```

In this case, the `findByProductId` method will return zero to many recommendation entities, so the return value is defined as a list.

Finally, the `Review` repository class looks like this:

```
public interface ReviewRepository extends CrudRepository<ReviewEntity,
Integer> {
    @Transactional(readOnly = true)
    List<ReviewEntity> findByProductId(int productId);
}
```

Since SQL databases are transactional, we have to specify the default transaction type—read-only in our case—for the query method, `findByProductId()`.

That's it—this is all it takes to establish a persistence layer for our core microservices.

For full source code of the repository classes, see the following:

- `se.magnus.microservices.core.product.persistence.ProductReposit ory` in the `product` project
- `se.magnus.microservices.core.recommendation.persistence.Recomme ndationRepository` in the `recommendation` project
- `se.magnus.microservices.core.review.persistence.ReviewRepositor y` in the `review` project

Let's start using them by writing some persistence tests to verify that they work as intended.

Writing automated tests that focus on persistence

When writing persistence tests, we want to start an embedded database when the tests begin and tear it down when the tests complete. However, we don't want the tests to wait for other resources to start up, for example, a web server such as Netty (which is required in runtime).

Spring Boot comes with two class level annotations tailored for this specific requirement:

- @DataMongoTest: This starts up an embedded MongoDB database when the test starts.
- @DataJpaTest: This starts up an embedded SQL database when the test starts:
  - Since we added a test dependency in the build file for the review microservice to the H2 database, it will be used as the embedded SQL database.
  - By default, Spring Boot configures the tests to roll back updates to the SQL database to minimize the risk of negative side effects on other tests. In our case, this behavior will cause some of the tests to fail. Therefore, automatic rollback is disabled with the class level annotation: @Transactional(propagation = NOT_SUPPORTED).

The persistence tests for the three core microservices are similar to each other, so we will only go through the persistence tests for the Product microservice.

The test class declares a method, setupDb(), annotated with @Before, which is executed before each test method. The setup method removes any entities from previous tests in the database and inserts an entity that the test methods can use as a base for their tests:

```
@RunWith(SpringRunner.class)
@DataMongoTest
public class PersistenceTests {

    @Autowired
    private ProductRepository repository;
    private ProductEntity savedEntity;

    @Before
    public void setupDb() {
        repository.deleteAll();
        ProductEntity entity = new ProductEntity(1, "n", 1);
        savedEntity = repository.save(entity);
        assertEqualsProduct(entity, savedEntity);
    }
```

Next comes the various test methods. First out is a `create` test:

```
@Test
public void create() {
    ProductEntity newEntity = new ProductEntity(2, "n", 2);
    savedEntity = repository.save(newEntity);

    ProductEntity foundEntity =
    repository.findById(newEntity.getId()).get();
    assertEqualsProduct(newEntity, foundEntity);

    assertEquals(2, repository.count());
}
```

This test creates a new entity and verifies that it can be found using the `findByProductId()` method and wraps up with asserting that there are two entities stored in the database, the one created by the `setup` method and the one created by the test itself.

The `update` test looks like this:

```
@Test
public void update() {
    savedEntity.setName("n2");
    repository.save(savedEntity);

    ProductEntity foundEntity =
    repository.findById(savedEntity.getId()).get();
    assertEquals(1, (long)foundEntity.getVersion());
    assertEquals("n2", foundEntity.getName());
}
```

This test updates the entity created by the setup method, reads it again from the database using the standard `findById()` method, and asserts that it contains expected values for some of its fields. Note that, when an entity is created, its `version` field is set to 0 by Spring Data.

The `delete` test looks like this:

```
@Test
public void delete() {
    repository.delete(savedEntity);
    assertFalse(repository.existsById(savedEntity.getId()));
}
```

This test deletes the entity created by the `setup` method and verifies that it no longer exists in the database.

The read test looks like this:

```
@Test
public void getByProductId() {
    Optional<ProductEntity> entity =
    repository.findByProductId(savedEntity.getProductId());
    assertTrue(entity.isPresent());
    assertEqualsProduct(savedEntity, entity.get());
}
```

This test uses the findByProductId() method to get the entity created by the setup method, verifies that it was found, and then uses the local helper method, assertEqualsProduct(), to verify that the entity returned by findByProductId() looks the same as the entity stored by the setup method.

Next, it follows two test methods that verify alternative flows—handling of error conditions. First, is a test that verifies that duplicates are handled correctly:

```
@Test(expected = DuplicateKeyException.class)
public void duplicateError() {
    ProductEntity entity = new
    ProductEntity(savedEntity.getProductId(), "n", 1);
    repository.save(entity);
}
```

The test tries to store an entity with the same business key as used by the entity saved by the setup method. The test will fail if the save operation succeeds or if the save fails with an exception other than the expected, DuplicateKeyException.

The other negative test is, in my opinion, the most interesting test in the test class. It is a test that verifies a correct error handling in the case of updates of stale data—it verifies that the optimistic locking mechanism works. It looks like this:

```
@Test
public void optimisticLockError() {

    // Store the saved entity in two separate entity objects
    ProductEntity entity1 =
    repository.findById(savedEntity.getId()).get();
    ProductEntity entity2 =
    repository.findById(savedEntity.getId()).get();

    // Update the entity using the first entity object
    entity1.setName("n1");
    repository.save(entity1);

    //  Update the entity using the second entity object.
```

```
    // This should fail since the second entity now holds a old version
    // number, that is, a Optimistic Lock Error
    try {
        entity2.setName("n2");
        repository.save(entity2);

        fail("Expected an OptimisticLockingFailureException");
    } catch (OptimisticLockingFailureException e) {}

    // Get the updated entity from the database and verify its new
    // state
    ProductEntity updatedEntity =
    repository.findById(savedEntity.getId()).get();
    assertEquals(1, (int)updatedEntity.getVersion());
    assertEquals("n1", updatedEntity.getName());
}
```

The following is observed from the preceding code:

1. First, the test reads the same entity twice and stores it in two different variables, entity1 and entity2.
2. Next, it uses one of the variables, entity1, to update the entity. The update of the entity in the database will cause the version field of the entity to be increased automatically by Spring Data. The other variable, entity2, now contains stale data, manifested by its version field that holds a lower value than the corresponding value in the database.
3. When the test tries to update the entity using the variable, entity2, that contains stale data, it is expected to fail by throwing an OptimisticLockingFailureException exception.
4. The test wraps up by asserting that the entity in the database reflects the first update, that is, contains the name "n1", and that the version field has the value 1, that is, only one update has been performed on the entity in the database.

Finally, the product service contains a test that demonstrates the usage of built-in support for sorting and paging in Spring Data:

```
@Test
public void paging() {
    repository.deleteAll();
    List<ProductEntity> newProducts = rangeClosed(1001, 1010)
        .mapToObj(i -> new ProductEntity(i, "name " + i, i))
        .collect(Collectors.toList());
    repository.saveAll(newProducts);

    Pageable nextPage = PageRequest.of(0, 4, ASC, "productId");
```

```
nextPage = testNextPage(nextPage, "[1001, 1002, 1003, 1004]",
true);
nextPage = testNextPage(nextPage, "[1005, 1006, 1007, 1008]",
true);
nextPage = testNextPage(nextPage, "[1009, 1010]", false);
}
```

The following is observed from the preceding code:

1. The test starts with removing any existing data, then inserts 10 entities with the productId field ranging from 1001 to 1010.

2. Next, it creates PageRequest, requesting a page count of 4 entities per page and a sort order based on ProductId in ascending order.

3. Finally, it uses a helper method, testNextPage, to read the expected three pages, verifying the expected product IDs in each page and verifying that Spring Data correctly reports back whether more pages exist or not.

The helper method testNextPage looks like this:

```
private Pageable testNextPage(Pageable nextPage, String expectedProductIds,
boolean expectsNextPage) {
    Page<ProductEntity> productPage = repository.findAll(nextPage);
    assertEquals(expectedProductIds, productPage.getContent()
    .stream().map(p -> p.getProductId()).collect(Collectors.
    toList()).toString());
    assertEquals(expectsNextPage, productPage.hasNext());
    return productPage.nextPageable();
}
```

The helper method uses the page request object, nextPage, to get the next page from the repository method, findAll(). Based on the result, it extracts the product IDs from the returned entities into a string and compares it to the expected list of product IDs. Finally, it returns a Boolean indicating whether more pages can be retrieved or not.

For full source code of the three persistence test classes, see the following:

- se.magnus.microservices.core.product.PersistenceTests in the product project
- se.magnus.microservices.core.recommendation.PersistenceTests in the recommendation project
- se.magnus.microservices.core.review.PersistenceTests in the review project

The persistence tests in the `product` microservice can be executed using Gradle with a command like this:

```
cd $BOOK_HOME/Chapter06
./gradlew microservices:product-service:test --tests PersistenceTests
```

After running the tests, it should respond with the following:

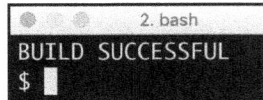

With a persistence layer in place, we can update the service layer in our core microservices to use the persistence layer.

Using the persistence layer in the service layer

In this section, we will learn how to use the persistence layer in the service layer to store data and retrieve data from a database. We will go through the following steps:

1. Log the database connection URL.
2. Add new APIs.
3. Use the persistence layer.
4. Declare a Java bean mapper.
5. Update the service tests.

Log the database connection URL

When scaling up the number of microservices where each microservice connects to its own database, I find myself, from time to time, in a situation where I'm not sure what database each microservice actually uses. Therefore, I usually add a log statement directly after the startup of a microservice that logs the connection URL that is used to connect to the database.

For example, the startup code for the `Product` service looks like this:

```
public class ProductServiceApplication {
    private static final Logger LOG =
    LoggerFactory.getLogger(ProductServiceApplication.class);

    public static void main(String[] args) {
        ConfigurableApplicationContext ctx =
        SpringApplication.run(ProductServiceApplication.class, args);
        String mongodDbHost =
        ctx.getEnvironment().getProperty("spring.data.mongodb.host");
        String mongodDbPort =
        ctx.getEnvironment().getProperty("spring.data.mongodb.port");
        LOG.info("Connected to MongoDb: " + mongodDbHost + ":" +
        mongodDbPort);
    }
}
```

In the log, the following type of output should be expected:

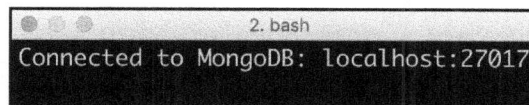

For the full source code, see the
`se.magnus.microservices.core.product.ProductServiceApplication` class in
the `product` project.

Adding new APIs

Before we can use the persistence layer for creating and deleting information in the
database, we need to create the corresponding API operations in our core service APIs.

The API operations for creating and deleting a product entity looks like this:

```
@PostMapping(
    value    = "/product",
    consumes = "application/json",
    produces = "application/json")
Product createProduct(@RequestBody Product body);

@DeleteMapping(value = "/product/{productId}")
void deleteProduct(@PathVariable int productId);
```

The implementation of the delete operation will be idempotent, that is, it will return the same result if called several times. This is a valuable characteristic in fault scenarios. For example, if a client experience a network timeout during a call to a delete operation, it can simply call the delete operation again without worrying about varying responses, for example, OK (200) in response the first time and Not Found (404) in response to consecutive calls, or any unexpected side effects. This implies that the operation should return the status code OK (200) even though the entity no longer exists in the database.

The API operations for the `recommendation` and `review` entities look similar; however, note that, when it comes to the delete operation for `recommendation` and `review` entities, it will delete all `recommendations` and `reviews` for the specified `productId`.

For the full source code, see the following classes in the `api` project:

- `se.magnus.api.core.product.ProductService`
- `se.magnus.api.core.recommendation.RecommendationService`
- `se.magnus.api.core.review.ReviewService`

The use of the persistence layer

The source code in the service layer for using the persistence layer is structured in the same way for all core microservices. Therefore, we will only go through the source code for the `Product` microservice.

First, we need to inject the repository class from the persistence layer and a Java bean mapper class into the constructor:

```
private final ServiceUtil serviceUtil;
private final ProductRepository repository;
private final ProductMapper mapper;

@Autowired
public ProductServiceImpl(ProductRepository repository, ProductMapper
mapper, ServiceUtil serviceUtil) {
    this.repository = repository;
    this.mapper = mapper;
    this.serviceUtil = serviceUtil;
}
```

In the next section, we will see how the Java mapper class is defined.

Next, the `createProduct` method is implemented as follows:

```
public Product createProduct(Product body) {
    try {
        ProductEntity entity = mapper.apiToEntity(body);
        ProductEntity newEntity = repository.save(entity);
        return mapper.entityToApi(newEntity);
    } catch (DuplicateKeyException dke) {
        throw new InvalidInputException("Duplicate key, Product Id: " +
        body.getProductId());
    }
}
```

The `create` method used the `save` method in the repository to store a new entity. It should be noted how the mapper class is used to convert Java beans between an API model class and an entity class using the two mapper methods, `apiToEntity()` and `entityToApi()`. The only error we handle for the `create` method is the `DuplicateKeyException` exception, which we convert into an `InvalidInputException` exception.

The `getProduct` method looks like this:

```
public Product getProduct(int productId) {
    if (productId < 1) throw new InvalidInputException("Invalid
    productId: " + productId);
    ProductEntity entity = repository.findByProductId(productId)
        .orElseThrow(() -> new NotFoundException("No product found for
            productId: " + productId));
    Product response = mapper.entityToApi(entity);
    response.setServiceAddress(serviceUtil.getServiceAddress());
    return response;
}
```

After some basic input validation (that is, ensuring that `productId` is not negative), the `findByProductId()` method in the repository is used to find the product entity. Since the repository method returns an `Optional` product, we can use the `orElseThrow()` method in the `Optional` class to conveniently throw a `NotFoundException` exception if no product entity is found. Before the product information is returned, the `serviceUtil` object is used to fill in the currently used address of the microservice.

Finally, let's see the `deleteProduct` method:

```
public void deleteProduct(int productId) {
    repository.findByProductId(productId).ifPresent(e ->
    repository.delete(e));
}
```

The `delete` method also uses the `findByProductId()` method in the repository and uses the `ifPresent()` method in the `Optional` class to conveniently delete the entity only if it exists. Note that the implementation is idempotent, that is, it will not report any failure if the entity is not found.

The source code for the three service implementation classes can be found at the following:

- `se.magnus.microservices.core.product.services.ProductServiceImpl` in the `product` project
- `se.magnus.microservices.core.recommendation.services.RecommendationServiceImpl` in the `recommendation` project
- `se.magnus.microservices.core.review.services.ReviewServiceImpl` in the `review` project

Declaring a Java bean mapper

So, what about the magic Java bean mapper?

As already mentioned, we use MapStruct to declare our mapper classes. The use of MapStruct is similar in all three core microservices, so we will only go through the source code for the mapper object in the `Product` microservice.

The mapper class for the `product` service looks like this:

```
@Mapper(componentModel = "spring")
public interface ProductMapper {

    @Mappings({
        @Mapping(target = "serviceAddress", ignore = true)
    })
    Product entityToApi(ProductEntity entity);

    @Mappings({
        @Mapping(target = "id", ignore = true),
        @Mapping(target = "version", ignore = true)
    })
    ProductEntity apiToEntity(Product api);
}
```

The following is observed from the preceding code:

- The `entityToApi()` method maps entity objects to the API model object. Since the entity class does not have a field for `serviceAddress`, the `entityToApi()` method is annotated to ignore `serviceAddress`.
- The `apiToEntity()` method maps API model objects to entity objects. In the same way, the `apiToEntity()` method is annotated to ignore the `id` and `version` fields that are missing in the API model class.

MapStruct does not only support mapping fields by name, but it can also be directed to map fields with different names. In the mapper class for the `Recommendation` service, the `rating` entity field is mapped to the API model field, `rate`, using the following annotations:

```
@Mapping(target = "rate", source="entity.rating"),
Recommendation entityToApi(RecommendationEntity entity);

@Mapping(target = "rating", source="api.rate"),
RecommendationEntity apiToEntity(Recommendation api);
```

After a successful Gradle build, the generated mapping implementation can be found in the `build/classes` folder, for example, the `Product` service: `$BOOK_HOME/Chapter06/microservices/product-service/build/classes/java/main/se/magnus/microservices/core/product/services/ProductMapperImpl.java`.

The source code for the three mapper classes can be found at the following:

- `se.magnus.microservices.core.product.services.ProductMapper` in the `product` project
- `se.magnus.microservices.core.recommendation.services.RecommendationMapper` in the `recommendation` project
- `se.magnus.microservices.core.review.services.ReviewMapper` in the `review` project

Updating the service tests

The tests of the APIs exposed by the core microservices have been updated since the previous chapter with tests on the create and delete API operations.

The added tests are similar in all three core microservices, so we will only go through the source code for the service tests in the `Product` microservice.

To ensure a known state for each test, a setup method, `setupDb()`, is declared and annotated with `@Before`, so it runs before each test runs. The setup method removes any previously created entities:

```
@Autowired
private ProductRepository repository;

@Before
public void setupDb() {
    repository.deleteAll();
}
```

The test method for the create API verifies that a product entity can be retrieved after it has been created and that creating another product entity with the same `productId` results in an expected error, `UNPROCESSABLE_ENTITY`, in the response to the API request:

```
@Test
public void duplicateError() {
    int productId = 1;
    postAndVerifyProduct(productId, OK);
    assertTrue(repository.findByProductId(productId).isPresent());

    postAndVerifyProduct(productId, UNPROCESSABLE_ENTITY)
        .jsonPath("$.path").isEqualTo("/product")
        .jsonPath("$.message").isEqualTo("Duplicate key, Product Id: " +
        productId);
}
```

The test method for the delete API verifies that a product entity can be deleted and that a second delete request is idempotent—it also returns the status code OK, even though the entity no longer exists in the database:

```
@Test
public void deleteProduct() {
    int productId = 1;
    postAndVerifyProduct(productId, OK);
    assertTrue(repository.findByProductId(productId).isPresent());

    deleteAndVerifyProduct(productId, OK);
    assertFalse(repository.findByProductId(productId).isPresent());

    deleteAndVerifyProduct(productId, OK);
}
```

To simplify sending the create, read, and delete requests to the API and verify the response status, three helper methods have been created:

- postAndVerifyProduct()
- getAndVerifyProduct()
- deleteAndVerifyProduct()

The postAndVerifyProduct() method looks like this:

```
private WebTestClient.BodyContentSpec postAndVerifyProduct(int productId,
HttpStatus expectedStatus) {
    Product product = new Product(productId, "Name " + productId,
    productId, "SA");
    return client.post()
        .uri("/product")
        .body(just(product), Product.class)
        .accept(APPLICATION_JSON_UTF8)
        .exchange()
        .expectStatus().isEqualTo(expectedStatus)
        .expectHeader().contentType(APPLICATION_JSON_UTF8)
        .expectBody();
}
```

Added to performing the actual HTTP request and verifying its response code, the helper method also returns the body of the response for further investigations by the caller, if required. The other two helper methods for read and delete requests are similar and can be found in the source code pointed out at the beginning of this section.

The source code for the three service tests classes can be found at the following:

- se.magnus.microservices.core.product.ProductServiceApplicationT ests in the product project
- se.magnus.microservices.core.recommendation.RecommendationServi ceApplicationTests in the recommendation project
- se.magnus.microservices.core.review.ReviewServiceApplicationTes ts in the review project

Now, lets move on to seeing how we extend a composite service API.

Extending the composite service API

In this section, we will see how we can extend the composite API with operations for creating and deleting composite entities. We will go through the following steps:

1. Adding new operations in the composite service API
2. Adding methods in the integration layer
3. Implementing the new composite API operations
4. Updating the composite service tests

Adding new operations in the composite service API

The composite versions of creating and deleting entities and handling aggregated entities are similar to the create and delete operations in the core service APIs. The major difference is that they have annotations added for Swagger-based documentation. For an explanation of the usage of the Swagger annotations, @ApiOperation and @ApiResponses, refer to *Chapter 5*, *Adding API Description Using OpenAPI/Swagger*, the section, *Adding API specific documentation in ProductCompositeService*. The API operation for creating a composite product entity is declared as follows:

```
@ApiOperation(
    value = "${api.product-composite.create-composite-
    product.description}",
    notes = "${api.product-composite.create-composite-product.notes}")
@ApiResponses(value = {
    @ApiResponse(code = 400, message = "Bad Request, invalid format of
    the request. See response message for more information."),
    @ApiResponse(code = 422, message = "Unprocessable entity, input
    parameters caused the processing to fail. See response message for
    more information.")
})
@PostMapping(
    value    = "/product-composite",
    consumes = "application/json")
void createCompositeProduct(@RequestBody ProductAggregate body);
```

The API operation for deleting a composite product entity is declared as follows:

```
@ApiOperation(
    value = "${api.product-composite.delete-composite-
    product.description}",
    notes = "${api.product-composite.delete-composite-product.notes}")
```

```
@ApiResponses(value = {
    @ApiResponse(code = 400, message = "Bad Request, invalid format of
    the request. See response message for more information."),
    @ApiResponse(code = 422, message = "Unprocessable entity, input
    parameters caused the processing to fail. See response message for
    more information.")
})
@DeleteMapping(value = "/product-composite/{productId}")
void deleteCompositeProduct(@PathVariable int productId);
```

For the full source code, see the Java
interface, se.magnus.api.composite.product.ProductCompositeService, in the
api project.

We also need to, as before, add the descriptive text of the API documentation to the
property file, application.yml:

```
create-composite-product:
  description: Creates a composite product
  notes: |
    # Normal response
    The composite product information posted to the API will be
    splitted up and stored as separate product-info, recommendation and
    review entities.

    # Expected error responses
    1. If a product with the same productId as specified in the posted
    information already exists, an <b>422 - Unprocessable Entity</b>
    error with a "duplicate key" error message will be returned

delete-composite-product:
  description: Deletes a product composite
  notes: |
    # Normal response
    Entities for product information, recommendations and reviews
    related to the specified productId will be deleted.
    The implementation of the delete method is idempotent, that is, it
    can be called several times with the same response.
    This means that a delete request of a non existing product will
    return <b>200 Ok</b>.
```

For details, see the configuration file, src/main/resources/application.yml, in
the product-composite project.

The updated Swagger documentation will look like this:

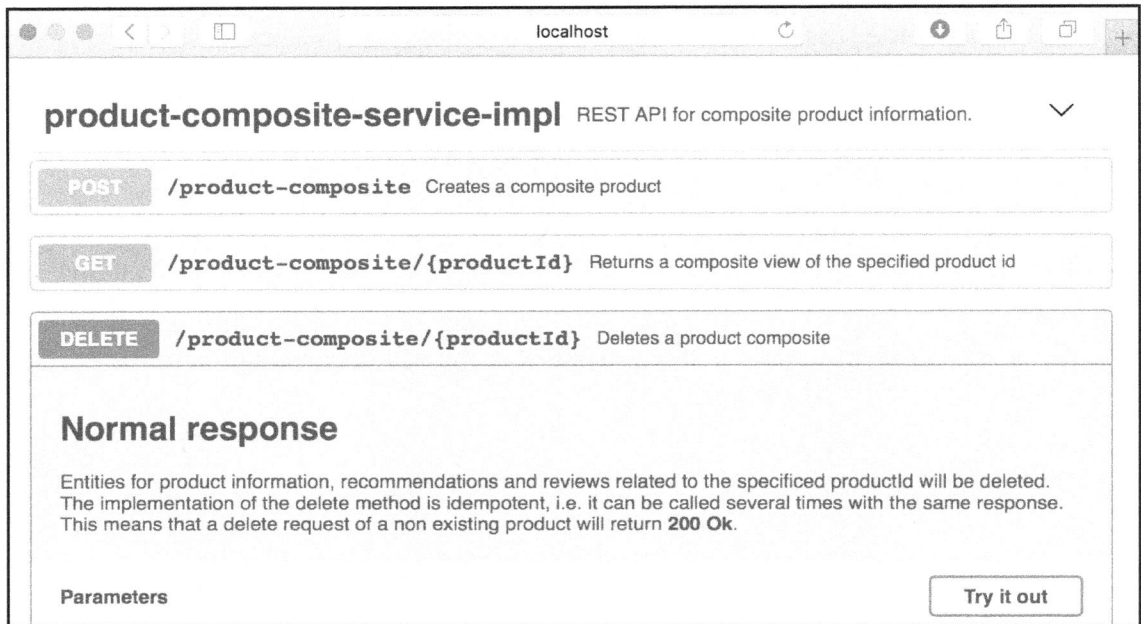

Later on in this chapter, we will user the Swagger UI to try out the new composite API operations.

Adding methods in the integration layer

Before we can implement the new create and delete APIs in the composite services, we need to extend the integration layer so it can call the underlying create and delete operations in the APIs of the core microservices.

The methods in the integration layer for calling the create and delete operations in the three core microservices are straightforward and similar to each other, so we will only go through the source code for the methods that call the `Product` microservice.

The `createProduct()` method looks like this:

```
@Override
public Product createProduct(Product body) {
    try {
        return restTemplate.postForObject(productServiceUrl, body,
```

```
            Product.class);
        } catch (HttpClientErrorException ex) {
            throw handleHttpClientException(ex);
        }
    }
```

It simply delegates the responsibility of sending the HTTP request to the `RestTemplate` object and delegates error handling to the helper method, `handleHttpClientException`.

The `deleteProduct()` method looks like this:

```
@Override
public void deleteProduct(int productId) {
    try {
        restTemplate.delete(productServiceUrl + "/" + productId);
    } catch (HttpClientErrorException ex) {
        throw handleHttpClientException(ex);
    }
}
```

It is implemented in the same way as for the create method, but performs an HTTP delete request instead.

The full source code for the integration layer can be seen in the `se.magnus.microservices.composite.product.services.ProductCompositeIntegration` class in the `product-composite` project.

Implementing the new composite API operations

Now, we can implement the composite create and delete methods!

The composite's create method will split up the aggregate product object into discrete objects for `product`, `recommendation`, and `review` and call the corresponding create methods in the integration layer:

```
@Override
public void createCompositeProduct(ProductAggregate body) {
    try {
        Product product = new Product(body.getProductId(),
        body.getName(), body.getWeight(), null);
        integration.createProduct(product);

        if (body.getRecommendations() != null) {
            body.getRecommendations().forEach(r -> {
                Recommendation recommendation = new
```

```
                    Recommendation(body.getProductId(),
                    r.getRecommendationId(), r.getAuthor(), r.getRate(),
                    r.getContent(), null);
                    integration.createRecommendation(recommendation);
                });
            }

            if (body.getReviews() != null) {
                body.getReviews().forEach(r -> {
                    Review review = new Review(body.getProductId(),
                    r.getReviewId(), r.getAuthor(), r.getSubject(),
                    r.getContent(), null);
                    integration.createReview(review);
                });
            }
        } catch (RuntimeException re) {
            LOG.warn("createCompositeProduct failed", re);
            throw re;
        }
    }
}
```

The composite's delete method simply calls the three delete methods in the integration layer to delete the corresponding entities in the underlying databases:

```
@Override
public void deleteCompositeProduct(int productId) {
    integration.deleteProduct(productId);
    integration.deleteRecommendations(productId);
    integration.deleteReviews(productId);
}
```

For full source code, see
the `se.magnus.microservices.composite.product.services.ProductCompositeS`
`erviceImpl` class in the `product-composite` project.

For happy day scenarios, this implementation will work fine, but if we consider various error scenarios this implementation will cause trouble!

What if, for example, one of the underlying core microservices temporarily is not available, for example, due to internal, network, or database problems?

This might result in partly created or deleted composite products. For the delete operation, this can be fixed if the requestor simply calls the composite's delete method until it succeeds. However, if the underlying problem remains for a while, the requestor will probably give up, resulting in an inconsistent state of the composite product—not acceptable in most cases!

In the next chapter, `Chapter 7`, *Developing Reactive Microservices,* we will see how we can address these types of shortcomings with synchronous APIs as a RESTful API!

For now, let's move on with this fragile design in mind.

Updating the composite service tests

Testing composite services, as already mentioned in `Chapter 3`, *Creating a Set of Cooperating Microservices* (refer to the *Automated tests of microservices in isolation* section), are limited to using simple mock components instead of the actual core services. This restricts us from testing more complex scenarios, for example, error handling when trying to create duplicates in the underlying databases. The tests of the composite create and delete API operations are therefore relatively simple:

```
@Test
public void createCompositeProduct1() {
    ProductAggregate compositeProduct = new ProductAggregate(1, "name",
    1, null, null, null);
    postAndVerifyProduct(compositeProduct, OK);
}

@Test
public void createCompositeProduct2() {
    ProductAggregate compositeProduct = new ProductAggregate(1, "name",
        1, singletonList(new RecommendationSummary(1, "a", 1, "c")),
        singletonList(new ReviewSummary(1, "a", "s", "c")), null);
    postAndVerifyProduct(compositeProduct, OK);
}

@Test
public void deleteCompositeProduct() {
    ProductAggregate compositeProduct = new ProductAggregate(1, "name",
        1, singletonList(new RecommendationSummary(1, "a", 1, "c")),
        singletonList(new ReviewSummary(1, "a", "s", "c")), null);
    postAndVerifyProduct(compositeProduct, OK);
    deleteAndVerifyProduct(compositeProduct.getProductId(), OK);
    deleteAndVerifyProduct(compositeProduct.getProductId(), OK);
}
```

For the full source code, see the test class, `se.magnus.microservices.composite.product.ProductCompositeServiceA pplicationTests`, in the `product-composite` project.

Next, we will see how to add databases to the landscape of Docker Compose.

Adding databases to the Docker Compose landscape

Now, we have all of the source code in place. Before we can start up the microservice landscape and try out the new APIs together with the new persistence layer, we must start up some databases.

We will bring MongoDB and MySQL into the system landscape controlled by Docker Compose and add configuration to our microservices so that they can find their databases when running, either with or without running as a Docker container.

The Docker Compose configuration

MongoDB and MySQL are declared as follows in the Docker Compose configuration file, `docker-compose.yml`:

```
mongodb:
  image: mongo:3.6.9
  mem_limit: 350m
  ports:
    - "27017:27017"
  command: mongod --smallfiles

mysql:
  image: mysql:5.7
  mem_limit: 350m
  ports:
    - "3306:3306"
  environment:
    - MYSQL_ROOT_PASSWORD=rootpwd
    - MYSQL_DATABASE=review-db
    - MYSQL_USER=user
    - MYSQL_PASSWORD=pwd
  healthcheck:
    test: ["CMD", "mysqladmin" ,"ping", "-uuser", "-ppwd", "-h",
"localhost"]
    interval: 10s
    timeout: 5s
    retries: 10
```

The following is observed from the preceding code:

1. We will use the official Docker image for MongoDB V3.6.9 and MySQL 5.7 and forward their default ports `27017` and `3306` to the Docker host, also made available on `localhost` when using Docker for Mac.

2. For MySQL, we also declare some environment variables, defining the following:
   - The root password
   - The name of the database that will be created on image startup
   - A username and password for a user that is set up for the database on image startup

3. For MySQL, we also declare a health check that Docker will run to determine the status of the MySQL database.

To avoid problems with microservices that try to connect to their databases before the database is up and running, the `product` and `recommendation` services are declared dependent on the `mongodb` database, as follows:

```
product/recommendation:
  depends_on:
  - mongodb
```

This means that Docker Compose will not start up the `product` and `recommendation` containers until the `mongodb` container is launched.

For the same reason, the `review` service is declared dependent on the `mysql` database:

```
review:
  depends_on:
    mysql:
      condition: service_healthy
```

In this case, the `review` service depends on the fact that the `mysql` container is not only launched, but also that the `mysql` containers health check reports are okay. The reason for this extra step is that the initialization of the `mysql` container includes setting up a database and creating a superuser for the database. This takes a few seconds and, to hold back the `review` service to startup before this is done, we direct Docker Compose to hold back the `review` container from being launched until the `mysql` container reports that it is operational through its health check.

Database connect configuration

With the database in place, we now need to set up the configuration for the core microservices so they know how to connect to their databases. This is set up in each core microservice's configuration file, `src/main/resources/application.yml`, in the `product`, `recommendation`, and `review` projects.

The configuration for the `product` and `recommendation` services are similar, so we will only look into the configuration of the `product` services. The following part of the configuration is of interest:

```
spring.data.mongodb:
  host: localhost
  port: 27017
  database: product-db

logging:
 level:
 org.springframework.data.mongodb.core.MongoTemplate: DEBUG

---
spring.profiles: docker

spring.data.mongodb.host: mongodb
```

The following is observed from the preceding code:

1. When running without Docker using the default Spring profile, the database is expected to be reachable on `localhost:27017`.
2. Setting the log level for `MongoTemplate` to `DEBUG` will allow us to see which MongoDB statements are executed in the log.
3. When running inside Docker using the Spring profile, `Docker`, the database is expected to be reachable on `mongodb:27017`.

The configuration for the `review` service, which affects how it connects to its SQL database, looks like the following:

```
spring.jpa.hibernate.ddl-auto: update

spring.datasource:
  url: jdbc:mysql://localhost/review-db
  username: user
  password: pwd

spring.datasource.hikari.initializationFailTimeout: 60000
```

```
logging:
 level:
 org.hibernate.SQL: DEBUG
 org.hibernate.type.descriptor.sql.BasicBinder: TRACE


 ---
 spring.profiles: docker

 spring.datasource:
 url: jdbc:mysql://mysql/review-db
```

The following is observed from the preceding code:

1. By default, Hibernate will be used by Spring Data JPA as the JPA Entity Manager.
2. The `spring.jpa.hibernate.ddl-auto` property is used to tell Spring Data JPA to create new or update existing SQL tables during startup.
   Note: It is strongly recommended to set the `spring.jpa.hibernate.ddl-auto` property to `none` in a production environment—this prevents Spring Data JPA to manipulate the structure of the SQL tables.
3. When running without Docker, using the default Spring profile, the database is expected to be reachable on `localhost` using the default port `3306`.
4. By default, HikariCP is used by Spring Data JPA as the JDBC connection pool. To minimize startup problems on computers with limited hardware resources, the `initializationFailTimeout` parameter is set to 60 seconds. This means that the Spring Boot application will wait for up to 60 seconds during startup to establish a database connection.
5. The log level settings for Hibernate will cause Hibernate to print the SQL statements used and the actual values used. Please note that, when used in a production environment, writing the actual values to the log should be avoided for privacy reasons.
6. When running inside Docker using the Spring profile, `Docker`, the database is expected to be reachable on the `mysql` hostname using the default port `3306`.

The MongoDB and MySQL CLI tools

To be able to run the database CLI tools, the Docker Compose `exec` command can be used.

The commands described in this section will be used when we get to the manual tests in the next section. Don't try to run them now; they will fail since we have no databases up and running yet!

To start the MongoDB CLI tool, `mongo`, inside the `mongodb` container, run the following command:

```
docker-compose exec mongodb mongo --quiet
>
```

Enter `exit` to leave the `mongo` CLI.

To start the MySQL CLI tool, `mysql`, inside the `mysql` container and log in to `review-db` using the user created at startup, run the following command:

```
docker-compose exec mysql mysql -uuser -p review-db
mysql>
```

> The `mysql` CLI tool will prompt you for a password; you can find it in the `docker-compose.yml` file. Look for the value of the environment variable, `MYSQL_PASSWORD`.

Enter `exit` to leave the `mysql` CLI.

We will see the usage of these tools in the next section.

> If you prefer graphical database tools, you can run them locally as well, since both the MongoDB and the MySQL containers expose their standard ports on localhost.

Manual tests of the new APIs and the persistence layer

Now, it is finally time to start everything up and test it manually using the Swagger UI.

Build and start the system landscape with the following command:

```
cd $BOOK_HOME/Chapter06
./gradlew build && docker-compose build && docker-compose up
```

Open the Swagger UI in a web browser, `http://localhost:8080/swagger-ui.html`, and perform the following steps on the web page:

1. Click on **product-composite-service-impl** and the **POST** method to expand them.
2. Click on the **Try it out** button and go down to the body field.
3. Replace the default value, 0, of the `productId` field with `123456`.
4. Scroll down to the **Execute** button and click on it.
5. Verify that the returned response code is `200`.

Following is a sample screenshot after hitting the **Execute** button:

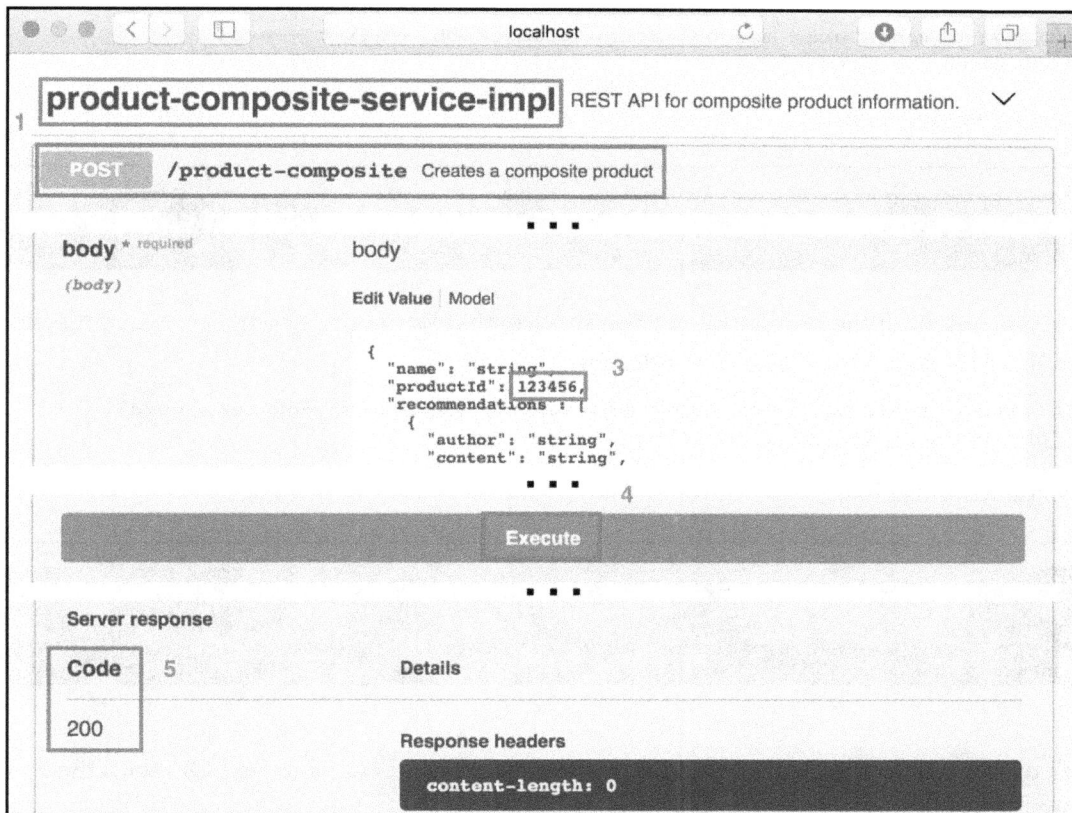

In the log output from the `docker-compose up` command, we should be able to see output like the following (abbreviated for increased readability):

```
product-composite_1 | ... createCompositeProduct: creates a new composite entity for productId: 123456
product_1 | ... createProduct: entity created for productId: 123456
recommendation_1 | ... createRecommendation: created a recommendation entity: 123456/0
review_1 | ... createReview: created a review entity: 123456/0
```

We can also use the database CLI tools to see the actual content in the different databases.

Look up content in the `product` service, that is, the `products` collection in MongoDB, with the following command:

```
docker-compose exec mongodb mongo product-db --quiet --eval
"db.products.find()"
```

Expect a response like:

```
{ "_id" : ObjectId("5c04ed370e8e3d000102ef94"), "version" : 0, "productId" : 123456, "name" : "string",
  "weight" : 0, "_class" : "se.magnus.microservices.core.product.persistence.ProductEntity" }
$
```

Look up content in the `recommendation` service, that is, the `recommendations` collection in MongoDB, with the following command:

```
docker-compose exec mongodb mongo recommendation-db --quiet --eval
"db.recommendations.find()"
```

Expect a response like:

```
{ "_id" : ObjectId("5c04ed378b87bc000133c349"), "version" : 0, "productId" : 123456,
  "recommendationId" : 0, "author" : "string", "rating" : 0, "content" : "string",
  "_class" : "se.magnus.microservices.core.recommendation.persistence.RecommendationEntity" }
$
```

10

Look up content in the `review` service, that is, the `reviews` table in MySQL, with the following command:

```
docker-compose exec mysql mysql -uuser -p review-db -e "select * from
reviews"
```

The `mysql` CLI tool will prompt you for a password; you can find it in the `docker-compose.yml` file. Look for the value of the environment variable, `MYSQL_PASSWORD`. Expect a response like the following:

Bring down the system landscape by interrupting the `docker-compose up` command with *Ctrl + C*, followed by the command, `docker-compose down`. After this, let us see how to update the automated tests in a microservice landscape.

Updating the automated tests of the microservice landscape

The automated tests of the microservice landscape, `test-em-all.bash`, needs to be updated so that they ensure that the database of each microservice has a known state before it runs the tests.

The script is extended with a setup function, `setupTestdata()`, which uses the composite's create and delete APIs to recreate the products that the tests use into a known state.

The `setupTestdata` function looks like this:

```
function setupTestdata() {

    body=\
    '{"productId":1,"name":"product 1","weight":1, "recommendations":[
        {"recommendationId":1,"author":"author
        1","rate":1,"content":"content 1"},
        {"recommendationId":2,"author":"author
        2","rate":2,"content":"content 2"},
        {"recommendationId":3,"author":"author
        3","rate":3,"content":"content 3"}
    ], "reviews":[
        {"reviewId":1,"author":"author 1","subject":"subject
        1","content":"content 1"},
        {"reviewId":2,"author":"author 2","subject":"subject
```

```
        2","content":"content 2"},
        {"reviewId":3,"author":"author 3","subject":"subject
        3","content":"content 3"}
    ]}'
    recreateComposite 1 "$body"

    body=\
    '{"productId":113,"name":"product 113","weight":113, "reviews":[
    {"reviewId":1,"author":"author 1","subject":"subject
     1","content":"content 1"},
    {"reviewId":2,"author":"author 2","subject":"subject
     2","content":"content 2"},
    {"reviewId":3,"author":"author 3","subject":"subject
     3","content":"content 3"}
    ]}'
    recreateComposite 113 "$body"

    body=\
    '{"productId":213,"name":"product 213","weight":213,
    "recommendations":[
        {"recommendationId":1,"author":"author
         1","rate":1,"content":"content 1"},
        {"recommendationId":2,"author":"author
         2","rate":2,"content":"content 2"},
        {"recommendationId":3,"author":"author
         3","rate":3,"content":"content 3"}
    ]}'
    recreateComposite 213 "$body"

}
```

It uses a helper function, `recreateComposite()`, to perform the actual requests to the create and delete APIs:

```
function recreateComposite() {
    local productId=$1
    local composite=$2

    assertCurl 200 "curl -X DELETE http://$HOST:$PORT/product-
    composite/${productId} -s"
    curl -X POST http://$HOST:$PORT/product-composite -H "Content-Type:
    application/json" --data "$composite"
}
```

The `setupTestdata` function is called directly after the `waitForService` function:

```
waitForService curl -X DELETE http://$HOST:$PORT/product-composite/13

setupTestdata
```

The main purpose of the `waitForService` function is to verify that all microservices are up and running. In the previous chapter, the get API on the composite product service was used. In this chapter, the delete API is used instead. When using the get API, only the product core microservice is called if the entity is not found; the recommendation and `review` services will not be called to verify that they are up and running. The call to the delete API will also ensure that the *Not Found*-test on `productId 13` will succeed. Later on in this book, we will see how we can define specific APIs for checking the health state of a microservice landscape.

Execute the updated test script with the following command:

```
cd $BOOK_HOME/Chapter06
./test-em-all.bash start stop
```

The execution should end by writing a log message like this:

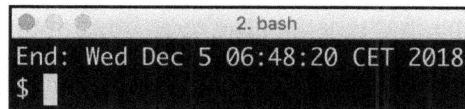

This ends updating of the automated tests of the microservice landscape.

Summary

In this chapter, we have seen how we can use Spring Data to add a persistence layer to the core microservices. We used the core concepts of Spring Data, repositories and entities, to store data in both MongoDB and MySQL using a programming model that is similar, even though not fully portable. We have also seen how Spring Boot's annotations, `@DataMongoTest` and `@DataJpaTest`, can be used to conveniently set up tests targeted for persistence; this is where an embedded database is started automatically before the test runs, but no other infrastructure that the microservice will need in runtime, for example, a web server such as Netty, is started up. This results in persistence tests that are easy to set up and that start with minimum overhead.

We have also seen how the persistence layer can be used by the service layer and how we can add APIs for creating and deleting entities, both core and composite entities.

Finally, we learned how convenient it is to start up databases such as MongoDB and MySQL in runtime using Docker Compose and how to use the new create and delete APIs to set up test data before running automated tests of the microservice-based system landscape.

However, one major concern was identified in this chapter. Updating (creating or deleting) a composite entity—an entity whose parts are stored in a number of microservices—using synchronous APIs can lead to inconsistencies, if not all involved microservices are updated successfully. This is, in general, not acceptable. This leads us into the next chapter, where we will look into why and how to build reactive microservices, that is, microservices that are scalable and robust.

Questions

1. Spring Data, a common programming model based on entities and repositories, can be used for different types of database engines. From the source code examples in this chapter, what are the most important differences in the persistence code for MySQL and MongoDB?
2. What is required to implement optimistic locking using Spring Data?
3. What is MapStruct used for?
4. What does it mean that an operation is idempotent and why is that useful?
5. How can we access the data that is stored in the MySQL and MongoDB databases without using the API?

7
Developing Reactive Microservices

In this chapter, we will learn how to develop reactive microservices, that is, how to develop non-blocking synchronous REST APIs and asynchronous event-driven services using Spring. We will also learn about how to choose between these two alternatives. Finally, we will see how to create and run manual and automated tests of a reactive microservice landscape.

As already described in the *Reactive microservices* section in `Chapter 1`, *Introduction to Microservices*, the foundations for reactive systems is that they are message-driven—they use asynchronous communication. This enables them to be elastic, that is, scalable and resilient, meaning that they will be tolerant to failures. Elasticity and resilience together will enable a reactive system to be responsive; they will be able to respond in a timely fashion.

The following topics will be covered in this chapter:

- Choosing between non-blocking synchronous APIs and event-driven asynchronous services
- Developing non-blocking synchronous REST APIs using Spring
- Developing event-driven asynchronous services
- Running manual tests of the reactive microservice landscape
- Running automated tests of the reactive microservice landscape

Technical requirements

All the commands described in this book are run on a MacBook Pro using macOS Mojave but should be straightforward to modify so that they can run on another platform such as Linux or Windows.

No new tools need to be installed in this chapter.

The source code for this chapter can be found on GitHub: `https://github.com/PacktPublishing/Hands-On-Microservices-with-Spring-Boot-and-Spring-Cloud/tree/master/Chapter07`.

To be able to run the commands as described in the book, download the source code to a folder and set up an environment variable, `$BOOK_HOME`, that points to that folder. Some sample commands are as follows:

```
export BOOK_HOME=~/Documents/Hands-On-Microservices-with-Spring-Boot-and-Spring-Cloud
git clone https://github.com/PacktPublishing/Hands-On-Microservices-with-Spring-Boot-and-Spring-Cloud $BOOK_HOME
cd $BOOK_HOME/Chapter07
```

The Java source code is written for Java 8 and tested on Java 12. This chapter uses Spring Cloud 2.1.0 (also known as the **Greenwich** release), Spring Boot 2.1.2, and Spring 5.1.4, which are the latest available versions of the Spring components at the time of writing this chapter.

The source code contains the following Gradle projects:

- `api`
- `util`
- `microservices/product-service`
- `microservices/review-service`
- `microservices/recommendation-service`
- `microservices/product-composite-service`

The code examples in this chapter all come from the source code in `$BOOK_HOME/Chapter07`, but are edited in many cases in order to remove irrelevant parts of the source code, such as comments and import and log statements.

In this chapter, you can take a look at the changes that ware applied to the source code and what it took to make the microservices reactive. This code can be compared to the source code for `Chapter 6`, *Adding Persistence*. You can use your favorite `diff`-tool and compare the two folders – `$BOOK_HOME/Chapter06` and `$BOOK_HOME/Chapter07`.

Choosing between non-blocking synchronous APIs and event-driven asynchronous services

When developing reactive microservices, it is not always obvious when to use non-blocking synchronous APIs and when to use event-driven asynchronous services. In general, to make a microservice robust and scalable, it is important to make it as autonomous as possible, for example, minimizing its runtime dependencies. This is also known as **loose coupling**. Therefore, asynchronous message passing of events, is preferable over synchronous APIs. This is because the microservice will only depend on access to the messaging system at runtime instead of being dependent on synchronous access to a number of other microservices.

There are, however, a number of cases where non-blocking synchronous APIs could be favorable to use, for example:

- For read operations where an end user is waiting for a response
- Where the client platforms are more suitable for consuming synchronous APIs, for example, mobile apps or SPA web applications
- Where the clients will connect to the service from other organizations—where it might be hard to agree over a common messaging system to use across organizations

For the system landscape used in this book, we will use the following:

- The create, read, and delete services exposed by the product composite microservice will be based on synchronous APIs. The composite microservice is assumed to have clients on both web and mobile platforms, as well as clients coming from other organizations rather than the ones that operate the system landscape. Therefore, synchronous APIs seem like a natural match.

- The read services provided by the core microservices will also be developed as non-blocking synchronous APIs since there is an end user waiting for their responses.
- The create and delete services provided by the core microservices will be developed as event-driven asynchronous services. The synchronous APIs provided by the composite microservices to create and delete aggregated product information will simply publish, create, and delete events on the topics that the core services listen on and then return with a 200 (OK) response.

This is illustrated by the following diagram:

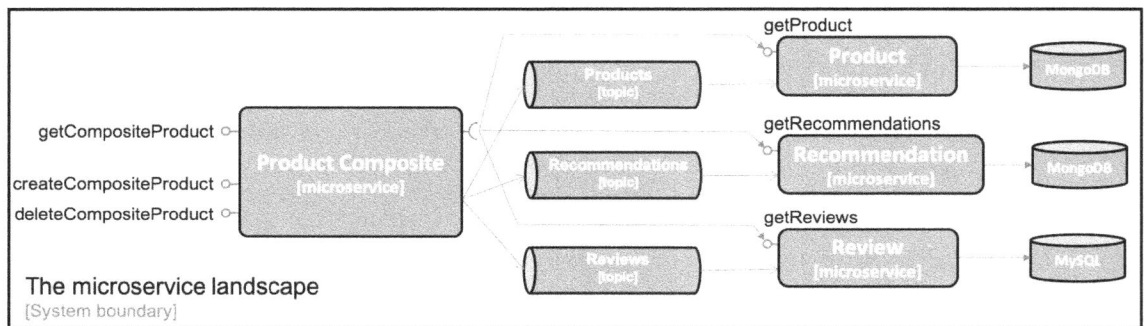

First, let's learn how we can develop non-blocking synchronous REST APIs, and thereafter, we will look at how to develop event-driven asynchronous services.

Developing non-blocking synchronous REST APIs using Spring

In this section, we will learn how to develop non-blocking versions of the read APIs. The composite service will make reactive, that is, non-blocking, calls in parallel to the three core services. When the composite service has received responses from the core services, it will create a composite response and send it back to the caller. This is illustrated in the following diagram:

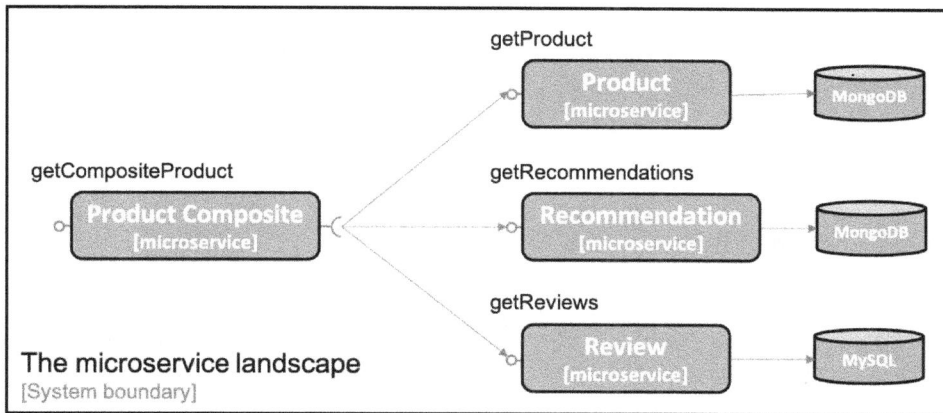

We will cover the following:

- An introduction to Spring Reactor
- Non-blocking persistence using Spring Data for MongoDB
- Non-blocking REST APIs in the core services, including how to handle blocking code for the JPA-based persistence layer
- Non-blocking REST APIs in the composite service

An introduction to Spring Reactor

As we mentioned in the *Beginning with Spring WebFlux* section in `Chapter 2`, *Introduction to Spring Boot*, the reactive support in Spring 5 is based on **Project Reactor** (`https://projectreactor.io`). Project Reactor is based on the *Reactive Streams specification* (`http://www.reactive-streams.org`), a standard for building reactive applications. Spring Reactor is fundamental and it is what Spring WebFlux, Spring WebClient, and Spring Data rely on to provide their reactive and non-blocking features.

The programming model is based on processing streams of data, and the core data types in Project Reactor are `Flux` and `Mono`. A `Flux` object is used to process a stream of *0...n* elements and a `Mono` object is used to process *0...1* elements. We will see numerous examples of its usage in this chapter. As a short introduction, let's look at the following test:

```
@Test
public void TestFlux() {

    List<Integer> list = new ArrayList<>();

    Flux.just(1, 2, 3, 4)
```

```
        .filter(n -> n % 2 == 0)
        .map(n -> n * 2)
        .log()
        .subscribe(n -> list.add(n));

  assertThat(list).containsExactly(4, 8);
}
```

Here is an explanation of the preceding source code:

1. We initiate the stream with the integers 1, 2, 3, and 4.

2. Next, we `filter` out the odd numbers—we only allow even numbers to proceed through the stream—in this test, these are 2 and 4.

3. Next, we transform (or `map`) the values in the stream by multiplying them by 2, that is, to 4 and 8.

4. Then, we `log` the data that flows through the stream after the `map` operation.

5. So far, we have only declared the processing of a stream. To actually get the stream processed, we need someone to subscribe to it. The final call to the `subscribe` method will register a subscriber and the subscriber will apply the lambda function specified in the call to the `subscribe` method on each element it gets from the stream. Thereafter, it will add them to the `list` element.

6. Finally, we can assert that `list` after the processing of the stream contains the expected result—the integers 4 and 8.

The log output will look like the following code:

```
20:01:45.714 [main] INFO reactor.Flux.MapFuseable.1 - |
onSubscribe([Fuseable] FluxMapFuseable.MapFuseableSubscriber)
20:01:45.716 [main] INFO reactor.Flux.MapFuseable.1 - | request(unbounded)
20:01:45.716 [main] INFO reactor.Flux.MapFuseable.1 - | onNext(4)
20:01:45.717 [main] INFO reactor.Flux.MapFuseable.1 - | onNext(8)
20:01:45.717 [main] INFO reactor.Flux.MapFuseable.1 - | onComplete()
```

Here is an explanation of the preceding source code:

1. The processing of the stream is started by a subscriber that subscribes to the stream and requests its content.

2. Next, the integers 4 and 8 pass through the `log` operation.

3. The processing concludes with a call to the `onComplete` method on the subscriber, notifying it that the stream has come to an end.

For the full source code, see the `se.magnus.util.reactor.ReactorTests` test class in the `util` project.

> Normally, we don't initiate the processing of the stream. Instead, we will only define how it shall be processed, and it will be the responsibility of an infrastructure component, such as Spring WebFlux, to initiate the processing, for example, as a response to an incoming HTTP request. An exception to this rule of thumb is the case where blocking code needs a response from the reactive stream. In these cases, the blocking code can call the `block()` method on the `Flux` or `Mono` object to get the response from the `Flux` or `Mono` object in a blocking way.

Non-blocking persistence using Spring Data for MongoDB

Making the MongoDB-based repositories for the `product` and `recommendation` services reactive is very simple:

- Change to the `ReactiveCrudRepository` base class for the repositories
- Change the custom finder methods to return a `Mono` or `Flux` object

The `ProductRepository` and `RecommendationRepository` look like the following after the change:

```
public interface ProductRepository extends
ReactiveCrudRepository<ProductEntity, String> {
    Mono<ProductEntity> findByProductId(int productId);
}

public interface RecommendationRepository extends
ReactiveCrudRepository<RecommendationEntity, String> {
    Flux<RecommendationEntity> findByProductId(int productId);
}
```

> No changes are applied to the persistence code for the `review` service, it will remain blocking using the JPA repository!

For the full source code, take a look at the following classes:

- `se.magnus.microservices.core.product.persistence.ProductReposit ory` in the `product` project.
- `se.magnus.microservices.core.recommendation.persistence.Recomme ndationRepository` in the `recommendation` project.

Changes in the test code

When it comes to testing the persistence layer, we have to make some changes. Since our persistence methods now return a `Mono` or `Flux` object, the test methods have to wait for the response to be available in the returned reactive objects. The test methods can either use an explicit call to the `block()` method on the `Mono/Flux` object to wait until a response is available or use the `StepVerifier` helper class from Project Reactor to declare a verifiable sequence of asynchronous events.

The following example shows how to change the test code to work for the reactive version of the repository:

```
ProductEntity foundEntity = repository.findById(newEntity.getId()).get();
assertEqualsProduct(newEntity, foundEntity);
```

We can use the `block()` method on the `Mono` object returned by the `repository.findById()` method and keep the imperative programming style, as shown here:

```
ProductEntity foundEntity = repository.findById(newEntity.getId()).block();
assertEqualsProduct(newEntity, foundEntity);
```

Alternatively, we can use the `StepVerifier` class to set up a sequence of processing steps that both execute the repository find operation and also verifies the result. The sequence is initialized by the final call to the `verifyComplete()` method like so:

```
StepVerifier.create(repository.findById(newEntity.getId()))
    .expectNextMatches(foundEntity -> areProductEqual(newEntity,
    foundEntity))
    .verifyComplete();
```

For examples of using the `StepVerifier` class to write tests, see the `se.magnus.microservices.core.product.PersistenceTests` test class in the `product` project.

For corresponding examples of using the `block()` method to write tests, see the `se.magnus.microservice.core.recommendation.PersistenceTests` test class in the `recommendation` project.

Non-blocking REST APIs in the core services

With a non-blocking persistence layer in place, it's time to make the APIs in the core services non-blocking as well. We need to make the following changes:

- Change the APIs so that they only return reactive data types
- Change the service implementations so they don't contain any blocking code
- Change our tests so that they can test the reactive services
- Deal with blocking code—isolate the code that still needs to be blocking from the non-blocking code

Changes in the APIs

To make the APIs of the core services reactive, we need to update their methods so that they return either a `Mono` or `Flux` object.

For example, `getProduct()` in the `product` service now returns `Mono<Product>` instead of a `Product` object:

```
Mono<Product> getProduct(@PathVariable int productId);
```

For the full source code, take a look at the following classes in the `api` project:

- `se.magnus.api.core.product.ProductService`
- `se.magnus.api.core.recommendation.RecommendationService`
- `se.magnus.api.core.review.ReviewService`

Changes in the service implementations

For the implementations of the services in the `product` and `recommendation` services that use a reactive persistence layer, we can use the fluent API in Project Reactor. For example, the implementation of the `getProduct()` method looks like the following code:

```
public Mono<Product> getProduct(int productId) {

    if (productId < 1) throw new InvalidInputException("Invalid
```

```
        productId: " + productId);

    return repository.findByProductId(productId)
        .switchIfEmpty(error(new NotFoundException("No product found
         for productId: " + productId)))
        .log()
        .map(e -> mapper.entityToApi(e))
        .map(e -> {e.setServiceAddress(serviceUtil.getServiceAddress());
    return e;});
}
```

Here is an explanation of the preceding source code:

1. The method will return a `Mono` object; the processing here is declared, not triggered. It is triggered by the web framework, `WebFlux`, once it receives a request to this service!
2. A product will be retrieved using its `productId` from the underlying database using the `findByProductId()` method in the persistence repository.
3. If no product is found for the given `productId`, `NotFoundException` will be thrown.
4. The `log` method will produce log output.
5. The `mapper.entityToApi()` method will be called to transform the returned entity from the persistence layer to an API model object.
6. The final `map` method will set the DNS name and IP address of the microservices that processed the request in the `serviceAddress` field of the model object.

Some sample log output for successful processing is as follows:

```
2019-02-06 10:09:47.006 INFO 62314 --- [ctor-http-nio-2]
reactor.Mono.SwitchIfEmpty.1 :
onSubscribe(FluxSwitchIfEmpty.SwitchIfEmptySubscriber)
2019-02-06 10:09:47.007 INFO 62314 --- [ctor-http-nio-2]
reactor.Mono.SwitchIfEmpty.1 : request(unbounded)
2019-02-06 10:09:47.034 INFO 62314 --- [ntLoopGroup-2-2]
reactor.Mono.SwitchIfEmpty.1 : onNext(ProductEntity: 1)
2019-02-06 10:09:47.048 INFO 62314 --- [ntLoopGroup-2-2]
reactor.Mono.SwitchIfEmpty.1 : onComplete()
```

The following is a sample of failed processing (throwing a not found exception):

```
2019-02-06 10:09:52.643 INFO 62314 --- [ctor-http-nio-3]
reactor.Mono.SwitchIfEmpty.2 :
onSubscribe(FluxSwitchIfEmpty.SwitchIfEmptySubscriber)
2019-02-06 10:09:52.643 INFO 62314 --- [ctor-http-nio-3]
reactor.Mono.SwitchIfEmpty.2 : request(unbounded)
```

```
2019-02-06 10:09:52.648 ERROR 62314 --- [ntLoopGroup-2-2]
reactor.Mono.SwitchIfEmpty.2 :
onError(se.magnus.util.exceptions.NotFoundException: No product found for
productId: 2)
2019-02-06 10:09:52.654 ERROR 62314 --- [ntLoopGroup-2-2]
reactor.Mono.SwitchIfEmpty.2 :

se.magnus.util.exceptions.NotFoundException: No product found for
productId: 2
   at
se.magnus.microservices.core.product.services.ProductServiceImpl.getProduct
(ProductServiceImpl.java:58) ~[classes/:na]
   . . .
```

For the full source code, see the following classes:

- se.magnus.microservices.core.product.services.ProductServiceImpl in the product project
- se.magnus.microservices.core.recommendation.services.RecommendationServiceImpl in the recommendation project

Changes in the test code

The test code for service implementations has been changed in the same way as the tests for the persistence layer we described previously. To handle the asynchronous behavior of the reactive return types, Mono and Flux, the tests use a mix of calling the block() method and using the StepVerifier helper class.

For the full source code, see the following test classes:

- se.magnus.microservices.core.product.ProductServiceApplicationTests in the product project
- se.magnus.microservices.core.recommendation.RecommendationServiceApplicationTests in the recommendation project

Dealing with blocking code

In the case of the review service, which uses JPA to access its data in a relational database, we don't have support for a non-blocking programming model. Instead, we can run the blocking code using Scheduler, which is capable of running the blocking code on a thread from a dedicated thread pool with a limited number of threads. Using a thread pool for the blocking code avoids draining the available threads in the microservice (avoids affecting the non-blocking processing in the microservice).

Let's see how this process works, as laid out in the following steps:

1. Firstly, we configure the thread pool in the main ReviewServiceApplication class, as follows:

```
@Autowired
public ReviewServiceApplication (
    @Value("${spring.datasource.maximum-pool-size:10}") Integer
    connectionPoolSize
) {
    this.connectionPoolSize = connectionPoolSize;
}

@Bean
public Scheduler jdbcScheduler() {
    LOG.info("Creates a jdbcScheduler with connectionPoolSize = " +
    connectionPoolSize);
    return Schedulers.fromExecutor(Executors.newFixedThreadPool
    (connectionPoolSize));
}
```

We can configure the size of the thread pool using the spring.datasource.maximum-pool-size parameter. If it is not set, it will default to 10 threads. For the full source code, see the se.magnus.microservices.core.review.ReviewServiceApplication class in the review project.

2. Next, we inject the scheduler into the review service implementation class, as shown here:

```
@RestController
public class ReviewServiceImpl implements ReviewService {

    private final Scheduler scheduler;

    @Autowired
    public ReviewServiceImpl(Scheduler scheduler, ...) {
```

```
        this.scheduler = scheduler;
    }
```

3. Finally, we use the thread pool in the reactive implementation of the
   getReviews() method, like so:

```
@Override
public Flux<Review> getReviews(int productId) {

    if (productId < 1) throw new InvalidInputException("Invalid
        productId: " + productId);

    return asyncFlux(getByProductId(productId)).log();
}

protected List<Review> getByProductId(int productId) {

    List<ReviewEntity> entityList =
    repository.findByProductId(productId);
    List<Review> list = mapper.entityListToApiList(entityList);
    list.forEach(e ->
            e.setServiceAddress(serviceUtil.getServiceAddress()));

    LOG.debug("getReviews: response size: {}", list.size());

    return list;
}

private <T> Flux<T> asyncFlux(Iterable<T> iterable) {
    return Flux.fromIterable(iterable).publishOn(scheduler);
}
```

Here is an explanation of the preceding code:

- The blocking code is placed in the getByProductId() method
- The getReviews() method uses the asyncFlux() method to run the blocking
  code in a thread from the thread pool

For the full source code, see the
se.magnus.microservices.core.review.services.ReviewServiceImpl class in
the review project.

Non-blocking REST APIs in the composite services

To make our REST API in the composite service non-blocking, we need to do the following:

- Change the APIs so that they only return reactive datatypes
- Change the integration layer so it uses a non-blocking HTTP client
- Change the service implementation so it calls the core services APIs in parallel and non-blocking
- Change our tests so that they can test the reactive service

Changes in the API

To make the API of the composite service reactive, we need to apply the same type of change that we applied for the APIs of the core services we described previously. This means that the return type of the `getCompositeProduct` method, `ProductAggregate`, needs to be replaced with `Mono<ProductAggregate>`.

For the full source code, see the `se.magnus.api.composite.product.ProductCompositeService` class in the `api` project.

Changes in the integration layer

In the `ProductCompositeIntegration` integration class, we have replaced the `RestTemplate` blocking HTTP client with the `WebClient` non-blocking HTTP client that comes with Spring 5.

A builder for the `WebClient` is auto-injected in to the constructor. If customization is required, for example, in setting up common headers or filters, it can be done in the constructor. For the available configuration options, see https://docs.spring.io/spring/docs/current/spring-framework-reference/web-reactive.html#webflux-client-builder. Please have a look at the following steps:

1. Here, we simply build the `WebClient` instance that we will use in our integration class, without any configuration:

```
public class ProductCompositeIntegration implements ProductService,
RecommendationService, ReviewService {
```

```
        private final WebClient webClient;

        @Autowired
        public ProductCompositeIntegration(
            WebClient.Builder webClient, ...
        ) {
            this.webClient = webClient.build();
        }
```

2. Next, we use the `webClient` instance to make our non-blocking requests for calling the `product` service:

```
        @Override
        public Mono<Product> getProduct(int productId) {
            String url = productServiceUrl + "/product/" + productId;

            return
        webClient.get().uri(url).retrieve().bodyToMono(Product.class).log()
            .onErrorMap(WebClientResponseException.class, ex ->
        handleException(ex));
        }
```

If the API call to the `product` service fails, the whole request will fail. The `WebClient onErrorMap()` method will call our `handleException(ex)` method, which maps the exceptions thrown previously by the HTTP layer to our own exceptions, for example, `NotFoundException` and `InvalidInputException`.

However, if calls to the `product` service succeed but the call to either the recommendation or review API fails, we don't want to let the whole request fail. Instead, we want to return as much information that is available, back to the caller. Therefore, instead of propagating an exception in these cases, we will instead return an empty list of recommendations or reviews using the `WebClient onErrorResume(error -> empty())` method. For this, consider the following code:

```
        @Override
        public Flux<Recommendation> getRecommendations(int productId) {

            String url = recommendationServiceUrl + "/recommendation?
        productId=" + productId;

            // Return an empty result if something goes wrong to make it
            // possible for the composite service to return partial responses
            return
        webClient.get().uri(url).retrieve().bodyToFlux(Recommendation.class).log().
        onErrorResume(error -> empty());
        }
```

For the full source code, see
the `se.magnus.microservices.composite.product.services.ProductCompositeI`
`ntegration` class in the `product-composite` project.

Changes in the service implementation

To be able to call the three APIs in parallel, the service implementation uses the
static `zip()` method on the `Mono` class. The `zip` method is capable of handling a number of
parallel requests and zipping them together once they all are complete. The code looks like
this:

```
@Override
public Mono<ProductAggregate> getCompositeProduct(int productId) {
    return Mono.zip(
        values -> createProductAggregate((Product) values[0],
        (List<Recommendation>) values[1], (List<Review>) values[2],
        serviceUtil.getServiceAddress()),
        integration.getProduct(productId),
        integration.getRecommendations(productId).collectList(),
        integration.getReviews(productId).collectList())
        .doOnError(ex -> LOG.warn("getCompositeProduct failed: {}",
         ex.toString()))
        .log();
}
```

Here is an explanation of the preceding source code:

1. The first parameter of the `zip` method is a lambda function that will receive the
   responses in an array. The actual aggregation of the responses from the three API
   calls is handled by the same helper method as
   before, `createProductAggregate`, without any changes.
2. The parameters after the lambda function are a list of the requests that the `zip`
   method will call in parallel, one `Mono` object per request. In our case, we send in
   three `Mono` objects that were created by the methods in the integration class, one
   for each request that's sent to each core microservice.

For the full source code, see
the `se.magnus.microservices.composite.product.services.ProductCompositeS erviceImpl` class in the `product-composite` project.

Changes in the test code

The only change that's required in the test classes is to update the setup of the mock of the integration class so that the `Mono` and `Flux` objects are returned using the `Mono.just()` helper methods and `Flux.fromIterable()`, as shown in the following code:

```
public class ProductCompositeServiceApplicationTests {

    @Before
    public void setUp() {

        when(compositeIntegration.getProduct(PRODUCT_ID_OK)).
            thenReturn(just(new Product(PRODUCT_ID_OK, "name", 1,
            "mock-address")));

        when(compositeIntegration.getRecommendations(PRODUCT_ID_OK)).
            thenReturn(Flux.fromIterable(singletonList(new
            Recommendation(PRODUCT_ID_OK, 1, "author", 1, "content",
            "mock address"))));

        when(compositeIntegration.getReviews(PRODUCT_ID_OK)).
            thenReturn(Flux.fromIterable(singletonList(new
            Review(PRODUCT_ID_OK, 1, "author", "subject", "content",
            "mock address"))));
```

For the full source code, see
the `se.magnus.microservices.composite.product.ProductCompositeServiceApp licationTests` test class in the `product-composite` project.

Now that we have developed non-blocking REST APIs with Spring, it is time to develop an event-driven synchronous service.

Developing event-driven asynchronous services

In this section, we will learn how to develop event-driven and asynchronous versions of the create and delete services. The composite service will publish create and delete events on each core service topic and then return a OK response back to the caller without waiting for processing to take place in the core services. This is illustrated in the following diagram:

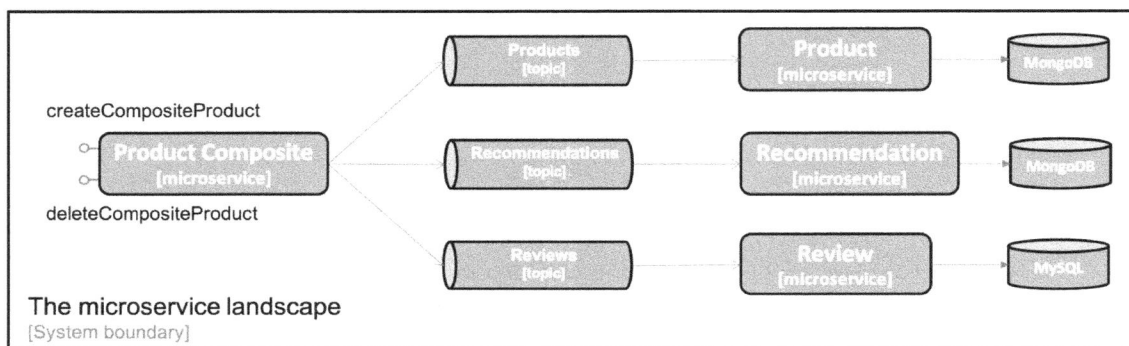

We will cover the following topics:

- Configuring Spring Cloud Stream to handle challenges with messaging
- Defining topics and events
- Changes in Gradle build files
- Publishing events in the composite service
- Consuming events in the core services

Configuring Spring Cloud Stream to handle challenges with messaging

To implement the event-driven create and delete services, we will use Spring Cloud Stream. In Chapter 2, *Introduction to Spring Boot*, in the *Spring Cloud Stream* section, we have already seen how easy it is to publish and consume messages on a topic using Spring Cloud Stream.

For example, to publish a message on a topic defined by `mysource`, we only have to write the following:

```
mysource.output().send(MessageBuilder.withPayload(message).build())
;
```

For consuming a message, we write the following code:

```
@StreamListener(target = Sink.INPUT)
 public void receive(MyMessage message) {
    LOG.info("Received: {}",message);
```

This programming model can be used independently of the messaging system used, for example, RabbitMQ or Apache Kafka!

Even though sending asynchronous messages is preferred over synchronous API calls, it comes with challenges. We will see how we can use Spring Cloud Stream to handle some of them. The following features in Spring Cloud Stream will be covered:

- Consumer groups
- Retries and dead-letter queues
- Guaranteed orders and partitions

We'll study each of these in the following sections.

Consumer groups

The problem here is, if we scale up the number of instances of a message consumer, for example, start two instances of the product microservice, both instances of the product microservice will consume the same messages, as illustrated by the following diagram:

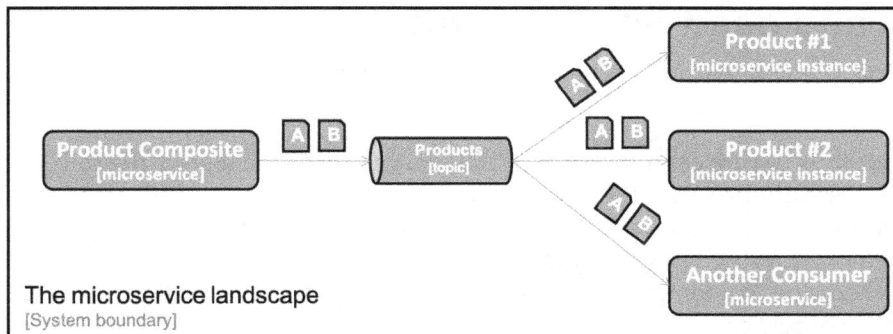

The solution to this is that we only want one instance per consumer to process each message. This can be solved by introducing a *consumer group*, as illustrated by the following diagram:

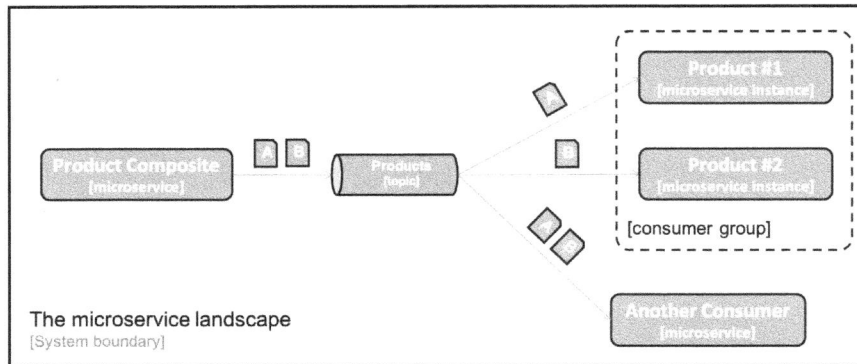

In Spring Cloud Stream, a consumer group can be configured on the consumer side, for example, for the product microservice, as shown here:

```
spring.cloud.stream:
  bindings.input:
    destination: products
    group: productsGroup
```

In the preceding configuration, Spring Cloud Stream will use the value of the `group` field to add instances of the `product` microservice to the consumer group called `productsGroup`. This means that messages sent to the `products` topic will only be delivered by Spring Cloud Stream to one of the instances of the product microservice.

Retries and dead-letter queues

In this section, we will learn how retries and dead-letter queues are used by message consumers.

If a consumer fails to process a message, it may lost or be requeued for the failing consumer until it is successfully processed. If the content of the message is invalid, also known as a **poisoned message**, it will block the consumer from processing other messages until it is manually removed. If the failure is due to a temporary problem, for example, the database can't be reached due to a temporary network error, the processing will probably succeed after a number of retries.

It must be possible to specify the number of retries until a message is moved to another storage for fault analysis and correction. A failing message is typically moved to a dedicated queue called a dead-letter queue. To avoid overloading the infrastructure during temporary failure, for example, a network error, it must be possible to configure how often retries are performed and preferably with increasing time between each retry.

In Spring Cloud Stream, this can be configured on the consumer side, for example, for the product microservice, as shown here:

```
spring.cloud.stream.bindings.input.consumer:
  maxAttempts: 3
  backOffInitialInterval: 500
  backOffMaxInterval: 1000
  backOffMultiplier: 2.0

spring.cloud.stream.rabbit.bindings.input.consumer:
  autoBindDlq: true
  republishToDlq: true

spring.cloud.stream.kafka.bindings.input.consumer:
  enableDlq: true
```

In the preceding example, we specify that Spring Cloud Stream shall perform 3 retries before placing a message on the dead-letter queue. The first retry shall be attempted after 500 ms and the two other attempts after 1000 ms.

Enabling the use of dead-letter queues is binding-specific; therefore, we have one configuration for RabbitMQ and one for Kafka.

Guaranteed order and partitions

We can use partitions to ensure that messages are delivered in the same order as they were sent but without losing performance and scalability.

If the business logic requires that messages are consumed and processed in the same order as they were sent, we cannot use multiple instances per consumer to increase processing performance; for example, we cannot use consumer groups. This might, in some cases, lead to an unacceptable latency in the processing of incoming messages.

In most cases, strict order in the processing of messages is only required for messages that affect the same business entities, for example, products.

For example, messages affecting the product with product ID 1 can, in many cases, be processed independently of messages that affect the product with product ID 2. This means that the order only needs to be guaranteed for messages that have the same product ID.

The solution to this is to make it possible to specify a key for each message that the messaging system can use in order to guarantee that the order is kept between messages with the same key. This can be solved by introducing sub-topics, also known as **partitions**, in a topic. The messaging system places messages in a specific partition based on its key. Messages with the same key are always placed in the same partition. The messaging system only needs to guarantee the delivery order for messages in one and the same partition. To ensure the order of the messages, we configure one consumer instance per partition within a consumer group. By increasing the number of partitions, we can allow a consumer to increase its number of instances. This increases its processing message performance without losing the delivery order. This is illustrated in the following diagram:

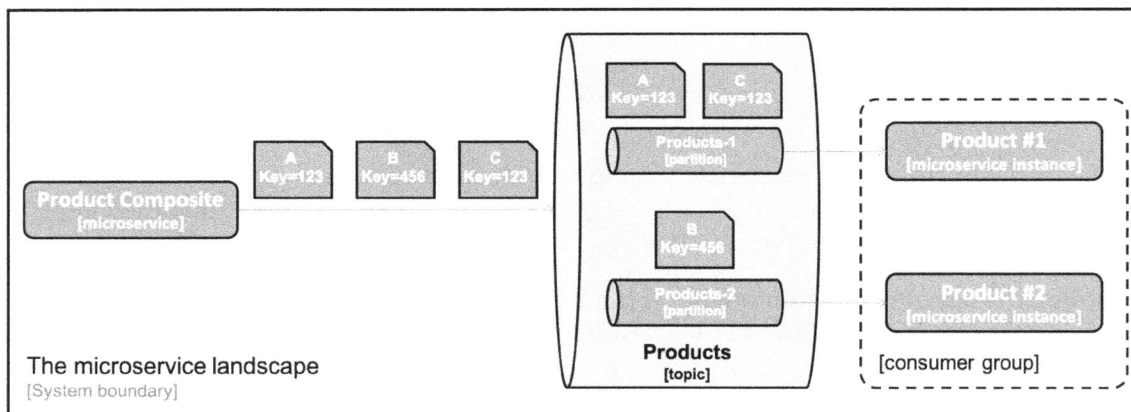

In Spring Cloud Stream, this needs to be configured on both the publisher and consumer side. On the publisher side, the key and number of partitions must be specified. For example, for the `product-composite` service, we have the following:

```
spring.cloud.stream.bindings.output:
  destination: products
  producer:
    partition-key-expression: payload.key
    partition-count: 2
```

The preceding configuration means that the key will be taken from the payload in the message using a field named `key` and that two partitions will be used.

Each consumer can specify which partition it wants to consume messages from. For example, for the `product` microservice, we have the following:

```
spring.cloud.stream.bindings.input:
  destination: products
  group:productsGroup
  consumer:
    partitioned: true
    instance-index: 0
```

The preceding configuration tells Spring Cloud Stream that this consumer will only consume messages from partition number 0, that is, the first partition.

Defining topics and events

As we already mentioned in the *Spring Cloud Stream* section in `Chapter 2`, *Introduction to Spring Boot*, Spring Cloud Stream is based on the publishing and subscribe pattern, where a publisher publishes messages to topics and subscribers subscribe to topics they are interested in to receive messages.

We will use one **topic** per type of entity: `products`, `recommendations`, and `reviews`.

Messaging systems handle **messages** that typically consist of headers and a body. An **event** is a message that describes something that has happened. For events, the message body can be used to describe the type of event, the event data, and a timestamp for when the event occurred.

An event is, for the scope of this book, defined by the following:

- The **type** of event, for example, create or delete an event
- A **key**, that identifies the data, for example, a product ID
- A **data** element, that is, the actual data in the event
- A **timestamp**, which describes when the event occurred

The event class we will use looks as follows:

```
public class Event<K, T> {

    public enum Type {CREATE, DELETE}

    private Event.Type eventType;
    private K key;
    private T data;
    private LocalDateTime eventCreatedAt;
```

```
    public Event() {
        this.eventType = null;
        this.key = null;
        this.data = null;
        this.eventCreatedAt = null;
    }

    public Event(Type eventType, K key, T data) {
        this.eventType = eventType;
        this.key = key;
        this.data = data;
        this.eventCreatedAt = now();
    }

    public Type getEventType() {
        return eventType;
    }

    public K getKey() {
        return key;
    }

    public T getData() {
        return data;
    }

    public LocalDateTime getEventCreatedAt() {
        return eventCreatedAt;
    }
}
```

Let's explain the preceding source code in detail:

- The Event class is a generic class parameterized over the types of its key and data field, K and T.
- The event type is declared as an enumerator with the allowed values, that is, CREATE and DELETE.
- The class defines two constructors, one empty and one that can be used to initialize the type, key, and value members.
- Finally, the class defines getter methods for its member variables.

For the full source code, see the se.magnus.api.event.Event class in the api project.

Changes in the Gradle build files

To bring in Spring Cloud Stream and its binders for RabbitMQ and Kafka, we need to add the two starter dependencies known as `spring-cloud-starter-stream-rabbit` and `spring-cloud-starter-stream-kafka`. We also need a test dependency, `spring-cloud-stream-test-support`, to bring in the test support. The following code shows this:

```
dependencies {
  implementation('org.springframework.cloud:spring-cloud-starter-stream-rabbit')
  implementation('org.springframework.cloud:spring-cloud-starter-stream-kafka')
  testImplementation('org.springframework.cloud:spring-cloud-stream-test-support')
}
```

To specify what version of Spring Cloud that we want to use, we first declare a variable for the version:

```
ext {
    springCloudVersion = "Greenwich.RELEASE"
}
```

To wrap up setting up dependency management for that version, we use the following code:

```
dependencyManagement {
    imports {
        mavenBom "org.springframework.cloud:spring-cloud-dependencies:${springCloudVersion}"
    }
}
```

For the full source code, see the `build.gradle` build file in the `product-composite` project.

Publishing events in the composite service

When the composite service receives requests for the creation or deletion of products, it shall publish the corresponding events to the core services on their topics. To be able to publish events in the composite service, we need to perform the following steps:

1. Declare message sources and publish events in the integration layer.
2. Add configuration for publishing events.
3. Change our tests so that they can test the publishing of events.

> No changes are required in the composite service implementation class!

Declaring message sources and publishing events in the integration layer

To be able to publish events to different topics, we need to declare one `MessageChannel` per topic in a Java interface and also declare that we want to use it with an `EnableBinding` annotation. Let's us see how to do this:

1. We declare our message channels in the `MessageSources` interface in the `ProductCompositeIntegration` class and ask Spring to inject an instance of it in the constructor, as follows:

```
@EnableBinding(ProductCompositeIntegration.MessageSources.class)
@Component
public class ProductCompositeIntegration implements ProductService,
RecommendationService, ReviewService {

    private MessageSources messageSources;

    public interface MessageSources {

        String OUTPUT_PRODUCTS = "output-products";
        String OUTPUT_RECOMMENDATIONS = "output-recommendations";
        String OUTPUT_REVIEWS = "output-reviews";

        @Output(OUTPUT_PRODUCTS)
        MessageChannel outputProducts();

        @Output(OUTPUT_RECOMMENDATIONS)
```

```
        MessageChannel outputRecommendations();

        @Output(OUTPUT_REVIEWS)
        MessageChannel outputReviews();
    }

    public ProductCompositeIntegration(
        MessageSources messageSources,
    ) {
        this.messageSources = messageSources;
    }
```

When we want to publish an event on a topic, we use the injected `messageSources` object. For example, to send a delete event for a product, we can use the `outputProducts()` method to get a message channel for the product's topic and then use its `send()` method to publish an event.

2. To create the message that contains the event, we can use the built-in `MessageBuilder` class, as follows:

```
@Override
public void deleteProduct(int productId) {
    messageSources.outputProducts().send(MessageBuilder.
    withPayload(new Event(DELETE, productId, null)).build());
}
```

For the full source code, see the `se.magnus.microservices.composite.product.services.ProductCompositeIntegration` class in the `product-composite` project.

Adding configuration for publishing events

We also need to set up a configuration for the messaging system to be able to publish events. To do this, we need to complete the following steps:

1. We declare that RabbitMQ is the default messaging system and that the default content type is JSON:

```
spring.cloud.stream:
  defaultBinder: rabbit
  default.contentType: application/json
```

2. Next, we bind our output channels to specific topic names, as follows:

```
bindings:
  output-products:
    destination: products
  output-recommendations:
    destination: recommendations
  output-reviews:
    destination: reviews
```

3. Finally, we declare connectivity information for both Kafka and RabbitMQ:

```
spring.cloud.stream.kafka.binder:
  brokers: 127.0.0.1
  defaultBrokerPort: 9092

spring.rabbitmq:
  host: 127.0.0.1
  port: 5672
  username: guest
  password: guest

---
spring.profiles: docker

spring.rabbitmq.host: rabbitmq
spring.cloud.stream.kafka.binder.brokers: kafka
```

In the default Spring profile, we specify hostnames to be used when we run our system landscape without Docker on `localhost` with the IP address `127.0.0.1`. In the `docker` Spring profile, we specify the hostnames we will use when running in Docker and using Docker Compose, that is, `rabbitmq` and `kafka`.

For the full source code, see the `src/main/resources/application.yml` configuration file in the `product-composite` project.

Changes in the test code

Testing asynchronous event-driven microservices is, by their nature, difficult. Tests typically need to synchronize on the asynchronous background processing in some way to be able to verify its result. Spring Cloud Stream comes with support, in terms of `TestSupportBinder`, for verifying what messages have been sent without using any messaging system during the tests!

The test support includes a `MessageCollector` helper class that can be used to get all the messages that were sent during a test. To see how it is done, check out these steps:

1. In the `MessagingTests` test class, we set up a queue that can be used to inspect the messages that are sent to each topic, as follows:

```
@Autowired
private MessageCollector collector;

BlockingQueue<Message<?>> queueProducts = null;
BlockingQueue<Message<?>> queueRecommendations = null;
BlockingQueue<Message<?>> queueReviews = null;

@Before
public void setUp() {
    queueProducts = getQueue(channels.outputProducts());
    queueRecommendations =
    getQueue(channels.outputRecommendations());
    queueReviews = getQueue(channels.outputReviews());
}

private BlockingQueue<Message<?>> getQueue(MessageChannel
messageChannel) {
    return collector.forChannel(messageChannel);
}
```

2. An actual test can verify the content in the queue like the following test can for the creation of a product:

```
@Test
public void createCompositeProduct1() {

    ProductAggregate composite = new ProductAggregate(1, "name", 1,
    null, null, null);
    postAndVerifyProduct(composite, OK);

    // Assert one expected new product events queued up
    assertEquals(1, queueProducts.size());

    Event<Integer, Product> expectedEvent = new Event(CREATE,
    composite.getProductId(), new Product(composite.getProductId(),
    composite.getName(), composite.getWeight(), null));
    assertThat(queueProducts,
    is(receivesPayloadThat (sameEventExceptCreatedAt
    (expectedEvent))));

    // Assert none recommendations and review events
```

```
                    assertEquals(0, queueRecommendations.size());
                    assertEquals(0, queueReviews.size());
    }
```

The `receivesPayloadThat()` method is a static method in another test support class in Spring Cloud Stream, `MessageQueueMatcher`. This class contains a set of methods that simplify the verification of messages in a queue.

The `sameEventExceptCreatedAt()` method is a static method in the `IsSameEvent` class that compares `Event` objects and treats them as equal if all the fields are equal, except for the `eventCreatedAt` field.

For the full source code, see the following test classes in the `product-composite` project:

- `se.magnus.microservices.composite.product.MessagingTests`
- `se.magnus.microservices.composite.product.IsSameEvent`

Consuming events in the core services

To be able to consume events in the core services, we need to do the following:

1. Declare message processors that listen for events on its topic.
2. Change our service implementations so it uses the reactive persistence layer correctly.
3. Add configuration for consuming events.
4. Change our tests so that they can test the asynchronous processing of the events.

Declaring message processors

The REST APIs for creating and deleting entities have been replaced with a message processor in each core microservice that listens for creating and deleting events on each entity's topic. To be able to consume messages that have been published to a topic, we need to bind to `SubscribableChannel`, similar to how we bind to `MessageChannel` when we want to publish messages. Since each message processor only listens to one topic, we can use the built-in `Sink` interface to bind to that topic. We use the `EnableBinding` annotation to declare the use of the `Sink` interface, as shown in the following source code:

```
@EnableBinding(Sink.class)
public class MessageProcessor {
```

To actually consume and process messages, we can annotate a method with the StreamListener annotation, where we specify what channel we shall listen to:

```
@StreamListener(target = Sink.INPUT)
public void process(Event<Integer, Product> event) {
```

The implementation of the process() method uses a switch statement to call the create method in the service component for creating events and the delete method for deleting events. The source code looks as follows:

```
switch (event.getEventType()) {

case CREATE:
    Product product = event.getData();
    LOG.info("Create product with ID: {}", product.getProductId());
    productService.createProduct(product);
    break;

case DELETE:
    int productId = event.getKey();
    LOG.info("Delete recommendations with ProductID: {}", productId);
    productService.deleteProduct(productId);
    break;

default:
    String errorMessage = "Incorrect event type: " +
    event.getEventType() + ", expected a CREATE or DELETE event";
    LOG.warn(errorMessage);
 throw new EventProcessingException(errorMessage);
}
```

Let's explain the preceding source code in detail:

1. The switch statement expects an event type that is either a CREATE or a DELETE event.
2. The productService.createProduct() method is called for create events.
3. The productService.deleteProduct() method is called for delete events.
4. If the event type is neither a CREATE or a DELETE event; an exception of the EventProcessingException type is thrown.

The service component is injected as usual using constructor injection, as shown here:

```
private final ProductService productService;

@Autowired
public MessageProcessor(ProductService productService) {
    this.productService = productService;
}
```

For the full source code, see the following classes:

- `se.magnus.microservices.core.product.services.MessageProcessor` in the `product` project
- `se.magnus.microservices.core.recommendation.services.MessageProcessor` in the `recommendation` project
- `se.magnus.microservices.core.review.services.MessageProcessor` in the `review` project

Changes in the service implementations

The service implementations of the create and delete methods for the `product` and `recommendation` service have been rewritten to use the non-blocking reactive persistence layer for MongoDB. For example, creating product entities is done as follows:

```
public class ProductServiceImpl implements ProductService {

    @Override
    public Product createProduct(Product body) {

        if (body.getProductId() < 1) throw new
        InvalidInputException("Invalid productId: " +
        body.getProductId());

        ProductEntity entity = mapper.apiToEntity(body);
        Mono<Product> newEntity = repository.save(entity)
            .log()
            .onErrorMap(
                DuplicateKeyException.class,
                ex -> new InvalidInputException("Duplicate key, Product
                Id: " + body.getProductId()))
            .map(e -> mapper.entityToApi(e));

        return newEntity.block();
    }
```

The onErrorMap() method is used to map the DuplicateKeyException persistence exception to our own InvalidInputException exception.

Since our message processor is based on a blocking programming model, we need to call the block() method on the returned Mono object from the persistence layer before we return it to the message processor. If we don't call the block() method, we won't be able to trigger the error handling in the messaging system if the processing in the service implementation fails; the event will not be requeued, and eventually, it will be moved to the dead-letter queue, as expected.

> The review service that uses the blocking persistence layer for JPA, as before, does not need to be updated.

For the full source code, see the following classes:

- se.magnus.microservices.core.product.services.ProductServiceImp l in the product project
- se.magnus.microservices.core.recommendation.services.Recommenda tionServiceImpl in the recommendation project

Adding configuration for consuming events

We also need to set up the configuration for the messaging system, to be able to consume events; this is similar to what we did for the publisher. Declaring RabbitMQ as the default messaging system, JSON as the default content type, and Kafka and RabbitMQ for connectivity information is the same as for the publisher. Added to the common parts, the consumer configuration specifies consumer groups; retry handling and dead-letter queues are as they were described earlier in the *Configuring Spring Cloud Stream to handle challenges with messaging* section.

For the full source code, see the following configuration files:

- src/main/resources/application.yml in the product project
- src/main/resources/application.yml in the recommendation project
- src/main/resources/application.yml in the review project

Changes in the test code

Since the core services now receive events for creating and deleting their entities, the tests need to be updated so that they send events instead of calling REST APIs, like they did previously. In the following source code, we can see how the `send()` method on the `input` method channel is used to send an event:

```
private void sendCreateProductEvent(int productId) {
    Product product = new Product(productId, "Name " + productId,
    productId, "SA");
    Event<Integer, Product> event = new Event(CREATE, productId,
    product);
    input.send(new GenericMessage<>(event));
}

private void sendDeleteProductEvent(int productId) {
    Event<Integer, Product> event = new Event(DELETE, productId, null);
    input.send(new GenericMessage<>(event));
}
```

The `input` channel is set up by the test class before any tests are run. It is based on the same built-in `Sink` interface that the message processor uses. In the following source code, we can see how the `input` channel is created in the `setupDb()` method. Since the `setupDb()` method is annotated with `@Before`, it will run before any tests are executed:

```
@Autowired
private Sink channels;

private AbstractMessageChannel input = null;

@Before
public void setupDb() {
    input = (AbstractMessageChannel) channels.input();
    repository.deleteAll().block();
}
```

This construction shortcuts the messaging system and the call to the `send()` method in the `input` channel will be processed synchronously by the message processor, that is, like a normal method call its `process()` method. This means that the test code doesn't need to implement any synchronization or *wait logic* for the asynchronous processing of an event. Instead, the test code can apply validation logic directly after calls to the `sendCreateProductEvent` and `sendDeleteProductEvent` send helper methods return.

For the full source code, see the following test classes:

- `se.magnus.microservices.core.product.ProductServiceApplicationTests` in the `product` project
- `se.magnus.microservices.core.recommendation.RecommendationServiceApplicationTests` in the `recommendation` project
- `se.magnus.microservices.core.review.ReviewServiceApplicationTests` in the `review` project

Running manual tests of the reactive microservice landscape

Now, we have fully reactive microservices, both in terms of non-blocking synchronous REST APIs and event-driven asynchronous services. Let's try them out!

Three different configurations are prepared as follows, each in a separate Docker Compose file:

- Using RabbitMQ without the use of partitions
- Using RabbitMQ with two partitions per topic
- Using Kafka with two partitions per topic

However, before testing these three configurations, we first need to simplify testing of the reactive microservice landscape. Once simplified, we can proceed with testing the microservices.

So accordingly, the following two features need to be checked:

- Saving events for later inspection when using RabbitMQ
- A health API that can be used to monitor the state of the landscape

Saving events

After running some tests on event-driven asynchronous services, it might be of interest to see what event was actually sent. When using Spring Cloud Stream with Kafka, events are retained in the topics, even after consumers have processed them. However, when using Spring Cloud Stream with RabbitMQ, the events are removed after they have been processed successfully.

To be able to see what events have been published on each topic, Spring Cloud Stream is configured to save published events in a separate `auditGroup` consumer group per topic. For the `products` topic, the configuration looks like the following:

```
spring.cloud.stream:
  bindings:
    output-products:
      destination: products
      producer:
        required-groups: auditGroup
```

When using RabbitMQ, this will result in extra queues being created where the events are stored for later inspection.

For the full source code, see the `src/main/resources/application.yml` configuration file in the `product-composite` project.

Adding a health API

Testing a system landscape of microservices that use a combination of synchronous APIs and asynchronous messaging is challenging. For example, how do we know when a newly started landscape of microservices, together with their databases and messaging system, are ready to process requests and messages?

To make it easier to know when all the microservices are ready to process requests and messages, we have added a health API in all the microservices. They are based on the support for health endpoints that comes with the Spring Boot module known as the Actuator. By default, a `health` endpoint based on the Actuator answers UP (and gives 200 as the HTTP return status) if the microservice itself and all the dependencies Spring Boot knows about are available, for example, dependencies to databases and messaging systems; otherwise, the health endpoint answers DOWN (and returns 500 as the HTTP return status).

We can also extend the `health` endpoint to cover dependencies that Spring Boot is not aware of. We will use this feature to extend to the product composite's `health` endpoint, which will also include the health of the three core services. This means that the product composite `health` endpoint will only respond with UP if itself and the three core microservices are healthy. This can be used either manually or automatically by the `test-em-all.bash` script to find out when all the microservices and their dependencies are up and running.

In the `ProductCompositeIntegration` integration class, we have added helper methods for checking the health of the three core microservices, as follows:

```
public Mono<Health> getProductHealth() {
    return getHealth(productServiceUrl);
}

public Mono<Health> getRecommendationHealth() {
    return getHealth(recommendationServiceUrl);
}

public Mono<Health> getReviewHealth() {
    return getHealth(reviewServiceUrl);
}

private Mono<Health> getHealth(String url) {
    url += "/actuator/health";
    LOG.debug("Will call the Health API on URL: {}", url);
    return webClient.get().uri(url).retrieve().bodyToMono(String.class)
        .map(s -> new Health.Builder().up().build())
        .onErrorResume(ex -> Mono.just(new
         Health.Builder().down(ex).build()))
        .log();
}
```

This code is similar to the code we used previously to call the core services to read APIs.

For the full source code, see the `se.magnus.microservices.composite.product.services.ProductCompositeInte gration` class in the `product-composite` project.

In the main `ProductCompositeServiceApplication` application class, we use these helper methods to register three health checks, one for each core microservice:

```
@Autowired
HealthAggregator healthAggregator;

@Autowired
ProductCompositeIntegration integration;

@Bean
ReactiveHealthIndicator coreServices() {

    ReactiveHealthIndicatorRegistry registry = new
    DefaultReactiveHealthIndicatorRegistry(new LinkedHashMap<>());

    registry.register("product", () -> integration.getProductHealth());
```

```
            registry.register("recommendation", () ->
            integration.getRecommendationHealth());
            registry.register("review", () -> integration.getReviewHealth());

            return new CompositeReactiveHealthIndicator(healthAggregator,
            registry);
        }
```

For the full source code, see
the `se.magnus.microservices.composite.product.ProductCompositeServiceApp
lication` class in the `product-composite` project.

Finally, in the `application.yml` file of all four microservices, we configure the Spring
Boot Actuator so that it does the following:

- Show details about the state of health, which not only includes UP or DOWN, but
  also information about its dependencies
- Expose all its endpoints over HTTP

The configuration for these two settings looks as follows:

```
management.endpoint.health.show-details: "ALWAYS"
management.endpoints.web.exposure.include: "*"
```

For an example of the full source code, see
the `src/main/resources/application.yml` configuration file in the `product-composite` project.

> **WARNING**: These configuration settings are good during development,
> but it can be a security issue to reveal too much information in actuator
> endpoints in production systems. Therefore, plan for minimizing the
> information exposed by the actuator endpoints in production!

For details regarding the endpoints that are exposed by Spring Boot Actuator, see `https://docs.spring.io/spring-boot/docs/current/reference/html/production-ready-endpoints.html`:

- Try it out (when you have all the microservices up and running using Docker
  Compose, as described in the next section):

```
curl localhost:8080/actuator/health -s | jq .
```

- This will result in the following response:

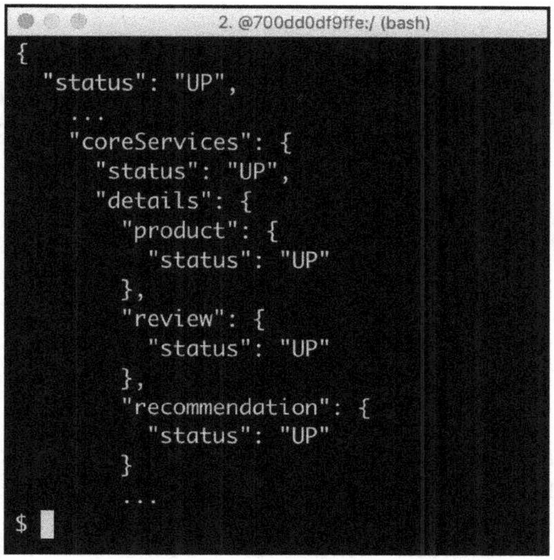

```
2. @700dd0df9ffe:/ (bash)
{
  "status": "UP",
  ...
    "coreServices": {
      "status": "UP",
      "details": {
        "product": {
          "status": "UP"
        },
        "review": {
          "status": "UP"
        },
        "recommendation": {
          "status": "UP"
        }
        ...
$
```

In the preceding output, we can see that the composite service reports that it is healthy, that is, its status is UP. At the end of the response, we can see that all three core microservices are also reported as healthy.

With a health API in place, we are ready to test our reactive microservices.

Using RabbitMQ without using partitions

In this section, we will test the reactive microservices together with RabbitMQ but without using partitions.

The default `docker-compose.yml` Docker Compose file is used in this configuration. The following changes have been applied to the file:

- RabbitMQ has been added, as shown here:

```
rabbitmq:
  image: rabbitmq:3.7.8-management
  mem_limit: 350m
  ports:
    - 5672:5672
    - 15672:15672
  healthcheck:
```

```
test: ["CMD", "rabbitmqctl", "status"]
interval: 10s
timeout: 5s
retries: 10
```

- The microservices now have a dependency declared to the RabbitMQ service. This means that Docker will not start the microservice containers until the RabbitMQ service is reported to be healthy:

```
depends_on:
  rabbitmq:
    condition: service_healthy
```

To run our tests, perform the following steps:

1. Build and start the system landscape with the following commands:

```
cd $BOOK_HOME/Chapter07
./gradlew build && docker-compose build && docker-compose up -d
```

2. Now, we have to wait for the microservice landscape to be up and running. Try running the following command a few times:

```
curl -s localhost:8080/actuator/health | jq -r .status
```

When it returns UP, we are ready to run our tests!

3. First, create a composite product with the following commands:

```
body='{"productId":1,"name":"product name C","weight":300,
"recommendations":[
 {"recommendationId":1,"author":"author
1","rate":1,"content":"content 1"},
 {"recommendationId":2,"author":"author
2","rate":2,"content":"content 2"},
 {"recommendationId":3,"author":"author
3","rate":3,"content":"content 3"}
], "reviews":[
 {"reviewId":1,"author":"author 1","subject":"subject
1","content":"content 1"},
 {"reviewId":2,"author":"author 2","subject":"subject
2","content":"content 2"},
 {"reviewId":3,"author":"author 3","subject":"subject
3","content":"content 3"}
]}'

curl -X POST localhost:8080/product-composite -H "Content-Type:
application/json" --data "$body"
```

When using Spring Cloud Stream together with RabbitMQ, it will create one RabbitMQ exchange per topic and a set of queues, depending on our configuration.

Let's see what queues that Spring Cloud Stream has created for us!

4. Open the following URL in a web browser: `http://localhost:15672/#/queues`. You should see the following queues:

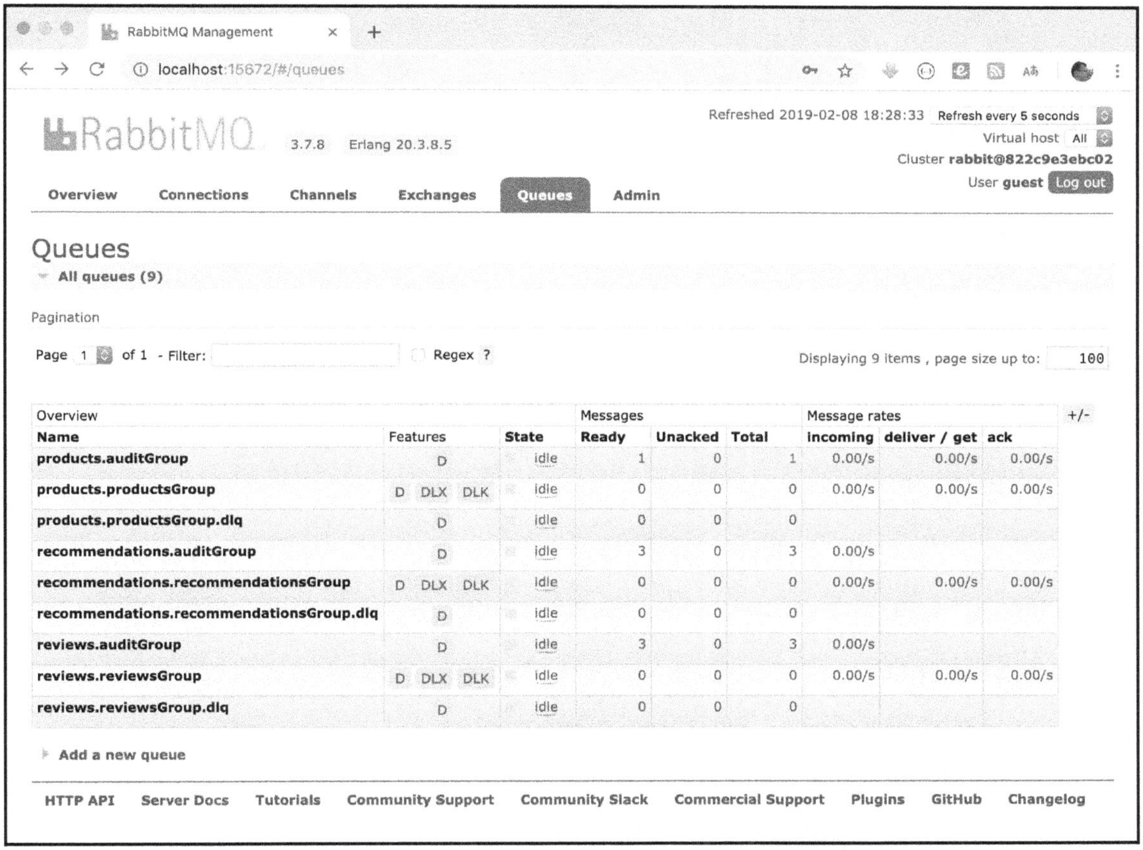

For each topic, we can see one queue for **auditGroup**, one for the consumer group that's used by the corresponding core microservice, and one dead-letter queue. We can also see that the **auditGroup** queues contain messages, as expected!

5. Click on the **products.auditGroup** queue and scroll down to **Get Message(s)**, expand it, and click on the button named **Get Message(s)** to see the message in the queue:

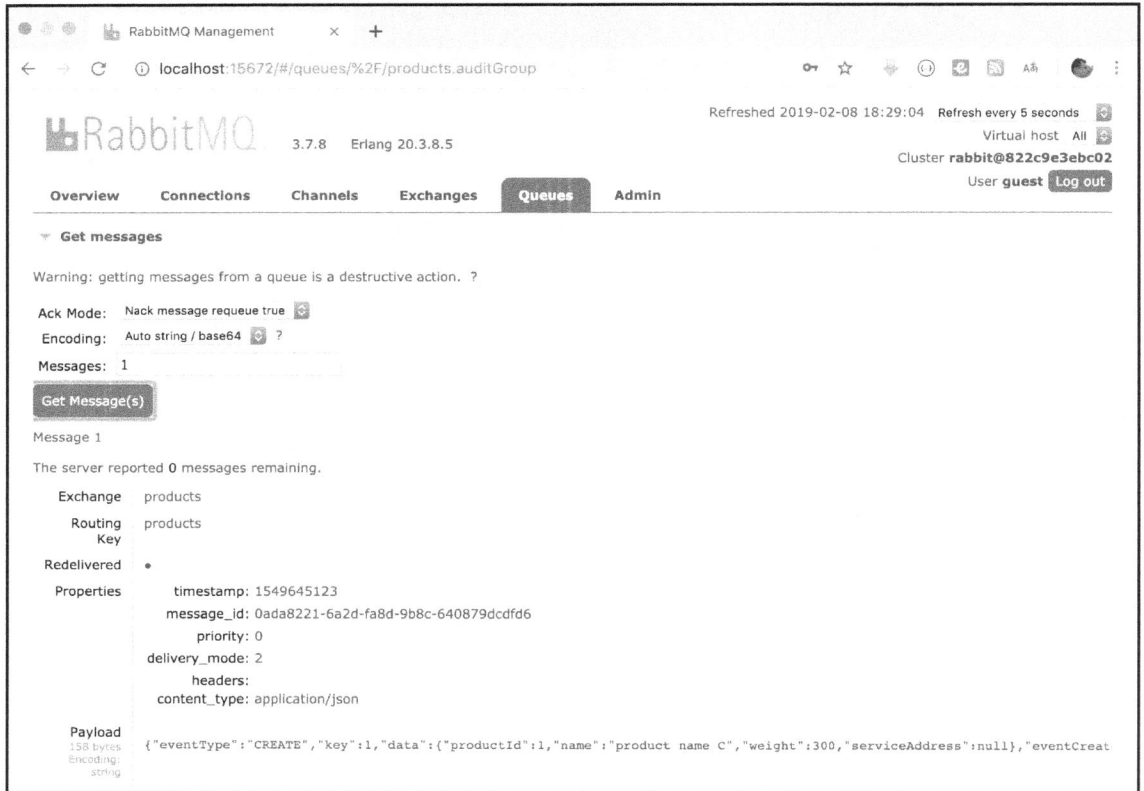

6. Next, try to get the product composite using the following code:

```
curl localhost:8080/product-composite/1 | jq
```

7. Finally, delete it, like so:

```
curl -X DELETE localhost:8080/product-composite/1
```

Trying to get the deleted product again should result in a `404 - "NotFound"` response!

If you look in the RabbitMQ audit queues again, you should be able to find new messages containing delete events.

8. Wrap up the test by bringing down the microservice landscape with the following command:

```
docker-compose down
```

This completes the tests where we use RabbitMQ without partitions. Now, let's move on and test RabbitMQ with partitions.

Using RabbitMQ with two partitions per topic

Now, let's try out the partitioning support in Spring Cloud Stream!

We have a separate Docker Compose file prepared for using RabbitMQ with two partitions per topic: `docker-compose-partitions.yml`. It will also start two instances per core microservice, one for each partition. For example, a second `product` instance is configured as follows:

```
product-p1:
  build: microservices/product-service
  mem_limit: 350m
  environment:
    - SPRING_PROFILES_ACTIVE=docker
    - SPRING_CLOUD_STREAM_BINDINGS_INPUT_CONSUMER_PARTITIONED=true
    - SPRING_CLOUD_STREAM_BINDINGS_INPUT_CONSUMER_INSTANCECOUNT=2
    - SPRING_CLOUD_STREAM_BINDINGS_INPUT_CONSUMER_INSTANCEINDEX=1
  depends_on:
    mongodb:
      condition: service_healthy
    rabbitmq:
      condition: service_healthy
```

Here is an explanation of the preceding source code:

- We use the same source code and Dockerfile that we did for the first `product` instance but configure them differently.
- Specifically, we assign the two `product` instances to different partitions using the `instance-index` property we described earlier in this chapter.
- When using system environment variables to specify Spring properties, we must use an uppercase format where dots are replaced with underscores.
- This `product` instance will only process asynchronous events; it will not respond to API calls. Since it has a different name, `product-p1` (also used as its DNS name), it will not respond to calls to a URL starting with `http://product:8080`.

Start up the microservice landscape with the following command:

```
export COMPOSE_FILE=docker-compose-partitions.yml
docker-compose build && docker-compose up -d
```

Repeat the tests from the previous section but also create a product with the product ID set to 2. If you take a look into the queues set up by Spring Cloud Stream, you will see one queue per partition and that the product audit queues now contain one message each, that is, the event for product ID 1 was placed in one partition and the event for product ID 2 was placed in the other partition. If you go back to `http://localhost:15672/#/queues` in your web browser, you should see something like the following:

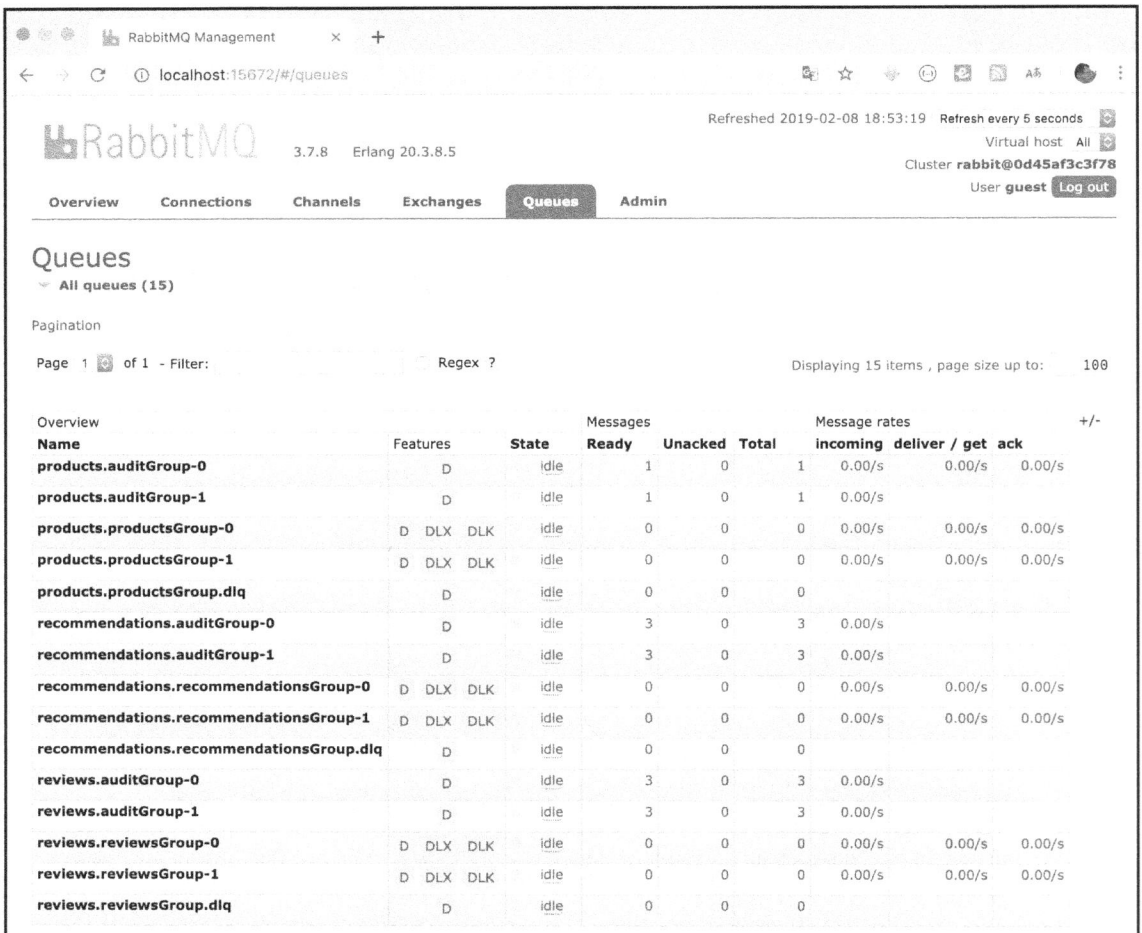

To end the test with RabbitMQ using partitions, bring down the microservice landscape with the following command:

```
docker-compose down
unset COMPOSE_FILE
```

We are now done with tests using RabbitMQ, both with and without partitions. The final test configuration we shall try out is testing the microservices together with Kafka.

Using Kafka with two partitions per topic

Now, we shall try out a very cool feature of Spring Cloud Stream: changing the messaging system from RabbitMQ to Apache Kafka!

This can be done simply by changing the value of the `spring.cloud.stream.defaultBinder` property from `rabbit` to `kafka`. This is handled by the `docker-compose-kafka.yml` Docker Compose file that has also replaced RabbitMQ with Kafka and Zookeeper. The configuration of Kafka and Zookeeper looks as follows:

```
kafka:
  image: wurstmeister/kafka:2.12-2.1.0
  mem_limit: 350m
  ports:
    - "9092:9092"
  environment:
    - KAFKA_ADVERTISED_HOST_NAME=kafka
    - KAFKA_ADVERTISED_PORT=9092
    - KAFKA_ZOOKEEPER_CONNECT=zookeeper:2181
  depends_on:
    - zookeeper

zookeeper:
  image: wurstmeister/zookeeper:3.4.6
  mem_limit: 350m
  ports:
    - "2181:2181"
  environment:
    - KAFKA_ADVERTISED_HOST_NAME=zookeeper
```

Kafka is also configured to use two partitions per topic, and like before, we start up two instances per core microservice, one for each partition. See the Docker Compose file, `docker-compose-kafka.yml`, for details!

Start up the microservice landscape with the following command:

```
export COMPOSE_FILE=docker-compose-kafka.yml
docker-compose build && docker-compose up -d
```

Repeat the tests from the previous section, for example, create two products, one with the product ID set to 1, and one with the product ID set to 2.

> Unfortunately, Kafka doesn't come with any graphical tools that can be used to inspect topics, partitions, and the messages that are placed within them. Instead, we can run CLI commands in the Kafka Docker container.

To see a list of topics, run the following command:

```
docker-compose exec kafka /opt/kafka/bin/kafka-topics.sh --zookeeper
zookeeper --list
```

Expect an output like the one shown here:

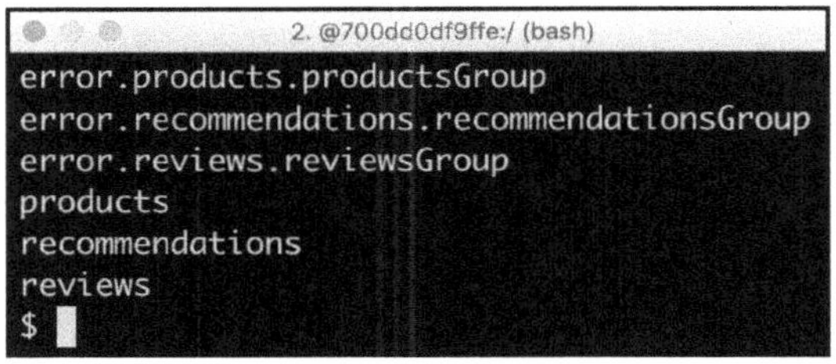

Here is an explanation of the preceding source code:

- The topics prefixed with `error` are the topics corresponding to dead-letter queues.
- You will not find any `auditGroup` in the case of RabbitMQ; instead, all messages the are available in the topics for any consumer to process.

To see the partitions in a specific topic, for example, the `products` topic, run the following command:

```
docker-compose exec kafka /opt/kafka/bin/kafka-topics.sh --describe --
zookeeper zookeeper --topic products
```

Expect an output like the one shown here:

```
2. @700dd0df9ffe:/ (bash)
Topic:products PartitionCount:2 ReplicationFactor:1 Configs:
    Topic: products Partition: 0 Leader: 1001 Replicas: 1001 Isr: 1001
    Topic: products Partition: 1 Leader: 1001 Replicas: 1001 Isr: 1001
$
```

To see all the messages in a specific topic, for example, the `products` topic, run the following command:

```
docker-compose exec kafka /opt/kafka/bin/kafka-console-consumer.sh --
bootstrap-server localhost:9092 --topic products --from-beginning --
timeout-ms 1000
```

Expect an output like the one shown here:

```
2. @700dd0df9ffe:/ (bash)
{"eventType":"CREATE","key":2,"data":{"productId":2,"name":"product name C","weight":300,
"serviceAddress":null},"eventCreatedAt":"2019-02-09T07:21:09.014259"}
{"eventType":"DELETE","key":2,"data":null,"eventCreatedAt":"2019-02-09T07:23:04.017709"}
{"eventType":"CREATE","key":1,"data":{"productId":1,"name":"product name C","weight":300,
"serviceAddress":null},"eventCreatedAt":"2019-02-09T07:18:11.600382"}
{"eventType":"DELETE","key":1,"data":null,"eventCreatedAt":"2019-02-09T07:23:02.359117"}
$
```

To see all the messages in a specific partition, for example, partition 1 in the `products` topic, run the following command:

```
docker-compose exec kafka /opt/kafka/bin/kafka-console-consumer.sh --
bootstrap-server localhost:9092 --topic products --from-beginning --
timeout-ms 1000 --partition 1
```

Expect an output like the one shown here:

```
2. @700dd0df9ffe:/ (bash)
{"eventType":"CREATE","key":1,"data":{"productId":1,"name":"product name C","weight":300,
"serviceAddress":null},"eventCreatedAt":"2019-02-09T07:18:11.600382"}
{"eventType":"DELETE","key":1,"data":null,"eventCreatedAt":"2019-02-09T07:23:02.359117"}
$
```

The output will end with a timeout exception since we stop the command by specifying a timeout for the command of `1000` ms.

Bring down the microservice landscape with the following command:

```
docker-compose down
unset COMPOSE_FILE
```

Now, we have learned how Spring Cloud Stream can be used to switch a message broker from RabbitMQ to Kafka without requiring any changes in the source code. It just requires a few changes in the Docker Compose file.

Running automated tests of the reactive microservice landscape

To be able to run tests of the reactive microservice landscape automatically instead of manually, the automated `test-em-all.bash` test script has been enhanced. The most important changes are as follows:

- The script uses the new `health` endpoint to know when the microservice landscape is operational, as shown here:

  ```
  waitForService curl http://$HOST:$PORT/actuator/health
  ```

- The script has a new `waitForMessageProcessing()` function, which is called after the test data is set up. Its purpose is simply to wait for the creation of the test data to be completed by the asynchronous create services.

  To use the test script to automatically run the tests with RabbitMQ and Kafka, perform the following steps:

1. Run the tests using the default Docker Compose file, that is, with RabbitMQ without partitions, with the following commands:

   ```
   unset COMPOSE_FILE
   ./test-em-all.bash start stop
   ```

2. Run the tests for RabbitMQ with two partitions per topic using the Docker Compose `docker-compose-partitions.yml` file with the following commands:

   ```
   export COMPOSE_FILE=docker-compose-partitions.yml
   ./test-em-all.bash start stop
   unset COMPOSE_FILE
   ```

3. Finally, run the tests with Kafka and two partitions per topic using the Docker Compose `docker-compose-kafka.yml` file with the following commands:

```
export COMPOSE_FILE=docker-compose-kafka.yml
./test-em-all.bash start stop
unset COMPOSE_FILE
```

In this section, we have learned how to use the `test-em-all.bash` test script to automatically run tests of the reactive microservice landscape that have been either configured to use RabbitMQ or Kafka as its message broker.

Summary

In this chapter, we have seen how we can develop reactive microservices!

Using Spring WebFlux and Spring WebClient, we can develop non-blocking synchronous APIs that can handle incoming HTTP requests and send outgoing HTTP requests without blocking any threads. Using Spring Data's reactive support for MongoDB, we can also access MongoDB databases in a non-blocking way, that is, without blocking any threads while waiting for responses from the database. Spring WebFlux, Spring WebClient, and Spring Data rely on Spring Reactor to provide their reactive and non-blocking features. When we must use blocking code, for example, when using Spring Data for JPA, we can encapsulate the processing of the blocking code by scheduling the processing of it in a dedicated thread pool.

We have also seen how Spring Data Stream can be used to develop event-driven asynchronous services that work on both RabbitMQ and Kafka as messing systems without requiring any changes in the code. By doing some configuration, we can use features in Spring Cloud Stream such as consumer groups, retries, dead-letter queues, and partitions to handle the various challenges of asynchronous messaging.

We have also learned how to manually and automatically test a system landscape consisting of reactive microservices.

This was the final chapter on how to use fundamental features in Spring Boot and Spring Framework.

Next up is an introduction to Spring Cloud and how it can be used to make our services production-ready, scalable, robust, configurable, secure, and resilient!

Questions

1. Why is it important to know how to develop reactive microservices?
2. How do you choose between non-blocking synchronous APIs and event/message-driven asynchronous services?
3. What makes a message different from an event?
4. Name some challenges with message-driven asynchronous services. How do we handle them?
5. Why is the following test failing?

```
@Test
public void TestFlux() {

    List<Integer> list = new ArrayList<>();

    Flux.just(1, 2, 3, 4)
        .filter(n -> n % 2 == 0)
        .map(n -> n * 2)
        .log();

    assertThat(list).containsExactly(4, 8);
```

6. What are the challenges of writing tests with reactive code using JUnit, and how can we handle them?

Section 2: Leveraging Spring Cloud to Manage Microservices

In this section, you'll gain an understanding of how Spring Cloud can be used to manage the challenges faced when developing microservices (that is, building a distributed system).

This section includes the following chapters:

- Chapter 8, *Introduction to Spring Cloud*
- Chapter 9, *Adding Service Discovery Using Netflix Eureka and Ribbon*
- Chapter 10, *Using Spring Cloud Gateway to Hide Microservices Behind an Edge Server*
- Chapter 11, *Securing Access to APIs*
- Chapter 12, *Centralized Configuration*
- Chapter 13, *Improving Resilience Using Resilience4j*
- Chapter 14, *Understanding Distributed Tracing*

Introduction to Spring Cloud

8

So far, we have seen how we can use Spring Boot to build microservices with well-documented APIs, along with Spring WebFlux and SpringFox; persist data in MongoDB and SQL databases using Spring Data for MongoDB and JPA; build reactive microservices either as non-blocking APIs using Project Reactor or as event-driven asynchronous services using Spring Cloud Stream with RabbitMQ or Kafka, together with Docker; and manage and test a system landscape consisting of microservices, databases, and messaging systems.

Now, it's time to see how we can use **Spring Cloud** to make our services production-ready, scalable, robust, configurable, secure, and resilient.

In this chapter, we will introduce you to how Spring Cloud can be used to implement the following design patterns from `Chapter 1`, *Introduction to Microservices*, the *Design patterns for microservices* section:

- Service discovery
- Edge server
- Centralized configuration
- Circuit breaker
- Distributed tracing

Technical requirements

This chapter does not contain any source code, and so no tools need to be installed.

The evolution of Spring Cloud

In its initial 1.0 release in March 2015, Spring Cloud was mainly a wrapper around the Netflix OSS tools, which are as follows:

- Netflix Eureka, a discovery server
- Netflix Ribbon, a client-side load balancer
- Netflix Zuul, an edge server
- Netflix Hystrix, a circuit breaker

The initial release of Spring Cloud also contained a configuration server and integration with Spring Security that provided OAuth 2.0 protected APIs. In May 2016, the Brixton release (V1.1) of Spring Cloud was made generally available. With the Brixton release, Spring Cloud got support for distributed tracing based on Spring Cloud Sleuth and Zipkin, which originated from Twitter. These initial Spring Cloud components could be used to implement the preceding design patterns. For more details, see `https://spring.io/blog/2015/03/04/spring-cloud-1-0-0-available-now` and `https://spring.io/blog/2016/05/11/spring-cloud-brixton-release-is-available`.

Since its inception, Spring Cloud has grown considerably over the years and has added support for the following, among others:

- Service discovery and centralized configuration based on HashiCorp Consul and Apache Zookeeper
- Event-driven microservices using Spring Cloud Stream
- Cloud providers such as Microsoft Azure, Amazon Web Services, and Google Cloud Platform

> See `https://spring.io/projects/spring-cloud` for a complete list of tools.

Since the release of Spring Cloud Greenwich (V2.1) in January 2019, some of the Netflix tools mentioned previously have been placed in maintenance mode in Spring Cloud. The following replacements are recommended by the Spring Cloud project:

Current component	Replaced by
Netflix Hystrix	Resilience4j
Netflix Hystrix Dashboard/Netflix Turbine	Micrometer and monitoring system
Netflix Ribbon	Spring Cloud load balancer
Netflix Zuul	Spring Cloud Gateway

For more details, for example on what maintenance mode means, see `https://spring.io/blog/2019/01/23/spring-cloud-greenwich-release-is-now-available`.

In this book, we will use the replacement alternatives to implement the design patterns mentioned previously. The following table maps each design pattern to the software components that will be used to implement them:

Design pattern	Software component
Service discovery	Netflix Eureka and Spring Cloud load balancer
Edge server	Spring Cloud Gateway and Spring Security OAuth
Centralized configuration	Spring Cloud Configuration Server
Circuit breaker	Resilience4j
Distributed tracing	Spring Cloud Sleuth and Zipkin

Now, let's go through the design patterns and introduce the software components that will be used to implement them!

Using Netflix Eureka as a discovery service

A discovery service is probably the most important support function required to make a landscape of cooperating microservices production-ready. As we already described in `Chapter 1`, *Introduction to Microservices*, in the *Service discovery* section, a discovery service can be used to keep track of existing microservices and their instances. The first discovery service that Spring Cloud supported was *Netflix Eureka*.

mn instance each.

With Netflix Eureka introduced, let's introduce how to use Spring Cloud Gateway as an
edge server.

tranipnit

Introduction to Spring Cloud

We will use this in Chapter 9, *Adding Service Discovery Using Netflix Eureka and Ribbon*, along with a load balancer and the new Spring Cloud load balancer.

We will see how easy it is to register microservices with Netflix Eureka when using Spring Cloud, and as a client sends HTTP requests such as a call to a RESTful API to one of the instances registered in Netflix Eureka. We will also see how to scale up the number of instances of a microservice, and how requests to a microservice will be load-balanced over its available instances (based on, by default, round-robin scheduling).

The following screenshot demonstrates the web UI from Eureka, where we can see what microservices we have registered:

The review service has three instances available, while the other two services only have one instance each.

With Netflix Eureka introduced, let's introduce how to use Spring Cloud Gateway as an edge server.

[246]

Using Spring Cloud Gateway as an edge server

Another very important support function is an edge server. As we already described in Chapter 1, *Introduction to Microservices*, in the *Edge server* section, it can be used to secure a microservice landscape, that is, hide private services from external usage and protect public services when they're used by external clients.

Initially, Spring Cloud used Netflix Zuul v1 as its edge server. Since the Spring Cloud Greenwich release, it's recommended to use **Spring Cloud Gateway** instead. Spring Cloud Gateway comes with similar support for critical features, such as URL path-based routing and the protection of endpoints via the use of OAuth 2.0 and **OpenID Connect** (**OIDC**).

One important difference between Netflix Zuul v1 and Spring Cloud Gateway is that Spring Cloud Gateway is based on non-blocking APIs that use Spring 5, Project Reactor, and Spring Boot 2, while Netflix Zuul v1 is based on blocking APIs. This means that Spring Cloud Gateway should be able to handle larger amounts of concurrent requests than Netflix Zuul v1, which is important for an edge server that all external traffic goes through.

The following diagram shows how all requests from external clients go through Spring Cloud Gateway as an edge server. Based on URL paths, it routes requests to the intended microservice:

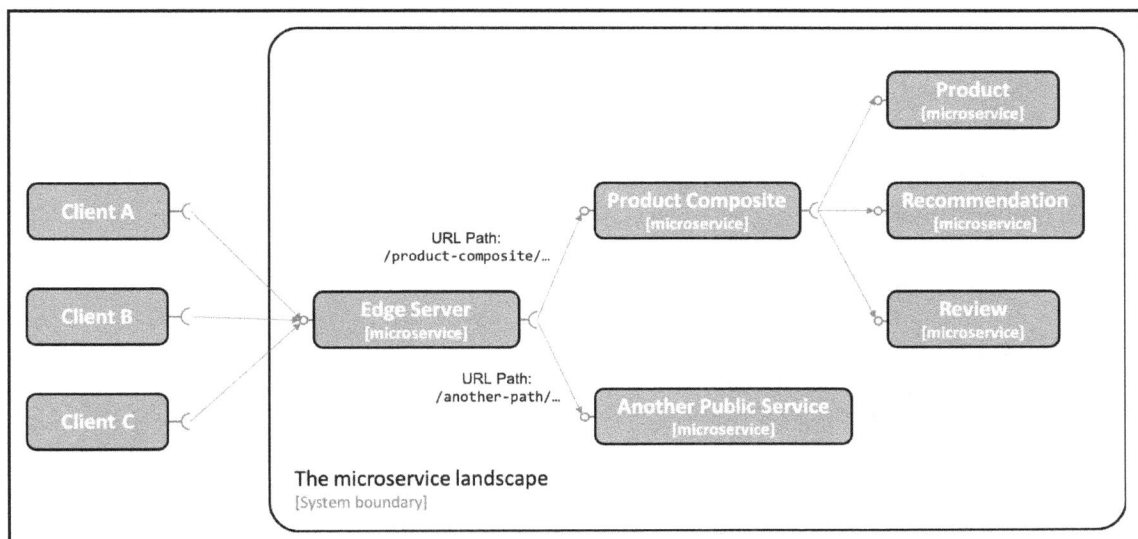

In the preceding diagram, we can see how the edge server will send external requests that have a URL path that starts with /product-composite/ to the **Product Composite** microservice. The core services **Product**, **Recommendation**, and **Review** are not reachable from external clients.

In Chapter 10, *Using Spring Cloud Gateway to Hide Microservices Behind an Edge Server*, we will look at how to set up Spring Cloud Gateway with our microservices.

In Chapter 11, *Secure Access to APIs*, we will see how we can use Spring Cloud Gateway together with Spring Security OAuth2 to protect access to the edge server using OAuth 2.0 and OIDC. We will also see how Spring Cloud Gateway can propagate identity information of the caller down to our microservices, for example, the username or email address of the caller.

With Spring Cloud Gateway introduced, let's introduce how to use Spring Cloud Config for centralized configuration.

Using Spring Cloud Config for centralized configuration

To manage the configuration of a system landscape of microservices, Spring Cloud contains Spring Cloud Config, which provides the centralized management of configuration files according to the requirements described in Chapter 1, *Introduction to Microservices*, in the *Central configuration* section.

Spring Cloud Config supports storing configuration files in a number of different backends, such as the following:

- A Git repository, for example, on GitHub or Bitbucket
- Local filesystem
- HashiCorp Vault
- A JDBC database

Spring Cloud Config allows us to handle configuration in a hierarchical structure; for example, we can place common parts of the configuration in a common file and microservice-specific settings in separate configuration files.

Spring Cloud Config also supports detecting changes in the configuration and pushing notifications to the affected microservices. It uses **Spring Cloud Bus** to transport the notifications. Spring Cloud Bus is an abstraction on top of Spring Cloud Stream that we already are familiar with; that is, it supports the use of either RabbitMQ or Kafka as the messaging system for transporting notifications out of the box.

The following diagram illustrates the cooperation between Spring Cloud Config, its clients, a Git repository, and Spring Cloud Bus:

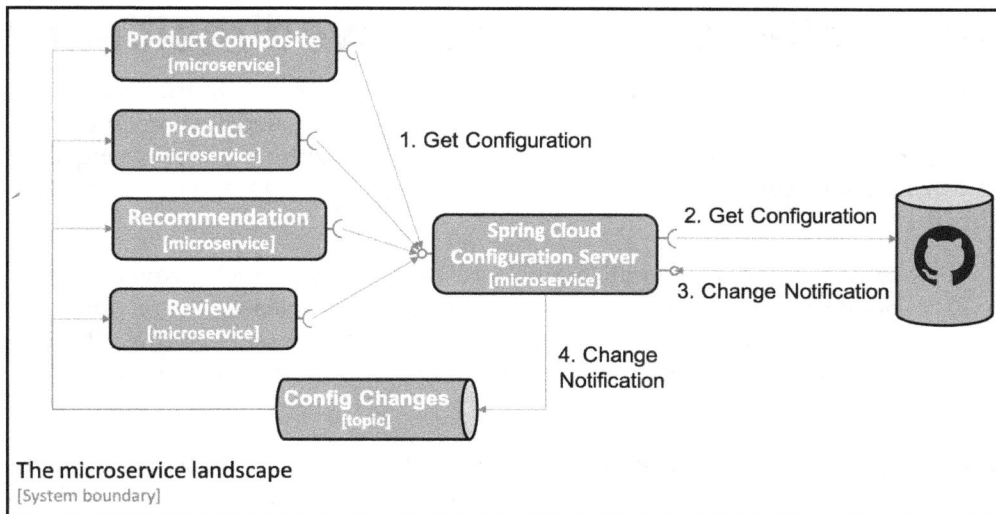

The diagram shows the following:

1. When the microservices starts up, they ask the configuration server for its configuration.
2. The configuration server gets the configuration from, in this case, a Git repository.
3. Optionally, the Git repository can be configured to send notifications to the configuration server when Git commits are pushed to the Git repository.
4. The configuration server will publish change events using Spring Cloud Bus. The microservices that are affected by the change will react and retrieve its updated configuration from the configuration server.

Finally, Spring Cloud Config also supports the encryption of sensitive information in the configuration, such as credentials.

We will learn about Spring Cloud Config in `Chapter 12`, *Centralized Configuration*.

With Spring Cloud Config introduced, let's get introduced to how to use Resilience4j for improved resilience.

Using Resilience4j for improved resilience

As we already mentioned in `Chapter 1`, *Introduction to Microservices*, in the *Circuit breaker* section, things go wrong occasionally. In a fairly large-scaled system landscape of cooperating microservices, we must assume that there is something going wrong all of the time. Failures must be seen as a normal state, and the system landscape must be designed to handle it!

> Initially, Spring Cloud came with Netflix Hystrix, a well-proven circuit breaker. But since the Spring Cloud Greenwich release, it is recommended to replace Netflix Hystrix with Resilience4j. The reason for this is that Netflix recently put Hystrix into maintenance mode. For more details, see `https://github.com/Netflix/Hystrix#hystrix-status`.

Resilience4j is an open source-based fault tolerance library. You can discover more about it at `https://github.com/resilience4j/resilience4j`. It comes with the following fault tolerance mechanisms built-in:

- **Circuit breaker** is used to prevent a chain of failure reactions if a remote service stops to respond.
- **Rate limiter** is used to limit the number of requests to service during a specified time period.
- **Bulkhead** is used to limit the number of concurrent requests to a service.
- **Retries** is used to handle random errors that might happen from time to time.
- **Timeout** is used to avoid waiting too long for a response from slow or not responding service.

In `Chapter 13`, *Improving Resilience Using Resilience4j*, we will focus on the circuit breaker in Resilience4j. It follows the classic design of a circuit breaker, as illustrated in the following state diagram:

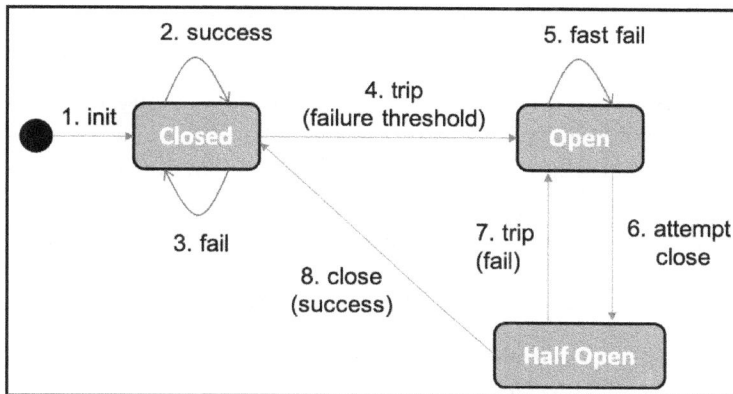

Let's take a look at the state diagram in more detail:

1. A circuit breaker starts as **Closed**, that is, allowing requests to be processed.
2. As long as the requests are processed successfully, it stays in the **Closed** state.
3. If failures start to happen, a counter starts to count up.
4. If a configured threshold of failures is reached, the circuit breaker will **trip**, that is, go to the **Open** state, not allowing further requests to be processed.
5. Instead, a request will **fast fail**, that is, return immediately with an exception.
6. After a configurable time, the circuit breaker will enter a **Half Open** state and allow one request to go through, such as a probe, to see whether the failure has been resolved.
7. If the probe request fails, the circuit breaker goes back to the **Open** state.
8. If the probe request succeeds, the circuit breaker goes to the initial **Closed** state, that is, allowing new requests to be processed.

Sample usage of the circuit breaker in Resilience4j

Let's assume we have a REST service that is protected by a circuit breaker via Resilience4j called `myService`.

If the service starts to produce internal errors, for example, because it can't reach a service it depends on, we might get a response from the service such as `500 Internal Server Error`. After a number of configurable attempts, the circuit will open and we will get a fast failure that returns an error message such as `CircuitBreaker 'myService' is open`. When the error is resolved and we make a new attempt (after the configurable wait time), the circuit breaker will allow a new attempt as a probe. If the call succeeds, the circuit breaker will be closed again; that is, it is operating normally.

When using Resilience4j together with Spring Boot, we will be able to monitor the state of the circuit breakers in a microservice using its Spring Boot Actuator `health` endpoint. We can, for example, use `curl` to see the state of the circuit breaker, that is, `myService`:

```
curl $HOST:$PORT/actuator/health -s | jq .details.myServiceCircuitBreaker
```

If it operates normally, that is, the circuit is `closed`, it will respond with something such as the following:

```
2. @700dd0df9ffe:/ (bash)
{
  "status": "UP",
  "details": {
    "failureRate": "-1.0%",
    "failureRateThreshold": "50.0%",
    "maxBufferedCalls": 5,
    "bufferedCalls": 3,
    "failedCalls": 0,
    "notPermittedCalls": 0
  }
}
$
```

If something is wrong and the circuit is **open**, it will respond with something such as the following:

```
2. @700dd0df9ffe:/ (bash)
{
    "status" : "DOWN",
    "details" : {
        "failureRate" : "100.0%",
        "failureRateThreshold" : "50.0%",
        "maxBufferedCalls" : 3,
        "bufferedCalls" : 3,
        "failedCalls" : 3,
        "notPermittedCalls" : 1
    }
}
$ 
```

With Resilience4j and specifically its circuit breaker introduced, we have seen an example of how the circuit breaker can be used to handle errors for a REST client. Let's get introduced to how to use Spring Cloud Sleuth and Zipkin for distributed tracing.

Using Spring Cloud Sleuth and Zipkin for distributed tracing

To understand what is going on in a distributed system such as a system landscape of cooperating microservices, it is crucial to be able to track and visualize how requests and messages flow between microservices when processing an external call to the system landscape.

> Refer to `Chapter 1`, *Introduction to Microservices*, the *Distributed tracing* section, for more information on this subject.

Spring Cloud comes with **Spring Cloud Sleuth**, which can mark requests and messages/events that are part of the same processing flow with a common *correlation ID*.

Spring Cloud Sleuth can also decorate log messages with correlation IDs to make it easier to track log messages from different microservices that come from the same processing flow. **Zipkin** is a distributed tracing system (http://zipkin.io) that Spring Cloud Sleuth can send tracing data to for storage and visualization.

The infrastructure for handling distributed tracing information in Spring Cloud Sleuth and Zipkin is based on Google Dapper (https://ai.google/research/pubs/pub36356). In Dapper, the tracing information from a complete workflow is called a **trace tree**, and subparts of the tree, such as the basic units of work, are called **spans**. Spans can, in turn, consist of sub-spans, which form the trace tree. A correlation ID is called TraceId, and a span is identified by its own unique SpanId, along with TraceId of the trace tree it belongs to.

Spring Cloud Sleuth can send requests to Zipkin either synchronously over HTTP or asynchronously using either RabbitMQ or Kafka. To avoid creating runtime dependencies to the Zipkin server from our microservices, we prefer sending trace information to Zipkin asynchronously using either RabbitMQ or Kafka. This is illustrated by the following diagram:

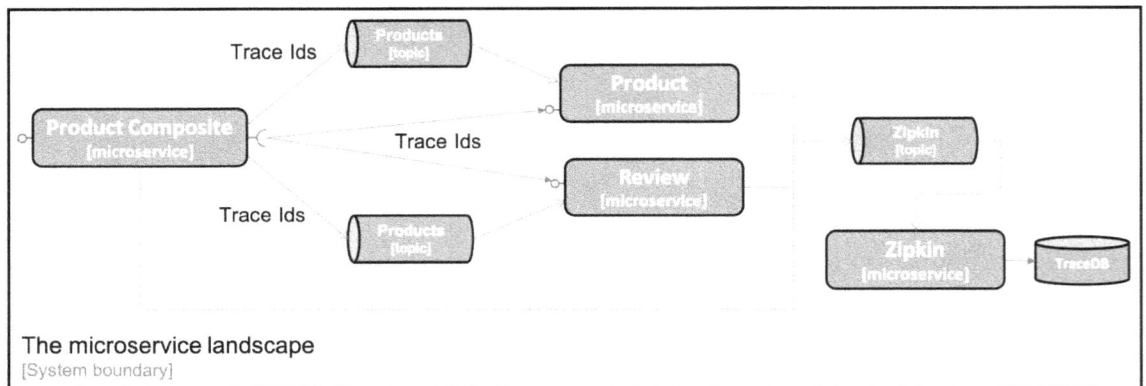

In Chapter 14, *Understanding Distributed Tracing*, we will see how we can use Spring Cloud Sleuth and Zipkin to trace the processing that goes on in our microservice landscape. The following is a screenshot from the Zipkin UI, which visualizes the trace tree that was created as a result of processing the creation of an aggregated product:

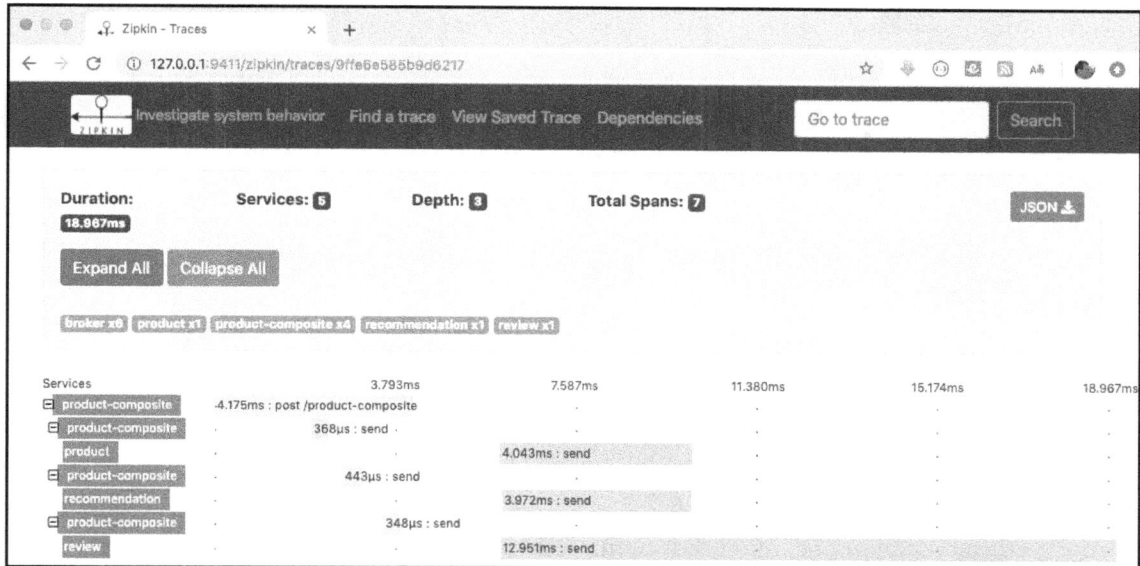

An HTTP POST request is sent to the **product-composite** service and responds by publishing create events to the topics for products, recommendations, and reviews. These events are consumed by the three core microservices in parallel and the data in the create events are stored in each microservice's database.

With Spring Cloud Sleuth and Zipkin for distributed tracing being introduced, we have seen an example of distributed tracing of the processing of an external synchronous HTTP request that includes asynchronous passing of events between the involved microservices.

Summary

In this chapter, we have seen how Spring Cloud has evolved from being rather Netflix OSS-centric to having a much larger scope as of today. We also introduced how components from the latest release of Spring Cloud Greenwich can be used to implement some of the design patterns we described in Chapter 1, *Introduction to Microservices*, in the *Design patterns for microservices* section. These design patterns are required to make a landscape of cooperating microservices production-ready.

Head over to the next chapter to see how we can implement service discovery using Netflix Eureka and Spring Cloud load balancer!

Questions

1. What is the purpose of Netflix Eureka?
2. What are the main features of Spring Cloud Gateway?
3. What backends are supported by Spring Cloud Config?
4. What are the capabilities that Resilience4j provides?
5. What are the concepts of trace tree and span used for in distributed tracing, and what is the paper called that defined them?

Adding Service Discovery Using Netflix Eureka and Ribbon

9

In this chapter, we will learn how to use Netflix Eureka as a discovery server for microservices based on Spring Boot. To allow our microservices to communicate with Netflix Eureka, we will use the Spring Cloud module for Netflix Eureka clients. Before we delve into the details, we will elaborate on why a discovery server is needed and why a DNS server isn't sufficient.

The following topics will be covered in this chapter:

- Introduction to service discovery
    - The problem with DNS-based service discovery
    - Challenges with service discovery
    - Service discovery with Netflix Eureka in Spring Cloud
- Setting up a Netflix Eureka server
- Connecting microservices to a Netflix Eureka server
- Setting up configuration for use in the development process
- Trying out the discovery service

Technical requirements

All of the commands that are described in this book have been run on a MacBook Pro using macOS Mojave, but it should be straightforward to modify it so that it can run on another platform, such as Linux or Windows.

No new tools need to be installed in this chapter.

The source code for this chapter can be found on GitHub: `https://github.com/PacktPublishing/Hands-On-Microservices-with-Spring-Boot-and-Spring-Cloud/tree/master/Chapter09`.

To be able to run the commands that are described in this book, download the source code to a folder and set up an environment variable, `$BOOK_HOME`, that points to that folder. Some sample commands are as follows:

```
export BOOK_HOME=~/Documents/Hands-On-Microservices-with-Spring-Boot-and-Spring-Cloud
git clone
https://github.com/PacktPublishing/Hands-On-Microservices-with-Spring-Boot-and-Spring-Cloud $BOOK_HOME
cd $BOOK_HOME/Chapter09
```

The Java source code is written for Java 8 and has been tested on Java 12. This chapter uses Spring Cloud 2.1.0 (also known as the **Greenwich** release), Spring Boot 2.1.3, and Spring 5.1.5—that is, the latest available version of the Spring components at the time of writing this chapter.

The source code contains the following Gradle projects:

- `api`
- `util`
- `microservices/product-service`
- `microservices/review-service`
- `microservices/recommendation-service`
- `microservices/product-composite-service`
- `spring-cloud/eureka-server`

The code examples in this chapter all come from the source code in the `$BOOK_HOME/Chapter09` directory but have been edited in several places in order to remove irrelevant parts of the source code, such as comments and import and log statements.

If you want to look at the changes that were applied to the source code in `Chapter 9`, *Adding Service Discovery Using Netflix Eureka and Ribbon*, to see what it took to add Netflix Eureka as a discovery service to the microservices landscape, you can compare it with the source code for `Chapter 7`, *Developing Reactive Microservices*. You can use your favorite `diff` tool and compare the two folders, `$BOOK_HOME/Chapter07` and `$BOOK_HOME/Chapter09`, respectively.

Introducing service discovery

The concept of service discovery was described in `Chapter 1`, *Introduction to Microservices*; please refer to the *Service discovery* section for more information. Netflix Eureka was introduced as a discovery service in `Chapter 8`, *Introduction to Spring Cloud*; please refer to the *Netflix Eureka as a discovery service* section for more information. Before we jump into the implementation details, we will look at the following topics:

- The problem with DNS-based service discovery
- Challenges with service discovery
- Service discovery with Netflix Eureka in Spring Cloud

The problem with DNS-based service discovery

So, what's the problem?

Why can't we simply start new instances of a microservice and rely on round-robin DNS? In essence, given that the microservice instances have the same DNS name, the DNS server will resolve it to a list of IP addresses for the available instances. Due to this, the client can call the service instances in a round-robin fashion.

Let's try it out and see what happens, shall we? Follow these steps:

1. Assuming that you have followed the instructions from `Chapter 7`, *Developing Reactive Microservices*, start the system landscape and insert some test data with the following command:

   ```
   cd $BOOK_HOME/chapter07
   ./test-em-all.bash start
   ```

2. Scale up the `review` microservice to two instances:

   ```
   docker-compose up -d --scale review=2
   ```

3. Ask the composite product service for the IP addresses it finds for the `review` microservice:

   ```
   docker-compose exec product-composite getent hosts review
   ```

4. Expect an answer like the following:

```
172.19.0.9 review
172.19.0.8 review
```

Great, the composite product service sees two IP addresses—in my case, `172.19.0.8` and `172.19.0.9`—one for each instance of the `review` microservice instances!

5. If you want to, you can verify that these are the correct IP addresses by using the following commands:

```
docker-compose exec --index=1 review cat /etc/hosts
docker-compose exec --index=2 review cat /etc/hosts
```

The last line in the output from each command should contain one of the IP addresses, as shown in the preceding code.

6. Now, let's try out a couple of calls to the composite product service and see whether it uses both instances of the `review` microservice:

```
curl localhost:8080/product-composite/2 -s | jq -r
.serviceAddresses.rev
```

Unfortunately, we will only get responses from one of the microservice instances, as in this example:

That was disappointing!

Okay, so what is going on here?

A DNS client typically caches the resolved IP addresses and hangs on to the first working IP address it tries out when it receives a list of IP addresses that have been resolved for a DNS name. Neither the DNS servers nor the DNS protocol is well-suited for handling volatile microservices instances that come and go all of the time. Because of this, DNS-based service discovery isn't very appealing from a practical standpoint.

Challenges with service discovery

So, we need something a bit more powerful than a plain DNS to keep track of available microservice instances!

We must take the following into consideration when we're keeping track of many small moving parts, that is, microservice instances:

- New instances can start up at any point in time.
- Existing instances can stop responding and eventually crash at any point in time.
- Some of the failing instances might be okay after a while and should start to receive traffic again, while others will not and should be removed from the service registry.
- Some microservice instances might take some time to start up; that is, just because they can receive HTTP requests doesn't mean that traffic should be routed to them.
- Unintended network partitioning and other network-related errors can occur at any time.

Building a robust and resilient discovery server is not an easy task, to say the least. Let's see how we can use Netflix Eureka to handle these challenges!

Service discovery with Netflix Eureka in Spring Cloud

Netflix Eureka implements client-side service discovery, meaning that the clients run software that talks to the discovery service, Netflix Eureka, to get information about the available microservice instances. This is illustrated in the following diagram:

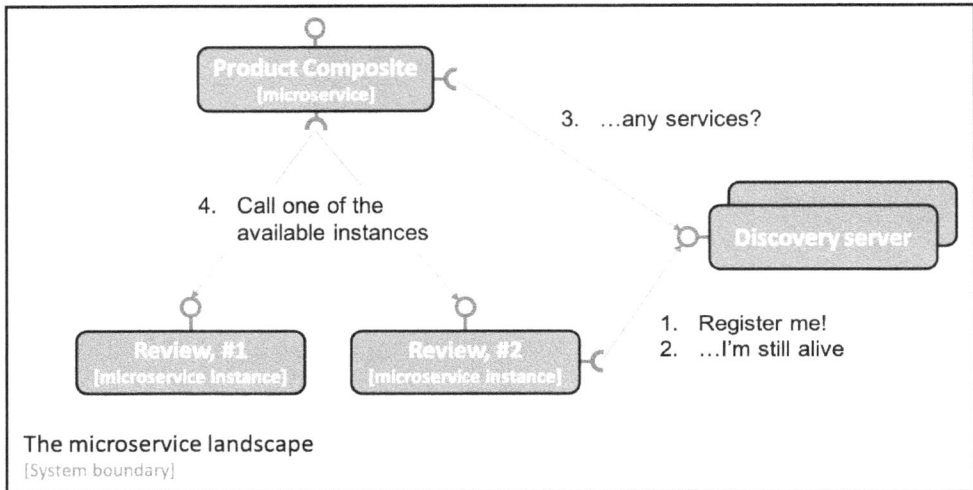

The process is as follows:

1. Whenever a microservice instance starts up—for example, the **Review** service—it registers itself to one of the Eureka servers.
2. On a regular basis, each microservice instance sends a heartbeat message to the Eureka server, telling it that the microservice instance is okay and is ready to receive requests.
3. Clients—for example, the **Product Composite** service—use a client library that regularly asks the Eureka service for information about available services.
4. When the client needs to send a request to another microservice, it already has a list of available instances in its client library and can pick one of them without asking the discovery server. Typically available instances are chosen in a round-robin fashion; that is, they are called one after another before the first one is called once more.

In Chapter 17, *Implementing Kubernetes Features as an Alternative*, we will look at an alternative approach to how to provide a discovery service using a server-side *service* concept in Kubernetes.

Spring Cloud comes with an abstraction of how to communicate with a discovery service such as Netflix Eureka and provides an interface called `DiscoveryClient`. This can be used to interact with a discovery service to get information regarding available services and instances. Implementations of the `DiscoveryClient` interface are also capable of automatically registering a Spring Boot application with the discovery server.

Spring Boot can find implementations of the `DiscoveryClient` interface automatically during startup, so we only need to bring in a dependency on the corresponding implementation to connect to a discovery server. In the case of Netflix Eureka, the dependency that's used by our microservices is `spring-cloud-starter-netflix-eureka-client`.

Spring Cloud also has `DiscoveryClient` implementations that support the use of either Apache Zookeeper or HashiCorp Consul as a discovery server.

Spring Cloud also comes with an abstraction—the `LoadBalancerClient` interface—for clients that want to make requests through a load balancer to registered instances in the discovery service. The standard reactive HTTP client, `WebClient`, can be configured to use the `LoadBalancerClient` implementation. By adding the `@LoadBalanced` annotation to an `@Bean` declaration that returns a `WebClient.Builder` object, a `LoadBalancerClient` implementation will be injected into the `Builder` instance as `ExchangeFilterFunction`. With the `spring-cloud-starter-netflix-eureka-client` dependency on the classpath, `RibbonLoadBalancerClient` will be automatically injected, that is, a load balancer based on Netflix Ribbon. So, even though a Netflix Ribbon is placed in maintenance mode, as described in Chapter 8, *Introduction to Spring Cloud*, it is still used under the hood. Later in this chapter in the *Connecting microservices to a Netflix Eureka server* section, we will look at some source code examples of how this can be used.

In summary, Spring Cloud makes it very easy to use Netflix Eureka as a discovery service. With this introduction to service discovery and its challenges and how Netflix Eureka can be used together with Spring Cloud, we are ready to learn how to set up a Netflix Eureka server.

Setting up a Netflix Eureka server

In this section, we will learn how to set up a Netflix Eureka server for service discovery. Setting up a Netflix Eureka server using Spring Cloud is really easy—just follow these steps:

1. Create a Spring Boot project using Spring Initializr, as described in `Chapter 3`, *Creating a Set of Cooperating Microservices*, in the *Using Spring Initializr to generate skeleton code* section.

2. Add a dependency to `spring-cloud-starter-netflix-eureka-server`.

3. Add the `@EnableEurekaServer` annotation to the application class.

4. Add a Dockerfile, similar to the Dockerfiles that are used for our microservices, with the exception that we export the Eureka default port, `8761`, instead of the default port for our microservices, `8080`.

5. Add the Eureka server to our three Docker Compose files, that is, `docker-compose.yml`, `docker-compose-partitions.yml`, and `docker-compose-kafka.yml`:

```
eureka:
  build: spring-cloud/eureka-server
  mem_limit: 350m
  ports:
    - "8761:8761"
```

6. Finally, add some configuration. Please go to the *Setting up configuration for use in the development process* section in this chapter, where we will go through the configuration for both the Eureka server and our microservices.

That's all it takes!

You can find the source code for the Eureka server in the `$BOOK_HOME/Chapter09/spring-cloud/eureka-server` folder.

Knowing how to set up a Netflix Eureka server for service discovery, we are ready to learn how to connect microservices to a Netflix Eureka server.

Connecting microservices to a Netflix Eureka server

In this section, we will learn how to connect microservice instances to a Netflix Eureka server. We will learn both how microservices instances register themselves to the Eureka server during their startup and how clients can use the Eureka server to find microservice instances it wants to call.

To be able to register a microservice instance in the Eureka server, we need to do the following:

1. Add a dependency to `spring-cloud-starter-netflix-eureka-client` in the build file, `build.gradle`:

   ```
   implementation('org.springframework.cloud:spring-cloud-starter-
   netflix-eureka-client')
   ```

2. When running tests on a single microservice, we don't want to depend on having the Eureka server up and running. Therefore, we will disable the use of Netflix Eureka in all Spring Boot tests, that is, JUnit tests annotated with `@SpringBootTest`. This can be done by adding the `eureka.client.enabled` property and setting it to `false` in the annotation, like so:

   ```
   @SpringBootTest(webEnvironment=RANDOM_PORT, properties =
   {"eureka.client.enabled=false"})
   ```

3. Finally, add some configuration. Please go to the *Setting up configuration for use in the development process* section, where we will go through the configuration for both the Eureka server and our microservices.

There is, however, one property in the configuration that is extra important: `spring.application.name`. It is used to give each microservice a virtual hostname, that is, a name used by the Eureka service to identify each microservice. Eureka clients will use this virtual hostname in the URLs that are used to make HTTP calls to the microservice, as we will see as we proceed.

To be able to look up available microservices instances through the Eureka server in the `product-composite` microservice, we also need to do the following:

1. Add a load balancer-aware `WebClient` builder, as described previously, in an application class, that is, `se.magnus.microservices.composite.product.ProductCompositeServiceApplication`:

```
@Bean
@LoadBalanced
public WebClient.Builder loadBalancedWebClientBuilder() {
    final WebClient.Builder builder = WebClient.builder();
    return builder;
}
```

2. Update how the `WebClient` object is created in the integration class, `se.magnus.microservices.composite.product.services.ProductCompositeIntegration`. The `@LoadBalanced` annotation will, as described previously, result in that Spring will inject a load balancer-aware filter into the `WebClient.Builder` bean. Unfortunately, this isn't done until after the constructor runs in the integration class. This means that we have to move the construction of `webClient` away from the constructor, as we did in *Chapter 7, Developing Reactive Microservices*, to a separate getter method that creates the `webClient` lazily, that is, once it's used for the first time. This is shown in the following code:

```
private WebClient getWebClient() {
    if (webClient == null) {
        webClient = webClientBuilder.build();
    }
    return webClient;
}
```

3. Whenever `WebClient` is used to create an outgoing HTTP request, it is accessed via the `getWebClient()` getter method (instead of using the `webClient` field directly). See the following example:

```
@Override
public Mono<Product> getProduct(int productId) {
    String url = productServiceUrl + "/product/" + productId;
    return getWebClient().get().uri(url).retrieve()
        .bodyToMono(Product.class).log()
        .onErrorMap(WebClientResponseException.class, ex ->
handleException(ex));
}
```

4. We can now get rid of our hardcoded configuration of available microservices in `application.yml`. For example, consider the following code:

```
app:
  product-service:
    host: localhost
    port: 7001
  recommendation-service:
    host: localhost
    port: 7002
  review-service:
    host: localhost
    port: 7003
```

The corresponding code in the integration class that handled the hardcoded configuration is replaced by a declaration of the base URLs to the APIs of the core microservices. This is shown in the following code:

```
private final String productServiceUrl = "http://product";
private final String recommendationServiceUrl = "http://recommendation";
private final String reviewServiceUrl = "http://review";
```

The hostnames in the preceding URLs are not actual DNS names. Instead, they are the virtual hostnames that are used by the microservices when they register themselves to the Eureka server, that is, the values of the `spring.application.name` property.

Knowing how to connect microservice instances to a Netflix Eureka server, we can move on and learn how to configure both a Eureka server and microservice instances that need to connect to a Eureka server.

Setting up configuration for use in the development process

Now, it's time for the trickiest part of setting up Netflix Eureka as a discovery service, that is, setting up a working configuration for both the Eureka server and its clients: our microservice instances.

Netflix Eureka is a highly configurable discovery server that can be set up for a number of different use cases, and it provides robust, resilient, and fault-tolerant runtime characteristics. One downside of this flexibility and robustness is that it has an almost overwhelming number of configuration options. Fortunately, Netflix Eureka comes with good default values for most of the configurable parameters—at least when it comes to using them in a production environment.

When it comes to using Netflix Eureka during development, the default values cause long startup times. For example, it can take a long time for a client to make an initial successful call to a microservices instance that is registered in the Eureka server.

Up to two minutes of wait time can be experienced when using the default configuration values. This wait time is added to the time it takes for the Eureka service and the microservices to start up. The reason for this wait time is that the involved processes need to synchronize registration information with each other.

The microservices instances need to register with the Eureka server, and the client needs to gather information from the Eureka server. This communication is mainly based on heartbeats, which happen every 30 seconds by default. A couple of caches are also involved, which slows down the propagation of updates.

We will use a configuration that minimizes this wait time, which is useful during development. For use in production environments, the default values should be used as a starting point!

> We will only use one Netflix Eureka server instance, which is okay in a development environment. In a production environment, you should always use two or more instances to ensure high availability for the Netflix Eureka server.

Let's start to learn what types of configuration parameters we need to know about.

Eureka configuration parameters

The configuration parameters for Eureka are divided into three groups:

- There are parameters for the Eureka server, prefixed with `eureka.server`.
- There are parameters for Eureka clients, prefixed with `eureka.client`. This is for clients who want to communicate with a Eureka server.

- There are parameters for Eureka instances, prefixed with `eureka.instance`. This is for the microservices instances that want to register themselves in the Eureka server.

> Some of the available parameters are described in the Spring Cloud documentation: *Service Discovery: Eureka Server*:
> `https://cloud.spring.io/spring-cloud-static/Greenwich.RELEASE/single/spring-cloud.html#spring-cloud-eureka-server`
> *Service Discovery: Eureka Clients*: `https://cloud.spring.io/spring-cloud-static/Greenwich.RELEASE/single/spring-cloud.html#_service_discovery_eureka_clients`

For an extensive list of available parameters, I recommend reading the source code:

- For Eureka server parameters, look at the `org.springframework.cloud.netflix.eureka.server.EurekaServerConfigBean` class for default values and the `com.netflix.eureka.EurekaServerConfig` interface for the relevant documentation.
- For Eureka client parameters, look at the `org.springframework.cloud.netflix.eureka.EurekaClientConfigBean` class for the default values anddocumentation.
- For Eureka instance parameters, look at the `org.springframework.cloud.netflix.eureka.EurekaInstanceConfigBean` class for default values and documentation.

Let's start to learn about configuration parameters for the Eureka server.

Configuring the Eureka server

To configure the Eureka server for use in a development environment, the following configuration can be used:

```
server:
  port: 8761

eureka:
  instance:
    hostname: localhost
  client:
    registerWithEureka: false
    fetchRegistry: false
    serviceUrl:
```

```
        defaultZone:
http://${eureka.instance.hostname}:${server.port}/eureka/

  server:
    waitTimeInMsWhenSyncEmpty: 0
    response-cache-update-interval-ms: 5000
```

The first part of the configuration, for a Eureka `instance` and `client` is a standard configuration of a standalone Eureka server. For details, see the Spring Cloud documentation that we referred to previously. The last two parameters used for the Eureka `server`, `waitTimeInMsWhenSyncEmpty` and `response-cache-update-interval-ms`, are used to minimize the startup time.

With the Eureka server configured, we are ready to see how clients to the Eureka server, that is, the microservice instances, can be configured.

Configuring clients to the Eureka server

To be able to connect to the Eureka server, the microservices have the following configuration:

```
eureka:
  client:
    serviceUrl:
 defaultZone: http://localhost:8761/eureka/
 initialInstanceInfoReplicationIntervalSeconds: 5
 registryFetchIntervalSeconds: 5
 instance:
 leaseRenewalIntervalInSeconds: 5
 leaseExpirationDurationInSeconds: 5


 ---

 spring.profiles: docker

 eureka.client.serviceUrl.defaultZone: http://eureka:8761/eureka/
```

The `eureka.client.serviceUrl.defaultZone` parameter is used to find the Eureka server, whereas the other parameters are used to minimize the startup time and the time it takes to deregister a microservice instance that is stopped.

The `product-composite` microservice, which uses the Eureka server to look up the other microservices, also has two Netflix Ribbon-specific parameters:

```
ribbon.ServerListRefreshInterval: 5000
ribbon.NFLoadBalancerPingInterval: 5
```

These two parameters are also used to minimize startup time.

Now, we have everything in place required to actually try out discovery service using the Netflix Eureka server together with our microservices.

Trying out the discovery service

With all of the details in place, we are ready to try out the service:

1. First, build the Docker images with the following commands:

   ```
   cd $BOOK_HOME/Chapter09
   ./gradlew build && docker-compose build
   ```

2. Next, start the system landscape and run the usual tests with the following command:

   ```
   ./test-em-all.bash start
   ```

   Expect output similar to what we have seen in previous chapters:

```
2. @700dd0df9ffe:/ (bash)
$ ./test-em-all.bash start
Start Tests: Fri Sep 6 19:46:54 CEST 2019
...
Creating chapter09_rabbitmq_1 ... done
...
Wait for: curl http://localhost:8080/actuator/health... , retry #1 ... Test OK (HTTP Code: 200)
Test OK ...
End, all tests OK: Fri Sep 6 19:47:54 CEST 2019
$
```

With the system landscape up and running, we can start with testing how to scale up the number of instances for one of the microservices.

Scaling up

Now, we can try out the discovery service by launching two extra `review` microservice instances:

```
docker-compose up -d --scale review=3
```

> With the preceding command, we ask Docker Compose to run three instances of the `review` service. Since one instance is already running, two new instances will be started up.

Once the new instances are up and running, browse to `http://localhost:8761/` and expect something like the following:

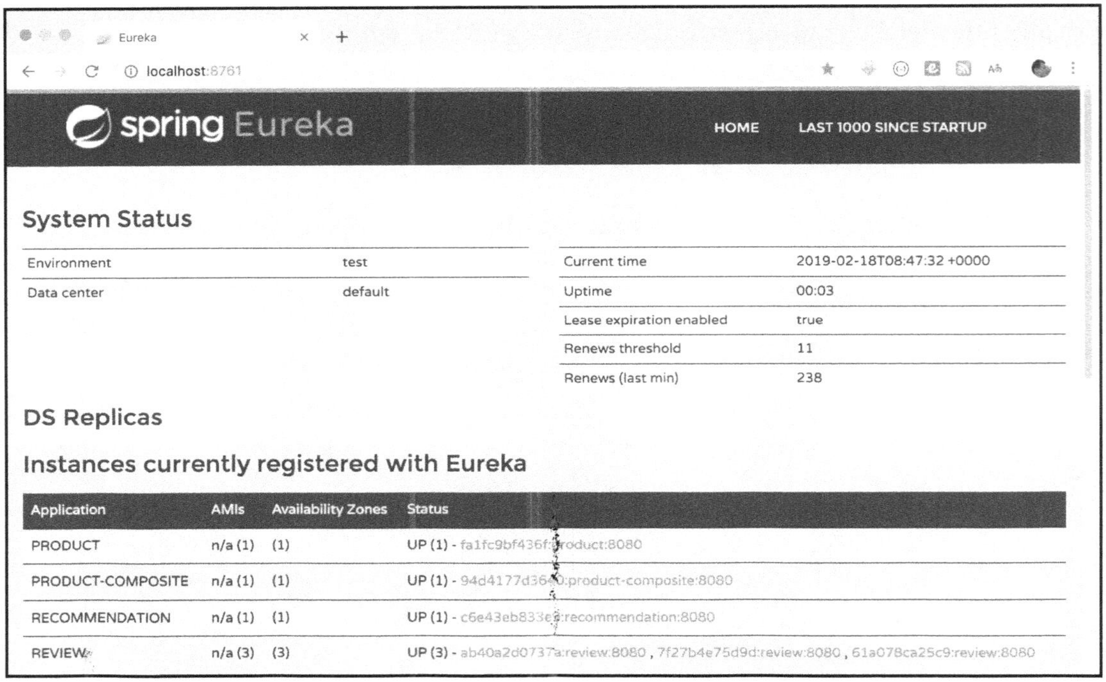

After running this localhost, verify that you can see three `review` instances in the Netflix Eureka web UI, as shown in the preceding screenshot.

One way of knowing when the new instances are up and running is to run the `docker-compose logs -f review` command and look for output that looks as follows:

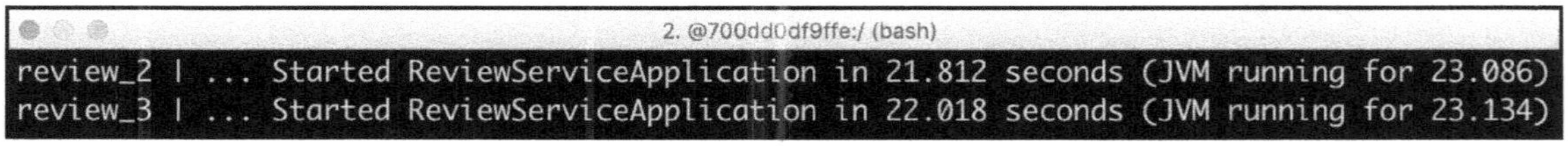

We can also use a REST API that the Eureka service exposes. To get a list of instance IDs, we can issue a `curl` command, like so:

```
curl -H "accept:application/json" localhost:8761/eureka/apps -s | jq -r
.applications.application[].instance[].instanceId
```

Expect a response that looks similar to the following:

```
● ● ●              2. @700dd0df9ffe:/ (bash)
3c7a676d8a5c:product-composite:8080
ac0a272e4488:product:8080
4034b100443e:review:8080
9599fead507d:review:8080
43d3788ce4e1:review:8080
f50156c9882a:recommendation:8080
$ ▌
```

Now that we have all of the instances up and running, let's try out the client-side load balancer by making some requests and focusing on the address of the `review` service in the responses, as follows:

```
curl localhost:8080/product-composite/2 -s | jq -r .serviceAddresses.rev
```

Expect responses similar to the following:

```
● ● ●              2. @700dd0df9ffe:/ (bash)
4034b100443e/192.168.96.9:8080
43d3788ce4e1/192.168.96.10:8080
9599fead507d/192.168.96.11:8080
$ ▌
```

Note that the address of the `review` service changes in each response; that is, the load balancer uses a round-robin to call the available `review` instances, one at a time!

We can also take a look into the `review` instances log with the following command:

```
docker-compose logs -f review
```

After this, you will see output that looks similar to the following:

```
● ● ●                      2. @700dd0df9ffe:/ (bash)
review_1 | 2019-03-02 12:20:45.420 DEBUG ... : getReviews: response size: 3
review_2 | 2019-03-02 12:20:46.059 DEBUG ... : getReviews: response size: 3
review_3 | 2019-03-02 12:21:12.500 DEBUG ... : getReviews: response size: 3
```

In the preceding output, we can see how the three review microservice instances, `review_1`, `review_2`, and `review_3`, in turn, have responded to the requests.

After trying out scaling up microservice instances we will try out what happens when we scale down the instances.

Scaling down

Let's also see what happens if we lose one instance of the `review` microservice. We can simulate that one instance stops unexpectedly by running the following command:

```
docker-compose up -d --scale review=2
```

After the shutdown of the `review` instance, there is a short time slot when calls to the API might fail. This is caused by the time it takes for information regarding the lost instance to propagate to the client, that is, the `product-composite` service. During this time frame, the client-side load balancer might choose the instance that no longer exists. To prevent this from occurring, resilience mechanisms such as timeouts and retries can be used. In Chapter 13, *Improving Resilience Using Resilience4j*, we will see how this can be applied. For now, let's specify a timeout on our `curl` command, using the `-m 2` switch to specify that we will wait no longer than two seconds for a response:

```
curl localhost:8080/product-composite/2 -m 2
```

If a timeout occurs, that is, the client-side load balancer tries to call an instance that no longer exists, the following response is expected from `curl`:

```
curl: (28) Operation timed out after 2003 milliseconds with 0 bytes
received
```

Besides that, we should expect normal responses from the two remaining instances; that is, the `serviceAddresses.rev` field should contain the addresses of the two instances, as in the following:

```
2. @700dd0df9ffe:/ (bash)
"rev": "4034b100443e/192.168.96.9:8080"
"rev": "9599fead507d/192.168.96.11:8080"
```

In the preceding sample output, we can see that two different container names and IP addresses are reported. This means that the requests have been served by different microservice instances.

After trying out the scaling down of microservice instances, we can try out something that is a bit more disruptive: stopping the Eureka server and seeing what happens when the discovery service is temporarily unavailable.

Disruptive tests with the Eureka server

Let's bring some disorder to our Eureka server and see how the system landscape manages it!

To start with, what happens if we crash the Eureka server?

As long as clients have read the information regarding available microservice instances from the Eureka server before it is stopped, the clients will be fine since they cache the information locally. However, new instances will not be made available to clients, and they will not be notified if any running instances are terminated. So, calls to instances that are no longer running will cause failures.

Let's try this out!

Stopping the Eureka server

To simulate that the Eureka server crashes, follow these steps:

1. First, stop the Eureka server and keep the two `review` instances up and running:

    ```
    docker-compose up -d --scale review=2 --scale eureka=0
    ```

2. Try a couple of calls to the API and extract the service address of the `review` service:

    ```
    curl localhost:8080/product-composite/2 -s | jq -r
    .serviceAddresses.rev
    ```

3. The response will—just like before we stopped the Eureka server—contain the addresses of the two `review` instances, like so:

```
2. @700dd0df9ffe:/ (bash)
4034b100443e/192.168.96.9:8080
9599fead507d/192.168.96.11:8080
```

This shows that the client can make calls to existing instances, even though the Eureka server is no longer running!

Stopping a review instance

To further investigate what the effects are of a crashed Eureka server, let's simulate that one of the remaining `review` microservice instances also crashes. Terminate one of the two `review` instances with the following command:

```
docker-compose up -d --scale review=1 --scale eureka=0
```

The client, that is, the `product-composite` service, will not be notified that one of the `review` instances has disappeared since no Eureka server is running. Due to this, it still thinks that there are two instances up and running. Every second call to the client will cause it to call a `review` instance that no longer exists, resulting in the response from the client not containing any information from the `review` service. The service address of the `review` service will be empty.

Try out the preceding `curl` command to verify that the service address of the `review` service will be empty every second time. This can be prevented, as described previously, by using resilience mechanisms such as timeouts and retries.

Starting up an extra instance of the product service

As a final test of the effects of a crashed Eureka server, let's see what happens if we start up a new instance of the `product` microservice. Perform the following steps:

1. Let's try starting a new instance of the `product` service:

```
docker-compose up -d --scale review=1 --scale eureka=0 --scale
product=2
```

2. Call the API a couple of times and extract the address of the `product` service with the following command:

```
curl localhost:8080/product-composite/2 -s | jq -r
.serviceAddresses.pro
```

3. Since no Eureka server is running, the client will not be notified of the new `product` instance, and so all calls will go to the first instance, as in the following example:

```
2. @700dd0df9ffe:/ (bash)
"pro": "0a20cc1efaae/172.18.0.9:8080"
```

Now we have seen some of the most important aspects of not having a Netflix Eureka server up and running. Let's conclude the section on disruptive tests by starting up the Netflix Eureka server again and seeing how the system landscape handles self-heals, that is, resilience.

Starting up the Eureka server again

In this section, we will wrap up the disruptive tests by starting up the Eureka server again. We shall also verify that the system landscape self-heals, that is, verify that the new instance of the `product` microservice gets registered with the Netflix Eureka server and that the client gets updated by the Eureka server. Perform the following steps:

1. Start the Eureka server with the following command:

```
docker-compose up -d --scale review=1 --scale eureka=1 --scale
product=2
```

Make some new calls to the API and verify that the following happens:

- All calls go to the remaining `review` instance, that is, the client has detected that the second `review` instance has gone.
- Calls to the `product` service are load-balanced over the two `product` instances, that is, the client has detected that there are two `product` instances available.

2. Make the following call a couple of times to extract the addresses of the product and the `review` service:

```
curl localhost:8080/product-composite/2 -s | jq -r
.serviceAddresses
```

3. Verify that the responses from the API calls contain addresses to the involved `product` and `review` instances, like so:

```
2. @700dd0df9ffe:/ (bash)
"pro":  "cbfd07416ddc/192.168.128.3:8080",
"rev":  "c5cc1f087afe/192.168.128.9:8080",
```

This is the second response:

```
2. @700dd0df9ffe:/ (bash)
"pro":  "18d6e52267c2/192.168.128.7:8080",
"rev":  "c5cc1f087afe/192.168.128.9:8080",
```

The `192.168.128.3` and `192.168.128.7` IP addresses belong to the two `product` instances. `192.168.128.9` is the IP address of the `review` instance.

To summarize, the Eureka server provides a very robust and resilient implementation of a discovery service. If even higher availability is desired, multiple Eureka servers can be launched and configured to communicate with each other. Details on how to set up multiple Eureka servers can be found in the Spring Cloud documentation: `https://cloud.spring.io/spring-cloud-static/Greenwich.RELEASE/single/spring-cloud.html#spring-cloud-eureka-server-peer-awareness`.

4. Finally, shut down the system landscape with the command:

```
docker-compose down
```

This completes the tests of the discovery server, Netflix Eureka, where we have learned both how to scale up and scale down microservice instances and learned what happens if a Netflix Eureka server crashes and later on comes back online.

Summary

In this chapter, we learned how to use Netflix Eureka for service discovery. First, we looked into the shortcomings of a simple DNS-based service discovery solution and the challenges that a robust and resilient service discovery solution must be able to handle.

Netflix Eureka is a very capable service discovery solution that provides robust, resilient, and fault-tolerant runtime characteristics. However, it can be challenging to configure correctly, especially for smooth developer experience. With Spring Cloud, it becomes easy to set up a Netflix Eureka server and adapt Spring Boot-based microservices, both so that they can register themselves to Eureka during startup and, when acting as a client to other microservices, to keep track of available microservices instances.

With a discovery service in place, it's time to see how we can handle external traffic using Spring Cloud Gateway as an edge server. Head over to the next chapter to find out how!

Questions

1. What is required to turn a Spring Boot application created with Spring Initializr into a fully-fledged Netflix Eureka Server?
2. What is required to make a Spring Boot-based microservice register itself automatically as a startup with Netflix Eureka?
3. What is required to make it possible for a Spring Boot-based microservice to call another microservice that is registered in a Netflix Eureka server?
4. Let's assume that you have a Netflix Eureka server up and running, along with one instance of microservice A and two instances of microservice B. All microservice instances register themselves with the Netflix Eureka server. Microservice A makes HTTP requests to microservice B based on the information it gets from the Eureka server. What will happen if, in turn, the following happens:
   - The Netflix Eureka server crashes
   - One of the instances of microservice B crashes
   - A new instance of microservice A starts up
   - A new instance of microservice B starts up
   - The Netflix Eureka server starts up again

10
Using Spring Cloud Gateway to Hide Microservices Behind an Edge Server

In this chapter, we will learn how to use Spring Cloud Gateway as an edge server, that is, to control what APIs are exposed from our microservices-based system landscape. We will see how microservices that have public APIs will be made accessible from the outside through the edge server, while microservices that have private APIs only will be accessible from the inside of the microservice landscape. In our system landscape, this means that the product composite service and the discovery service, Netflix Eureka, will be exposed through the edge server. The three core services—product, recommendation, and review—will be hidden from the outside.

The following topics will be covered in this chapter:

- Adding an edge server to our system landscape
- Setting up a Spring Cloud Gateway, including configuring routing rules
- Trying out the edge server

Technical requirements

All commands described in this book are run on a MacBook Pro using macOS Mojave, but should be straightforward to modify in order to run on another platform such as Linux or Windows.

No new tools need to be installed in this chapter.

The source code for this chapter can be found on GitHub: `https://github.com/ PacktPublishing/Hands-On-Microservices-with-Spring-Boot-and-Spring-Cloud/tree/ master/Chapter10`.

To be able to run the commands as described in this book, download the source code to a folder and set up an environment variable, `$BOOK_HOME`, that points to that folder. The following are sample commands:

```
export BOOK_HOME=~/Documents/Hands-On-Microservices-with-Spring-Boot-and-
Spring-Cloud
git clone
https://github.com/PacktPublishing/Hands-On-Microservices-with-Spring-Boot-
and-Spring-Cloud $BOOK_HOME
cd $BOOK_HOME/Chapter10
```

The Java source code is written for Java 8 and tested on Java 12. This chapter uses Spring Cloud 2.1.0, SR1 (also known as the **Greenwich** release), Spring Boot 2.1.3, and Spring 5.1.5, which is the latest available version of the Spring components at the time of writing this chapter.

The source code contains the following Gradle projects:

- `api`
- `util`
- `microservices/product-service`
- `microservices/review-service`
- `microservices/recommendation-service`
- `microservices/product-composite-service`
- `spring-cloud/eureka-server`
- `spring-cloud/gateway`

The code examples in this chapter all come from source code in `$BOOK_HOME/Chapter10` but are, in several cases, edited to remove non-relevant parts of the source code, such as comments, and import and log statements.

If you want to see the changes applied to the source code in `Chapter 10`, *Using Spring Cloud Gateway to Hide Microservices Behind an Edge Server*, that is, see what it took to add Spring Cloud Gateway as an edge server to the microservices landscape, you can compare it with the source code for `Chapter 9`, *Adding Service Discovery Using Netflix Eureka and Ribbon*. You can use your favorite `diff` tool and compare the two folders, `$BOOK_HOME/Chapter09` and `$BOOK_HOME/Chapter10`.

Adding an edge server to our system landscape

In this section we will see how the edge server is added to the system landscape and how it affects the way external clients access the public APIs that the microservices expose. All incoming requests will now be routed through the edge server, as illustrated by the following diagram:

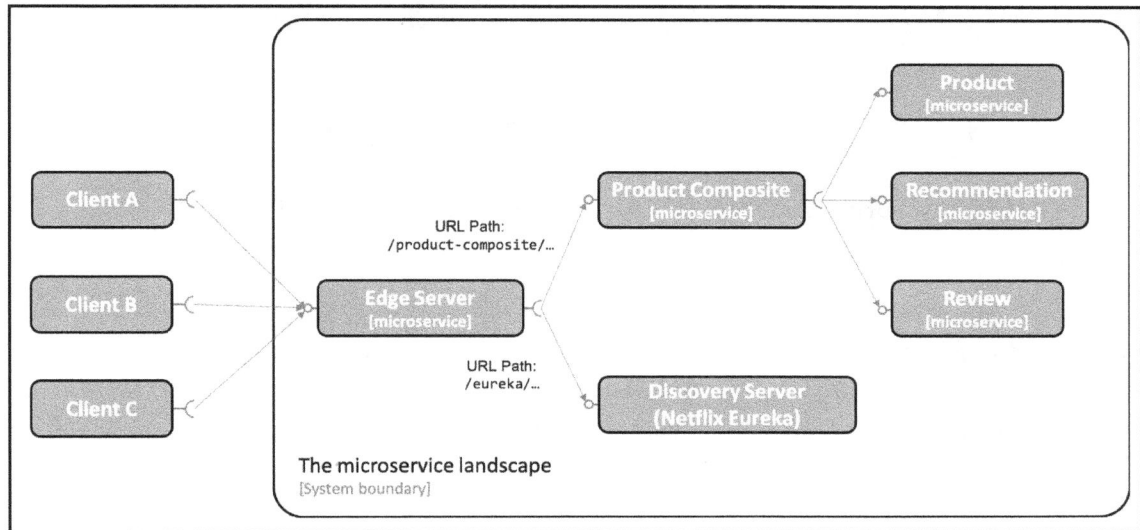

As we can see from the preceding diagram, external clients send all their requests to the edge server. The edge server can route the incoming requests based on the URL path. For example, requests with a URL that starts with /product-composite/ are routed to the **Product Composite** microservice, and a request with a URL that starts with /eureka/ is routed to the **Discovery Server** based on Netflix Eureka.

In the previous chapter 9, *Adding Service Discovery Using Netflix Eureka and Ribbon*, we exposed both the product-composite service and the discovery service, Netflix Eureka, to the outside. When we introduce the edge server in this chapter, this will no longer be the case. This is implemented by removing the following port declarations for the two services in the Docker Compose files:

```
product-composite:
  build: microservices/product-composite-service
  ports:
    - "8080:8080"
```

```
eureka:
  build: spring-cloud/eureka-server
  ports:
    - "8761:8761"
```

With the edge serve added to the system landscape, we will learn how to set up an edge server based on Spring Cloud Gateway in the next section.

Setting up a Spring Cloud Gateway

In this section, we will learn how to set up an edge server based on Spring Cloud Gateway.

Setting up a Spring Cloud Gateway as an edge server is straightforward and can be done by means of the following steps:

1. Create a Spring Boot project using Spring Initializr as described in Chapter 3, *Creating a Set of Cooperating Microservices*—refer to the *Using Spring Initializr to generate skeleton code* section.
2. Add a dependency to spring-cloud-starter-gateway.
3. To be able to locate microservices instances though Netflix Eureka, also add the spring-cloud-starter-netflix-eureka-client dependency.
4. Add the edge server to the common build file, settings.gradle:

   ```
   include ':spring-cloud:gateway'
   ```

5. Add a Dockerfile with the same content as for our microservices.
6. Add the edge server to our three Docker Compose files:

   ```
   gateway:
     environment:
       - SPRING_PROFILES_ACTIVE=docker
     build: spring-cloud/gateway
     mem_limit: 350m
     ports:
       - "8080:8080"
   ```

> **TIP**
>
> Port 8080 of the edge server is exposed outside the Docker engine. The memory limit of 350 MB is to ensure that all containers in this and the coming chapters will fit in the 6 GB of memory that we have allocated to the Docker engine

7. Add configuration for routing rules and more; refer to the *Configuring a Spring Cloud Gateway* section as we proceed in this chapter.

8. Since the edge server will handle all incoming traffic, we will move the composite health check from the product composite service to the edge server. This is described in *Adding a composite health check* section.

You can find the source code for the Spring Cloud Gateway in `$BOOK_HOME/Chapter10/spring-cloud/gateway`.

Adding a composite health check

With an edge server in place, external health check requests also have to go through the edge server. Therefore, the composite health check that checks the status of all microservices been moved from the `product-composite` service to the edge server. See `Chapter 7`, *Developing Reactive Microservices*—refer to the *Adding a health API* section for implementation details of the composite health check.

The following has been added to the edge server:

1. The `se.magnus.springcloud.gateway.HealthCheckConfiguration` class has been added, which declares the health indicator:

```
@Bean
ReactiveHealthIndicator healthcheckMicroservices() {

    ReactiveHealthIndicatorRegistry registry =
        new DefaultReactiveHealthIndicatorRegistry
            (new LinkedHashMap<>());

    registry.register("product",() ->
        getHealth("http://product"));
    registry.register("recommendation", () ->
        getHealth("http://recommendation"));
    registry.register("review", () ->
        getHealth("http://review"));
    registry.register("product-composite", () ->
        getHealth("http://product-composite"));

    return new CompositeReactiveHealthIndicator
        (healthAggregator, registry);
}

private Mono<Health> getHealth(String url) {
    url += "/actuator/health";
```

```
LOG.debug("Will call the Health API on URL: {}", url);
return getWebClient().get().uri(url)
    .retrieve().bodyToMono(String.class)
    .map(s -> new Health.Builder().up().build())
    .onErrorResume(ex ->
        Mono.just(new Health.Builder().down(ex).build()))
    .log();
}
```

We have added the `product-composite` service to the composite health check!

2. The main application class,
`se.magnus.springcloud.gateway.GatewayApplication`, declares
a `WebClient.builder` bean to be used by the implementation of the
health indicator as follows:

```
@Bean
@LoadBalanced
public WebClient.Builder loadBalancedWebClientBuilder() {
    final WebClient.Builder builder = WebClient.builder();
    return builder;
}
```

From the preceding source code, we see that `WebClient.builder` is annotated with
`@LoadBalanced`, which makes it aware of microservice instances registered in the
discovery server, Netflix Eureka. Refer to the *Service discovery with Netflix Eureka in Spring Cloud* section in `Chapter 9`, *Adding Service Discovery Using Netflix Eureka and Ribbon*, for details.

With a composite health check in place in the edge server, we are ready to look at the configuration that can be set up for a Spring Cloud Gateway.

Configuring a Spring Cloud Gateway

When it comes to configuring a Spring Cloud Gateway, the most important thing is setting up the routing rules. We also need to set up a few other things in the configuration:

1. Since Spring Cloud Gateway will use Netflix Eureka to find the microservices it will route traffic to, so it must be configured as a Eureka client in the same way as described in `Chapter 9`, *Adding Service Discovery Using Netflix Eureka and Ribbon*—refer to the *Configuration of clients to the Eureka server* section.

2. Configure Spring Boot Actuator for development usage as described in `Chapter 7`, *Developing Reactive Microservices*—refer to the *Adding a health API* section:

```
management.endpoint.health.show-details: "ALWAYS"
management.endpoints.web.exposure.include: "*"
```

3. Configure log levels so that we can see log messages from interesting parts of the internal processing in the Spring Cloud Gateway, for example, how it decides where to route incoming requests to:

```
logging:
  level:
    root: INFO
org.springframework.cloud.gateway.route.RouteDefinitionRouteLocator
: INFO
    org.springframework.cloud.gateway: TRACE
```

For the full source code, refer to the configuration file: `src/main/resources/application.yml`.

Routing rules

Setting up routing rules can be done in two ways; programmatically, using a Java DSL, or by configuration. Using the Java DSL to set up the routing rules programmatically can be useful in cases where the rules are stored in external storage, such as a database, or are given at runtime, for example, via a RESTful API or a message sent to the gateway. In most cases, I find it convenient to declare the routes in the configuration file, `src/main/resources/application.yml`.

A **route** is defined by the following:

1. **Predicates**, which select a route based on information in the incoming HTTP request
2. **Filters**, which can modify both the request and/or the response
3. A **destination URI**, which describes where to send a request
4. An **ID**, that is, the name of the route

For a full list of available predicates and filters, refer to the reference documentation: `https://cloud.spring.io/spring-cloud-gateway/single/spring-cloud-gateway.html`.

Routing requests to the product-composite API

If we, for example, want to route incoming requests where the URL path starts with /product-composite/ to our product-composite service, we can specify a routing rule like this:

```
spring.cloud.gateway.routes:
- id: product-composite
  uri: lb://product-composite
  predicates:
  - Path=/product-composite/**
```

The following are some points to take from the preceding code:

- id: product-composite: The name of the route is product-composite.
- uri: lb://product-composite: If the route is selected by its predicates, the request will be routed to the service that is named product-composite in the discovery service, that is, Netflix Eureka. lb:// is used to direct Spring Cloud Gateway to use the client-side load balancer to look up the destination in the discovery service.
- predicates:- Path=/product-composite/** is used to specify what requests this route should match. ** matches zero or more elements in the path.

Routing requests to the Eureka server's API and web page

Eureka exposes both an API and a web page for its clients. To provide a clean separation between the API and the web page in Eureka, we will set up routes as follows:

- Requests sent to the edge server with the path starting with /eureka/api/ should be handled as a call to the Eureka API.
- Requests sent to the edge server with the path starting with /eureka/web/ should be handled as a call to the Eureka web page.

API requests will be routed to http://${app.eureka-server}:8761/eureka. The route rule for the Eureka API looks like this:

```
- id: eureka-api
  uri: http://${app.eureka-server}:8761
  predicates:
  - Path=/eureka/api/{segment}
  filters:
  - SetPath=/eureka/{segment}
```

The `{segment}` part in the `Path` value matches zero or more elements in the path and will be used to replace the `{segment}` part in the `SetPath` value.

Web page requests will be routed to `http://${app.eureka-server}:8761`. The web page will load several web resources, such as `.js`, `.css`, and `.png` files. These requests will be routed to `http://${app.eureka-server}:8761/eureka`. The route rules for the Eureka web page look like this:

```
- id: eureka-web-start
  uri: http://${app.eureka-server}:8761
  predicates:
  - Path=/eureka/web
  filters:
  - SetPath=/

- id: eureka-web-other
  uri: http://${app.eureka-server}:8761
  predicates:
  - Path=/eureka/**
```

From the preceding configuration, we can take the following notes: The `${app.eureka-server}` property is resolved by Spring's property mechanism depending on what Spring profile is activated:

1. When running the services on the same host without using Docker, for example, for debugging purposes, the property will be translated to `localhost` using the `default` profile.
2. When running the services as Docker containers, the Netflix Eureka server will run in a container with the DNS name `eureka`. Therefore, the property will be translated into `eureka` using the `docker` profile.

The relevant parts in the `application.yml` file that defines this translation look like this:

```
app.eureka-server: localhost
---
spring.profiles: docker
app.eureka-server: eureka
```

Routing requests with predicates and filters

To learn a bit more about the routing capabilities in Spring Cloud Gateway, we will try out host-based routing; that is, where Spring Cloud Gateway uses the hostname of the incoming request to determine where to route the request. We will use one of my favorite websites for testing HTTP codes: `http://httpstat.us/`.

A call to `http://httpstat.us/${CODE}` simply returns a response with the `${CODE}` HTTP code and a response body containing the HTTP code and a corresponding descriptive text. For example, see the following `curl` command:

```
curl http://httpstat.us/200 -i
```

This will return the HTTP code 200, and a response body with the text, 200 OK.

Let's assume that we want to route calls to `http://${hostname}:8080/headerrouting` as follows:

- Calls to the `i.feel.lucky` host should return 200 OK.
- Calls to the `im.a.teapot` host should return `418 I'm a teapot`.
- Calls to all other hostnames should return `501 Not Implemented`.

To implement these routing rules in Spring Cloud Gateway, we can use the `Host` route predicate to select requests with specific hostnames, and the `SetPath` filter to set the desired HTTP code in the request path. This can be done as follows:

1. To make calls to `http://i.feel.lucky:8080/headerrouting` return 200 OK, we can set up the following route:

   ```
   - id: host_route_200
     uri: http://httpstat.us
     predicates:
     - Host=i.feel.lucky:8080
     - Path=/headerrouting/**
     filters:
     - SetPath=/200
   ```

2. To make calls to `http://im.a.teapot:8080/headerrouting` return `418 I'm a teapot`, we can set up the following route:

   ```
   - id: host_route_418
     uri: http://httpstat.us
     predicates:
     - Host=im.a.teapot:8080
     - Path=/headerrouting/**
     filters:
     - SetPath=/418
   ```

3. Finally, to make calls to all other hostnames return `501 Not Implemented`, we can set up the following route:

   ```
   - id: host_route_501
     uri: http://httpstat.us
   ```

```
predicates:
- Path=/headerrouting/**
filters:
- SetPath=/501
```

Okay, that was quite a bit of configuration, so now let's try it out!

Trying out the edge server

To try out the edge server, we perform the following steps:

1. First, build the Docker images with the following commands:

   ```
   cd $BOOK_HOME/Chapter10
   ./gradlew build && docker-compose build
   ```

2. Next, start the system landscape in Docker and run the usual tests with the following command:

   ```
   ./test-em-all.bash start
   ```

   Expect output similar to what we have seen in previous chapters:

```
                              2. @700dd0df9ffe:/ (bash)
$ ./test-em-all.bash start
Start Tests: Fri Sep 6 19:46:54 CEST 2019
...
Creating chapter09_rabbitmq_1 ... done
...
Wait for: curl http://localhost:8080/actuator/health... , retry #1 ... Test OK (HTTP Code: 200)
Test OK ...
End, all tests OK: Fri Sep 6 19:47:54 CEST 2019
$
```

With the system landscape including the edge server, let's explore the following topics:

- Examine what is exposed by the edge server outside of the system landscape running in the Docker engine.
- Try out some of the most frequently used routing rules as follows:
    - Use URL-based routing to call our APIs through the edge server.
    - Use URL-based routing to call Netflix Eureka through the edge server, both using its API and web-based UI.
    - Use header-based routing to see how we can route requests based on the hostname in the request.

Examining what is exposed outside the Docker engine

To understand what the edge server exposes to the outside of the system landscape, perform the following steps:

1. Use the `docker-compose ps` command to see that what ports are exposed by our services:

   ```
   docker-compose ps gateway eureka product-composite product
   recommendation review
   ```

2. As we can see in the following output, only the edge server (named `gateway`) exposes its port (`8080`) outside the Docker engine:

3. If we want to see what routes the edge server has set up, we can use the `/actuator/gateway/routes` API. The response from this API is rather verbose. To limit the response to information we are interested in, we can apply a `jq` filter. In the following example, I have selected the `id` of the route and the first predicate in the route:

   ```
   curl localhost:8080/actuator/gateway/routes -s | jq '.[] |
   {"\(.route_id)":
   "\(.route_definition.predicates[0].args._genkey_0)"}'
   ```

4. This command will respond with the following:

```
● ● ●                2. @700dd0df9ffe;/ (bash)
{
    "eureka-api": "/eureka/api/{segment}"
}
{
    "eureka-web-start": "/eureka/web"
}
{
    "eureka-web-other": "/eureka/**"
}
{
    "product-composite": "/product-composite/**"
}
{
    "host_route_200": "i.feel.lucky:8080"
}
{
    "host_route_418": "im.a.teapot:8080"
}
{
    "host_route_501": "/headerrouting/**"
}
$
```

This gives us a good overview of the actual routes configured in the edge server. Now, let's try out the routes!

Trying out the routing rules

In this section, we will try out the edge server and the routes it exposes to the outside of the system landscape. Let's start with calling the product composite API, then call the Eureka API and visit its web page, and conclude with testing the routes that are based on hostnames.

Calling the product composite API through the edge server

Let's perform the following steps to call the product composite API through the edge server as follows:

1. To be able to see what is going on in the edge server, we can follow its log output:

   ```
   docker-compose logs -f --tail=0 gateway
   ```

2. Now, make the call to the product composite API through the edge server:

   ```
   curl http://localhost:8080/product-composite/2
   ```

3. Expect the normal type of response from the composite product API:

```
2. @700dd0df9ffe:/ (bash)
{"productId":2, ... "recommendations":[...],"reviews":[...],"serviceAddresses":{...}}
$
```

4. We should be able to find the following interesting information in the log output:

```
Pattern "/product-composite/**" matches against value "/product-
composite/2"
Route matched: product-composite
LoadBalancerClientFilter url chosen:
http://b8013440aea0:8080/product-composite/2
```

From the log output, we can see the pattern matching based on the predicate we specified in the configuration, and we can see what microservice instance the edge server selected from the available instances in the discovery server—in this case, `http://b8013440aea0:8080/product-composite/2`.

Calling Eureka through the edge server

To call Eureka through an edge server, perform the following steps:

1. First, call the Eureka API through the edge server to see what instances are currently registered in the discovery server:

```
curl -H "accept:application/json" localhost:8080/eureka/api/apps -s
| \ jq -r .applications.application[].instance[].instanceId
```

2. Expect a response along the lines of the following:

```
2. @700dd0df9ffe:/ (bash)
b91cde7148d9:gateway:8080
b8013440aea0:product-composite:8080
7c9a92146991:product:8080
21668e72a668:review:8080
ffcbdb9f32a4:recommendation:8080
$
```

> Note that the edge server (named `gateway`) is also present in the response.

3. Next, open the Eureka web page in a web browser using the URL, `http://localhost:8080/eureka/web`:

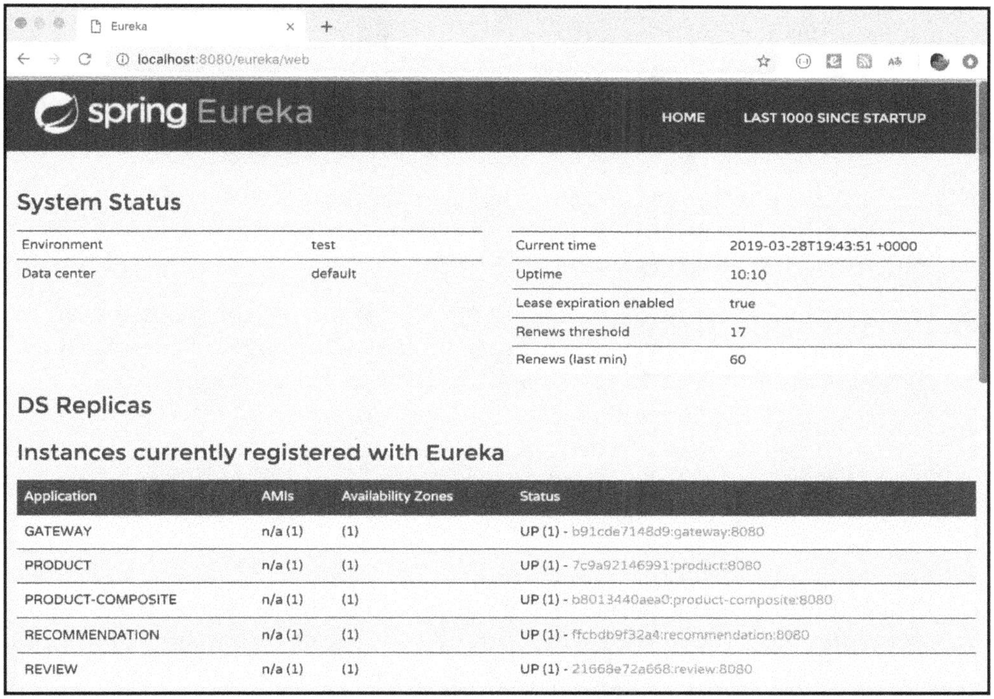

From the preceding screenshot, we can see the Eureka web page reporting the same available instances as the API response in the previous step.

Routing based on the host header

Let's wrap up by testing the route setup based on the hostname used in the requests!

Normally, the hostname in the request is set automatically in the `Host` header by the HTTP client. When testing the edge server locally, the hostname will be `localhost`—that is not so useful when testing hostname-based routing. But we can cheat by specifying another hostname in the `Host` header in the call to the API. Let's see how this can be done:

1. To call for the `i.feel.lucky` hostname, use this code:

```
curl http://localhost:8080/headerrouting -H "Host:
i.feel.lucky:8080"
```

2. Expect the response 200 OK. For the hostname `im.a.teapot`, use the following command:

```
curl http://localhost:8080/headerrouting -H "Host:
im.a.teapot:8080"
```

Expect the response `418 I'm a teapot`.

3. Finally, if not specifying any `Host` header, use `localhost` as the `Host` header:

```
curl http://localhost:8080/headerrouting
```

Expect the response `501 Not Implemented`.

4. We can also use `i.feel.lucky` and `im.a.teapot` as real hostnames in the requests if we add them to the local `/etc/hosts` file and specify that they should be translated into the same IP address as `localhost`, that is `127.0.0.1`. Run the following command to add a row to the `/etc/hosts` file with the required information:

```
sudo bash -c "echo '127.0.0.1 i.feel.lucky im.a.teapot' >>
/etc/hosts"
```

5. We can now perform the same routing based on the hostname, but without specifying the `Host` header. Try it out by running the following commands:

```
curl http://i.feel.lucky:8080/headerrouting
curl http://im.a.teapot:8080/headerrouting
```

Expect the same response as previously, that is, 200 OK and `418 I'm a teapot`.

6. Wrap up the tests by shutting down the system landscape with the following command:

```
docker-compose down
```

7. Also, clean up the `/etc/hosts` file from the DNS name translation we added for the hostnames, `i.feel.lucky` and `im.a.teapot`. Edit the `/etc/hosts` file and remove the line we added: `127.0.0.1 i.feel.lucky im.a.teapot`.

These tests of the routing capabilities in the system landscape's edge server end the chapter.

Summary

In this chapter, we have seen how Spring Cloud Gateway can be used as an edge server to control what services are allowed to be called from the outside of the system landscape. Based on predicates, filters, and destination URIs, we can define routing rules in a very flexible way. If we want to, we can configure Spring Cloud Gateway to use a discovery service such as Netflix Eureka to look up the target microservice instances.

One important question still unanswered is how we prevent unauthorized access to the APIs exposed by the edge server and how we can prevent third parties from intercepting the traffic.

In the next chapter, we will see how we can secure access to the edge server using standard security mechanisms such as HTTPS, OAuth, and OpenID Connect.

Questions

1. What are the elements used to build a routing rule in Spring Cloud Gateway called?
2. What are they used for?
3. How can we instruct Spring Cloud Gateway to locate microservice instances through a discovery service such as Netflix Eureka?
4. In a Docker environment, how can we ensure that external HTTP requests to the Docker engine can only reach the edge server?
5. How do we change the routing rules so that the edge server accepts calls to the `product-composite` service on the `http://$HOST:$PORT/api/product` URL instead of the currently used `http://$HOST:$PORT/product-composite`?

Securing Access to APIs

11

In this chapter, we will see how we can secure access to the APIs and web pages exposed by the edge server introduced in the previous chapter. We will learn to use HTTPS to protect against eavesdropping on external access to our APIs and also how to use OAuth 2.0 and OpenID Connect to authenticate and authorize users and client applications to access our APIs. Finally, we will study the use of HTTP basic authentication to secure access to the discovery service, Netflix Eureka.

The following topics will be covered in this chapter:

- An introduction to the OAuth 2.0 and OpenID Connect standards
- A general discussion on how to secure the system landscape
- Adding an authorization server to our system landscape
- Protecting external communication with HTTPS
- Securing access to the discovery service, Netflix Eureka
- Authenticating and authorizing API access using OAuth 2.0 and OpenID Connect
- Testing with the local authorization server
- Testing with an OpenID Connect provider, Auth0

Technical requirements

All commands described in this book are run on a MacBook Pro using macOS Mojave but modifying them so they run on another platform such as Linux or Windows should be straightforward.

No new tools need to be installed in this chapter.

The source code for this chapter can be found on GitHub at `https://github.com/PacktPublishing/Hands-On-Microservices-with-Spring-Boot-and-Spring-Cloud/tree/master/Chapter11`.

To be able to run the commands as described in the book, download the source code to a folder and set up an environment variable, $BOOK_HOME, that points to that folder. The following commands can be used to perform these steps:

```
export BOOK_HOME=~/Documents/Hands-On-Microservices-with-Spring-Boot-and-
Spring-Cloud
git clone
https://github.com/PacktPublishing/Hands-On-Microservices-with-Spring-Boot-
and-Spring-Cloud $BOOK_HOME
cd $BOOK_HOME/Chapter11
```

The Java source code is written for Java 8 and tested on Java 12. This chapter uses Spring Cloud 2.1.0, SR1 (also known as the **Greenwich** release), Spring Boot 2.1.3, and Spring 5.1.5, that is, the latest available version of the Spring components at the time of writing.

The source code contains the following Gradle projects:

- api
- util
- microservices/product-service
- microservices/review-service
- microservices/recommendation-service
- microservices/product-composite-service
- spring-cloud/eureka-server
- spring-cloud/gateway
- spring-cloud/authorization-server

The code examples in this chapter all come from source code in $BOOK_HOME/Chapter11, but are, in several cases, edited to remove non-relevant parts of the source code, such as comments, imports, and log statements.

If you want to see the changes applied to the source code in Chapter 11, *Secure Access to APIs*, that is, to see what it took to secure access to the APIs in the microservice landscape, you can compare it with the source code for Chapter 10, *Using Spring Cloud Gateway to Hide Microservices Behind an Edge Server*. You can use your favorite diff tool and compare the two folders, $BOOK_HOME/Chapter10 and $BOOK_HOME/Chapter11.

Introduction to OAuth 2.0 and OpenID Connect

Before introducing OAuth 2.0 and OpenID Connect, let's clarify what we mean with authentication and authorization. **Authentication** means identifying a user by validating credentials supplied by the user, such as a username and password. **Authorization** is about giving access to various parts of, in our case, an API to an authenticated, that is, an identified user. In our case, a user will be assigned a set of privileges based on OAuth 2.0 scopes, as explained hereinafter. The microservices will be based on these privileges determine whether the user is allowed to access an API.

OAuth 2.0 is an open standard for authorization, and **OpenID Connect** is an add-on to OAuth 2.0 that enables client applications to verify the identity of users based on the authentication performed by the authorization server. Let's look briefly at OAuth 2.0 and OpenID Connect separately to get an initial understanding of their purposes!

Introduction to OAuth 2.0

OAuth 2.0 is a widely accepted open standard for authorization that enables a user to give consent for a third-party client application to access protected resources in the name of the user.

So, what does this mean?

Let's start with sorting out the concepts used:

- **Resource owner**: The end user.
- **Client**: The third-party client application, for example, a web app or a native mobile app, that wants to call some protected APIs in the name of the end user.
- **Resource server**: The server that exposes the APIs that we want to protect.
- **Authorization server:** The authorization server issues tokens to the client after the resource owner, that is, the end user, has been authenticated. The management of user information and the authentication of users are typically delegated, behind the scenes, to an **Identity Provider (IdP)**.

A client is registered in the authorization server and is given a **client ID** and a **client secret**. The client secret must be protected by the client, like a password. A client also gets registered with a set of allowed **redirect-URIs** that the authorization server will use after a user has been authenticated to send **grant codes** and **tokens** that have been issued back to the client application.

The following is an example by way of illustration. Let's say that a user accesses a third-party client application and the client application wants to call a protected API to serve the user. To be allowed to access these APIs, the client application needs a way to tell the APIs that it is acting in the name of the user. To avoid solutions where the user must share their credentials with the client application for authentication, an **access token** is issued by an authorization server that gives the client application limited access to a selected set of APIs in the name of the user.

This means that the user never has to reveal their credentials to the client application. The user can also give consent to the client application to access specific APIs on behalf of the user. An access token represents a time-constrained set of access rights, expressed as a *scope* in OAuth 2.0 terms. A **refresh token** can also be issued to a client application by the authorization server. A refresh token can be used by the client application to obtain new access tokens without having to involve the user.

The OAuth 2.0 specification defines four authorization grant flows for issuing access tokens, explained as follows:

- **Authorization Code grant flow**: This is the safest, but also the most complex, grant flow. This grant flow requires that the user interact with the authorization server using a web browser for authentication and giving consent to the client application, as illustrated by the following diagram:

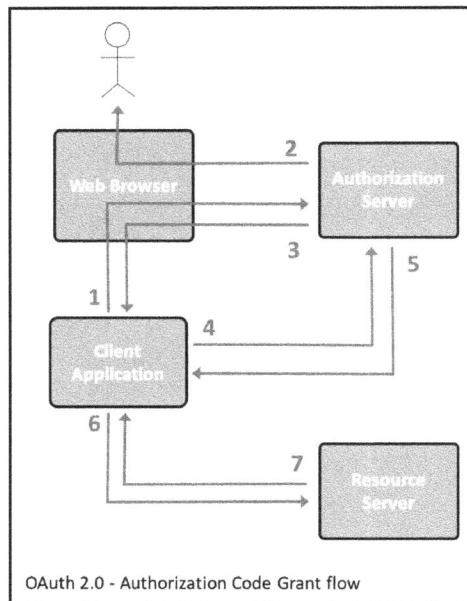

OAuth 2.0 - Authorization Code Grant flow

Explanations for this diagram are as follows:

1. The client application initiates the grant flow by sending the user to the authorization server in the web browser.
2. The authorization server will authenticate the user and ask for the user's consent.
3. The authorization server will redirect the user back to the client application with a grant code. The authorization server will use the redirect-URI specified by the client in step 1 to know where to send the grant code. Since the grant code is passed back to the client application using the web browser, that is, to an insecure environment where malicious JavaScript code potentially can pick up the grant code, it is only allowed to be used once and only during a short time period.
4. To exchange the grant code for an access token, the client application is expected to call the authorization server again, using server-side code. The client application must present its client ID and client secret together with the grant code for the authorization server.
5. The authorization server issues an access token and sends it back to the client application. The authorization server can also, optionally, issue and return a refresh token.
6. Using the access token, the client can send a request to the protected API exposed by the resource server.
7. The resource server validates the access token and serves the request in the event of a successful validation. Steps 6 and 7 can be repeated as long as the access token is valid. When the lifetime of the access token has expired, the client can use their refresh token to acquire a new access token.

- **Implicit grant flow**: This flow is also web browser-based, but intended for client applications that are not able to keep a client secret protected, for example, a single-page web application. It gets an access token back from the authorization server instead of a grant code, but cannot request a refresh token, since it is using the implicit grant flow that is less secure than the code grant flow.
- **Resource Owner Password Credentials grant flow**: If a client application can't interact with a web browser, it can fall back on this grant flow. In this grant flow, the user must share their credentials with the client application and the client application will use these credentials to acquire an access token.
- **Client Credentials grant flow:** In the case where a client application needs to call an API unrelated to a specific user, it can use this grant flow to acquire an access token using its own client ID and client secret.

> When it comes to automating tests against APIs that are protected by OAuth 2.0, the **Resource Owner Password Credentials grant flow** is very handy since it doesn't require manual interaction using a web browser. We will use this later on in this chapter with our test script; see the *Changes in the test script* section.

The full specification can be found here: `https://tools.ietf.org/html/rfc6749`. There are also a number of additional specifications that detail various aspects of OAuth 2.0; for an overview, refer to `https://www.oauth.com/oauth2-servers/map-oauth-2-0-specs/`.

> One additional specification that is worth some extra attention is *RFC 7636 – Proof Key for Code Exchange by OAuth Public Clients (PKCE)*, `https://tools.ietf.org/html/rfc7636`. This specification describes how an otherwise insecure public client, such as a mobile native app or desktop application, can utilize the code grant flow by adding an extra layer of security.

Introducing OpenID Connect

OpenID Connect (abbreviated to **OIDC**) is, as has already been mentioned, an add-on to OAuth 2.0 that enables client applications to verify the identity of users. OIDC adds an extra token, an ID token, that the client application gets back from the authorization server after a completed grant flow.

The ID token is encoded as a **JSON Web Token (JWT)** and contains a number of claims, such as the ID and email address of the user. The ID token is digitally signed using JSON web signatures. This makes it possible for a client application to trust the information in the ID token by validating the digital signature using public keys from the authorization server.

Optionally, access tokens can also be encoded and signed in the same way as ID tokens, but it is not mandatory according to the specification. Finally, OIDC defines a **discovery endpoint**, which is a standardized way to establish URLs to important endpoints, such as initiating a grant flow, getting the public keys to verify a digitally signed JWT token, and a **user-info endpoint**, which can be used to get extra information about an authenticated user given an access token for that user.

For an overview of the available specifications, see `https://openid.net/developers/specs/`.

This concludes our introduction to the OAuth 2.0 and OpenID Connect standards. In the next section, we will get a high-level view of how the system landscape will be secured.

Securing the system landscape

To secure the system landscape as described in the introduction to this chapter, we will perform the following steps:

- Encrypt external requests and responses to and from our external API using HTTPS to protect against eavesdropping
- Authenticate and authorize users and client applications that access our APIs using OAuth 2.0 and OpenID Connect
- Secure access to the discovery service, Netflix Eureka, using HTTP basic authentication

We will only apply HTTPS for external communication to our edge server, using plain HTTP for communication inside our system landscape.

> In the chapter on service mesh (`Chapter 18`, *Using a Service Mesh to Improve Observability and Management*) that will appear later in this book, we will see how we can get help from a service mesh product to automatically provision HTTPS to secure communication inside a system landscape.

For test purposes, we will add a local OAuth 2.0 authorization server to our system landscape. All external communication with the authorization server will be routed through the edge server. The edge server and the product-composite service will act as OAuth 2.0 resource servers; that is, they will require a valid OAuth 2.0 access token to allow access.

To minimize the overhead of validating access tokens, we will assume that they are encoded as signed JWT tokens and that the authorization server exposes an endpoint that the resource servers can use to access the public keys, also known as `jwk-set`, required to validate the signing.

The system landscape will look like the following:

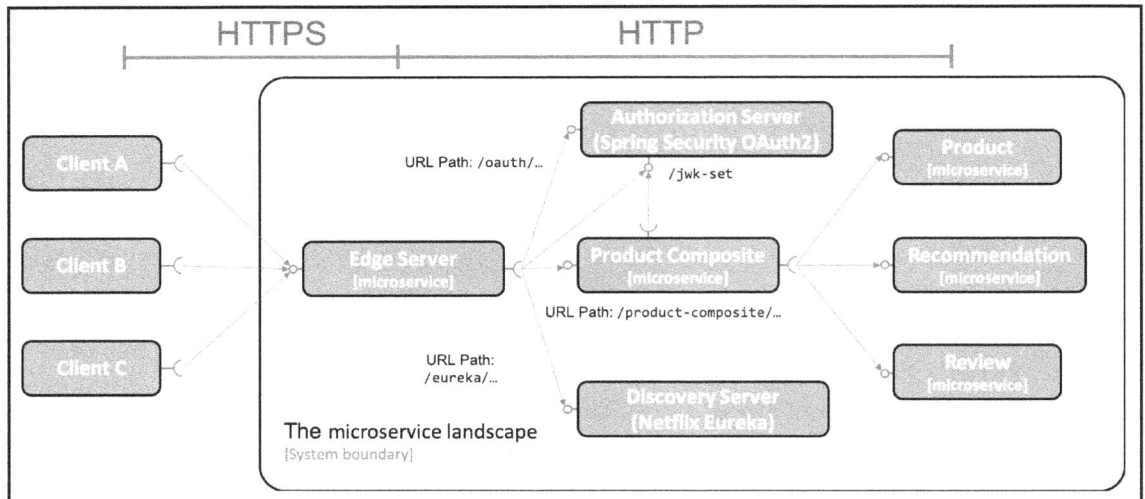

From the preceding diagram, we can note that:

1. HTTPS is used for external communication, while plain text HTTP is used inside the system landscape.
2. The local OAuth 2.0 authorization server will be accessed externally through the edge server.
3. Both the edge server and the product composite microservice will validate access tokens as signed JWT tokens.
4. The edge server and the product composite microservice will get the authorization server's public keys from its `jwk-set` endpoint, and use them to validate the signature of the JWT-based access tokens.

> Note that we will focus on securing access to APIs over HTTP, not on covering general best practices for securing web applications, for example, managing web application security risks pointed out by the *Category:OWASP Top Ten Project*. Refer to `https://www.owasp.org/index.php/Category:OWASP_Top_Ten_Project` for more information on the OWASP Top Ten.

With this overview of how the system landscape will be secured, let's start by adding a local authorization server to the system landscape.

Adding an authorization server to our system landscape

To be able to run tests locally and fully automated with APIs that are secured using OAuth 2.0 and OpenID Connect, we will add an OAuth 2.0-based authorization server to our system landscape. Spring Security 5.1 does not, unfortunately, provide an authorization server out of the box. But there is a legacy project (currently in maintenance mode), Spring Security OAuth, that provides an authorization server that we can use.

In fact, in the samples provided by Spring Security 5.1, a project using the authorization server from Spring Security OAuth is available. It is configured to use JWT-encoded access tokens, and it also exposes an endpoint for a **JSON Web Key Set** (**JWKS**) (part of the OpenID Connect Discovery standard), a set of keys containing the public keys that can be used by resource servers to verify JWT tokens issued by the authorization server.

So, even if it isn't a full-blown OpenID Connect provider, it is suitable for use together with tests that we want to be able to run locally and in a fully automated manner.

> For more details on planned support for OAuth 2.0 in Spring Security, refer to `https://spring.io/blog/2018/01/30/next-generation-oauth-2-0-support-with-spring-security`.
> The authorization server in the Spring Security sample projects is available here: `https://github.com/spring-projects/spring-security/tree/master/samples/boot/oauth2authorizationserver`.

The Spring Security sample project configures two OAuth clients, `reader` and `writer`, where the `reader` client is granted a read scope, and the `writer` client is granted both a read and a write scope. Both clients are configured to have the secret set to `secret`; refer to the `configure()` method in the `sample.AuthorizationServerConfiguration` class.

The following changes have been applied to the sample project:

- A Eureka client has been added in the same way as for the other microservices. See `Chapter 9`, *Adding Service Discovery Using Netflix Eureka and Ribbon*; refer to the *Connecting microservices to a Netflix Eureka server* section.
- Spring Boot Actuator has been added to get access to the `health` endpoint.
- A Dockerfile has been added to be able to run the authorization server as a Docker container.

- The Gradle build file, `spring-security-samples-boot-oauth2authorizationserver.gradle`, has been changed to become more like the `build.gradle` files used in the source code of this book.
- The configuration in the `sample/AuthorizationServerConfiguration` class has been changed as follows:
  - Support has been added for the grant types: `code`, `authorization_code`, and `implicit`.
  - The names of the scopes, `message:read` and `message:write`, have been changed to `product:read` and `product:write`.
  - The username of the user registered in the authorization server has been changed to `magnus`, with the password `password`; refer to the `userDetailsService()` method in the `UserConfig` class (found in the `sample/AuthorizationServerConfiguration.java` file).

The source code for the authorization server is available in `$BOOK_HOME/Chapter11/spring-cloud/authorization-server`.

To incorporate the authorization server in the system landscape, a number of changes have been applied. The authorization server has been added to the following:

- The common build file, `settings.gradle`
- The three Docker Compose files, `docker-compose*.yml`
- The edge server, `spring-cloud/gateway`:
  - A health check has been added to `HealthCheckConfiguration`.
  - A route for URIs starting with `/oauth/` has been added.

With an understanding of how a local authorization server is added to the system landscape, let's move on and see how we can protect external communication from eavesdropping using HTTPS.

Protecting external communication with HTTPS

In this section, we will learn how to prevent eavesdropping on external communication, for example from the internet, via the public APIs exposed by the edge server. We will use HTTPS to encrypt communication. To use HTTPS, we need to do the following:

- **Create a certificate**: We will create our own self-signed certificate, sufficient for development purposes.
- **Configure the edge server**: It has to be configured to accept only HTTPS-based external traffic using the certificate.

The self-signed certificate is created with the following command:

```
keytool -genkeypair -alias localhost -keyalg RSA -keysize 2048 -storetype
PKCS12 -keystore edge.p12 -validity 3650
```

> The source code comes with a sample certificate file, so you don't need to run this command to run the following examples.

The command will ask for a number of parameters. When asked for a password, I entered `password`. For the rest of the parameters, I simply entered an empty value to accept the default value. The certificate file created, `edge.p12`, is placed in the `gateway` projects folder, `src/main/resources/keystore`. This means that the certificate file will be placed in the `.jar` file when it is built and will be available on the classpath in runtime at: `keystore/edge.p12`.

> Providing certificates using the classpath is sufficient during development, but not applicable to other environments, for example, a production environment. The following shows how we can replace this certificate with an external certificate at runtime!

To configure the edge server to use the certificate and HTTPS, the following is added to `application.yml` in the `gateway` project:

```
server.port: 8443

server.ssl:
  key-store-type: PKCS12
  key-store: classpath:keystore/edge.p12
  key-store-password: password
  key-alias: localhost
```

The following are the explanations for the preceding source code:

- The path to the certificate is specified in the `server.ssl.key-store` parameter, and is set to the `classpath:keystore/edge.p12` value. This means that the certificate will be picked up on the classpath from the location, `keystore/edge.p12`.
- The password for the certificate is specified in the `server.ssl.key-store-password` parameter.
- To indicate that the edge server talks HTTPS and not HTTP, we also change the port from `8080` to `8443` in the `server.port` parameter.

In addition to these changes in the edge server, changes are also required in the following files to reflect the changes to the port and HTTP protocol:

- The three Docker Compose files, `docker-compose*.yml`
- The test script, `test-em-all.bash`

Providing certificates using the classpath is as already mentioned previously only sufficient during development; let's see how we can replace this certificate with an external certificate in runtime!

Replacing a self-signed certificate in runtime

Placing a self-signed certificate in the `.jar` file is only useful for development. For a working solution in runtime environments, for example, for test or production, it must be possible to use certificates signed by authorized **CAs** (short for **Certificate Authorities**).

It must also be possible to specify the certificates to be used during runtime without the need to rebuild the .jar files and, when using Docker, the Docker image that contains the .jar file. When using Docker Compose to manage the Docker container, we can map a volume in the Docker container to a certificate that resides on the Docker host. We can also set up environment variables for the Docker container that points to the new certificate in the Docker volume.

> In Chapter 15, *Introduction to Kubernetes*, we will learn about Kubernetes, where we will see more powerful solutions for how to handle secrets, such as certificates, that are suitable for running Docker containers in a cluster; that is, where containers are scheduled on a group of Docker hosts and not on a single Docker host.
>
> The changes described in this topic have **not** been applied to the source code in the book's GitHub repository; that is, you need to make them yourself to see them in action!

To replace the certificate packaged in the .jar file, perform the following steps:

1. Create a second certificate and set the password to testtest, when asked for it:

```
cd $BOOK_HOME/Chapter11
mkdir keystore

keytool -genkeypair -alias localhost -keyalg RSA -keysize 2048 -
storetype PKCS12 -keystore keystore/edge-test.p12 -validity 3650
```

2. Update the Docker Compose file, docker-compose.yml, with environment variables for the location and password for the new certificate and a volume that maps to the folder where the new certificate is placed. The configuration of the edge server will look like the following after the change:

```
gateway:
  environment:
    - SPRING_PROFILES_ACTIVE=docker
    - SERVER_SSL_KEY_STORE=file:/keystore/edge-test.p12
    - SERVER_SSL_KEY_STORE_PASSWORD=testtest
  volumes:
    - $PWD/keystore:/keystore
  build: spring-cloud/gateway
  mem_limit: 350m
  ports:
    - "8443:8443"
```

3. If the edge server is up and running, it needs to be restarted with the following commands:

```
docker-compose up -d --scale gateway=0
docker-compose up -d --scale gateway=1
```

The `docker-compose restart gateway` command might look like a good candidate for restarting the `gateway` service, but it actually does not take changes in `docker-compose.yml` into consideration. Hence, it is not a useful command in this case.

The new certificate is now in use!

This concludes the section on how to protect external communication with HTTPS. In the next section we will learn how to secure access to the discovery service, Netflix Eureka, using HTTP basic authentication.

Securing access to the discovery service, Netflix Eureka

Previously, we learned to protect external communication with HTTPS. Now we will use HTTP basic authentication to restrict access to the APIs and web pages on the discovery server, Netflix Eureka; that is, we will require a user to supply a username and password to get access. Changes are required both on the Eureka server and in the Eureka clients described as follows.

Changes in the Eureka server

To protect the Eureka servers, the following changes have been applied:

1. A dependency in `build.gradle` has been added to Spring Security:

```
implementation 'org.springframework.boot:spring-boot-starter-
security'
```

2. Security configuration has been added
   to the `se.magnus.springcloud.eurekaserver.SecurityConfig` class:

   - The user is defined as follows:

     ```
     public void configure(AuthenticationManagerBuilder auth) throws
     Exception {
       auth.inMemoryAuthentication()
         .passwordEncoder(NoOpPasswordEncoder.getInstance())
         .withUser(username).password(password)
         .authorities("USER");
     }
     ```

   - The `username` and `password` are injected into the constructor from the
     configuration file:

     ```
     @Autowired
     public SecurityConfig(
       @Value("${app.eureka-username}") String username,
       @Value("${app.eureka-password}") String password
     ) {
       this.username = username;
       this.password = password;
     }
     ```

   - All APIs and web pages are protected using HTTP basic authentication by
     means of the following definition:

     ```
     protected void configure(HttpSecurity http) throws Exception {
       http
         .authorizeRequests()
           .anyRequest().authenticated()
           .and()
           .httpBasic();
     }
     ```

3. Credentials for the user are set up in the configuration file, `application.yml`:

   ```
   app:
    eureka-username: u
    eureka-password: p
   ```

4. Finally, the test class,
   `se.magnus.springcloud.eurekaserver.EurekaServerApplicationTests`
   , uses the credentials from the configuration file when testing the APIs of the
   Eureka server:

```
@Value("${app.eureka-username}")
private String username;

@Value("${app.eureka-password}")
private String password;

@Autowired
public void setTestRestTemplate(TestRestTemplate testRestTemplate)
{
    this.testRestTemplate = testRestTemplate.withBasicAuth(username,
password);
}
```

The preceding are the steps required for restricting access to the APIs and web pages of the discovery server, Netflix Eureka. It will now use HTTP basic authentication and require a user to supply a username and password to get access. In the next section, we will learn how to configure Netflix Eureka clients so that they pass credentials when accessing the Netflix Eureka server.

Changes in Eureka clients

For Eureka clients, the credentials have to be specified in the connection URL for the Eureka server. This is specified in each client's configuration file, `application.yml`, as follows:

```
app:
  eureka-username: u
  eureka-password: p

eureka:
  client:
    serviceUrl:
      defaultZone: "http://${app.eureka-username}:${app.eureka-
                    password}@${app.eureka-server}:8761/eureka/"
```

We will see this configuration in use by Netflix Eureka clients when we test the secured system landscape in the *Testing with the local authorization server* section.

In the next section, we will learn how to add credentials when we manually access the Netflix Eureka server, either using its API or its Web pages.

Testing the protected Eureka server

Once the protected Eureka server is up and running, we have to supply valid credentials to be able to access its APIs and web pages.

For example, asking the Eureka server for registered instances can be done by means of the following `curl` command:

```
curl -H "accept:application/json"
https://u:p@localhost:8443/eureka/api/apps -ks | jq -r
.applications.application[].instance[].instanceId
```

A sample response is as follows:

```
2. @700dd0df9ffe:/ (bash)
abe7ee8d450c:gateway:8443
1fbb5fcd7864:auth-server:9999
6cdb02a5ad71:product-composite:8080
9975baef8ae7:product:8080
e7b8ac60ae6e:review:8080
d300f3e31c1f:recommendation:8080
$
```

When accessing the web page on `https://localhost:8443/eureka/web`, we first have to accept an insecure connection, since our certificate is self-signed, and next we have to supply valid credentials, as specified in the preceding configuration files:

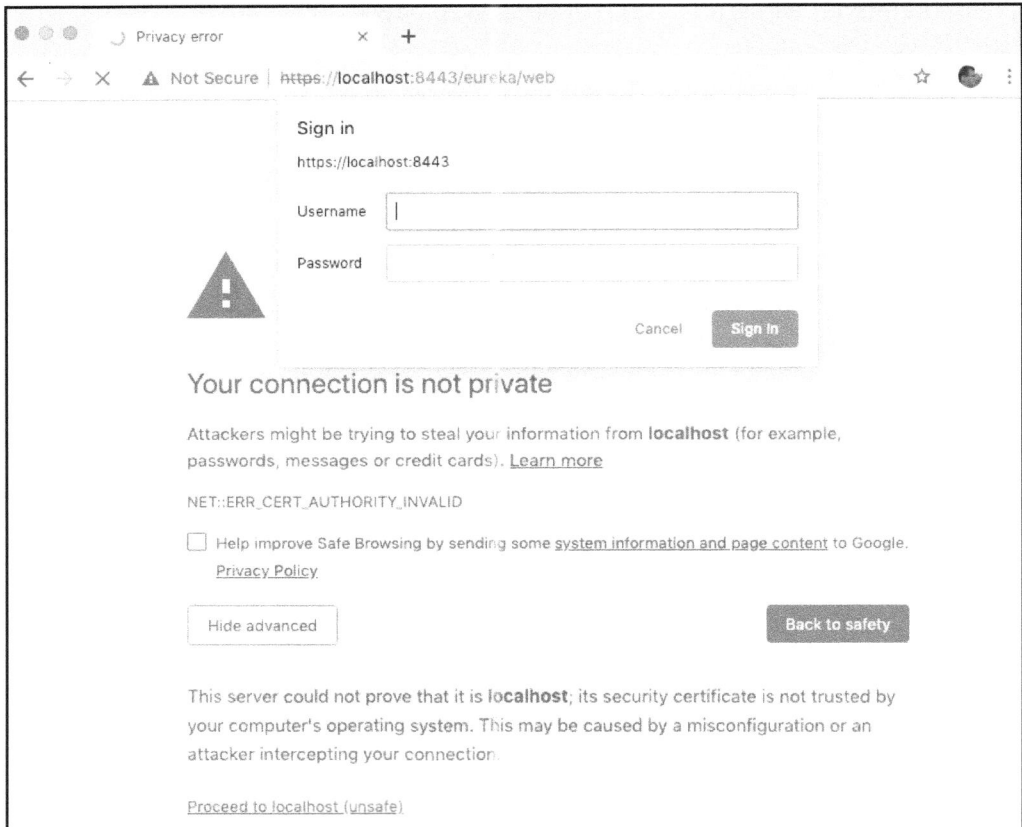

Following a successful login, we will see the familiar web page from the Eureka server:

This concludes the section on how to restrict access to the Netflix Eureka server. In the next section we will learn how to use OAuth 2.0 and OpenID Connect to authenticate and authorize access to APIs.

Authenticating and authorizing API access using OAuth 2.0 and OpenID Connect

With the authorization server in place, we can enhance the edge server and the `product-composite` service so they become OAuth 2.0 resource servers; that is, they require a valid access token to allow access. We will configure the edge server to accept any access token it can validate using the signature provided by the authorization server. The `product-composite` service will also require the access token to contain some OAuth 2.0 scopes:

- The `product:read` scope will be required for accessing the read-only APIs.
- The `product:write` scope will be required for accessing the create and delete APIs.

We also need to enhance our test script, `test-em-all.bash`, so that it acquires access tokens before it runs the tests.

Changes in both the edge server and the product-composite service

The following changes have been applied:

- Spring Security 5.1 dependencies have been added to `build.gradle` to support OAuth 2.0 resource servers:

```
implementation('org.springframework.boot:spring-boot-starter-
security')
implementation('org.springframework.security:spring-security-
oauth2-resource-server')
implementation('org.springframework.security:spring-security-
oauth2-jose')
```

- Security configurations have been added to the `se.magnus.springcloud.gateway.SecurityConfig` and `se.magnus.microservices.composite.product.SecurityConfig` classes:

```
@EnableWebFluxSecurity
public class SecurityConfig {

  @Bean
  SecurityWebFilterChain
springSecurityFilterChain(ServerHttpSecurity http) {
    http
      .authorizeExchange()
        .pathMatchers("/actuator/**").permitAll()
        .anyExchange().authenticated()
        .and()
      .oauth2ResourceServer()
        .jwt();
    return http.build();
  }
}
```

Explanations for the preceding source code are as follows:

- `.pathMatchers("/actuator/**").permitAll()` is used to allow access to URLs that should be unprotected, for example, the `actuator` endpoints in this case. Refer to the source code for URLs that are treated as unprotected. Be careful about which URLs are exposed unprotected. For example, the `actuator` endpoints should be protected before going to production:
  - `.anyExchange().authenticated()` ensures that the user is authenticated before being allowed access to all other URLs.
  - `.oauth2ResourceServer().jwt()` specifies that authentication and authorization will be based on a JWT-encoded OAuth 2.0 access token.
- The endpoint of the authorization server's `jwk-set` endpoint has been registered in the configuration file, `application.yml`:

```
spring.security.oauth2.resourceserver.jwt.jwk-set-uri:
http://${app.auth-server}:9999/.well-known/jwks.json
```

With these changes applied to both the edge server and the `product-composite` service to make them act as OAuth 2.0 resource servers, we also need to make some changes that only apply to the `product-composite` service.

Changes in the product-composite service

In addition to the common changes applied in the previous section, the following changes have also been applied to the `product-composite` service:

- The security configuration has been refined by requiring OAuth 2.0 scopes in the access token in order to allow access:

```
.pathMatchers(POST, "/product-
composite/**").hasAuthority("SCOPE_product:write")
.pathMatchers(DELETE, "/product-
composite/**").hasAuthority("SCOPE_product:write")
.pathMatchers(GET, "/product-
composite/**").hasAuthority("SCOPE_product:read")
```

By convention, OAuth 2.0 scopes should be prefixed with SCOPE_ when
checked for authority using Spring Security.

- A method, logAuthorizationInfo(), has been added to log relevant parts
  from the JWT-encoded access token upon each call to the API. The access token
  can be acquired using the standard Spring Security, SecurityContext, which,
  in a reactive environment, can be acquired using the static helper method,
  ReactiveSecurityContextHolder.getContext(). Refer to the
  se.magnus.microservices.composite.product.services.ProductCompo
  siteServiceImpl class for details.
- The use of OAuth has been disabled when running Spring-based integration
  tests. To prevent the OAuth machinery from kicking in when we are running
  integration tests, we disable it as follows:
    - A security configuration, TestSecurityConfig, is added to be used during
      tests that permit access to all resources:

      ```
      http.csrf().disable().authorizeExchange().anyExchange().permitA
      ll();
      ```

    - In each Spring integration test class, we configure TestSecurityConfig to
      override the existing security configuration with the following:

      ```
      @SpringBootTest( classes =
      {ProductCompositeServiceApplication.class,
      TestSecurityConfig.class },
       properties = {"spring.main.allow-bean-definition-
      overriding=true"})
      ```

With these changes in place, both the edge server and the product-composite service can
act as OAuth 2.0 resource servers. The last step we need to take to introduce the usage of
OAuth 2.0 and OpenID Connect is to update the test script so it acquires access tokens and
uses them when running the tests.

Changes in the test script

To start with, we need to acquire an access token before we can call any of the APIs, except the health API. This is done using the OAuth 2.0 password flow. To be able to call the create and delete APIs, we acquire an access token as the `writer` client, as follows:

```
ACCESS_TOKEN=$(curl -k https://writer:secret@$HOST:$PORT/oauth/token -d
grant_type=password -d username=magnus -d password=password -s | jq
.access_token -r)
```

To verify that the scope-based authorization works, two tests have been added to the test script:

- The first test calls an API without supplying an access token. The API is expected to return the 401 Unauthorized HTTP status.
- The other test calls an updating API using the `reader` client, which is only granted a read scope. The API is expected to return the 403 Forbidden HTTP status.

For the full source code, see `test-em-all.bash`:

```
# Verify that a request without access token fails on 401, Unauthorized
assertCurl 401 "curl -k
https://$HOST:$PORT/product-composite/$PROD_ID_REVS_RECS -s"

# Verify that the reader - client with only read scope can call the read
API but not delete API.
READER_ACCESS_TOKEN=$(curl -k https://reader:secret@$HOST:$PORT/oauth/token
-d grant_type=password -d username=magnus -d password=password -s | jq
.access_token -r)
 READER_AUTH="-H \"Authorization: Bearer $READER_ACCESS_TOKEN\""

assertCurl 200 "curl -k
https://$HOST:$PORT/product-composite/$PROD_ID_REVS_RECS $READER_AUTH -s"
assertCurl 403 "curl -k
https://$HOST:$PORT/product-composite/$PROD_ID_REVS_RECS $READER_AUTH -X
DELETE -s"
```

With the test scripts updated to acquire and use OAuth 2.0 access tokens, we are ready to try them out in the next section!

Testing with the local authorization server

In this section we will try out the secured system landscape; that is, we will test all the security components together. We will use the local authorization server to issue access tokens. The following tests will be performed:

1. First, we build from source and run the test script to ensure that everything fits together.
2. Next, we learn how to acquire access tokens using OAuth 2.0 grant flows: password, implicit, and code grant flows.
3. Finally, we will use access tokens to call APIs. We will also verify that an access token issued for a reader client can't be used to call an updating API.

Building and running the automated tests

To build and run automated tests, we perform the following steps:

1. First, build Docker images with the following commands:

```
cd $BOOK_HOME/Chapter11
./gradlew build && docker-compose build
```

2. Next, start the system landscape in Docker and run the usual tests with the following command:

```
./test-em-all.bash start
```

> Note the new negative tests at the end that verify that we get a 401 Unauthorized code back when not authenticated, and 403 Forbidden when not authorized.

Acquiring access tokens

Now we can acquire access tokens using the various grant flows defined by OAuth 2.0. We will try out the following grant flows: password, implicit, and code grant.

Acquiring access tokens using the password grant flow

To get an access token for the `writer` client, that is, with both the `product:read` and `product:write` scopes, issue the following command:

```
curl -k https://writer:secret@localhost:8443/oauth/token -d
grant_type=password -d username=magnus -d password=password -s | jq .
```

The client identifies itself using HTTP basic authentication, passing its `writer` client ID, and its secret, `secret`. It sends the credentials of the resource owners, that is the end user, using the `username` and `password` parameters.

A sample response is as follows:

```
 ● ● ●                    2. @700dd0df9ffe:/ (bash)
{
  "access_token": "eyJ...SyI1Q",
  "token_type": "bearer",
  "expires_in": 599999999,
  "scope": "product:read product:write",
  "jti": "57502ce2-d325-4ffc-98cb-5dcccc0a53df"
}
$
```

Set the value of the `access_token` field in the response as the access token in an environment variable:

```
ACCESS_TOKEN=eyJ...SyI1Q
```

To get an access token for the `reader` client, that is, with only the `product:read` scope, simply replace `writer` with `reader` in the preceding command:

```
curl -k https://reader:secret@localhost:8443/oauth/token -d
grant_type=password -d username=magnus -d password=password -s | jq .
```

Acquiring access tokens using the implicit grant flow

To acquire an access token using the implicit grant flow, we need to involve a web browser. Open the URL in a web browser that accepts the use of self-signed certificates, for example, Chrome. Then perform the following steps:

1. To get an access token for the `reader` client open the URL,
   `https://localhost:8443/oauth/authorize?response_type=token&clie`
   `nt_id=reader&redirect_uri=http://my.redirect.uri&scope=product:`
   `read&state=48532`. When asked to login by the web browser, use the
   credentials specified in the configuration of the authorization server, for
   example, `magnus` and `password`:

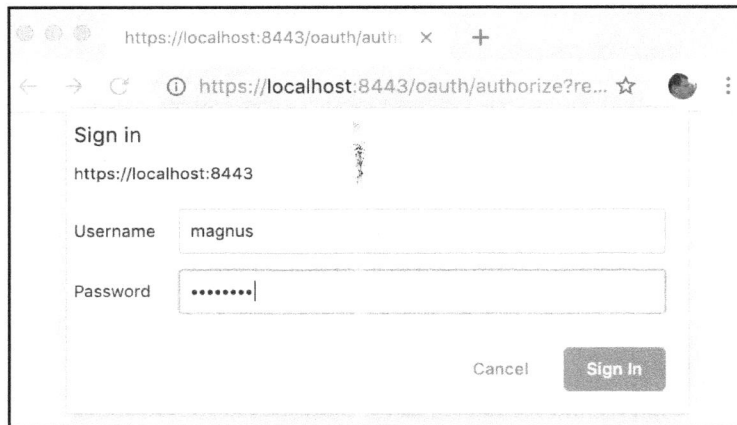

2. Next, you will be asked to authorize the `reader` client to call the APIs in your
   name:

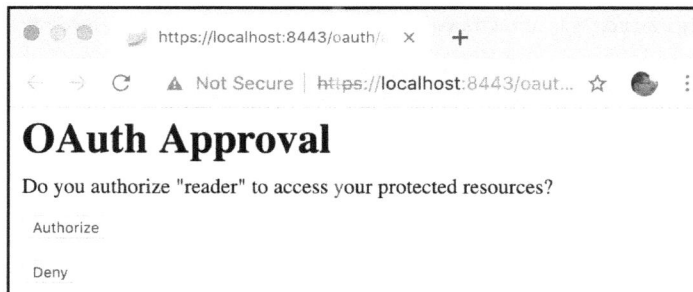

3. Finally, we will get the following response:

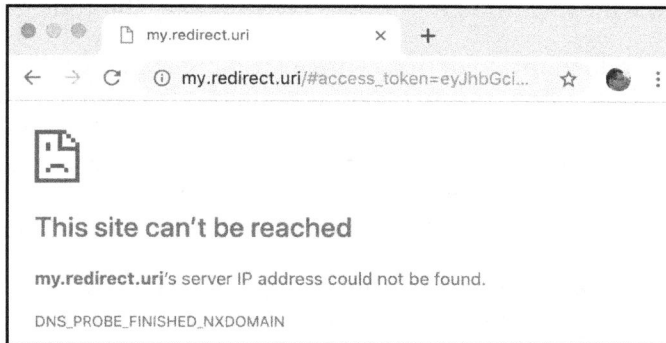

This might, at first glance, look a bit disappointing. The URL that the authorization server sent back to the web browser is based on the redirect-URI specified by the client in the initial request. Copy the URL into a text editor and you will find something similar to the following:

```
http://my.redirect.uri/#access_token=eyJh...C8pw&token_type=bearer&stat
e=48532&expires_in=599999999&jti=8956b38b-36ea-4888-80dc-685b49f20f91
```

Great! We can find the access token in the new URL in the `access_token` request parameter.

Save the access token in an environment variable, as shown:

```
ACCESS_TOKEN=eyJh...C8pw
```

To get an access token for the `writer` client, you can use the following URL:

```
https://localhost:8443/oauth/authorize?response_type=token&client_id=wr
iter&redirect_uri=http://my.redirect.uri&scope=product:read+product:wri
te&state=95372.
```

You are already authenticated, so you do not need to log in again, but you must give your consent to the `writer` client.

> Note that no client secret is required; that is, the implicit grant flow is not very secure.
> Any application can claim that it is the `writer` client and can ask for the user's consent to use the requested scopes to access APIs in the name of the user, so beware!

Acquiring access tokens using the code grant flow

Finally, let's try out the most secure grant flow in OAuth 2.0 – the code grant flow!

When it comes to the code grant flow, things are a bit more complicated in order to make the flow more secure. In the first insecure step, we will use the web browser to acquire a code that can be used only once, when it is exchanged with an access token. The code shall be passed from the web browser to a secure layer, for example, server-side code, which can make a new request the authorization server again to exchange the code with an access token. In this exchange, the server has to supply a client secret to verify its origin.

To get a code for the `reader` client, use the following URL in the web browser: `https://localhost:8443/oauth/authorize?response_type=code&client_id=reader&redirect_uri=http://my.redirect.uri&scope=product:read&state=35725`.

This time, you will get back a much shorter URL, for example, `http://my.redirect.uri/?code=T2pxvW&state=72489`.

Extract the authorization code from the `code` parameter and define an environment variable, `CODE`, with its value:

```
CODE=T2pxvW
```

Next, pretend you are the backend server that exchanges the authorization code with an access token using the following `curl` command:

```
curl -k https://reader:secret@localhost:8443/oauth/token \
  -d grant_type=authorization_code \
  -d client_id=reader \
  -d redirect_uri=http://my.redirect.uri \
  -d code=$CODE -s | jq .
```

A sample response is as follows:

```
2. @700dd0df9ffe:/ (bash)
{
  "access_token": "eyJh...KUBA",
  "token_type": "bearer",
  "expires_in": 599999999,
  "scope": "product:read",
  "jti": "998764d2-b940-4aeb-b381-bbfd37c84282"
}
$
```

Finally, save the access token in an environment variable as previously:

```
ACCESS_TOKEN=eyJh...KUBA
```

To get a code for the `writer` client, use the following
URL: https://localhost:8443/oauth/authorize?response_type=code&client_id=writer&redirect_uri=http://my.redirect.uri&scope=product:read+product:write&state=72489.

Calling protected APIs using access tokens

Now, let's use the access tokens we have acquired to call the protected APIs!

1. First, call an API to retrieve a composite product without a valid access token:

```
ACCESS_TOKEN=an-invalid-token
curl https://localhost:8443/product-composite/2 -k -H
"Authorization: Bearer $ACCESS_TOKEN" -i
```

2. It should return the following response:

The error message clearly states that the access token is invalid!

3. Next, try using the API to retrieve a composite product using one of the access tokens acquired for the `reader` client from the previous section:

```
ACCESS_TOKEN={a-reader-access-token}
curl https://localhost:8443/product-composite/2 -k -H
"Authorization: Bearer $ACCESS_TOKEN" -i
```

4. Now we will get the `200 OK` status code and the expected response body will be returned:

If we try to access an updating API, for example, the delete API, with an access token acquired for the `reader` client, the call will fail:

```
ACCESS_TOKEN={a-reader-access-token}
curl https://localhost:8443/product-composite/999 -k -H "Authorization:
Bearer $ACCESS_TOKEN" -X DELETE -i
```

It will fail with a response similar to the following:

```
                              2. @700dd0df9ffe:/ (bash)
HTTP/1.1 403 Forbidden
WWW-Authenticate: Bearer error="insufficient_scope",
error_description="The token provided has insufficient scope [product:read] for this request",
error_uri="https://tools.ietf.org/html/rfc6750#section-3.1", scope="product:read"
$
```

If we repeat the call to the delete API, but with an access token acquired for the `writer` client, the call will succeed with 200 OK in the response.

> The delete operation should return `200` even if the product with the specified product ID does not exist in the underlying database, since the delete operation is idempotent, as described in `Chapter 6`, *Adding Persistence*. Refer to the *Adding new APIs* section.

If you look into the log output using the `docker-compose logs -f product-composite` command, you should be able to find authorization information such as the following:

```
                              2. @700dd0df9ffe:/ (bash)
product-composite_1 ...
Authorization info: Subject: magnus, scopes: ["product:read","product:write"],
expires Tue Apr 13 06:36:41 UTC 2038: issuer: null, audience: null
```

This information was extracted by the new method, `logAuthorizationInfo()`, in the `product-composite` service from the JWT-encoded access token; that is, the `product-composite` service did not need to communicate with the authorization server to get this information!

With these tests, we have seen how to acquire an access token with the various grant flows, that is, password, implicit, and code grant flow. We have also seen how scopes can be used to limit what a client can do with a specific access token, for example only use is for reading operations.

In the next section, we will replace the local authorization server used in this section to an external OpenID Connect provider.

Testing with an OpenID Connect provider – Auth0

So, the OAuth dance works fine with an authorization server we control ourselves. But what happens if we replace it with a certified OpenID Connect provider? In theory, it should work out of the box. Let's find out, shall we?

For a list of certified implementations of OpenID Connect, refer to `https://openid.net/developers/certified/`. We will use Auth0, `https://auth0.com/`, for our tests with an OpenID provider. To be able to use Auth0 instead of our own authorization server, we will go through the following topics:

- Setting up an account with an OAuth client and a user in Auth0
- Applying the changes required to use Auth0 as an OpenID provider and running the test script to verify whether it is working
- Acquiring access tokens using the following:
    - Password grant flow
    - Implicit grant flow
    - Authorization code grant flow
- Calling protected APIs using the access tokens.
- Using the **user info** endpoint to get more information about a user.

Let us understand each of them in the following sections.

Setting up an account and OAuth 2.0 client in Auth0

Perform the following steps to sign up for a free account in Auth0, configure both an OAuth 2.0 client and the `product-composite` API, and finally register a user:

1. Open the URL, `https://auth0.com`, in your browser.
2. Click on the **SIGN UP** button:
    1. Sign up with an account of your choice.
    2. After a successful sign-up, you will be asked to create a tenant domain. Enter the name of the tenant of your choice, in my case: `dev-ml.eu.auth0.com`.
    3. Fill in information about your account as requested.

3. Following sign-up, you will be directed to your dashboard. Select the **Applications** tab (on the left) to see the default client application that was created for you during the sign-up process.
4. Click on the **Default App** to configure it:
    1. Copy the **Client ID** and **Client Secret**; you will need them later on.
    2. As **Application Type**, select **Machine to Machine**.
    3. As **Token Endpoint Authentication Method**, select **POST**.
    4. Enter `http://my.redirect.uri` as the allowed callback URL.
    5. Click on **Show Advanced Settings**, go to the **Grant Types** tab, deselect **Client Credentials**, and select the **Password** box.
    6. Click on **SAVE CHANGES**.
5. Now define authorizations for our API:
    1. Click on the **APIs** tab (on the left) and click on the **+ CREATE API** button.
    2. Name the API `product-composite`, give it the identifier `https://localhost:8443/product-composite`, and click on the **CREATE** button.
    3. Click on the **Permissions** tab and create two permissions (that is, OAuth scopes) for `product:read` and `product:write`.

6. Next, create a user:
    1. Click on the **Users & Roles** and **-> Users** tab (on the left) and then on the **+ CREATE YOUR FIRST USER** button.
    2. Enter an `email` and `password` of your preference and click on the **SAVE** button.
    3. Look for a verification mail from Auth0 in the **Inbox** for the email address you supplied.
7. Finally, validate your **Default Directory** setting, used for the password grant flow:
    1. Click on your tenant profile in the upper-right corner and select **Settings**.
    2. In the tab named **General**, scroll down to the field named **Default Directory** and verify that it contains the `Username-Password-Authentication` value. If not, update the field and save the change.
8. That's it! Note that both the default app and the API get a client ID and secret. We will use the client ID and secret for the default app; that is, the OAuth client.

With an Auth0 account created and configured we can move on and apply the necessary configuration changes in the system landscape.

Applying the necessary changes to use Auth0 as an OpenID provider

In this section we will learn what configuration changes are required to be able to replace the local authorization server with Auth0. We only need to change the configuration for the two services that act as OAuth resource servers, the `product-composite`, and the `gateway` services. We also need to change our test script a bit, so that it acquires the access tokens from Auth0 instead of from our local authorization server. Let's start with the OAuth resource servers, that is, the `product-composite` and the `gateway` services.

> The changes described in this topic have **not** been applied to the source code in the book's Git repository; that is, you need to make them yourself to see them in action!

Changing the configuration in the OAuth resource servers

When using an OpenID Connect provider, we only have to configure the base URI to the standardized discovery endpoint in the OAuth resource servers, that is, the `product-composite` and the `gateway` service. Spring Security will use the information in the response from the discovery endpoint to configure the resource server.

In the `product-composite` and `gateway` projects, make the following change to the `resource/application.yml` file:

Now find the following property setting:

```
spring.security.oauth2.resourceserver.jwt.jwk-set-uri: http://${app.auth-server}:9999/.well-known/jwks.json
```

Replace it with:

```
spring.security.oauth2.resourceserver.jwt.issuer-uri:
https://${TENANT_DOMAIN_NAME}/
```

Note: Replace `${TENANT_DOMAIN_NAME}` in the preceding configuration with your tenant domain name; in my case, it is `dev-ml.eu.auth0.com`, and do not forget the trailing `/`!

> If you are curious, you can see what's in the discovery document by running the following command:
>
> ```
> curl https://${TENANT_DOMAIN_NAME}/.well-known/openid-configuration -s | jq
> ```

Rebuild the `product-composite` and `gateway` services as follows:

```
cd $BOOK_HOME/Chapter11
./gradlew build && docker-compose up -d --build product-composite gateway
```

With the `product-composite` and the `gateway` service updated, we can move on and also update the test script.

Changing the test script so it acquires access tokens from Auth0

We also need to update the test script so it acquires access tokens from the Auth0 OIDC provider. This is done by performing the following changes in `test-em-all.bash`.

Take the following command:

```
ACCESS_TOKEN=$(curl http://writer:secret@$HOST:$PORT/oauth/token -d
grant_type=password -d username=magnus -d password=password -s | jq
.access_token -r)
```

Replace it with this command:

```
ACCESS_TOKEN=$(curl --request POST \
  --url 'https://${TENANT_DOMAIN_NAME}/oauth/token' \
  --header 'content-type: application/json' \
  --data '{"grant_type":"password", "username":"${USER_EMAIL}",
"password":"${USER_PASSWORD}",
"audience":"https://localhost:8443/product-composite", "scope":"openid
email product:read product:write", "client_id": "${CLIENT_ID}",
"client_secret": "${CLIENT_SECRET}"}' -s | jq -r .access_token)
```

Now, replace ${TENANT_DOMAIN_NAME}, ${USER_EMAIL}, ${USER_PASSWORD}, ${CLIENT_ID}, and ${CLIENT_SECRET} in the preceding command with the values you collected during the registration process in Auth0, as described previously. Then, take the following command:

```
READER_ACCESS_TOKEN=$(curl -k https://reader:secret@$HOST:$PORT/oauth/token
-d grant_type=password -d username=magnus -d password=password -s | jq
.access_token -r)
```

Replace it with this command:

```
READER_ACCESS_TOKEN=$(curl --request POST \
  --url 'https://${TENANT_DOMAIN_NAME}/oauth/token' \
  --header 'content-type: application/json' \
  --data '{"grant_type":"password", "username":"${USER_EMAIL}",
"password":"${USER_PASSWORD}",
"audience":"https://localhost:8443/product-composite", "scope":"openid
email product:read", "client_id": "${CLIENT_ID}", "client_secret":
"${CLIENT_SECRET}"}' -s | jq -r .access_token)
```

Apply the preceding changes to the command. Also note that we only require the product:read scope and not the product:write scope. This is to simulate a client with read-only access.

Now access tokens are issued by Auth0 instead of our local authorization server, and our API implementations can verify that the access tokens (have been correctly signed by Auth0 and have not expired), using information from Auth0's discovery service flagged in the `application.yml` files. The API implementations can, as before, use the scopes in the access tokens to authorize the client to perform the call to the API, or not.

Now we have all the required changes in place, let's run some tests to verify that we can acquire access tokens from Auth0.

Running the test script with Auth0 as the OpenID Connect provider

Now, we are ready to give Auth0 a try!

Run the usual tests against Auth0 with the following command:

```
./test-em-all.bash
```

In the logs (using the `docker-compose logs -f product-composite` command), you will be able to find authorization information from the access tokens issued by Auth0:

From calls using an access token with both the `product:read` and `product:write` scopes, we will see that both scopes are listed as follows:

```
                              2. @700dd0df9ffe:/ (bash)
product-composite_1 ...
Authorization info: Subject: auth0|5ca0b73c97f31e11bc85a5e6,
scopes: openid email product:read product:write,
expires Mon Apr 08 10:46:35 UTC 2019: issuer: https://dev-ml.eu.auth0.com/,
audience: [https://localhost:8443/product-composite, https://dev-ml.eu.auth0.com/userinfo]
```

From calls using an access token with only the `product:read` scope, we will see that only that scope is listed as follows:

```
                              2. @700dd0df9ffe:/ (bash)
product-composite_1 ...
Authorization info: Subject: auth0|5ca0b73c97f31e11bc85a5e6,
scopes: openid email product:read,
expires Mon Apr 08 10:46:41 UTC 2019: issuer: https://dev-ml.eu.auth0.com/,
audience: [https://localhost:8443/product-composite, https://dev-ml.eu.auth0.com/userinfo]
```

As we can see from the log output, we now get information regarding the intended audience for this access token. To strengthen security, we could add a test to our service that verifies that its URL, `https://localhost:8443/product-composite` in this case, is part of the audience list. This would prevent the situation where someone tries to use an access token issued for another purpose to get access to our API.

With the automated tests working together with Auth0, we can move on and learn how to acquire access tokens using the different types of grant flow. Let's start with the password grant flow.

Acquiring access tokens using the password grant flow

In this section we will learn how to acquire an access token from Auth0 using the password grant flow.

If you want to acquire an access token from Auth0 yourself, you can do so by running the following command:

```
curl --request POST \
 --url 'https://${TENANT_DOMAIN_NAME}/oauth/token' \
 --header 'content-type: application/json' \
 --data '{"grant_type":"password", "username":"${USER_EMAIL}",
"password":"${USER_PASSWORD}",
"audience":"https://localhost:8443/product-composite", "scope":"openid
email product:read", "client_id": "${CLIENT_ID}", "client_secret":
"${CLIENT_SECRET}"}' -s | jq
```

Following the instruction in the *Calling protected APIs using the access tokens* section, you should be able to call the APIs using the acquired access token. The next grant flow we'll try out is the implicit grant flow.

Acquiring access tokens using the implicit grant flow

In this section, we will learn how to acquire an access token from Auth0 using the implicit grant flow.

If you want to try out the more involved implicit grant flow, you can open the following URL in a web browser:

```
https://${TENANT_DOMAIN_NAME}/authorize?response_type=token&scope=openid
email product:read
product:write&client_id=${CLIENT_ID}&state=98421&&nonce=jxdlsjfi0fa&redirec
t_uri=http://my.redirect.uri&audience=https://localhost:8443/product-compos
ite
```

> **TIP**
> Replace `${TENANT_DOMAIN_NAME}` and `${CLIENT_ID}` in the preceding URL with the tenant domain name and client ID you collected during the registration process in Auth0 as described previously.

Let's have a look at the following steps:

1. Auth0 should present the following login screen:

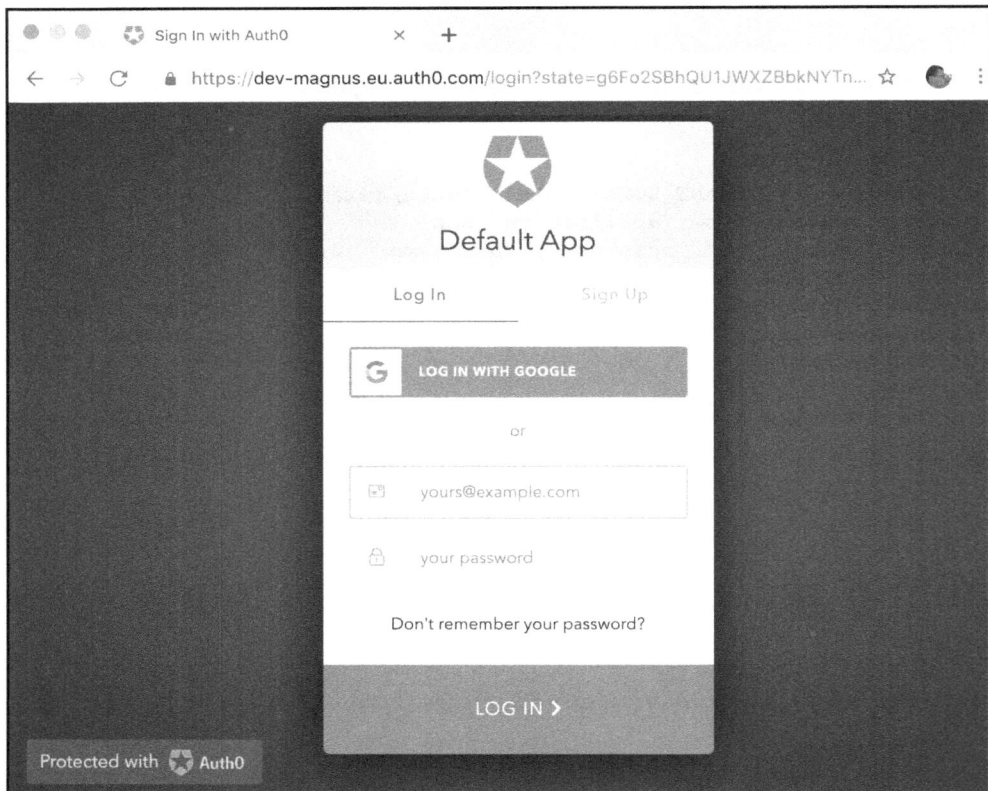

2. Following a successful login, Auth0 will ask you to give the client application your consent:

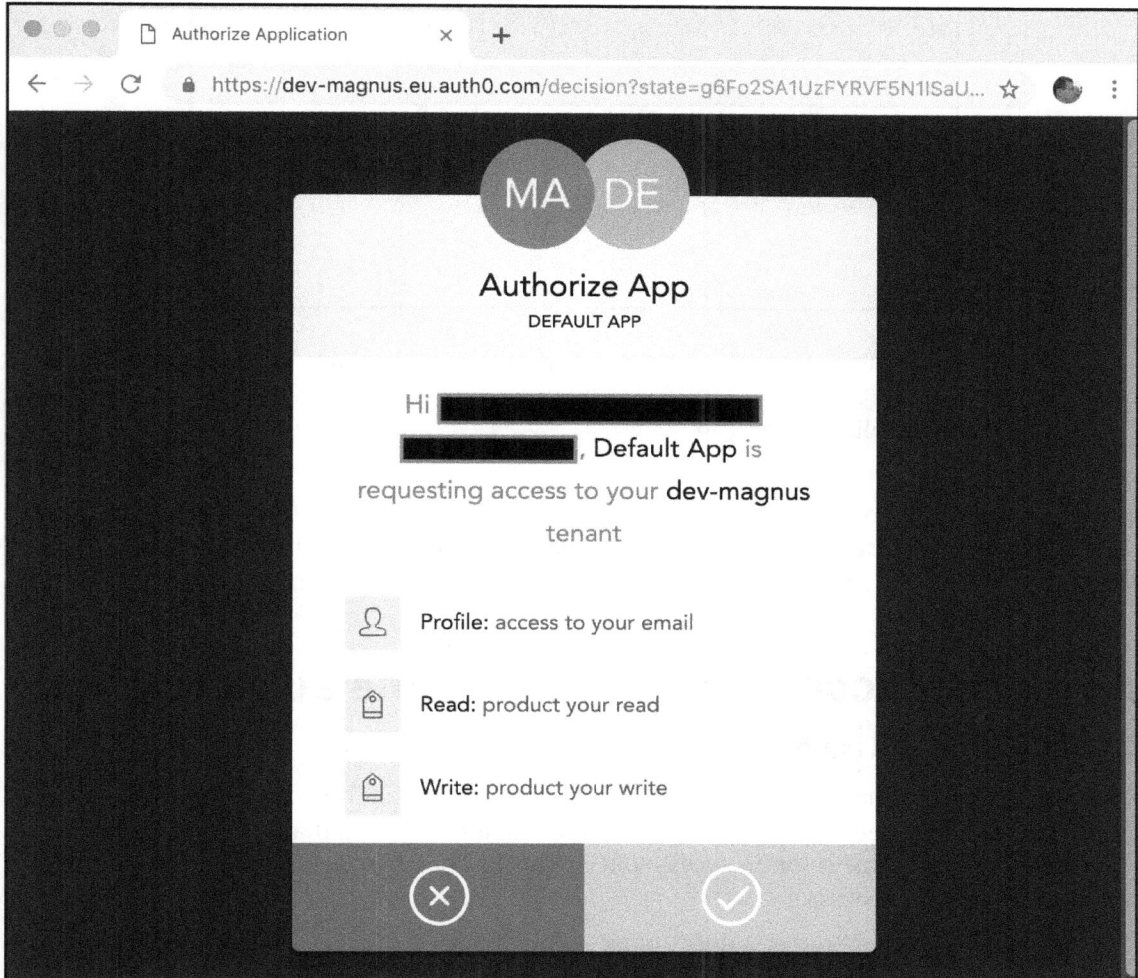

The access token is now in the URL in the browser, just like when we tried out the implicit flow in our local authorization server:

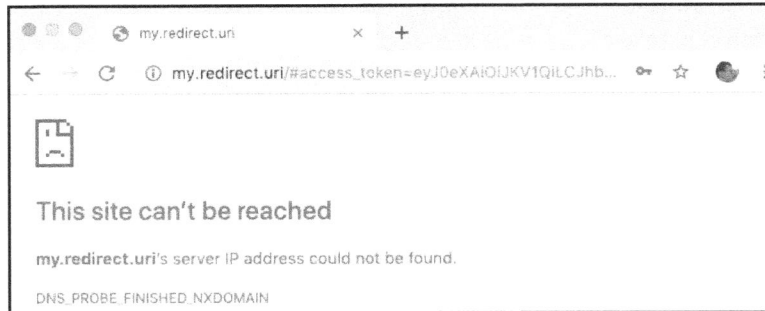

To get an access token that corresponds to the `reader` client, remove the `product:write` scope from the preceding URL that we used to initiate the implicit grant flow.

Now that we know how to acquire an access token using the implicit grant flow, we can move on to the third and last grant flow that we will try out, the authorization code grant flow.

Acquiring access tokens using the authorization code grant flow

Finally, we come to the most secure grant flow – the authorization code grant flow. We will follow the same procedure as with the local authorization server; that is, we first acquire code and then exchange it for an access token. Get the code by opening the following URL in a web browser, as follows:

```
https://${TENANT_DOMAIN_NAME}/authorize?audience=https://localhost:8443/pro
duct-composite&scope=openid email product:read
product:write&response_type=code&client_id=${CLIENT_ID}&redirect_uri=http:/
/my.redirect.uri&state=845361
```

Replace `${TENANT_DOMAIN_NAME}` and `${CLIENT_ID}` in the preceding URL with the tenant domain name and client ID you collected during the registration process in Auth0 as described previously.

Expect a redirect attempt in the web browser to a URL as follows:

```
http://my.redirect.uri/?code=6mQ7HK--WyX9fMnv&state=845361
```

Extract the code and run the following command to get the access token:

```
curl --request POST \
    --url 'https://${TENANT_DOMAIN_NAME}/oauth/token' \
    --header 'content-type: application/json' \
    --data '{"grant_type":"authorization_code","client_id":
"${CLIENT_ID}","client_secret": "${CLIENT_SECRET}","code":
"${CODE}","redirect_uri": "http://my.redirect.uri"}' -s | jq .
```

Replace ${TENANT_DOMAIN_NAME}, ${CLIENT_ID}, ${CLIENT_SECRET}, and ${CODE} in the preceding URL with the tenant domain name, client ID, and the client code you collected during the registration process in Auth0 as described previously.

Now that we have learned how to acquire access tokens using all three types of grant flows, we are ready to try calling the external API using an access token acquired from Auth0 in the next section.

Calling protected APIs using the Auth0 access tokens

In this section, we will see how we can use an access token acquired from Auth0 to call the external API.

We can use access tokens issued by Auth0 to call our APIs just like when we used access tokens issued by our local authorization server.

For a read-only API, execute the following command:

```
ACCESS_TOKEN=...
curl https://localhost:8443/product-composite/2 -k -H "Authorization:
Bearer $ACCESS_TOKEN" -i
```

For an updating API, execute the following command:

```
ACCESS_TOKEN=...
curl https://localhost:8443/product-composite/999 -k -H "Authorization:
Bearer $ACCESS_TOKEN" -X DELETE -i
```

Since we have requested both scopes, product:read and product:write, both the preceding API calls are expected to return 200 OK.

Getting extra information about the user

As you can see in the log output, the ID of the subject, that is, the user, is a bit cryptic, for example, `auth0|5ca0b73c97f31e11bc85a5e6`.

If you want your API implementation to know a bit more about the user, it can call Auth0's `userinfo_endpoint` as described in the response to the discovery request made previously:

```
curl -H "Authorization: Bearer $ACCESS_TOKEN"
https://${TENANT_DOMAIN_NAME}/userinfo -s | jq
```

Replace `${TENANT_DOMAIN_NAME}` in the preceding command with the tenant domain name you collected during the registration process in Auth0 as described previously.

A sample response is as follows:

> This endpoint can also be used to verify that the user hasn't revoked the access token in Auth0.

Wrap up the tests by shutting down the system landscape with the following command:

```
docker-compose down
```

This concludes the section where we have learned how to replace the local OAuth 2.0 Authorization server, only used for tests, with an external alternative. We have also seen how to reconfigure the microservice landscape to validate access tokens using an external OIDC provider.

Summary

In this chapter, we have learned how to use Spring Security to protect our APIs.

We have seen how easy it is to enable HTTPS to prevent eavesdropping by third parties using Spring Security. With Spring Security, we have also learned that it is straightforward to restrict access and the discovery server, Netflix Eureka, using HTTP basic authentication. Finally, we have seen how we can use Spring Security to simplify the use of OAuth 2.0 and OpenID Connect to allow third-party client applications to access our APIs in the name of a user, but without requiring that the user share credentials with the client application. We have learned both how to set up a local OAuth 2.0 authorization server based on Spring Security and also how to change the configuration so that an external OpenID Connect provider, Auth0, can be used instead.

One concern, however, is how to manage the configuration required. Many small pieces of configuration must be set up for the microservices involved and the configuration must be synchronized to match. Added to the scattered configuration is the fact that some of the configuration contains sensitive information, such as credentials or certificates. It seems like we need a better way to handle the configuration for a number of cooperating microservices and also a solution for how to handle sensitive parts of the configuration.

In the next chapter, we will explore the Spring Cloud Configuration server and see how it can be used to handle these types of requirement.

Questions

1. What are the benefits and shortcomings of using self-signed certificates?
2. What is the purpose of OAuth 2.0 authorization codes?
3. What is the purpose of OAuth 2.0 scopes?
4. What does it mean when a token is a JWT token?
5. How can we trust the information that is stored in a JWT token?
6. Is it suitable to use the OAuth 2.0 authorization code grant flow with a native mobile app?
7. What does OpenID Connect add to OAuth 2.0?

12
Centralized Configuration

In this chapter, we will learn how to use the Spring Cloud Configuration server to centralize managing the configuration of our microservices. As already described in `Chapter 1`, *Introduction to Microservices*, in the *Central configuration* section, an increasing number of microservices typically come with an increasing number of configuration files that need to be managed and updated.

With the Spring Cloud Configuration server, we can place the configuration files for all our microservices in a central configuration repository that will make it much easier to handle them. Our microservices will be updated to retrieve their configuration from the configuration server at startup.

The following topics will be covered in this chapter:

- Introduction to the Spring Cloud Configuration server
- Setting up a config server
- Configuring clients of a config server
- Structuring the configuration repository
- Trying out the Spring Cloud Configuration server

Technical requirements

All the commands described in this book are run on a MacBook Pro using macOS Mojave but should be straightforward enough to modify in order to be able to run on another platform such as Linux or Windows.

No new tools need to be installed in this chapter.

The source code for this chapter can be found on GitHub at `https://github.com/ PacktPublishing/Hands-On-Microservices-with-Spring-Boot-and-Spring-Cloud/tree/ master/Chapter12`.

To be able to run the commands as described in the book, download the source code to a folder and set up an environment variable, $BOOK_HOME, that points to that folder. Sample commands include the following:

```
export BOOK_HOME=~/Documents/Hands-On-Microservices-with-Spring-Boot-and-
Spring-Cloud
git clone
https://github.com/PacktPublishing/Hands-On-Microservices-with-Spring-Boot-
and-Spring-Cloud $BOOK_HOME
cd $BOOK_HOME/Chapter12
```

The Java source code is written for Java 8 and tested on Java 12. This chapter uses Spring Cloud 2.1.0, SR1 (also known as the **Greenwich** release), Spring Boot 2.1.4, and Spring 5.1.6, that is, the latest available versions of the Spring components at the time of writing this chapter.

The base Docker image, openjdk:12.0.2, is used in all Dockerfiles.

The source code contains the following Gradle projects:

- api
- util
- microservices/product-service
- microservices/review-service
- microservices/recommendation-service
- microservices/product-composite-service
- spring-cloud/eureka-server
- spring-cloud/gateway
- spring-cloud/authorization-server
- spring-cloud/config-server

All source code examples in this chapter come from the source code in $BOOK_HOME/Chapter12, but are, in several cases, edited to remove non-relevant parts of the source code, such as comments, import statements, and log statements.

If you want to see the changes applied to the source code in Chapter 12, *Centralized Configuration*, that is, see what it took to add a configuration server, you can compare that with the source code for Chapter 11, *Securing Access to APIs*. You can use your favorite diff tool and compare the two folders, $BOOK_HOME/Chapter11 and $BOOK_HOME/Chapter12.

Introduction to the Spring Cloud Configuration server

The Spring Cloud Configuration server (shortened to *config server*) will be added to the existing microservice landscape behind the edge server in `Chapter 10`, *Using Spring Cloud Gateway to Hide Microservices Behind an Edge Server*, in the same way as for the other microservices:

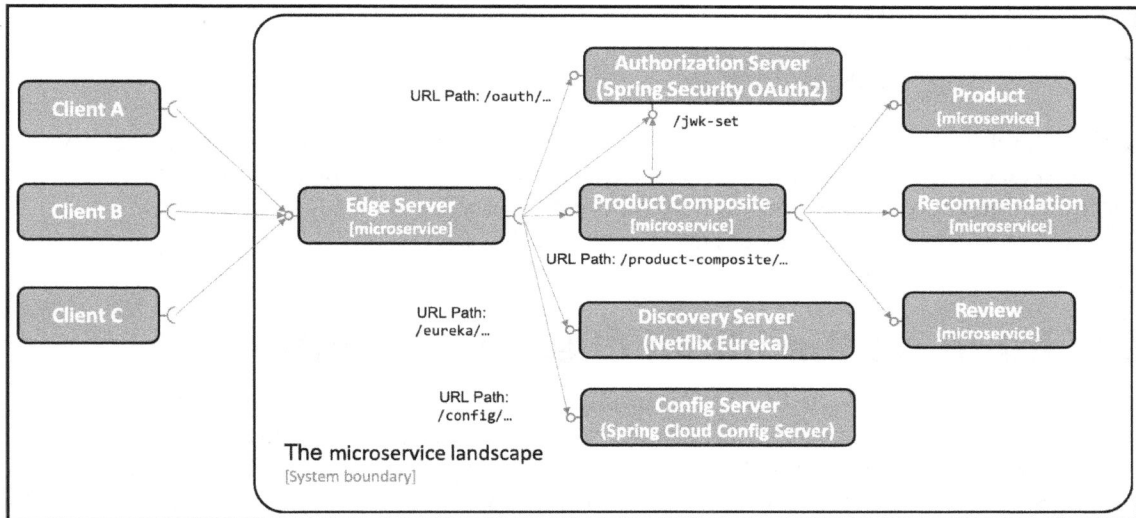

When it comes to setting up a config server, there are a number of options to consider:

- Selecting a storage type for the configuration repository
- Deciding on the initial client connection, either to the config server or to the discovery server
- Securing the configuration, both against unauthorized access to the API and avoiding storing sensitive information in plain text in the configuration repository

Let's go through each option one by one and also introduce the API exposed by the config server.

Selecting the storage type of the configuration repository

As already described in Chapter 8, *Introduction to Spring Cloud*, in the *Spring Cloud Config for centralized configuration* section, the config server supports storing configuration files in a number of different backends, for example:

- Git repository
- Local filesystem
- HashiCorp Vault
- A JDBC database

In this chapter, we will use a local filesystem. To use the local filesystem, the config server needs to be launched with the Spring profile, native, enabled. The location of the configuration repository is specified using the property, spring.cloud.config.server.native.searchLocations.

Deciding on the initial client connection

By default, a client connects first to the config server to retrieve its configuration. Based on the configuration, it connects to the discovery server, that is, Netflix Eureka in our case, to register itself. It is also possible to do this the other way around, that is, the client first connects to the discovery server to find a config server instance and then connects to the config server to get its configuration. There are pros and cons to both approaches.

In this chapter, the clients will first connect to the config server. With this approach, it will be possible to store the configuration of the discovery server, that is, Netflix Eureka, in the config server.

To learn more about the other alternative, see https://cloud.spring.io/spring-cloud-static/spring-cloud-config/2.1.0.RELEASE/single/spring-cloud-config.html#discovery-first-bootstrap.

One concern with connecting to the config server first is that the config server can become a single point of failure. If the clients connect first to a discovery service, such as Netflix Eureka, there can be multiple config server instances registered, so that a single point of failure can be avoided. When, later on in this book, we learn about the *service* concept in Kubernetes, we will see how we can avoid a single point of failure by running multiple containers, for example, config servers, behind each Kubernetes service.

Securing the configuration

Configuration information will, in general, be handled as sensitive information. This means that we need to secure the configuration information both in transit and at rest. From a runtime perspective, the config server does not need to be exposed to the outside through the edge server. During development, it is, however, useful to be able to access the API of the config server to check the configuration. In production environments, it is recommended to lock down external access to the config server.

Securing the configuration in transit

When the configuration information is asked for by a microservice, or anyone using the API of the config server, it will be protected against eavesdropping by the edge server since it already uses HTTPS.

To ensure that the API user is a known client, we will use HTTP basic authentication. We can set up HTTP basic authentication by using Spring Security in the config server and specifying the environment variables, SPRING_SECURITY_USER_NAME and SPRING_SECURITY_USER_PASSWORD, with the permitted credentials.

Securing the configuration at rest

To avoid a situation whereby anyone with access to the configuration repository can steal sensitive information, such as passwords, the config server supports encryption of configuration information when stored on disk. The config server supports using both symmetric and asymmetric keys. Asymmetric keys are more secure but harder to manage.

In this chapter, we will use a symmetric key. The symmetric key is given to the config server at startup by specifying an environment variable, ENCRYPT_KEY. The encrypted key is just a plain text string that needs to be protected in the same way as any sensitive information.

To learn more about the use of asymmetric keys, see https://cloud.spring.io/spring-cloud-static/spring-cloud-config/2.1.0.RELEASE/single/spring-cloud-config.html#_key_management.

Introducing the config server API

The config server exposes a REST API that can be used by its clients to retrieve their configuration. In this chapter, we will use the following endpoints in the API:

- /actuator: The standard actuator endpoints exposed by all microservices. As always, these should be used with care. They are very useful during development but must be locked down before being used in production.
- /encrypt and /decrypt: Endpoints for encrypting and decrypting sensitive information. These must also be locked down before being used in production.
- /{microservice}/{profile}: Returns the configuration for the specified microservice and the specified Spring profile.

We will see some sample uses for the APIs when we try out the config server.

Setting up a config server

Setting up a config server on the basis of the decisions discussed is straightforward:

1. Create a Spring Boot project using Spring Initializr as described in Chapter 3, *Creating a Set of Cooperating Microservices*. Refer to the *Using Spring Initializr to generate skeleton code* section.
2. Add the dependencies, spring-cloud-config-server and spring-boot-starter-security, to the Gradle build file, build.gradle.
3. Add the annotation, @EnableConfigServer, to the application class, ConfigServerApplication:

```
@EnableConfigServer
@SpringBootApplication
public class ConfigServerApplication {
```

4. Add the configuration for the config server to the default property file, `application.yml`:

```
server.port: 8888

spring.cloud.config.server.native.searchLocations:
file:${PWD}/config-repo

management.endpoint.health.show-details: "ALWAYS"
management.endpoints.web.exposure.include: "*"

logging.level.root: info
---
spring.profiles: docker
spring.cloud.config.server.native.searchLocations: file:/config-
repo
```

The most important configuration is to specify where to find the configuration repository, specified by the `spring.cloud.config.server.native.searchLocations` property.

5. Add a routing rule to the edge server to make the API of the config server accessible from outside the microservice landscape.
6. Add a Dockerfile and a definition of the config server to the three Docker Compose files.
7. Externalize sensitive configuration parameters to the standard Docker Compose environment file, `.env`
8. Add the config server to the common build file, `settings.gradle`:

```
include ':spring-cloud:config-server'
```

The source code for the Spring Cloud Configuration server can be found in `$BOOK_HOME/Chapter12/spring-cloud/config-server`.

Now, let's look a bit more into how to set up the routing rule and how to configure the config server for use in Docker.

Setting up a routing rule in the edge server

To be able to access the API of the config server from outside the microservice landscape, we add a routing rule to the edge server. All requests to the edge server that begin with /config will be routed to the config server with the following routing rule:

```
- id: config-server
  uri: http://${app.config-server}:8888
 predicates:
 - Path=/config/**
 filters:
 - RewritePath=/config/(?<segment>.*), /$\{segment}
```

The RewritePath filter in the preceding routing rule will remove the leading part, /config, from the incoming URL before it sends it to the config server.

With this routing rule in place, we can use the API of the config server; for example, run the following command to ask for the configuration of the product service when it uses the Docker Spring profile:

```
curl https://dev-usr:dev-pwd@localhost:8443/config/product/docker -ks | jq
```

We will run the preceding command when we try out the config server.

Configuring the config server for use with Docker

The Dockerfile of the config server looks the same as for the other microservices, except for the fact that it exposes port 8888 instead of port 8080.

When it comes to adding the config server to the Docker Compose files, it looks a bit different from what we have seen for the other microservices:

```
config-server:
  environment:
    - SPRING_PROFILES_ACTIVE=docker,native
    - ENCRYPT_KEY=${CONFIG_SERVER_ENCRYPT_KEY}
    - SPRING_SECURITY_USER_NAME=${CONFIG_SERVER_USR}
    - SPRING_SECURITY_USER_PASSWORD=${CONFIG_SERVER_PWD}
  volumes:
    - $PWD/config-repo:/config-repo
  build: spring-cloud/config-server
  mem_limit: 350m
```

Here are the explanations for the preceding source code:

1. The Spring profile, `native`, is added to signal to the config server that the config repository is based on plain files; in other words, it is not a Git repository.
2. The environment variable `ENCRYPT_KEY` is used to specify the symmetric encryption key that shall be used by the config server to encrypt and decrypt sensitive configuration information.
3. The environment variables, `SPRING_SECURITY_USER_NAME` and `SPRING_SECURITY_USER_PASSWORD`, are used to specify the credentials to be used for protecting the APIs using basic HTTP authentication.
4. The volume declaration will make the `config-repo` folder accessible in the Docker container at `/config-repo`.

The values of the three preceding environment variables defined are fetched by Docker Compose from the `.env` file:

```
CONFIG_SERVER_ENCRYPT_KEY=my-very-secure-encrypt-key
CONFIG_SERVER_USR=dev-usr
CONFIG_SERVER_PWD=dev-pwd
```

> The information stored in the `.env` file, that is, the username, password, and encryption key, is sensitive information and must be protected if used for something other than development and testing. Also, note that losing the encryption key will lead to a situation whereby the encrypted information in the config repository cannot be decrypted!

Configuring clients of a config server

To be able to get their configurations from the config server, our microservices need to be updated. This can be done through the following steps:

1. Add the `spring-cloud-starter-config`, and `spring-retry` dependencies to the Gradle build file, `build.gradle`.
2. Move the configuration file, `application.yml`, to the config repository and rename it to the name of the client as specified by the property, `spring.application.name`.

3. Add a file named `bootstrap.yml` to the `src/main/resources` folder. This file holds the configuration required to connect to the config server. Refer to the following for an explanation of its content.

4. Add credentials for accessing the config server to the Docker Compose files, for example, the `product` service:

```
product:
  environment:
  - CONFIG_SERVER_USR=${CONFIG_SERVER_USR}
  - CONFIG_SERVER_PWD=${CONFIG_SERVER_PWD}
```

5. Disable the use of the config server when running Spring Boot-based automated tests. This is done by adding `spring.cloud.config.enabled=false` to the `@DataMongoTest`, `@DataJpaTest`, and `@SpringBootTest` annotations. For example, execute the following command:

```
@DataMongoTest(properties = {"spring.cloud.config.enabled=false"})

@DataJpaTest(properties = {"spring.cloud.config.enabled=false"})

@SpringBootTest(webEnvironment=RANDOM_PORT, properties =
{"eureka.client.enabled=false",
"spring.cloud.config.enabled=false"})
```

Configuring connection information

As mentioned previously, the `src/main/resources/bootstrap.yml` file holds the client configuration that is required in order to be able to connect to the config server. This file has the same content for all clients of the config server, except for the application name as specified by the property called, `spring.application.name` (in the following example, set to `product`):

```
app.config-server: localhost

spring:
  application.name: product
  cloud.config:
    failFast: true
    retry:
      initialInterval: 3000
      multiplier: 1.3
      maxInterval: 10000
      maxAttempts: 20
    uri: http://${CONFIG_SERVER_USR}:${CONFIG_SERVER_PWD}@${app.config-
```

```
server}:8888

---
spring.profiles: docker

app.config-server: config-server
```

This configuration will make the client do the following:

1. Connect to the config server using the `http://localhost:8888` URL when it runs outside Docker, and using the `http://config-server:8888` URL when running in a Docker container.
2. Use HTTP basic authentication using the value of the `CONFIG_SERVER_USR` and `CONFIG_SERVER_PWD` properties, as its username and password.
3. Try to reconnect to the config server during startup up to 20 times, if required.
4. If the connection attempt fails, the client will initially wait for 3 seconds before trying to reconnect.
5. The wait time for subsequent retries will increase by a factor of 1.3.
6. The maximum wait time between connection attempts will be 10 seconds.
7. If the client can't connect to the config server after 20 attempts, its startup will fail.

This configuration is generally good for resilience against temporary connectivity problems with the config server. It is especially useful when the whole landscape of microservices and its config server are started up at once, for example, when using the `docker-compose up` command. In this scenario, many of the clients will be trying to connect to the config server before it is ready, and the retry logic will make the clients connect to the config server successfully once it is up and running.

Moving the partitioning configuration from Docker Compose files to the configuration repository

The Docker Compose files, `docker-compose-partitions.yml`, and `docker-compose-kafka.yml`, contain some extra configuration for handling partitions in the message brokers, RabbitMQ and Kafka. For details, refer to the *Guaranteed order and partitions* section in `Chapter 7`, *Developing Reactive Microservices*. This configuration has also been moved to the centralized configuration repository.

For example, in `docker-compose-kafka.yml`, the configuration for the product consumer that reads messages from the first partition in the product topic in Kafka appears as follows:

```
product:
  environment:
    - SPRING_PROFILES_ACTIVE=docker
    - MANAGEMENT_HEALTH_RABBIT_ENABLED=false
    - SPRING_CLOUD_STREAM_DEFAULTBINDER=kafka
    - SPRING_CLOUD_STREAM_BINDINGS_INPUT_CONSUMER_PARTITIONED=true
    - SPRING_CLOUD_STREAM_BINDINGS_INPUT_CONSUMER_INSTANCECOUNT=2
    - SPRING_CLOUD_STREAM_BINDINGS_INPUT_CONSUMER_INSTANCEINDEX=0
```

This configuration has been structured into a number of Spring profiles for increased reusability and moved to the corresponding configuration files in the configuration repository. The Spring profiles added are as follows:

- `streaming_partitioned` contains properties for enabling the use of partitions in a message broker.
- `streaming_instance_0` contains properties required for consuming messages from the first partition.
- `streaming_instance_1` contains properties required for consuming messages from the second partition.
- `kafka` contains properties that are specific for the use of Kafka as the messaging broker.

The following configuration has been added to the configuration files of the message consumers, that is, the product, review, and recommendation services:

```
---
spring.profiles: streaming_partitioned
spring.cloud.stream.bindings.input.consumer:
  partitioned: true
  instanceCount: 2

---
spring.profiles: streaming_instance_0
spring.cloud.stream.bindings.input.consumer.instanceIndex: 0

---
spring.profiles: streaming_instance_1
spring.cloud.stream.bindings.input.consumer.instanceIndex: 1

---
spring.profiles: kafka
```

```
management.health.rabbit.enabled: false
spring.cloud.stream.defaultBinder: kafka
```

The following configuration has been added to the configuration file of the message producer, that is, the product-composite service:

```
---
spring.profiles: streaming_partitioned

spring.cloud.stream.bindings.output-products.producer:
  partition-key-expression: payload.key
  partition-count: 2

spring.cloud.stream.bindings.output-recommendations.producer:
  partition-key-expression: payload.key
  partition-count: 2

spring.cloud.stream.bindings.output-reviews.producer:
  partition-key-expression: payload.key
  partition-count: 2

---
spring.profiles: kafka

management.health.rabbit.enabled: false
spring.cloud.stream.defaultBinder: kafka
```

The Docker Compose files are now cleaner and only contain the configuration of credentials for accessing the configurations server and a list of Spring profiles to activate. For example, the configuration for the product consumer that read messages from the first partition in the product topic in Kafka is now reduced to the following:

```
product:
    environment:
      -
SPRING_PROFILES_ACTIVE=docker,streaming_partitioned,streaming_instance_0,ka
fka
        - CONFIG_SERVER_USR=${CONFIG_SERVER_USR}
        - CONFIG_SERVER_PWD=${CONFIG_SERVER_PWD}
```

For the full source code, refer to the following:

- docker-compose-partitions.yml
- docker-compose-kafka.yml
- config-repo/product-composite.yml
- config-repo/product.yml

- config-repo/recommendation.yml
- config-repo/review.yml

Structuring the configuration repository

After moving the configuration files from each client to the configuration repository, we will have some level of consistent configuration in many of the configuration files, for example, for the configuration of actuator endpoints and how to connect to Eureka, RabbitMQ, and Kafka. The common parts have been placed in a configuration file named application.yml that is shared by all clients. The configuration repository contains the following files:

- application.yml
- eureka-server.yml
- product-composite.yml
- recommendation.yml
- auth-server.yml
- gateway.yml
- product.yml
- review.yml

The configuration repository can be found in $BOOK_HOME/Chapter12/config-repo.

Trying out the Spring Cloud Configuration server

Now it is time to try out the config server:

1. First, we build from source and run the test script to ensure that everything fits together.
2. Next, we will try out the config server API to retrieve the configuration for our microservices.
3. Finally, we will see how we can encrypt and decrypt sensitive information, for example, passwords.

Building and running automated tests

So now we build and run, as follows:

1. First, build the Docker images with the following commands:

```
cd $BOOK_HOME/Chapter12
./gradlew build && docker-compose build
```

2. Next, start the system landscape in Docker and run the usual tests with the following command:

```
./test-em-all.bash start
```

Getting the configuration using the config server API

As already described previously, we can reach the API of the config server through the edge server by using the URL prefix, /config. We also have to supply credentials as specified in the .env file for HTTP basic authentication. For example, to retrieve the configuration used for the product service when it runs as a Docker container, that is, having activated the Spring profile docker, run the following command:

```
curl https://dev-usr:dev-pwd@localhost:8443/config/product/docker -ks | jq
```

Expect a response with the following structure (many of the properties in the response are replaced by . . . to increase readability):

```
{
  "name": "product",
  "profiles": [
    "docker"
  ],
  ...
  "propertySources": [
    {
      "name": "file:/config-repo/product.yml (document #1)",
      "source": {
        "spring.profiles": "docker",
        "server.port": 8080,
        ...
      }
    },
```

```
  {
    "name": "file:/config-repo/application.yml (document #1)",
    "source": {
      "spring.profiles": "docker",
      ...
    }
  },
  {
    "name": "file:/config-repo/product.yml (document #0)",
    "source": {
      "server.port": 7001,
      ...
    }
  },
  {
    "name": "file:/config-repo/application.yml (document #0)",
    "source": {
      ...
      "app.eureka-password": "p",
      "spring.rabbitmq.password": "guest"
    }
  }
 ]
}
```

The explanations for the preceding response are as follows:

- The response contains properties from a number of *property sources*, one per the Spring profile and property file that matched the API request. The property sources are returned in priority order; that is, if a property is specified in multiple property sources, the first property in the response takes precedence. The preceding sample response contains the following property sources:
  - /config-repo/product.yml, for the docker Spring profile
  - /config-repo/application.yml, for the docker Spring profile
  - /config-repo/product.yml, for the default Spring profile
  - /config-repo/application.yml, for the default Spring profile docker
- For example, the port used will be 8080 and not 7001, since "server.port": 8080 is specified before "server.port": 7001 in the preceding response.

- Sensitive information, such as the passwords to Eureka and RabbitMQ, are returned in plain text, for example, `"p"` and `"guest"`, but they are encrypted on disk. In the configuration file, `application.yml`, they are specified as follows:

```
app:
  eureka-password:
'{cipher}bf298f6d5f878b342f9e44bec08cb9ac00b4ce57e98316f030194a225f
ac89fb'

spring.rabbitmq:
  password:
'{cipher}17fcf0ae5b8c5cf87de6875b699be4a1746dd493a99d926c7a26a68c42
2117ef'
```

Encrypting and decrypting sensitive information

Information can be encrypted and decrypted using the /encrypt, and /decrypt endpoints exposed by the config server. The /encrpyt endpoint can be used to create encrypted values to be placed in the property file in the config repository. Refer to the preceding example where the passwords to Eureka and RabbitMQ are stored encrypted on disk. The /decrypt endpoint can be used to verify encrypted information that is stored on disk in the config repository.

To encrypt the `hello world` string, run the following command:

```
curl -k https://dev-usr:dev-pwd@localhost:8443/config/encrypt --data-
urlencode "hello world"
```

It is important to use the `--data-urlencode` flag when using `curl` to call the /encrypt endpoint, so as to ensure the correct handling of special characters such as `'+'`.

Expect a response along the lines of the following:

```
9eca39e823957f37f0f0f4d8b2c6c46cd49ef461d1cab20c65710823a8b412ce
$
```

To decrypt the encrypted value, run the following command:

```
curl -k https://dev-usr:dev-pwd@localhost:8443/config/decrypt -d
9eca39e823957f37f0f0f4d8b2c6c46cd49ef461d1cab20c65710823a8b412ce
```

Expect the `hello world` string as the response:

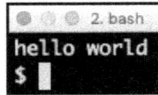

If you want to use an encrypted value in a configuration file, you need to prefix it with `{cipher}` and wrap it in `''`. For example, to store the encrypted version of `hello world`, execute the following command:

```
my-secret:'{cipher}9eca39e823957f37f0f0f4d8b2c
6c46cd49ef461d1cab20c65710823a8b412ce'
```

These tests conclude the chapter on centralized configuration. Wrap it up by shutting down the system landscape:

```
docker-compose down
```

Summary

In this chapter, we have seen how we can use the Spring Cloud Configuration server to centralize managing the configuration of our microservices. We can place the configuration files in a common configuration repository and share common configurations in a single configuration file while keeping microservice-specific configuration in microservice specific configuration files. The microservices have been updated to retrieve their configuration from the config server at startup and are configured to handle temporary outages while retrieving their configuration from the config server.

The config server can protect configuration information by requiring authenticated usage of its API with basic HTTP authentication, and can prevent eavesdropping by exposing its API externally through the edge server that uses HTTPS. To prevent intruders who obtained access to the configuration files on disk from gaining access to sensitive information such as passwords, we can use the config server `/encrypt` endpoint to encrypt the information and store it encrypted on disk.

While exposing the APIs from the config server externally is useful during development, they should be locked down before use in production.

In the next chapter, we will learn how we can use *Resilience4j* to mitigate the potential drawbacks of overusing synchronous communication between microservices. If we, for example, establish chains of microservices that call each other synchronously using REST APIs, and the last microservice stops responding, bad things can happen that affect many of the microservices involved. Resilience4j comes with an implementation of the circuit breaker pattern, which can be used to handle these types of problem.

Questions

1. What API call can we expect from a review service to the config server during startup to retrieve its configuration? The review service was started up using the following command: `docker compose up -d`.
2. What configuration information should we expect back from an API call to the config server using this command:

   ```
   curl
   https://dev-usr:dev-pwd@localhost:8443/config/application/default -
   ks | jq
   ```

3. What types of repository backend does Spring Cloud Config support?
4. How can we encrypt sensitive information on disk using Spring Cloud Config?
5. How can we protect the config server API from misuse?
6. Mention some pros and cons for clients that first connect to the config server as opposed to those that first connect to the discovery server.

13
Improving Resilience Using Resilience4j

In this chapter, we will learn how to use Resilience4j to make our microservices more resilient, that is, how to mitigate and recover from errors. As we already discussed in Chapter 1, *Introduction to Microservices*, in the *Circuit breaker* section, and Chapter 8, *Introduction to Spring Cloud*, the *Resilience4j for improved resilience* section, a circuit breaker can be used to minimize the damage that a slow or not-responding downstream microservice can cause in a large-scale system landscape of synchronously communicating microservices. We will see how the circuit breaker in Resilience4j can be used together with a timeout and retry mechanism to prevent two—in my experience—of the most common error situations:

- Microservices that start to respond slowly or not at all
- Requests that randomly fail from time to time, for example, due to temporary network problems

The following topics will be covered in this chapter:

- Introducing the Resilience4j circuit breaker and retry mechanism
- Adding a circuit breaker and retry mechanism to the source code
- Trying out the circuit breaker and retry mechanism

Technical requirements

All the commands that are described in this book are run on a MacBook Pro using macOS Mojave but should be straightforward to modify if you want to run them on another platform such as Linux or Windows.

No new tools need to be installed in this chapter.

The source code for this chapter can be found in this book's GitHub repository: `https://github.com/PacktPublishing/Hands-On-Microservices-with-Spring-Boot-and-Spring-Cloud/tree/master/Chapter13`.

To be able to run the commands that are described in this book, download the source code to a folder and set up an environment variable, `$BOOK_HOME`, that points to that folder. Some sample commands are as follows:

```
export BOOK_HOME=~/Documents/Hands-On-Microservices-with-Spring-Boot-and-
Spring-Cloud
git clone
https://github.com/PacktPublishing/Hands-On-Microservices-with-Spring-Boot-
and-Spring-Cloud $BOOK_HOME
cd $BOOK_HOME/Chapter13
```

The Java source code is written for Java 8 and tested on Java 12. This chapter uses Spring Cloud 2.1.0, SR1 (also known as the **Greenwich** release), Spring Boot 2.1.4, and Spring 5.1.6, that is, the latest available version of the Spring components at the time of writing this chapter.

The `openjdk:12.0.2` base Docker image is used in all the Dockerfiles.

The source code contains the following Gradle projects:

- `api`
- `util`
- `microservices/product-service`
- `microservices/review-service`
- `microservices/recommendation-service`
- `microservices/product-composite-service`
- `spring-cloud/eureka-server`
- `spring-cloud/gateway`
- `spring-cloud/authorization-server`
- `spring-cloud/config-server`

The configuration files can be found in the config repository, `config-repo`.

All the source code examples in this chapter come from the source code in `$BOOK_HOME/Chapter13` but in several cases have been edited to remove irrelevant parts of the source code, such as comments, imports, and log statements.

If you want to see the changes that were applied to the source code in this chapter, that is, see what it took to add resilience using Resilience4j, you can compare it with the source code for `Chapter 12`, *Centralized Configuration*. You can use your favorite `diff` tool and compare the two folders, `$BOOK_HOME/Chapter12` and `$BOOK_HOME/Chapter13`.

Introducing the Resilience4j circuit breaker and retry mechanism

Retries and circuit breakers are potentially useful in any synchronous communication between two software components, for example, microservices. Resilience4j can be used by all our microservices except for the edge server since Spring Cloud Gateway currently only supports the older circuit breaker, Netflix Hystrix. In this chapter, we will apply a circuit breaker and a retry mechanism in one place, in calls to the `product` service from the `product-composite` service. This is illustrated in the following diagram:

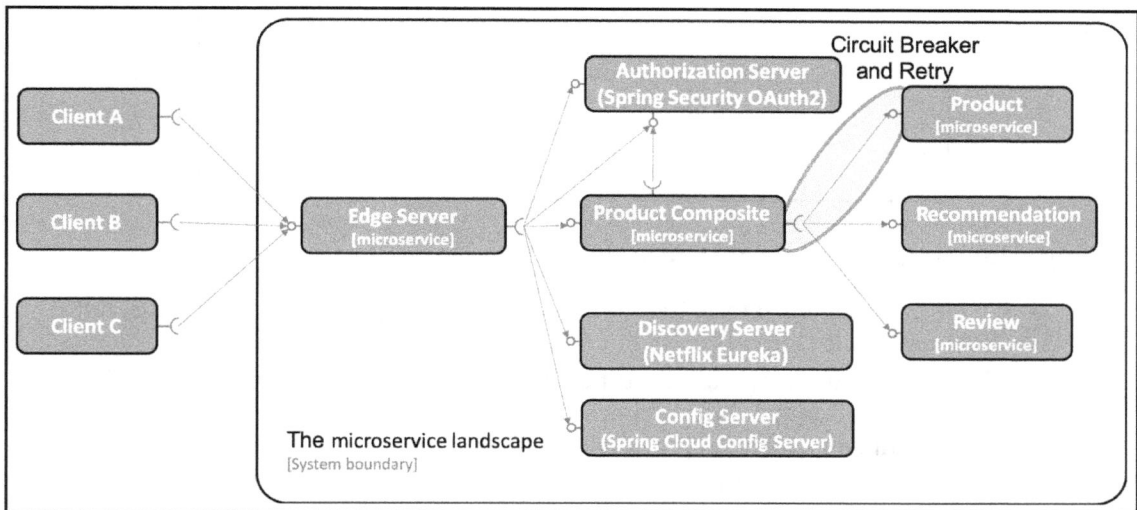

Note that the synchronous calls to the discovery and config servers from the other microservices are not shown in the preceding diagram (to make it easier to read).

> Work is ongoing as this chapter was written to add an abstraction layer for circuit breakers in Spring Cloud, something Spring Cloud Gateway will probably be able to benefit from. For details, see `https://spring.io/blog/2019/04/16/introducing-spring-cloud-circuit-breaker`.

Introducing the circuit breaker

Let's quickly revisit the state diagram for a circuit breaker from `Chapter 8`, *Introduction to Spring Cloud*, in the *Resilience4j for improved resilience* section:

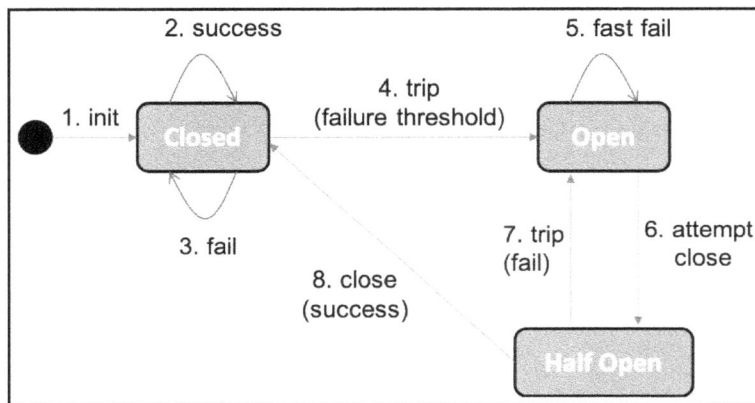

The key features of a circuit breaker are as follows:

- If a circuit breaker detects too many faults, it will open its circuit, that is, not allow new calls.
- When the circuit is open, a circuit breaker will perform fast failure logic. This means that it doesn't wait for a new fault, for example, a timeout, to happen on subsequent calls. Instead, it directly redirects the call to a **fallback method**. The fallback method can apply various business logic to produce the best effort response. For example, a fallback method can return data from a local cache or simply return an immediate error message. This will prevent a microservice from getting unresponsive if the services it depends on stop responding normally. This is specifically useful under high load.

- After a while, the circuit breaker will be half-open, allowing new calls to see whether the issue that caused the failures is gone. If new failures are detected by the circuit breaker, it will open the circuit again and go back to the fast failure logic. Otherwise, it will close the circuit and go back to normal operation. This makes a microservice resilient to faults, a capability that is indispensable in a system landscape of microservices that communicate synchronously with each other!

Resilience4j exposes information about circuit breakers at runtime in a number of ways:

- The current state of a circuit breaker can be monitored using the microservice's actuator `health` endpoint, `/actuator/health`.
- The circuit breaker also publishes events on an `actuator` endpoint, for example, state transitions, `/actuator/circuitbreakerevents`.
- Finally, circuit breakers are integrated with Spring Boot's metrics system and can use it to publish metrics to monitoring tools such as Prometheus.

We will try out the `health` and `event` endpoints in this chapter. In `Chapter 20`, *Monitoring Microservices*, we will see Prometheus in action and how it can collect metrics that are exposed by Spring Boot, for example, metrics from our circuit breaker.

To control the logic in a circuit breaker, Resilience4J can be configured using standard Spring Boot configuration files. We will use the following configuration parameters:

- `ringBufferSizeInClosedState`: Number of calls in a closed state, which are used to determine whether the circuit shall be opened.
- `failureRateThreshold`: The threshold, in percent, for failed calls that will cause the circuit to be opened.
- `waitInterval`: Specifies how long the circuit stays in an open state, that is, before it transitions to the half-open state.
- `ringBufferSizeInHalfOpenState`: The number of calls in the half-open state that are used to determine whether the circuit shall be opened again or go back to the normal, closed state.
- `automaticTransitionFromOpenToHalfOpenEnabled`: Determines whether the circuit automatically will transition to half-open once the wait period is over or wait for the first call after the waiting period until it transitions to the half-open state.

- `ignoreExceptions`: Can be used to specify exceptions that should not be counted as faults. Expected business exceptions such as not found or invalid input are typical exceptions that the circuit breaker should ignore, that is, users that search for non-existing data or enter invalid input should not cause the circuit to open.

> Resilience4j keeps track of successful and failed calls when in the closed and half-open state using a ring buffer, hence the parameter names `ringBufferSizeInClosedState` and `ringBufferSizeInHalfOpenState`.

In this chapter, we will use the following settings:

- `ringBufferSizeInClosedState = 5` and `failureRateThreshold = 50%`, meaning that if three or more of the last five calls are faults, then the circuit will open.
- `waitInterval = 10000` and `automaticTransitionFromOpenToHalfOpenEnabled = true`, meaning that the circuit breaker will keep the circuit open for 10 seconds and then transition to the half-open state.
- `ringBufferSizeInHalfOpenState = 3`, meaning that the circuit breaker will decide whether the circuit shall be opened or closed based on the three first calls after the circuit has transitioned to the half-open state. Since the `failureRateThreshold` parameters are set to 50%, the circuit will be open again if two or all three calls fail. Otherwise, the circuit will be closed.
- `ignoreExceptions = InvalidInputException` and `NotFoundException`, meaning that our two business exceptions will not be counted as faults in the circuit breaker.

Introducing the retry mechanism

The **retry** mechanism is very useful for random and infrequent faults, such as temporary network glitches. The retry mechanism can simply retry a failed request a number of times with a configurable delay between the attempts. One very important restriction on the use of the retry mechanism is that the services that it retries must be **idempotent**, that is, calling the service one or many times with the same request parameters gives the same result. For example, reading information is idempotent but creating information is typically not. You don't want a retry mechanism to accidentally create two orders just because the response from the first order's creation got lost in the network.

Resilience4j exposes retry information in the same way as it does for circuit breakers when it comes to events and metrics but does not provide any health information. Retry events are accessible on the `actuator` endpoint, `/actuator/retryevents`. To control the retry logic, Resilience4J can be configured using standard Spring Boot configuration files. We will use the following configuration parameters:

- `maxRetryAttempts`: Number of retries before giving up, including the first call
- `waitDuration`: Wait time before the next retry attempt
- `retryExceptions`: A list of exceptions that shall trigger a retry

In this chapter, we will use the following values:

- `maxRetryAttempts = 3`: We will make a maximum of two retry attempts.
- `waitDuration= 1000`: We will wait one second between retries.
- `retryExceptions = InternalServerError`: We will only trigger retries on `InternalServerError` exceptions, that is, when HTTP requests respond with a 500 status code.

> Be careful when configuring retry and circuit breaker settings so that, for example, the circuit breaker doesn't open the circuit before the intended number of retries have been completed!

Adding a circuit breaker and retry mechanism to the source code

Before we add a circuit breaker and a retry mechanism to the source code, we will add code that makes it possible to force an error to occur—either a delay and/or a random fault. Next, we will add a circuit breaker to handle slow or not responding APIs, as well as a retry mechanism that can handle faults that happens randomly. Adding these features from Resilience4j follows the traditional Spring Boot way:

- Add a starter dependency for Resilience4j in the build file.
- Add annotations in the source code where the circuit breaker and retry mechanism shall be applied.
- Add configuration that controls the behavior of the circuit breaker and retry mechanism.

Once we have the circuit breaker and retry mechanism in place, we will extend our test script, `test-em-all.bash`, with the tests of the circuit breaker.

Adding programmable delays and random errors

To be able to test our circuit breaker and retry mechanism, we need a way to control when errors happen. A simple way to achieve this is by adding optional query parameters in the API in order to retrieve a product and a composite product. The composite product API will simply pass on the parameters to the product API. The following query parameters have been added to the two APIs:

- `delay`: Causes the `getProduct` API on the `product` microservice to delay its response. The parameter is specified in seconds. For example, if the parameter is set to 3, it will cause a delay of three seconds before the response is returned.

- `faultPercentage`: Causes the `getProduct` API on the `product` microservice to throw an exception randomly with the probability specified by the query parameter, from 0 to 100%. For example, if the parameter is set to 25, it will cause every fourth call to the API, on average, to fail with an exception. It will return an HTTP error 500 internal server error in these cases.

Changes in the API definitions

The two query parameters that we introduced previously, `delay` and `faultPercentage`, have been defined in the `api` project in the following two Java interfaces:

- `se.magnus.api.composite.product.ProductCompositeService`:

```
Mono<ProductAggregate> getCompositeProduct(
    @PathVariable int productId,
    @RequestParam(value = "delay", required = false, defaultValue =
    "0") int delay,
    @RequestParam(value = "faultPercent", required = false,
    defaultValue = "0") int faultPercent
);
```

- `se.magnus.api.core.product.ProductService`:

```
Mono<Product> getProduct(
    @PathVariable int productId,
    @RequestParam(value = "delay", required = false, defaultValue
    = "0") int delay,
    @RequestParam(value = "faultPercent", required = false,
```

```
        defaultValue = "0") int faultPercent
);
```

Changes in the product composite microservice

The `product-composite` microservice simply passes the parameters to the product API. The service implementation receives the API request and passes on the parameters to the integration component that makes the call to the product API:

- The call to the
  `se.magnus.microservices.composite.product.services.ProductCompo`
  `siteServiceImpl` class:

  ```java
  public Mono<ProductAggregate> getCompositeProduct(int productId,
  int delay, int faultPercent) {
      return Mono.zip(
          ...
          integration.getProduct(productId, delay, faultPercent),
          ....
  ```

- The call to the
  `se.magnus.microservices.composite.product.services.ProductCompo`
  `siteIntegration` class:

  ```java
  public Mono<Product> getProduct(int productId, int delay, int
  faultPercent) {
      URI url = UriComponentsBuilder
          .fromUriString(productServiceUrl + "/product/{pid}?delay=
          {delay}&faultPercent={fp}")
          .build(productId, delay, faultPercent);
      return getWebClient().get().uri(url)...
  ```

Changes in the product microservice

The `product` microservice implements actual delay and random error generator in `se.magnus.microservices.core.product.services.ProductServiceImpl` as follows:

```java
public Mono<Product> getProduct(int productId, int delay, int faultPercent)
{
    if (delay > 0) simulateDelay(delay);
    if (faultPercent > 0) throwErrorIfBadLuck(faultPercent);
    ...
}
```

The delay function, `simulateDelay()`, uses the `Thread.sleep()` function to simulate a delay:

```
private void simulateDelay(int delay) {
    LOG.debug("Sleeping for {} seconds...", delay);
    try {Thread.sleep(delay * 1000);} catch (InterruptedException e) {}
    LOG.debug("Moving on...");
}
```

The random error generator, `throwErrorIfBadLuck()`, creates a random number between 1 and 100 and throws an exception if it is higher or equal to the specified fault percentage:

```
private void throwErrorIfBadLuck(int faultPercent) {
    int randomThreshold = getRandomNumber(1, 100);
    if (faultPercent < randomThreshold) {
        LOG.debug("We got lucky, no error occurred, {} < {}",
        faultPercent, randomThreshold);
    } else {
        LOG.debug("Bad luck, an error occurred, {} >= {}",
        faultPercent, randomThreshold);
        throw new RuntimeException("Something went wrong...");
    }
}

private final Random randomNumberGenerator = new Random();
private int getRandomNumber(int min, int max) {
    if (max < min) {
        throw new RuntimeException("Max must be greater than min");
    }
    return randomNumberGenerator.nextInt((max - min) + 1) + min;
}
```

Adding a circuit breaker

As we mentioned previously, we need to add dependencies, annotations, and configuration. We also need to add some code for handling timeouts and fallback logic. We will see how to do this in the following sections.

Adding dependencies to the build file

To add a circuit breaker, we have to add dependencies to the appropriate Resilience4j libraries in the build file, `build.gradle`:

```
ext {
    resilience4jVersion = "0.14.1"
}
dependencies {
    implementation("io.github.resilience4j:resilience4j-spring-
    boot2:${resilience4jVersion}")
    implementation("io.github.resilience4j:resilience4j-
    reactor:${resilience4jVersion}")
    ...
```

Adding the circuit breaker and timeout logic

The circuit breaker can be applied by annotating the method it is expected to protect with `@CircuitBreaker(name="nnn")`, which in this case is the `getProduct()` method in the `se.magnus.microservices.composite.product.services.ProductCompositeIntegration` class. The circuit breaker is triggered by an exception, not by a timeout itself. To be able to trigger the circuit breaker after a timeout, we have to add code that generates an exception after a timeout. Using `WebClient`, which is based on Project Reactor, allows us to do that conveniently by using its `timeout(Duration)` method. The source code looks as follows:

```
@CircuitBreaker(name = "product")
public Mono<Product> getProduct(int productId, int delay, int faultPercent)
{
    ...
    return getWebClient().get().uri(url)
        .retrieve().bodyToMono(Product.class).log()
        .onErrorMap(WebClientResponseException.class, ex ->
        handleException(ex))
        .timeout(Duration.ofSeconds(productServiceTimeoutSec));
}
```

The name of the circuit breaker, `"product"`, is used to identify the configuration that we will go through. The timeout parameter, `productServiceTimeoutSec`, is injected into the constructor as a configurable parameter value:

```
private final int productServiceTimeoutSec;

@Autowired
public ProductCompositeIntegration(
    ...
    @Value("${app.product-service.timeoutSec}") int
productServiceTimeoutSec
) {
    ...
    this.productServiceTimeoutSec = productServiceTimeoutSec;
}
```

> To activate the circuit breaker, the annotated method must be invoked as a Spring Bean. In our case, it's the integration class that's injected by Spring into the service implementation class and therefore used as a Spring Bean:
>
> ```
> private final ProductCompositeIntegration integration;
>
> @Autowired
> public ProductCompositeServiceImpl(...
> ProductCompositeIntegration integration) {
>     this.integration = integration;
> }
>
> public Mono<ProductAggregate> getCompositeProduct(int
> productId, int delay, int faultPercent) {
>     return Mono.zip(..., integration.getProduct(productId,
> delay, faultPercent), ...
> ```

Adding fast fail fallback logic

To be able to apply fallback logic when the circuit breaker is open, that is, when a request fast fails, we can catch an exception, `CircuitBreakerOpenException`, that is thrown by the circuit breaker when it is open and call a fallback method. This has to be done outside of the circuit breaker, that is, in the caller. In our case, it is the `product-composite` service's implementation that calls the integration class.

Here, we use the `onErrorReturn` method to call the `getProductFallbackValue()` method when we catch `CircuitBreakerOpenException`:

```
public Mono<ProductAggregate> getCompositeProduct(int productId, int delay,
int faultPercent) {
    return Mono.zip(
        ...
        integration.getProduct(productId, delay, faultPercent)
            .onErrorReturn(CircuitBreakerOpenException.class,
            getProductFallbackValue(productId)),
        ...
```

The fallback logic can be based on `productId` lookup information on the product from alternative sources, for example, an internal cache. In our case, we return a hardcoded value unless `productId` is `13`; otherwise, we throw a not found exception:

```
private Product getProductFallbackValue(int productId) {
    if (productId == 13) {
        throw new NotFoundException("Product Id: " + productId + " not
        found in fallback cache!");
    }
    return new Product(productId, "Fallback product" + productId,
    productId, serviceUtil.getServiceAddress());
}
```

Adding configuration

Finally, the configuration of the circuit breaker is added to the `product-composite.yml` file in the config repository, as follows:

```
app.product-service.timeoutSec: 2

resilience4j.circuitbreaker:
  backends:
    product:
      registerHealthIndicator: true
      ringBufferSizeInClosedState: 5
      failureRateThreshold: 50
      waitInterval: 10000
      ringBufferSizeInHalfOpenState: 3
      automaticTransitionFromOpenToHalfOpenEnabled: true
      ignoreExceptions:
        - se.magnus.util.exceptions.InvalidInputException
        - se.magnus.util.exceptions.NotFoundException
```

Most of the values in the configuration have already been described in *Introducing the circuit breaker* section, except for the following:

- `app.product-service.timeoutSec`: Used to configure the timeout we introduced previously. This is set to two seconds.
- `registerHealthIndicator`: Determines whether the circuit breaker shall display information in the `health` endpoint or not. This is set to `true`.

Adding a retry mechanism

In the same way as for the circuit breaker, a retry mechanism is set up by adding dependencies, annotations, and configuration. The dependencies were added previously, so we only need to add the annotation and set up some configuration. We, however, also need to add some error handling logic due to retry-specific exceptions that the retry mechanism throws.

Adding the retry annotation

The retry mechanism can be applied to a method by annotating it with `@Retry(name="nnn")`, where `nnn` is the name of the configuration entry to be used for this method. See the *Adding configuration* section for details on the configuration. The method, in our case, is the same as it is for the circuit breaker, that is, `getProduct()` in the `se.magnus.microservices.composite.product.services.ProductCompositeIntegration` class:

```
@Retry(name = "product")
@CircuitBreaker(name = "product")
public Mono<Product> getProduct(int productId, int delay, int faultPercent)
{
```

Handling retry-specific exceptions

Exceptions that are thrown by a method annotated with `@Retry` can be wrapped by the retry mechanism with a `RetryExceptionWrapper` exception. To be able to handle the actual exception that the method threw, for example, to apply a fallback method when `CircuitBreakerOpenException` is thrown, the caller needs to add logic that unwraps `RetryExceptionWrapper` exceptions and replaces them with the actual exception.

In our case, it is the `getCompositeProduct` method in the `ProductCompositeServiceImpl` class that makes the call using the Project Reactor API for `Mono` objects. The `Mono` API has a convenient method, `onErrorMap`, that can be used to unwrap `RetryExceptionWrapper` exceptions. It is used in the `getCompositeProduct` method like so:

```
public Mono<ProductAggregate> getCompositeProduct(int productId, int delay,
int faultPercent) {
    return Mono.zip(
        ...
        integration.getProduct(productId, delay, faultPercent)
            .onErrorMap(RetryExceptionWrapper.class, retryException ->
            retryException.getCause())
            .onErrorReturn(CircuitBreakerOpenException.class,
            getProductFallbackValue(productId)),
```

Adding configuration

Configuration for the retry mechanism is added in the same way as it is for the circuit breaker, that is, in the `product-composite.yml` file in the config repository, like so:

```
resilience4j.retry:
  backends:
    product:
      maxRetryAttempts: 3
      waitDuration: 1000
      retryExceptions:
      -
org.springframework.web.reactive.function.client.WebClientResponseException
$InternalServerError
```

The actual values were discussed in *Introducing the retry mechanism* section.

Adding automated tests

Automated tests for the circuit breaker have been added to the `test-em-all.bash` test script in a separate function, `testCircuitBreaker()`:

```
...
function testCircuitBreaker() {
    echo "Start Circuit Breaker tests!"
    ...
```

```
}
...
testCircuitBreaker
echo "End, all tests OK:" `date`
```

To be able to perform some of the required verifications, we need to have access to the `actuator` endpoints of the `product-composite` microservice, which are not exposed through the edge server. Therefore, we will access the `actuator` endpoints through a separate Docker container that will be attached to the internal network that was set up by Docker Compose for our microservices.

By default, the name of the network is based on the name of the folder where the Docker Compose file is placed. To avoid that uncertain dependency, an explicit network name, `my-network`, is defined in the `docker-compose` files. All container definitions have been updated to specify that they shall attach to the `my-network` network. The following is an example from `docker-compose.yml`:

```
...
  product:
    build: microservices/product-service
    networks:
      - my-network
...
networks:
  my-network:
    name: my-network
```

Since the container is attached to the internal network, it can access the `actuator` endpoints of the product composite without going through the edge server. We will use Alpine as our Docker image and use `wget` instead of `curl` since `curl` isn't included in the Alpine distribution by default. For example, to be able to find out the state of the circuit breaker named `product` in the `product-composite` microservice, we can run the following command:

```
docker run --rm -it --network=my-network alpine wget product-
composite:8080/actuator/health -qO - | jq -r
.details.productCircuitBreaker.details.state
```

The command is expected to return a value of CLOSED.

> Since we have created the Docker container with the `--rm` flag, it will be stopped and destroyed by the Docker engine after the `wget` command completes.

The test starts by doing exactly this, that is, verifying that the circuit breaker is closed before the tests are executed:

```
EXEC="docker run --rm -it --network=my-network alpine"
assertEqual "CLOSED" "$($EXEC wget product-composite:8080/actuator/health -
qO - | jq -r .details.productCircuitBreaker.details.state)"
```

Next, the test will force the circuit breaker to open up by running three commands in a row, all of which will fail on a slow response from the `product` service:

```
for ((n=0; n<3; n++))
do
    assertCurl 500 "curl -k https://$HOST:$PORT/product-
    composite/$PROD_ID_REVS_RECS?delay=3 $AUTH -s"
    message=$(echo $RESPONSE | jq -r .message)
    assertEqual "Did not observe any item or terminal signal within
    2000ms" "${message:0:57}"
done
```

> **Quick repetition of the configuration**: The timeout of the `product` service is set to two seconds so that a delay of three seconds will cause a timeout. The circuit breaker is configured to evaluate the last five last calls when closed. The tests in the script that precede the circuit breaker-specific tests have already performed a couple of successful calls. The failure threshold is set to 50%, that is, three calls with a three-second delay is enough to open the circuit.

With the circuit open, we expect a fast failure, that is, we won't need to wait for the timeout before we get a response. We also expect the `fallback` method to be called to return a best-effort response. This should also apply for a normal call, that is, without requesting a delay. This is verified with the following code:

```
assertCurl 200 "curl -k
https://$HOST:$PORT/product-composite/$PROD_ID_REVS_RECS?delay=3 $AUTH -s"
assertEqual "Fallback product2" "$(echo "$RESPONSE" | jq -r .name)"

assertCurl 200 "curl -k
https://$HOST:$PORT/product-composite/$PROD_ID_REVS_RECS $AUTH -s"
assertEqual "Fallback product2" "$(echo "$RESPONSE" | jq -r .name)"
```

We can also verify that the simulated not found error logic works as expected in the fallback method, that is, the fallback method returns 404, NOT_FOUND for product ID 13:

```
assertCurl 404 "curl -k
https://$HOST:$PORT/product-composite/$PROD_ID_NOT_FOUND $AUTH -s"
assertEqual "Product Id: $PROD_ID_NOT_FOUND not found in fallback cache!"
"$(echo $RESPONSE | jq -r .message)"
```

As configured, the circuit breaker will change its state to half-open after 10 seconds. To be able to verify that, the test waits for 10 seconds:

```
echo "Will sleep for 10 sec waiting for the CB to go Half Open..."
sleep 10
```

After verifying the expected state (half-closed), the test runs three normal requests to make the circuit breaker go back to its normal state, which is also verified:

```
assertEqual "HALF_OPEN" "$($EXEC wget product-
composite:8080/actuator/health -qO - | jq -r
.details.productCircuitBreaker.details.state)"

for ((n=0; n<3; n++))
do
    assertCurl 200 "curl -k https://$HOST:$PORT/product-
    composite/$PROD_ID_REVS_RECS $AUTH -s"
    assertEqual "product name C" "$(echo "$RESPONSE" | jq -r .name)"
done

assertEqual "CLOSED" "$($EXEC wget product-composite:8080/actuator/health -
qO - | jq -r .details.productCircuitBreaker.details.state)"
```

> **Quick repetition of the configuration:** The circuit breaker is configured to evaluate the first three calls when in the half-open state. Therefore, we need to run three requests where more than 50% are successful before the circuit is closed.

The test wraps up by using the /actuator/circuitbreakerevents actuator API, which is exposed by the circuit breaker to reveal internal events. It can, for example, be used to find out what state transitions the circuit breaker has performed. We expect the last three state transitions to be as follows:

- First state transitions: Closed to open
- Next state transitions: Open to half-closed
- Last state transitions: Half-closed to closed

This is verified by the following code:

```
assertEqual "CLOSED_TO_OPEN"        "$($EXEC wget product-
composite:8080/actuator/circuitbreakerevents/product/STATE_TRANSITION -qO -
| jq -r .circuitBreakerEvents[-3].stateTransition)"
assertEqual "OPEN_TO_HALF_OPEN"     "$($EXEC wget product-
composite:8080/actuator/circuitbreakerevents/product/STATE_TRANSITION -qO -
| jq -r .circuitBreakerEvents[-2].stateTransition)"
assertEqual "HALF_OPEN_TO_CLOSED" "$($EXEC wget product-
composite:8080/actuator/circuitbreakerevents/product/STATE_TRANSITION -qO -
| jq -r .circuitBreakerEvents[-1].stateTransition)"
```

> The `jq` expression, `circuitBreakerEvents[-1]`, means the last entry in the array of circuit breaker events, `[-2]`, is the second to last event, while `[-3 ]` is the third to last event. Together, they are the three latest events, that is, the ones we are interested in. By default, Resilience4j keeps the last 100 events per circuit breaker. This can be customized using the `eventConsumerBufferSize` configuration parameter.

We added quite a lot of steps to the test script, but with this, we can automatically verify that the expected basic behavior of our circuit breaker is in place. In the next section, we will try it out!

Trying out the circuit breaker and retry mechanism

Now, it's time to try out the circuit breaker and retry mechanism. We will start, as usual, by building the Docker images and running the test script, `test-em-all.bash`. After that, we will run through the tests we described previously manually to ensure that we understand what's going on! We will perform the following manual tests:

- Happy days tests of the circuit breaker, that is, to verify that the circuit is closed under normal operations
- Negative tests of the circuit breaker, that is, to verify that the circuit opens up when things start to go wrong
- Going back to normal operation, that is, to verify that the circuit goes back to its closed state once the problems are resolved
- Trying out the retry mechanism with random errors

Building and running the automated tests

In order to build and run the automated tests, we need to do the following:

1. First, build the Docker images with the following commands:

```
cd $BOOK_HOME/Chapter13
./gradlew build && docker-compose build
```

2. Next, start the system landscape in Docker and run the usual tests with the following command:

```
./test-em-all.bash start
```

> When the test script prints out Start Circuit Breaker tests!, the tests we described previously are executed!

Verifying that the circuit is closed under normal operations

Before we can call the API, we need an access token. Run the following commands to acquire an access token:

```
unset ACCESS_TOKEN
ACCESS_TOKEN=$(curl -k https://writer:secret@localhost:8443/oauth/token -d
grant_type=password -d username=magnus -d password=password -s | jq -r
.access_token)
echo $ACCESS_TOKEN
```

Try a normal request and verify that it returns the HTTP response code 200:

```
curl -H "Authorization: Bearer $ACCESS_TOKEN" -k
https://localhost:8443/product-composite/2 -w "%{http_code}\n" -o /dev/null
-s
```

> The -w "%{http_code}\n" switch is used to print the HTTP return status. As long as the command returns 200, we are not interested in the response body, and so we suppress it with the switch, that is, -o /dev/null.

Verify that the circuit breaker is closed using the `health` API:

```
docker run --rm -it --network=my-network alpine wget product-
composite:8080/actuator/health -qO - | jq -r
.details.productCircuitBreaker.details.state
```

We expect it to respond with CLOSED.

Forcing the circuit breaker to open when things go wrong

Now, it's time to make things go wrong! By that, I mean it's time to try out some negative tests in order to verify that the circuit opens up when things start to go wrong. Call the API three times and direct the `product` service to cause a timeout on every call, that is, delay the response with 3 seconds. This should be enough to trip the circuit breaker:

```
curl -H "Authorization: Bearer $ACCESS_TOKEN" -k
https://localhost:8443/product-composite/2?delay=3 -s | jq .
```

We expect a response such as the following each time:

```
{
    "timestamp": "2019-05-03T15:12:57.554+0000",
    "path": "/product-composite/2",
    "status": 500,
    "error": "Internal Server Error",
    "message": "Did not observe any item or terminal signal within 2000ms
     in 'onErrorResume' (and no fallback has been configured)"
}
```

The circuit breaker is now open, so if you make a fourth attempt (within `waitInterval`, that is, 10 seconds), you will see a fast fail and the `fallback` method in action. You will get a response back immediately, instead of an error message once the timeout kicks in after 2 seconds:

```
{
    "productId": 2,
    "name": "Fallback product2",
    ...
}
```

The response will come from the fallback method. This can be recognized by looking at the value in the name field, that is, `Fallback product2`.

> Fast fail and fallback methods are key capabilities of a circuit breaker! Given our configuration with a wait time set to only 10 seconds requires you to be rather quick to be able to see fast fail and fallback methods in action! Once in a half-open state, you can always submit three new requests that cause a timeout, forcing the circuit breaker back to the open state, and then quickly try the fourth request. Then, you should get a fast fail response from the fallback method! You can also increase the wait time to a minute or two, but it can be rather boring to wait that amount of time before the circuit switches to the half-open state.

Wait 10 seconds, for the circuit breaker to transition to half-open and then run the following command to verify that the circuit now is in a half-open state:

```
docker run --rm -it --network=my-network alpine wget product-composite:8080/actuator/health -qO - | jq -r
.details.productCircuitBreaker.details.state
```

Expect it to respond with HALF_OPEN.

Closing the circuit breaker again

Once the circuit breaker is in a half-open state, it waits for three calls to see whether it should open the circuit again or go back to normal, that is, close it.

Let's submit three normal requests to close the circuit breaker:

```
curl -H "Authorization: Bearer $ACCESS_TOKEN" -k
https://localhost:8443/product-composite/2 -w "%{http_code}\n" -o /dev/null
-s
```

They should all response with 200. Verify that the circuit is closed again by using the health API:

```
docker run --rm -it --network=my-network alpine wget product-composite:8080/actuator/health -qO - | jq -r
.details.productCircuitBreaker.details.state
```

We expect it to respond with CLOSED.

Wrap this up by listing the last three state transitions using the following command:

```
docker run --rm -it --network=my-network alpine wget product-
composite:8080/actuator/circuitbreakerevents/product/STATE_TRANSITION -qO -
| jq -r '.circuitBreakerEvents[-3].stateTransition,
.circuitBreakerEvents[-2].stateTransition,
.circuitBreakerEvents[-1].stateTransition'
```

Expect it to respond with the following command:

```
CLOSED_TO_OPEN
OPEN_TO_HALF_OPEN
HALF_OPEN_TO_CLOSED
```

This response tells us that we have taken our circuit breaker through a full lap of its state diagram:

- From closed to open when an error starts to prevent requests from succeeding
- From open to half-open to see whether the error is gone
- From half-open to closed when the error is gone, that is, when we are back to normal operation

Trying out retries caused by random errors

Let's simulate that there is a – hopefully temporary – random issue with our `product` service or the communication with it.

We can do this by using the `faultPercent` parameter. If we set it to `25`, we expect every fourth request to fail. We hope that the retry mechanism will kick in to help us by automatically retrying the request. One way of noticing that the retry mechanism has kicked in is to measure the response time of the `curl` command. A normal response should take no more than 100 ms. Since we have configured the retry mechanism to wait one second (see the `waitDuration` parameter in the configuration of the preceding retry mechanism), we expect the response time to increase with one second per retry attempt. To force a random error to occur, run the following command a couple of times:

```
time curl -H "Authorization: Bearer $ACCESS_TOKEN" -k
https://localhost:8443/product-composite/2?faultPercent=25 -w
"%{http_code}\n" -o /dev/null -s
```

The command should respond with 200, indicating that the request succeeded. A response time prefixed with real, for example, real 0m0.078s means that the response time was 0.078 s or 78 ms. A normal response, that is, without any retries, should look as follows:

```
200
real  0m0.078s
...
```

A response after one retry should look as follows:

```
200
real  0m1.077s
```

> The HTTP status code 200 indicates that the request has succeeded, even though it required one retry before succeeding!

After you have noticed a response time of one second, that is, the request required one retry to succeed, run the following command to see the last two retry events:

```
docker run --rm -it --network=my-network alpine wget product-
composite:8080/actuator/retryevents -qO - | jq '.retryEvents[-2],
.retryEvents[-1]'
```

You should be able to see the failed request and the next successful attempt. The creationTime timestamps are expected to differ by one second. Expect a response such as the following:

```
{
  "retryName": "product",
  "type": "RETRY",
  "creationTime": "2019-05-01T05:40:18.458858Z[Etc/UTC]",
  "errorMessage": "org.springframework.web.reactive.
    function.client.WebClientResponseException$InternalServerError: 500
    Internal Server Error",
  "numberOfAttempts": 1
}
{
  "retryName": "product",
  "type": "SUCCESS",
  "creationTime": "2019-05-01T05:40:19.471136Z[Etc/UTC]",
  "numberOfAttempts": 1
}
```

If you are really unlucky, you will get two faults in a row, and then you will get a response time of two seconds instead of one. If you repeat the preceding command, you will be able to see that the `numberOfAttempts` field is counted for each retry attempt, which is set to 2 in this case: `"numberOfAttempts": 2`. If calls continue to fail, the circuit breaker will kick in and open its circuit, that is, subsequent calls will fast fail and the fallback method will be applied!

That's it!

Feel free to elaborate with the parameters in the configuration to learn about the circuit breaker and retry mechanisms better!

Summary

In this chapter, we have seen Resilience4j and its circuit breaker and retry mechanism in action.

A circuit breaker can, using fast fail and `fallback` methods when it is open, prevent a microservice from becoming unresponsive if the synchronous services it depends on stop responding normally. A circuit breaker can also make a microservice resilient by allowing requests when it is half-open to see whether the failing service operates normally again and close the circuit if so.

A retry mechanism can retry requests that randomly fail from time to time, for example, due to temporary network problems. It is very important to only apply retry requests on idempotent services, that is, services that can handle that the same request is sent two or more times.

Circuit breakers and retry mechanisms are implemented by following Spring Boot conventions, that is, declaring dependencies, and adding annotations and configuration. Resilience4j exposes information about its circuit breakers and retry mechanisms at runtime, using `actuator` endpoints for health, events, and metrics for circuit breakers and events and metrics for retries.

We have seen the usage of both endpoints for health and events in this chapter, but we will have to wait until Chapter 20, *Monitoring Microservices*, before we use any of the metrics.

In the next chapter, we will cover the last part of using Spring Cloud, where we will learn how to trace call chains through a set of cooperating microservices using Spring Cloud Sleuth and Zipkin. Head over to Chapter 14, *Understanding Distributed Tracing*, to get started!

Questions

- What are the states of a circuit breaker and how are they used?
- How can we handle timeout errors in the circuit breaker?
- How can we apply fallback logic when a circuit breaker fast fails?
- How can a retry mechanism and a circuit breaker interfere with each other?
- Provide an example of a service that you can't apply a retry mechanism for.

14
Understanding Distributed Tracing

In this chapter, we will learn how to use distributed tracing to better understand how our microservices cooperate; for example, fulfilling a request sent to the external API. Being able to utilize distributed tracing is essential for being able to manage a system landscape of cooperating microservices. As already described in Chapter 8, *Introduction to Spring Cloud*, in reference to the *Spring Cloud Sleuth and Zipkin for distributed tracing* section, Spring Cloud Sleuth will be used to collect trace information, and Zipkin will be used for the storage and visualization of said trace information.

In this chapter, we will learn about the following topics:

- Introducing distributed tracing with Spring Cloud Sleuth and Zipkin
- How to add distributed tracing to the source code
- How to perform distributed tracing:
    - We will learn how to visualize trace information using Zipkin in relation to the following:
        - Successful and unsuccessful API requests
        - Synchronous and asynchronous processing of API requests
    - We will use both RabbitMQ and Kafka to send trace events from our microservices to the Zipkin server

Technical requirements

All commands described in this book are run on a MacBook Pro using macOS Mojave but should be straightforward to modify so that they can be run on another platform such as Linux or Windows.

No new tools need to be installed in this chapter.

The source code for this chapter can be found on GitHub at `https://github.com/PacktPublishing/Hands-On-Microservices-with-Spring-Boot-and-Spring-Cloud/tree/master/Chapter14`.

To be able to run the commands as described in the book, download the source code to a folder and set up an environment variable, `$BOOK_HOME`, that points to that folder. Some sample commands are as follows:

```
export BOOK_HOME=~/Documents/Hands-On-Microservices-with-Spring-Boot-and-
Spring-Cloud
git clone
https://github.com/PacktPublishing/Hands-On-Microservices-with-Spring-Boot-
and-Spring-Cloud $BOOK_HOME
cd $BOOK_HOME/Chapter14
```

The Java source code is written for Java 8 and tested on Java 12. This chapter uses Spring Cloud 2.1.0, SR1 (also known as the **Greenwich** release), Spring Boot 2.1.4, and Spring 5.1.6, that is, the latest available version of the Spring components at the time of writing this chapter.

The base Docker image, `openjdk:12.0.2`, is used in all Dockerfiles.

All source code examples in this chapter come from the source code in `$BOOK_HOME/Chapter14` but are, in several cases, edited to remove non-relevant parts of the source code, such as comments and import and log statements.

If you want to see the changes applied to the source code in this chapter, that is, see what it took to add distributed tracing using Spring Cloud Sleuth and Zipkin, you can compare it with the source code for `Chapter 13`, *Improving Resilience Using Resilience4j*. You can use your favorite `diff` tool and compare the two folders
– `$BOOK_HOME/Chapter13` and `$BOOK_HOME/Chapter14`.

Introducing distributed tracing with Spring Cloud Sleuth and Zipkin

To recapitulate from Chapter 8, *Introduction to Spring Cloud*, in reference to the *Spring Cloud Sleuth and Zipkin for distributed tracing* section, the tracing information from a complete workflow is called a **trace** or a **trace tree**, and sub-parts of the tree, for example, the basic units of work, are called a **span**. Spans can consist of sub spans forming the trace tree. The Zipkin UI can visualize a trace tree and its spans as follows:

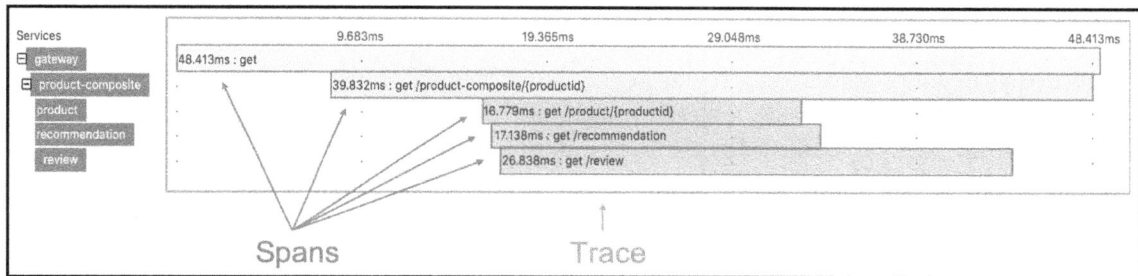

Spring Cloud Sleuth can send trace information to Zipkin either synchronously over HTTP, or asynchronously using a message broker such as RabbitMQ or Kafka. To avoid creating runtime dependencies on the Zipkin server from the microservices, it is preferable to send trace information to Zipkin asynchronously using either RabbitMQ or Kafka. This is illustrated in the following diagram:

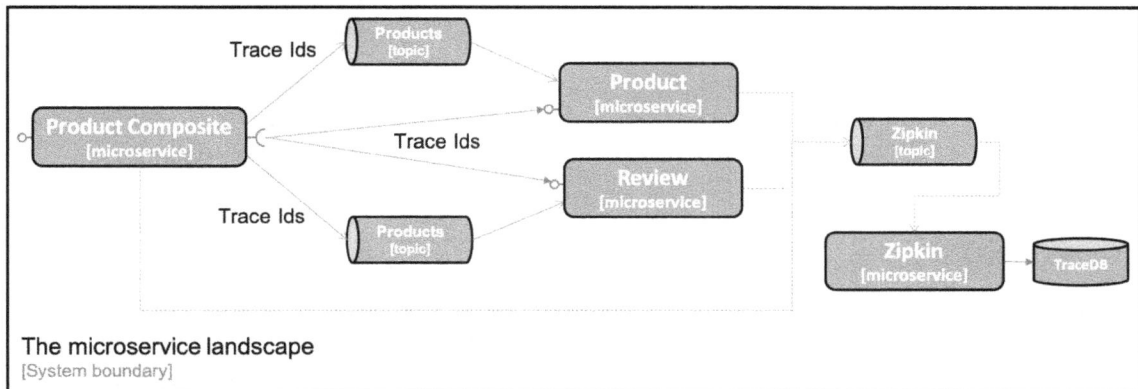

Zipkin comes with native support for storing trace information either in memory, or in Apache Cassandra, Elasticsearch, or MySQL. Added to this, a number of extensions are available. For details, refer to `https://zipkin.apache.org/pages/extensions_choices.html`. In this chapter, we will store the trace information in memory.

Adding distributed tracing to the source code

In this section, we will learn how to update the source code to enable distributed tracing using Spring Cloud Sleuth and Zipkin. This can be done through the following steps:

1. Add dependencies to the build files to bring in Spring Cloud Sleuth and the capability of sending trace information to Zipkin.
2. Add dependencies to RabbitMQ and Kafka for the projects that haven't used them before, that is, the Spring Cloud projects `authorization-server`, `eureka-server`, and `gateway`.
3. Configure the microservices to send trace information to Zipkin using either RabbitMQ or Kafka.
4. Add a Zipkin server to the Docker compose files.
5. Add the `kafka` Spring profile in `docker-compose-kafka.yml` to the Spring Cloud projects `authorization-server`, `eureka-server`, and `gateway`.

Adding the Zipkin server will be effected using a Docker image from Docker Hub that has been published by the Zipkin project. Refer to `https://hub.docker.com/r/openzipkin/zipkin` for details.

> Zipkin is itself a Spring Boot application and is, at the time of writing, undergoing incubation at the **Apache Software Foundation** (**ASF**). Refer to `https://zipkin.apache.org/` for more information.

Adding dependencies to build files

To be able to utilize Spring Cloud Sleuth and the ability to send trace information to Zipkin, we need to add a couple of dependencies to the Gradle project build files, `build.gradle`.

This is accomplished by adding the following two lines:

```
implementation('org.springframework.cloud:spring-cloud-starter-sleuth')
implementation('org.springframework.cloud:spring-cloud-starter-zipkin')
```

For the Gradle projects that haven't used RabbitMQ and Kafka before, that is, the Spring Cloud projects `authorization-server`, `eureka-server`, and `gateway`, the following dependencies have to be added:

```
implementation('org.springframework.cloud:spring-cloud-starter-stream-
rabbit')
implementation('org.springframework.cloud:spring-cloud-starter-stream-
kafka')
```

Adding configuration for Spring Cloud Sleuth and Zipkin

Configuration for using Spring Cloud Sleuth and Zipkin is added to the common configuration file, `config-repo/application.yml`. In the default profile, it is specified that trace information shall be sent to Zipkin using RabbitMQ:

```
spring.zipkin.sender.type: rabbit
```

By default, Spring Cloud Sleuth only sends 10% of the traces to Zipkin. To ensure that all traces are sent to Zipkin, the following property is added in the default profile:

```
spring.sleuth.sampler.probability: 1.0
```

When sending traces to Zipkin using Kafka, the Spring profile `kafka` will be used. In earlier chapters, the `kafka` Spring profile was defined in the configuration files specific to the composite and core microservices. In this chapter, where the Spring Cloud services will also use Kafka to send trace information to Zipkin, the `kafka` Spring profile is moved to the common configuration file, `config-repo/application.yml`. The following two properties have also been added to the `kafka` Spring profile:

- `spring.zipkin.sender.type: kafka` tells Spring Cloud Sleuth to send trace information to Zipkin using Kafka.
- `spring.kafka.bootstrap-servers: kafka:9092` specifies where to find the Kafka server.

All in all, the `kafka` Spring profile appears as follows:

```
---
spring.profiles: kafka

management.health.rabbit.enabled: false
spring.cloud.stream.defaultBinder: kafka
spring.zipkin.sender.type: kafka
spring.kafka.bootstrap-servers: kafka:9092
```

Adding Zipkin to the Docker Compose files

As we mentioned previously, the Zipkin server is added to the Docker Compose files using an already existing Docker image, `openzipkin/zipkin`, published by the Zipkin project. In `docker-compose.yml` and `docker-compose-partitions.yml`, where RabbitMQ is used, the definition of the Zipkin server appears as follows:

```
zipkin:
  image: openzipkin/zipkin:2.12.9
  networks:
    - my-network
  environment:
    - RABBIT_ADDRESSES=rabbitmq
    - STORAGE_TYPE=mem
  mem_limit: 512m
  ports:
    - 9411:9411
  depends_on:
    rabbitmq:
      condition: service_healthy
```

Let's explain the preceding source code:

- The version of the Docker image, `openzipkin/zipkin`, is specified to be version `2.12.19`.
- The `RABBIT_ADDRESSES=rabbitmq` environment variable is used to specify that Zipkin shall receive trace information using RabbitMQ and that Zipkin shall connect to RabbitMQ using the hostname `rabbitmq`.
- The `STORAGE_TYPE=mem` environment variable is used to specify that Zipkin shall keep all trace information in memory.

- The memory limit for Zipkin is increased to 512 MB, compared to 350 MB for all other containers. The reason for this is that since Zipkin is configured to keep all trace information in memory, it will consume more memory than the other containers after a while.
- Zipkin exposes the HTTP port `9411` for web browsers to access its web user interface.
- Docker will wait to start up the Zipkin server until the RabbitMQ service reports being healthy to Docker.

> While this is OK to store the trace information in Zipkin in memory for development and test activities, Zipkin should be configured to store trace information in a database such as Apache Cassandra, Elasticsearch, or MySQL in a production environment.

In `docker-compose-kafka.yml`, where Kafka is used, the definition of the Zipkin server appears as follows:

```
zipkin:
  image: openzipkin/zipkin:2.12.9
  networks:
    - my-network
  environment:
    - KAFKA_BOOTSTRAP_SERVERS=kafka:9092
    - STORAGE_TYPE=mem
  mem_limit: 512m
  ports:
    - 9411:9411
  depends_on:
    - kafka
```

Let's explain for the preceding source code in detail:

- The configuration for using Zipkin together with Kafka is similar to the configuration when using Zipkin with RabbitMQ previously.
- The main difference it the use of the `KAFKA_BOOTSTRAP_SERVERS=kafka:9092` environment variable, which is used to specify that Zipkin shall use Kafka to receive trace information and that Zipkin shall connect to Kafka using the hostname `kafka` and the port `9092`.

In `docker-compose-kafka.yml`, the `kafka` Spring profile is added to the Spring Cloud services `eureka`, `gateway`, and `auth-server`:

```
environment:
    - SPRING_PROFILES_ACTIVE=docker,kafka
```

That's what it takes to add distributed tracing using Spring Cloud Sleuth and Zipkin, so let's try it out in the next section!

Trying out distributed tracing

With the necessary changes to the source code in place, we can try out distributed tracing! We will do this by performing the following steps:

1. Build, start, and verify the system landscape with RabbitMQ as the queue manager.
2. Send a successful API request and see what trace information we can find in Zipkin related to this API request.
3. Send an unsuccessful API request and see what the trace information in Zipkin looks like.
4. Send a successful API request that triggers asynchronous processing and see how its trace information is represented in Zipkin.
5. Investigate how we can monitor trace information that's passed to Zipkin in RabbitMQ.
6. Switch the queue manager to Kafka and repeat the preceding steps.

We will discuss these steps in detail in the upcoming sections.

Starting up the system landscape with RabbitMQ as the queue manager

Let's start up the system landscape. Build the Docker images with the following commands:

```
cd $BOOK_HOME/Chapter14
./gradlew build && docker-compose build
```

Start the system landscape in Docker and run the usual tests with the following command:

```
./test-em-all.bash start
```

Before we can call the API, we need an access token. Run the following commands to acquire an access token:

```
unset ACCESS_TOKEN
ACCESS_TOKEN=$(curl -k https://writer:secret@localhost:8443/oauth/token -d
grant_type=password -d username=magnus -d password=password -s | jq -r
.access_token)
echo $ACCESS_TOKEN
```

Sending a successful API request

Now, we are ready to send a normal request to the API. Run the following command:

```
curl -H "Authorization: Bearer $ACCESS_TOKEN" -k
https://localhost:8443/product-composite/2 -w "%{http_code}\n" -o /dev/null
-s
```

Expect the command to returns the HTTP status code for success, 200.

We can now launch the Zipkin UI to look into what trace information has been sent to Zipkin:

1. Open the following URL in your web browser: http://localhost:9411/zipkin/.
2. To find the trace information for our request, implement the following steps:
    1. Select **Service Name**: **gateway**.
    2. Set **Sort** order: to **Newest First**.
    3. Click on the **Find Traces** button.

The response from finding traces should look like the following screenshot:

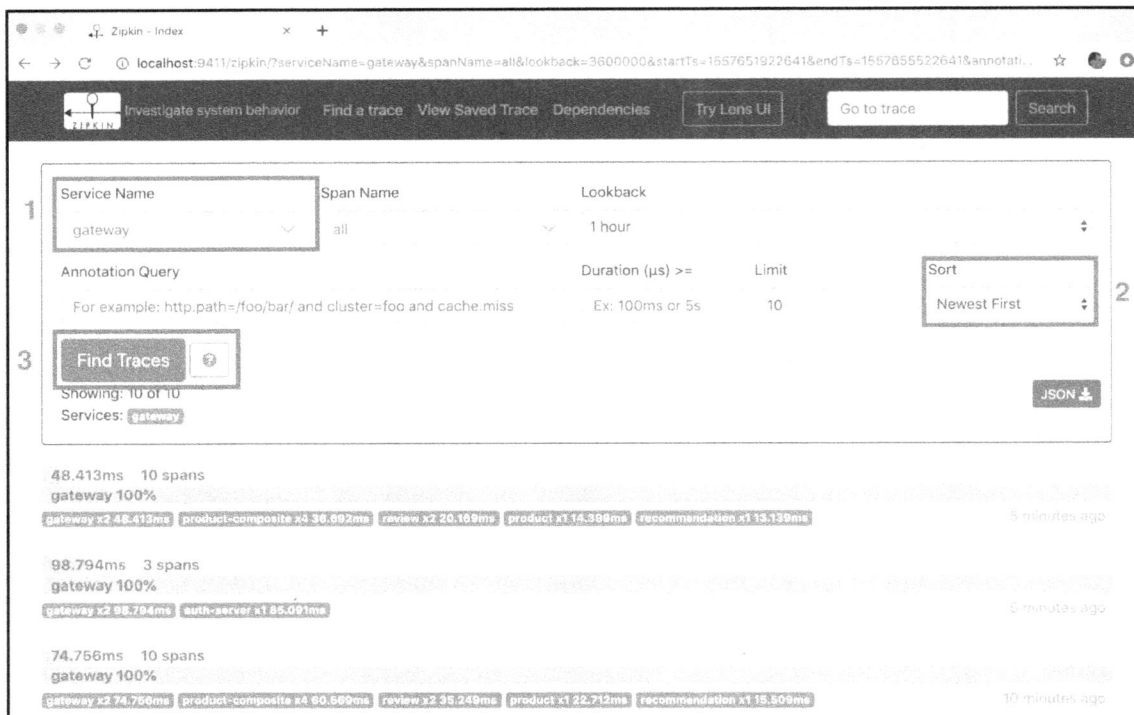

The trace information from our preceding API request is the first one in the list. Click on it to see details pertaining to the trace:

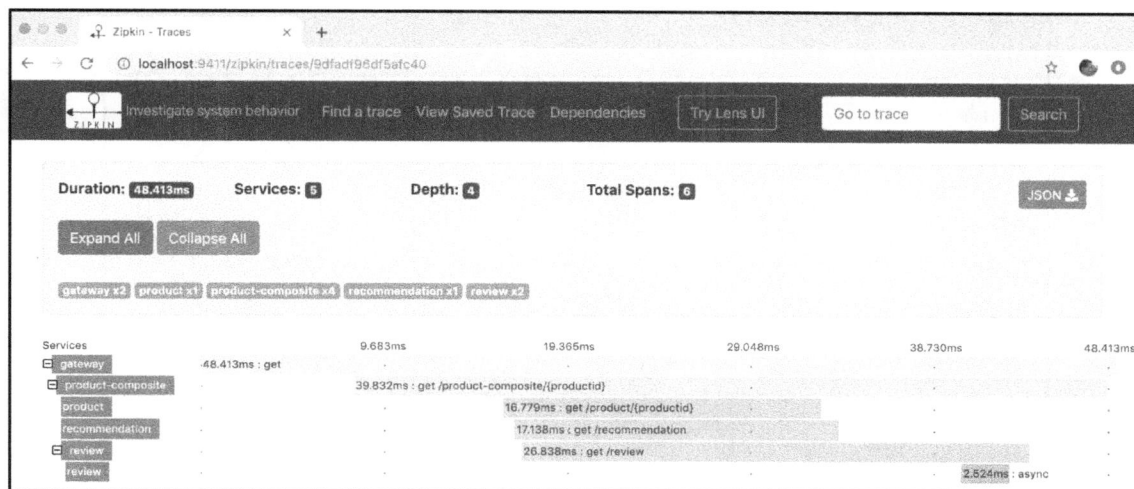

In the detailed trace information view, we can observe the following:

1. The request was received by the **gateway** service.
2. It delegated the processing of the request to the **product-composite** service.
3. The **product-composite** service, in turn, sent three parallel requests to the core services: **product**, **recommendation**, and **review**.
4. Once the **product-composite** service received the response from all three core services, it created a composite response.
5. The composite response was sent back to the caller through the **gateway** service.

> When using Safari, I have noticed that the trace tree isn't always rendered correctly. Switching to either Chrome or Firefox resolved the issue.

If we click on the first span, **gateway**, we can see even more details:

```
gateway.get: 48.413ms                                              ×


    Services:   gateway


  Date Time                  Relative Time    Annotation      Address

  12/05/2019, 12:04:29                        Server Start    192.168.176.2 (gateway)

  12/05/2019, 12:04:29       48.413ms         Server Finish   192.168.176.2 (gateway)


  Key                              Value

  http.method                      GET

  http.path                        /product-composite/2

  [Show IDs]
```

Here, we can see the actual request we sent: **product-composite/2**. This is very valuable when analyzing traces that, for example, take a long time to complete!

Sending an unsuccessful API request

Let's see what the trace information looks like if we make an unsuccessful API request; for example, searching for a product that does not exist:

1. Send an API request for product ID `12345` and verify that it returns the HTTP status code for Not Found, 404:

```
curl -H "Authorization: Bearer $ACCESS_TOKEN" -k
https://localhost:8443/product-composite/12345 -w "%{http_code}\n"
-o /dev/null -s
```

2. In the Zipkin UI, go back to the search page (use the back button in the web browser) and click on the **Find Traces** button. You should see the failed request at the top of the returned list, in red:

3. Click on the top trace marked in red:

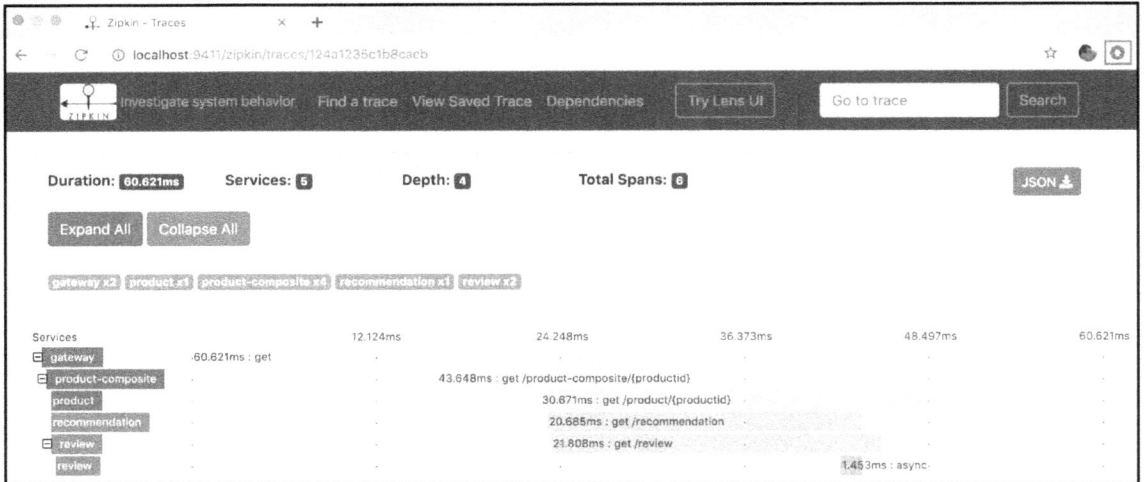

4. In the detailed trace view, we can see by the color-coding that the request went wrong when **product-composite** called the **product** service. Click on the **product** span to see details of what went wrong:

Here, we can see what request caused the error, **product/12345**, as well as the error code and the reason returned: **404** Not Found. This is very useful when analyzing the root cause of a failure!

Sending an API request that triggers asynchronous processing

The third type of request that is interesting to see how it is represented in the Zipkin UI is a request where parts of its processing are done asynchronously. Let's try a delete request, where the delete process in the core services is done asynchronously. The `product-composite` service sends a delete event to each of the three core services over the message broker and each core service picks up the delete event and processes it asynchronously. Thanks to Spring Cloud Sleuth, trace information is added to the events that are sent to the message broker, resulting in a coherent view of the total processing of the delete request.

Run the following command to delete the product with a product ID of `12345` and verify that it returns the HTTP status code for success, 200:

```
curl -X DELETE -H "Authorization: Bearer $ACCESS_TOKEN" -k
https://localhost:8443/product-composite/12345 -w "%{http_code}\n" -o
/dev/null -s
```

Remember that the delete operation is idempotent, that is, it will succeed even if the product doesn't exist!

In the Zipkin UI, go back to the search page (use the back button in the web browser) and click on the **Find Traces** button. You should see the trace from the delete request at the top of the returned list:

Click on the first trace to see its trace information:

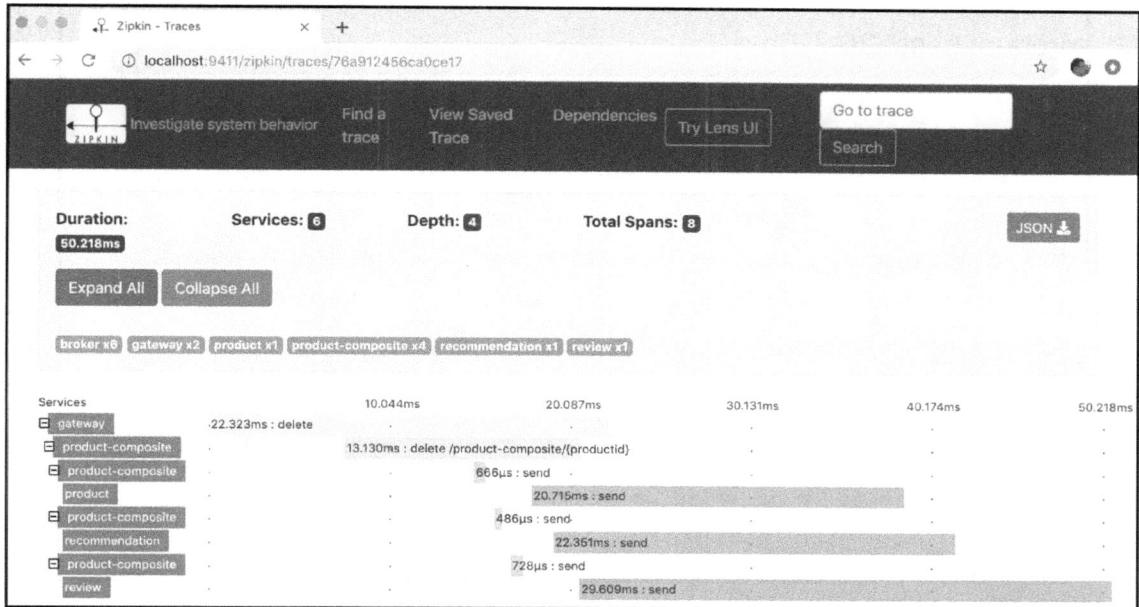

Here, we can see the trace information for processing the delete request:

1. The request was received by the **gateway** service.
2. It delegated the processing of the request to the **product-composite** service.
3. The **product-composite** service, in turn, published three events on the message broker (RabbitMQ, in this case).
4. The **product-composite** service is now done and returns a success HTTP status code, **200**, through the **gateway** service back to the caller.
5. The core services, **product**, **recommendation**, and **review**, receive the delete events and start to process them asynchronously, that is, independent of one another.

To see more detailed information, click on the **product** span:

product.send: 20.715ms			✕

Services: broker,product

Date Time	Relative Time	Annotation	Address
12/05/2019, 12:21:08	17.945ms	Producer Start	192.168.176.9 (product)
12/05/2019, 12:21:08	38.660ms	Producer Finish	192.168.176.9 (product)

Key	Value
channel	input
Broker Address	broker

`Show IDs`

Here, we can see that the **product** service was triggered by an event coming in to its **input** channel, which was sent from the message broker.

> The Zipkin UI contains much more functionality for finding traces of interest!
> To get more accustomed to the Zipkin UI, try out the `Annotation Query` parameter; for example, search for a specific request using `http.path=/product-composite/214` or `error=401` to find requests that failed due to authorization failures. Watch out for the `Limit` parameter, which is set to `10` by default; this can hide results of interest if not raised. Also, ensure that the `Lookback` parameter doesn't remove traces of interest!

Monitoring trace information passed to Zipkin in RabbitMQ

To monitor trace information that's sent to Zipkin over RabbitMQ, we can use the RabbitMQ management web UI. Open the following URL in your web browser: `http://localhost:15672/#/queues/%2F/zipkin`. If required, log in using the username `guest` and the password `guest`. Expect a web page that looks like the following:

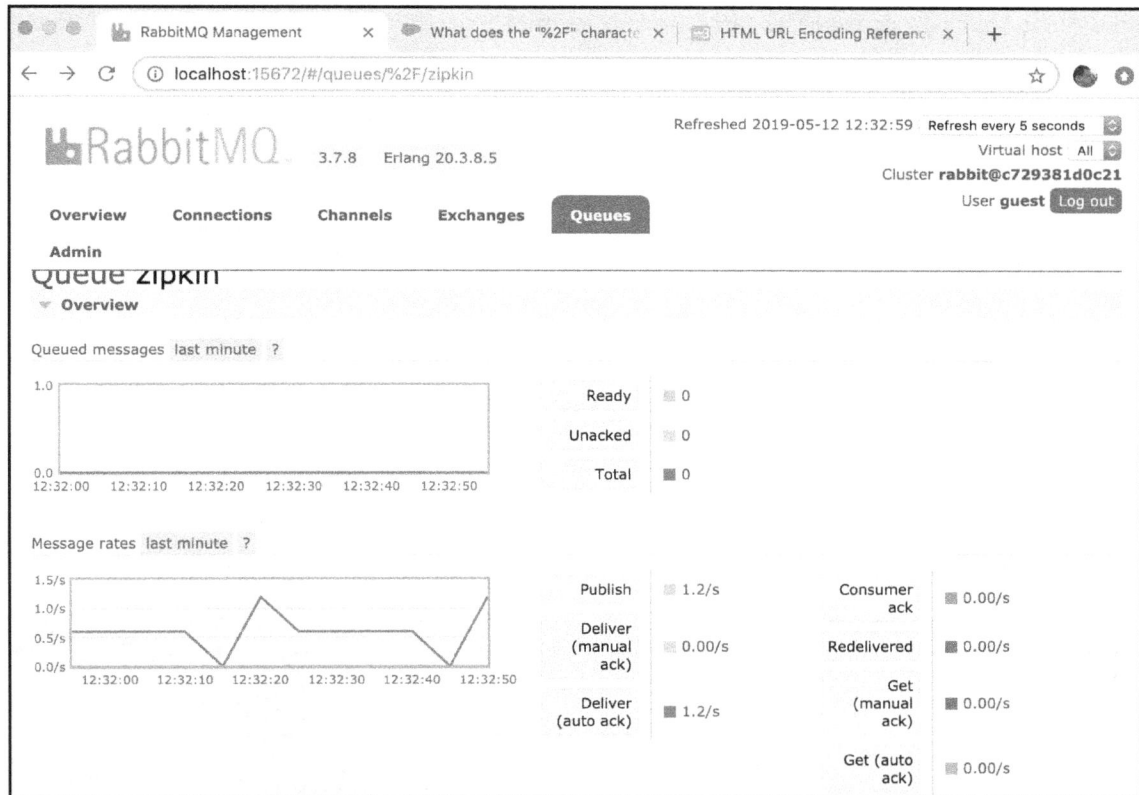

In the graph named `Message Rates`, we can see that trace messages are sent to Zipkin, currently at an average rate of 1.2 messages per second.

Wrap up the tests of distributed tracing using RabbitMQ by bringing down the system landscape. Run the following command:

```
docker-compose down
```

Using Kafka as a message broker

Let's also verify that we can send trace information to Zipkin using Kafka instead of RabbitMQ!

Start up the system landscape using the following commands:

```
export COMPOSE_FILE=docker-compose-kafka.yml
./test-em-all.bash start
```

Repeat the commands we performed in the previous sections, where we used RabbitMQ, and verify that you can see the same trace information in the Zipkin UI when using Kafka!

Kafka doesn't come with a management web UI like RabbitMQ. Therefore, we need to run a few Kafka commands to be able to verify that the trace events actually were passed to the Zipkin server using Kafka:

> For a recap on how to run Kafka commands when running Kafka as a Docker container, refer to the *Using Kafka with two partitions per topic* section in Chapter 7, *Developing Reactive Microservices*.

1. First, list the available topics in Kafka:

   ```
   docker-compose exec kafka /opt/kafka/bin/kafka-topics.sh --
   zookeeper zookeeper --list
   ```

2. Expect to find a topic named `zipkin`:

```
2. bash
 (bash)
$ docker-compose exec kafka /opt/kafka/bin/kafka-topics.sh --zookeeper zookeeper --list
__consumer_offsets
error.products.productsGroup
error.recommendations.recommendationsGroup
error.reviews.reviewsGroup
products
recommendations
reviews
zipkin
$
```

3. Next, ask for trace events that were sent to the `zipkin` topic:

```
docker-compose exec kafka /opt/kafka/bin/kafka-console-consumer.sh
--bootstrap-server localhost:9092 --topic zipkin --from-beginning -
-timeout-ms 1000
```

4. Expect a lot of events similar to the following:

The details of a trace event are not important. The Zipkin server sorts that out for us and makes the information presentable in the Zipkin UI. The important point here is that we can see that the trace events actually were sent to the Zipkin server using Kafka.

Now, bring down the system landscape and unset the `COMPOSE_FILE` environment variable:

```
docker-compose down
unset COMPOSE_FILE
```

That concludes this chapter on distributed tracing!

Summary

In this chapter, we have learned how to use distributed tracing to understand how our microservices cooperate. We have learned how to use Spring Cloud Sleuth to collect trace information, and how to use Zipkin to store and visualize the trace information.

To promote the decoupling of runtime components, we have learned how to configure microservices to send trace information to the Zipkin server asynchronously while using RabbitMQ and Kafka as message brokers. We have seen how adding Spring Cloud Sleuth to microservices is effected by adding a couple of dependencies to the build files and setting up a few configuration parameters. We have also seen how the Zipkin UI makes it very easy to identify what part of a complex workflow caused either an unexpectedly long response time or an error. Both synchronous and asynchronous workflows can be visualized by Zipkin UI.

In the next chapter, we will learn about container orchestrators, specifically Kubernetes. We will learn how to use Kubernetes to deploy and manage microservices, while also improving important runtime characteristics such as scalability, high availability, and resilience.

Questions

1. What configuration parameter is used to control how trace information is sent to Zipkin?
2. What is the purpose of the `spring.sleuth.sampler.probability` configuration parameter?
3. How can you identify the longest-running request after executing the `test-em-all.bash` test script?
4. How can we find requests that have been interrupted by the timeout introduced in `Chapter 13`, *Improving Resilience Using Resilience4j*?
5. What does the trace look like for an API request when the circuit breaker introduced in `Chapter 13`, *Improving Resilience Using Resilience4j*, is open?
6. How can we locate APIs that failed on the caller not being authorized to perform the request?

3
Section 3: Developing Lightweight Microservices Using Kubernetes

This section will help you to understand the importance of Kubernetes as a runtime platform for containerized workloads. You will learn how to set up Kubernetes in a local development environment and deploy microservices on Kubernetes. Finally, you will learn how to use some of the most important features in Kubernetes instead of the corresponding Spring Cloud features to provide a more lightweight microservice system landscape (for example, that is easier to maintain and manage).

This section includes the following chapters:

- Chapter 15, *Introduction to Kubernetes*
- Chapter 16, *Deploying Our Microservices in Kubernetes*
- Chapter 17, *Implementing Kubernetes Features as an Alternative*
- Chapter 18, *Using a Service Mesh to Improve Observability and Management*
- Chapter 19, *Centralized Logging with the EFK Stack*
- Chapter 20, *Monitoring Microservices*

15
Introduction to Kubernetes

In this chapter, we will start to learn about Kubernetes, the most popular and widely used container orchestrator at the time of writing this book. Since the subjects on container orchestrators in general and Kubernetes itself are too big to be covered in one chapter, I will focus on introducing the areas that I have found to be the most important when I used Kubernetes over the last few years.

The following topics will be covered in this chapter:

- Introducing Kubernetes concepts
- Introducing Kubernetes API objects
- Introducing Kubernetes runtime components
- Creating a local Kubernetes cluster
- Trying out a sample deployment and getting used to the `kubectl` Kubernetes CLI tool
- Managing a Kubernetes cluster

Technical requirements

To work with Kubernetes locally, we will use Minikube running on VirtualBox. We will also use the Kubernetes CLI tool known as `kubectl` a lot. `kubectl` comes with Docker for macOS, but unfortunately with a version that's too old (at least as of when this chapter was written). Therefore, we need to install a newer version. In total, we need the following:

- Minikube version 1.2 or later
- kubectl version 1.15 or later
- VirtualBox version 6.0 or later

These tools can be installed using Homebrew with the following commands:

```
brew install kubectl
brew cask install minikube
brew cask install virtualbox
```

After installing `kubectl`, run the following command to ensure that the newer version of `kubectl` is used:

```
brew link --overwrite kubernetes-cli
```

The installation of VirtualBox will ask you to rely on the system extensions that come with VirtualBox:

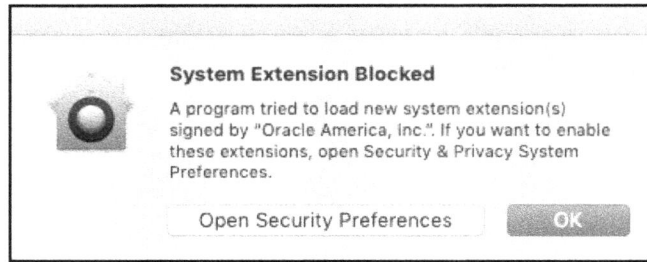

Click on the **OK** button and then on the **Allow** button in the next dialog window:

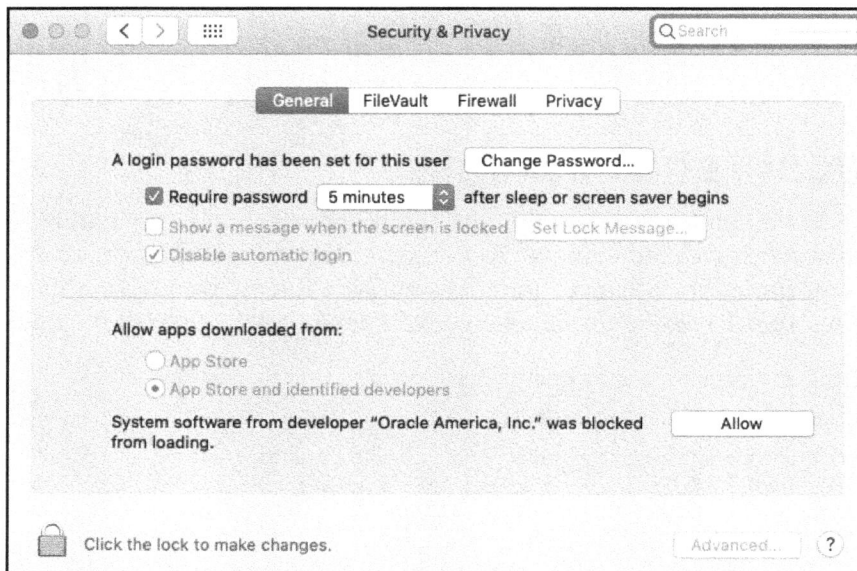

Conclude the tool's installation by verifying the versions of the installed tools with the following commands:

```
kubectl version --client --short
minikube version
vboxmanage --version
```

Expect a response such as the following:

The source code for this chapter can be found in this book's GitHub repository: https://github.com/PacktPublishing/Hands-On-Microservices-with-Spring-Boot-and-Spring-Cloud/tree/master/Chapter15.

To be able to run the commands that are described in this book, you need to download the source code to a folder and set up an environment variable, $BOOK_HOME, that points to that folder. Some sample commands are as follows:

```
export BOOK_HOME=~/Documents/Hands-On-Microservices-with-Spring-Boot-and-
Spring-Cloud
git clone
https://github.com/PacktPublishing/Hands-On-Microservices-with-Spring-Boot-
and-Spring-Cloud $BOOK_HOME
cd $BOOK_HOME/Chapter15
```

All the source code examples in this chapter come from the source code in $BOOK_HOME/Chapter15 and have been tested using Kubernetes 1.15.

Introducing Kubernetes concepts

At a high level, as a container orchestrator, Kubernetes makes a cluster of servers (physical or virtual) that run containers appear as one big logical server running containers. As an operator, we declare a desired state to the Kubernetes cluster by creating objects using the Kubernetes API. Kubernetes continuously compares the desired state with the current state. If it detects differences, it takes actions to ensure that the current state is the same as the desired state.

One of the main purposes of a Kubernetes cluster is to deploy and run containers, but also to support zero-downtime rolling upgrades using techniques such as green/blue and canary deployments. Kubernetes can schedule containers, that is, **pods** that contain one or more co-located containers, to the available nodes in the cluster. To be able to monitor the health of running containers, Kubernetes assumes that containers implement a **liveness probe**. If a liveness probe reports an unhealthy container, Kubernetes will restart the container. Containers can be scaled in the cluster manually or automatically using a horizontal autoscaler. To optimize the use of the available hardware resources in a cluster, for example, memory and CPU, containers can be configured with **quotas** that specify how much resources a container needs. On the other hand, limits regarding how much a group of containers is allowed to consume can be specified on a **namespace** level. Namespaces will be introduced as we proceed through this chapter. This is of extra importance if several teams share a common Kubernetes cluster.

Another main purpose of Kubernetes is to provide service discovery of the running pods and its containers. Kubernetes `Service` objects can be defined for services discovery and will also load balance incoming requests over the available pods. `Service` objects can be exposed externally of a Kubernetes cluster. However, as we will see, an Ingress object is, in many cases, better suited to handling externally incoming traffic to a group of services. To help Kubernetes find out whether a container is ready to accept incoming requests, a container can implement a **readiness probe**.

Internally, a Kubernetes cluster provides one big flat IP network where each pod gets its own IP address and can reach all the other pods, independent of what node they run on. To support multiple network vendors, Kubernetes allows the use of network plugins that comply with the **Container Network Interface** (**CNI**) specification (`https://github.com/containernetworking/cni`). Pods are not isolated by default, that is, they accept all incoming requests. CNI plugins that support the use of network policy definitions can be used to lock down access to pods, for example, only allowing traffic from pods in the same namespace.

To allow multiple teams to work on the same Kubernetes cluster in a safe way, **Role-Based Access Control** (**RBAC**, `https://kubernetes.io/docs/reference/access-authn-authz/rbac/`) can be applied. For example, administrators can be authorized to access resources on a cluster level, while the access of team members can be locked down to resources that are created in a namespace owned by the teams.

In total, these concepts provide a platform for running containers that is scalable, secure, highly available, and resilient.

Let's look a bit more into API objects that are available in Kubernetes and after that, what runtime components make up a Kubernetes cluster.

Introducing Kubernetes API objects

Kubernetes defines an API that is used to manage different types of *objects* or *resources*, as they are also known as. Some of the most commonly used types, or *kinds*, as they are referred to in the API, are as follows in my experience:

- **Node:** A node represents a server, virtual or physical, in the cluster.
- **Pod:** A pod represents the smallest possible deployable component in Kubernetes, consisting of one or more co-located containers. Typically, a pod consists of one container, but there are use cases for extending the functionality of the main container by running the second container in a pod. In Chapter 18, *Using a Service Mesh to Improve Observability and Management,* a second container will be used in the pods, running a sidecar that makes the main container join the service mesh.
- **Deployment**: Deployment is used to deploy and upgrade pods. The deployment objects hand over the responsibility of creating and monitoring the pods to a ReplicaSet. When creating a deployment for the first time, the work performed by the deployment object is no much more than creating the ReplicaSet object. When performing a rolling upgrade of deployment, the role of the deployment object is more involved.
- **ReplicaSet**: A ReplicaSet is used to ensure that a specified number of pods are running at all times. If a pod is deleted, it will be replaced with a new pod by the ReplicaSet.
- **Service**: A service is a stable network endpoint that you can use to connect to one or multiple pods. A service is assigned an IP address and a DNS name in the internal network of the Kubernetes cluster. The IP address of the service will stay the same for the lifetime of the service. Requests that are sent to a service will be forwarded to one of the available pods using round-robin-based load balancing. By default, a service is only exposed inside the cluster using a cluster IP address. It is also possible to expose a service outside the cluster, either on a dedicated port on each node in the cluster or – even better – through an external load balancer that is aware of Kubernetes, that is, it can automatically provision a public IP address and/or DNS name for the service. Cloud providers that offer Kubernetes as a service, in general, support this type of load balancer.

- **Ingress:** Ingress can manage external access to services in a Kubernetes cluster, typically using HTTP. For example, it can route traffic to the underlying services based on URL paths or HTTP headers such as the hostname. Instead of exposing a number of services externally, either using node ports or through load balancers, it is, in general, more convenient to set up an Ingress in front of the services. To handle the actual communication defined by the Ingress objects, an Ingress controller must be running in the cluster. We will see an example of an Ingress controller as we proceed.

- **Namespace**: A namespace is used to group and, on some levels, isolate resources in a Kubernetes cluster. The names of resources must be unique in their namespaces, but not between namespaces.

- **ConfigMap**: ConfigMap is used to store configuration that's used by containers. ConfigMaps can be mapped into a running container as environment variables or files.

- **Secret:** This is used to store sensitive data used by containers, such as credentials. Secrets can be made available to containers in the same way as ConfigMaps. Anyone with full access to the API server can access the values of created secrets, so they are not as safe as the name might imply.

- **DaemonSet**: This ensures that one pod is running on each node in a set of nodes in the cluster. In `Chapter 19`, *Centralized Logging with the EFK Stack*, we will see an example of a log collector, Fluentd, that will run on each worker node.

For a full list of resource objects that the Kubernetes API covers in v1.15, see `https://kubernetes.io/docs/reference/generated/kubernetes-api/v1.15/`.

The following diagram summarizes the Kubernetes resources that are involved in handling incoming requests:

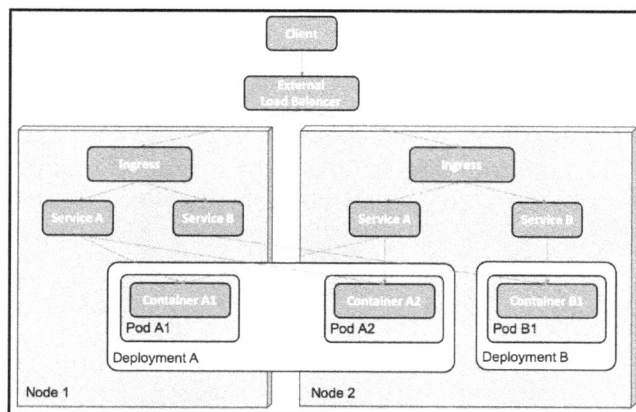

In the preceding diagram, we can see the following:

- Two deployments, **Deployment A** and **Deployment B**, have been deployed to a cluster with two nodes, **Node 1** and **Node 2**.
- **Deployment A** contains two pods, **Pod A1** and **Pod A2**.
- **Deployment B** contains one **Pod B1**.
- **Pod A1** is scheduled to **Node 1**.
- **Pod A2** and **Pod B1** are scheduled to **Node 2**.
- Each deployment has a corresponding service deployed, **Service A** and **Service B**, and they are available on all nodes.
- An Ingress is defined to route incoming requests to the two services.
- A client typically sends requests to the cluster via an external load balancer.

These objects are not, by themselves, running components; instead, they are definitions of different types of desired states. To reflect the desired state in the cluster's current state, Kubernetes comes with an architecture consisting of a number of runtime components, as described in the next section.

Introducing Kubernetes runtime components

A Kubernetes cluster contains two types of nodes: master nodes and worker nodes. Master nodes manage the cluster, while the main purpose of worker nodes is to run the actual workload, for example, the containers we deploy in the cluster. Kubernetes is built up by a number of runtime components. The most important components are as follows:

- There are components that run on master nodes, constituting the control plane:
  - `api-server`, the entry point to the control plane. This exposes a RESTful API, which, for example, the Kubernetes CLI tool known as `kubectl` uses.
  - `etcd`, a highly available and distributed key/value store, used as a database for all cluster data.
  - A controller manager, which contains a number of controllers that continuously evaluate the desired state versus the current state for the objects defined in the `etcd` database.

- Whenever the desired or the current state changes, a controller that's responsible for that type of state takes actions to move the current state to the desired state. For example, a replication controller that's responsible for managing pods will react if a new pod is added through the API server or a running pod dies and ensures that new pods are started. Another example of a controller is the node controller. It is responsible for acting if a node becomes unavailable, ensuring that pods running on a failing node are rescheduled on other nodes in the cluster.

- A **Scheduler**, which is responsible for assigning newly created pods to a node with available capacity, for example, in terms of memory and CPU. Affinity rules can be used to control how pods are assigned to nodes. For example, pods that perform a lot of disks I/O can be assigned to a group of worker nodes that have fast SSD disks. Anti-affinity rules can be defined to separate pods, for example, to avoid scheduling pods from the same deployment to the same worker node.

- Components that run on all the nodes that constitute the data plane are as follows:

    - `kubelet`, a node agent that executes as a process directly in the nodes operating system and not as a container. It is responsible for that the containers that are up and running in the pods being assigned to the node where `kubelet` runs. It acts as a conduit between the `api-server` and the container runtime on its node.

    - `kube-proxy`, a network proxy that enables the service concept in Kubernetes and is capable of forwarding requests to the appropriate pods, typically in a round-robin fashion if more than one pod is available for the specific service. `kube-proxy` is deployed as a DaemonSet.

    - **Container runtime**, which is the software that runs containers on the node. Typically, this is Docker, but any implementation of the Kubernetes **Container Runtime Interface (CRI)** can be used, for example, `cri-o` (`https://cri-o.io`), `containerd` (`https://containerd.io/`), or `rktlet` (`https://github.com/kubernetes-incubator/rktlet`).

- **Kubernetes DNS**, which is a DNS server that's used in the cluster's internal network. Services and pods are assigned a DNS name, and pods are configured to use this DNS server to resolve the internal DNS names. The DNS server is deployed as a deployment object and a service object.

The following diagram summarizes the Kubernetes runtime components:

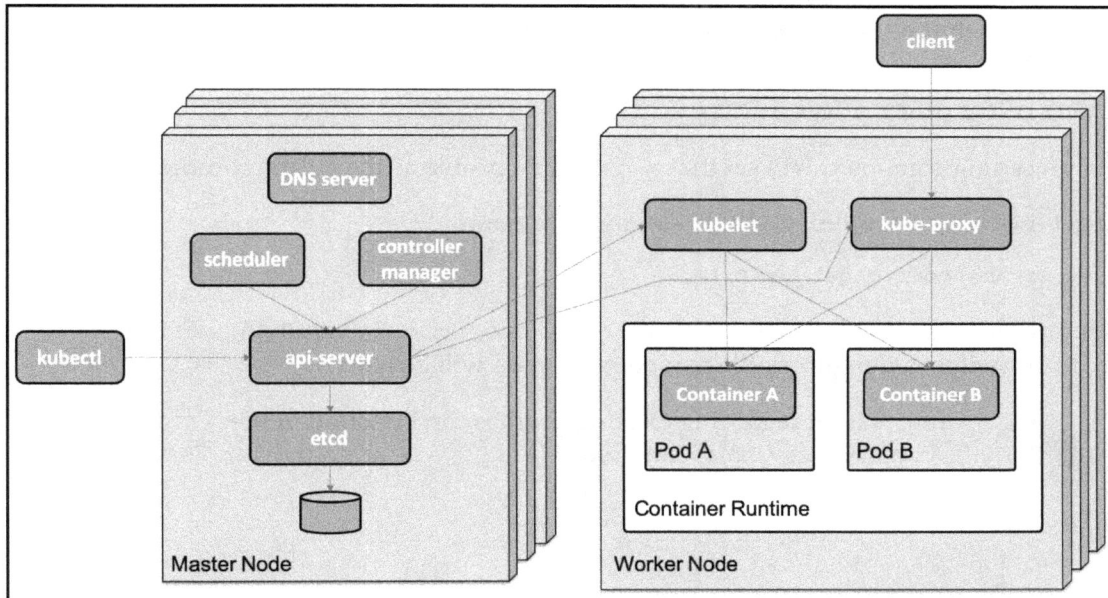

Now that we understand the Kubernetes runtime components and what they support and run on, let's move on to creating a Kubernetes cluster with Minikube.

Creating a Kubernetes cluster using Minikube

Now, we are ready to create a Kubernetes cluster! We will use Minikube to create a local single-node cluster running on VirtualBox.

Before creating the Kubernetes cluster, we need to learn a bit about Minikube profiles, the Kubernetes CLI tool known as kubectl, and its use of contexts.

Working with Minikube profiles

In order to run multiple Kubernetes clusters locally, Minikube comes with the concept of profiles. For example, if you want to work with multiple versions of Kubernetes, you can create multiple Kubernetes clusters using Minikube. Each cluster will be assigned a separate Minikube profile. Most of the Minikube commands accept a `--profile` flag (or `-p` for short) that can be used to specify which of the Kubernetes clusters the command shall be applied to. If you plan to work with one specific profile for a while, a more convenient alternative exists, where you specify the current profile with the following command:

```
minikube profile my-profile
```

The preceding command will set the `my-profile` profile as the current profile.

To get the current profile, run the following command:

```
minikube config get profile
```

If no profile is specified, neither using the `minikube profile` command nor the `--profile` switch, a default profile named `minikube` will be used.

> Information regarding existing profiles can be found in the `~/.minikube/profiles` folder.

Working with Kubernetes CLI, kubectl

`kubectl` is the Kubernetes CLI tool. Once a cluster has been set up, this is usually the only tool you need to manage the cluster!

For managing the API objects we described earlier in this chapter, the `kubectl apply` command is the only command you need to know about. It is a declarative command; that is, as an operator, we ask Kubernetes to apply the object definition we give to the command. It is then up to Kubernetes to figure out what actually needs to be done.

> Another example of a declarative command that's hopefully familiar to many readers of this book is a SQL SELECT statement that joins information from several database tables. We only declare the expected result in the SQL query, and it is up to the database query optimizer to figure out in what order the tables shall be accessed and what indexes to use to retrieve the data in the most efficient way.

In some cases, imperative statements that explicitly tell Kubernetes what to do are preferred. One example is the kubectl delete command, where we explicitly tell Kubernetes to delete some API objects. Creating a namespace object can also be conveniently done with an explicit kubectl create namespace command.

Repetitive usage of the imperative statements will make them fail, for example, deleting the same API object twice using kubectl delete or creating the same namespace twice using kubectl create. A declarative command, that is, using kubectl apply, will not fail on repetitive usage—it will simply state that there is no change and exit without taking any action.

Some commonly used commands for retrieving information about a Kubernetes cluster are as follows:

- kubectl get shows information about the specified API object.
- kubectl describe gives more detail about the specified API object.
- kubectl logs display log output from containers.

We will see a lot of examples of these and other kubectl commands in this and the upcoming chapters!

If in doubt about how to use the kubectl tool, the kubectl help and kubectl <command> --help commands are always available and provide very useful information on how to use the kubectl tool.

Working with kubectl contexts

To be able to work with more than one Kubernetes cluster, using either Minikube locally or Kubernetes clusters set up on-premises servers or in the cloud, kubectl comes with the concept of contexts. A context is a combination of the following:

- A Kubernetes cluster
- Authentication information for a user
- A default namespace

By default, contexts are saved in the `~/.kube/config` file, but the file can be changed using the `KUBECONFIG` environment variable. In this book, we will use the default location, so we will unset `KUBECONFIG` using the `unset KUBECONFIG` command.

When a Kubernetes cluster is created in Minikube, a context is created with the same name as the Minikube profile and is then set as the current context. So, `kubectl` commands that are issued after the cluster is created in Minikube will be sent to that cluster.

To list the available contexts, run the following command:

```
kubectl config get-contexts
```

The following is a sample response:

```
8. bash
$ kubectl config get-contexts
CURRENT   NAME                           CLUSTER                        AUTHINFO                       NAMESPACE
*         handson-spring-boot-cloud      handson-spring-boot-cloud      handson-spring-boot-cloud      first-attempts
          minikube                       minikube                       minikube
$
```

The wildcard, `*`, in the first column, mark the current context.

> You will only see the `handson-spring-boot-cloud` context in the preceding response once the cluster has been created, which we will describe here.

If you want to switch the current context to another context, that is, work with another Kubernetes cluster, run the following command:

```
kubectl config use-context my-cluster
```

In the preceding example, the current context will be changed to `my-cluster`.

To update a context, for example, switching the default namespace used by `kubectl`, use the `kubectl config set-context` command.

For example, to change the default namespace of the current context to `my-namespace`, use the following command:

```
kubectl config set-context $(kubectl config current-context) --namespace
my-namespace
```

In the preceding command, `kubectl config current-context` is used to get the name of the current context.

Creating a Kubernetes cluster

To create a Kubernetes cluster using Minikube, we need to run a few commands:

- Unset the KUBECONFIG environment variable to ensure that the kubectl context is created in the default config file, ~/.kube/config.
- Specify the Minikube profile to be used for the cluster. We will use handson-spring-boot-cloud as the profile name.
- Create the cluster using the minikube start command, where we can also specify how much hardware resources we want to allocate to the cluster. To be able to complete the examples in the remaining chapters of this book, allocate at least 10 GB of memory, that is, 10,240 MB, to the cluster.
- After the cluster has been created, we will use the add-on manager in Minikube to enable an Ingress controller and a metrics server that comes out of the box with Minikube. The Ingress controller and the metrics will be used in the next two chapters.

> Before you create a Kubernetes cluster using Minikube, it might be a good idea to shut down Docker for macOS to avoid running out of memory.

Run the following commands to create the Kubernetes cluster:

```
unset KUBECONFIG

minikube profile handson-spring-boot-cloud

minikube start \
  --memory=10240 \
  --cpus=4 \
  --disk-size=30g \
  --kubernetes-version=v1.15.0 \
  --vm-driver=virtualbox

minikube addons enable Ingress
minikube addons enable metrics-server
```

After the preceding commands complete, you should be able to communicate with the cluster. Try the `kubectl get nodes` command. It should respond with something that looks similar to the following:

```
8. bash
$ kubectl get nodes
NAME       STATUS   ROLES    AGE     VERSION
minikube   Ready    master   3m10s   v1.14.1
$
```

Once created, the cluster will initialize itself in the background, starting up a number of system pods in the `kube-system` namespace. We can monitor its progress by issuing the following command:

```
kubectl get pods --namespace=kube-system
```

Once the startup is complete, the preceding command should report the status for all pods as `Running` and the **READY** count should be `1/1`, meaning that a single container in each pod is up and running:

```
8. bash
$ kubectl get pods --namespace=kube-system
NAME                                           READY   STATUS    RESTARTS   AGE
coredns-fb8b8dccf-2fbkp                        1/1     Running   0          3m4s
coredns-fb8b8dccf-chctl                        1/1     Running   0          3m4s
default-http-backend-6864bbb7db-wdb62          1/1     Running   0          3m4s
etcd-minikube                                  1/1     Running   0          2m12s
kube-addon-manager-minikube                    1/1     Running   0          2m1s
kube-apiserver-minikube                        1/1     Running   0          2m11s
kube-controller-manager-minikube               1/1     Running   0          119s
kube-proxy-dmhsh                               1/1     Running   0          3m5s
kube-scheduler-minikube                        1/1     Running   0          118s
nginx-ingress-controller-586cdc477c-rctnr      1/1     Running   0          3m3s
storage-provisioner                            1/1     Running   0          3m4s
$
```

We are now ready for some action!

Trying out a sample deployment

Let's see how we can do the following:

- Deploy a simple web server based on NGINX in our Kubernetes cluster.
- Apply some changes to the deployment:
    - Delete a pod and verify that the ReplicaSet creates a new one.
    - Scale the web server to three pods to verify that the ReplicaSet fills the gap.
- Route external traffic to it using a service with a node port.

First, create a namespace, `first-attempts`, and update the `kubectl` context to use this namespace by default:

```
kubectl create namespace first-attempts
kubectl config set-context $(kubectl config current-context) --
namespace=first-attempts
```

We can now create a deployment of NGINX in the namespace using the `kubernetes/first-attempts/nginx-deployment.yaml` file. This file looks as follows:

```
apiVersion: apps/v1
kind: Deployment
metadata:
  name: nginx-deploy
spec:
  replicas: 1
  selector:
    matchLabels:
    app: nginx-app
  template:
    metadata:
      labels:
        app: nginx-app
    spec:
      containers:
      - name: nginx-container
        image: nginx:latest
        ports:
        - containerPort: 80
```

Let's explain the preceding source code in more detail:

- The `kind` and `apiVersion` attributes are used to specify that we are declaring a deployment object.
- The `metadata` section is used to describe the deployment object, for example, when we give it a name of `nginx-deploy`.
- Next comes a `spec` section that defines our desired state of the deployment object:
  - `replicas: 1` specifies we want to have one pod up and running.
  - A `selector` section that specifies how the deployment will find the pods it manages. In this case, the deployment will look for pods that have the `app` label set to `nginx-app`.
  - The `template` section is used to specify how pods shall be created:
    - The `metadata` section specifies the `label`, `app: nginx-app`, which is used to identify the pods, thereby matching the selector.
    - The `spec` section specifies details for the creation of the single container in the pod, that is, `name` and `image` and what `ports` it uses.

Create the deployment with the following commands:

```
cd $BOOK_HOME/Chapter15
kubectl apply -f kubernetes/first-attempts/nginx-deployment.yaml
```

Let's see what we got with the `kubectl get all` command:

```
$ kubectl get all
NAME                                      READY   STATUS    RESTARTS   AGE
pod/nginx-deploy-59b8c5f7cd-mt6pg         1/1     Running   0          8s

NAME                                READY   UP-TO-DATE   AVAILABLE   AGE
deployment.apps/nginx-deploy        1/1     1            1           8s

NAME                                          DESIRED   CURRENT   READY   AGE
replicaset.apps/nginx-deploy-59b8c5f7cd       1         1         1       8s
$
```

As expected, we got a deployment, ReplicaSet, and pod object. After a short while, which mainly depends on the time it takes to download the NGINX Docker image, the pod will be up and running, and the desired state will be equal to the current state!

Change the current state by deleting the pod with the following command:

```
kubectl delete pod --selector app=nginx-app
```

> Since the pod has a random name (`nginx-deploy-59b8c5f7cd-mt6pg` in the preceding example), the pod is selected based on the `app` label, which is set to `nginx-app` in the pod.

Running a subsequent `kubectl get all` command will reveal that the difference between the desired and current state was detected and handled by the ReplicaSet in just a few seconds, that is, a new pod was launched almost immediately.

Change the desired state by setting the number of desired pods to three replicas in the `kubernetes/first-attempts/nginx-deployment.yaml` deployment file. Apply the change in the desired state by simply repeating the `kubectl apply` command, as we mentioned previously.

Quickly run the `kubectl get all` command a couple of times to monitor how Kubernetes takes action to ensure that the current state meets the new desired state. After a few seconds, two new NGINX pods will be up and running. The desired state is, again, equal to the current state with three running NGINX pods. Expect a response that looks similar to the following:

```
                                                    8. bash
$ kubectl get all
NAME                                     READY   STATUS    RESTARTS   AGE
pod/nginx-deploy-59b8c5f7cd-mt6pg        1/1     Running   0          46s
pod/nginx-deploy-59b8c5f7cd-pmns9        1/1     Running   0          12s
pod/nginx-deploy-59b8c5f7cd-vtstj        1/1     Running   0          12s

NAME                              READY   UP-TO-DATE   AVAILABLE   AGE
deployment.apps/nginx-deploy      3/3     3            3           46s

NAME                                        DESIRED   CURRENT   READY   AGE
replicaset.apps/nginx-deploy-59b8c5f7cd     3         3         3       46s
$
```

To enable external communication with the web servers, create a service using the `kubernetes/first-attempts/nginx-service.yaml` file:

```
apiVersion: v1
kind: Service
metadata:
  name: nginx-service
spec:
  type: NodePort
  selector:
    app: nginx-app
  ports:
    - targetPort: 80
      port: 80
      nodePort: 30080
```

Let's explain the preceding source code in more detail:

- The `kind` and `apiVersion` attributes are used to specify that we are declaring a `Service` object.
- The `metadata` section is used to describe the `Service` object, for example, to give it a name: `nginx-service`.
- Next comes a `spec` section, which defines the desired state of the `Service` object:
    - With the `type` field, we specify that we want `NodePort`, that is, something that's accessible externally on a dedicated port on each node in the cluster. This means that an external caller can reach the pods using this port on any of the nodes in the cluster, independent of which nodes the pods actually run on.
    - The selector is used by the service to find available pods, which, in our case, is pods labeled with `app: nginx-app`.
    - Finally, `ports` are declared as follows:
        - `port: 80` specifies on which port the services will be accessible on, that is, internally in the cluster.
        - `nodePort: 30080` specifies on what port the service will be externally accessible on using any of the nodes in the cluster. By default, a node port must be in the range of `30000` to `32767`.
        - `targetPort: 80` specifies the port in the pod where the requests shall be forwarded to.

This port range is used to minimize the risk of colliding with other ports in use. In a production system, a load balancer is typically placed in front of the Kubernetes cluster, shielding the external users both from the knowledge of these ports and the IP numbers of the nodes in the Kubernetes cluster. See `Chapter 18`, *Using a Service Mesh to Improve Observability and Management*, the *Setting up port forwarding required by Istio* section, for more on the usage of a `LoadBalanced` Kubernetes service.

Create the service with the following command:

```
kubectl apply -f kubernetes/first-attempts/nginx-service.yaml
```

To see what we got, run the `kubectl get svc` command. Expect a response such as the following:

```
8. bash
$ kubectl get svc
NAME            TYPE       CLUSTER-IP      EXTERNAL-IP   PORT(S)        AGE
nginx-service   NodePort   10.111.232.48   <none>        80:30080/TCP   56m
$
```

`kubectl` supports short names for many of the API objects as an alternative to their full name. For example, `svc` was used in the preceding command instead of the full name, `service`.

To try this out, we need to know the IP address of the single node in our cluster. We can get that by issuing the `minikube ip` command. In my case, it is `192.168.99.116`. With this IP address and the node port `30080`, we can direct our web browser to the deployed web server. In my case, the address is `http://192.168.99.116:30080`. Expect a response such as the following:

Great! But what about the internal cluster IP address and port?

One way to verify this is to launch a small pod inside the cluster that we can use to run `curl` from the inside, that is, we are able to use the internal cluster IP address and port. We don't need to use the IP address; instead, we can use a DNS name that is created for the service in the internal DNS server. The short name of the DNS name is the same as the name of the service, that is, `nginx-service`.

Run the following command:

```
kubectl run -i --rm --restart=Never curl-client --image=tutum/curl:alpine --command -- curl -s 'http://nginx-service:80'
```

The preceding command looks a bit complex, but it will only do the following:

1. Create a pod with a small container based on the `tutum/curl:alpine` Docker image, which contains the `curl` command.
2. Run the `curl -s 'http://nginx-service:80'` command inside the container and redirect the output to the Terminal using the `-i` option.
3. Delete the pod using the `--rm` option.

Expect the output from the preceding command to contain the following information (we are only showing parts of the response here):

```
8. bash
$ cat run-curl.txt
$ kubectl run -i --rm --restart=Never curl-client --image=tutum/curl:alpine --command -- curl -s 'http://nginx-service:80'
...
<h1>Welcome to nginx!</h1>
...
pod "curl-client" deleted
$
```

This means that the web server is also accessible internally in the cluster!

This is basically all we need to know to be able to deploy our system landscape.

Wrap this up by removing the namespace containing the `nginx` deployment:

```
kubectl delete namespace first-attempts
```

Before we end this introductory chapter on Kubernetes, we need to learn how to manage our Kubernetes cluster.

Managing a Kubernetes cluster

A running Kubernetes cluster consumes a lot of resources, mostly memory. So, when we are done working with a Kubernetes cluster in Minikube, we must be able to hibernate it in order to release the resources allocated to it. We also need to know how to resume the cluster when we want to continue working with it. Eventually, we must also be able to permanently remove the cluster when we don't want to keep it on disk anymore.

Minikube comes with a `stop` command that can be used to hibernate a Kubernetes cluster. The `start` command we used to initially create the Kubernetes cluster can also be used to resume the cluster from its hibernated state. To permanently remove a cluster, we can use the `delete` command from Minikube.

Hibernating and resuming a Kubernetes cluster

Run the following command to hibernate (that is, `stop`) the Kubernetes cluster:

```
minikube stop
```

Run the following command to resume (that is, `start`) the Kubernetes cluster again:

```
minikube start
```

> When resuming an already existing cluster, the `start` command ignores switches that were used when you were creating the cluster.

After resuming the Kubernetes cluster, the `kubectl` context will be updated to use this cluster with the currently used namespace set to `default`. If you are working with another namespace, for example, the `hands-on` namespace that we will use in the upcoming chapter, that is, `Chapter 16`, *Deploying Our Microservices to Kubernetes*, you can update the `kubectl` context with the following command:

```
kubectl config set-context $(kubectl config current-context) --
namespace=hands-on
```

Subsequent `kubectl` commands will be applied to the `hands-on` namespace when applicable.

Terminating a Kubernetes cluster

Run the following command to terminate a Kubernetes cluster:

```
minikube delete --profile handson-spring-boot-cloud
```

You can actually run the `delete` command without specifying the profile, but I find it safer to be explicit regarding the profile when it comes to the `delete` command. Otherwise, you may accidentally delete the wrong Kubernetes cluster!

Neither the Minikube profile definition under `~/.minikube/profiles/` nor the `kubectl` context in `~/.kube/config` is deleted by this command. If they are no longer required, they can be deleted with the following commands:

```
rm -r ~/.minikube/profiles/handson-spring-boot-cloud
kubectl config delete-context handson-spring-boot-cloud
```

> The `kubectl config delete-context` command will warn you about deleting the active context, but that's okay.

We've successfully learned how to manage a Kubernetes cluster that runs in Minikube. We now know how to suspend and resume a cluster and, when no longer needed, we know how to permanently remove it.

Summary

In this chapter, we have been introduced to Kubernetes as a container orchestrator. Kubernetes makes a cluster of servers that run containers appear as one big logical server. As an operator, we declare a desired state to the cluster and Kubernetes continuously compares the desired state with the current state. If it detects differences, it takes actions to ensure that the current state is the same as the desired state.

The desired state is declared by creating resources using the Kubernetes API server. The controller manager in Kubernetes and its controllers react to the various resources that were created by the API server and takes actions to ensure that the current state meets the new desired state. The scheduler assigns nodes to newly created containers, that is, pods that contain one or more containers. On each node, an agent, `kubelet`, runs and ensures that the pods that were scheduled to its node are up and running. `kube-proxy` acts as a network proxy, enabling a service abstraction by forwarding requests that are sent to the service to available pods in the cluster. External requests can be handled either by a service that specifies a node port that's available on all of the nodes in the cluster or through a dedicated Ingress resource.

We have also tried out Kubernetes by creating a local single-node cluster using Minikube and VirtualBox. Using the Kubernetes CLI tool known as `kubectl`, we deployed a simple web server based on NGINX. We tried out resilience capabilities by deleting the web server, and we observed it being recreated automatically and scaled it by requesting three pods running on the web server. Finally, we created a service with a node port and verified that we could access it both externally and from the inside of the cluster.

Finally, we learned how to manage a Kubernetes cluster running in Minikube on VirtualBox in terms of how to hibernate, resume, and terminate a Kubernetes cluster.

We are now ready to deploy our system landscape from the earlier chapters in Kubernetes. Head over to the next chapter to find out how to do this!

Questions

1. What happens if you run the same `kubectl create` command twice?
2. What happens if you run the same `kubectl apply` command twice?
3. In terms of questions *1* and *2*, why do they act differently the second time they are run?
4. What is the purpose of a ReplicaSet, and what other resource creates a ReplicaSet?
5. What is the purpose of `etcd` in a Kubernetes cluster?
6. How can a container find out the IP address of another container that runs in the same pod?
7. What happens if you create two deployments with the same name but in different namespaces?
8. What can you make the creation of two services with the same name fail if they are created in two different namespaces?

Deploying Our Microservices to Kubernetes

16

In this chapter, we will deploy the microservices in this book to Kubernetes. We will also learn about some of the core features of Kubernetes, such as using **Kustomize** to configure deployments for different runtime environments and using Kubernetes deployments object for rolling upgrades. Before we do that, we need to review how we use service discovery. Since Kubernetes comes with built-in support for service discovery, it seems unnecessary to deploy our own since we have been using Netflix Eureka up to this point.

The following topics will be covered in this chapter:

- Replacing Netflix Eureka with Kubernetes `Service` objects and `kube-proxy` for service discovery
- Using Kustomize to prepare the microservices to be deployed in different environments
- Testing the deployments with a version of the test script, `test-em-all.bash`
- Performing rolling upgrades
- Learning how to roll back a failed upgrade

Technical requirements

All the commands that are described in this book are run on a MacBook Pro using macOS Mojave but should be straightforward to modify if you want to run them on another platform such as Linux or Windows.

The only new tool that's required for this chapter is the `siege` command-line tool, which is used for HTTP-based load testing and benchmarking. We will use `siege` to put some load on the Kubernetes cluster while performing rolling upgrades. The tool can be installed using Homebrew with the following commands:

```
brew install siege
```

The source code for this chapter can be found in this book's GitHub repository: https://github.com/PacktPublishing/Hands-On-Microservices-with-Spring-Boot-and-Spring-Cloud/tree/master/Chapter16.

To be able to run the commands that are described in this book, you need to download the source code to a folder and set up an environment variable, $BOOK_HOME, that points to that folder. Some sample commands are as follows:

```
export BOOK_HOME=~/Documents/Hands-On-Microservices-with-Spring-Boot-and-
Spring-Cloud
git clone
https://github.com/PacktPublishing/Hands-On-Microservices-with-Spring-Boot-
and-Spring-Cloud $BOOK_HOME
cd $BOOK_HOME/Chapter16
```

All the source code examples in this chapter come from the source code in $BOOK_HOME/Chapter16 and have been tested using Kubernetes 1.15.

If you want to see the changes that were applied to the source code in this chapter, that is, see the changes that are required to be able to deploy the microservices on Kubernetes, you can compare it with the source code for Chapter 15, *Introduction to Kubernetes*. You can use your favorite `diff` tool and compare the two folders, $BOOK_HOME/Chapter15 and $BOOK_HOME/Chapter16.

Replacing Netflix Eureka with Kubernetes services

As shown in the previous chapter, Chapter 15, *Introduction to Kubernetes*, Kubernetes comes with a built-in discovery service based on Kubernetes Service objects and the kube-proxy runtime component. This makes it unnecessary to deploy a separate discovery service such as Netflix Eureka, which we used in the previous chapters. An advantage of using Kubernetes discovery service is that it doesn't require a client library such as Netflix Ribbon, which we have been using together with Netflix Eureka. This makes the Kubernetes discovery service easy to use, independent of which language or framework a microservice is based on. A drawback of using the Kubernetes discovery service is that it only works in a Kubernetes environment. However, since the discovery service is based on kube-proxy, which accepts requests to the DNS name or IP address of a service object, it should be fairly simple to replace it with a similar discovery service, for example, one that comes bundled with another container orchestrator.

To summarize this, we will remove the discovery server based on Netflix Eureka from our microservice landscape, as illustrated in the following diagram:

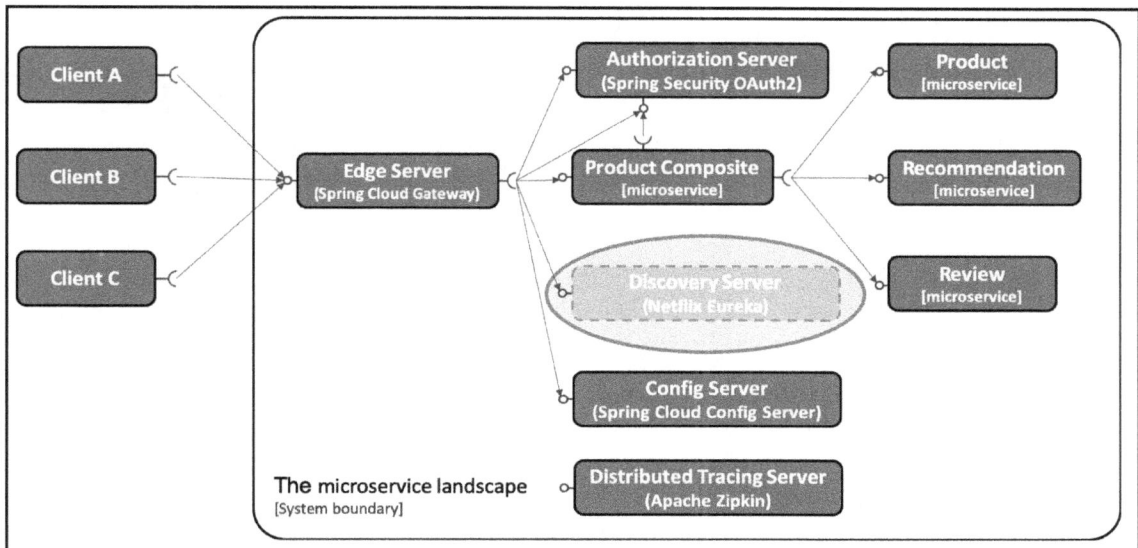

To replace the discovery server based on Netflix Eureka with the Kubernetes built-in discovery service, the following changes have been applied to the source code:

- Netflix Eureka and the Ribbon-specific configuration (client and server) have been removed from the configuration repository, `config-repo`.
- Routing rules in the gateway service to the Eureka server have been removed from the `config-repo/gateway.yml` file.
- We've removed the Eureka server project, that is, we've removed the `spring-cloud/eureka-server` folder.
- We've removed the Eureka server from the Docker Compose files and the `settings.gradle` Gradle file.
- We've removed the dependency to `spring-cloud-starter-netflix-eureka-client` in all of Eureka's client build files, that is, `build.gradle`.
- We've removed the no-longer-required `eureka.client.enabled=false` property setting from all of Eureka's client integration tests.
- The gateway service no longer uses routing based on the client-side load balancer in Spring Cloud using the `lb` protocol. For example, the `lb://product-composite` routing destination has been replaced by the `http://product-composite` in the `config-repo/gateway.yml` file.
- The HTTP port used by the microservices and the authorization server has been changed from port the `8080` port (`9999` in the case of the authorization server) to the default HTTP port `80`. This has been configured in `config-repo` for each affected service like so:

```
spring.profiles: docker
server.port: 80
```

None of the HTTP addresses that we are using are affected by the replacement of Netflix Eureka with Kubernetes services. For example, addresses used by the composite service are unaffected:

```
private final String productServiceUrl = "http://product";
private final String recommendationServiceUrl = "http://recommendation";
private final String reviewServiceUrl = "http://review";
```

This is achieved by changing the HTTP port used by the microservices and the authorization server to the default HTTP port, `80`, as described previously.

Using Docker Compose still works, even though Netflix Eureka has been removed. This can be used for running functional tests of the microservices without deploying them to Kubernetes, for example, running `test-em-all.bash` together with Docker for macOS in the same way as in the previous chapters. Removing Netflix Eureka, however, means that we no longer have a discovery service in place when using plain Docker and Docker Compose. Therefore, scaling microservices will only work when deploying to Kubernetes.

Now that we've familiarized ourselves with Kubernetes services, let's move on to Kustomize, a tool that's used for customizing Kubernetes objects.

Introducing Kustomize

Kustomize is a tool that's used for creating environment-specific customizations of the Kubernetes definitions files, that is, the YAML files, for example, for development, test, staging, and production environments. Common definition files are stored in a `base` folder, while environment-specific additions are kept in environment-specific `overlay` folders. Environment-specific information can, for example, be any of the following:

- What version of the Docker images to use
- Number of replicas to run
- Resource quotas in terms of CPU and memory

Each folder contains a `kustomization.yml` file that describes its content for Kustomize. When deploying to a specific environment, Kustomize will take the content from the `base` folder and the environment-specific `overlay` folder and send the combined result to `kubectl`. Properties from the files in the `overlay` folder will override the corresponding properties in the `base` folder, if any.

In this chapter, we will set up customizations for two sample environments: development and production.

The folder structure under $BOOK_HOME/Chapter16 looks as follows:

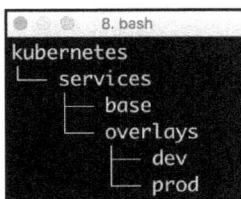

Since Kubernetes 1.14, kubectl comes with built-in support for Kustomize using the -k flag. As we will see as we proceed, deploying to the development environment using Kustomize will be done with the kubectl apply -k kubernetes/services/overlays/dev command.

Setting up common definitions in the base folder

In the base folder, we will have one definition file for each microservice, but none for the resource managers (MongoDB, MySQL, and RabbitMQ). The resource managers will only be deployed in Kubernetes in the development environment and are expected to run outside of Kubernetes in the production environment—for example, in an existing database and queue manager service on premises or as a managed service in the cloud.

The definition files in the base folder contain a deployment object and a service object for each microservice. Let's go through a typical deployment object in kubernetes/services/base/product.yml. It is geared toward what is required in a development environment. It starts with the following code:

```
apiVersion: apps/v1
kind: Deployment
metadata:
  name: product
spec:
  replicas: 1
  selector:
    matchLabels:
      app: product
  template:
    metadata:
      labels:
        app: product
    spec:
      containers:
        - name: pro
```

This part looks exactly the same as it does for the NGINX deployment we used in the previous chapter, `Chapter 15`, *Introduction to Kubernetes*, in the *Trying out a sample deployment* section, so we don't need to go through it again.

The next part looks a bit different:

```
image: hands-on/product-service
imagePullPolicy: Never
env:
- name: SPRING_PROFILES_ACTIVE
  value: "docker"
envFrom:
- secretRef:
    name: config-client-credentials
ports:
- containerPort: 80
resources:
  limits:
    memory: 350Mi
```

Let's explain the preceding source code in more detail:

- The Docker image specified, `hands-on/product-service`, will be created underneath where we build our microservices. See the *Building Docker images* section for more information.
- The `imagePullPolicy: Never` declaration tells Kubernetes to not try to download the Docker image from a Docker registry. See the *Building Docker images* section for further information.
- The `SPRING_PROFILES_ACTIVE` environment variable is defined to tell the Spring application to use the `docker` Spring profile in the configuration repository.
- A secret, `config-client-credentials`, is used to provide the container with credentials for accessing the configuration server.
- The HTTP port that's used is the default HTTP port `80`.
- A resource limit is defined to maximize the available memory to 350 MB, that is, in the same way as when we used Docker Compose in the previous chapters.

The last part of the declaration of the deployment object contains liveness and readiness probes:

```
livenessProbe:
  httpGet:
    scheme: HTTP
    path: /actuator/info
    port: 80
  initialDelaySeconds: 10
  periodSeconds: 10
  timeoutSeconds: 2
  failureThreshold: 20
  successThreshold: 1
readinessProbe:
  httpGet:
    scheme: HTTP
    path: /actuator/health
    port: 80
  initialDelaySeconds: 10
  periodSeconds: 10
  timeoutSeconds: 2
  failureThreshold: 3
  successThreshold: 1
```

Let's explain the preceding source code in more detail:

- The **liveness probe** is based on an HTTP request that's sent to the Spring Boot Actuator `info` endpoint. This means that if the microservice instance is in such bad shape that it is not capable of responding 200 (OK) to a request that's sent to the lightweight `info` endpoint, it is time for Kubernetes to restart the microservice instance.
- The **readiness probe** is based on an HTTP request that's sent to the Spring Boot Actuator `health` endpoint. Kubernetes will only send requests to the microservice instance if its `health` endpoint responds with the HTTP status 200 (OK). Not responding with 200 (OK) typically means that the microservice instance has problems with reaching some of the resources it depends on, and so it makes sense to not send any requests to a microservice instance when it does not respond with 200 (OK) on the `health` endpoint.
- The liveness and the readiness probes can be configured using the following properties:
    - `initialDelaySeconds` specifies how long Kubernetes waits to probe a container after it's started up.
    - `periodSeconds` specifies the time between probe requests sent by Kubernetes.

- `timeoutSeconds` specifies how long Kubernetes waits on a response before it treats the probe as failed.
- `failureThreshold` specifies how many failed attempts Kubernetes makes before giving up. In the case of a liveness probe, this means restarting the pod. In the case of a readiness probe, it means that Kubernetes will not send any more requests to the container.
- `successThreshold` specifies the number of successful attempts that are required for a probe to be considered successful again after a failure. This only applies to readiness probes since they must be set to `1` if specified for liveness probes.

Finding optimal settings for the probes can be challenging, that is, finding a proper balance between getting a swift reaction from Kubernetes when the availability of a pod changes and not overloading the pods with probe requests. Specifically configuring a liveness probe with values that are too low can result in Kubernetes restarting pods that just take some time to start, that is, that don't need to be restarted. Starting a large number of pods with values that have been set too low on the liveness probes can result in a lot of unnecessary restarts. Setting the configuration values too high on the probes (except for the `successThreshold` value) makes Kubernetes react slower, which can be annoying in a development environment. Proper values also depend on the available hardware, which affects the startup times for the pods. For the scope of this book, `failureThreshold` for the liveness probes is set to a high value, `20`, to avoid unnecessary restarts on computers with limited hardware resources.

The service object in `kubernetes/services/base/product.yml` looks as follows:

```
apiVersion: v1
kind: Service
metadata:
  name: product
spec:
  selector:
    app: product
  ports:
  - port: 80
    targetPort: 80
```

The service object looks similar to the NGINX service object we used in the previous chapter, Chapter 15, *Introduction to Kubernetes*, in the *Trying out a sample deployment* section. One difference is that the service type is ClusterIP (which is the default type and therefore not specified). The service object will receive internal requests on port 80 and forward them to the target port, 80, on the selected pod. The only exception to this is the gateway microservice that is exposed externally using a NodePort service on the host's port, that is, 31443:

```
apiVersion: v1
kind: Service
metadata:
 name: gateway
spec:
 type: NodePort
 selector:
 app: gateway
 ports:
 - port: 443
 nodePort: 31443
 targetPort: 8443
```

Finally, we have the Kustomize file that binds everything together in the base folder:

```
resources:
- auth-server.yml
- config-server.yml
- gateway.yml
- product-composite.yml
- product.yml
- recommendation.yml
- review.yml
- zipkin-server.yml
```

It simply lists the YAML definition files that Kustomize shall use in the base folder.

Now, we will see how we can use these base definitions with the definitions in the overlay folders, and see how they are applied using the -k switch with the kubectl apply command.

Deploying to Kubernetes for development and test

In this section, we will deploy the microservices in an environment to be used for development and test activities, for example, system integration tests. This type of environment is used primarily for functional tests and is therefore configured to use minimal system resources.

Since the deployment objects in the `base` folder are configured for a development environment, they don't need any further refinement in the overlay for development. We only have to add deployment and service objects for the three resource managers for RabbitMQ, MySQL, and MongoDB in the same way as when using Docker Compose. We will deploy the resource managers in the same Kubernetes namespace as the microservices. This is illustrated by the following diagram:

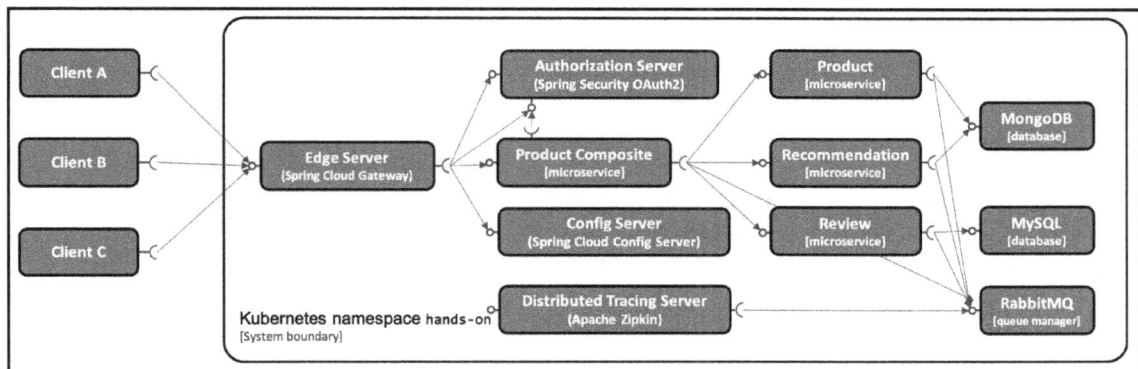

The definition files for the resource managers can be found in the `kubernetes/services/overlays/dev` folder.

The `kustomization.yml` file looks like this:

```
bases:
- ../../base
resources:
- mongodb-dev.yml
- rabbitmq-dev.yml
- mysql-dev.yml
```

It defines that the `base` folder shall be used as the base and adds the three resources we mentioned previously.

Building Docker images

Normally, we have to push images to a Docker registry and configure Kubernetes to pull images from the registry. In our case, where we have a local single node cluster, we can shortcut this process by pointing our Docker client to the Docker engine in Minikube and then run the `docker-compose build` command. This will result in the Docker images being immediately available to Kubernetes. For development, we will be using `latest` as the Docker image version for the microservices.

> You might be wondering how we can update a pod that uses the `latest` Docker image.
>
> From Kubernetes 1.15, this is very simple. Just change the code and rebuild the Docker image, for example, using the `build` command that's described here. Then, update a pod with the `kubectl rollout restart` command.
>
> For example, if the `product` service has been updated, run the `kubectl rollout restart deploy product` command.

You can build Docker images from source as follows:

```
cd $BOOK_HOME/Chapter16
eval $(minikube docker-env)
./gradlew build && docker-compose build
```

The `eval $(minikube docker-env)` command directs the local Docker client to communicate with the Docker engine in Minikube, for example, when building the Docker images.

The `docker-compose.yml` file has been updated to specify a name for the Docker images it builds. For example, for the `product` service, we have the following:

```
product:
  build: microservices/product-service
  image: hands-on/product-service
```

> `latest` is the default tag for a Docker image name, so it is not specified.

With the Docker images built, we can start creating the Kubernetes resource objects!

Deploying to Kubernetes

Before we can deploy the microservices to Kubernetes, we need to create a namespace, the required config maps, and secrets. After the deployment is performed, we will wait for the deployments to be up and running, and also verify that we got the expected result in terms of deployed pods and Docker images that were used per pod.

Create a namespace, hands-on, and set it as the default namespace for kubectl:

```
kubectl create namespace hands-on
kubectl config set-context $(kubectl config current-context) --
namespace=hands-on
```

All application configuration is kept in the configuration repository that's managed by the configuration server. The only configuration information that needs to be stored outside of the configuration repository is the credentials for connecting to the configuration server and an encryption key. The encryption key is used by the configuration server to keep sensitive information in the configuration repository encrypted at rest, that is, on disk.

We will store the configuration repository in a config map with all the sensitive information encrypted; see Chapter 12, *Centralized Configuration*, for details. The credentials for connecting to the configuration server and the encryption key will be stored in two secrets, one for the configuration server and one for its clients.

To check this, perform the following steps:

1. Create the config map for the configuration repository based on the files in the config-repo folder with the following command:

```
kubectl create configmap config-repo --from-file=config-repo/ --
save-config
```

2. Create the secret for the configuration server with the following command:

```
kubectl create secret generic config-server-secrets \
  --from-literal=ENCRYPT_KEY=my-very-secure-encrypt-key \
  --from-literal=SPRING_SECURITY_USER_NAME=dev-usr \
  --from-literal=SPRING_SECURITY_USER_PASSWORD=dev-pwd \
  --save-config
```

3. Create the secret for the clients of the configuration server with the following command:

```
kubectl create secret generic config-client-credentials \
--from-literal=CONFIG_SERVER_USR=dev-usr \
--from-literal=CONFIG_SERVER_PWD=dev-pwd --save-config
```

Since we have just entered commands that contain sensitive information in clear text, for example, passwords and an encryption key, it is a good idea to clear the history command. To clear the history command both in memory and on disk, run the history -c; history -w command.

See the discussion at https://unix.stackexchange.com/a/416831 for details on the history command.

4. To avoid a slow deployment due to Kubernetes downloading Docker images (potentially causing the liveness probes we described previously to restart our pods), run the following docker pull commands to download the images:

```
docker pull mysql:5.7
docker pull mongo:3.6.9
docker pull rabbitmq:3.7.8-management
docker pull openzipkin/zipkin:2.12.9
```

5. Deploy the microservices for the development environment, based on the dev overlay, using the -k switch to activate Kustomize, as described previously:

```
kubectl apply -k kubernetes/services/overlays/dev
```

6. Wait for the deployments and their pods to be up and running by running the following command:

```
kubectl wait --timeout=600s --for=condition=ready pod --all
```

Expect each command to respond with deployment.extensions/... condition met. ... will be replaced with the name of the actual deployment.

7. To see the Docker images that are used for development, run the following command:

```
kubectl get pods -o json | jq .items[].spec.containers[].image
```

The response should look similar to the following:

```
● ○ ○                          8. bash
$ kubectl get pods -o json | jq .items[].spec.containers[].image
"hands-on/auth-server"
"hands-on/config-server"
"hands-on/gateway"
"mongo:3.6.9"
"mysql:5.7"
"hands-on/product-service"
"hands-on/product-composite-service"
"rabbitmq:3-management"
"hands-on/recommendation-service"
"hands-on/review-service"
"openzipkin/zipkin:2.12.9"
$
```

We are now ready to test our deployment!

But before we can do that, we need to go through changes that are required in the test script for use with Kubernetes.

Changes in the test script for use with Kubernetes

To test the deployment we will, as usual, run the test script, that is, test-em-all.bash. To work with Kubernetes, the circuit breaker tests have been slightly modified. Take a look at the testCircuitBreaker() function for more details. The circuit breaker tests call the actuator endpoints on the product-composite service to check their health state and get access to circuit breaker events. The actuator endpoints are not exposed externally, so the test script needs to use different techniques to access the internal endpoints when using Docker Compose and Kubernetes:

- When using Docker Compose, the test script will launch a Docker container using a plain docker run command that calls the actuator endpoints from the inside of the network created by Docker Compose.
- When using Kubernetes, the test script will launch a Kubernetes pod that it can use to run the corresponding commands inside Kubernetes.

Let's see how this is done when using Docker Compose and Kubernetes.

Reaching the internal actuator endpoint using Docker Compose

The base command that's defined for Docker Compose is as follows:

```
EXEC="docker run --rm -it --network=my-network alpine"
```

Note that the container will be killed using the `--rm` switch after each execution of a test command.

Reaching the internal actuator endpoint using Kubernetes

Since launching a pod in Kubernetes is slower than starting a container, the test script will launch a single pod, `alpine-client`. The pod will be launched at the start of the `testCircuitBreaker()` function, and the tests will use the `kubectl exec` command to run the test commands in this pod. This will be much faster than creating and deleting a pod for each test command.

Launching the single pod is handled at the beginning of the `testCircuitBreaker()` function:

```
echo "Restarting alpine-client..."
local ns=$NAMESPACE
if kubectl -n $ns get pod alpine-client > /dev/null ; then
    kubectl -n $ns delete pod alpine-client --grace-period=1
fi
kubectl -n $ns run --restart=Never alpine-client --image=alpine --command -
- sleep 600
echo "Waiting for alpine-client to be ready..."
kubectl -n $ns wait --for=condition=Ready pod/alpine-client

EXEC="kubectl -n $ns exec alpine-client --"
```

At the end of the circuit breaker tests, the pod is deleted by using the following command:

```
kubectl -n $ns delete pod alpine-client --grace-period=1
```

Choosing between Docker Compose and Kubernetes

To make the test script work with both Docker Compose and Kubernetes, it assumes that Docker Compose will be used if the HOST environment variable is set to localhost; otherwise, it assumes that Kubernetes will be used. See the following code:

```
if [ "$HOST" = "localhost" ]
then
    EXEC="docker run --rm -it --network=my-network alpine"
else
    echo "Restarting alpine-client..."
    ...
    EXEC="kubectl -n $ns exec alpine-client --"
fi
```

The default value for the HOST environment variable in the test script is localhost.

Once the EXEC variable has been set up, depending on whether the tests are running on Docker Compose or on Kubernetes, it is used in the testCircuitBreaker() test function. The test starts by verifying that the circuit breaker is closed with the following statement:

```
assertEqual "CLOSED" "$($EXEC wget product-
composite:${MGM_PORT}/actuator/health -qO - | jq -r
.details.productCircuitBreaker.details.state)"
```

A final change in the test script occurs because our services are now reachable on the 80 port inside the cluster; that is, they are no longer on the 8080 port.

> If the various ports that we've used seem confusing, review the definitions of the services in the *Setting up common definitions in the base folder* section.

Testing the deployment

When launching the test script, we have to give it the address of the host that runs Kubernetes, that is, our Minikube instance, and the external port where our gateway service listens for external requests. The minikube ip command can be used to find the IP address of the Minikube instance and, as mentioned in the *Setting up common definitions in the base folder* section, we have assigned the external NodePort 31443 to the gateway service.

Start the tests with the following command:

```
HOST=$(minikube ip) PORT=31443 ./test-em-all.bash
```

In the output from the script we will see how the IP address of the Minikube instance is used and also how the `alpine-client` pod is created and destroyed:

```
3. bash
$ HOST=$(minikube ip) PORT=31443 ./test-em-all.bash
Start Tests: Sat Jun 29 08:29:05 CEST 2019
HOST=192.168.99.116
PORT=31443
Wait for: curl -k https://192.168.99.116:31443/actuator/health... DONE, continues...
Test OK (HTTP Code: 200)
...
Start Circuit Breaker tests!
Restarting alpine-client...
Error from server (NotFound): pods "alpine-client" not found
pod/alpine-client created
Waiting for alpine-client to be ready...
pod/alpine-client condition met
Test OK (actual value: CLOSED)
...
Test OK (actual value: HALF_OPEN_TO_CLOSED)
pod "alpine-client" deleted
End, all tests OK: Sat Jun 29 08:29:33 CEST 2019
$
```

Before we move on and look at how to set up a corresponding environment for staging and production use, let's clean up what we have installed in the development environment to preserve resources in the Kubernetes cluster. We can do this by simply deleting the namespace. Deleting the namespace will recursively delete the resources that exist in the namespace.

Delete the namespace with the following command:

```
kubectl delete namespace hands-on
```

With the development environment removed, we can move on and set up an environment targeting staging and production.

Deploying to Kubernetes for staging and production

In this section, we will deploy the microservices in an environment for staging and production usage. A staging environment is used for performing **quality assurance (QA)** and **user acceptance tests (UAT)** as the last step before taking a new release into production. To be able to verify that the new release not only meets functional requirements but also non-functional requirements, for example, in terms of performance, robustness, scalability, and resilience, a staging environment is configured to be as similar as possible to the production environment.

When deploying to an environment for staging or production, there are a number of changes required compared to when deploying for development or tests:

- **Resource managers should run outside of the Kubernetes cluster**: It is technically feasible to run databases and queue managers for production use on Kubernetes as stateful containers using `StatefulSets` and `PersistentVolumes`. At the time of writing this chapter, I recommend against it, mainly because the support for stateful containers is relatively new and unproven in Kubernetes. Instead, I recommend using the existing database and queue manager services on premises or managed services in the cloud, leaving Kubernetes to do what it is best for, that is, running stateless containers. For the scope of this book, to simulate a production environment, we will run MySQL, MongoDB, and RabbitMQ as plain Docker containers outside of Kubernetes using the already existing Docker Compose files.
- **Lockdown:**
  - For security reasons, things like `actuator` endpoints and log levels need to be constrained in a production environment.
  - Externally exposed endpoints should also be reviewed from a security perspective. For example, access to the configuration server should most probably be locked down in a production environment, but we will keep it exposed in this book for convenience.
  - Docker image tags must be specified to be able to track which versions of the microservices have been deployed.

- **Scale up available resources**: To meet the requirements of both high availability and higher load, we need to run at least two pods per deployment. We might also need to increase the amount of memory and CPU that are allowed to be used per pod. To avoid running out of memory in the Minikube instance, we will keep one pod per deployment but increase the maximum memory allowed in the production environment.
- **Set up a production-ready Kubernetes cluster**: This is outside the scope of this book, but, if feasible, I recommend using one of the managed Kubernetes services provided by the leading cloud providers. For the scope of this book, we will deploy to our local Minikube instance.

> This is not meant to be an exhaustive list of things that have to be considered when setting up an environment for production, but it's a good start.

Our simulated production environment will look as follows:

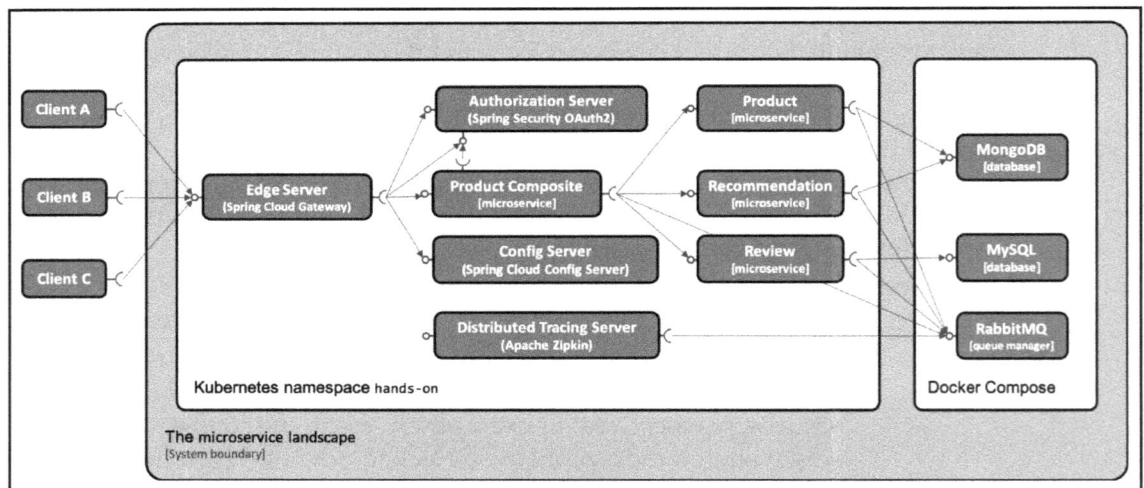

Changes in the source code

The following changes have been applied to the source code to prepare for deployment in an environment that's used for production:

- A Spring profile named `prod` has been added to the configuration files in the `config-repo` configuration repository:

  ```
  spring.profiles: prod
  ```

- In the `prod` profiles, the following has been added:
  - URLs to the resource managers that run as plain Docker containers:

    ```
    spring.rabbitmq.host: 172.17.0.1
    spring.data.mongodb.host: 172.17.0.1
    spring.datasource.url: jdbc:mysql://172.17.0.1:3306/review-db
    ```

    We are using the `172.17.0.1` IP address to address the Docker engine in the Minikube instance. This is the default IP address for the Docker engine when creating it with Minikube, at least for Minikube up to version 1.2.

    There is work ongoing for establishing a standard DNS name for containers to use if they need to access the Docker host they are running on, but at the time of writing this chapter, this work effort hasn't been completed.

  - Log levels have been set to warning or higher, that is, error or fatal. For example:

    ```
    logging.level.root: WARN
    ```

  - The only `actuator` endpoints that are exposed over HTTP are the `info` and `health` endpoints that are used by the liveness and readiness probes in Kubernetes, as well as the `circuitbreakerevents` endpoint that's used by the test script, `test-em-all.bash`:

    ```
    management.endpoints.web.exposure.include:
    health,info,circuitbreakerevents
    ```

- In the production `overlay` folder, `kubernetes/services/overlays/prod`, one deployment object for each microservice has been added with the following content so that it can be merged with the base definition:
    - For all microservices, `v1` is specified as the Docker `image` tag, and the `prod` profile is added to the active Spring profiles. For example, we have the following for the `product` service:

      ```
      image: hands-on/product-service:v1
      env:
      - name: SPRING_PROFILES_ACTIVE
        value: "docker,prod"
      ```

    - For the Zipkin and configuration server, which don't keep their configuration in the configuration repository, environment variables have been added in their deployment definitions with the corresponding configuration:

      ```
      env:
      - name: LOGGING_LEVEL_ROOT
        value: WARN
      - name: MANAGEMENT_ENDPOINTS_WEB_EXPOSURE_INCLUDE
        value: "health,info"
      - name: RABBIT_ADDRESSES
        value: 172.17.0.1
      ```

    - Finally, a `kustomization.yml` file defines that the files in the `prod` `overlay` folder shall be merged by specifying the `patchesStrategicMerge` patch mechanism with the corresponding definition in the `base` folder:

      ```
      bases:
      - ../../base
      patchesStrategicMerge:
      - auth-server-prod.yml
      - ...
      ```

In a real-world production environment, we should have also changed the `imagePullPolicy: Never` setting to `IfNotPresent`, that is, to download Docker images from a Docker registry. But since we will be deploying the production setup to the Minikube instance where we manually build and tag the Docker images, we will not update this setting.

Deploying to Kubernetes

To simulate production-grade resource managers, MySQL, MongoDB, and RabbitMQ will run outside of Kubernetes using Docker Compose. We start them up as we did in the previous chapters:

```
eval $(minikube docker-env)
docker-compose up -d mongodb mysql rabbitmq
```

We also need to tag the existing Docker images with v1 using the following commands:

```
docker tag hands-on/auth-server hands-on/auth-server:v1
docker tag hands-on/config-server hands-on/config-server:v1
docker tag hands-on/gateway hands-on/gateway:v1
docker tag hands-on/product-composite-service hands-on/product-composite-
service:v1
docker tag hands-on/product-service hands-on/product-service:v1
docker tag hands-on/recommendation-service hands-on/recommendation-
service:v1
docker tag hands-on/review-service hands-on/review-service:v1
```

From here, the commands are very similar to how we deployed to the development environment.

We will use another Kustomize overlay and use different credentials for the configuration server, but, otherwise, it will be the same (which, of course, is a good thing!). We will use the same configuration repository but configure the pods to use the prod Spring profile, as described previously. Follow these steps to do so:

1. Create a namespace, hands-on, and set this as the default namespace for kubectl:

```
kubectl create namespace hands-on
kubectl config set-context $(kubectl config current-context) --
namespace=hands-on
```

2. Create the config map for the configuration repository based on the files in the config-repo folder with the following command:

```
kubectl create configmap config-repo --from-file=config-repo/ --
save-config
```

3. Create the secret for the configuration server with the following command:

```
kubectl create secret generic config-server-secrets \
   --from-literal=ENCRYPT_KEY=my-very-secure-encrypt-key \
   --from-literal=SPRING_SECURITY_USER_NAME=prod-usr \
   --from-literal=SPRING_SECURITY_USER_PASSWORD=prod-pwd \
   --save-config
```

4. Create the secret for the clients of the configuration server with the following command:

```
kubectl create secret generic config-client-credentials \
--from-literal=CONFIG_SERVER_USR=prod-usr \
--from-literal=CONFIG_SERVER_PWD=prod-pwd --save-config
```

5. Remove the clear text encryption key and passwords from the command history:

```
history -c; history -w
```

6. Deploy the microservices for the development environment, based on the prod overlay, using the -k switch to activate Kustomize, as described previously:

```
kubectl apply -k kubernetes/services/overlays/prod
```

7. Wait for the deployments to be up and running:

```
kubectl wait --timeout=600s --for=condition=ready pod --all
```

8. To see the Docker images that are currently being used for production, run the following command:

```
kubectl get pods -o json | jq .items[].spec.containers[].image
```

The response should look something like the following:

```
● ○ ●                            8. bash
$ kubectl get pods -o json | jq .items[].spec.containers[].image
"hands-on/auth-server:v1"
"hands-on/config-server:v1"
"hands-on/gateway:v1"
"hands-on/product-composite-service:v1"
"hands-on/product-service:v1"
"hands-on/recommendation-service:v1"
"hands-on/review-service:v1"
"openzipkin/zipkin:2.12.9"
$ 
```

Note the `v1` version of the Docker images!

Also note that the resource manager pods for MySQL, MongoDB, and RabbitMQ are gone; these can be found with the `docker-compose ps` command.

Run the test script, `thest-em-all.bash`, to verify the simulated production environment:

```
HOST=$(minikube ip) PORT=31443 ./test-em-all.bash
```

Expect the same type of output that we got when the test script was run against the development environment.

Performing a rolling upgrade

Historically, updates often result in some downtime of the component that is updated. In a system landscape with an increasing number of autonomous microservices that are updated independently of each other, recurring downtimes due to frequent updates of the microservices is not acceptable. Being able to deploy an update without downtime becomes crucial.

In this section, we will see how we can perform a rolling upgrade, updating a microservice to a new version of its Docker image without requiring any downtime. Performing a rolling upgrade means that Kubernetes first starts the new version of the microservice in a new pod, and when it reports as being healthy, Kubernetes will terminate the old one. This ensures that there is always a pod up and running, ready to serve incoming requests during the upgrade. A prerequisite for a rolling upgrade to work is that the upgrade is backward compatible, both in terms of APIs and message formats that are used to communicate with other services and database structures. If the new version of the microservice requires changes to either the external APIs, message formats, or database structures that the old version can't handle, a rolling upgrade can't be applied. A deployment object is configured to perform any updates as a rolling upgrade by default.

To try this out, we will create a v2 version of the Docker image for the `product` service and then start up a test client, `siege`, that will submit one request per second during the rolling upgrade. The assumption is that the test client will report 200 (OK) for all the requests that it sends during the upgrade.

Preparing the rolling upgrade

To prepare for the rolling upgrade, first, verify that we have the v1 version of the product pod deployed:

```
kubectl get pod -l app=product -o
jsonpath='{.items[*].spec.containers[*].image} '
```

The expected output should reveal that v1 of the Docker image is in use:

```
8. bash
$ kubectl get pod -l app=product -o jsonpath='{.items[*].spec.containers[*].image} '
hands-on/product-service:v1 $
```

Create a v2 tag on the Docker image for the `product` service with the following command:

```
docker tag hands-on/product-service:v1 hands-on/product-service:v2
```

> To try out a rolling upgrade from a Kubernetes perspective, we don't need to change any code in the `product` service. Deploying a Docker image with another tag than the existing one will start up a rolling upgrade.

To be able to observe whether any downtime occurs during the upgrade, we will start a low volume load test using `siege`. The following command starts a load test that simulates one user (`-c1`) that submits one request per second on average (`-d1`):

```
siege https://$(minikube ip):31443/actuator/health -c1 -d1
```

Since the test calls the gateways health endpoint, it verifies that all the services are healthy.

You should receive an output that looks similar to the following screenshot:

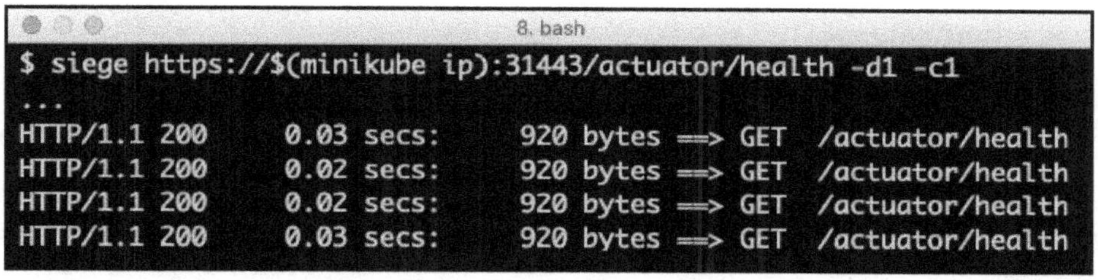

The interesting part in the response is the HTTP status code, which we expect to be 200 at all times.

Also, monitor changes to the state of the product pods with the following command:

```
kubectl get pod -l app=product -w
```

Upgrading the product service from v1 to v2

To upgrade the `product` service, edit the `kubernetes/services/overlays/prod/product-prod.yml` file and change `image: hands-on/product-service:v1` to `image: hands-on/product-service:v2`.

Apply the update with the following command:

```
kubectl apply -k kubernetes/services/overlays/prod
```

Expect a response from the command that reports that most of the objects are left unchanged, except for the product deployment that should be reported to be updated to `deployment.apps/product configured`.

Kubernetes comes with some shorthand commands. For example, `kubectl set image deployment/product pro=hands-on/product-service:v2` can be used to perform the same update that we did by updating the definitions file and running the `kubectl apply` command. A major benefit of using the `kubectl apply` command is that we can keep track of the changes by pushing the changes in the source code to a version control system such as Git. This is very important if we want to be able to handle our infrastructure as code. When playing around with a Kubernetes cluster, only use it to test shorthand commands, as this can be very useful.

In the output from the `kubectl get pod -l app=product -w` command we launched in the *Preparing the rolling upgrade* section, we will see some action occurring. Take a look at the following screenshot:

```
●  ○  ●                          8. bash
$ kubectl get pods -l app=product -w
NAME                       READY   STATUS             RESTARTS   AGE
product-5d45f8bcd-ffrdh    1/1     Running            0          20s
product-d4f789cc-t8mcl     0/1     Pending            0          0s
product-d4f789cc-t8mcl     0/1     Pending            0          0s
product-d4f789cc-t8mcl     0/1     ContainerCreating  0                     0s
product-d4f789cc-t8mcl     0/1     Running            0                     2s
product-d4f789cc-t8mcl     1/1     Running            0                     16s
product-5d45f8bcd-ffrdh    1/1     Terminating        0                     2m5s
product-5d45f8bcd-ffrdh    0/1     Terminating        0                     2m10s
product-5d45f8bcd-ffrdh    0/1     Terminating        0                     2m17s
product-5d45f8bcd-ffrdh    0/1     Terminating        0                     2m17s
```

Here, we can see how the existing pod (`ffrdh`) initially reported that it was up and running and also reported to be healthy when a new pod was launched (`t8mcl`). After a while (`16s`, in my case), it is reported as up and running as well. During a certain time period, both pods will be up and running and processing requests. After a while, the first pod is terminated (2 minutes, in my case).

When looking at the `siege` output, we can sometimes find a few errors being reported in terms of the `503` service unavailable errors:

```
●  ○  ○                          8. bash
HTTP/1.1 200      0.02 secs:     920 bytes ==> GET /actuator/health
HTTP/1.1 503      0.03 secs:    1068 bytes ==> GET /actuator/health
HTTP/1.1 503      0.03 secs:    1068 bytes ==> GET /actuator/health
HTTP/1.1 200      0.03 secs:     920 bytes ==> GET /actuator/health
```

This typically happens when the old pod is terminated. Before the old pod is reported unhealthy by the readiness probe, it can receive a few requests during its termination, that is, when it is no longer capable of serving any requests.

> In `Chapter 18`, *Using a Service Mesh to Improve Observability and Management*, we will see how we can set up routing rules that move traffic in a smoother way from an old pod to a newer one without causing 503 errors. We will also see how we can apply retry mechanisms to stop temporary failures from reaching an end user.

Wrap this up by verifying that the pod is using the new `v2` version of the Docker image:

```
kubectl get pod -l app=product -o
jsonpath='{.items[*].spec.containers[*].image} '
```

The expected output reveals that `v2` of the Docker image is in use:

```
●  ○  ○                          8. bash
$ kubectl get pod -l app=product -o jsonpath='{.items[*].spec.containers[*].image} '
hands-on/product-service:v2 $
```

After performing this upgrade, we can move on to learning what happens when things fail. In the next section, we will see how we can roll back a failed deployment.

Rolling back a failed deployment

From time to time, things don't go according to plan, for example, an upgrade of deployments and pods can fail for various reasons. To demonstrate how to roll back a failed upgrade, let's try to upgrade to `v3` without creating a `v3` tag on the Docker image!

Let's try out the following shorthand command to perform the update:

```
kubectl set image deployment/product pro=hands-on/product-service:v3
```

Expect to see the following changes reported by the `kubectl get pod -l app=product -w` command we launched in the *Preparing the rolling upgrade* section:

```
8. bash
product-7549b597b-m2dtn    0/1    Pending            0        0s
product-7549b597b-m2dtn    0/1    Pending            0        0s
product-7549b597b-m2dtn    0/1    ContainerCreating  0             0s
product-7549b597b-m2dtn    0/1    ErrImageNeverPull  0             1s
```

We can clearly see that the new pod (ending with `m2dtn`, in my case) has failed to start because of a problem finding its Docker image (as expected). If we look at the output from the `siege` test tool, no errors are reported, only 200 (OK)! Here, the deployment hangs since it can't find the requested Docker image, but no errors are affecting end users since the new pod couldn't even start.

Let's see what history Kubernetes has regarding the product's deployment. Run the following command:

```
kubectl rollout history deployment product
```

You will receive output similar to the following:

```
8. bash
$ kubectl rollout history deployment product
deployment.extensions/product
REVISION   CHANGE-CAUSE
1          <none>
2          <none>
3          <none>

$
```

We can guess that revision 2 is the one with the latest successful deployment, that is, `v2` of the Docker image. Let's check this with the following command:

```
kubectl rollout history deployment product --revision=2
```

In the response, we can see that `revision #2` is the one with Docker image `v2`:

```
                            8. bash
$ kubectl rollout history deployment product --revision=2
deployment.extensions/product with revision #2
Pod Template:
  Labels:        app=product
         pod-template-hash=d4f789cc
  Containers:
   pro:
    Image:      hands-on/product-service:v2
  ...
$
```

Let's roll back our deployment to `revision=2` with the following command:

```
kubectl rollout undo deployment product --to-revision=2
```

Expect a response that confirms the rollback, like so:

```
                            8. bash
$ kubectl rollout undo deployment product --to-revision=2
deployment.extensions/product rolled back
$
```

The `kubectl get pod -l app=product -w` command we launched in the *Preparing the rolling upgrade* section will report that the new (not working) pod has been removed by the `rollback` command:

```
                            8. bash
product-7549b597b-m2dtn    0/1    Terminating    0    7m40s
product-7549b597b-m2dtn    0/1    Terminating    0    7m40s
product-7549b597b-m2dtn    0/1    Terminating    0    7m43s
product-7549b597b-m2dtn    0/1    Terminating    0    7m43s
```

We can wrap this up by verifying that the current image version is still `v2`:

```
kubectl get pod -l app=product -o
jsonpath='{.items[*].spec.containers[*].image} '
```

Cleaning up

To delete the resources that we used, run the following commands:

1. Stop the watch command, `kubectl get pod -l app=product -w`, and the load test program, `siege`, with *Ctrl + C*.
2. Delete the namespace:

   ```
   kubectl delete namespace hands-on
   ```

3. Shut down the resource managers that run outside of Kubernetes:

   ```
   eval $(minikube docker-env)
   docker-compose down
   ```

The `kubectl delete namespace` command will recursively delete all Kubernetes resources that existed in the namespace, and the `docker-compose down` command will stop MySQL, MongoDB, and RabbitMQ. With the production environment removed, we have reached the end of this chapter.

Summary

In this chapter, we learned how to deploy the microservices in this book on Kubernetes. We also introduced some core features in Kubernetes, such as using Kustomize to configure deployments for different runtime environments, using Kubernetes deployment objects for rolling upgrades, and how to roll back a failed update if required. To help Kubernetes understand when the microservices need to be restarted and if they are ready to accept requests, we implemented liveness and readiness probes.

Finally, to be able to deploy our microservices, we had to replace Netflix Eureka with the built-in discovery service in Kubernetes. Changing the discovery service was done without any code changes – all we had to do was apply changes to the build dependencies and some of the configuration.

In the next chapter, we will see how we can further utilize Kubernetes to reduce the number of supporting services we need to deploy in Kubernetes. Head over to the next chapter to see how we can eliminate the need for the configuration server and how our edge server can be replaced by a Kubernetes ingress controller.

Questions

1. Why did we remove the Eureka server from the microservices landscape when deploying it on Kubernetes?
2. What did we replace the Eureka server with and how was the source code of the microservices affected by this change?
3. How are base and overlay folders used with Kustomize?
4. How can we get a running pod updated with changes in a config map or secret?
5. If we are using the latest tag on a Docker image, how can we get running pods using a new build of the Docker image?
6. What commands can we use to roll back a failed deployment?
7. What's the purpose of liveness and readiness probes?
8. What are the different ports that are being used in the following service definition?

```
apiVersion: v1
kind: Service
spec:
  type: NodePort
  ports:
    - port: 80
      nodePort: 30080
      targetPort: 8080
```

17
Implementing Kubernetes Features as an Alternative

The current microservice landscape contains a number of supportive services that implement important design patterns required in a large-scale microservice landscape; for example an edge, config, and authorization server, and a service for distributed tracing. For details, see Chapter 1, *Introduction to Microservices*, and refer to the *Design patterns for microservices* section. In the previous chapter, we replaced the implementation of the design pattern for service discovery, based on Netflix Eureka, with the built-in discovery service in Kubernetes. In this chapter, we will further simplify the microservice landscape by reducing the number of supportive services required to be deployed. Instead, the corresponding design patterns will be handled by built-in capabilities in Kubernetes. The Spring Cloud Config Server will be replaced with Kubernetes config maps and secrets. The Spring Cloud Gateway will be replaced by a Kubernetes ingress resource, which can act as an edge server in the same way as Spring Cloud Gateway.

In Chapter 11, *Securing Access to APIs*, refer to the *Protecting the external communication with HTTPS* section, where we use certificates to protect the external API. Manual handling of certificates is both time-consuming and error-prone. As an alternative, we will be introduced to the Cert Manager, which can automatically provide new certificates and replace expired ones for the external HTTPS endpoint exposed by the ingress. We will configure cert-manager to use **Let's Encrypt** to issue the certificates. Let's Encrypt is a free Certificate Authority that can be used to automatically issue certificates. Let's Encrypt must be able to verify that we own the DNS name that the certificate will be issued for. Since our Kubernetes cluster runs locally in Minikube, we have to make it possible for Let's Encrypt to access our cluster during the provisioning. We will use ngrok to create a temporary HTTP tunnel from the internet to our local Kubernetes cluster to be used by Let's Encrypt.

When using more and more features in a platform such as Kubernetes, it is important to ensure that the source code of the microservices isn't dependent on the platform; that is, should ensure that the microservices can still be used without Kubernetes. To ensure that we can still use the microservices outside Kubernetes, the chapter will conclude by deploying the microservice landscape using Docker Compose and executing the `test-em-all.bash` test script to verify that the microservices still work without using Kubernetes.

The following topics will be covered in this chapter:

- Replacing Spring Cloud Config Server with Kubernetes config maps and secrets
- Replacing Spring Cloud Gateway with a Kubernetes ingress resource
- Adding the Cert Manager to automatically provide certificates issued by Let's Encrypt
- Using `ngrok` to establish an HTTP tunnel from the internet to our local Kubernetes cluster
- Deploying and testing the microservice landscape using Docker Compose to ensure that the source code in the microservices isn't locked into Kubernetes

Technical requirements

All commands described in this book are run on a MacBook Pro using macOS Mojave but modifying this so that it can run on other platforms, such as Linux or Windows, should be straightforward.

The only new tool required for this chapter is the command-line `ngrok` tool used for establishing an HTTP tunnel from the internet to our local environment. It can be installed using Homebrew with the following command:

```
brew cask install ngrok
```

To use `ngrok`, a free account has to be created and an authorization token also has to be registered by taking the following steps:

1. Sign up here: `https://dashboard.ngrok.com/signup`.
2. After the account is created, run the following command:

   ngrok authtoken <YOUR_AUTH_TOKEN>

   Here, `<YOUR_AUTH_TOKEN>` is replaced with the authorization token found on the following page—`https://dashboard.ngrok.com/auth`.

The source code for this chapter can be found on GitHub: `https://github.com/PacktPublishing/Hands-On-Microservices-with-Spring-Boot-and-Spring-Cloud/tree/master/Chapter17`.

To be able to run the commands as described in the book, you need to download the source code to a folder and set up an environment variable, `$BOOK_HOME`, that points to that folder. Sample commands are as follows:

```
export BOOK_HOME=~/Documents/Hands-On-Microservices-with-Spring-Boot-and-Spring-Cloud
git clone
https://github.com/PacktPublishing/Hands-On-Microservices-with-Spring-Boot-and-Spring-Cloud $BOOK_HOME
cd $BOOK_HOME/Chapter17
```

The Java source code is written for Java 8 and tested on Java 12. This chapter uses Spring Cloud 2.1, SR2 (also known as the **Greenwich** release), Spring Boot 2.1.6, and Spring 5.1.8—the latest available versions of the Spring components at the time of writing this chapter. The source code has been tested using Kubernetes v1.15.

All source code examples in this chapter come from the source code in `$BOOK_HOME/Chapter17` but have been edited in several cases to remove non-relevant parts of the source code, such as comments, imports, and log statements.

If you want to see the changes applied to the source code in Chapter 17, *Implementing Kubernetes Features as an Alternative*, that is, the changes required to replace the Spring Cloud Config Server and Spring Cloud Gateway with corresponding features in Kubernetes, you can compare it with the source code for Chapter 16, *Deploying Our Microservices to Kubernetes*. You can use your favorite `diff` tool and compare the `$BOOK_HOME/Chapter16` and `$BOOK_HOME/Chapter17` folders.

Replacing the Spring Cloud Config Server

As we have seen in the previous chapter, `Chapter 16`, *Deploying Our Microservices to Kubernetes*, in the *Deploying to Kubernetes* section, config maps and secrets can be used to hold configuration information for our microservices. The Spring Cloud Config Server adds values such as keeping all configuration in one place, optional version control using Git, and the ability to encrypt sensitive information on the disk. But it also consumes a non-negligible amount of memory (as with any Java and Spring-based application) and adds significant overhead during startup. For example, when running automated integration tests such as the test script we are using in this book, `test-em-all.bash`, all microservices are started up at the same time, including the configuration server. Since the other microservices must get their configuration from the configuration server before they can start up, they all have to wait for the configuration server to be up and running before they can start up. This leads to a significant delay when running integration tests. If we use Kubernetes config maps and secrets instead, this delay is eliminated, making automated integration tests run faster. To me, it makes sense to use the Spring Cloud Config Server where the underlying platform doesn't provide a similar capability, but when deploying to Kubernetes, it is better to use config maps and secrets.

Using Kubernetes config maps and secrets instead of the Spring Cloud Config Server will make the microservice landscape start up faster and it will require less memory. It will also simplify the microservice landscape by eliminating one supportive service, the configuration server. This is illustrated by the following diagram:

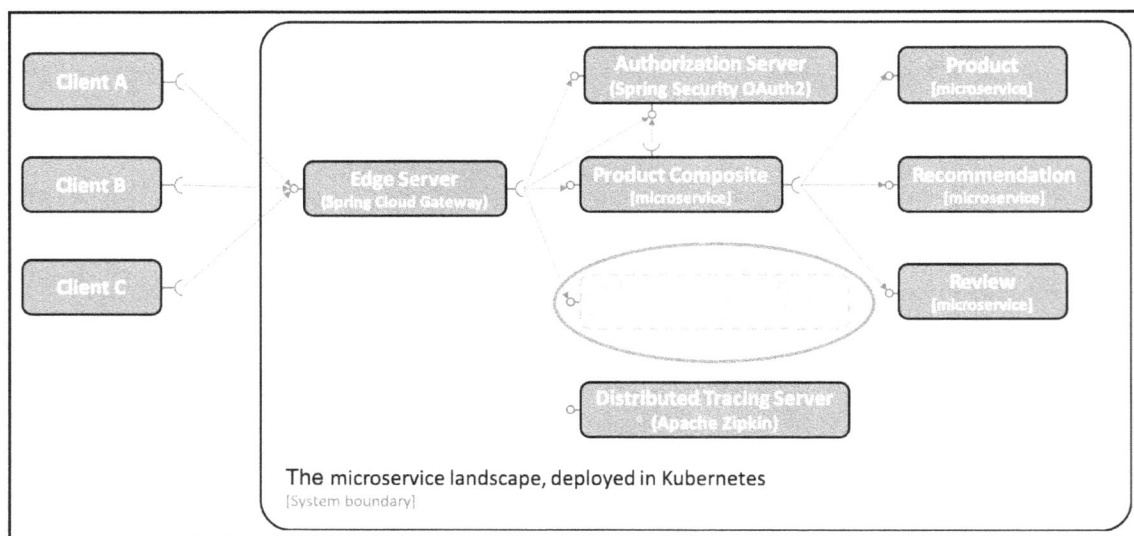

The microservice landscape, deployed in Kubernetes
[System boundary]

Let's see what is required to replace the Spring Cloud Config Server with Kubernetes config maps and secrets!

> Note especially that we only change the configuration; that is, no changes are required in the Java source code!

Changes in the source code to replace the Spring Cloud Config Server

The following changes have been applied in the configuration of the source code to replace the Spring Cloud Config Server with Kubernetes config maps and secrets:

- Removed the project `spring-cloud/config-server`, also including:
    - Removed the project in the `settings.gradle` build file.
    - Removed the configuration server YAML files and its declaration in the `kustomization.yml` files in the `kubernetes/services/base` and `kubernetes/services/overlays/prod` folders.
- Removed configuration from all microservices:
    - Removed the `spring-cloud-starter-config` dependency in the `build.gradle` build files
    - Removed the `bootstrap.yml` files in the `src/main/resource` folders in each project
    - Removed the `spring.clod.config.enabled=false` property setting in integration tests
- Changes in the configuration files in the `config-repo` folder:
    - Removed properties with sensitive information, that is, credentials for MongoDB, MySQL, RabbiMQ, and the password for the TLS certificate used by the edge server. They will be replaced by Kubernetes secrets.
    - The route to the configuration server API is removed in the configuration of the edge server

- Changes in the Kubernetes definition files for deployment resources in the `kubernetes/services/base` folder:
  - Config maps are mounted as volumes, that is, as folders in the filesystem of the container. Each microservice gets its own config maps, which contain the configuration files applicable for the specific microservice.
  - Define the `SPRING_CONFIG_LOCATION` environment variable to point out the configuration files in the volume.
  - Define credentials for access to resource managers using secrets.

Most changes are in the Kubernetes definitions files for the deployment resources. Let's look at the definition of the deployment resource for the `product` microservice as an example:

```
apiVersion: apps/v1
kind: Deployment
metadata:
  name: product
spec:
  template:
    spec:
      containers:
      - name: pro
        env:
        - name: SPRING_PROFILES_ACTIVE
          value: "docker"
        - name: SPRING_CONFIG_LOCATION
          value: file:/config-repo/application.yml,file:/config-
            repo/product.yml
        envFrom:
        - secretRef:
            name: rabbitmq-credentials
        - secretRef:
            name: mongodb-credentials
        volumeMounts:
        - name: config-repo-volume
          mountPath: /config-repo
      volumes:
      - name: config-repo-volume
        configMap:
          name: config-repo-product
```

Note that parts of the definition that have not been affected by the changes are left out for improved readability. See `kubernetes/services/base/product.yml` for the full source code.

The following explains the preceding source code:

- The `config-repo-product` config map is mapped in a volume named `config-repo-volume`.
- The `config-repo-volume` volume is mounted in the filesystem at `/config-repo`.
- The `SPRING_CONFIG_LOCATION` environment variable tells Spring where to find the property files, in this case, the `/config-repo/application.yml` and `/config-repo/product.yml` files.
- Credentials for accessing RabbitMQ and MongoDB are set up as environment variables based on the content in the `rabbitmq-credentials` and `mongodb-credentials` secrets.

The Kubernetes config maps and secrets will be created in the *Testing with ConfigMaps, secrets, and ingress* section.

That is what is required to replace the configuration server with Kubernetes config maps and secrets. In the next section, we will learn about how we can replace the Spring Cloud Gateway with a Kubernetes ingress resource.

Replacing the Spring Cloud Gateway

In this section, we will further simplify the microservice landscape by replacing the Spring Cloud Gateway with the built-in ingress resource in Kubernetes, reducing the number of supportive services required to be deployed.

As introduced in `Chapter 15`, *Introduction to Kubernetes*, an ingress resource can be used in Kubernetes to act as an edge server in the same way as a Spring Cloud Gateway. The Spring Cloud Gateway comes with a richer routing functionality compared to an ingress resource. But the ingress feature is part of the Kubernetes platform and can also be extended using the Cert Manager to automatically provide certificates, as we will see later on in this chapter.

We have also used the Spring Cloud Gateway to protect our microservices from unauthenticated requests; that is, the microservices require a valid OAuth 2.0/OIDC access token from a trusted OAuth Authorization Server or OIDC Provider. See `Chapter 11`, *Securing Access to APIs*, if a recap is required. Generally, Kubernetes ingress resources do not have support for that. Specific implementations of the ingress controller might, however, support it.

Finally, the composite health check we added to the gateway in `Chapter 10`, *Using Spring Cloud Gateway to Hide Microservices Behind an Edge Server* can be replaced by the Kubernetes liveness and readiness probes defined in each microservices deployment resource. To me, it makes sense to use the Spring Cloud Gateway where the underlying platform doesn't provide a similar capability, but when deploying to Kubernetes, it is better to use ingress resources.

In this chapter, we will delegate the responsibility for validating that the request contains a valid access token to the `product-composite` microservice. The next chapter will introduce the concept of a Service Mesh, where we will see an alternate implementation of an ingress that fully supports validating JWT-encoded access tokens, that is, the type of access tokens that we are using in this book.

> In the *Verifying that the microservices work without Kubernetes* section, we will still use the Spring Cloud Gateway together with Docker Compose, so we will not remove the project.

The following diagram shows how to remove the Spring Cloud Gateway from the microservice landscape when deploying to Kubernetes:

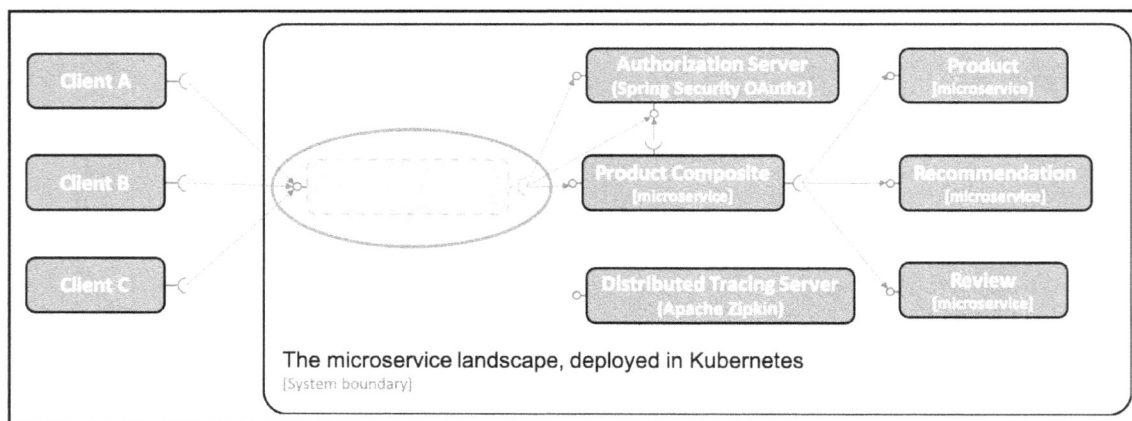

The microservice landscape, deployed in Kubernetes
[System boundary]

Let's see what is required to replace the Spring Cloud Gateway with a Kubernetes ingress resource!

> Note especially that we only change the configuration; that is, no changes are required in the Java source code!

Changes in the source code for Spring Cloud Gateway

The following changes have been applied in the configuration of the source code to replace the Spring Cloud Gateway with a Kubernetes ingress resource:

- Changes in the Kubernetes definition files for deployment resources in the `kubernetes/services` folder.
    - Removed the gateway YAML files and its declaration in the `kustomization.yml` files in the `base` and `overlays/prod` folders
    - Added the ingress resource in `base/ingress-edge-server.yml` and added a reference to it in `base/kustomization.yml`

The definition of the ingress resource looks like the following code:

```yaml
apiVersion: extensions/v1beta1
kind: Ingress
metadata:
  name: edge
spec:
  tls:
    - hosts:
      - minikube.me
      secretName: tls-certificate
  rules:
  - host: minikube.me
    http:
      paths:
      - path: /oauth
        backend:
          serviceName: auth-server
          servicePort: 80
      - path: /product-composite
        backend:
          serviceName: product-composite
          servicePort: 80
      - path: /actuator/health
        backend:
          serviceName: product-composite
          servicePort: 80
```

The following are the explanations for the preceding source code:

- The ingress resource is named `edge`.
- The `tls` section specifies that the ingress will require the use of HTTPS and that it will use a certificate issued for the `minikube.me` hostname.
- The certificate is stored in a secret named `tls-certificate`
  The `tls-certificate` secret will be created in *step 4* in the *Testing with Kubernetes ConfigMaps, secrets, and ingress resource* section.
- Routing rules are defined for requests to the `minikube.me` hostname.
  The DNS name `minikube.me` will be mapped to the IP address of the Minikube instance in the next topic.
- Routes are defined for the following:
    - The `auth-server` on the `/oauth` path
    - The `product-composite` microservice on the `/product-composite` path
    - The `health` endpoint in the `product-composite` microservice on the `/actuator/health` path

The Kubernetes ingress resource will be created in the next section where we will test the microservice landscape together with Kubernetes config maps, secrets, and an ingress resource.

Testing with Kubernetes ConfigMaps, secrets, and ingress resource

With the preceding changes described, we are ready to test the system landscape with the Spring Cloud Config Server and the Spring Cloud Gateway replaced by Kubernetes config maps, secrets, and an ingress resource. As before, when we used the Spring Cloud Gateway as the edge server, the external API will be protected by HTTPS. With this deployment, we will configure the ingress resource to reuse the self-signed certificate we used with the Spring Cloud Gateway for HTTPS. This is illustrated by the following diagram:

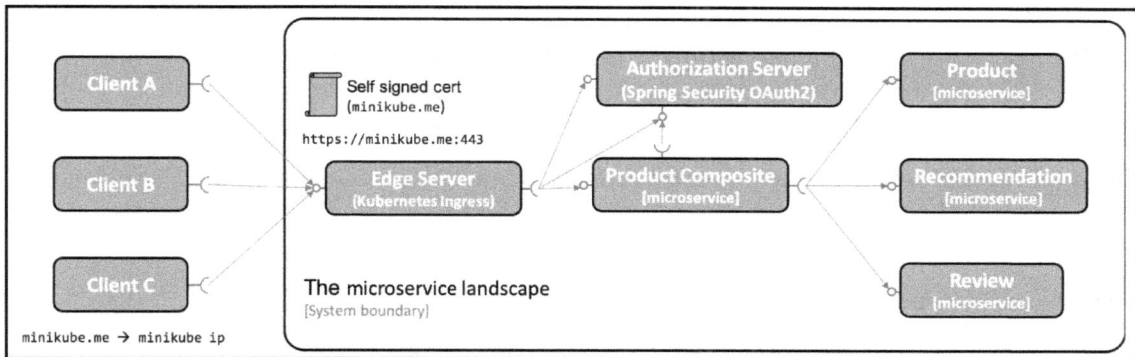

In the next section, we will enhance the certificate usage and replace
the self-signed certificate with certificates issued by Let's Encrypt.

The ingress will be exposed on the default HTTPS port, 443, on the Minikube instance. This
is handled by the ingress controller that was installed when we performed the minikube
addons enable ingress command; see Chapter 15, *Introduction to Kubernetes* and refer
to the *Creating a Kubernetes cluster* section for a recap. The ingress controller consists of a
deployment, nginx-ingress-controller, in the kube-system namespace. The
deployment configures its pod using a hostPort to map port 443 in the host, that is, the
Minikube instance, to port 443 in the container that runs in the pod. The central parts in the
definition of the deployment look like the following:

```
apiVersion: extensions/v1beta1
kind: Deployment
metadata:
  name: nginx-ingress-controller
spec:
  template:
    spec:
      containers:
        image: quay.io/kubernetes-ingress-controller/nginx-ingress-
          controller:0.23.0
        ports:
        - containerPort: 443
          hostPort: 443
```

> This setup works for a single-node Kubernetes cluster used for development and testing. In a multi-node Kubernetes cluster, external load balancers are used to expose an ingress controller for high availability and scalability.

The deployment uses the same type of commands as we used in `Chapter 16`, *Deploying Our Microservices to Kubernetes*; refer to the *Deploying to Kubernetes for development and test* section.

The major differences are that this deployment will:

- Create one config map for each microservice instead of one config map for the configuration server
- Create secrets for credentials to the resource managers and a secret for the TLS certificate used by the ingress instead of creating secrets for the credentials to the configuration server
- Create one ingress instead of using Spring Cloud Gateway

To simplify the deployment, deploy scripts for the development and production environments have been added to the source code. Let's go through the deploy script for the development environment that we will use in this section.

Walking through the deploy script

The `kubernetes/scripts/deploy-dev-env.bash` script, contains the necessary commands for performing the deployment. The script will perform the following steps:

1. It will create config maps, one per microservice. For example, for the `product` microservice, we have the following:

   ```
   kubectl create configmap config-repo-product --from-file=config-
   repo/application.yml --from-file=config-repo/product.yml --save-
   config
   ```

2. Then, it will create the required secrets. For example, credentials for accessing RabbitMQ are created with the following command:

   ```
   kubectl create secret generic rabbitmq-credentials \
       --from-literal=SPRING_RABBITMQ_USERNAME=rabbit-user-dev \
       --from-literal=SPRING_RABBITMQ_PASSWORD=rabbit-pwd-dev \
       --save-config
   ```

3. Secrets are also created for the resource managers; their names are suffixed with `server-credentials`. They are used in the Kubernetes definitions files in the `kubernetes/services/overlays/dev` folder. For example, credentials used by RabbitMQ are created with the following command:

```
kubectl create secret generic rabbitmq-server-credentials \
    --from-literal=RABBITMQ_DEFAULT_USER=rabbit-user-dev \
    --from-literal=RABBITMQ_DEFAULT_PASS=rabbit-pwd-dev \
    --save-config
```

4. The secret that contains the TLS certificate for the ingress, `tls-certificate`, is based on the already existing self-signed certificate in the `kubernetes/cert` folder. It is created with the following command:

```
kubectl create secret tls tls-certificate --key
kubernetes/cert/tls.key --cert kubernetes/cert/tls.crt
```

The self-signed certificate has been created with the following command: `openssl req -x509 -sha256 -nodes -days 365 -newkey rsa:2048 -keyout kubernetes/cert/tls.key -out kubernetes/cert/tls.crt -subj "/CN=minikube.me/O=minikube.me"`

5. Deploy the microservices for the development environment, based on the `dev` overlay, using the `-k` switch to activate Kustomize:

```
kubectl apply -k kubernetes/services/overlays/dev
```

6. Wait for the deployment and its pods to be up and running:

```
kubectl wait --timeout=600s --for=condition=ready pod --all
```

After this walkthrough, we are ready to run the commands required for deploying and testing!

Running commands for deploying and testing

Before we can perform the deployment, we need to make the following preparations:

- Map the DNS name used by the ingress, `minikube.me`, to the IP address of the Minikube instance
- Build Docker images from source
- Create a namespace in Kubernetes

Run the following commands to prepare, deploy, and test:

1. Map `minikube.me` to the IP address of the Minikube instance by adding a line to the file `/etc/hosts` with the following command:

   ```
   sudo bash -c "echo $(minikube ip) minikube.me | tee -a /etc/hosts"
   ```

   Verify the result with the `cat /etc/hosts` command. Expect a line that contains the IP address of your Minikube instance followed by `minikube.me` as shown in the following screenshot:

2. Build Docker images from source with the following commands:

   ```
   cd $BOOK_HOME/Chapter17
   eval $(minikube docker-env)
   ./gradlew build && docker-compose build
   ```

3. Recreate the namespace, `hands-on`, and set it as the default namespace:

   ```
   kubectl delete namespace hands-on
   kubectl create namespace hands-on
   kubectl config set-context $(kubectl config current-context) --namespace=hands-on
   ```

4. Execute the deployment by running the script with the following command:

   ```
   ./kubernetes/scripts/deploy-dev-env.bash
   ```

5. Once the deployment is complete, start the tests with the following command:

   ```
   HOST=minikube.me PORT=443 ./test-em-all.bash
   ```

Expect the normal output that we have seen from the previous chapters as shown in the following screenshot:

```
                            3. bash
$ HOST=minikube.me PORT=443 ./test-em-all.bash
Start Tests: Wed Jul 10 13:05:51 CEST 2019
HOST=minikube.me
PORT=443
Wait for: curl -k https://minikube.me:443/actuator/health... DONE, continues...
Test OK (HTTP Code: 200)
...
End, all tests OK: Wed Jul 10 13:06:33 CEST 2019
$
```

6. You can try out the APIs manually by performing the same steps as in the earlier chapters: just replace the host and port with `minikube.me`. Get an OAuth/OIDC access token and use it to call an API with the following commands:

```
ACCESS_TOKEN=$(curl -k
https://writer:secret@minikube.me/oauth/token -d
grant_type=password -d username=magnus -d password=password -s | jq
.access_token -r)

curl -ks https://minikube.me/product-composite/2 -H "Authorization:
Bearer $ACCESS_TOKEN" | jq .productId
```

Expect the requested product ID, 2, in the response.

> The deployment we have set up in this section is based on an environment aimed at developing and testing. If you want to set up an environment aimed at staging and production, such as the one described in `Chapter 16`, *Deploying Our Microservices to Kubernetes*, refer to the *Deploying to Kubernetes for staging and production* section. For this, you can use the `./kubernetes/scripts/deploy-prod-env.bash` script. Use it in *step 4* as previously outlined instead of the `deploy-dev-env.bash` script. Note that the `deploy-prod-env.bash` script will launch the three resource managers for MySQL, MongoDB, and RabbitMQ using Docker Compose; that is, they will run as Docker containers outside Kubernetes (in the same way as in `Chapter 16`, *Deploying Our Microservices to Kubernetes*).

This deployment uses a self-signed certificate that was exposed by the Kubernetes ingress and that requires manual provisioning. Manual handling of certificates is both time-consuming and error-prone. It is, for example, very easy to forget to renew a certificate in time. In the next section, we will learn how to use the Cert Manager and Let's Encrypt to automate this provisioning process!

Automating the provision of certificates

As mentioned in the introduction to this chapter, we will use the Cert Manager to automate the provision of certificates used by the external HTTPS endpoint exposed by the ingress. The Cert Manager will run as an add-on in Kubernetes and will be configured to request the issuing of certificates from Let's Encrypt with a free Certificate Authority that can be used to automate the issuing of certificates. To be able to verify that we own the DNS name that the certificate shall be issued for, Let's Encrypt requires access to the endpoint we want to issue the certificate for. Since our Kubernetes cluster runs locally in Minikube, we must make it possible for Let's Encrypt to access our cluster during the provisioning. We will use the ngrok tool to create a temporary HTTP tunnel from the internet to our local Kubernetes cluster to be used by Let's Encrypt.

For more information on each product, see the following:

- Cert Manager: `http://docs.cert-manager.io/en/latest/index.html`
- Let's Encrypt: `https://letsencrypt.org/docs/`
- ngrok: `https://ngrok.com/docs`

All this together might seem a bit overwhelming, so let's take it step by step:

1. Deploy the Cert Manager and define issuers in Kubernetes based on Let's Encrypt.
2. Create an HTTP tunnel using ngrok.
3. Provision certificates with the Cert Manager and Let's Encrypt.
4. Verify that we got certificates from Let's Encrypt.
5. Clean up.

> The HTTP tunnel is only required if your Kubernetes cluster isn't reachable on the internet. If its ingress resource can be accessed directly from the internet, the use of ngrok can be skipped.

Deploying the Cert Manager and defining Let's Encrypt issuers

To deploy the Cert Manager, we can execute a single Kubernetes definition file that will create a namespace, `cert-manager`, and then deploy the Cert Manager into the namespace. We will install version 0.8.1, the latest available version when writing this chapter. Run the following command:

```
kubectl apply -f
https://github.com/jetstack/cert-manager/releases/download/v0.8.1/cert-mana
ger.yaml
```

If you get an error message such as `unable to recognize "https://github.com/jetstack/cert-manager/releases/download/v0.8.1/cert-manager.yaml": no matches for kind "Issuer" in version "certmanager.k8s.io/v1alpha1"`, then simply rerun the command again.

Wait for the deployment and its pods to be available:

```
kubectl wait --timeout=600s --for=condition=ready pod --all -n cert-manager
```

Expect output similar to the following from the command:

```
● ● ●                              4. bash
$ kubectl wait --timeout=600s --for=condition=ready pod --all -n cert-manager
pod/cert-manager-5d5cc69d6-5f9wb condition met
pod/cert-manager-cainjector-7688bf9689-9md7k condition met
pod/cert-manager-webhook-dfcbcc64b-vh5qh condition met
$
```

With the Cert Manager in place, we can define issuers in Kubernetes that are based on Let's Encrypt.

Let's Encrypt exposes the following issuers:

- **Staging environment**, to be used during development and test phases where it can be expected that a lot of short-lived certificates are requested. The staging environment allows for the creation of many certificates but the root **CA** (short for **Certificate Authority**) in the certificate is not trusted. This means that certificates from the staging environment can't be used to protect web pages or APIs used by a web browser. A web browser won't trust its root CA and will complain when a user opens a web page protected by certificates from the staging environment.

- **Production environment**, it uses a trusted root CA to issue certificates. It can, therefore, be used to issue certificates that are trusted by web browsers. The production environment limits the number of certificates that can be issued. For example, only 50 new certificates per week can be issued per registered domain, for instance, in case `ngrok.io`.

We will register two issuers in Kubernetes, one for the staging environment and one for the production environment. Issuers can be registered either globally in the cluster or locally in a namespace. To keep things together, we will use namespace local issuers.

Communication between the Cert Manager and Let's Encrypt during the provision of certificates is based on a standard protocol, **Automated Certificate Management Environment v2**, or **ACME v2** for short. Let's Encrypt will act as a CA and the Cert Manager will act as an ACME client. To validate the ownership of a DNS name, the ACME protocol specifies two types of challenge that a CA can use:

- `http-01`: The CA asks the ACME client for a randomly named file to be made available under the following
  URL: `http://<domainname>/.well-known/acme-challenge/<randomfile name>`. If the CA succeeds in accessing the file using this URL, the ownership of the domain is validated.
- `dns-01`: The CA asks the ACME client for a specified value to be placed in a TXT record, `_acme-challenge.<YOUR_DOMAIN>`, under the domain in the DNS server. This is typically achieved by using an API of the DNS provider. If the CA succeeds in accessing the specified content in the TXT record in the DNS server, the ownership of the domain is validated.

Automating a `dns-01` based challenge is harder to achieve than automating an `http-01` challenge in most cases; however, it is preferred, for example, if the HTTP endpoint isn't available on the internet. A `dns-01` challenge also supports issuing wildcard certificates, which an `http-01` challenge can't be used for. In this chapter, we will configure the Cert Manager to use an `http-01`—based challenge.

The definition of the issuer for the Let's Encrypt staging environment looks like the following:

```
apiVersion: certmanager.k8s.io/v1alpha1
kind: Issuer
metadata:
  name: letsencrypt-issuer-staging
spec:
  acme:
    email: <your email address>
```

```
server: https://acme-staging-v02.api.letsencrypt.org/directory
privateKeySecretRef:
  name: letsencrypt-issuer-staging-account-key
solvers:
- http01:
    ingress:
      class: nginx
```

The following explains the preceding source code:

- The `name` of the issuer, `letsencrypt-issuer-staging`, will be used in the ingress when referring to the issuer to be used when provisioning certificates for the ingress.
- The `email` must be filled in with your email address. Let's Encrypt will use the email address to contact you about expiring certificates and issues, if any, related to your account.
- The `server` field points out the URL for the Let's Encrypt staging environment.
- The `privateKeySecretRef` field contains the name of a secret. This secret will be created by the Cert Manager and will contain an ACME/Let's Encrypt `account private key`. This key identifies you (or your company) as a user of the ACME service, that is, Let's Encrypt. It is used to sign requests sent to Let's Encrypt to validate your identity.
- The `solver` definition declares that an `http-01` challenge shall be used to verify the ownership of the domain name.

The definition of the issuer for the Let's Encrypt production environment looks the same, the major difference is the ACME server URL used: `https://acme-v02.api.letsencrypt.org/directory`.

Edit the following files and replace `<your email address>` with your email address:

- `kubernetes/services/base/letsencrypt-issuer-staging.yaml`
- `kubernetes/services/base/letsencrypt-issuer-prod.yaml`

Apply the definitions with the following commands:

```
kubectl apply -f kubernetes/services/base/letsencrypt-issuer-staging.yaml
kubectl apply -f kubernetes/services/base/letsencrypt-issuer-prod.yaml
```

We now have the Cert Manager in place and have registered issuers for the Let's Encrypt staging and production environment. The next step is to create an HTTP tunnel using `ngrok`.

Creating an HTTP tunnel using ngrok

The free subscription to ngrok can be used to create an HTTP tunnel where ngrok terminates the HTTPS traffic using its own wildcard certificate for *.ngrok.io, that is, before the HTTP requests reach the ingress resource in Kubernetes. The client that sends the HTTPS request will only see the ngrok certificate and not the certificate exposed by the ingress resource in Kubernetes. This means that we can't use the HTTP tunnel to test a certificate that has been issued by Let's Encrypt and is used by the ingress resource in Kubernetes. This is illustrated in the following diagram:

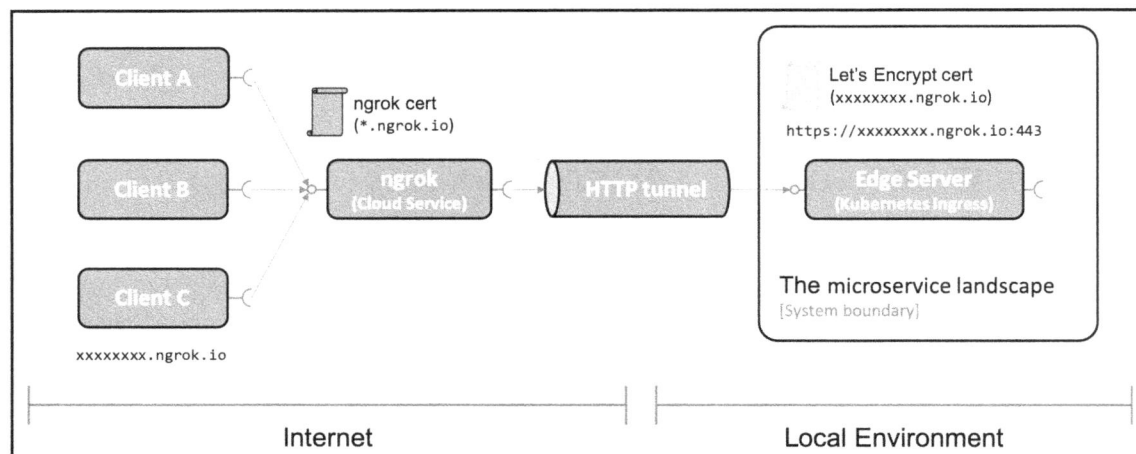

But the HTTP tunnel can be used during the provisioning phase where Let's Encrypt needs to verify that the ACME client owns the DNS name it is requested to issue a certificate for. The DNS name will be the hostname that ngrok assigns to the HTTP tunnel, for example, 6cc09528.ngrok.io. Once the provisioning is performed, we can shut down the HTTP tunnel and redirect the hostname to the IP address of the Minikube instance (using the local /etc/hosts file). This is illustrated in the following diagram:

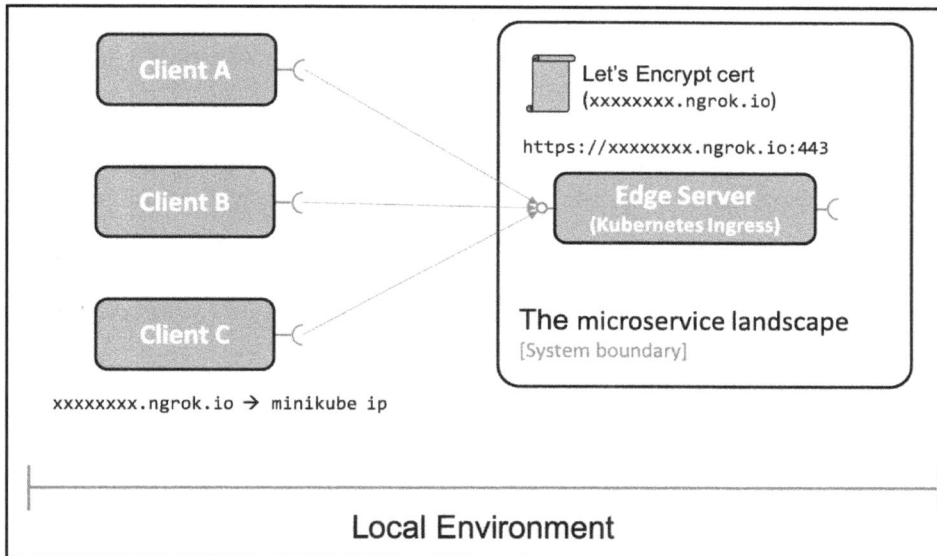

For paying customers, `ngrok` provides a TLS tunnel that passes through HTTPS traffic instead of terminating it; that is, a client that sends an HTTPS request will be able to see and verify the certificate exposed by the ingress resource in Kubernetes. Using a TLS tunnel instead of the HTTP tunnel should make this extra step unnecessary.

Perform the following steps to create the HTTP tunnel:

1. Create the HTTP tunnel with the following command:

   ngrok http https://minikube.me:443

2. Expect output similar to the following screenshot:

3. Pick up the hostname for the HTTP tunnel, `6cc09528.ngrok.io` in the preceding example, and save it in an environment variable such as the following:

```
NGROK_HOST=6cc09528.ngrok.io
```

With the HTTP tunnel in place, we can prepare the definition of the ingress resource for automatic provisioning of its certificate using the Cert Manager and Let's Encrypt!

Provisioning certificates with the Cert Manager and Let's Encrypt

Before configuring the ingress resource, it might be good to have a high level understanding of how the provisioning is performed. The automated provisioning of a certificate using the Cert Manager and Let's Encrypt looks like the following:

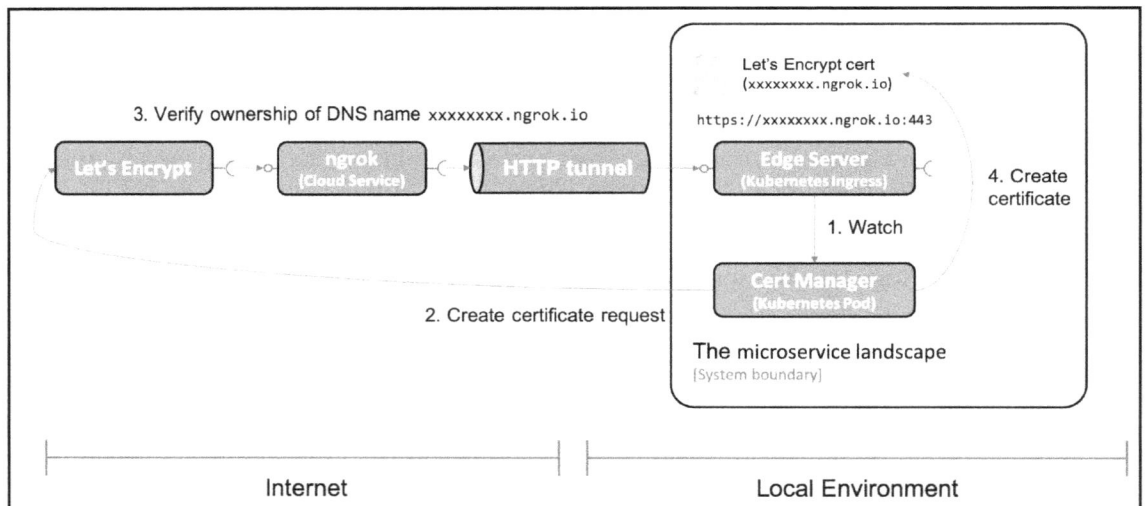

The following steps will be taken during the provisioning:

1. An ingress is created annotated with `certmanager.k8s.io/issuer: "name of a Let's Encrypt issuer"`.
2. This annotation will trigger the Cert Manager to start to provide a certificate for the ingress using Let's Encrypt.

3. During the provisioning process, Let's Encrypt will perform an `http-01` challenge and use the HTTP tunnel to verify that the Cert Manager owns the DNS name.

4. Once the provisioning is complete, the Cert Manager will store the certificate in Kubernetes and create a secret with the name specified by the ingress.

We will add a new ingress, `edge-ngrok`, defined in the `ingress-edge-server-ngrok.yml` file, which will route requests to the hostname of the HTTP tunnel. This ingress will have the same routing rules as the existing ingress. The part that differs looks like the following:

```
apiVersion: extensions/v1beta1
kind: Ingress
metadata:
  name: edge-ngrok
  annotations:
    certmanager.k8s.io/issuer: "letsencrypt-issuer-staging"
spec:
  tls:
  - hosts:
    - xxxxxxxx.ngrok.io
    secretName: tls-ngrok-letsencrypt-certificate
  rules:
  - host: xxxxxxxx.ngrok.io
```

Here is an explanation for the preceding source code:

- Using the `certmanager.k8s.io/issuer: "letsencrypt-issuer-staging"` annotation, we ask the Cert Manager to provision a certificate for this ingress using the issuer named `letsencrypt-issuer-staging`.
- The `xxxxxxxx.ngrok.io` hostname in the `tls` and `rules` declarations must be replaced with the actual hostname of your HTTP tunnel.
- The secret with the name `tls-ngrok-letsencrypt-certificate` is where the certificate will be stored once the provisioning is complete.

With this high level of understanding of the provisioning process and an ingress resource prepared for using it in place, we can start to provision certificates using the two environments that Let's Encrypt supports. Let's start with the staging environment, suitable for development and test activities.

Using Let's Encrypt's staging environment

Perform the following steps to provision a certificate from Let's Encrypt staging environment and verify that it works:

1. Edit the `kubernetes/services/base/ingress-edge-server-ngrok.yml` file and replace `xxxxxxxx.ngrok.io` with the hostname of your HTTP tunnel in two places!
   (`6cc09528.ngrok.io` in the preceding example.)

2. Before starting up the provisioning, run a watch command in a separate Terminal window to monitor the provisioning of the certificate. Run the following command:

   ```
   kubectl get cert --watch
   ```

3. Initiate the provisioning by applying the new ingress definition with the following command:

   ```
   kubectl apply -f kubernetes/services/base/ingress-edge-server-ngrok.yml
   ```

4. The Cert Manager will now detect the new ingress and start to provide a certificate with Let's Encrypt staging environment as the issuer using the ACME v2 protocol via the HTTP tunnel set up by `ngrok`.

5. After a while, you should notice the `http-01` challenge in the Terminal window where the HTTP tunnel runs. Expect a request like the following in the output:

   ```
   3. bash
   HTTP Requests
   -------------

   GET /.well-known/acme-challenge/FtYgFcTeAekq1NGt06 200 OK
   ```

6. A `tls-ngrok-letsencrypt-certificate` certificate will be created and it will be stored in the `tls-ngrok-letsencrypt-certificate` secret, as specified in the ingress. Expect output from the `kubectl get cert --watch` command similar to the following:

```
● ○ ●                            3. bash
$ kubectl get cert -w
NAME                                     READY   SECRET                                     AGE
tls-ngrok-letsencrypt-certificate        False   tls-ngrok-letsencrypt-certificate          1s
tls-ngrok-letsencrypt-certificate        True    tls-ngrok-letsencrypt-certificate          44s
```

7. After a while the READY state of the certificate will be changed to True, meaning that the certificate is provisioned and we are ready to try it out!

8. To try out the certificate provisioned by Let's Encrypt, we need to redirect the ngrok hostname to point directly to the Minikube IP address. We will add the hostname of the HTTP tunnel to the /etc/hosts file resolved to the IP address of the Minikube instance. This will result in local requests sent to the hostname of the HTTP tunnel being directed to the Minikube instance as illustrated by the following diagram:

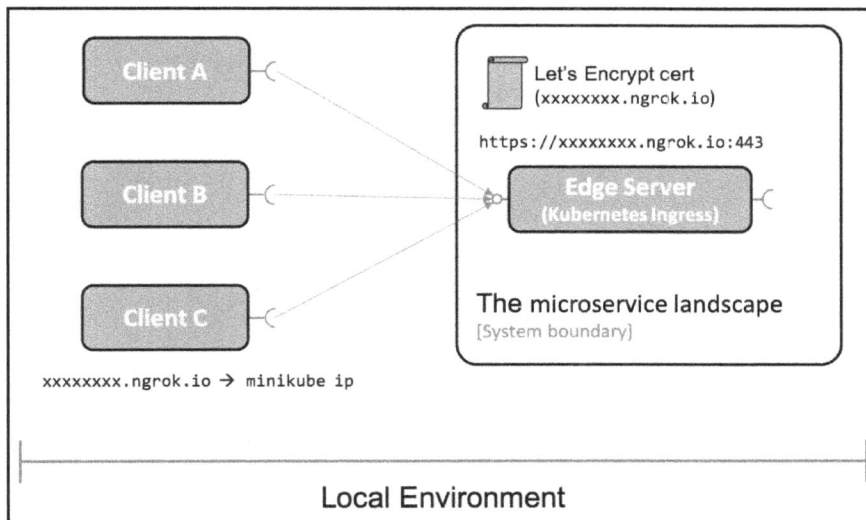

9. Edit the /etc/hosts file and add the hostname of your HTTP tunnel after minikube.me in the line we added earlier in the chapter. After the edit, the line should look similar to the following:

```
● ○ ●                            3. bash
$ cat /etc/hosts
...
192.168.99.121 minikube.me 6cc09528.ngrok.io
$ ▊
```

10. Use the `keytool` command to see what certificate the hostname of the HTTP tunnel exposes:

```
keytool -printcert -sslserver $NGROK_HOST:443 | grep -E
"Owner:|Issuer:"
```

11. Expect a response such as the following:

```
3. bash
$ keytool -printcert -sslserver $NGROK_HOST:443 | grep -E "Owner:|Issuer:"
Owner: CN=6cc09528.ngrok.io
Issuer: CN=Fake LE Intermediate X1
Owner: CN=Fake LE Intermediate X1
Issuer: CN=Fake LE Root X1
$
```

> If your `keytool` is localized, that is, it prints its output in another language rather than English, you will need to change the `Owner:|Issuer:` string used by the preceding `grep` command, to the localized version.

12. The certificate is issued for the hostname of the HTTP tunnel (`6cc09528.ngrok.io` in the preceding example) and it is issued by `Fake LE Intermediate X1` using `Fake LE Root X1` as its Root CA. This verifies that the ingress uses the Let's Encrypt staging certificate!

13. Wrap up by running the `test-em-all.bash` test script using the same command:

```
HOST=$NGROK_HOST PORT=443 ./test-em-all.bash
```

Expect the usual output from the test script; check that it concludes with the following:

```
3. bash
End, all tests OK: Wed Jul 10 13:06:33 CEST 2019
$
```

Certificates provisioned by Let's Encrypt staging environment are, as mentioned previously, good for development and test activities. But since its root CA is not trusted by web browsers, they can't be used in production scenarios. Let's also try out Let's Encrypt's production environment, which is capable of provisioning trusted certificates, albeit in limited numbers.

Using Let's Encrypt's production environment

To provision a certificate from Let's Encrypt production environment, instead of the staging environment, we have to change the issuer in the ingress definition and then apply the updated definition. Perform the following steps:

1. Edit the `kubernetes/services/base/ingress-edge-server-ngrok.yml` file and change the following code:

   ```
   certmanager.k8s.io/issuer: "letsencrypt-issuer-staging"
   ```

   The preceding code should now be as follows:

   ```
   certmanager.k8s.io/issuer: "letsencrypt-issuer-prod"
   ```

2. Apply the change by running the following command:

   ```
   kubectl apply -f kubernetes/services/base/ingress-edge-server-ngrok.yml
   ```

3. Monitor the output from the `kubectl get cert --watch` command and wait for the new certificate to be provisioned. Its ready state will change to `False` immediately after the apply command, and after a short while it will go back to `True`. This means that the Cert Manager has provisioned a certificate issued by Let's Encrypt production environment!

4. Check the certificate with the following `keytool` command:

   ```
   keytool -printcert -sslserver $NGROK_HOST:443 | grep -E "Owner:|Issuer:"
   ```

   Expect output such as the following:

   ```
   $ keytool -printcert -sslserver $NGROK_HOST:443 | grep -E "Owner:|Issuer:"
   Owner: CN=6cc09528.ngrok.io
   Issuer: CN=Let's Encrypt Authority X3, O=Let's Encrypt, C=US
   Owner: CN=Let's Encrypt Authority X3, O=Let's Encrypt, C=US
   Issuer: CN=DST Root CA X3, O=Digital Signature Trust Co.
   $
   ```

5. The new certificate is like the one previously issued for the hostname of the HTTP tunnel (`6cc09528.ngrok.io` in the preceding example), but this time the issuer and Root CA are from the production environment. This means that the certificate should be trusted by a web browser.

6. Open the `https://6cc09528.ngrok.io/actuator/health` URL
(replace `6cc09528.ngrok.io` with the hostname of your HTTP tunnel) in a local
web browser. If you use Google Chrome and click on the certificate icon (the
padlock in front of the URL) you should see something like the following output:

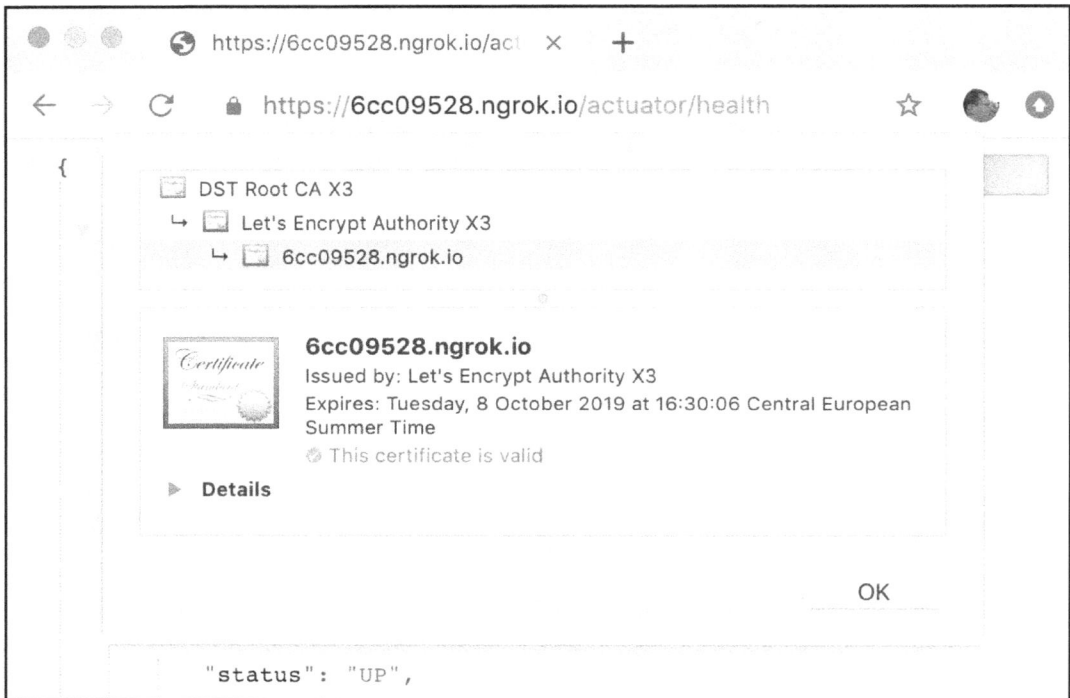

As seen in the preceding screenshot Chrome reports: **This certificate is valid**!

7. Wrap up by verifying that the `test-em-all.bash` test script also works with
this certificate as follows:

```
HOST=$NGROK_HOST PORT=443 ./test-em-all.bash
```

Expect the usual output from the test script; check that it concludes with the
following output:

You can switch back to the staging issuer by following the same procedure but also change back to the staging issuer in the ingress definition.

Cleaning up

When you are done, clean up the resources created in Kubernetes (and optionally in Docker) using Docker Compose by running the following commands:

1. Stop the `kubectl get cert --watch` command with *Ctrl + C*.
2. Stop the HTTP tunnel with *Ctrl + C*.
3. Delete the namespace in Kubernetes with the following command:

   ```
   kubectl delete namespace hands-on
   ```

4. If you tried out the production environment deployment using the `./kubernetes/scripts/deploy-prod-env.bash` script, you also need to stop the resource managers that were launched as Docker containers using Docker Compose. Run the following command to stop them:

   ```
   docker-compose down mongodb mysql rabbitmq
   ```

Now that we are done automating the certificates to provision them, let's see how to verify that microservices work without Kubernetes. Let's see how this is done.

Verifying that microservices work without Kubernetes

In this chapter and the previous one, we have seen how features in the Kubernetes platform, such as config maps, secrets, services, and ingress resources, can simplify the effort of developing a landscape of cooperating microservices. But it is important to ensure that the source code of the microservices doesn't get dependent on the platform from a functional perspective. Avoiding such a lock-in makes it possible to change to another platform in the future, if required, with minimal effort. Changing the platform should not require changes in the source code but only in the configuration of the microservices.

Testing the microservices using Docker Compose and the `test-em-all.bash` test script will ensure that they work from a functional perspective, meaning that they will verify that the functionality in the microservice source code still works without Kubernetes. When running microservices without Kubernetes, we will lack the non-functional features that Kubernetes provides us with, for example, monitoring, scaling, and restarting containers.

When using Docker Compose, we will map the following Kubernetes features:

- Instead of config maps, we use volumes that map the configuration files directly from the host filesystem.
- Instead of using secrets, we keep sensitive information such as credentials in the `.env` file.
- Instead of an ingress, we will use the Spring Cloud Gateway.
- Instead of services, we will map hostnames used by the clients directly to the hostnames of the containers, meaning that we will not have any service discovery in place and will not be able to scale containers.

Using Docker Compose this way will result in significant disadvantages from a non-functional perspective compared to using Kubernetes. But it is acceptable, given that Docker Compose will only be used to run functional tests.

Let's go through the code changes in the `docker-compose*.yml` files before we run the tests using Docker Compose.

Changes in the source code for Docker Compose

To run microservices outside Kubernetes, using Docker Compose, the following changes have been applied to the `docker-compose*.yml` files:

- Removed the configuration server definition
- Removed the use of the following configuration server environment variables: `CONFIG_SERVER_USR` and `CONFIG_SERVER_PWD`
- Mapped the `config-repo` folder as a volume in each container that needs to read configuration files from the configuration repository
- Defined the `SPRING_CONFIG_LOCATION` environment variable to point to the configuration files in the configuration repository

- Stored sensitive information such as credentials and passwords in TLS certificates in the Docker Compose `.env` file
- Defined environment variables with credentials for access to resource managers using the variables defined in the `.env` file

For example, the configuration of the `product` microservice looks like the following in `docker-compose.yml`:

```
product:
  build: microservices/product-service
  image: hands-on/product-service
  environment:
    - SPRING_PROFILES_ACTIVE=docker
    - SPRING_CONFIG_LOCATION=file:/config-
repo/application.yml,file:/config-repo/product.yml
    - SPRING_RABBITMQ_USERNAME=${RABBITMQ_USR}
    - SPRING_RABBITMQ_PASSWORD=${RABBITMQ_PWD}
    - SPRING_DATA_MONGODB_AUTHENTICATION_DATABASE=admin
    - SPRING_DATA_MONGODB_USERNAME=${MONGODB_USR}
    - SPRING_DATA_MONGODB_PASSWORD=${MONGODB_PWD}
  volumes:
    - $PWD/config-repo:/config-repo
```

Here is an explanation for the preceding source code:

- The `config-repo` folder is mapped as a volume into the container at `/config-repo`.
- The `SPRING_CONFIG_LOCATION` environment variable tells Spring where to find the property files, in this case, the `/config-repo/application.yml` and `/config-repo/product.yml` files.
- Credentials for accessing RabbitMQ and MongoDB are set up as environment variables based on the content in the `.env` file.

The credentials referred to in the preceding source code are defined in the `.env` file as:

```
RABBITMQ_USR=rabbit-user-prod
RABBITMQ_PWD=rabbit-pwd-prod
MONGODB_USR=mongodb-user-prod
MONGODB_PWD=mongodb-pwd-prod
```

Testing with Docker Compose

To test with Docker Compose, we will use Docker Desktop (earlier named Docker for macOS) instead of Minikube. Perform the following steps:

1. To direct the Docker client to use Docker Desktop instead of Minikube run the following command:

```
eval $(minikube docker-env --unset)
```

2. To save memory, you might want to stop the Minikube instance:

```
minikube stop
```

3. Start Docker Desktop (if not already running).
4. Build the Docker images in Docker Desktop with the following command:

```
docker-compose build
```

5. Run the tests using RabbitMQ (with one partition per topic):

```
COMPOSE_FILE=docker-compose.yml ./test-em-all.bash start stop
```

The tests should begin by starting all the containers, run the tests, and finally stop all the containers. Expect output like the following:

```
3. bash
$ COMPOSE_FILE=docker-compose.yml ./test-em-all.bash start stop
Start Tests: Sat Jul 13 16:40:19 CEST 2019
HOST=localhost
PORT=8443
Restarting the test environment...
$ docker-compose down --remove-orphans
$ docker-compose up -d
Creating network "my-network" with the default driver
Creating book-source-code_mongodb_1       ... done
...
Creating book-source-code_product-composite_1 ... done
Wait for: curl -k https://localhost:8443/actuator/health... , retry #1 ... DONE, continues...
Test OK (HTTP Code: 200)
...
End, all tests OK: Sat Jul 13 16:42:05 CEST 2019
Stopping the test environment...
$ docker-compose down --remove-orphans
Stopping book-source-code_product-composite_1 ... done
...
Removing book-source-code_mongodb_1       ... done
Removing network my-network
$
```

6. Optionally, run the tests using RabbitMQ with multiple partitions per topic:

```
COMPOSE_FILE=docker-compose-partitions.yml ./test-em-all.bash start
stop
```

Expect output that's similar to the preceding test.

7. Alternatively, run the test using Kafka with multiple partitions per topic:

```
COMPOSE_FILE=docker-compose-kafka.yml ./test-em-all.bash start stop
```

Expect output that's similar to the preceding test.

8. Stop Docker Desktop to save memory.
9. Start the Minikube instance, if it was stopped previously, and set the default namespace to hands-on:

```
minikube start
kubectl config set-context $(kubectl config current-context) --
namespace=hands-on
```

10. Point the Docker client back to the Kubernetes cluster in the Minikube instance:

```
eval $(minikube docker-env)
```

With the successful execution of these tests, we have verified that the microservices work without Kubernetes.

Summary

In this chapter, we have seen how capabilities in Kubernetes can be used to simplify a microservice landscape, meaning that we reduce the number of support services to be developed and deployed together with the microservices. We have seen how Kubernetes config maps and secrets can be used to replace the Spring Cloud Config Server and how a Kubernetes ingress can replace an edge service based on Spring Cloud Gateway.

Using the Cert Manager together with Let's Encrypt allowed us to automatically provision certificates for HTTPS endpoints exposed by the ingress, eliminating the need for manual and cumbersome work. Since our Kubernetes cluster running in a local Minikube instance isn't available from the internet, we used ngrok to establish an HTTP tunnel from the internet to the Minikube instance. The HTTP tunnel was used by Let's Encrypt to verify that we are the owner of the DNS name we requested a certificate for.

To verify that the source code of the microservices can run on other platforms, that is, isn't locked into Kubernetes, we deployed the microservices using Docker Compose and ran the `test-em-all.bash` test script.

In the next chapter, we will be introduced to the concept of a service mesh and learn how a service mesh product, **Istio**, can be used to improve observability, security, resilience, and routing in a landscape of cooperating microservices that are deployed on Kubernetes.

Head over to the next chapter!

Questions

1. How was the Spring Cloud Config Server replaced by Kubernetes resources?
2. How was the Spring Cloud Gateway replaced by Kubernetes resources?
3. What does ACME stand for and what is it used for?
4. What role does the Cert Manager and Let's Encrypt play in automating the provision of certificates?
5. What Kubernetes resources are involved in automating the provision of certificates?
6. Why did we use `ngrok` and what is required to be added to remove the use of ngrok?
7. Why did we run the tests using Docker Compose?

18
Using a Service Mesh to Improve Observability and Management

In this chapter, you will be introduced to the concept of a service mesh and see how its capabilities can be used to handle challenges in a system landscape of microservices in areas including security, policy enforcement, resilience, and traffic management. A service mesh can also be used to provide observability, that is, the capability to visualize how traffic flows between microservices in a service mesh.

A service mesh overlaps partly with the capabilities of Spring Cloud and Kubernetes we learned about earlier in this book. But most of the functionality in a service mesh complements Spring Cloud and Kubernetes, as we will see in this chapter.

The following topics will be covered in this chapter:

- An introduction to the service mesh concept and Istio, a popular open source implementation
- You will also learn how to do the following:
    - Deploy Istio in Kubernetes
    - Create a service mesh
    - Observe a service mesh
    - Secure a service mesh
    - Ensure that a service mesh is resilient
    - Perform zero downtime deployments using a service mesh
    - Test the microservice landscape using Docker Compose to ensure that the source code in the microservices is not locked into either Kubernetes or Istio

Technical requirements

All commands described in this book are run on a MacBook Pro using macOS Mojave, but modifying these commands should be sufficiently straightforward to run them on another platform such as Linux or Windows.

The only new tool required for this chapter is Istio's command-line tool, `istioctl`. This can be installed using Homebrew with the following command:

```
brew install istioctl
```

The source code for this chapter can be found on GitHub at `https://github.com/PacktPublishing/Hands-On-Microservices-with-Spring-Boot-and-Spring-Cloud/tree/master/Chapter18`.

To be able to run the commands as described in the book, you need to download the source code to a folder and set up an environment variable, `$BOOK_HOME`, that points to that folder. Examples of sample commands include the following:

```
export BOOK_HOME=~/Documents/Hands-On-Microservices-with-Spring-Boot-and-Spring-Cloud
git clone https://github.com/PacktPublishing/Hands-On-Microservices-with-Spring-Boot-and-Spring-Cloud $BOOK_HOME
cd $BOOK_HOME/Chapter18
```

The Java source code is written for Java 8 and tested on Java 12. This chapter uses Spring Cloud 2.1, SR2 (also known as the **Greenwich** release), Spring Boot 2.1.6, and Spring 5.1.8, that is, the latest available version of the Spring components at the time of writing this chapter. The source code has been tested using Kubernetes V1.15.

All source code examples in this chapter come from the source code in `$BOOK_HOME/Chapter18`, but are, in several cases, edited to remove non-relevant parts of the source code, such as comments, and import and log statements.

If you want to see the changes applied to the source code in Chapter 18, *Using a Service Mesh to Improve Observability and Management*, that is, the changes required to create a service mesh using Istio, you can compare it with the source code for Chapter 17, *Implementing Kubernetes Features as an Alternative*. You can use your favorite diff tool and compare the two folders, `$BOOK_HOME/Chapter17` and `$BOOK_HOME/Chapter18`.

Introduction to service mesh using Istio

A service mesh is an infrastructure layer that controls and observes the communication between services, for example, microservices. The capabilities in a service mesh, for example, observability, security, policy enforcement, resilience, and traffic management, are implemented by controlling and monitoring all internal communication inside the service mesh, that is, between the microservices in the service mesh. One of the core components in a service mesh is a lightweight **proxy** component that is injected into all microservices that will be part of the service mesh. All traffic in and out of a microservice is configured to go through its proxy component. The proxy components are configured in runtime by a **control plane** in the service mesh using API's exposed by the proxy. The control plane also collects telemetry data through these APIs from the proxies to visualize how the traffic flows in the service mesh.

A service mesh also contains a **data plane**, consisting of the proxy components in all microservices in the service mesh together with separate components for handling external incoming and outgoing traffic to and from the service mesh. This is illustrated by the following diagram:

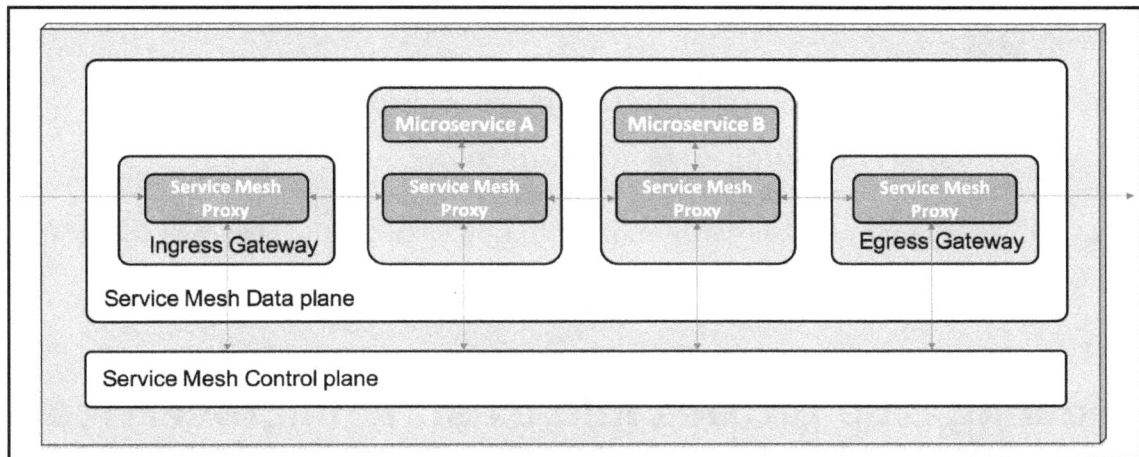

The first publicly available implementation of a service mesh was the open source project Linkerd, managed by Buoyant (https://linkerd.io), having its origins in Twitter's Finagle project (http://twitter.github.io/finagle). It was launched during 2016 and, one year later, in 2017, IBM, Google, and Lyft launched the open source project, Istio (https://istio.io).

One of the core components in Istio, the proxy component, is based on Lyft's Envoy proxy (`https://www.envoyproxy.io`). Linkerd and Istio are, at the time of writing this chapter, the two most popular and widely used service mesh implementations. In this chapter, we will use Istio.

Istio can be deployed in various environments, including Kubernetes (see `https://istio.io/docs/setup`). When deploying Istio on Kubernetes, its runtime components are deployed into a separate Kubernetes namespace, `istio-system`. Istio also comes with a set of Kubernetes **Custom Resources Definitions** (**CRDs**). CRDs are used in Kubernetes to extend its API, that is, to add new objects to its API. The Istio objects added are used to configure how Istio will be used. Finally, Istio comes with a CLI tool, `istioctl`, which will be used to inject Istio proxies into the microservices that participate in the service mesh.

Istio is, as explained previously, divided into a control plane and a data plane. As an operator, we will define a desired state by creating Istio objects in the Kubernetes API server, for example, declaring routing rules. The control plane will read these objects and send commands to the proxies in the data plane to take actions according to the desired state, for example, configuring routing rules. The proxies handle the actual communication between the microservices and report back telemetry data to the control plane. The telemetry data is used by various components in a control plane to visualize what's going on in the service mesh.

In the following subsections, we will cover the following topics:

- How Istio proxies are injected into microservices
- The Istio API objects that we will use in this chapter
- The runtime components in Istio that constitute the control plane and the data plane
- Changes in the microservice landscape as a result of the introduction of Istio

Injecting Istio proxies into existing microservices

The microservices we have deployed in Kubernetes in the previous chapters run as a single container in a Kubernetes pod (refer to the *Introducing Kubernetes API objects* section in `Chapter 15`, *Introduction to Kubernetes*, for a recap). To make a microservice join an Istio-based service mesh, an Istio proxy is injected into each microservice. This is done by adding an extra container to the pod that runs the Istio proxy.

> Containers added to a pod with the aim of supporting the main container, such as an Istio proxy, are referred to as a *sidecar*.

The following diagram shows how an Istio proxy has been injected into a sample pod, **Pod A**, as a sidecar:

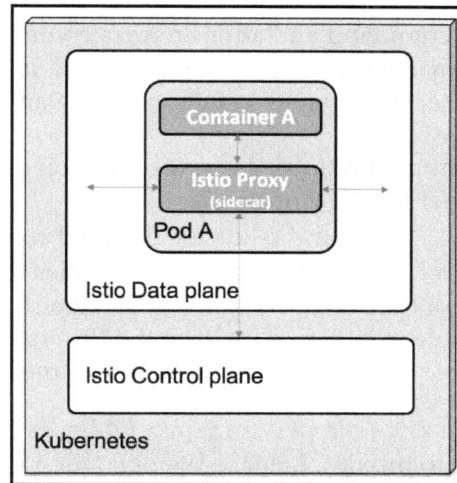

The main container in the pod, **Container A**, is configured to route all its traffic through the Istio proxy.

Istio proxies can be injected either automatically when a deployment object is created or manually using the istioctl tool.

In this chapter, we will inject the Istio proxies manually. The reason for this is that Istio proxies do not support the protocols used by MySQL, MongoDB, and RabbitMQ, so we will only inject Istio proxies into pods where the HTTP protocol is used. An Istio proxy can be injected into the pods of an existing deployment object by means of the following command:

```
kubectl get deployment sample-deployment -o yaml | istioctl kube-inject -f
- | kubectl apply -f -
```

This command may, at first glance, appear somewhat daunting, but it is actually just three separate commands. The previous command sends its output to the next command using pipes, that is, the | character. Let's go through each command:

1. The `kubectl get deployment` command gets the current definition of a deployment named `sample-deployment` from the Kubernetes API server and returns its definition in the YAML format.
2. The `istioctl kube-inject` command reads the definition from the `kubectl get deployment` command and adds an extra container for an Istio proxy in pods that the deployment handles. The configuration for the existing container in the deployment object is updated so that incoming and outgoing traffic goes through the Istio proxy.
   The `istioctl` command returns the new definition of the deployment object, including a container for the Istio proxy.
3. The `kubectl apply` command reads the updated configuration from the `istioctl kube-inject` command and applies the updated configuration. A rolling upgrade of the pods belonging to the deployment will start up in the same way as we have seen before (refer to the *Performing a rolling upgrade* section in `Chapter 16`, *Deploying Our Microservices to Kubernetes*).

The deployment scripts in the `kubernetes/scripts` folder have been extended to use `istioctl` to inject the Istio proxies. Refer to the upcoming *Creating the service mesh* section for details.

Introducing Istio API objects

Istio extends the Kubernetes API with a number of objects using its CRDs. Refer to the *Introducing Kubernetes API objects* section in `Chapter 15`, *Introduction to Kubernetes*, for a recap of the Kubernetes API. In this chapter we will use the following Istio objects:

* `Gateway` is used to configure how to handle incoming traffic to, and outgoing traffic from, the service mesh. A gateway depends on a virtual service routing the incoming traffic to Kubernetes services. We will use a gateway object to accept incoming traffic to the DNS name, `minikube.me`, using HTTPS. Refer to the *Kubernetes Ingress resource replaced with Istio Ingress Gateway as an edge server* section for details.

- `VirtualService` is used to define routing rules in the service mesh. We will use virtual services to describe how to route incoming traffic from an Istio gateway to the Kubernetes services and between services. We will also use virtual services to inject faults and delays in order to test the reliability and resilience capabilities of the service mesh.
- `DestinationRule` is used to define policies and rules for traffic that is routed (using a virtual service) to a specific service (that is, a destination). We will use destination rules to set up encryption policies to encrypt internal HTTP traffic and define service subsets that describe available versions of the services. We will use service subsets when performing zero downtime (blue/green) deployments from an existing version of a microservice to a new version.
- `Policy` is used to define how requests will be authenticated. We will use policies to require incoming requests to the service mesh to be authenticated using a JWT-based OAuth 2.0/OIDC access token. Refer to the *Authenticating external requests using OAuth 2.0/OIDC access tokens* section of this chapter. A policy can also be used to define how to secure parts of the internal communication in the service mesh. For example, a policy can require that internal requests are encrypted using HTTPS or allow plain text requests. Finally, a `MeshPolicy` object can be used to define global policies that apply to the whole service mesh.

Introducing runtime components in Istio

Istio contains a number of runtime components, is highly configurable in terms of what components to use, and provides fine-grained control over the configuration of each component. Refer to the *Deploying Istio in a Kubernetes cluster* section of this chapter for information on the configuration we will use in this chapter.

In the configuration used in this chapter, the Istio control plane consists of the following runtime components:

- **Pilot**: responsible for supplying all sidecars with updates of the service mesh configuration.
- **Mixer**: consists of two different runtime components:
  - **Policy** – enforces network policies such as authentication, authorization, rate limits, and quotas.
  - **Telemetry** – collects telemetry information and sends it to Prometheus, for example.

- **Galley**: responsible for collecting and validating configuration information and distribution to the other Istio components in the control plane.
- **Citadel**: responsible for issuing and rotating internally used certificates.
- **Kiali**: provides observability to the service mesh, visualizing what is going on in the mesh. Kiali is a separate open source project (see `https://www.kiali.io`)
- **Prometheus**: performs data ingestion and storage for time series-based data, for example, performance metrics.
  Prometheus is a separate open source project (refer to `https://prometheus.io`).
- **Grafana**: visualizes performance metrics and other time series-related data collected in Prometheus. Grafana is a separate open source project (see `https://grafana.com`).
- **Tracing**: handles and visualizes distributed tracing information. Based on Jaeger, it is an open source project for distributed tracing (refer to `https://www.jaegertracing.io`). Jaeger provides the same type of functionality as Zipkin, which we used in `Chapter 14`, *Understanding Distributed Tracing*.

Kiali is accessed using a web browser and integrates Grafana for viewing performance metrics and Jaeger for visualizing distributed tracing information.

The Istio data plane consists of the following runtime components:

- **Ingress Gateway**: handles incoming traffic to the service mesh
- **Egress Gateway**: handles outgoing traffic from the service mesh
- All pods with an Istio proxy are injected as a sidecar

The runtime components in Istio's control plane and data plane are summarized in the following diagram:

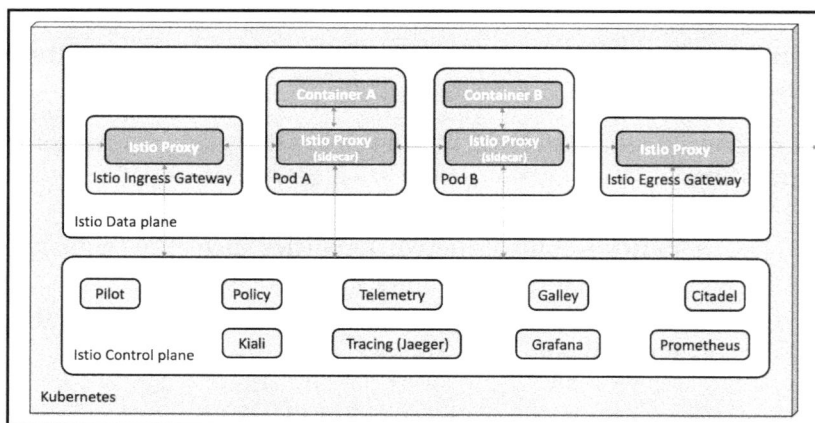

In the next section, we will go through changes applied to the microservice landscape arising from the introduction of Istio.

Changes in the microservice landscape

As we have seen in the preceding section, Istio comes with components that overlap with components currently used in the microservice landscape in terms of functionality:

- The Istio Ingress Gateway can act as an edge server, an alternative to the Kubernetes Ingress resources.
- The Jaeger component that comes bundled with Istio can be used for distributed tracing instead of Zipkin.

In the following two subsections, we will learn why and how Kubernetes Ingress resources are replaced with Istio Ingress Gateway, and how and why Zipkin is replaced with Jaeger.

Kubernetes Ingress resources are replaced with Istio Ingress Gateway as an edge server

In the previous chapter, we introduced Kubernetes Ingress resources as edge servers (refer to the *Replacing the Spring Cloud Gateway* section in `Chapter 17`, *Implementing Kubernetes Features as an Alternative*). Unfortunately, ingress resources cannot be configured to handle the fine-grained routing rules that come with Istio. Instead, Istio has its own edge server, the Istio ingress Gateway, introduced previously in the *Introducing runtime components in Istio* section. The Istio Ingress Gateway is used by creating `Gateway` and `VisualService` resources described previously in the *Introducing Istio API objects* section.

The definition files for the following Kubernetes Ingress resources, `kubernetes/services/base/ingress-edge-server.yml` and `kubernetes/services/base/ingress-edge-server-ngrok.yml`, have therefore been removed. Definition files for Istio `Gateway` and `VirtualService` resources will be added in the *Creating the service mesh* section.

The Istio Ingress Gateway is reached using a different IP address than the IP address used to access Kubernetes Ingress resources, so we also need to update the IP address mapped to the hostname, `minikube.me`, which we use when running tests. This is handled in the *Setting up access to Istio services* section in this chapter.

Simplifying the system landscape and replacing Zipkin with Jaeger

As mentioned in the *Introducing runtime components in Istio* section, Istio comes with built-in support for distributed tracing using Jaeger. Using Jaeger, we can offload and simplify the microservice landscape by removing the Zipkin server we introduced in `Chapter 14`, *Understanding Distributed Tracing*.

The following changes have been applied to the source code to remove the Zipkin server:

- The dependency to `org.springframework.cloud:spring-cloud-starter-zipkin` in all microservice build files, `build.gradle`, has been removed.
- The definition of the Zipkin server in the three Docker Compose files, `docker-compose.yml`, `docker-compose-partitions.yml`, and `docker-compose-kafka.yml`, has been removed.
- The following Kubernetes definition files for Zipkin have been removed:
  - `kubernetes/services/base/zipkin-server.yml`
  - `kubernetes/services/overlays/prod/zipkin-server-prod.yml`

Jaeger will be installed in the *Creating the service mesh* section.

The changes were made to the microservice landscape due to the introduction of Istio. We are now ready to deploy Istio in the Kubernetes cluster.

Deploying Istio in a Kubernetes cluster

In this section, we will learn how to deploy Istio in a Kubernetes cluster and how to access Istio services in it.

We will use v1.2.4 of Istio, the latest release available when this chapter was written.

We will be using a demo configuration of Istio that is suitable for testing Istio in a development environment, that is, with most features enabled but configured for minimalistic resource usage.

> This configuration is unsuitable for production usage and for performance testing.

For other installation options, see `https://istio.io/docs/setup/kubernetes/install`.

To deploy Istio, perform the following steps:

1. Download Istio as follows:

```
cd $BOOK_HOME/Chapter18
curl -L https://git.io/getLatestIstio | ISTIO_VERSION=1.2.4 sh -
```

2. Ensure that your Minikube instance is up-and-running with the following command:

```
minikube status
```

Expect a response along the lines of the following, provided it is up and running:

```
$ minikube status
host: Running
kubelet: Running
apiserver: Running
kubectl: Correctly Configured: pointing to minikube-vm at 192.168.99.125
$
```

3. Install Istio-specific custom resource definitions (CRDs) in Kubernetes:

```
for i in istio-1.2.4/install/kubernetes/helm/istio-
init/files/crd*yaml; do kubectl apply -f $i; done
```

4. Install Istio demo configurations in Kubernetes as follows:

```
kubectl apply -f istio-1.2.4/install/kubernetes/istio-demo.yaml
```

5. Wait for the Istio deployments to become available:

```
kubectl -n istio-system wait --timeout=600s --
for=condition=available deployment --all
```

The command will report deployment resources in Istio as available, one after another. Expect 12 messages such as `deployment.extensions/NNN condition met` before the command ends. It can take a couple of minutes (or more) depending on your hardware and internet connectivity.

6. Update Kiali's config map with URLs to Jaeger and Grafana with the following commands:

```
kubectl -n istio-system apply -f kubernetes/istio/setup/kiali-
configmap.yml && \
kubectl -n istio-system delete pod -l app=kiali && \
kubectl -n istio-system wait --timeout=60s --for=condition=ready
pod -l app=kiali
```

The config map, `kubernetes/istio/setup/kiali-configmap.yml`, contains URLs to Jaeger and Grafana that utilize the DNS names set up by the `minikube tunnel` command used in the next section.

Istio is now deployed in Kubernetes, but before we move on and create the service mesh, we need to learn a bit about how to access Istio services in a Minikube environment.

Setting up access to Istio services

The demo configuration used in the previous section to install Istio comes with a few connectivity-related issues that we need to resolve. The Istio Ingress Gateway is configured as a load-balanced Kubernetes service; that is, its type is `LoadBalancer`.

It can also be reached using its node port, in the port range `30000-32767`, on the IP address of the Minikube instance. Unfortunately, HTTPS-based routing in Istio can't include port numbers; that is, Istio's Ingress Gateway must be reached over the default port for HTTPS (`443`). Therefore, a node port can't be used. Instead, a load balancer must be used to be able to use Istio's routing rules with HTTPS.

Minikube contains a command that can be used to simulate a local load balancer, `minikube tunnel`. This command assigns an external IP address to each load-balanced Kubernetes service, including the Istio Ingress Gateway. This gives you what we need to update the translation of the hostname `minikube.me`, which we use in our tests. The hostname, `minikube.me`, now needs to be translated to the external IP address of the Istio Ingress Gateway, instead of to the IP address of the Minikube instance that we used in the previous chapters.

The `minikube tunnel` command also makes cluster-local Kubernetes services accessible using their DNS name. The DNS name is based on the naming convention: `{service-name}.{namespace}.svc.cluster.local`. For example, Istio's Kiali service can be reached from a local web browser using the DNS name, `kiali.istio-system.svc.cluster.local`, when the tunnel is up and running.

The following diagram summarizes how Istio services are accessed:

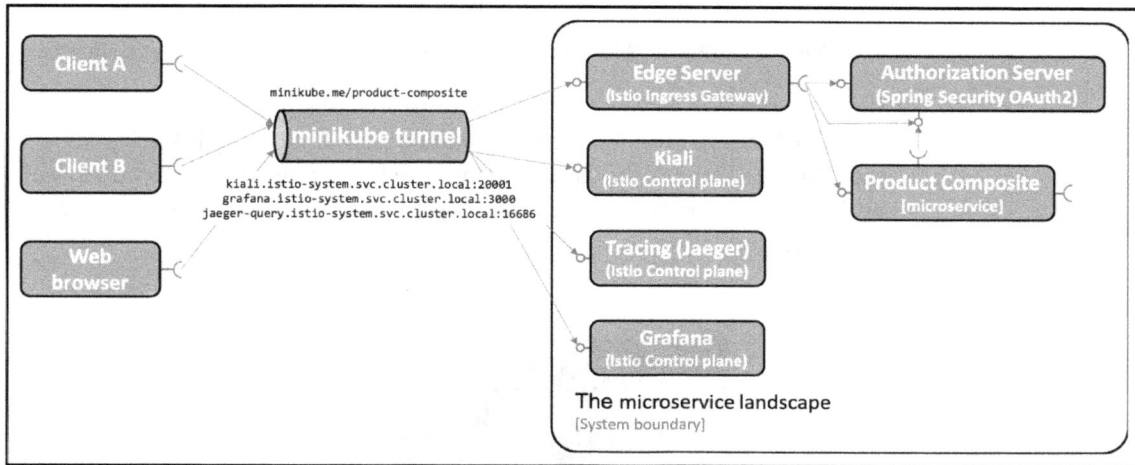

Perform the following steps to set up the Minikube tunnel:

1. Make Kubernetes services available locally. Run the following command in a separate terminal window (the command locks the terminal window when the tunnel is up and running):

```
minikube tunnel
```

Note that this command requires that your user has `sudo` privileges and that you enter your password during startup and shutdown. It takes a couple of seconds before the command asks for the password, so it is easy to miss!

2. Config `minikube.me` to be resolved to the IP address of the Istio Ingress Gateway as follows:
    1. Get the IP address exposed by the `minikube tunnel` command for the Istio Ingress Gateway and save it in an environment variable named INGRESS_HOST:

```
INGRESS_HOST=$(kubectl -n istio-system get service istio-
ingressgateway -o
jsonpath='{.status.loadBalancer.ingress[0].ip}')
```

2. Update `/etc/hosts` so that `minikube.me` points to the Istio Ingress Gateway:

```
echo "$INGRESS_HOST minikube.me" | sudo tee -a /etc/hosts
```

3. Remove the line in `/etc/hosts` where `minikube.me` that points to the IP address of the Minikube instance (`minikube ip`). Verify that `/etc/hosts` only contains one line that translates `minikube.me` and that it points to the IP address of the Istio Ingress Gateway; for example, the value of `$INGRESS_HOST`:

```
● ● ●              6. bash
$ cat /etc/hosts
...
10.102.72.36 minikube.me
$
```

3. Verify that Kiali, Jaeger, and Grafana can be reached through the tunnel with the following commands:

```
curl -o /dev/null -s -L -w "%{http_code}"
http://kiali.istio-system.svc.cluster.local:20001/kiali/
curl -o /dev/null -s -L -w "%{http_code}"
http://grafana.istio-system.svc.cluster.local:3000
curl -o /dev/null -s -L -w "%{http_code}"
http://jaeger-query.istio-system.svc.cluster.local:16686
```

Each command should return `200` (OK).

> The `minikube tunnel` command can stop running if, for example, your computer or the Minikube instance in the virtual machine is paused or restarted. The command needs to be restarted manually in these cases. So, if you fail to call API's on the `https://minikube.me` URL or if Kiali's web UI can't reach Jaeger to visualize distributed tracing, or Grafana to visualize performance metrics, always check whether the Minikube tunnel is running and restart it if required.

An added bonus from using the minikube tunnel command

Running the `minikube tunnel` command also makes it possible to access some other cluster-internal Kubernetes services that may be of interest. Once the environment is up and running as described in the *Running commands to create the service mesh* section, the following can be achieved:

- The `health` endpoint of the `product-composite` microservice can be checked with the following command:

```
curl -k
http://product-composite.hands-on.svc.cluster.local:4004/actuator/h
ealth
```

  Refer to the *Observing the service mesh* section for an explanation of the use of port `4004`.

- MySQL tables in the review database can be accessed with the following command:

```
mysql -umysql-user-dev -pmysql-pwd-dev review-db -e "select * from
reviews" -h mysql.hands-on.svc.cluster.local
```

- MongoDB collections in the `product` and `recommendations` databases can be accessed with the following commands:

```
mongo --host mongodb.hands-on.svc.cluster.local -u mongodb-user-dev
-p mongodb-pwd-dev --authenticationDatabase admin product-db --eval
"db.products.find()"
```

```
mongo --host mongodb.hands-on.svc.cluster.local -u mongodb-user-dev
-p mongodb-pwd-dev --authenticationDatabase admin recommendation-db
--eval "db.recommendations.find()"
```

- RabbitMQ's web UI can be accessed using the following URL: `http://rabbitmq.hands-on.svc.cluster.local:15672`. Log in using the credentials `rabbit-user-dev` and `rabbit-pwd-dev`.

With the Minikube tunnel in place, we are now ready to create the service mesh.

Creating the service mesh

With Istio deployed, we are ready to create the service mesh. We will use the `kubernetes/scripts/deploy-dev-env.bash` script to set up an environment for development and testing.

The steps required to create the service mesh are basically the same as those we used in `Chapter 17`, *Implementing Kubernetes Features as an Alternative* (refer to the *Testing with Kubernetes ConfigMaps, secrets, and ingress* section). Let's first see what additions have been made to the Kubernetes definition files to set up the service mesh before we run the commands to create the service mesh.

Source code changes

To be able to run the microservices in a service mesh managed by Istio, the following changes have been applied to the Kubernetes definition files:

- The deployment scripts have been updated to inject Istio proxies
- The file structure of the Kubernetes definition files has been changed
- Kubernetes definition files for Istio have been added

Let's go through them one by one.

Updating the deployment scripts to inject Istio proxies

The scripts used to deploy microservices in Kubernetes, `deploy-dev-env.bash` and `deploy-prod-env.bash`, both in the `kubernetes/scripts` folder, have been updated to inject Istio proxies into the five microservices, that is, the `auth-server`, `product-composite`, `product`, `recommendation`, and `review` services.

> The `deploy-prod-env.bash` script will be used in the *Performing zero downtime deploys* section.

The `istioctl kube-inject` command previously described in the *Injecting Istio proxies in existing microservices* section has been added to both deployment scripts as follows:

```
kubectl get deployment auth-server product product-composite recommendation
review -o yaml | istioctl kube-inject -f - | kubectl apply -f -
```

Since the `kubectl apply` command will start a rolling upgrade, the following command has been added to wait for the upgrade to be completed:

```
waitForPods 5 'version=<version>'
```

During the rolling upgrade, we will have two pods running for each microservice: an old one without an Istio proxy and a new one with the Istio proxy injected. The `waitForPods` function will wait until the old pods are terminated; that is, the rolling upgrade is complete, and only the five new pods are running. To identify what pods to wait for, a label named `version` is used. In a development environment, all microservice pods are labeled with `version=latest`.

For example, the deployment file for the product microservice, `kubernetes/services/base/deployments/product-deployment.yml`, has the following definition of the `version` label:

```
metadata:
  labels:
    version: latest
```

> In the *Performing zero downtime deployments* section, where we will upgrade microservices from version v1 to v2, the version label will be set to v1 and v2.

Finally, the following command has been added to the scripts to make them wait until the deployments and their pods are ready:

```
kubectl wait --timeout=120s --for=condition=Ready pod --all
```

After reviewing the updates in the deployment scripts, let's see how the file structure of the Kubernetes definition files has been affected as a result of the introduction of Istio.

Changing the file structure of the Kubernetes definition files

The file structure for the Kubernetes definition files in `kubernetes/services` has been expanded a bit since `Chapter 16`, *Deploying Our Microservices to Kubernetes* (refer to the *Introduction to Kustomize* section) and this now appears as follows:

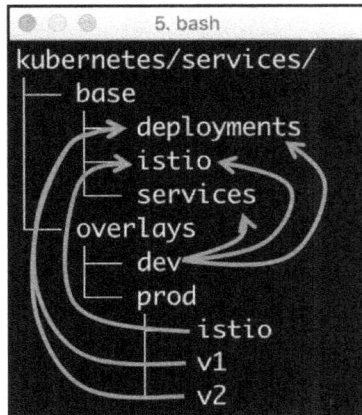

The `base` folder consists of three subfolders. The reason for this is that we will run two versions of the microservices concurrently in the *Performing zero downtime deploys* section, that is, one pod per microservice version. Since pods are managed by the deployment object, we also need two deployment objects per microservice. To be able to achieve this, the base version of the deployment objects has been placed in a separate folder, `deployments`. The service objects and the Istio definitions are placed in their own base folders: `services` and `istio`, respectively.

In the development environment, we will only run one version per microservice. Its kustomization file, `kubernetes/services/overlays/dev/kustomization.yml`, has been updated to include all three folders as base folders:

```
bases:
 - ../../base/deployments
 - ../../base/services
 - ../../base/istio
```

Refer to the following *Performing zero downtime deploys* section for details on how two concurrent versions of the microservices will be deployed using the setup for the production environment.

For now, let's also go through the new files in the Istio folder.

Adding Kubernetes definition files for Istio

Istio definitions have been added to the `istio` folder. The Istio files of interest in this section are the gateway definition and its corresponding virtual services. The other Istio files will be explained in the *Authenticating external requests using OAuth 2.0/OIDC access tokens* and *Protecting internal communication using mutual authentication (mTLS)* sections.

The Istio gateway is declared in the `kubernetes/services/base/istio/gateway.yml` file and appears as follows:

```
apiVersion: networking.istio.io/v1alpha3
kind: Gateway
metadata:
  name: hands-on-gw
spec:
  selector:
    istio: ingressgateway
  servers:
  - hosts:
    - "minikube.me"
    port:
      number: 443
      name: https
      protocol: HTTPS
    tls:
      mode: SIMPLE
      serverCertificate: /etc/istio/ingressgateway-certs/tls.crt
      privateKey: /etc/istio/ingressgateway-certs/tls.key
```

The following are some explanations of the preceding source code:

- The gateway is named `hands-on-gw`; this name is used by the virtual services underneath.
- The `selector` field specifies that the gateway resource will be handled by the built-in Istio Ingress Gateway.
- The `hosts` and `port` fields specify that the gateway will handle incoming requests for the `minikube.me` hostname using HTTPS over port `443`.
- The `tls` field specifies where the Istio Ingress Gateway can find the certificate and private key used for HTTPS communication. Refer to the *Protecting external endpoints with HTTPS and certificates* section for details on how these certificate files are created.

The virtual service object for routing requests from the gateway to the product-composite service, kubernetes/services/base/istio/product-composite-virtual-service.yml, appears as follows:

```
apiVersion: networking.istio.io/v1alpha3
kind: VirtualService
metadata:
  name: product-composite-vs
spec:
  hosts:
  - "minikube.me"
  gateways:
  - hands-on-gw
  http:
  - match:
    - uri:
        prefix: /product-composite
    route:
    - destination:
        port:
          number: 80
        host: product-composite
```

Explanations for the preceding source code are as follows:

- The hosts field specifies that the virtual service will route requests sent to the host, minikube.me.
- The match and route blocks specify that requests that contain a URI starting with /product-composite will be forwarded to the Kubernetes service named product-composite.

> In the preceding source code, the destination host is specified using its short name, in other words, product-composite. This works since the example in this chapter keeps all Kubernetes definitions in one and the same namespace, hands-on. If that is not the case, it is recommended in the Istio documentation using the host's **fully qualified domain name** (**FQDN**) instead, that is, product-composite.hands-on.svc.cluster.local.

Finally, the virtual service object for routing requests from the gateway to the auth server, kubernetes/services/base/istio/auth-server-virtual-service.yml, looks very similar, the difference being that it routes requests that start with /oauth to the Kubernetes service, auth-server.

With these changes in the source code in place, we are now ready to create the service mesh.

Running commands to create the service mesh

Create the service mesh by running the following commands:

1. Build Docker images from source with the following commands:

```
cd $BOOK_HOME/Chapter18
eval $(minikube docker-env)
./gradlew build && docker-compose build
```

2. Recreate the hands-on namespace, and set it as the default namespace:

```
kubectl delete namespace hands-on
kubectl create namespace hands-on
kubectl config set-context $(kubectl config current-context) --
namespace=hands-on
```

3. Execute the deployment by running the deploy-dev-env.bash script with the following command:

```
./kubernetes/scripts/deploy-dev-env.bash
```

4. Once the deployment is complete, verify that we have two containers in each of the microservice pods:

```
kubectl get pods
```

Expect a response along the lines of the following:

```
● ● ●                                    4. bash
$ kubectl get pods
NAME                                 READY   STATUS    RESTARTS   AGE
auth-server-78c9b85c9b-9sjs4         2/2     Running   0          8m4s
mongodb-75d7df8bd7-7s9f6             1/1     Running   0          9m33s
mysql-754d8f7584-26lxd               1/1     Running   0          9m33s
product-8695c57758-64q7x             2/2     Running   0          8m4s
product-composite-74f4dc9b4f-vkvbd   2/2     Running   0          8m4s
rabbitmq-855fb78bcc-5mcq7            1/1     Running   0          9m33s
recommendation-7bc5446b4c-btpqx      2/2     Running   0          8m4s
review-546bb44f8d-hpll7              2/2     Running   0          8m4s$
$ 
```

Note that the pods that run our microservices report two containers per pod; that is, they have the Istio proxy injected as a sidecar!

5. Run the usual tests with the following command:

    ```
    ./test-em-all.bash
    ```

    The default values for `script test-em-all.bash` have been updated from previous chapters to accommodate Kubernetes running in Minikube.

Expect the output to be similar to what we have seen in previous chapters:

```
4. bash
$ ./test-em-all.bash
...
Wait for: curl -k http://product-composite.hands-on.svc.cluster.local:4004/actuator/health...
 DONE, continues...
Test OK (HTTP Code: 200)
...
End, all tests OK: Sun Jul 28 11:47:44 CEST 2019
$
```

6. You can try out the APIs manually by running the following commands:

    ```
    ACCESS_TOKEN=$(curl -k
    https://writer:secret@minikube.me/oauth/token -d
    grant_type=password -d username=magnus -d password=password -s | jq
    .access_token -r)

    curl -ks https://minikube.me/product-composite/2 -H "Authorization:
    Bearer $ACCESS_TOKEN" | jq .productId
    ```

Expect the requested product ID, 2, in the response.

With the service mesh up and running, let's see how we can observe what's going on in the service mesh using Kiali!

Observing the service mesh

In this section, we will use Kiali together with Jaeger to observe what's going on in the service mesh. For performance monitoring using Grafana, refer to Chapter 20, *Monitoring Microservices*.

Before we do that, we need to get rid of some noise created by the health checks performed by Kubernetes' liveness and readiness probes. In the previous chapters, they have been using the same port as the API requests. This means that Istio will collect telematics data for both health checks and requests sent to the API. This will cause the graphs shown by Kiali to become unnecessarily cluttered. Kiali can filter out traffic that we are not interested in, but a simpler solution is to use a different port for the health checks.

Microservices can be configured to use a separate port for requests sent to the actuator endpoints, for example, health checks sent to the `/actuator/health` endpoint. The following line has been added to the common configuration file for all microservices, `config-repo/application.yml`:

```
management.server.port: 4004
```

This will make all microservices use port `4004` to expose the health endpoints. All deployment files in the `kubernetes/services/base/deployments` folder have been updated to use port `4004` in their liveness and readiness probes.

The Spring Cloud Gateway (this is retained so we can run tests in Docker Compose) will continue to use the same port for requests to the API and the `health` endpoint. In the `config-repo/gateway.yml` configuration file, the management port is reverted to the port used for the API:

```
management.server.port: 8443
```

With the requests sent to the health endpoint out of the way, we can start to send some requests through the service mesh.

We will start a low-volume load test using `siege`, which we got to know in Chapter 16, *Deploying Our Microservices to Kubernetes* (refer to the *Performing a rolling upgrade* section). After that, we will go through some of the most important parts of Kiali to see how Kiali can be used to observe a service mesh. We will also explore Kiali's integration with Jaeger and how Jaeger is used for distributed tracing:

Start the test with the following commands:

```
ACCESS_TOKEN=$(curl -k https://writer:secret@minikube.me/oauth/token -d
grant_type=password -d username=magnus -d password=password -s | jq
.access_token -r)

siege https://minikube.me/product-composite/2 -H "Authorization: Bearer
$ACCESS_TOKEN" -c1 -d1
```

The first command will get an OAuth 2.0/OIDC access token that will be used in the next command, where `siege` is used to submit one HTTP request per second to the product-composite API.

Expect output from the `siege` command as follows:

```
                                          4. bash
$ siege https://minikube.me/product-composite/2 -H "Authorization: Bearer $ACCESS_TOKEN" -c1 -d1
...
The server is now under siege...
HTTP/1.1 200     0.08 secs:      772 bytes ==> GET  /product-composite/2
HTTP/1.1 200     0.03 secs:      772 bytes ==> GET  /product-composite/2
HTTP/1.1 200     0.05 secs:      772 bytes ==> GET  /product-composite/2
```

1. Open Kiali's web UI using the `http://kiali.istio-system.svc.cluster.local:20001/kiali` URL in a web browser and log in with the following username and password: `admin` and `admin`. Expect a web page similar to the following:

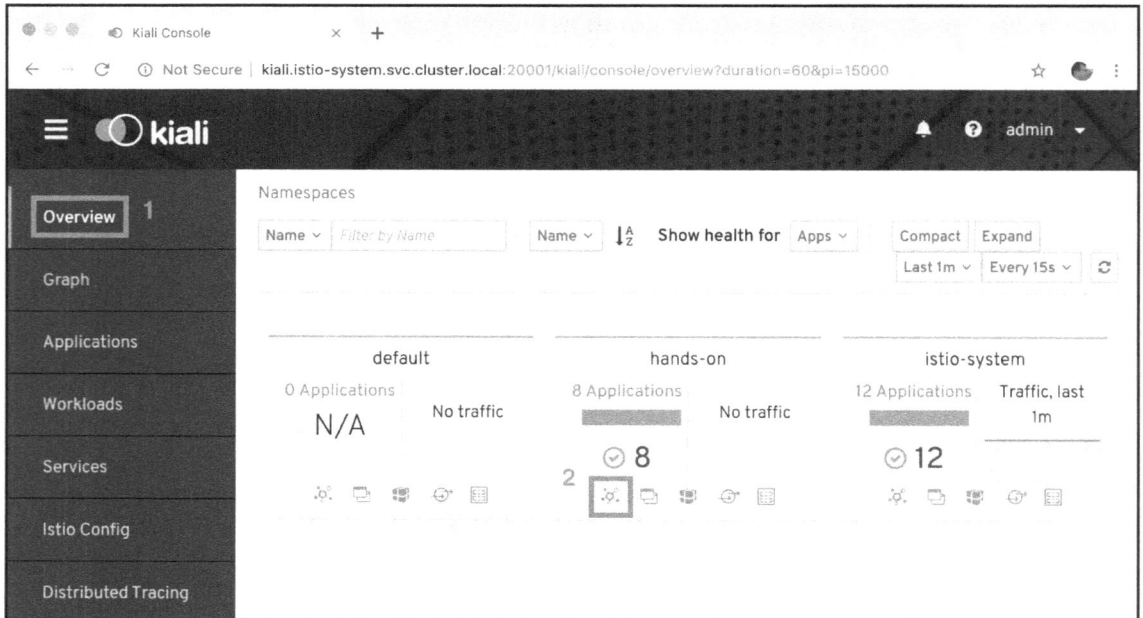

2. Click on the **Overview** tab, if not already active.

3. Click on the graph icon in the **hands-on** namespace. Expect a graph to be shown, representing the current traffic flow through the service mesh, along the lines of the following:

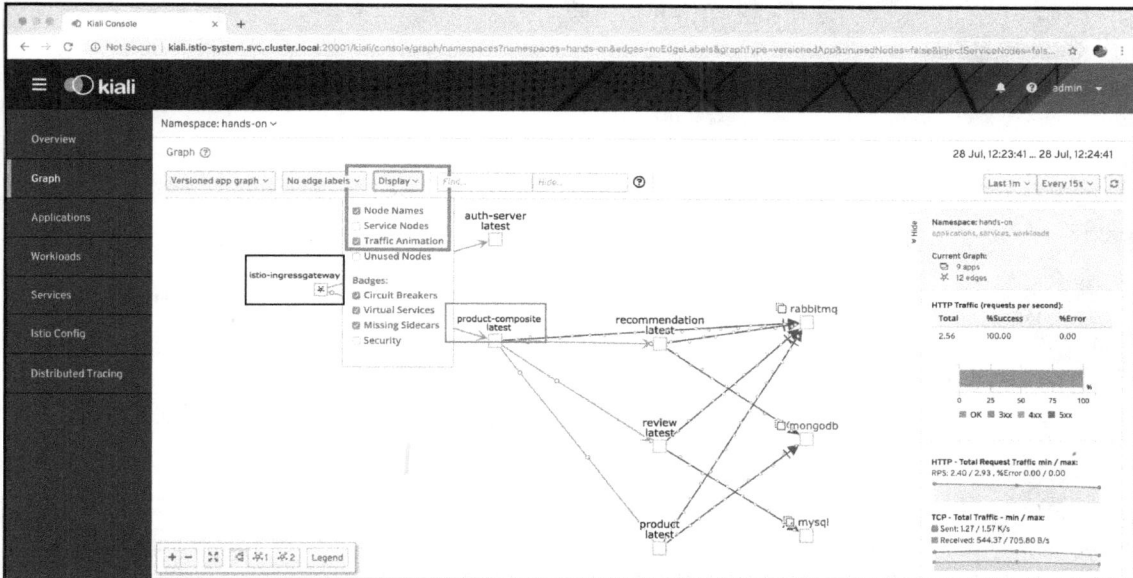

4. Click on the **Display**-button, unselect **Service Nodes**, and select **Traffic Animation**.

Kiali displays a graph representing requests that are currently sent through the service mesh, where active requests are represented by small moving circles along with arrows.

This gives a pretty good initial overview of what's going on in the service mesh!

5. Let's now look at some distributed tracing using Jaeger:

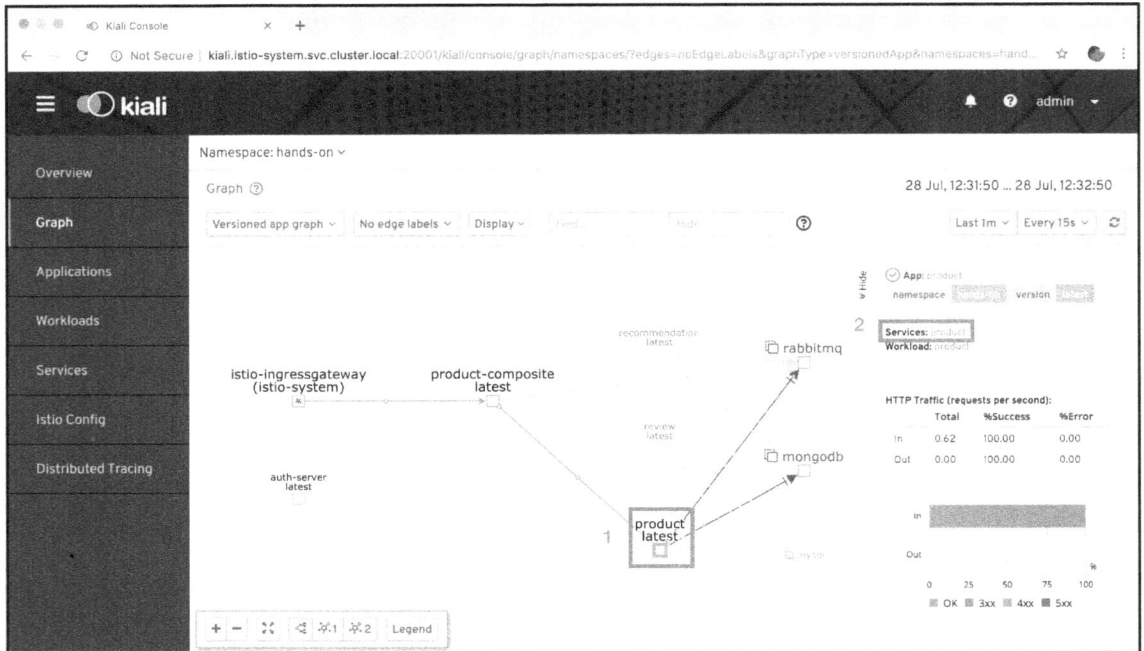

6. Click on the **product** node.

7. Click on the **Service: product** link. On the web page for the service, click on the
   Traces tab in the menu and Kiali will use Jaeger to show an embedded view of
   traces that the product service is involved in. Expect a web page such as the
   following:

8. Click on one of the traces to examine it. Expect a web page such as the following:

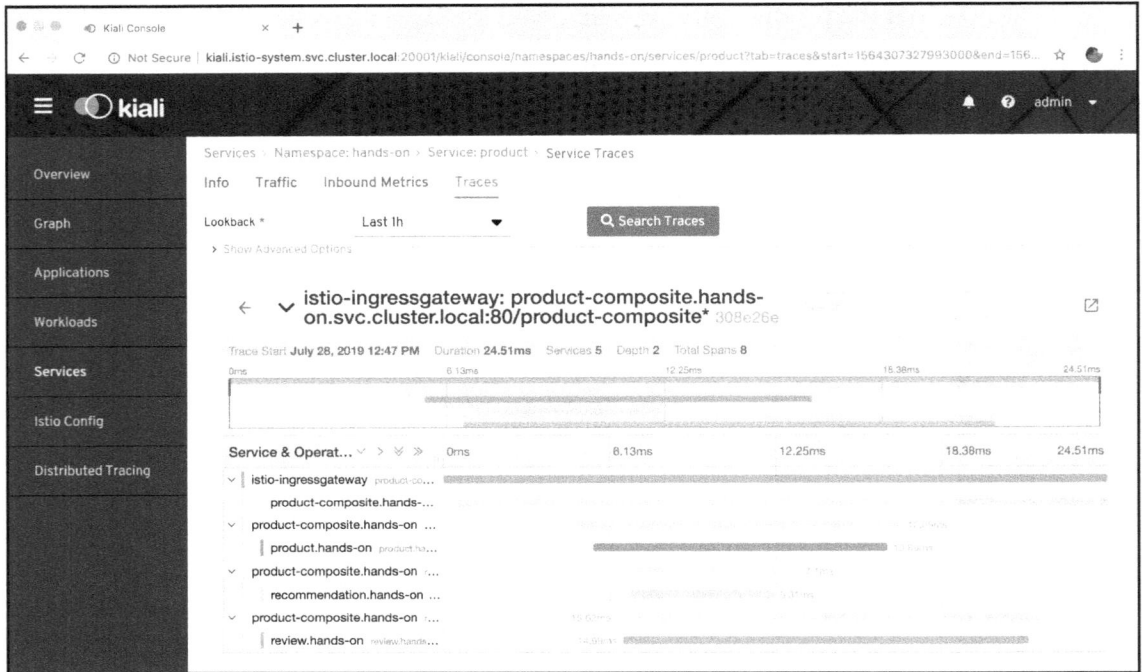

This is basically the same tracing information as Zipkin, made available in `Chapter 14`, *Understanding Distributed Tracing*.

There is much more to explore, but this is enough by way of an introduction. Feel free to explore the web UI in Kiali, Jaeger, and Grafana on your own.

> In `Chapter 20`, *Monitoring Microservices*, we will explore performance monitoring capabilities further.

Let's move on and learn how Istio can be used to improve security in the service mesh!

Securing a service mesh

In this section, we will learn how to use Istio to improve the security of a service mesh. We will cover the following topics:

- How to protect external endpoints with HTTPS and certificates
- How to require that external requests are authenticated using OAuth 2.0/OIDC access tokens
- How to protect internal communication using mutual authentication (mTLS)

Let's now understand each of these in the following sections.

Protecting external endpoints with HTTPS and certificates

In the *Creating the service mesh* section, we saw how the Istio Ingress Gateway is configured to use the following certificate files to protect external requests sent to `minikube.me` using HTTPS. The Istio Ingress Gateway is configured as follows:

```
spec:
  servers:
  - hosts:
    - "minikube.me"
    ...
    tls:
      mode: SIMPLE
      serverCertificate: /etc/istio/ingressgateway-certs/tls.crt
      privateKey: /etc/istio/ingressgateway-certs/tls.key
```

But where did these files come from, you may ask?

We can see how the Istio Ingress Gateway is configured by running the following command:

```
kubectl -n istio-system get deploy istio-ingressgateway -o json
```

We will find that it is prepared to mount an optional secret named `istio-ingressgateway-certs` and that it will be mapped to the folder, `/etc/istio/ingressgateway-certs/`:

This results in certificate files, `tls.crt` and `tls.key`, from a secret named `istio-ingressgateway-certs` being made available to the Istio Ingress Gateway on the `/etc/istio/ingressgateway-certs/tls.crt` and `/etc/istio/ingressgateway-certs/tls.key` file paths.

Creating of this secret is handled by means of the `deploy-dev-env.bash` and `deploy-prod-env.bash` deployment scripts, found in the `kubernetes/scripts` folder, by means of the following command:

```
kubectl create -n istio-system secret tls istio-ingressgateway-certs \
--key kubernetes/cert/tls.key --cert kubernetes/cert/tls.crt
```

The certificate files were created in `Chapter 17`, *Implementing Kubernetes Features as an Alternative* (refer to the *Testing with Kubernetes ConfigMaps, secrets, and ingress* section).

To verify that it is these certificates that are used by the Istio Ingress Gateway, we can run the following command:

```
keytool -printcert -sslserver minikube.me:443 | grep -E "Owner:|Issuer:"
```

Expect the following output:

```
● ● ●                            4. bash
$ keytool -printcert -sslserver minikube.me:443 | grep -E "Owner:|Issuer:"
Owner: O=minikube.me, CN=minikube.me
Issuer: O=minikube.me, CN=minikube.me
$
```

The output shows that the certificate is issued for `minikube.se` and that it is self-signed; that is, the issuer is also `minikube.me`.

This self-signed certificate can be replaced with a certificate bought by a trusted certificate authority (CA) for production use cases. Istio has recently added support for the automated provisioning of trusted certificates using, for example, the cert manager and Let's Encrypt, as we did in `Chapter 17`, *Implementing Kubernetes Features as an Alternative* (refer to the *Provisioning certificates with the cert manager and Let's Encrypt* section). This support is currently a bit too complex to fit into this chapter.

With the certificate configuration verified, let's now move on to see how the Istio Ingress Gateway can protect microservices from unauthenticated requests.

Authenticating external requests using OAuth 2.0/OIDC access tokens

Istio Ingress Gateway is capable of requiring and validating JWT-based OAuth 2.0/OIDC access tokens, in other words, protecting the microservices in the service mesh from external unauthenticated requests. For a recap on JWT, OAuth 2.0, and OIDC, refer to `Chapter 11`, *Secure Access to APIs* (see the *Authenticating and authorizing API access using OAuth 2.0 and OpenID Connect* section).

To enable authentication, we need to create an Istio `Policy` object that specifies which targets should be protected and which access token issuers, that is, OAuth 2.0/OIDC providers, should be trusted. This is done in the `kubernetes/services/base/istio/jwt-authentication-policy.yml` file and appears as follows:

```
apiVersion: "authentication.istio.io/v1alpha1"
kind: "Policy"
metadata:
  name: "jwt-authentication-policy"
spec:
  targets:
  - name: product-composite
```

```
peers:
- mtls:
    mode: PERMISSIVE
origins:
- jwt:
    issuer: "http://auth-server.local"
    jwksUri:
"http://auth-server.hands-on.svc.cluster.local/.well-known/jwks.json"
    principalBinding: USE_ORIGIN
```

Explanations for the preceding source code are as follows:

- The `targets` list specifies that the authentication check will be performed for requests sent to the `product-composite` microservice.
- The `origins` list specifies the OAuth 2.0/OIDC providers we rely on. For each issuer, the name of the issuer and the URL for its JSON web key set are specified. For a recap, see Chapter 11, *Securing Access to APIs* (refer to the *Introducing OpenId Connect* section). We have specified the local auth server, `http://auth-server.local`.

The policy file was applied by the `kubernetes/scripts/deploy-dev-env.bash` deployment script, when it was used in the *Running commands to create the service mesh* section.

The easiest way to verify that an invalid request is rejected by the Istio Ingress Gateway and not the `product-composite` microservice is to make a request without an access token and observe the error message that is returned. The Istio Ingress Gateway returns the following error message, `Origin authentication failed.`, in the event of a failed authentication, while the `product-composite` microservice returns an empty string. Both return the HTTP code `401` (Unauthorized).

Try it out with the following commands:

1. Make a request without an access token along the lines of the following:

   ```
   curl https://minikube.me/product-composite/2 -kw " HTTP Code:
   %{http_code}\n"
   ```

   Expect a response saying `Origin authentication failed. HTTP Code:`
   `401`.

2. Temporarily delete the policy with the following command:

   ```
   kubectl delete -f kubernetes/services/base/istio/jwt-
   authentication-policy.yml
   ```

Wait a minute to allow that policy change to be propagated to the Istio Ingress Gateway and then retry the request without an access token. The response should now only contain the HTTP code: `HTTP Code: 401`.

3. Enable the policy again with the following command:

```
kubectl apply -f kubernetes/services/base/istio/jwt-authentication-
policy.yml
```

Suggested additional exercise: Try out the Auth0 OIDC provider, as described in `Chapter 11`, *Securing Access to APIs* (refer to the *Testing with an OpenID Connect provider, Auth0*, section. Add your Auth0 provider to `jwt-authentication-policy.yml`. In my case, it appears as follows:

```
- jwt:
    issuer: "https://dev-magnus.eu.auth0.com/"
    jwksUri:
"https://dev-magnus.eu.auth0.com/.well-known/jwks.json"
```

Now, let's move on to the last security mechanism that we will cover in Istio – the automatic protection of internal communication in the service mesh using mutual authentication, mTLS.

Protecting internal communication using mutual authentication (mTLS)

In this section, we will learn how Istio can be configured to automatically protect internal communication within the service mesh using *mutual authentication*, mTLS. When using mutual authentication, not only does the service side prove its identity by exposing a certificate, but also the clients prove their identity to the servers by exposing a client-side certificate. This provides a higher level of security compared to normal TLS/HTTPS usage, where only the identity of the server is proven. Setting up and maintaining mutual authentication; that is, the provision of new, and the rotating of outdated, certificates, is known to be complex and is therefore seldom used. Istio fully automates the provisioning and rotation of certificates for mutual authentication used for internal communication inside the service mesh. This makes it much easier to use mutual authentication compared to setting it up manually.

So, why should we use mutual authentication? Isn't it sufficient to protect external APIs with HTTPS and OAuth 2.0/OIDC access tokens?

As long as the attacks come through the external API, it might be sufficient. But what if a pod inside the Kubernetes cluster becomes compromised? For example, if an attacker gains control over a pod, then the attacker can start listening to traffic between other pods in the Kubernetes cluster. If the internal communication is sent as plain text, it will be very easy for the attacker to gain access to sensitive information sent between pods in the cluster. To minimize the damage caused by such an intrusion, mutual authentication can be used to prevent an attacker from eavesdropping on internal network traffic.

To enable the use of mutual authentication managed by Istio, Istio needs to be configured both on the server side, using a policy, and on the client side, using a destination rule.

When using the demo configuration of Istio, as we did in the *Deploying Istio in a Kubernetes cluster* section, we got a global mesh policy created that configures the server side to use a permissive mode, meaning the Istio proxies will allow both plain text and encrypted requests. This can be verified with the following command:

```
kubectl get meshpolicy default -o yaml
```

Expect a response similar to the following:

```
6. bash
$ kubectl get meshpolicy default -o yaml
apiVersion: authentication.istio.io/v1alpha1
kind: MeshPolicy
  ...
  name: default
spec:
  peers:
  - mtls:
      mode: PERMISSIVE
$
```

To configure microservices to use mutual authentication when sending requests internally to other microservices, a destination rule is created for each microservice. This is done in the kubernetes/services/base/istio/internal_mtls_destination_rules.yml file. The destination rules all look the same; for example, for the product-composite service, they appear as follows:

```
apiVersion: networking.istio.io/v1alpha3
kind: DestinationRule
metadata:
  name: product-composite-dr
spec:
  host: product-composite
  trafficPolicy:
```

```
tls:
    mode: ISTIO_MUTUAL
```

`trafficPolicy` is set to use `tls` with `ISTIO_MUTUAL`, meaning mutual authentication is managed by Istio.

The destination rules were applied by the `kubernetes/scripts/deploy-dev-env.bash` deployment script, when it was used in the preceding *Running commands to create the service mesh* section.

To verify that the internal communication is protected, perform the following steps:

1. Ensure that the load tests started in the preceding *Observing the service mesh* section are still running.
2. Go to the Kiali graph in a web browser (`http://kiali.istio-system.svc.cluster.local:20001/kiali`).
3. Click on the **Display** button to enable the **Security** label. The graph will show a padlock on all communication links that are protected by Istio's automated mutual authentication, as follows:

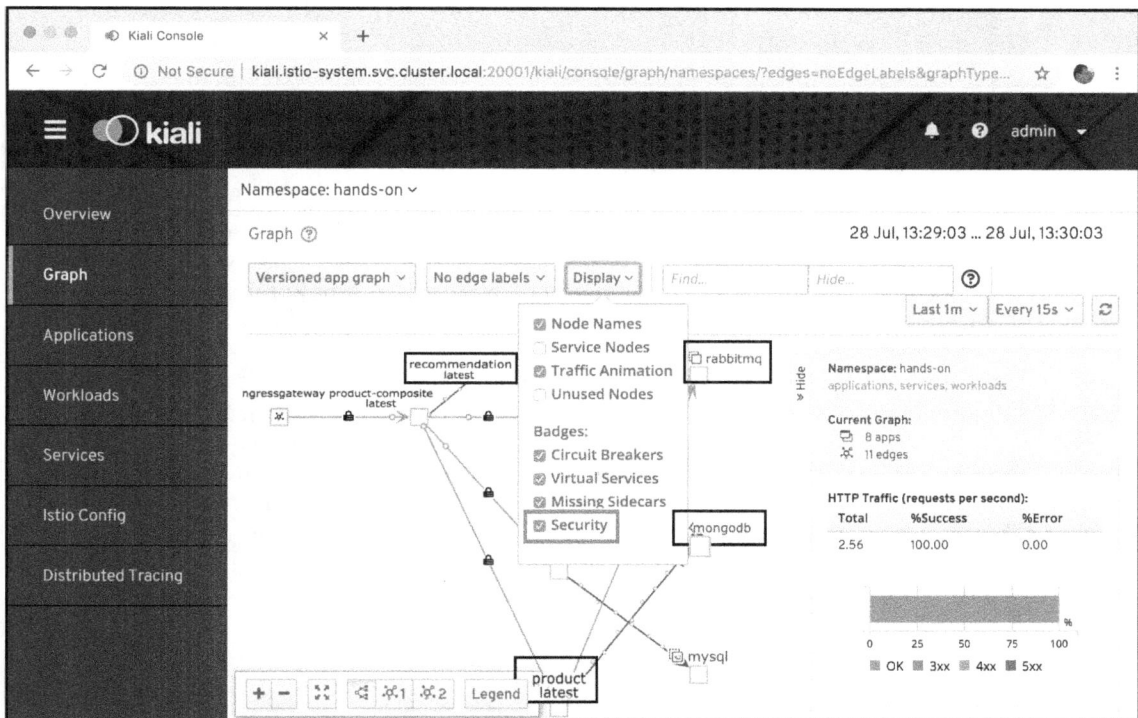

Expect a padlock on all links except for those to resource managers – RabbitMQ, MySQL, and MongoDB.

> Calls to RabbitMQ, MySQL, and MongoDB are not handled by Istio proxies, and therefore require manual configuration to be protected using TLS.

With this, we have seen all three security mechanisms in Istio in action, and it's now time to see how Istio can help us to verify that a service mesh is resilient.

Ensuring that a service mesh is resilient

In this section, we will learn how to use Istio to ensure that a service mesh is resilient; that is, it can handle temporary faults in a service mesh. Istio comes with mechanisms similar to what the Spring Framework offers in terms of timeouts, retries, and a type of circuit breaker called **outlier detection** to handle temporary faults. When it comes to deciding whether language-native mechanisms should be used to handle temporary faults, or whether this should be delegated to a service mesh such as Istio, I tend to favor using language-native mechanisms, as in the examples in Chapter 13, *Improving Resilience Using Resilience4J*. In many cases, it is important to keep the logic for handling errors, for example, handling fallback alternatives for a circuit breaker, together with other business logic for a microservice.

There are cases when the corresponding mechanisms in Istio could be of great help. For example, if a microservice is deployed and it is determined that it can't handle temporary faults that occur in production from time to time, then it can be very convenient to add a timeout or a retry mechanism using Istio instead of waiting for a new release of the microservice with corresponding error handling features put in place.

Another capability in the area of resilience that comes with Istio is the capability to inject faults and delays into an existing service mesh. Why would anyone want to do that?

Injecting faults and delays in a controlled way is very useful for verifying that the resilient capabilities in the microservices work as expected! We will try them out in this section, verifying that the retry, timeout, and circuit breaker in the product-composite microservice work as expected.

In Chapter 13, *Improving Resilience Using Resilience4j* (refer to the *Adding programmable delays and random errors* section), we added support for injecting faults and delays in the microservices source code. That source code can preferably be replaced by using Istio's capabilities for injecting faults and delays at runtime, as demonstrated in the following.

We will begin by injecting faults to see whether the retry mechanisms in the product-composite microservice work as expected. After that, we will delay the responses from the product service and verify that the circuit breaker handles the delay as expected.

Testing resilience by injecting faults

Let's make the product service throw random errors and verify that the microservice landscape handles this correctly. We expect the retry mechanism in the product-composite microservice to kick in and retry the request until it succeeds or its limit of max numbers of retries is reached. This will ensure that a shortlived fault does not affect the end user more than the delay introduced by the retry attempts. Refer to the *Adding a retry mechanism* section in Chapter 13, *Improving Resilience Using Resilience4j*, for a recap on the retry mechanism in the product-composite microservice.

Faults can be injected using kubernetes/resilience-tests/product-virtual-service-with-faults.yml. This appears as follows:

```
apiVersion: networking.istio.io/v1alpha3
kind: VirtualService
metadata:
  name: product-vs
spec:
  hosts:
    - product
  http:
  - route:
    - destination:
        host: product
    fault:
  abort:
        httpStatus: 500
        percent: 20
```

The definition says that 20% of the requests sent to the product service shall be aborted with the HTTP status code 500 (Internal Server Error).

Perform the following steps to test this:

1. Ensure that the load tests using `siege`, as started in the *Observing the service mesh* section, are running.
2. Apply fault injection with the following command:

```
kubectl apply -f kubernetes/resilience-tests/product-virtual-
service-with-faults.yml
```

3. Monitor the output from the `siege` load tests tool. Expect output similar to the following:

```
                                      4. bash
HTTP/1.1 200     0.03 secs:     772 bytes ==> GET  /product-composite/2
HTTP/1.1 200     1.08 secs:     772 bytes ==> GET  /product-composite/2
HTTP/1.1 200     0.03 secs:     772 bytes ==> GET  /product-composite/2
HTTP/1.1 200     0.05 secs:     772 bytes ==> GET  /product-composite/2
HTTP/1.1 200     1.03 secs:     772 bytes ==> GET  /product-composite/2
HTTP/1.1 200     0.06 secs:     772 bytes ==> GET  /product-composite/2
```

From the sample output, we can see that all requests are still successful, in other words, status 200 (OK) is returned; however, some of them (20%) take an extra second to complete. This indicates that the retry mechanism in the `product-composite` microservice has kicked in and has retried a failed request to the product service.

4. Kiali will also indicate that something is wrong with requests sent to the product service, as follows:
   1. Go to the call graph in Kiali's web UI that we used earlier to observe the traffic in our namespace, `hands-on`.
   2. Click on the **Display** menu button and select **Service Nodes**.
   3. Click on the menu button to the left of the **Display** button, named **No edge labels**, and select the **Response time** option.

4. The graph will show something like the following:

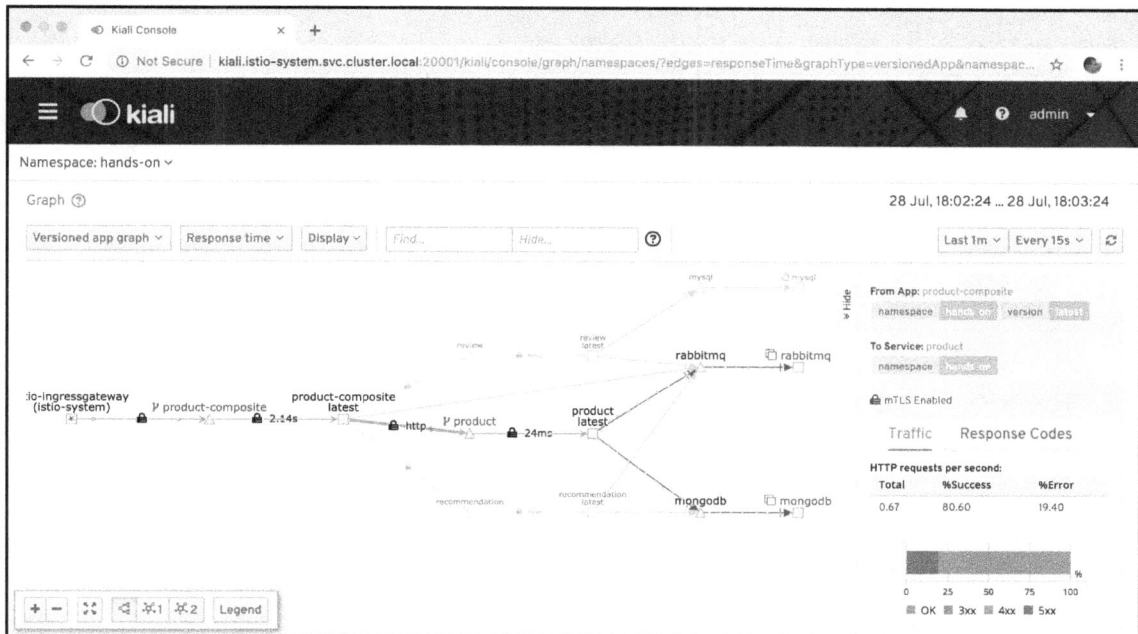

The arrow to the Service Node product will be shown in red to indicate that failed requests are detected. If we click on the arrow, we can see fault statistics to the right.

In the preceding sample screenshot, an error rate of 19.4% is reported, which corresponds well with the 20% we asked for. Note that the arrow from the Istio Gateway to the product-composite service is still green. This means that the retry mechanism in the product-composite service protects the end user; in other words, the faults do not propagate to the end user.

Conclude the removal of the fault injection with the following command:

```
kubectl delete -f kubernetes/resilience-tests/product-virtual-
service-with-faults.yml
```

Let's now move on to the next section, where we will inject delays to trigger the circuit breaker.

Testing resilience by injecting delays

From Chapter 13, *Improving Resilience Using Resilience4j* (refer to the *Introducing the circuit breaker* section), we know that a circuit breaker can be used to prevent problems due to the slow response of services, or the fact that the services do not respond at all.

Let's verify that the circuit breaker in the product-composite service works as expected by injecting a delay into the product service using Istio. A delay can be injected using a virtual service.

Refer to kubernetes/resilience-tests/product-virtual-service-with-delay.yml. Its code appears as follows:

```
apiVersion: networking.istio.io/v1alpha3
kind: VirtualService
metadata:
  name: product-vs
spec:
  hosts:
    - product
  http:
  - route:
    - destination:
        host: product
    fault:
      delay:
        fixedDelay: 3s
        percent: 100
```

The preceding definition says that all requests sent to the product service shall be delayed by 3 seconds.

Requests sent to the product service from the product-composite service are configured to timeout after 2 seconds. The circuit breaker is configured to open its circuit if 3 consecutive requests fail. When the circuit is open, it will fast-fail; in other words, it will immediately throw an exception, not attempting to call the underlying service. The business logic in the product-composite microservice will catch this exception and apply fallback logic. For a recap, see Chapter 13, *Improving Resilience Using Resilience4j* (refer to the *Adding a circuit breaker* section).

Perform the following steps to test the circuit breaker by injecting a delay:

1. Stop the load test run by means of the `siege` command by pressing *Ctrl + C* in the terminal window where `siege` is running.

2. Create a temporary delay in the product service with the following command:

```
kubectl apply -f kubernetes/resilience-tests/product-virtual-
service-with-delay.yml
```

3. Acquire an access token as follows:

```
ACCESS_TOKEN=$(curl -k
https://writer:secret@minikube.me/oauth/token -d
grant_type=password -d username=magnus -d password=password -s | jq
.access_token -r)
```

4. Send six requests in a row. Expect the circuit to open up after the first three failed calls, that the circuit breaker applies fast-fail logic for the three last calls, and that a fallback response is returned, as follows:

```
for i in {1..6}; do time curl -k
https://minikube.me/product-composite/2 -H "Authorization: Bearer
$ACCESS_TOKEN"; done
```

The responses from the first 3 calls are expected to be a timeout-related error message, and a response time of 2 seconds, in other words, the timeout time. Expect responses for the first 3 calls along the lines of the following:

```
4. bash
{..."message":"Did not observe any item or terminal signal within 2000ms in ..."}
real    0m2.051s
$
```

The responses from the last 3 calls are expected to be a response from the fallback logic with a short response time. Expect responses for the last 3 calls as follows:

```
6. bash
{"productId":2,"name":"Fallback product2"...
real    0m0.083
```

1. Simulate the fact that the delay problem is fixed by removing the temporary delay with the following command:

```
kubectl delete -f kubernetes/resilience-tests/product-virtual-
service-with-delay.yml
```

2. Verify that correct answers are returned again and without any delay by sending a new request using the preceding command.

> If you want to check the state of the circuit breaker, you can do it with the following command:
>
> ```
> curl product-composite.hands-
> on.svc.cluster.local:4004/actuator/health -s | jq -r
> .details.productCircuitBreaker.details.state
> ```
> It should report CLOSED, OPEN, or HALF_OPEN, depending on its state.

This proves that the circuit breaker reacts as expected when we inject a delay using Istio. This concludes testing features in Istio that can be used to verify that the microservice landscape is resilient. The final feature we will explore in Istio is its support for traffic management; we will establish how it can be used to enable deployments with zero downtime.

Performing zero-downtime deployments

As already mentioned in Chapter 16, *Deploying Our Microservices to Kubernetes* (refer to the *Performing a rolling upgrade* section), being able to deploy an update without downtime becomes crucial with a growing number of autonomous microservices that are updated independently of one another.

In this section, we will learn about Istio's traffic management and routing capabilities and how they can be used to perform deployments of new versions of microservices without requiring any downtime. In Chapter 16, *Deploying Our Microservices to Kubernetes* (refer to the *Performing a rolling upgrade* section), we saw how Kubernetes can be used to perform a rolling upgrade without requiring any downtime. Using the Kubernetes rolling upgrade mechanism automates the entire process, but unfortunately provides no option to test the new version before all users are routed to the new version.

Using Istio, we can deploy the new version, but initially route all users to the existing version (called the old version in this chapter). After that, we can use Istio's fine-grained routing mechanism to control how users are routed to the new and the old versions. We will see how two popular upgrade strategies can be implemented using Istio:

- **Canary deploys:** When using canary deploys, most users are routed to the old version, except for a group of selected test users who are routed to the new version. When the test users have approved the new version, regular users can be routed to the new version using a blue/green deploy.
- **Blue/green deploys:** Traditionally, a blue/green deploy means that all users are switched to either the blue or the green version, one being the new version and the other being the old version. If something goes wrong when switching over to the new version, it is very simple to switch back to the old version. Using Istio, this strategy can be refined by gradually shifting users over to the new version, for example, starting with 20% of the users and then slowly increasing the percentage of users who are routed to the new version. At all times, it is very easy to route all users back to the old version if a fatal error is revealed in the new version.

As already stated in `Chapter 16`, *Deploying Our Microservices to Kubernetes* (refer to the *Performing a rolling upgrade* section), it is important to remember that a prerequisite for these types of upgrade strategies is that the upgrade is backward-compatible. Such an upgrade is compatible both in terms of APIs and message formats, which are used to communicate with other services and database structures. If the new version of the microservice requires changes to external APIs, message formats, or database structures that the old version can't handle, these upgrade strategies can't be applied.

We will go through the following deploy scenario in the following subsections:

- We will start by deploying the `v1` and `v2` versions of the microservices, with routing configured to send all requests to the `v1` version of the microservices.
- Next, we will allow a test group to run canary tests; that is, we'll verify the new `v2` versions of the microservices. To simplify the tests somewhat, we will only route test users to the new versions of the core microservices, that is, the `product`, `recommendation`, and `review` microservices.
- Finally, we will start to move regular users over to the new versions using a blue/green deploy: initially, a small percentage of users and then, over time, more and more users until, eventually, they are all routed to the new version. We will also see how we can quickly switch back to the `v1` versions if a fatal error is detected in the new v2 version.

Let's first see what changes have been applied to the source code to deploy two concurrent versions, v1 and v2, of the microservices.

Source code changes

As already mentioned in the *Changing the file structure of the Kubernetes definition files* section, the file structure for the Kubernetes definition files in kubernetes/services has been expanded in this chapter to support the deployment of concurrent versions of the microservices in the production environment. The expanded file structure appears as follows:

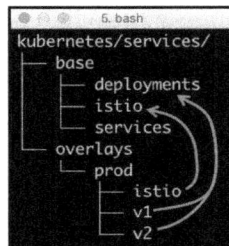

> Details regarding the development environment have been removed from the preceding diagram.

Let's first see how service and deployment objects for the v1 and v2 versions of the microservices are configured and created. After that, we will go through additional definition files for Istio objects used to control the routing.

Service and deployment objects for concurrent versions of microservices

To be able to run multiple versions of a microservice concurrently, the deployment objects and their corresponding pods must have different names, for example, product-v1 and product-v2. There must, however, be only one Kubernetes service object per microservice. All traffic to a specific microservice always goes through one and the same service object, irrespective of what version of the pod the request will be routed to in the end. This is achieved using Kustomize by splitting up deployment objects and service objects into different folders.

To give deployment objects and their pods version-dependent names, the `kustomization.yml` file can use the `nameSuffix` directive to tell Kustomize to add the given suffix to all Kubernetes objects it creates. For example, the `kustomization.yml` file used for the `v1` version of the microservices in the `kubernetes/services/overlays/prod/v1` folder appears as follows:

```
nameSuffix: -v1
bases:
- ../../../base/deployments
patchesStrategicMerge:
- ...
```

The `nameSuffix: -v1` setting will result in all objects created using this `kustomization.yml` file being named with the `-v1` suffix.

To create the objects without a version suffix, and the deployment objects and their pods with the `v1` and `v2` version suffixes, the `kubernetes/scripts/deploy-prod-env.bash` deployment script executes separate `kubectl apply` commands as follows:

```
kubectl apply -k kubernetes/services/base/services
kubectl apply -k kubernetes/services/overlays/prod/v1
kubectl apply -k kubernetes/services/overlays/prod/v2
```

Let's also see what Istio definition files we have added to configure routing rules.

Added Kubernetes definition files for Istio

To configure routing rules, we will add Istio objects to the `kubernetes/services/overlays/prod/istio` folder. Each microservice has a virtual service object that defines the weight distribution for the routing between the old and the new versions. Initially, it is set to route 100% of the traffic to the old version. For example, the routing rule for the product microservice in `product-routing-virtual-service.yml` appears as follows:

```
http:
- route:
  - destination:
      host: product
      subset: old
    weight: 100
  - destination:
      host: product
      subset: new
    weight: 0
```

The virtual service defines subsets for the old and the new versions. To define what actual versions the old and new versions are, each microservice also has a destination rule defined. The destination rule details how the old subset and the new subset shall be identified, for example, in the case of the product microservice in `old_new_subsets_destination_rules.yml`:

```
apiVersion: networking.istio.io/v1alpha3
kind: DestinationRule
metadata:
  name: product-dr
spec:
  host: product
  subsets:
  - name: old
    labels:
      version: v1
  - name: new
    labels:
      version: v2
```

The subset named `old` points to product pods that have the `version` label set to `v1`, while the subset named `new` points to pods with the `version` label set to `v2`.

> To route traffic to a specific version, Istio documentation recommends that pods are labeled with a label named `version` to identify its version. Refer to `https://istio.io/docs/setup/kubernetes/additional-setup/requirements/` for details.

Finally, to support canary testers, an extra routing rule has been added to the virtual services for the three core microservices: product, recommendation, and review. This routing rule states that any incoming request that has an HTTP header named `X-group` set to the value `test` will always be routed to the new version of the service. This appears as follows:

```
http:
- match:
  - headers:
      X-group:
        exact: test
  route:
  - destination:
      host: product
      subset: new
```

The `match` and `route` sections specify that requests with the HTTP header, `X-group`, set to the value, `test`, shall be routed to the subset named `new`.

To create these Istio objects, the `kubernetes/scripts/deploy-prod-env.bash` deployment script executes the following command:

```
kubectl apply -k kubernetes/services/overlays/prod/istio
```

Finally, to be able to route canary testers to the new version based on header-based routing, the `product-composite` microservice has been updated to forward the HTTP header `X-group`. Refer to the `getCompositeProduct()` method in the `se.magnus.microservices.composite.product.services.ProductCompositeServiceImpl` class for details.

Now, we have seen all the changes to the source code and we are ready to deploy v1 and v2 versions of the microservices.

Deploying v1 and v2 versions of the microservices with routing to the v1 version

To be able to test the `v1` and `v2` versions of the microservices, we need to remove the development environment we have been using earlier in this chapter and create a production environment where we can deploy the v1 and v2 versions of the microservices.

To achieve this, run the following commands:

1. Recreate the `hands-on` namespace:

```
kubectl delete namespace hands-on
kubectl create namespace hands-on
```

2. Execute the deployment by running the script with the following command:

```
./kubernetes/scripts/deploy-prod-env.bash
```

The command takes a couple of minutes and should eventually list all the v1 or v2 versions of the pods as follows:

```
                              4. bash
$ ./kubernetes/scripts/deploy-prod-env.bash
...
+ kubectl wait --timeout=120s --for=condition=Ready pod --all
pod/auth-server-v1-5f75968f7f-v7j8p condition met
pod/auth-server-v2-97b4b5cb4-lcvx4 condition met
pod/product-composite-v1-7f87fd87cb-2vmjl condition met
pod/product-composite-v2-99855f749-lz44j condition met
pod/product-v1-b8d48477c-qvl9f condition met
pod/product-v2-657cd6749d-xdh9c condition met
pod/recommendation-v1-545fb976cd-jfq9w condition met
pod/recommendation-v2-66d475fbf7-swdhs condition met
pod/review-v1-868c87cc95-ww2hv condition met
pod/review-v2-f4c97c748-2mlwm condition met
$ ▊
```

3. Run the usual tests to verify that everything works:

```
SKIP_CB_TESTS=true ./test-em-all.bash
```

If this command is executed immediately after the `deploy` command, it sometimes fails. Simply rerun the command and it should run fine!

> Since we now have two pods (version V1 and V2) running for each microservice, the circuit breaker tests no longer work. The reason for this is that the test script can't control which pod it talks to, through the Kubernetes service. The test script asks about the state of the circuit breaker in the `product-composite` microservice using the actuator endpoint on port `4004`. This port is not managed by Istio, so its routing rules do no apply. The test script will therefore not know whether it is checking the state of the circuit breaker in V1 or V2 of the `product-composite` microservice. We can skip circuit breaker tests by using the `SKIP_CB_TESTS=true` flag.

Expect output that is similar to what we have seen from the previous chapters, but excluding the circuit breaker tests:

```
                                    4. bash
$ SKIP_CB_TESTS=true ./test-em-all.bash
...
Wait for: curl -k http://product-composite.hands-on.svc.cluster.local:4004/actuator/health...
 DONE, continues...
Test OK (HTTP Code: 200)
...
End, all tests OK: Mon Aug 5 09:19:37 CEST 2019
$
```

We are now ready to run some *zero-downtime deploy* tests. Let's begin by verifying that all traffic goes to the v1 version of the microservices!

Verifying that all traffic initially goes to the v1 version of the microservices

To verify that all requests are routed to the v1 version of the microservices, we will start up the load test tool, `siege`, and then observe the traffic that flows through the service mesh using Kiali.

Perform the following steps:

1. Get a new access token and start the `siege` load test tool, with the following commands:

   ```
   ACCESS_TOKEN=$(curl -k
   https://writer:secret@minikube.me/oauth/token -d
   grant_type=password -d username=magnus -d password=password -s | jq
   .access_token -r)

   siege https://minikube.me/product-composite/2 -H "Authorization:
   Bearer $ACCESS_TOKEN" -c1 -d1
   ```

2. Go to the graph view in Kiali's web UI (`http://kiali.istio-system.svc.cluster.local:20001/kiali`):
   1. Click on the **Display** menu button and deselect **Service Nodes**.
   2. After a minute or two, expect only traffic to the **v1** version of the microservices as follows:

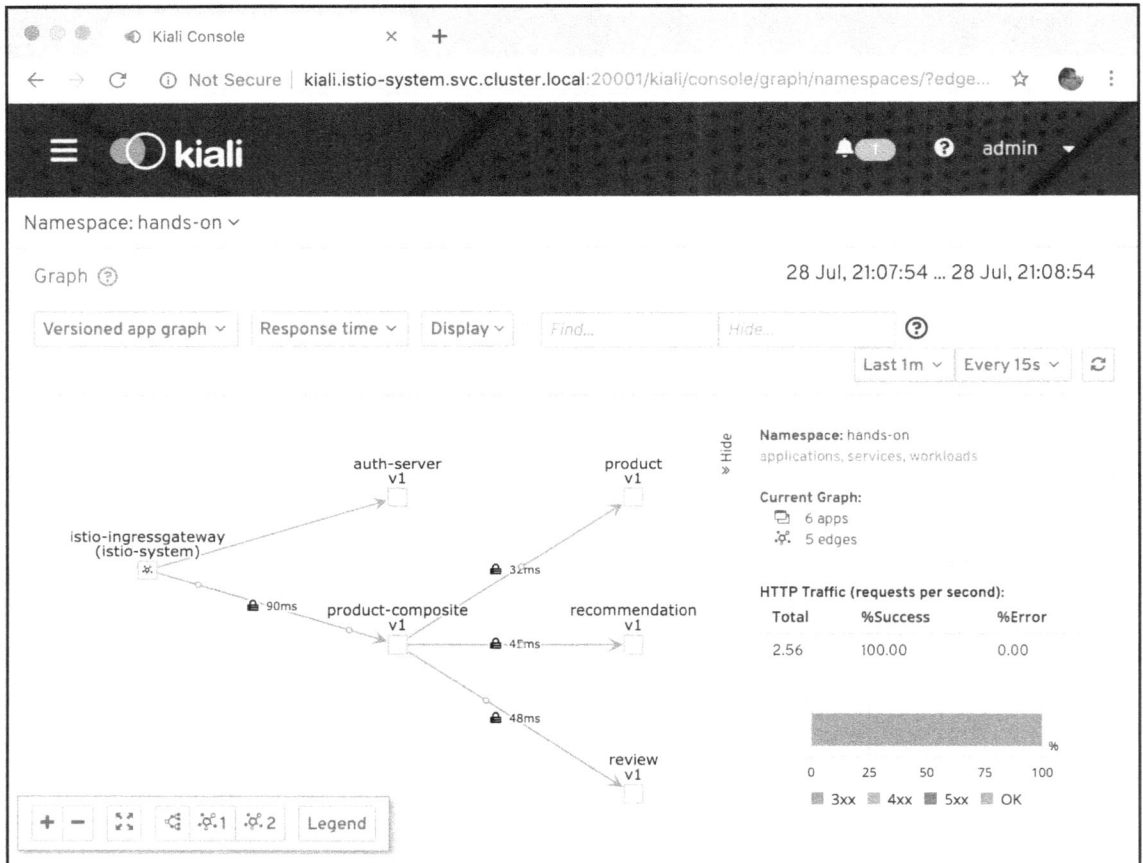

Good! This means that, even though the v2 versions of the microservices are deployed, they do not get any traffic routed to them. Let's now try out canary tests where selected test users are allowed to try out the v2 versions of the microservices!

Running canary tests

To run a canary test, in other words, in order to be routed to the new versions while all other users are still routed to the old versions of the deployed microservices, we need to add the X-group HTTP header set to the value test in our requests sent to the external API.

To see which version of a microservice served a request, the serviceAddresses field in the response can be inspected. The serviceAddresses field contains the hostname of each service that took part in creating the response. The hostname is equal to the name of the pod, so we can find the version in the hostname; for example, product-v1-... for a product service of version V1, and product-v2-... for a product service of version V2.

Let's begin by sending a normal request and verify that it is the v1 versions of the microservices that respond to our request. Next, send a request with the X-group HTTP header set to the value test, and verify that the new v2 versions are responding.

To do this, perform the following steps:

1. Perform a normal request to verify that the request is routed to the v1 version of the microservices by using jq to filter out the serviceAddresses field in the response:

   ```
   curl -ks https://minikube.me/product-composite/2 -H "Authorization:
   Bearer $ACCESS_TOKEN" | jq .serviceAddresses
   ```

   Expect a response along the lines of the following:

   ```
   $ curl -ks https://minikube.me/product-composite/2 -H "Authorization: Bearer $ACCESS_TOKEN" | jq .serviceAddresses
   {
     "cmp": "product-composite-v1-7f87fd87cb-2vmjl/172.17.0.25:80",
     "pro": "product-v1-b8d48477c-qvl9f/172.17.0.27:80",
     "rev": "review-v1-868c87cc95-ww2hv/172.17.0.29:80",
     "rec": "recommendation-v1-545fb976cd-jfq9w/172.17.0.28:80"
   }
   $
   ```

As expected, all three core services are v1 versions of the microservices.

2. If we add the `X-group=test` header, we expect the request to be served by v2 versions of the core microservices. Run the following command:

```
curl -ks https://minikube.me/product-composite/2 -H "Authorization:
Bearer $ACCESS_TOKEN" -H "X-group: test" | jq .serviceAddresses
```

Expect a response similar to the following:

```
4. bash
$ curl -ks https://minikube.me/product-composite/2 \
  -H "Authorization: Bearer $ACCESS_TOKEN" -H "X-group: test" | jq .serviceAddresses
{
  "cmp": "product-composite-v1-7f87fd87cb-2vmjl/172.17.0.25:80",
  "pro": "product-v2-657cd6749d-xdh9c/172.17.0.32:80",
  "rev": "review-v2-f4c97c748-2mlwm/172.17.0.33:80",
  "rec": "recommendation-v2-66d475fbf7-swdhs/172.17.0.34:80"
}
$
```

As expected, all three core microservices that respond are now v2 versions; that is, as a canary tester, we are routed to the new v2 versions!

Given that the canary tests returned the expected results, we are ready to allow normal users to be routed to the new v2 versions using blue/green deployment.

Running blue/green tests

To route parts of the normal users to the new v2 versions of the microservices, we have to modify the weight distribution in the virtual services. They are currently 100/0; in other words, all traffic is routed to the old v1 versions. We can achieve this as we did before, that is, by editing the definition files of the virtual services in the `kubernetes/services/overlays/prod/istio` folder and then running a `kubectl apply` command to make the change take effect. As an alternative, we can use the `kubectl patch` command to change the weight distribution directly on the virtual service objects in the Kubernetes API server.

I find the patch command useful when making a number of changes to the same objects to try something out, for example, to change the weight distribution in the routing rules. In this section, we will use the `kubectl patch` command to quickly change the weight distribution in the routing rules between the v1 and v2 versions of the microservices. To get the state of a virtual service after a number of `kubectl patch` commands have been executed, a command such as `kubectl get vs NNN -o yaml` can be issued. For example, to get the state of the virtual service of the product microservice, issue the following command: `kubectl get vs product-vs -o yaml`.

Since we haven't used the `kubectl patch` command before and it can be a bit involved to start with, let's undertake a short introduction to how it works before we perform the green/blue deploy.

A short introduction to the kubectl patch command

The `kubectl patch` command can be used to update specific fields in an existing object in the Kubernetes API server. We will try the patch command on the virtual service for the review microservice, named `review-vs`. The relevant parts of the definition for the virtual service, `review-vs`, appear as follows:

```
spec:
  http:
  - match:
    . . .
  - route:
    - destination:
        host: review
        subset: old
      weight: 100
    - destination:
        host: review
        subset: new
      weight: 0
```

For the full source code, refer to `kubernetes/services/overlays/prod/istio/review-routing-virtual-service.yml`.

A sample patch command that changes the weight distribution of the routing to the v1 and v2 pods in the `review` microservice appears as follows:

```
kubectl patch virtualservice review-vs --type=json -p='[
  {"op": "add", "path": "/spec/http/1/route/0/weight", "value": "80"},
  {"op": "add", "path": "/spec/http/1/route/1/weight", "value": "20"}
]'
```

The command will configure the routing rules of the review microservice to route 80% of the requests to the old version, and 20% of the requests to the new version.

To specify that the `weight` value shall be changed in the `review-vs` virtual service, the `/spec/http/1/route/0/weight` path is given for the old version and `/spec/http/1/route/1/weight` for the new version.

The `0` and `1` in the path are used to specify the index of array elements in the definition of the virtual service. For example, `http/1` means the second element in the array under the `http` element. See the definition of the preceding `review-vs` virtual service.

From the preceding definition we can see that the second element is the `route` element. The first element with index `0` being the match element.

Now that we know a bit more about the `kubectl patch` command, we are ready to test a blue/green deployment.

Performing the blue/green deployment

Now, it is time to gradually move more and more users to the new versions using blue/green deployment. To perform the deployment, run the following steps:

1. Ensure that the load test tool, `Siege`, is still running.
   It was started in the preceding *Verifying that all traffic initially goes to the v1 version of the microservices* section.
2. To allow 20% of the users to be routed to the new v2 version of the review microservice, we can patch the virtual service and change weights with the following command:

   ```
   kubectl patch virtualservice review-vs --type=json -p='[
     {"op": "add", "path": "/spec/http/1/route/0/weight", "value":
     "80"},
     {"op": "add", "path": "/spec/http/1/route/1/weight", "value":
     "20"}
     ]'
   ```

3. To observe the change in the routing rule, go to the Kiali web UI (`http://kiali.istio-system.svc.cluster.local:20001/kiali`) and select the graph view.

4. Change the edge label to `Requests percentage`.

5. Wait for a minute before the statics are updated in Kiali so that we can observe the change. Expect the graph in Kiali to show something like the following:

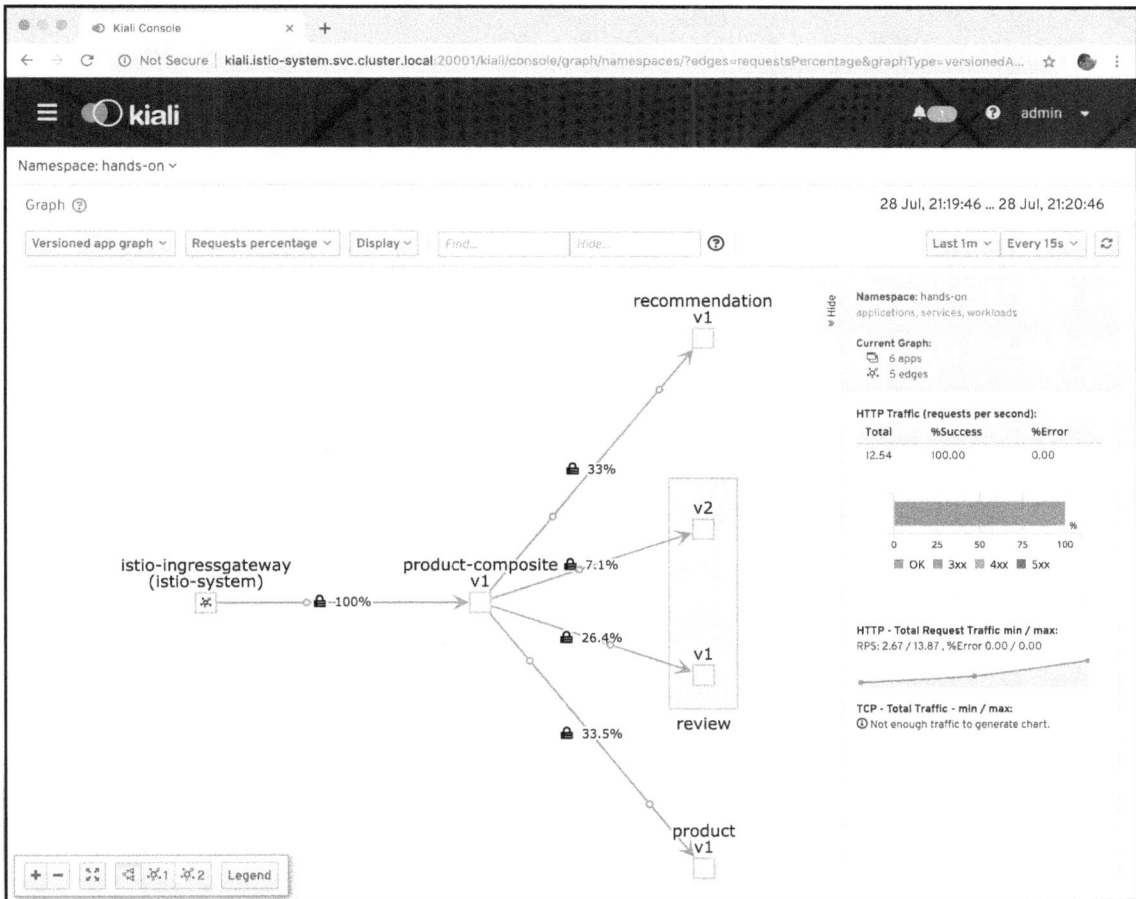

Depending on how long you have waited, the graph might look a bit different!
In the screenshot, we can see that Istio now routes traffic to both the v1 and v2 versions of the `review` microservice.

Of the 33% of the traffic that is sent to the `review` microservice from the `product-composite` microservice, 7% are routed to the new v2 pod, and 26% to the old v1 pod. This means that 7/33 (= 21%) of the requests are routed to the v2 pod, and 26/33 (= 79%) to the v1 pod. This is in line with the 20/80 distribution we have requested:

1. Please feel free to try out the preceding `kubectl patch` command to affect the routing rules for the other core microservices: `product` and `recommendation`.

2. If you want to route all traffic to the v2 version of all microservices, you can run the following script:

```
./kubernetes/scripts/route-all-traffic-to-v2-services.bash
```

You have to give Kiali a minute or two to collect metrics before it can visualize the changes in routing between the v1 and v2 versions of the microservices, but remember that the change in the actual routing is immediate!

Expect only v2 versions of the microservices to show up in the graph after a while:

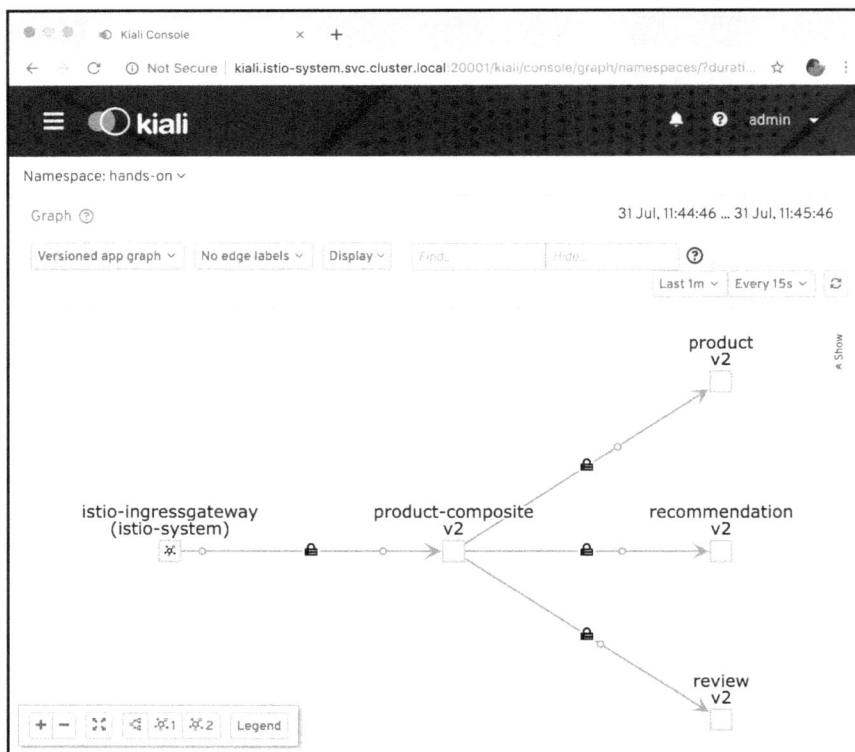

Depending on how long you have waited, the graph might look a bit different!

3. If something goes terribly wrong after the upgrade to v2, the following command can be executed to revert all traffic back to the v1 version of all microservices:

```
./kubernetes/scripts/route-all-traffic-to-v1-services.bash
```

After a short while, the graph in Kiali should look like the screenshot in the previous *Verifying that all traffic initially goes to the v1 version of the microservices* section; that is, visualize that all requests go to the v1 version of all microservices again.

This concludes the introduction to the service mesh concept and Istio as an implementation of the concept.

Before we wrap up the chapter, let's recap how we can run tests in Docker Compose to ensure that the source code of our microservices does not rely on deployment in Kubernetes.

Running tests with Docker Compose

As mentioned in Chapter 17, *Implementing Kubernetes Features as an Alternative* (refer to the *Verifying that the microservices work without Kubernetes* section), it is important to ensure that the source code of the microservices doesn't become dependent on a platform such as Kubernetes or Istio from a functional perspective.

To verify that the microservices work as expected without the presence of Kubernetes and Istio, run the tests as described in Chapter 17, *Implementing Kubernetes Features as an Alternative* (refer to the *Testing with Docker Compose* section). Since the default values of the test script, test-em-all.bash, are changed, as described previously in the *Running commands to create the service mesh* section, the following parameters must be set when using Docker Compose: HOST=localhost PORT=8443 HEALTH_URL=https://localhost:8443. For example, to run the tests using the default Docker Compose file, docker-compose.yml, run the following command:

```
HOST=localhost PORT=8443 HEALTH_URL=https://localhost:8443 ./test-em-all.bash start stop
```

The tests should, as before, begin by starting all containers; it should then run the tests, and finally stop all containers. For details of the expected output, see `Chapter 17`, *Implementing Kubernetes Features as an Alternative* (refer to the *Verifying that the microservices work without Kubernetes* section).

After successfully executing the tests using Docker Compose, we have verified that the microservices are dependent neither on Kubernetes nor Istio from a functional perspective. These tests conclude the chapter on using Istio as a service mesh.

Summary

In this chapter, we learned about the service mesh concept and Istio, an open source project that implements it. A service mesh provides capabilities for handling challenges in a system landscape of microservices in areas such as security, policy enforcement, resilience, and traffic management. A service mesh can also be used to make a system landscape of microservices observable by visualizing the traffic that flows through the microservices.

For observability, Istio uses Kiali, Jaeger, and Grafana (more on Grafana in `Chapter 20`, *Monitoring Microservices*). When it comes to security, Istio can be configured to use a certificate to protect external APIs with HTTPS and require that external requests contain valid JWT-based OAuth 2.0/OIDC access tokens. Finally, Istio can be configured to automatically protect internal communication using **mutual authentication** (**mTLS**).

For resilience and robustness, Istio comes with mechanisms for handling retries, timeouts, and an outlier detection mechanism similar to a circuit breaker. In many cases, it is preferable to implement these resilience capabilities in the source code of the microservices, if possible. The ability in Istio to inject faults and delays is very useful for verifying that the microservices in the service mesh work together as a resilient and robust system landscape. Istio can also be used to handle zero-downtime deployments. Using its fine-grained routing rules, both canary and blue/green deployments can be performed.

One important area that we haven't covered yet is how to collect and analyze log files created by all microservice instances. In the next chapter, we will see how this can be done using a popular stack of tools, known as the EFK stack, based on Elasticsearch, Fluentd, and Kibana.

Questions

1. What is the purpose of a proxy component in a service mesh?
2. What's the difference between a control plane and a data plane in a service mesh?
3. What is the `istioctl kube-inject` command used for?
4. What is the `minikube tunnel` command used for?
5. What tools are used in Istio for observability?
6. What configuration is required to make Istio protect communication within the service mesh using mutual authentication?
7. What can the `abort` and `delay` elements in a virtual service be used for?
8. What configuration is required to set up a blue/green deploy scenario?

19
Centralized Logging with the EFK Stack

In this chapter, we will learn how to collect and store log records from microservice instances, as well as how to search and analyze log records. As we mentioned in Chapter 1, *Introduction to Microservices* (refer to the *Centralized log analysis* section), it is difficult to get an overview of what is going on in a system landscape of microservices when each microservice instance writes log records to its local filesystem. We need a component that can collect the log records from the microservice's local filesystem and store them in a central database for analysis, search, and visualization. A popular open source-based solution for this builds on the following tools:

- **Elasticsearch**, a distributed database with great capabilities for the search and analysis of large datasets
- **Fluentd**, a data collector that can be used to collect log records from various sources, filter and transform the collected information, and finally send it to various consumers, for example, Elasticsearch
- **Kibana**, a graphical frontend to Elasticsearch that can be used to visualize search results and run analyses of the collected log records

Together, these tools are called the **EFK stack**, named after the initials of each tool.

The following topics will be covered in this chapter:

- Configuring Fluentd
- Deploying the EFK stack on Kubernetes for development and test usage
- Trying out the EFK stack by:
    - Analyzing the collected log records
    - Discovering log records from the microservices and finding related log records
    - Performing root cause analysis

Technical requirements

All of the commands that are described in this book have been run on a MacBook Pro using macOS Mojave but should be straightforward to modify so that they can be run on another platform, such as Linux or Windows.

No new tools need to be installed in this chapter.

The source code for this chapter can be found in this book's GitHub repository: `https://github.com/PacktPublishing/Hands-On-Microservices-with-Spring-Boot-and-Spring-Cloud/tree/master/Chapter19`.

To be able to run the commands that are described in this book, you need to download the source code to a folder and set up an environment variable, `$BOOK_HOME`, which points to that folder. Some sample commands are as follows:

```
export BOOK_HOME=~/Documents/Hands-On-Microservices-with-Spring-Boot-and-
Spring-Cloud
git clone
https://github.com/PacktPublishing/Hands-On-Microservices-with-Spring-Boot-
and-Spring-Cloud $BOOK_HOME
cd $BOOK_HOME/Chapter19
```

All of the source code examples in this chapter come from the source code in `$BOOK_HOME/Chapter19` and have been tested using Kubernetes 1.15.

If you want to take a look at the changes we applied to the source code in this chapter, that is, look at the changes we made so that we can use the EFK stack for centralized log analyses, you can compare it with the source code for `Chapter 18`, *Using a Service Mesh to Improve Observability and Management*. You can use your favorite `diff` tool and compare the two folders, `$BOOK_HOME/Chapter18` and `$BOOK_HOME/Chapter19`.

Configuring Fluentd

In this section we will learn the basics for how to configure Fluentd. Before we do that, let's learn a bit about the background of Fluentd and how it works on a high level.

Introducing Fluentd

Historically, one of the most popular open source stacks for handling log records has been the ELK stack from Elastic (`https://www.elastic.co`), based on Elasticsearch, Logstash (used for log collection and transformation), and Kibana. Since Logstash runs on a Java VM, it requires a relatively large amount of memory. Over the years, a number of open source alternatives have been developed that require significantly less memory than Logstash, one of them being Fluentd (`https://www.fluentd.org`).

Fluentd is managed by the **Cloud Native Computing Foundation** (**CNCF**) (`https://www.cncf.io`), that is, the same organization that manages the Kubernetes project. Therefore, Fluentd has become a natural choice as an open source-based log collector that runs in Kubernetes. Together with Elastic and Kibana, it forms the EFK stack.

Fluentd is written in a mix of C and Ruby, using C for the performance-critical parts and Ruby where flexibility is of more importance, for example, allowing the simple installation of third-party plugins using Ruby's `gem install` command.

A log record is processed as an event in Fluentd and consists of the following information:

* A `time` field describing when the log record was created
* A `tag` field that identifies what type of log record it is—the tag is used by Fluentd's routing engine to determine how a log record shall be processed
* A **record** that contains the actual log information, which is stored as a JSON object

A Fluentd configuration file is used to tell Fluentd how to collect, process, and finally send log records to various targets, such as Elasticsearch. A configuration file consists of the following types of core elements:

* `<source>`: Source elements describe where Fluentd will collect log records. For example, tailing log files that have been written to by Docker containers. Source elements typically tag the log records, describing the type of log record. It could, for example, be used to tag log records to state that they come from containers running in Kubernetes.

- `<filter>`: Filter elements are used to process the log records, for example, a filter element can parse log records that come from Spring Boot-based microservices and extract interesting parts of the log message into separate fields in the log record. Extracting information into separate fields in the log record makes the information searchable by Elasticsearch. A filter element selects what log records to process based on their tags.
- `<match>`: Output elements are used to perform two main tasks:
    - Send processed log records to targets such as Elasticsearch.
    - Routing is to decide how to process log records. A routing rule can rewrite the tag and reemit the log record into the Fluentd routing engine for further processing. A routing rule is expressed as an embedded `<rule>` element inside the `<match>` element. Output elements decide what log records to process, in the same way as a filter: based on the tag of the log records.

Fluentd comes with a number of built-in and external third-party plugins that are used by the source, filter, and output elements. We will see some of them in action when we walk through the configuration file in the next section. For more information on the available plugins, see Fluentd's documentation, which is available at `https://docs.fluentd.org`.

With this introduction to Fluentd out of the way, we are ready to see how Fluentd can be configured to process the log records from our microservices.

Configuring Fluentd

The configuration of Fluentd is based on the configuration files from a Fluentd project on GitHub, `fluentd-kubernetes-daemonset`. The project contains Fluentd configuration files for how to collect log records from containers that run in Kubernetes and how to send them to Elasticsearch once they have been processed. We can reuse this configuration without changes and it will simplify our own configuration to a great extent. The Fluentd configuration files can be found at `https://github.com/fluent/fluentd-kubernetes-daemonset/tree/master/docker-image/v1.4/debian-elasticsearch/conf`.

The configuration files that provide this functionality are `kubernetes.conf` and `fluent.conf`. The `kubernetes.conf` configuration file contains the following information:

- Source elements that tail container log files and log files from processes that run outside of Kubernetes, for example, the `kubelet` and the Docker daemon. The source elements also tag the log records from Kubernetes with the full name of the log file with / replaced by . and prefixed with `kubernetes`. Since the tag is based on the full filename, the name contains the name of the namespace, pod, and container, among other things. So, the tag is very useful for finding log records of interest by matching the tag. For example, the tag from the `product-composite` microservice could be something like `kubernetes.var.log.containers.product-composite-7...s_hands-on_comp-e...b.log`, while the tag for the corresponding `istio-proxy` in the same pod could be something like `kubernetes.var.log.containers.product-composite-7...s_hands-on_istio-proxy-1...3.log`.
- A filter element that enriches the log records that come from containers running inside Kubernetes, along with Kubernetes-specific fields that contain information such as the names of the containers and the namespace they run in.

The main configuration file, `fluent.conf`, contains the following information:

- `@include` statements for other configuration files, for example, the `kubernetes.conf` file we described previously. It also includes custom configuration files that are placed in a specific folder, making it very easy for us to reuse these configuration files without any changes and provide our own configuration file that only handles processing related to our own log records. We simply need to place our own configuration file in the folder specified by the `fluent.conf` file.
- An output element that sends log records to Elasticsearch.

As we described in the *Deploying Fluentd* section, these two configuration files will be packaged into the Docker image we will build for Fluentd.

What's left to cover in our own configuration file is the following:

- Detect and parse Spring Boot formatted log records from our microservices.
- Handling multiline stack traces. Stack traces, for example, are written to log files using multiple lines. This makes it hard for Fluentd to handle a stack trace as a single log record.

- Separating log records from the `istio-proxy` sidecars from the log records that were created by the microservices running in the same pod. The log records that are created by `istio-proxy` don't follow the same pattern as the log patterns that are created by our Spring Boot-based microservices. Therefore, they must be handled separately so that Fluentd doesn't try to parse them as Spring Boot formatted log records.

To achieve this, the configuration is, to a large extent, based on using the `rewrite_tag_filter` plugin. This plugin can be used for routing log records based on the concept of changing the name of a tag and then reemitting the log record to the Fluentd routing engine.

This processing is summarized by the following UML activity diagram:

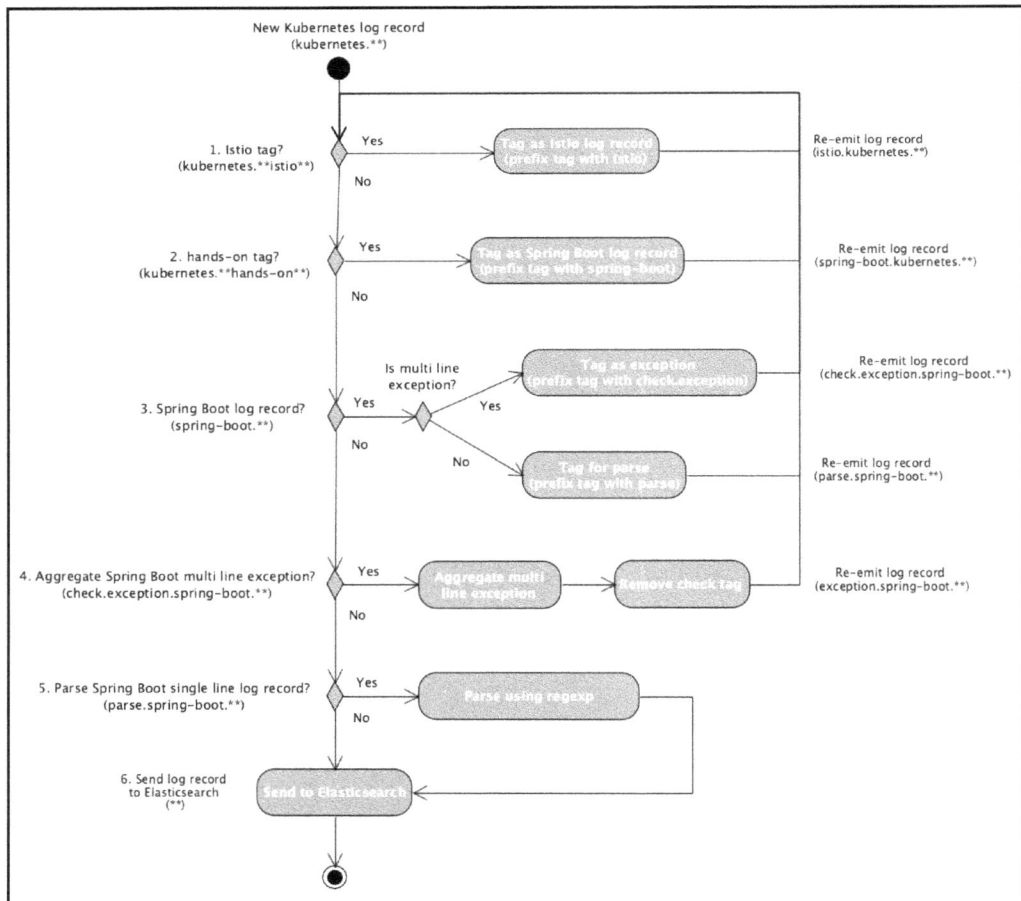

At a high level, the design of the configuration file looks as follows:

- The tags of all of the log records from Istio, including istio-proxy, are prefixed with istio so that they can be separated from the Spring Boot-based log records.
- The tags of all of the log records from the hands-on namespace (except for the log records from istio-proxy) are prefixed with spring-boot.
- The log records from Spring Boot are checked for the presence of multiline stack traces. If the log record is part of a multiline stack trace, it is processed by the third-party detect-exceptions plugin to recreate the stack trace. Otherwise, it is parsed using a regular expression to extract information of interest. See the *Deploying Fluentd* section for details on this third-party plugin.

The fluentd-hands-on.conf configuration file follows this activity diagram closely. The configuration file is placed inside a Kubernetes config map (see kubernetes/efk/fluentd-hands-on-configmap.yml). Let's go through this step by step, as follows:

1. First comes the definition of the config map and the filename of the configuration file, fluentd-hands-on.conf. It looks as follows:

```
apiVersion: v1
kind: ConfigMap
metadata:
  name: fluentd-hands-on-config
  namespace: kube-system
data:
  fluentd-hands-on.conf: |
```

From the preceding source code, we understand that the data element will contain the configuration of Fluentd. It starts with the filename and uses a vertical bar | to mark the beginning of the embedded configuration file for Fluentd.

2. The first <match> element matches the log records from Istio, that is, tags that are prefixed with kubernetes and contain either istio as part of its namespace or part of its container name. It looks like this:

```
<match kubernetes.**istio**>
  @type rewrite_tag_filter
  <rule>
    key log
    pattern ^(.*)$
    tag istio.${tag}
  </rule>
</match>
```

Let's explain the preceding source code in more detail:

- The <match> element matches any tags that follow the kubernetes.**istio** pattern, that is, it starts with kubernetes and then contains the word istio somewhere in the tag name. istio can either come from the name of the namespace or the container; both are part of the tag.
- The <match> element contains only one <rule> element, which prefixes the tag with istio. The ${tag} variable holds the current value of the tag.
- Since this is the only <rule> element in the <match> element, it is configured to match all of the log records like so:
  - Since all of the log records that come from Kubernetes have a log field, the key field is set to log, that is, the rule looks for a log field in the log records.
  - To match any string in the log field, the pattern field is set to the ^(.*)$ regular expression. ^ marks the beginning of a string, while $ marks the end of a string. (.*) matches any number of characters, except for line breaks.
  - The log records are reemitted to the Fluentd routing engine. Since no other elements in the configuration file match tags starting with istio, they will be sent directly to the output element for Elasticsearch, which is defined in the fluent.conf file we described previously.

3. The second <match> element matches all of the log records from the hands-on namespace, that is, the log records that are emitted by our microservices. It looks like this:

```
<match kubernetes.**hands-on**>
  @type rewrite_tag_filter
  <rule>
    key log
    pattern ^(.*)$
    tag spring-boot.${tag}
  </rule>
</match>
```

From the preceding source code we can see that:

- The log records emitted by our microservices use formatting rules for the log message defined by Spring Boot so their tags are prefixed with `spring-boot`. Then, they are re-emitted for further processing.
- The `<match>` element is configured in the same way as the `<match kubernetes.**istio**>` element we looked at previously.

4. The third `<match>` element matches `spring-boot` log records and determines whether they are ordinary Spring Boot log records or are part of a multiline stack trace. It looks like this:

```
<match spring-boot.**>
  @type rewrite_tag_filter
  <rule>
    key log
    pattern /^\d{4}-\d{2}-\d{2}\s\d{2}:\d{2}:\d{2}\.\d{3}.*/
    tag parse.${tag}
  </rule>
  <rule>
    key log
    pattern /^.*/
    tag check.exception.${tag}
  </rule>
</match>
```

As seen in the preceding source code, this is determined by using two `<rule>` elements:

- The first uses a regular expression to check whether the `log` field in the log element starts with a timestamp or not.
- If the `log` field starts with a timestamp, the log record is treated as an ordinary Spring Boot log record and its tag is prefixed with `parse`.
- Otherwise, the second `<rule>` element will match and the log record is handled as a multiline log record. Its tag is prefixed with `check.exception`.
- The log record is re-emitted in either case and its tag will either start with `check.exception.spring-boot.kubernetes` or `parse.spring-boot.kubernetes` after this process.

5. In the fourth `<match>` element, the selected log records have a tag that starts with `check.exception.spring-boot`, that is, log records that are part of a multiline stack trace. It looks like this:

```
<match check.exception.spring-boot.**>
  @type detect_exceptions
  languages java
  remove_tag_prefix check
  message log
  multiline_flush_interval 5
</match>
```

The source code for the `detect_exceptions` plugin works like:

- The `detect_exceptions` plugin is used to combine multiple one-line log records into a single log record that contains a complete stack trace.
- Before a multiline log record is reemitted into the routing engine, the `check` prefix is removed from the tag to prevent a never-ending processing loop of the log record.

6. Finally, the configuration file consists of a filter element that parses Spring Boot log messages using a regular expression, extracting information of interest. It looks like this:

```
<filter parse.spring-boot.**>
  @type parser
  key_name log
  time_key time
  time_format %Y-%m-%d %H:%M:%S.%N
  reserve_data true
  format /^(?<time>\d{4}-\d{2}-
  \d{2}\s\d{2}:\d{2}:\d{2}\.\d{3})\s+
  (?<spring.level>[^\s]+)\s+
  (\[(?<spring.service>[^,]*),(?<spring.trace>[^,]*),(?
  <spring.span>[^,]*),[^\]]*\])\s+
  (?<spring.pid>\d+)\s+---\s+\[\s*(?<spring.thread>[^\]]+)\]\s+
  (?<spring.class>[^\s]+)\s*:\s+
  (?<log>.*)$/
</filter>
```

Let's explain the preceding source code in more detail:

- Note that filter elements don't re-emit log records; instead, they just pass them on to the next element in the configuration file that matches the log record's tag.
- The following fields are extracted from the Spring Boot log message that's stored in the `log` field in the log record:
  - `<time>`: The timestamp for when the log record was created
  - `<spring.level>`: The log level of the log record, for example, FATAL, ERROR, WARN, INFO, DEBUG, or TRACE
  - `<spring.service>`: The name of the microservice
  - `<spring.trace>`: The trace ID used to perform distributed tracing
  - `<spring.span>`: The span ID, the ID of the part of the distributed processing that this microservice executed
  - `<spring.pid>`: The process ID
  - `<spring.thread>`: The thread ID
  - `<spring.class>`: The name of the Java class
  - `<log>`: The actual log message

> The names of Spring Boot-based microservices are specified using the `spring.application.name` property. This property has been added to each microservice-specific property file in the config repository, in the `config-repo` folder.

Getting regular expressions right can be challenging, to say the least. Thankfully, there are several websites that can help. When it comes to using regular expressions together with Fluentd, I recommend using the following site: `https://fluentular.herokuapp.com/`.

Now that you've been introduced to how Fluentd works and how the configuration file is constructed, we are ready to deploy the EKF stack.

Deploying the EFK stack on Kubernetes

Deploying the EFK stack on Kubernetes will be done in the same way as we have deployed our own microservices: using Kubernetes definition files for objects such as deployments, services, and configuration maps.

The deployment of the EFK stack is divided into two parts:

- One part where we deploy Elasticsearch and Kibana
- One part where we deploy Fluentd

But first, we need to build and deploy our own microservices.

Building and deploying our microservices

Building, deploying, and verifying the deployment using the `test-em-all.bash` test script is done in the same way as it was done in Chapter 18, *Using a Service Mesh to Improve Observability and Management*, in the *Running commands to create the service mesh* section. Run the following commands to get started:

1. First, build the Docker images from the source with the following commands:

    ```
    cd $BOOK_HOME/Chapter19
    eval $(minikube docker-env)
    ./gradlew build && docker-compose build
    ```

2. Recreate the namespace, `hands-on`, and set it as the default namespace:

    ```
    kubectl delete namespace hands-on
    kubectl create namespace hands-on
    kubectl config set-context $(kubectl config current-context) --
    namespace=hands-on
    ```

3. Execute the deployment by running the `deploy-dev-env.bash` script with the following command:

    ```
    ./kubernetes/scripts/deploy-dev-env.bash
    ```

4. Start the Minikube tunnel, if it's not already running (see `Chapter 18`, *Using a Service Mesh to Improve Observability and Management*, the *Setting up access to Istio services* section for a recap, if required):

```
minikube tunnel
```

Remember that this command requires that your user has `sudo` privileges and that you enter your password during startup and shutdown. It takes a couple of seconds before the command asks for the password, so it is easy to miss!

5. Run the normal tests to verify the deployment with the following command:

```
./test-em-all.bash
```

Expect the output to be similar to what we have seen from the previous chapters:

```
4. bash
$ ./test-em-all.bash
...
Wait for: curl -k http://product-composite.hands-on.svc.cluster.local:4004/actuator/health...
 DONE, continues...
Test OK (HTTP Code: 200)
...
End, all tests OK: Sun Jul 28 11:47:44 CEST 2019
$ 
```

6. You can also try out the APIs manually by running the following commands:

```
ACCESS_TOKEN=$(curl -k
https://writer:secret@minikube.me/oauth/token -d
grant_type=password -d username=magnus -d password=password -s | jq
.access_token -r)

curl -ks https://minikube.me/product-composite/2 -H "Authorization:
Bearer $ACCESS_TOKEN" | jq .productId
```

Expect the requested product ID, 2, in the response.

With the microservices deployed, we can move on and deploy Elasticsearch and Kibana!

Deploying Elasticsearch and Kibana

We will deploy Elasticsearch and Kibana to its own namespace, `logging`. Both
Elasticsearch and Kibana will be deployed for development and test usage using a
Kubernetes deployment object. This will be done with a single pod and a Kubernetes node
port service. The services will expose the standard ports for Elasticsearch and
Kibana internally in the Kubernetes cluster, that is, port `9200` for Elasticserach and port
`5601` for Kibana. Thanks to the `minikube tunnel` command, we will be able to access
these services locally using the following URLs:

- `elasticsearch.logging.svc.cluster.local:9200` for Elasticserch
- `kibana.logging.svc.cluster.local:5601` for Kibana

> For the recommended deployment in a production environment on
> Kubernetes, see `https://www.elastic.co/elasticsearch-kubernetes`.

We will use the versions that were available when this chapter was written:

- Elasticsearch version 7.3.0
- Kibana version 7.3.0

Before we perform the deployments, let's look at the most interesting parts of the definition
files.

A walkthrough of the definition files

The definition file for Elasticsearch, `kubernetes/efk/elasticsearch.yml`, contains a
standard Kubernetes deployment and service object that we have seen multiples times
before, for example, in Chapter 15, *Introduction to Kubernetes*, in the *Trying out a sample
deployment* section. The most interesting part, as we explained previously, of
the definition file is the following:

```
apiVersion: extensions/v1beta1
kind: Deployment
...
    containers:
    - name: elasticsearch
      image: docker.elastic.co/elasticsearch/elasticsearch-oss:7.3.0
      resources:
        limits:
          cpu: 500m
```

```
      memory: 2Gi
    requests:
      cpu: 500m
      memory: 2Gi
```

Let's explain the preceding source code in detail:

- We use an official Docker image from Elastic that's available at `docker.elastic.co` with a package that only contains open source components. This is ensured by using the `-oss` suffix on the name of the Docker image, `elasticsearch-oss`. The version is set to `7.3.0`.
- The Elasticsearch container is allowed to allocate a relatively large amount of memory—2 GB—to be able to perform queries with good performance. The more memory, the better the performance.

The definition file for Kibana, `kubernetes/efk/kibana.yml`, also contains a standard Kubernetes deployment and service object. The most interesting parts in the definition file are as follows:

```
apiVersion: extensions/v1beta1
kind: Deployment
...
        containers:
        - name: kibana
          image: docker.elastic.co/kibana/kibana-oss:7.3.0
          env:
          - name: ELASTICSEARCH_URL
            value: http://elasticsearch:9200
```

Let's explain the preceding source code in detail:

- For Kibana, we also use an official Docker image from Elastic that's available at `docker.elastic.co`, along with a package that only contains open source components, `kibana-oss`. The version is set to `7.3.0`.
- To connect Kibana with the Elasticsearch pod, an environment variable, `ELASTICSEARCH_URL`, is defined to specify the address to the Elasticsearch service, `http://elasticsearch:9200`.

With these insights, we are ready to perform the deployment of Elasticsearch and Kibana.

Running the deploy commands

Deploy Elasticsearch and Kibana by performing the following steps:

1. Create a namespace for Elasticsearch and Kibana with the following command:

   ```
   kubectl create namespace logging
   ```

2. To make the deploy steps run faster, prefetch the Docker images for Elasticsearch and Kibana with the following commands:

   ```
   eval $(minikube docker-env)
   docker pull docker.elastic.co/elasticsearch/elasticsearch-oss:7.3.0
   docker pull docker.elastic.co/kibana/kibana-oss:7.3.0
   ```

3. Deploy Elasticsearch and wait for its pod to be ready with the following commands:

   ```
   kubectl apply -f kubernetes/efk/elasticsearch.yml -n logging
   kubectl wait --timeout=120s --for=condition=Ready pod -n logging --all
   ```

4. Verify that Elasticsearch is up and running with the following command:

   ```
   curl http://elasticsearch.logging.svc.cluster.local:9200 -s | jq -r .tagline
   ```

Expect `You Know, for Search` as a response.

> Depending on your hardware, you might need to wait for a minute or two before Elasticsearch responds with this message.

5. Deploy Kibana and wait for its pod to be ready with the following commands:

   ```
   kubectl apply -f kubernetes/efk/kibana.yml -n logging
   kubectl wait --timeout=120s --for=condition=Ready pod -n logging --all
   ```

6. Verify that Kibana is up and running with the following command:

```
curl -o /dev/null -s -L -w "%{http_code}\n"
http://kibana.logging.svc.cluster.local:5601
```

Expect 200 as the response.

With Elasticsearch and Kibana deployed, we can start to deploy Fluentd.

Deploying Fluentd

Deploying Fluentd is a bit more complex compared to deploying Elasticsearch and Kibana. To deploy Fluentd, we will use a Docker image that's been published by the Fluentd project on Docker Hub, fluent/fluentd-kubernetes-daemonset, and sample the Kubernetes definition files from a Fluentd project on GitHub, fluentd-kubernetes-daemonset. It is located at https://github.com/fluent/fluentd-kubernetes-daemonset. As it's implied by the name of the project, Fluentd will be deployed as a daemon set, running one pod per node in the Kubernetes cluster. Each Fluentd pod is responsible for collecting log output from processes and containers that run on the same node as the pod. Since we are using Minikube, that is, a single node cluster, we will only have one Fluentd pod.

To handle multiline log records that contain stack traces from exceptions, we will use a third-party Fluentd plugin provided by Google, fluent-plugin-detect-exceptions, which is available at https://github.com/GoogleCloudPlatform/fluent-plugin-detect-exceptions. To be able to use this plugin, we will build our own Docker image where the fluent-plugin-detect-exceptions plugin will be installed. Fluentd's Docker image, fluentd-kubernetes-daemonset, will be used as the base image.

We will use the versions that were available when this chapter was written:

- Fluentd version 1.4.2
- fluent-plugin-detect-exceptions version 0.0.12

Before we perform the deployments, let's look at the most interesting parts of the definition files.

A walkthrough of the definition files

The Dockerfile that's used to build the Docker image, `kubernetes/efk/Dockerfile`, looks as follows:

```
FROM fluent/fluentd-kubernetes-daemonset:v1.4.2-debian-elasticsearch-1.1

RUN gem install fluent-plugin-detect-exceptions -v 0.0.12 \
 && gem sources --clear-all \
 && rm -rf /var/lib/apt/lists/* \
         /home/fluent/.gem/ruby/2.3.0/cache/*.gem
```

Let's explain the preceding source code in detail:

- The base image is Fluentd's Docker image, `fluentd-kubernetes-daemonset`. The `v1.4.2-debian-elasticsearch-1.1` tag specifies that version v1.4.2 shall be used with a package that contains built-in support for sending log records to Elasticsearch. The base Docker image contains the Fluentd configuration files that were mentioned in the *Configuring Fluentd* section.
- The Google plugin, `fluent-plugin-detect-exceptions`, is installed using Ruby's package manager, `gem`.

The definition file of the daemon set, `kubernetes/efk/fluentd-ds.yml`, is based on a sample definition file in the `fluentd-kubernetes-daemonset` project, which can be found at `https://github.com/fluent/fluentd-kubernetes-daemonset/blob/master/fluentd-daemonset-elasticsearch.yaml`. This file is a bit complex, so let's go through the most interesting parts separately:

1. First, here's the declaration of the daemon set:

   ```
   apiVersion: extensions/v1beta1
   kind: DaemonSet
   metadata:
     name: fluentd
     namespace: kube-system
   ```

   Let's explain the preceding source code in detail:

   - The `kind` key specifies that this is a daemon set.
   - The `namespace` key specifies that the daemon set shall be created in the `kube-system` namespace and not in the `logging` namespace where Elasticseach and Kibana are deployed.

2. The next part specifies the template for the pods that are created by the daemon set. The most interesting parts are as follows:

```
spec:
  template:
    spec:
      containers:
      - name: fluentd
        image: hands-on/fluentd:v1
        env:
          - name: FLUENT_ELASTICSEARCH_HOST
            value: "elasticsearch.logging"
          - name: FLUENT_ELASTICSEARCH_PORT
            value: "9200"
```

Let's explain the preceding source code in detail:

- The Docker image that's used for the pods is `hands-on/fluentd:v1`. We will build this Docker image after walking through the definition files using the Dockerfile we described previously.
- A number of environment variables are supported by the Docker image and are used to customize it. The two most important ones are as follows:
  - `FLUENT_ELASTICSEARCH_HOST`, which specifies the hostname of the Elasticsearch service, that is, `elasticsearch.logging`
  - `FLUENT_ELASTICSEARCH_PORT`, which specifies the port that's used to communicate with Elasticsearch, that is, `9200`

Since the Fluentd pod runs in another namespace than Elasticsearch, the hostname cannot be specified using its short name, that is, `elasticsearch`. Instead, the namespace part of the DNS name must also be specified, that is, `elasticsearch.logging`. As an alternative, the **fully qualified domain name (FQDN)**, `elasticsearch.logging.svc.cluster.local`, can also be used. But since the last part of the DNS name, `svc.cluster.local`, is shared by all DNS names inside a Kubernetes cluster, it does not need to be specified.

3. Finally, a number of volumes, that is, filesystems, are mapped into the pod, as follows:

```
          volumeMounts:
          - name: varlog
            mountPath: /var/log '
          - name: varlibdockercontainers
            mountPath: /var/lib/docker/containers
            readOnly: true
          - name: journal
            mountPath: /var/log/journal
            readOnly: true
          - name: fluentd-extra-config
            mountPath: /fluentd/etc/conf.d
      volumes:
      - name: varlog
        hostPath:
          path: /var/log
      - name: varlibdockercontainers
        hostPath:
          path: /var/lib/docker/containers
      - name: journal
        hostPath:
          path: /run/log/journal
      - name: fluentd-extra-config
        configMap:
          name: "fluentd-hands-on-config"
```

Let's explain the preceding source code in detail:

- Three folders on the host (that is, the node) are mapped into the Fluentd pod. These folders contain the log files that Fluentd will tail and collect log records from. The folders are: `/var/log`, `/var/lib/docker/containers` and `/run/log/journal`.

- Our own configuration file that specifies how Fluentd shall process log records from our microservices is mapped using a config map called `fluentd-hands-on-config` to the `/fluentd/etc/conf.d` folder. The base Docker image that's used for preceding Fluentd, `fluentd-kubernetes-daemonset`, configures Fluentd to include any configuration file that's found in the `/fluentd/etc/conf.d` folder. See the *Configuring Fluentd* section for details.

For the full source code of the definition file for the daemon set, see the `kubernetes/efk/fluentd-ds.yml` file.

Now that we've walked through everything, we are ready to perform the deployment of Fluentd.

Running the deploy commands

To deploy Fluentd, we have to build the Docker image, create the config map, and finally deploy the daemon set. Run the following commands to perform these steps:

1. Build the Docker image and tag it with `hands-on/fluentd:v1` using the following command:

```
eval $(minikube docker-env)
docker build -f kubernetes/efk/Dockerfile -t hands-on/fluentd:v1
kubernetes/efk/
```

2. Create the config map, deploy Fluentd's daemon set, and wait for the pod to be ready with the following commands:

```
kubectl apply -f kubernetes/efk/fluentd-hands-on-configmap.yml
kubectl apply -f kubernetes/efk/fluentd-ds.yml
kubectl wait --timeout=120s --for=condition=Ready pod -l
app=fluentd -n kube-system
```

3. Verify that the Fluentd pod is healthy with the following command:

```
kubectl logs -n kube-system $(kubectl get pod -l app=fluentd -n
kube-system -o jsonpath={.items..metadata.name}) | grep "fluentd
worker is now running worker"
```

Expect a response of `2019-08-16 15:11:33 +0000 [info]: #0 fluentd worker is now running worker=0`.

4. Fluentd will start to collect a considerable amount of log records from the various processes and containers in the Minkube instance. After a minute or so, you can ask Elasticsearch how many log records have been collected with the following command:

```
curl
http://elasticsearch.logging.svc.cluster.local:9200/_all/_count
```

The command can be a bit slow the first time it is executed, but should return a response similar to the following:

```
4. bash
$ curl http://elasticsearch.logging.svc.cluster.local:9200/_all/_count
{"count":144750,"_shards":{"total":7,"successful":7,"skipped":0,"failed":0}}
$
```

In this example, Elasticsearch contains 144750 log records.

This completes the deployment of the EFK stack. Now, it's time to try it out and find out what all of the collected log records are about!

Trying out the EFK stack

The first thing we need to do before we can try out the EFK stack is initialize Kibana so it knows what search indices to use in Elasticsearch. Once that is done, we will try out the following, in my experience, common tasks:

1. We will start by analyzing of what types of log records Fluentd has collected and stored in Elasticsearch. Kibana has a very useful visualization capability that can be used for this.
2. Next, we will learn how to discover log records from different microservices that belong to one and the same processing of an external request to the API. We will use the **trace ID** in the log records as a correlation ID to find related log records.
3. Thirdly, we will learn how to use Kibana to perform **root cause analysis**, that is, find the actual reason for an error.

Initializing Kibana

Before we start to use Kibana, we must specify what search indices to use in Elasticsearch and what field in the indices holds the timestamps for the log records.

Perform the following steps to initialize Kibana:

1. Open Kibana's web UI using the `http://kibana.logging.svc.cluster.local:5601` URL in a web browser.
2. On the welcome page, **Welcome to Kibana**, click on the **Explore on my own** button.

3. Click on the **Expand** button in the lower-left corner to view the names of the menu choices. These will be shown on the left-hand side.

4. Click on **Discover** in the menu to the left. You will be asked to define a pattern that's used by Kibana to identify what Elasticsearch indices it shall retrieve log records from.

5. Enter the `logstash-*` index pattern and click on **Next Step**.

6. On the next page, you will be asked to specify the name of the field that contains the timestamp for the log records. Click on the drop-down list for the **Time Filter** field name and select the only available field, **@timestamp**.

7. Click on the **Create index pattern** button.

8. Kibana will show a page that summarizes the fields that are available in the selected indices.

> Indices are, by default, named `logstash` for historical reasons, even though it is Flutentd that is used for log collection.

With Kibana initialized, we are ready to examine the log records we have collected.

Analyzing the log records

From the deployment of Fluentd, we know that it immediately started to collect a significant number of log records. So, the first thing we need to do is get an understanding of what types of log records Fluentd has collected and stored in Elasticsearch.

We will use Kibana's visualization feature to divide the log records per Kubernetes namespace and then ask Kibana to show us how the log records are divided per type of container within each namespace. A pie chart is a suitable chart type for this type of analysis. Perform the following steps to create a pie chart:

1. In Kibana's web UI, click on **Visualize** in the menu to the left.

2. Click on the **Create new visualization** button.

3. Select **Pie** as the visualization type.

4. Select **logstash-*** as the source.

5. In the time picker (a date interval selector) above the pie chart, set a date interval of your choice (set to the last 7 days in the following screenshot). Click on its calendar icon to adjust the time interval.

6. Click on **Add** to create the first bucket, as follows:
    1. Select the bucket type, that is, **Split slices.**
    2. For the aggregation type, select **Terms** from the drop-down list.
    3. As the field, select **kubernetes.namespace_name.keyword.**
    4. For the size, select **10.**
    5. Enable **Group other values in separate bucket.**
    6. Enable **Show missing values.**
    7. Press the **Apply changes** button (the blue play icon above the **Bucket** definition). Expect a pie chart that looks similar to the following:

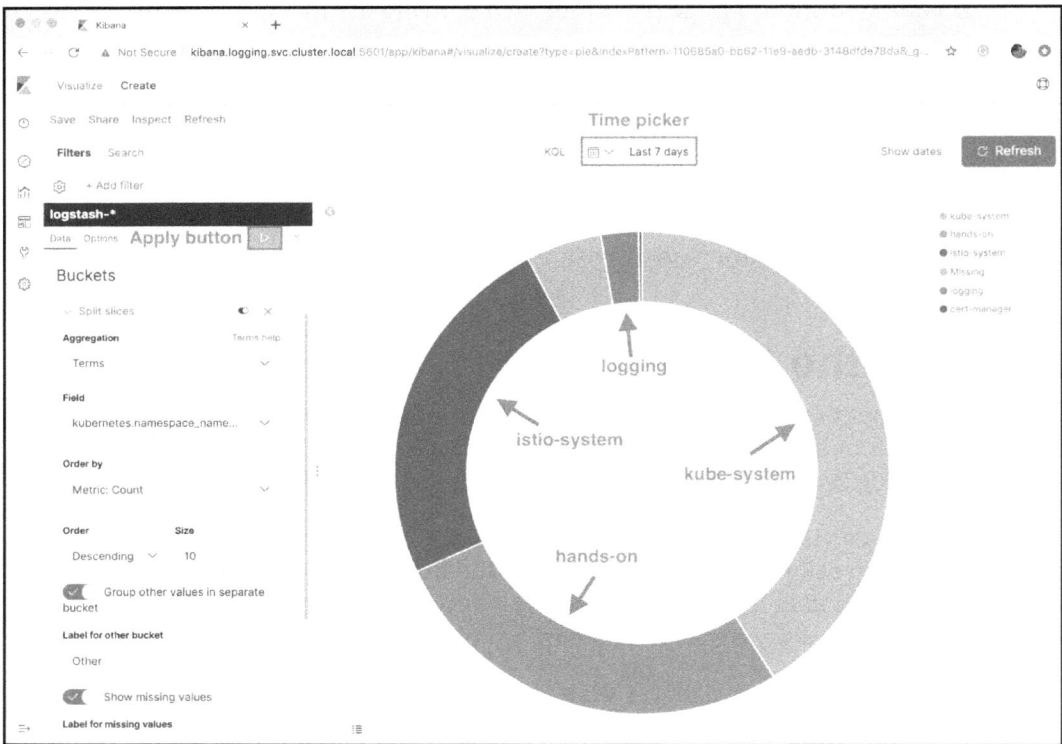

We can see that the log records are divided over the namespaces we have been working with in the previous chapters: `kube-system`, `istio-system`, `logging`, `cert-manager`, and our own `hands-on` namespace. To see what containers have created the log records divided per namespace, we need to create a second bucket.

7. Click on **Add** again to create a second bucket:
    1. Select the bucket type, that is, **Split slices.**
    2. As the sub-aggregation type, select **Terms** from the drop-down list.
    3. As the field, select **kubernetes.container_name.keyword.**
    4. For the size, select **10.**
    5. Enable **Group other values in separate bucket.**
    6. Enable **Show missing values**.
    7. Press the **Apply changes** button again. Expect a pie chart that looks similar to the following:

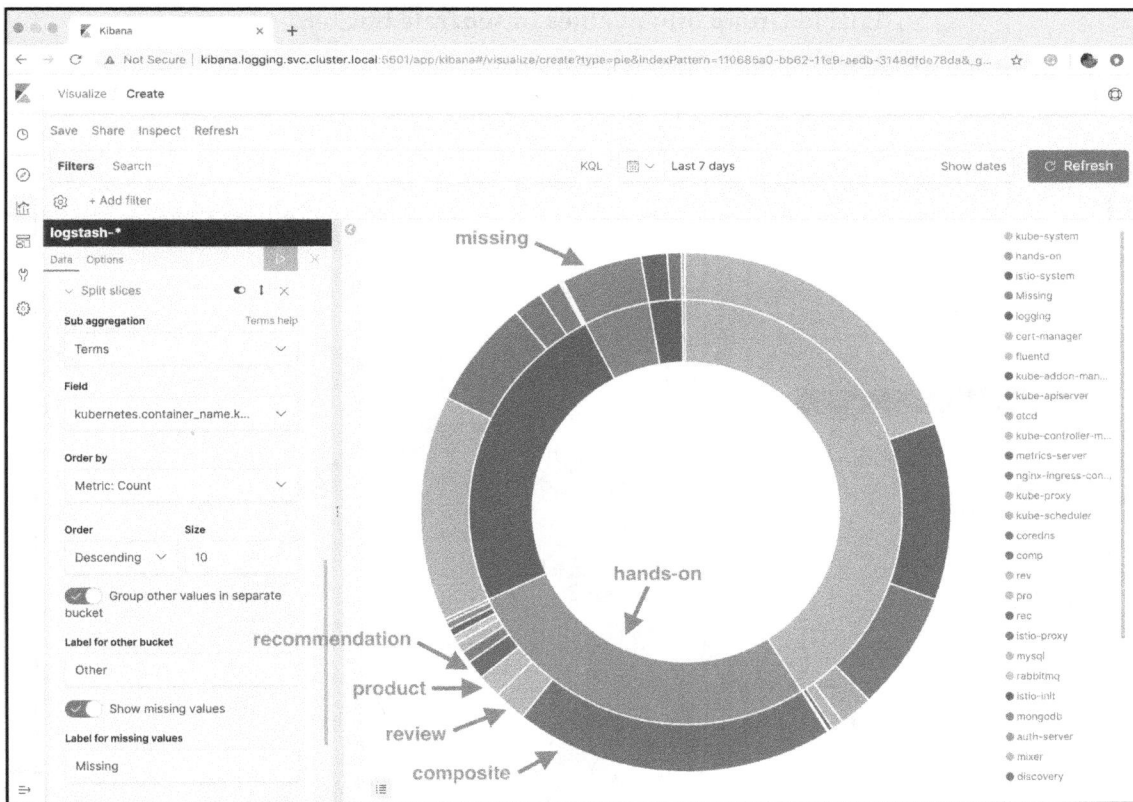

Here, we can find the log records from our microservices. Most of the log records come from the `product-composite` microservice.

8. At the top of the pie chart, we have a group of log records labeled `missing`, that is, they neither have a Kubernetes namespace nor a container name specified. What's behind these missing log records? These log records come from processes running outside of the Kubernetes cluster in the Minikube instance and they are stored using Syslog. They can be analyzed using Syslog-specific fields, specifically the *identifier field*. Let's create a third bucket that divides log records based on their Syslog identifier field, if any.

9. Click on `Add` again to create a third bucket:
    1. Select the bucket type, that is, **Split slices.**
    2. As the sub-aggregation type, select **Terms** from the drop-down list.
    3. As the field, select **SYSLOG_IDENTIFIER.keyword.**
    4. Enable **Group other values in separate bucket.**
    5. Enable **Show missing values.**
    6. Press the **Apply changes** button and expect a pie chart that looks similar to the following:

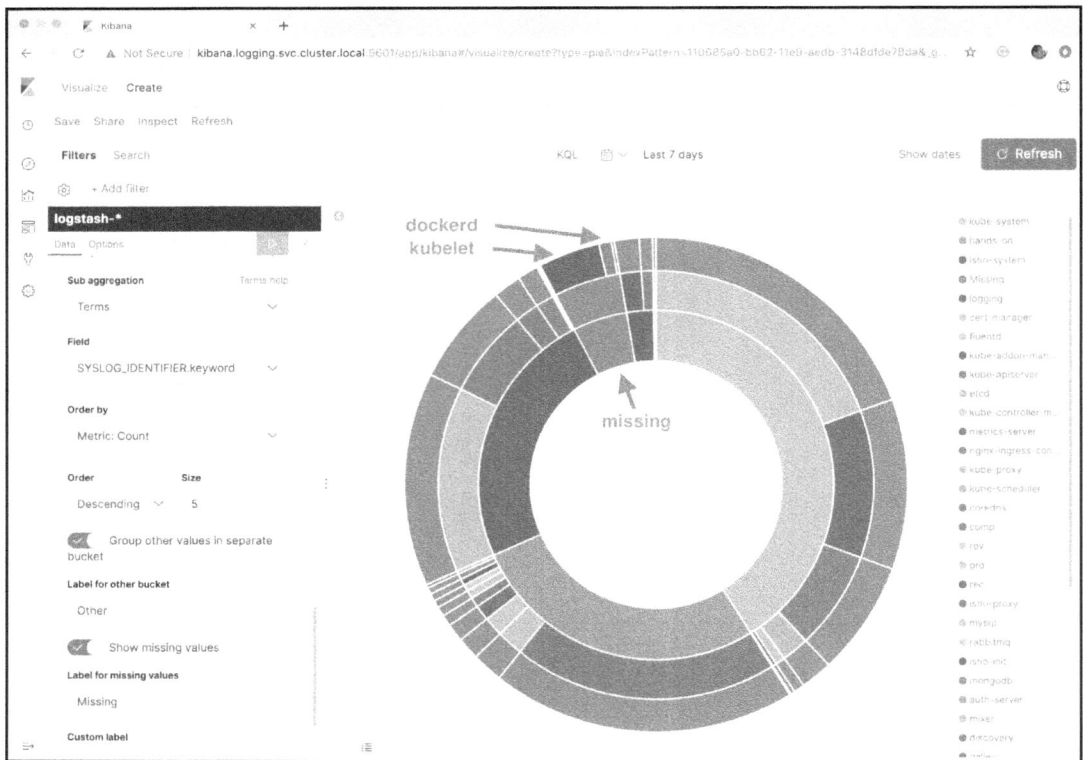

The `missing` log records turn out to come from the `kubelet` process, which manages the node from a Kubernetes perspective, and `dockerd`, the Docker daemon that manages all of the containers.

Now that we have found out where the log records come from, we can start to locate the actual log records from our microservices.

Discovering the log records from microservices

In this section, we will learn how to utilize one of the main features of centralized logging, that is, finding log records from our microservices. We will also learn how to use the trace ID in the log records to find log records from other microservices that belong to one and the same process, for example, a request to the API.

Let's start by creating some log records that we can look up with the help of Kibana. We will use the API to create a product with a unique product ID and then retrieve information about the product. After that, we can try to find the log records that were created when retrieving the product information.

The creation of log records in the microservices has updated a bit from the previous chapter so that the product composite and the three core microservices, `product`, `recommendation`, and `review`, all write a log record with the log level set to `INFO` when they begin processing a get request. Let's go over the source code that's been added to each microservice:

- Product composite microservice log creation:

```
LOG.info("Will get composite product info for product.id={}",
productId);
```

- Product microservice log creation:

```
LOG.info("Will get product info for id={}", productId);
```

- Recommendation microservice log creation:

```
LOG.info("Will get recommendations for product with id={}",
productId)
```

- Review microservice log creation:

```
LOG.info("Will get reviews for product with id={}", productId);
```

For more details, see the source code in the `microservices` folder.

Perform the following steps to use the API to create log records and then use Kibana to look up the log records:

1. Get an access token with the following command:

```
ACCESS_TOKEN=$(curl -k
https://writer:secret@minikube.me/oauth/token -d
grant_type=password -d username=magnus -d password=password -s | jq
.access_token -r)
```

2. As mentioned in the introduction to this section we will start by creating a product with a unique product ID. Create a minimalistic product (without recommendations and reviews) for "productId" :1234 by executing the following command:

```
curl -X POST -k https://minikube.me/product-composite \
  -H "Content-Type: application/json" \
  -H "Authorization: Bearer $ACCESS_TOKEN" \
  --data '{"productId":1234,"name":"product name
1234","weight":1234}'
```

3. Read the product with the following command:

```
curl -H "Authorization: Bearer $ACCESS_TOKEN" -k
'https://minikube.me/product-composite/1234'
```

Expect a response similar to the following:

```
4. bash
$ curl -H "Authorization: Bearer $ACCESS_TOKEN" -k 'https://minikube.me/product-composite/1234'
{"productId":1234,"name":"product name 1234","weight":1234,"recommendations":[],"reviews":[],
"serviceAddresses":{"cmp":"product-composite-74f4dc9b4f-4s9bk/172.17.0.39:80","pro":"product-869
5c57758-ttmsg/172.17.0.40:80","rev":"","rec":""}}
$
```

Hopefully, we got some log records created by these API calls. Let's jump over to Kibana and find out!

4. On the Kibana web page, click on the Discover menu on the left. You will see something like the following:

On the left-top corner, we can see that Kibaba has found **326,642** log records. The time picker shows that they are from the last 7 days. In the histogram, we can see how the log records are spread out over time. Following that is a table showing the most recent log events that were found by the query.

5. If you want to change the time interval, you can use the time picker. Click on its calendar icon to adjust the time interval.

6. To get a better view of the content in the log records, add some fields from the log records to the table under the histogram. Select the fields from the list of available fields to the left. Scroll down until the field is found. Hold the cursor over the field and an add button will appear; click on it to add the field as a column in the table. Select the following fields, in order:
   1. **spring.level**, the log level
   2. **kubernetes.container_name**, the name of the container
   3. **spring.trace**, the trace ID used for distributed tracing

4. **log**, the actual log message. The web page should look something similar to the following:

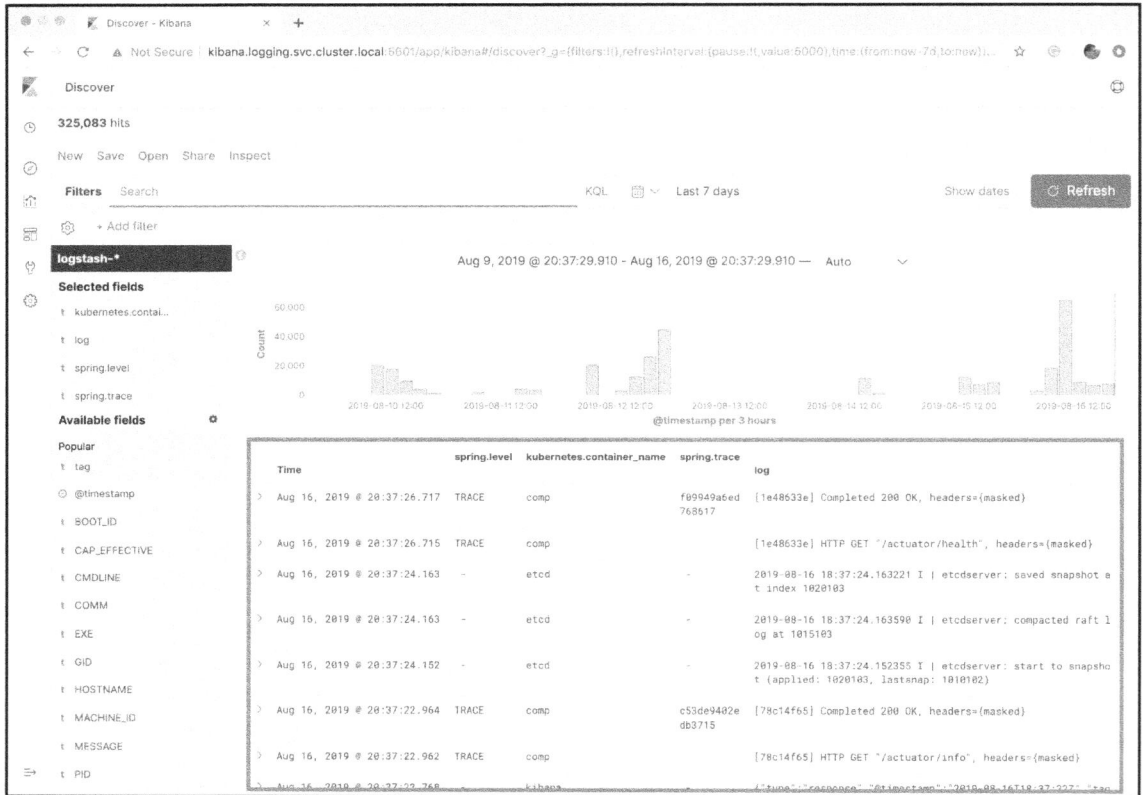

The table now contains information that is of interest regarding the log records!

7. To find log records from the call to the GET API, we can ask Kibana to find log records where the log field contains the text **product.id=1234**. This matches the log output from the product composite microservice that was shown previously. This can be done by entering log:"product.id=1234" in the **Search** field and clicking on the **Update** button (this button can also be labeled **Refresh**). Expect one log record to be found:

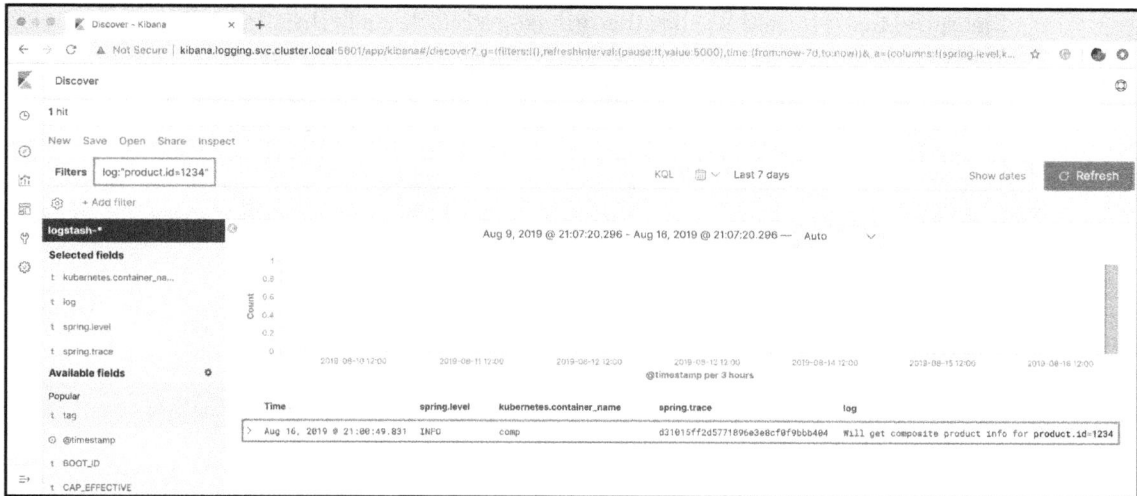

8. Verify that the timestamp is from when you called the GET API and verify that the name of the container that created the log record is **comp**, that is, verify that the log record was sent by the product composite microservice.

9. Now, we want to see the related log records from the other microservices that participated in the process of returning information about the product with **productId 1234**, that is, finding log records with the same trace ID as that of the log record we found. To do that, place the cursor over the spring.trace field for the log record. Two small magnifying glasses will be shown to the right of the field, one with a + sign and one with a – sign. Click on the magnifying glass with the + sign to filter on the trace ID.

10. Clean the **Search** field so that the only search criteria is the filter of the trace field. Then, click on the **Update** button to see the result. Expect a response similar to the following:

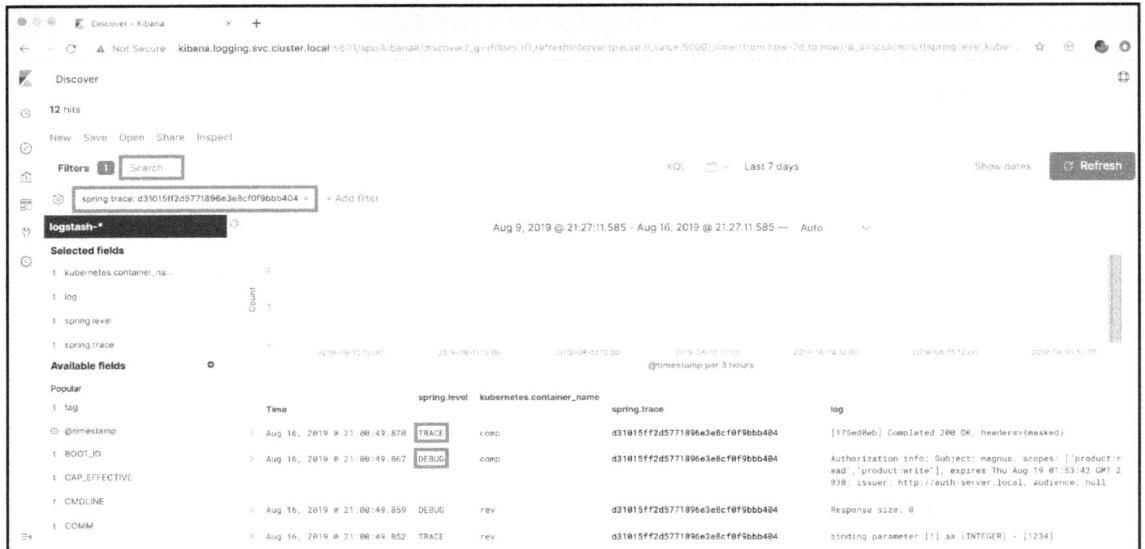

We can see a lot of detailed debug and trace messages that clutter the view; let's get rid of them!

11. Place the cursor over a **TRACE** value and click on the magnifying glass with the - sign to filter out log records with the log level set to **TRACE**.

12. Repeat the preceding step for the **DEBUG** log record.

13. We should now be able to see the four expected log records, one for each microservice involved in the lookup of product information for the product with product ID 1234:

Also, note the filters that were applied included the trace ID but excluded log records with the log level set to **DEBUG** or **TRACE**.

Now that we know how to find the expected log records, we are ready to take the next step. This will be to learn how to find unexpected log records, that is, error messages, and how to perform root cause analysis, that is, find the reason for these error messages.

Performing root cause analyses

One of the most important features of centralized logging is that it makes it possible to analyze errors using log records from many sources and, based on that, perform root cause analysis, that is, find the actual reason for the error message.

In this section, we will simulate an error and see how we can find information about it, all of the way down to the line of source code that caused the error in one of the microservices in the system landscape. To simulate an error, we will reuse the fault parameter we introduced in Chapter 13, *Improving Resilience Using Resilience4j*, in the *Adding programmable delays and random errors* section. We can use this to force the product microservice to throw an exception. Perform the following steps:

1. Run the following command to generate a fault in the product microservice while searching for product information on the product with product ID 666:

```
curl -H "Authorization: Bearer $ACCESS_TOKEN" -k
https://minikube.me/product-composite/666?faultPercent=100
```

Expect the following error in response:

```
$ curl -H "Authorization: Bearer $ACCESS_TOKEN" -k https://minikube.me/product-composite/666?faultPercent=100
{"timestamp":"2019-08-16T19:59:36.509+0000","path":"/product-composite/666","status":500,"error":"Internal Server Error","message":"500 Internal Server Error"}
$
```

Now, we have to pretend that we have no clue about the reason for this error! Otherwise, the root cause analysis wouldn't be very exciting, right? Let's assume that we work in a support organization and have been asked to investigate some problems that just occurred while an end user tried to look up information regarding a product with product ID 666.

2. Before we start to analyze the problem, let's delete the previous search filters in the Kibana web UI so that we can start from scratch. For each filter we defined in the previous section, click on their close icon (an **x**) to remove them. After all of the filters have been removed, the web page should look similar to the following:

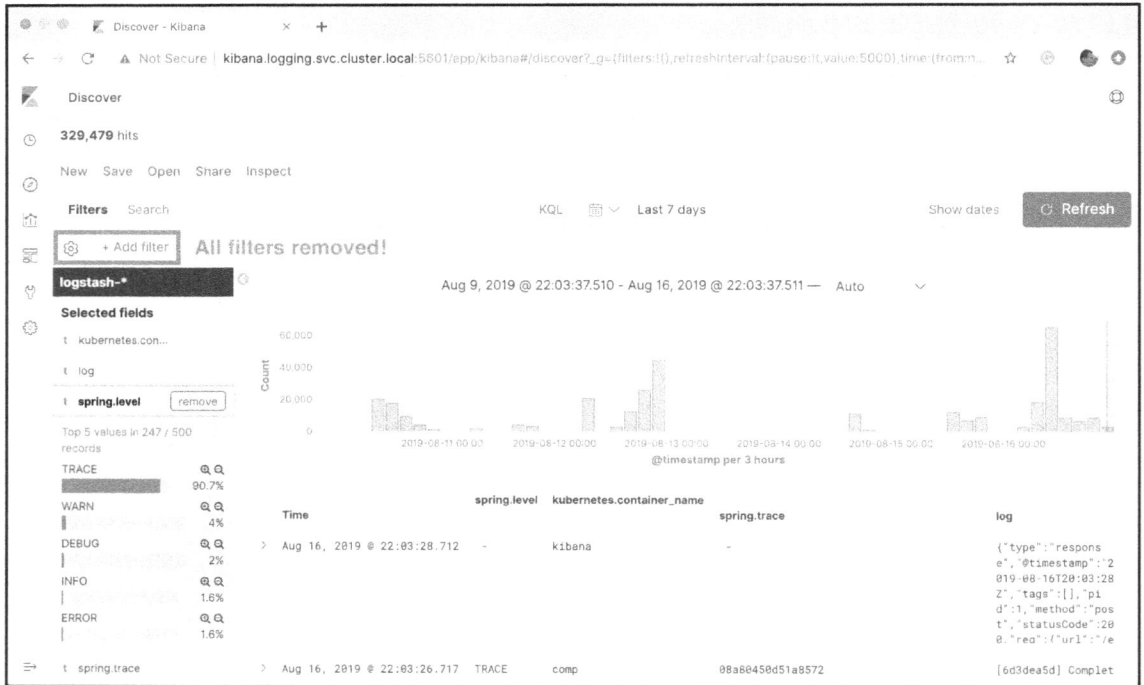

3. Start by selecting a time interval that includes the point in time when the problem occurred using the time picker. For example, search the last seven days if you know that the problem occurred within the last seven days.

4. Next, search for log records with the log level set to **ERROR** within this timeframe. This can be done by clicking on the **spring.level** field in the list of selected fields. When you click on this field, its most commonly used values will be displayed under it. Filter on the **ERROR** value by clicking on its magnifier, shown with the + sign. Kibana will now show log records within the selected time frame with its log level set to **ERROR**, like so:

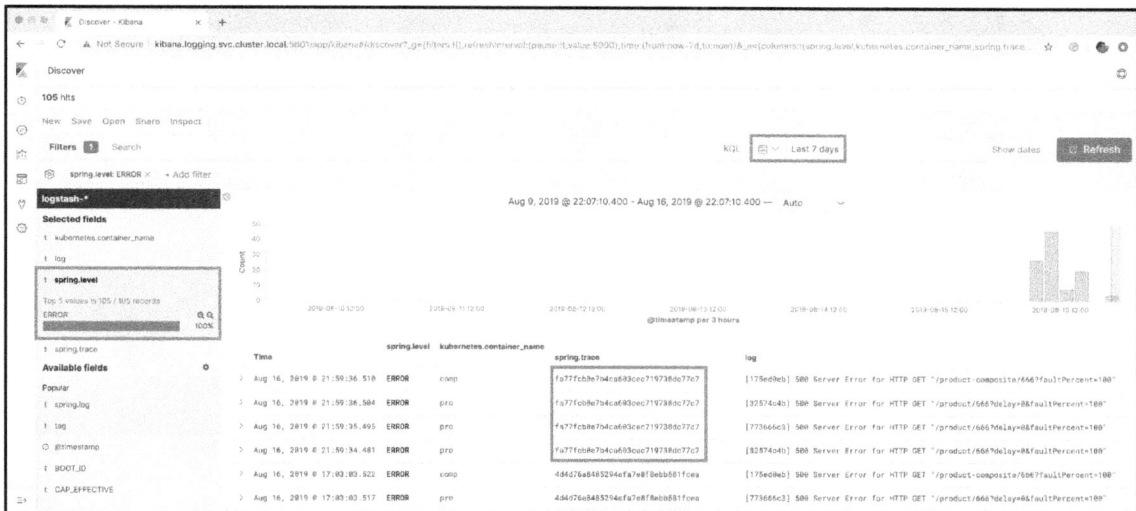

5. We can see a number of error messages related to product ID 666. The top four have the same trace ID, so this seems like a trace ID of interest to use for further investigation.

6. We can also see more error messages below the top four that seem to be related to the same error but with different trace IDs. Those are caused by the retry mechanism in the product composite microservice, that is, it retries the request a couple of times before giving up and returning an error message to the caller.

7. Filter on the trace ID of the first log record in the same way we did in the previous section.

8. Remove the filter of the **ERROR** log level to be able to see all of the records belonging to this trace ID. Expect Kibana to respond with a lot of log records. Look to the oldest log record, that is, the one that occurred first, that looks suspicious. For example, it may have a **WARN** or **ERROR** log level or a strange log message. The default sort order is showing the latest log record at the top, so scroll down to the end and search backward (you can also change the sort order to show the oldest log record first by clicking on the small up/down arrow next to the `Time` column header). The **WARN** log message that says `Bad luck, and error occurred` looks like it could be the root cause of the problem. Let's investigate it further:

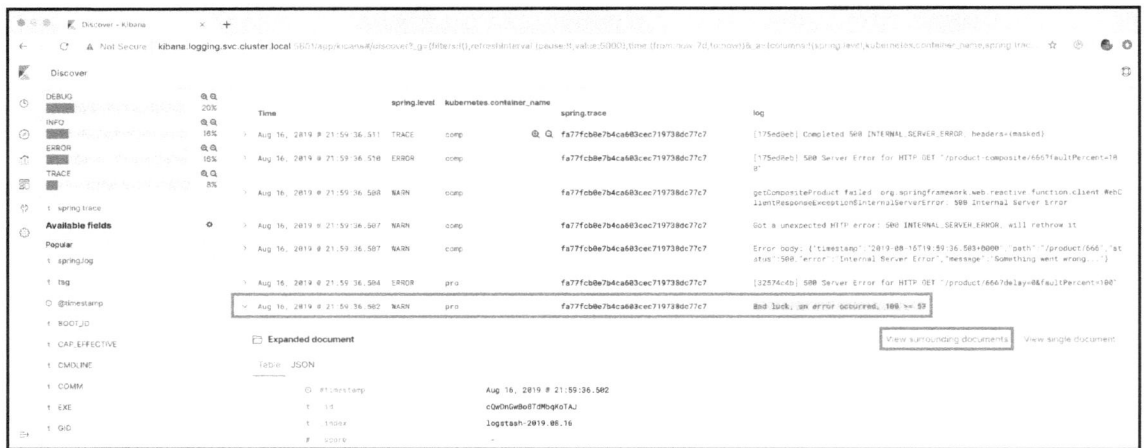

9. Once a log record has been found that might be the root cause of the problem, it is of great interest to be able to find the nearby stack trace describing where exceptions were thrown in the source code. Unfortunately, the Fluentd plugin we use for collecting multiline exceptions, `fluent-plugin-detect-exceptions`, is unable to relate stack traces to the trace ID that was used. Therefore, stack traces will not show up in Kibana when we filter on a trace ID. Instead, we can use a feature in Kibana for finding surrounding log records that show log records that have occurred in near time to a specific log record.

10. Expand the log record that says bad luck using the arrow to the left of the log record. Detailed information about this specific log record will be revealed. There is also a link named **View surrounding documents**; click on it to see nearby log records. Expect a web page similar to the following:

11. The log record above the bad luck log record with the stack trace for the error message **Something went wrong...** looks interesting and was logged by the product microservice just two milliseconds after it logged the *bad luck* log record. They seem to be related! The stack trace in that log record points to line 96 in `ProductServiceImpl.java`. Looking in the source code (see `microservices/product-service/src/main/java/se/magnus/microservices/core/product/services/ProductServiceImpl.java`), line 96 looks as follows:

```
throw new RuntimeException("Something went wrong...");
```

This is the root cause of the error. We did know this in advance, but now we have seen how we can navigate to it as well.

> In this case, the problem is quite simple to resolve: simply omit the `faultPercent` parameter in the request to the API. In other cases, the resolution of the root cause can be much harder to figure out!

This concludes this chapter on using the EFK stack for centralized logging.

Summary

In this chapter, we learned about the importance of collecting log records from microservices in a system landscape into a common centralized database where analysis and searches among the stored log records can be performed. We used the EFK stack, that is, Elasticsearch, Fluentd, and Kibana, to collect, process, store, analyze, and search for log records.

Fluentd was used to collect log records not only from our microservices but also from the various supporting containers and processes in the Kubernetes cluster. Elasticsearch was used as a text search engine. Together with Kibana, we saw how easy it is to get an understanding of what types of log records we have collected.

We also learned how to use Kibana to perform important tasks such as finding related log records from cooperating microservices and how to perform root cause analysis, that is, finding the real problem for an error message. Finally, we learned how to update the configuration of Fluentd and how to get the change reflected by the executing Fluentd pod.

Being able to collect and analyze log records in this way is an important capability in a production environment, but these types of activities are always done afterward, once the log record has been collected. Another important capability is to be able to monitor the current health of the microservices, that is, collect and visualize runtime metrics in terms of the use of hardware resources, response times, and so on. We touched on this subject in the previous chapter, Chapter 18, *Using a Service Mesh to Improve Observability and Management*, and in the next chapter, Chapter 20, *Monitoring Microservices*, we will learn more about monitoring microservices.

Questions

1. A user searched for **ERROR** log messages in the hands-on namespace for the last 30 days using the search criteria shown in the following screenshot, but none were found. Why?

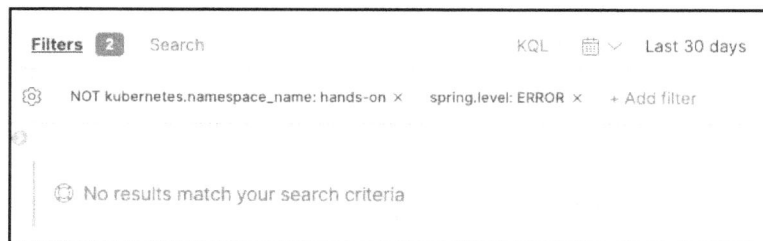

2. A user has found a log record of interest. How can the user find related log records from this and other microservices, for example, that come from processing an external API request?

3. A user has found a log record that seems to indicate the root cause of a problem that was reported by an end user. How can the user find the stack trace that shows wherein the source code the error occurred?

Time	log
Aug 25, 2019 @ 18:35:33.255	onError(se.magnus.util.exceptions.InvalidInputException: Invalid productId: -1)

📂 **Expanded document**   View surrounding documents   View single document

Table JSON

○ @timestamp	Aug 25, 2019 @ 18:35:33.255
t _id	FheiyWwBo8TdMbqKDumU
t _index	logstash-2019.08.25

4. Why doesn't the following Fluentd configuration element work?

```
<match kubernetes.**hands-on**>
  @type rewrite_tag_filter
  <rule>
    key log
    pattern ^(.*)$
    tag spring-boot.${tag}
  </rule>
</match>
```

5. How can you determine whether Elasticsearch is up and running?

6. Suddenly, you lose connection to Kibana from your web browser. What caused this problem?

20
Monitoring Microservices

In this chapter, we will learn how to use Prometheus and Grafana to collect, monitor, and alert about performance metrics. As we mentioned in `Chapter 1`, *Introduction to Microservices*, in the *Centralized monitoring and alarms* section, in a production environment, it is crucial to be able to collect metrics for application performance and hardware resource usage. Monitoring these metrics is required in order to avoid long response times or outages for API requests and other processes.

To be able to monitor a system landscape of microservices in a cost-efficient and proactive way, we need to define alarms that are triggered automatically if the metrics exceed the configured limits.

In this chapter, we will cover the following topics:

- Introduction to performance monitoring using Prometheus and Grafana
- Changes in source code for collecting application metrics
- Building and deploying microservices
- Monitoring microservices using Grafana dashboards
- Setting up alarms in Grafana

Technical requirements

All of the commands that are described in this book have been run on a MacBook Pro using macOS Mojave but should be straightforward to modify so that they can be run on another platform, such as Linux or Windows.

The source code for this chapter can be found in this book's GitHub repository: `https://github.com/PacktPublishing/Hands-On-Microservices-with-Spring-Boot-and-Spring-Cloud/tree/master/Chapter20`.

To be able to run the commands as described in this book, you need to download the source code to a folder and set up an environment variable, $BOOK_HOME, that points to that folder. Some sample commands are as follows:

```
export BOOK_HOME=~/Documents/Hands-On-Microservices-with-Spring-Boot-and-
Spring-Cloud
git clone
https://github.com/PacktPublishing/Hands-On-Microservices-with-Spring-Boot-
and-Spring-Cloud $BOOK_HOME
cd $BOOK_HOME/Chapter20
```

All of the source code examples in this chapter come from the source code in $BOOK_HOME/Chapter20 and have been tested using Kubernetes 1.15.

If you want to see the changes that we applied to the source code for this chapter so that you can use Prometheus and Grafana to monitor an alert on performance metrics, you can compare it with the source code for Chapter 19, *Centralized Logging with the EFK Stack*. You can use your favorite differentiating tool and compare the two folders $BOOK_HOME/Chapter19 and $BOOK_HOME/Chapter20.

Introduction to performance monitoring using Prometheus and Grafana

In this chapter, we will reuse the deployment of Prometheus and Grafana that we created in Chapter 18, *Using a Service Mesh to Improve Observability and Management*, in the *Deploying Istio in the Kubernetes cluster* section. Also in that chapter, in the *Introducing the runtime components in Istio* section, we were briefly introduced to Prometheus, a popular open source database for time series such as performance metrics. We were also introduced to Grafana as an open source tool for visualizing performance metrics. Istio's console for observability, Kiali, is integrated with Grafana. A user can navigate from a service of interest in Kiali to its corresponding performance metrics in Grafana. Kiali can also render some performance-related graphs without the use of Grafana. In this chapter, we will get some hands-on experience with this integration by using these tools together.

The Istio configuration we deployed in Chapter 18, *Using a Service Mesh to Improve Observability and Management*, includes a configuration of Prometheus, where it automatically collects metrics from pods in Kubernetes. All we need to do is set up an endpoint in our microservice that produces metrics in a format Prometheus can consume. We also need to add annotations to the Kubernetes pods so that Prometheus can find the address of the endpoints. See the *Changes in source code for collecting application metrics* section of this chapter for details on how to set this up.

The following diagram illustrates the relationship between the runtime components we just discussed:

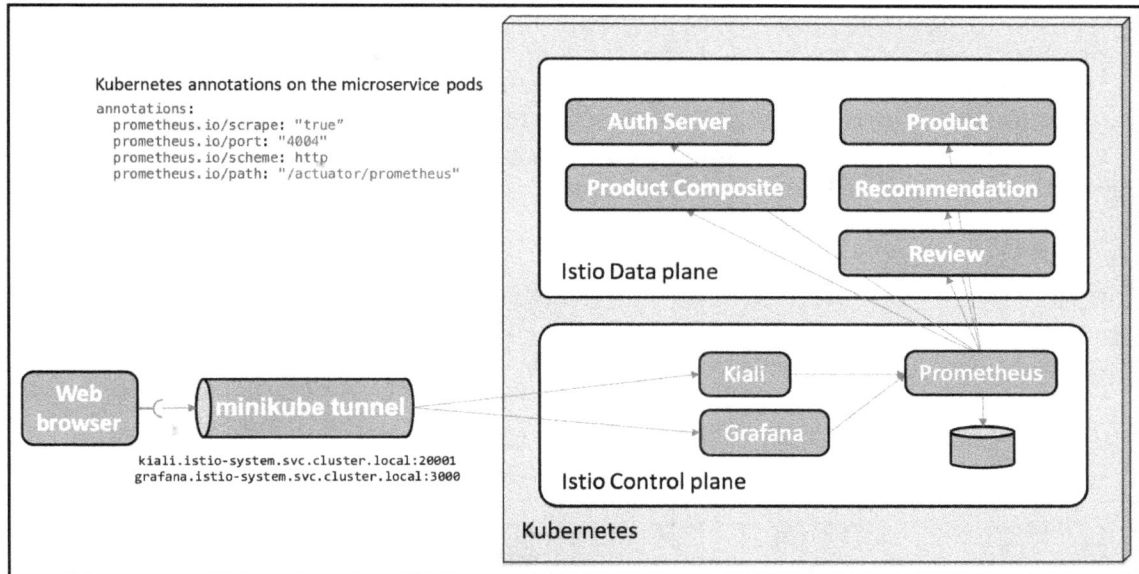

Here, we can see how Prometheus uses the annotations in the definitions of the Kubernetes pods to be able to collect metrics from our microservices. It then stores these metrics in its database. A user can access the web UIs of Kiali and Grafana to monitor these metrics in a **web browser**. The **web browser** uses the **minikube tunnel** that was introduced in Chapter 18, *Using a Service Mesh to Improve Observability and Management,* in the *Setting up access to Istio services* section, to access Kiali and Grafana.

> Please remember that the configuration that was used for deploying Istio from Chapter 18, *Using a Service Mesh to Improve Observability and Management,* is only intended for development and test, not production. For example, performance metrics stored in the Prometheus database will not survive the Prometheus pod being restarted!

In the next section, we will look at what changes have been applied to the source code to make the microservices produce performance metrics that Prometheus can collect.

Changes in source code for collecting application metrics

Spring Boot 2 supports producing performance metrics in a Prometheus format using the Micrometer library (https://micrometer.io). There's only one change we need to make to the source code: we need to add a dependency to the Micrometer library, `micrometer-registry-prometheus`, in the Gradle build files, `build.gradle`, for each microservice. Here, the following dependency has been added:

```
implementation("io.micrometer:micrometer-registry-prometheus")
```

This will make the microservices produce Prometheus metrics on port `4004` using the `"/actuator/prometheus"` URI. To let Prometheus know about these endpoints, each microservice's pod is annotated with the following code:

```
annotations:
  prometheus.io/scrape: "true"
  prometheus.io/port: "4004"
  prometheus.io/scheme: http
  prometheus.io/path: "/actuator/prometheus"
```

View the deployment definitions in the `kubernetes/services/base/deployments` folder for more details.

To make it easier to identify the source of the metrics once they have been collected by Prometheus, they are tagged with the name of the microservice that produced the metric. This is achieved by adding the following configuration to the common configuration file, `config-repo/application.yml`:

```
management.metrics.tags.application: ${spring.application.name}
```

This will result in each metric that's produced having an extra label named `application`. It will contain the value of the standard Spring property for the name of a microservice, `spring.application.name`.

These are all the changes that are required to prepare the microservices to produce performance metrics and to make Prometheus aware of what endpoints to use to start collecting these metrics. In the next section, we will build and deploy the microservices.

Building and deploying the microservices

Building, deploying, and verifying the deployment using the `test-em-all.bash` test script is done in the same way it was done in Chapter 19, *Centralized Logging with the EFK Stack*, in the *Building and deploying the microservices* section. Run the following commands:

1. Build the Docker images from the source with the following commands:

   ```
   cd $BOOK_HOME/Chapter20
   eval $(minikube docker-env)
   ./gradlew build && docker-compose build
   ```

2. Recreate the namespace, `hands-on`, and set it as the default namespace:

   ```
   kubectl delete namespace hands-on
   kubectl create namespace hands-on
   kubectl config set-context $(kubectl config current-context) --
   namespace=hands-on
   ```

3. Execute the deployment by running the `deploy-dev-env.bash` script with the following command:

   ```
   ./kubernetes/scripts/deploy-dev-env.bash
   ```

4. Start the Minikube tunnel, if it's not already running, as follows (see Chapter 18, *Using a Service Mesh to Improve Observability and Management*, the *Setting up access to Istio services* section, for a recap if you need one):

   ```
   minikube tunnel
   ```

5. Run the normal tests to verify the deployment with the following command:

   ```
   ./test-em-all.bash
   ```

   Expect the output to be similar to what we've seen in the previous chapters:

   ```
   $ ./test-em-all.bash
   ...
   Wait for: curl -k http://product-composite.hands-on.svc.cluster.local:4004/actuator/health...
     DONE, continues...
   Test OK (HTTP Code: 200)
   ...
   End, all tests OK: Sun Jul 28 11:47:44 CEST 2019
   $
   ```

With the microservices deployed, we can move on and start monitoring our microservices using Grafana!

Monitoring microservices using Grafana dashboards

As we already mentioned in the introduction, Kiali is integrated with Grafana and provides some very useful dashboards out of the box. In general, they are focused on application-level performance metrics such as requests per second, response times, and fault percentages for processing requests. They are, as we will see shortly, very useful on an application level. But if we want to understand the usage of the underlying hardware resources, we need more detailed metrics, for example, Java VM-related metrics.

Grafana has an active community that, among other things, shares reusable dashboards. We will try out a dashboard from the community that's tailored for getting a lot of valuable Java VM-related metrics from a Spring Boot 2 application such as our microservices. Finally, we will see how we can build our own dashboards in Grafana. But let's start by exploring the integration between Kiali and Grafana.

Before we do that, we need to make two preparations:

1. Install a local mail - server for tests and configure Grafana to be able to send emails to it.
   We will use the mail server in the section "Setting up alarms in Grafana".
2. To be able to monitor some metrics, we will start the load test tool we used in previous chapters.

Installing a local mail server for tests

In this section, we will set up a local test mail server and configure Grafana to send alert emails to the mail server.

Grafana can send emails to any SMPT mail server, but to keep the tests local, we will deploy a test mail server named `maildev`. Consider the following steps:

1. Install the test mail server with the following commands:

```
kubectl create deployment mail-server --image
djfarrelly/maildev:1.1.0
kubectl expose deployment mail-server --port=80,25 --type=ClusterIP
kubectl wait --timeout=60s --for=condition=ready pod -l app=mail-server
```

2. Verify that the test mail server is up and running by visiting its web page at `http://mail-server.hands-on.svc.cluster.local`. Expect a web page such as the following to be rendered:

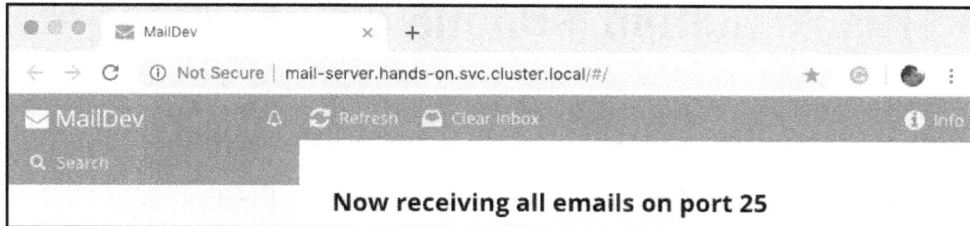

3. Configure Grafana to send emails to the test mail server by setting up a number of environment variables. Run the following commands:

```
kubectl -n istio-system set env deployment/grafana \
    GF_SMTP_ENABLED=true \
    GF_SMTP_SKIP_VERIFY=true \
    GF_SMTP_HOST=mail-server.hands-on.svc.cluster.local:25 \
    GF_SMTP_FROM_ADDRESS=grafana@minikube.me
kubectl -n istio-system wait --timeout=60s --for=condition=ready
pod -l app=grafana
```

> **TIP**
>
> For more details, see `https://hub.docker.com/r/djfarrelly/maildev`.

Now, we have a test mail server up and running and Grafana has been configured to send emails to it. In the next section we will start the load test tool.

Starting up the load test

To have something to monitor, let's start up the load test using Siege, which we used in previous chapters. Run the following commands:

```
ACCESS_TOKEN=$(curl -k https://writer:secret@minikube.me/oauth/token -d
grant_type=password -d username=magnus -d password=password -s | jq
.access_token -r)
siege https://minikube.me/product-composite/2 -H "Authorization: Bearer
$ACCESS_TOKEN" -c1 -d1
```

Now, we are ready to learn about the integration between Kiali and Grafana and explore the Grafana dashboards that come with Istio.

Using Kiali's built-in Grafana dashboards

In `Chapter 18`, *Using a Service Mesh to Improve Observability and Management*, in the *Observing the service mesh* section, we learned about Kiali, but we skipped the part where Kiali shows performance metrics. Now, it's time to get back to that subject!

Execute the following steps to learn about Kiali's integration with Grafana:

1. Open the Kiali web UI in a web browser using the `http://kiali.istio-system.svc.cluster.local:20001` URL. Log in with `admin`/`admin` if required.
2. Go to the service page by clicking on the **Services** tab from the menu on the left-hand side.
3. Select the **Product** service page by clicking on it.
4. On the **Service:product** page, select the **Inbound Metrics** tab. You will see the following page:

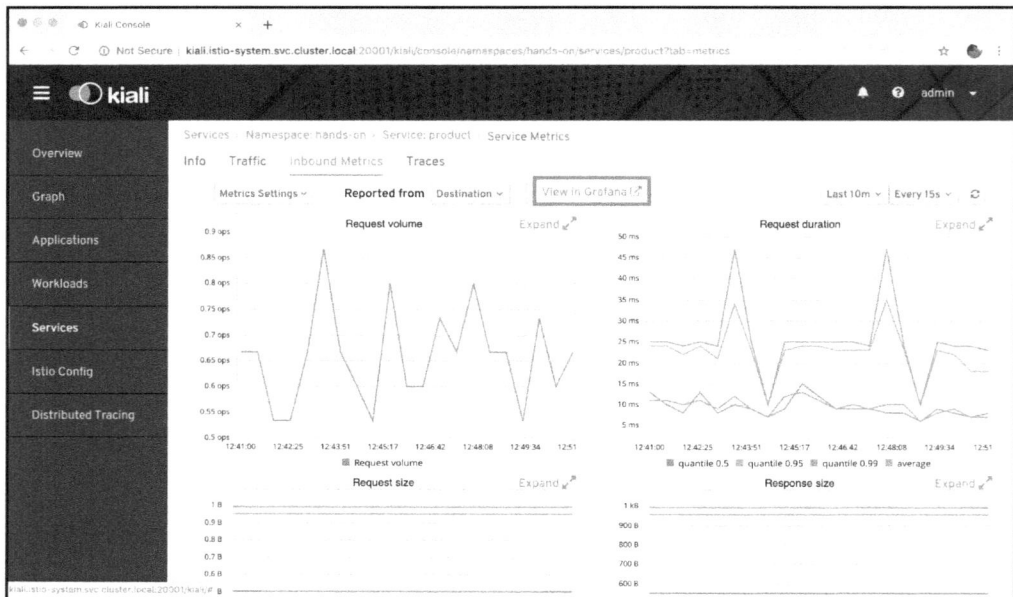

5. Kiali will visualize some overall performance graphs. However, far more detailed performance metrics are available in Grafana. Click on the **View in Grafana** link and Grafana will open up in a new tab. Expect a web page like the following:

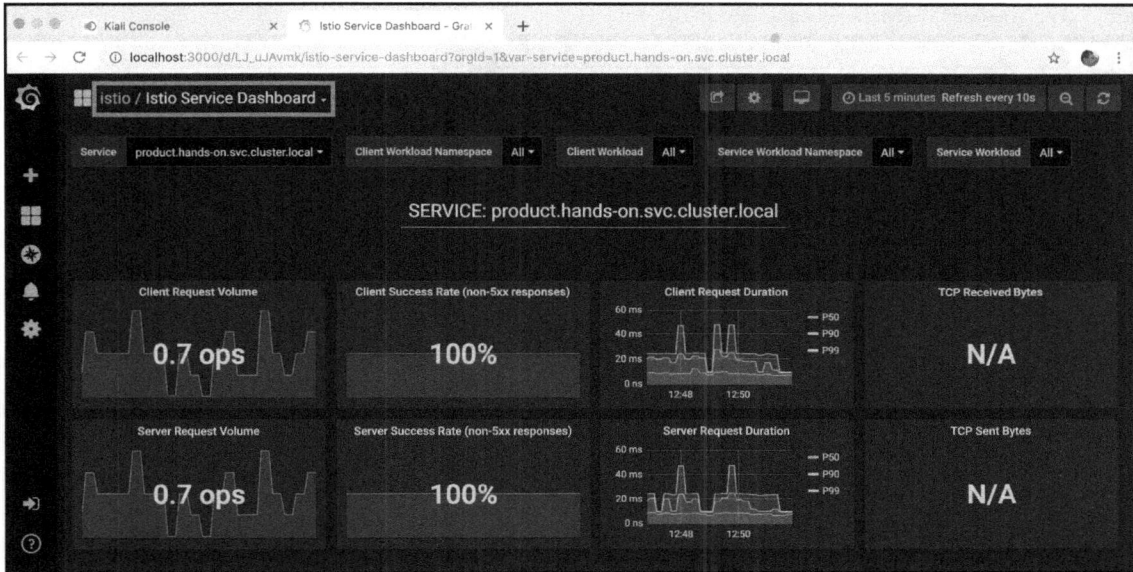

6. There are a lot of performance metrics at an application-level being presented here, such as HTTP request rates, response times, and error rates. The metrics are presented for the **Product** service, that is, the service that was selected in Kiali. Click on the **Service** drop-down menu in the top left corner of the page to select another service. Feel free to look around!

Istio comes with a set of pre-installed Grafana dashboards; click on **Istio/Istio Service Dashboard** to view a list of available dashboards. Now, select the **Istio Mesh Dashboard**. You will see a web page that looks similar to the following:

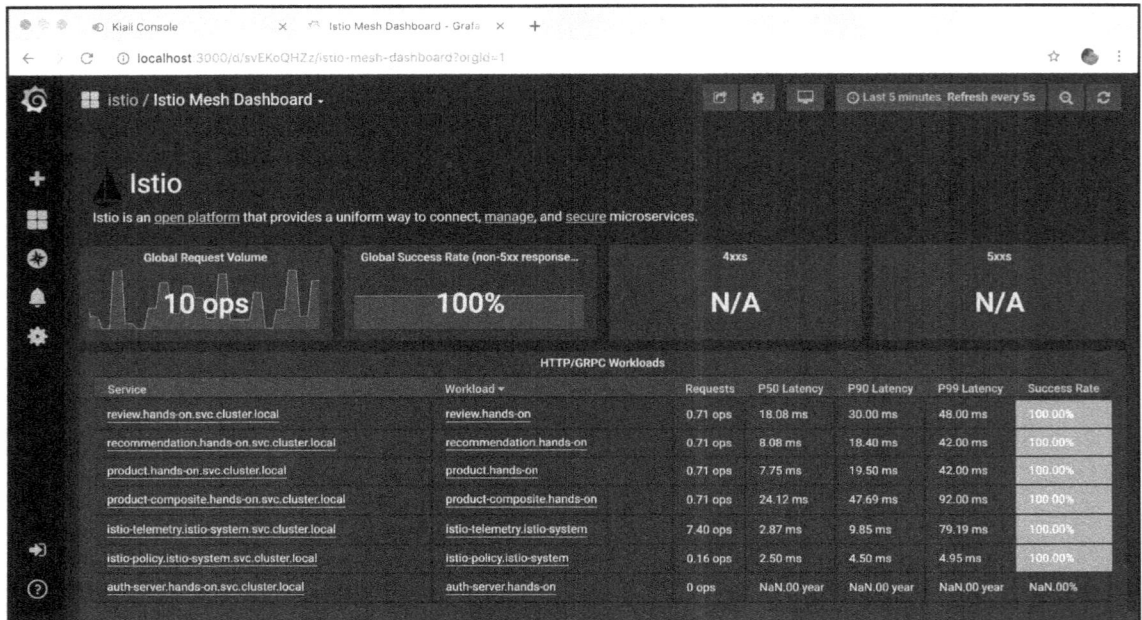

> This dashboard gives a very good overview of the microservices that are parts of the service mesh, as well as their current status in terms of requests per second, response times, and success rate.

As we've already mentioned, the Istio dashboards give a very good overview at an application level. But there is also a need for monitoring the metrics of hardware usage per microservice. In the next section, we will learn about how existing dashboards can be imported—specifically, a dashboard showing Java VM metrics for a Spring Boot 2-based application.

Importing existing Grafana dashboards

As we've already mentioned, Grafana has an active community that shares reusable dashboards. They can be explored at `https://grafana.com/grafana/dashboards`. We will try out a dashboard, called **JVM (Micrometer)**, that's tailored for getting a lot of valuable JVM-related metrics from Spring Boot 2 applications. The URL to the dashboard is `https://grafana.com/grafana/dashboards/4701`. It is very easy to import a dashboard in Grafana. Perform the following steps to import this dashboard:

1. Import the dashboard named **JVM (Micrometer)** by following these steps:
    1. On the Grafana web page, click on the + sign in the left-hand side menu and then select **Import**.
    2. On the **Import** page, paste the dashboard ID `4701` into the **Grafana.com Dashboard** field and press the Tab key to leave the field.
    3. On the **Import** page that will be displayed, click on the **Prometheus** drop-down menu and select **Prometheus**.
    4. Now, by clicking on the **Import** button, the **JVM (Micrometer)** dashboard will be imported and rendered.

2. Inspect the **JVM (Micrometer)** dashboard by following these steps:
    1. To get a good view of the metrics, click on the time picker on the top-right. This will allow you to select a proper time interval:
        1. Select **Last 5 minutes** as the range. Click on the time picker again and set the refresh rate to **5 seconds.**
        2. Click on the **Apply** button after specifying the refresh rate.
    2. In the **Application** drop-down menu, which can be found on the top-left of the page, select the **product-composite** microservice.

3. Since we are running a load test using Siege in the background, we will see a lot of metrics. The following is a sample screenshot:

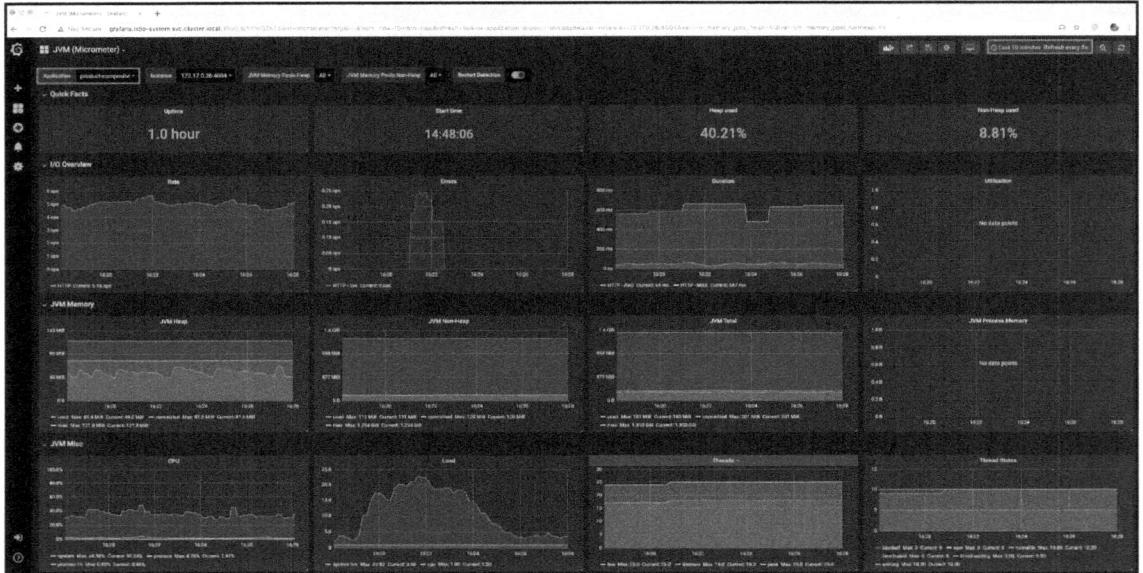

In this dashboard, we can find all types of Java VM relevant metrics for, among others, CPU, memory, and I/O usage, as well as HTTP-related metrics such as requests/second, average duration, and error rates. Feel free to explore these metrics on your own!

Being able to import existing dashboards is of great value when we want to get started quickly. However, what's even more important is to know how to create our own dashboard. We will learn about this in the next section.

Developing your own Grafana dashboards

Getting started with developing Grafana dashboards is straightforward. The important thing for us to understand is what metrics Prometheus makes available for us.

In this section, we will learn how to examine the available metrics. Based on these, we will create a dashboard that can be used to monitor some of the more interesting metrics.

Examining Prometheus metrics

In the *Changes in source code for collecting application metrics* section, we configured Prometheus to collect metrics from our microservices. We can actually make a call to the same endpoint and see what metrics Prometheus collects. Run the following command:

```
curl
http://product-composite.hands-on.svc.cluster.local:4004/actuator/prometheu
s -s
```

Expect a lot of output from the command, as in the following example:

```
$ curl http://product-composite.hands-on.svc.cluster.local:4004/actuator/prometheus -s
...
resilience4j_retry_calls{application="product-composite",kind="successful_with_retry",name="product",} 0.0
resilience4j_retry_calls{application="product-composite",kind="failed_with_retry",name="product",} 0.0
resilience4j_retry_calls{application="product-composite",kind="successful_without_retry",name="product",} 5610.0
resilience4j_retry_calls{application="product-composite",kind="failed_without_retry",name="product",} 75.0
...
resilience4j_circuitbreaker_state{application="product-composite",name="product",} 0.0
...
$
```

Among all of the metrics that are reported, there are two very interesting ones:

- `resilience4j_retry_calls`: Resilience4j reports on how its retry mechanism operates. It reports four different values for successful and failed requests, with and without retries.
- `resilience4j_circuitbreaker_state`: Resilience4j reports on the state of the circuit breaker.

Note that the metrics have a label named `application`, which contains the name of the microservice. This field comes from the configuration of the `management.metrics.tags.application` property, which we did in the *Changes in source code for collecting application metrics* section.

These metrics seem interesting to monitor. None of the dashboards we have used so far use metrics from Resilience4j. In the next section, we will create a dashboard for these metrics.

Creating the dashboard

In this section, we will learn how to create a dashboard that visualizes the Resilience4j metrics we described in the previous section.

We will set up the dashboard in the following subsections:

- Creating an empty dashboard
- Creating a new panel for the circuit breaker metric
- Creating a new panel for the retry metric
- Arranging the panels

Creating an empty dashboard

Perform the following steps to create an empty dashboard:

1. In the Grafana web page, click on the + sign in the left-hand menu and then select dashboard.
2. A web page named **New dashboard** will be displayed:

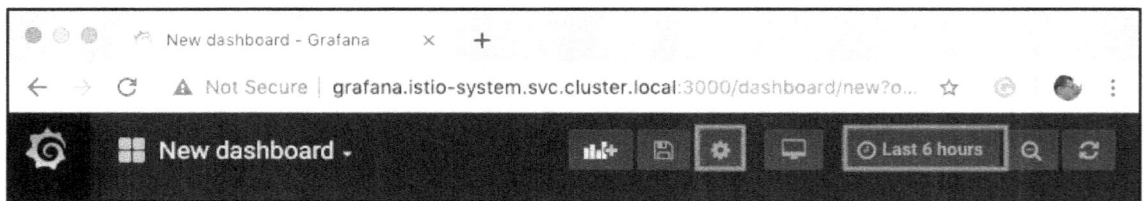

3. Click on the dashboard settings button (it has a gear as its icon), as shown in the preceding screenshot. Then, follow these steps:
   1. Specify the name of the dashboard in the **Name** field and set the value to **Hands-on Dashboard**.
   2. Click on the **Save** button.
4. Click on the time picker to select the default values for the dashboard, as follows:
   1. Select **Last 5 minutes** as the range.
   2. Click on the time picker again and specify **5 seconds** as the refresh rate in the **Refreshing every** field at the bottom of the panel.
   3. Click on the **Apply** button after specifying a refresh rate.
   4. Click on the **Save** button from the menu at the top of the page.
   5. Enable **Save current time range** and click on the **Save** button in the **Save Changes** dialog window.

Creating a new panel for the circuit breaker metric

Perform the following steps to create a new panel for the circuit breaker metric:

1. Click on the **Add panel** button at the top-left of the page (it has an icon of a graph with a + sign next to it).
2. Click on the **Add Query** button. A page will be displayed where the new panel can be configured.
3. In the query field, under the **A** letter, specify the name of the circuit breaker metric, that is, **resilience4j_circuitbreaker_state**.
4. In the **Legend** field, specify the format, that is, **{{application}}.{{namespace}}**. This will create a legend in the panel where the involved microservices will be labeled with its name and namespace.
5. The filled in values should look as follows:

6. Click on the third tab, named **General**, from the left-hand side menu and set the **Title** field to **Circuit Breaker**.
7. Press the back button on the top-left of the page to get back to the dashboard.

Creating a new panel for the retry metric

Here, we will repeat the same procedure that we went through for adding a panel for the preceding circuit breaker metric, but instead, we will specify the values for the retry metrics:

1. In the query field, specify `rate(resilience4j_retry_calls[30s])`. Since the retry metric is a counter, its value will only go up. An ever-increasing metric is rather uninteresting to monitor. The **rate** function is used to convert the retry metric into a rate per second metric. The time window specified, that is, 30 s, is used by the rate function to calculate the average values of the rate.
2. For the legend, specify `{{application}}.{{namespace}} ({{kind}})`. Just like the output for the preceding Prometheus endpoint, we will get four metrics for the retry mechanism. To separate them in the legend, the `kind` attribute needs to be added.

3. Note that Grafana immediately starts to render a graph in the panel editor based on the specified values.

4. Specify `Retry` as the title.

5. Press the back button to get back to the dashboard.

Arranging the panels

Perform the following steps to arrange the panels on the dashboard:

1. You can resize a panel by dragging its lower right-hand corner to the preferred size.

2. You can also move a panel by dragging its header to the desired position.

3. The following is an example layout of the two panels:

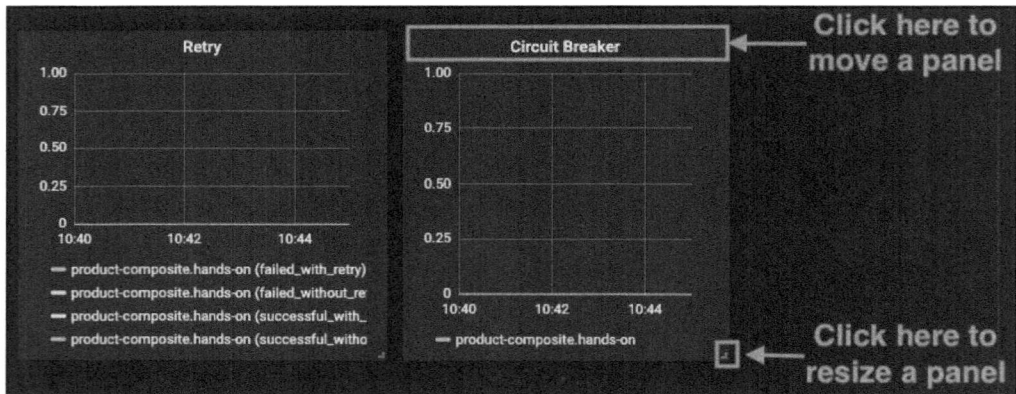

4. Finally, click on the **Save** button at the top of the page. A **Save Changes** dialog will show up; enter an optional description and hit the **Save** button.

With the dashboard created we are ready to try it out: in the next section, we will try out both metrics.

Trying out the new dashboard

Before we start testing the new dashboard, we must stop the load test tool, Siege. For this, go to the command window where Siege is running and press *Ctrl + C* to stop it.

Let's start by testing how to monitor the circuit breaker. Afterward, we will try out the retry metrics.

Testing the circuit breaker metrics

If we force the circuit breaker to open up, its state will change from **closed** to **open**, and then eventually to the **half-open** state. This should be reported in the **circuit breaker** panel.

Open the circuit, just like we did in Chapter 13, *Improving Resilience Using Resilience4j*, in the *Trying out the circuit breaker and retry mechanism* section; that is, make three requests to the API in a row, all of which will fail. Run the following commands:

```
ACCESS_TOKEN=$(curl -k https://writer:secret@minikube.me/oauth/token -d
grant_type=password -d username=magnus -d password=password -s | jq
.access_token -r)
for ((n=0; n<3; n++)); do curl -o /dev/null -skL -w "%{http_code}\n"
https://minikube.me/product-composite/2?delay=3 -H "Authorization: Bearer
$ACCESS_TOKEN" -s; done
```

We can expect three 500 as a response, indicating three errors in a row, that is, what it takes to open the circuit breaker!

> At some rare occasions, I have noticed that the circuit breaker metrics are not reported in Grafana. If they don't show up after a minute, simply rerun the preceding command to reopen the circuit breaker again.

Expect the value for the circuit breaker metric to rise to 1, indicating that the circuit is open. After a while, it should rise to 2, indicating that the circuit is now half-open. This demonstrates that we can monitor that the circuit breaker opens up if there are problems. Close the circuit breaker again by issuing three successful requests to the API with the following command:

```
for ((n=0; n<3; n++)); do curl -o /dev/null -skL -w "%{http_code}\n"
https://minikube.me/product-composite/2?delay=0 -H "Authorization: Bearer
$ACCESS_TOKEN" -s; done
```

We will get three 200 as responses. Note that the circuit breaker metric goes back to 0 again in the dashboard; that is, it's closed.

After this test, the Grafana dashboard should look as follows:

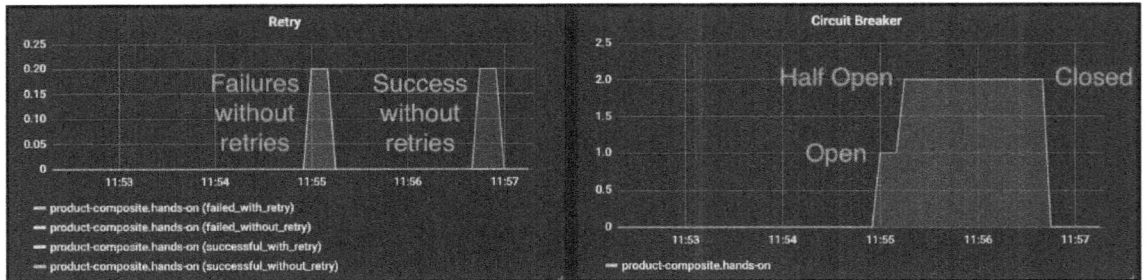

From the preceding screenshot, we can see that the retry mechanism also reports metrics that succeeded and failed.

Now that we have seen the circuit breaker metrics in action, let's see the retry metrics in action!

Testing the retry metrics

To trigger the retry mechanism, we will use the `faultPercentage` parameter we used in previous chapters. To avoid triggering the circuit breaker, we need to use relatively low values for the parameter. Run the following command:

```
while true; do curl -o /dev/null -s -L -w "%{http_code}\n" -H
"Authorization: Bearer $ACCESS_TOKEN" -k
https://minikube.me/product-composite/2?faultPercent=10; sleep 3; done
```

The preceding command will call the API once every third second. It specifies that 10% of the requests shall fail so that the retry mechanism kicks in and retries the failed request. After a few minutes, the dashboard should report metrics such as the following:

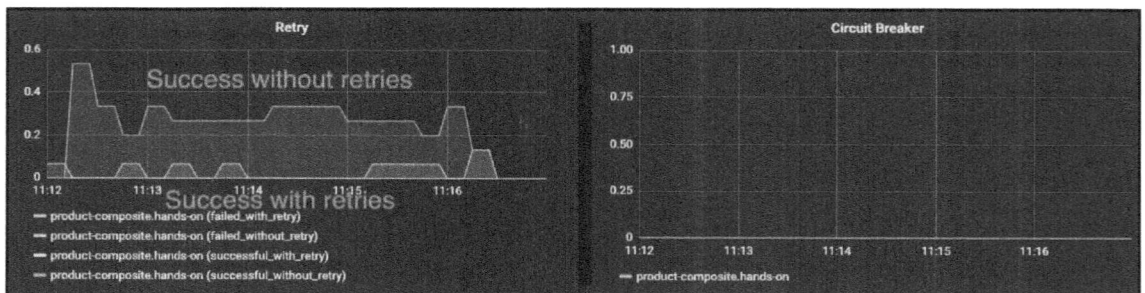

In the preceding screenshot, we can see that the majority of the requests have been executed successfully, without any retries. Approximately 10% of the requests have been retried by the retry mechanism and successfully executed after the retry. Before proceeding to the next section, remember to stop the request loop that we started for the preceding retry test!

In the next section, we will learn how to set up alarms in Grafana, based on these metrics.

Setting up alarms in Grafana

Being able to monitor the circuit breaker and retry metrics is of great value, but even more important is the capability to define automated alarms on these metrics. Automated alarms relieve us from monitoring the metrics manually.

Grafana comes with built-in support for defining alarms and sending notifications to a number of destinations. In this section we will define alerts on the circuit breaker and configure Grafana to send emails to the test mail server when alerts are raised. The local test mail server was installed in section *Installing a local mail server for tests*.

In the next section, we will define a mail-based notification channel that will be used by the alert in the section after this.

Setting up a mail-based notification channel

To configure a mail-based notification channel in Grafana, perform the following steps:

1. On the Grafana web page, on the menu to the left, click on the **Alerting** menu choice (with an alarm bell as its icon) and select **Notification channels.**
2. Click on the **Add channel** button.
3. Set the name to `mail`.
4. Select the type to `Email`.
5. Enable **Send on all alerts.**
6. Enable **Include image.**

7. Enter an email address of your choice. Emails will only be sent to the local test mail server, independent of what email address that's specified. The configuration of the notification channel should look as follows:

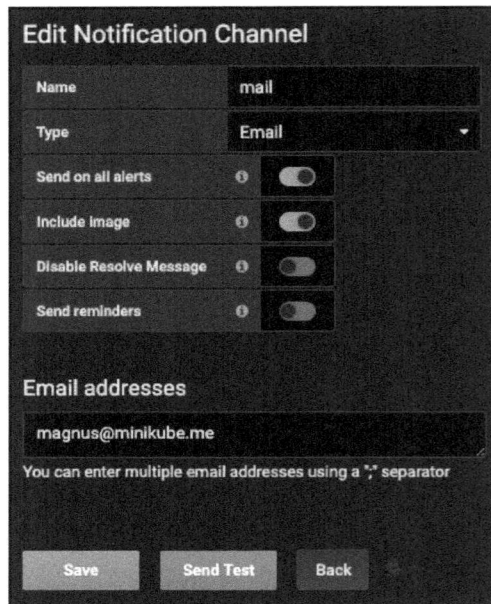

8. Click on the **Send Test** button to send a test mail.
9. Click on the **Save** button.
10. Click on the **Dashboard** button in the left-hand side menu and then on the home button.
11. Select **Hands-on Dashboard** from the list to get back to the dashboard.
12. Check the test mail server's web page to ensure that we have received a test email. You should receive the following output:

With a notification channel in place, we are ready to define an alert on the circuit breaker.

Setting up an alarm on the circuit breaker

To create an alarm on the circuit breaker, we need to create the alert and then add an alert list to the dashboard, where we can see what alert events have occurred over time.

Perform the following steps to create an alert for the circuit breaker:

1. In the **Hands-on Dashboard**, click on the header of the **circuit breaker** panel. A drop-down menu will appear.
2. Select the **Edit** menu option.
3. Select the **Alert** tab in the tab list to the left (shown as an alarm bell icon).
4. Click on the **Create Alert** button.
5. In the **Evaluate every** field, set the value to 10s.
6. In the **For** field, set the value to 0m.
7. In the **Conditions** section, specify the following values:
   - Set the **WHEN** field to max().
   - Set the **OF** field to query(A, 1m, now).
   - Set the **IS ABOVE** field to 0.5.
8. Scroll down to confirm that the notification has been sent to the default notification channel, that is, the mail channel we defined previously. The alarm definition should look as follows:

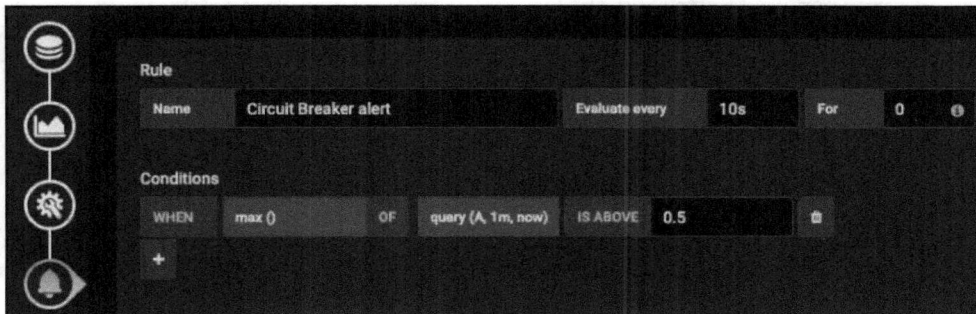

9. Click on the back button (left arrow) to get back to the dashboard.

Then, we need to perform the following steps to create an alarm list:

1. Click on the **Add panel** button at the top of the page.
2. Select **Choose Visualization** in the **New Panel** page.

3. Among the presented visualizations, select **Alert List**. Click on it twice to display an **Options** list.

4. Select the **Show** option called **Recent state changes.**

5. Enable **Alerts from this dashboard**. The settings should look as follows:

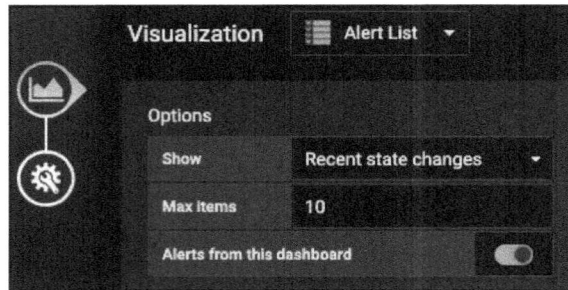

6. Click on the back button to get back to the dashboard.

7. Rearrange the panel to suit your needs.

8. Save the changes to the dashboard.

Here is a sample layout with the alarm list added:

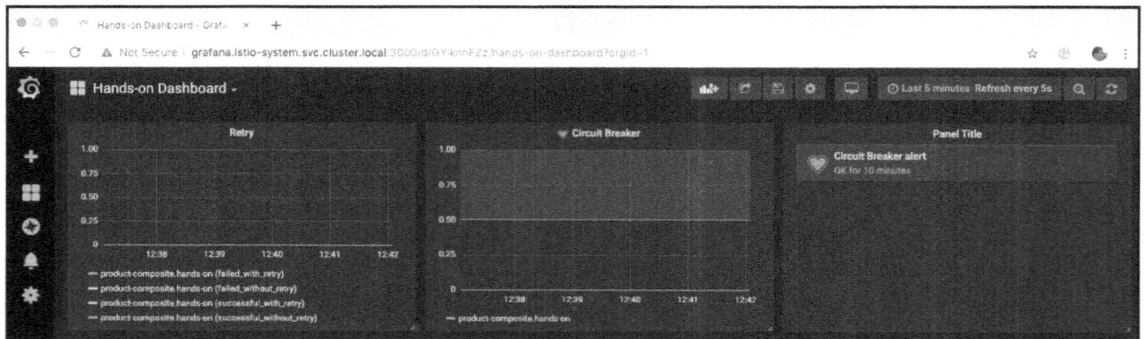

We can see that the circuit breaker reports the metrics as healthy (with a green heart) and that the alert list contains an OK event for the circuit breaker.

Now, it's time to try out the alarm!

Trying out the circuit breaker alarm

Here, we will repeat the tests from the *Testing the circuit breaker metrics* section, but this time, we expect alarms to be raised and emails to be sent as well! Let's get started:

1. Start by opening the circuit breaker:

```
for ((n=0; n<3; n++)); do curl -o /dev/null -skL -w
"%{http_code}\n" https://minikube.me/product-composite/2?delay=3 -H
"Authorization: Bearer $ACCESS_TOKEN" -s; done
```

The dashboard should report the circuit as open as it did previously. After a minute, an alarm should be raised and an email should also be sent. Expect the dashboard to look similar to the following screenshot:

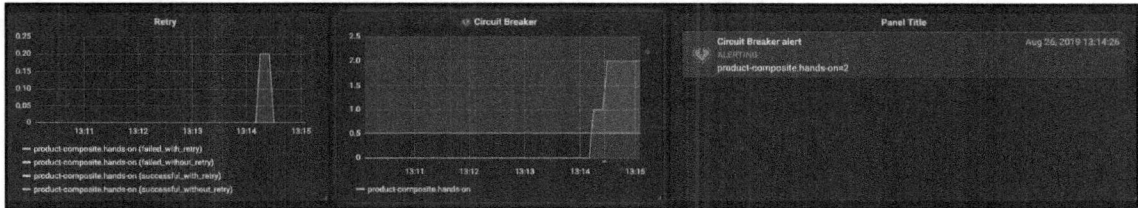

Take note of the alarm icon in the header of the **circuit breaker** panel (a red broken heart). The red line marks the time of the alert event and that an alert has been added to the alert list.

2. In the test mail server, you should see an email, as shown in the following screenshot:

3. Great; we got alarms, just like we expected! Now, close the circuit, making the problem go away with the following command:

```
for ((n=0; n<3; n++)); do curl -o /dev/null -skL -w
"%{http_code}\n" https://minikube.me/product-composite/2?delay=0 -H
"Authorization: Bearer $ACCESS_TOKEN" -s; done
```

The metric should go back to normal, that is 0, and after a minute, the alert should go green again.

Expect the dashboard to look like the following screenshot:

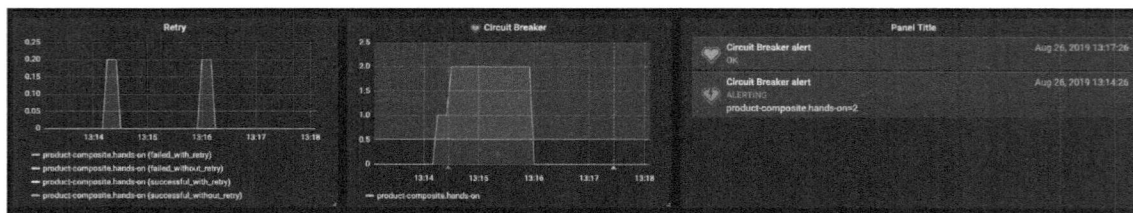

Note that the alarm icon in the header of the **circuit breaker** panel is green again; the green line marks the time for the OK event and that an OK event has been added in the alert list.

In the test mail server, you should see an email, as shown in the following screenshot:

That completes how to monitor microservices using Prometheus and Grafana.

Summary

In this chapter, we have learned how to use Prometheus and Grafana to collect and monitor alerts on performance metrics.

We saw that, for collecting performance metrics, we can use Prometheus in a Kubernetes environment. We then learned how Prometheus can automatically collect metrics from a pod when a few Prometheus annotations are added to the pod's definition. In order to produce metrics in our microservices, we used Micrometer.

Then, we saw how we can monitor the collected metrics using Grafana dashboards. Both of the dashboards that come with Kiali, as well as the dashboards that were shared by the Grafana community. We also learned how to develop our own dashboards where we used metrics from Resilience4j to monitor the usage of its circuit breaker and retry mechanisms.

Finally, we learned how to define alerts on metrics in Grafana and how to use Grafana to send out alert notifications. We used a local test mail server to receive alert notifications from Grafana as emails.

I hope this book has helped you learn how to develop microservices using all the amazing features of Spring Boot, Spring Cloud, Kubernetes, and Istio and that you feel encouraged to try them out!

Questions

1. What changes did we need to make to the source code in the microservices to make them produce metrics that are consumed by Prometheus?
2. What is the `management.metrics.tags.application` config parameter used for?
3. If you want to analyze a support case regarding high CPU consumption, which of the dashboards in this chapter would you start with?
4. If you want to analyze a support case regarding slow API responses, which of the dashboards in this chapter would you start with?
5. What is the problem with counter-based metrics such as Resilience4J's retry metrics and what can be done so that we can monitor them in a useful way?

6. Why does the metric for the circuit breaker report **1** for a short while before it reports **2**? See the following screenshot:

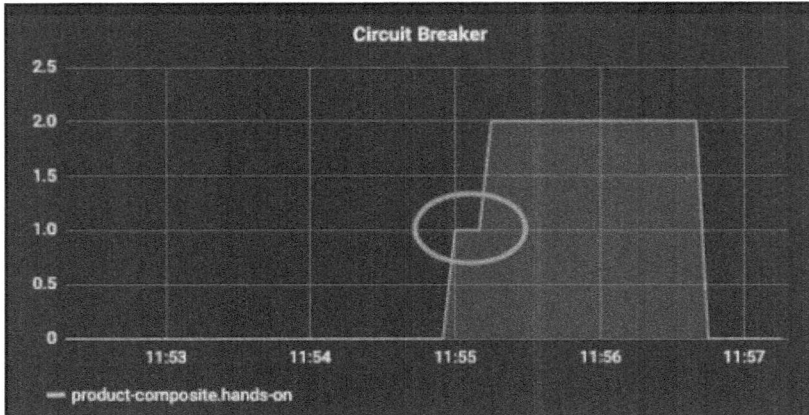

Other Books You May Enjoy

If you enjoyed this book, you may be interested in these other books by Packt:

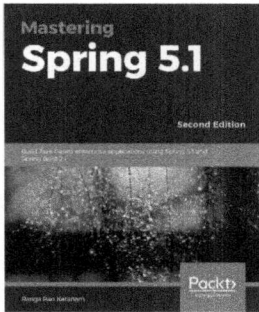

Mastering Spring 5 - Second Edition
Ranga Rao Karanam

ISBN: 978-1-78961-569-2

- Explore Spring Framework 5.1 features such as AOP, transaction management, task scheduling, and scripting
- Build REST APIs and microservices with Spring and Spring Boot
- Develop a secure REST API with Spring Security
- Build your first full stack React application
- Write efficient unit tests with Spring and Spring Boot
- Understand the advanced features that Spring Boot offers for developing and monitoring applications
- Use Spring Cloud to deploy and manage applications on the cloud

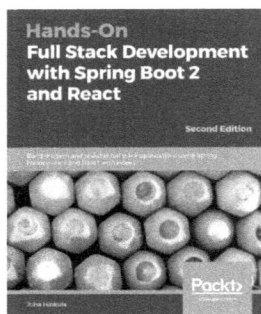

Hands-On Full Stack Development with Spring Boot 2 and React - Second Edition
Juha Hinkula

ISBN: 978-1-83882-236-1

- Create a RESTful web service with Spring Boot
- Grasp the fundamentals of dependency injection and how to use it for backend development
- Discover techniques for securing the backend using Spring Security
- Understand how to use React for frontend programming
- Benefit from the Heroku cloud server by deploying your application to it
- Delve into the techniques for creating unit tests using JUnit
- Explore the Material UI component library to make more user-friendly user interfaces

Leave a review - let other readers know what you think

Please share your thoughts on this book with others by leaving a review on the site that you bought it from. If you purchased the book from Amazon, please leave us an honest review on this book's Amazon page. This is vital so that other potential readers can see and use your unbiased opinion to make purchasing decisions, we can understand what our customers think about our products, and our authors can see your feedback on the title that they have worked with Packt to create. It will only take a few minutes of your time, but is valuable to other potential customers, our authors, and Packt. Thank you!

Index

www.ingramcontent.com/pod-product-compliance
Lightning Source LLC
Chambersburg PA
CBHW081210220326
41598CB00037B/6740